The FCLD Learning Disabilities Resource Guide

A STATE-BY-STATE DIRECTORY OF SPECIAL PROGRAMS, SCHOOLS, AND SERVICES

Library of Congress Cataloging in Publication Data
Main entry under title:

The FCLD learning disabilities resource guide.

    "Created and published for the Foundation for Children
with Learning Disabilities by Education Systems, Inc."--
T.p.verso
    "Revised and greatly expanded"--P.
    Rev. ed. of: The FCLD guide for parents of children with
learning disabilities.   c 1984.
    Bibliography: p.
    Includes index.
    1. Learning disabled children--Education--United
States--Directories. 2. Learning disabled children--
Education--Information services--United States--
Directories. 3. Learning disabled children--Services
for--United States--Directories. I. Foundation for
Children with Learning Disabilities (U.S.)
II. Education Systems, Inc. III. FCLD guide for
parents of children with learning disabilities.
LC 4704.6.F35   1985   371.9'025'73   85-13874
ISBN 0-8147-2579-1
New York University Press hardcover edition
ISBN 0-931112-03-8 pbk.

Table of Contents

Preface

How to Use This Guide   1

Learning Disabilities: The Hidden Handicap   5

    What Are Learning Disabilities?
    The Causes of Learning Disabilities
    The Effects of Learning Disabilities
    The Prevalence of Learning Disabilities
    Learning Disability Warning Signs
    The Outlook for Persons with Learning Disabilities

The Rights of Children with Learning Disabilities   16

    Questions and Answers about IEPs
    Due Process in Brief
    Filing a Discrimination Complaint

Beyond High School: Alternatives for LD Adults   25

    College, Vocational Training, Entering the Work Force
    National Organizations and Services for Adults
    State and Regional Adult Programs and Services

Sources of Information and Help   46

    National Organizations Concerned with Learning
       Disabilities
    United States Government Agencies
    Canadian Organizations Concerned with Learning
       Disabilities
    Learning Disability Information Centers
    Special Materials for the Learning Disabled

State-by-State Listings   57

    Offices of Organizations Concerned with Learning
        Disabilities
    State Department of Education Learning Disabilities
        Personnel
    Private and Day Schools
    Summer Camps and Programs
    College and University Special Programs and Services
    Hospital Clinics and Other Services

Books and Other Materials   366

    An Annotated List of Materials Related to Learning
        Disabilities

A Dictionary of LD Terms   382

    Definitions of Words and Terms

Index   392

Order Form for Additional Guides   409

Preface

It is with pleasure that I introduce this revised and much larger second edition of the FCLD Guide. In the preface to the first edition, I promised that with your help, future editions would be better, more comprehensive, and more useful.

As a result of your suggestions, this edition includes nearly twice as much information on special programs, schools, and services for children and adults with learning disabilities.

To make it easier to locate appropriate resources, new, separate listings for summer camps and programs, hospital clinics, and other services have been added. College and university programs that are designed specifically for students with learning disabilities are now highlighted in the listings.

The field of learning disabilities is now almost 25 years old and the first children recognized and diagnosed as learning disabled are now adults with adult needs and concerns. In response, several sections of this Guide have been revised to help meet the growing needs of older persons with learning disabilities. For example, when a private and day school offers services to adults with learning disabilities, this is now indicated. Also, the section on alternatives for learning disabled adults has been revised and greatly expanded.

Although these changes and additions for adults are important, the major emphasis of this Guide continues to be on helping children. Nearly two million children in the United States have been diagnosed as learning disabled. Unfortunately, many more are still undiagnosed—unable to understand why they cannot learn as other children do.

As a parent, it is my fondest wish to bring hope to these intelligent, often "gifted" children and their families. Early and accurate diagnosis, proper remediation, and the informed and caring support of parents and professionals can make the difference that will assure these children the productive, happy life that they deserve. The information in this Guide is intended to help in the difficult and ongoing task of finding appropriate schools, services, and support for children who must cope with this baffling hidden handicap.

The Foundation for Children with Learning Disabilities was established in 1977 with two primary goals: to promote public awareness of learning disabilities, and to provide funding for programs that serve children with learning disabilities and their families. The Foundation also publishes *Their World*, an annual magazine for parents and professionals. The magazine tells real-life stories about the ways that families cope with learning disabilities.

The Foundation's public awareness campaign makes maximum use of public service advertising. Visual and print ads created and donated by Grey Advertising, Inc. appear in weekly news magazines and on all major radio and television networks. You may have first learned about FCLD and this Guide through one of these public service announcements.

We are extremely proud of the Foundation's ongoing grants program. FCLD supports innovative, action-oriented programs that specifically address the needs of persons with learning disabilities. These programs often cannot get funding from any other source. Many are models for similar programs in other locations and settings. Foundation grantees include schools, camps, after school recreation programs, and day care centers.

Cultural institutions such as the Boston Children's Museum, Capital Children's Museum in Washington, D.C., and the Metropolitan Museum of Art in New York City have received FCLD funding. LD Teenline, the national toll free information hotline operated by the Parents' Campaign for Handicapped Children and Youth, is supported by FCLD grants. Because undetected learning disabilities and delinquent behavior are often linked, FCLD funds a number of projects for youth at risk.

The Foundation has granted a total of more than one million dollars to projects all over the United States.

FCLD is committed to supporting and facilitating the efforts of parents and professionals to help children and adults with learning disabilities. This second edition of the FCLD Guide is evidence of that continuing commitment.

Carrie Rozelle (Mrs. Pete)
Founder and President,
Foundation for Children
with Learning Disabilities

How to Use This Guide

The search for appropriate programs and services for children and adults with learning disabilities is often a time-consuming and frustrating task. This second FCLD Guide, revised and greatly expanded, can be an important aid in that search.

Extensive state-by-state listings of special programs, schools, and services for persons with learning disabilities are a major feature of this Guide. The programs and services listed cover all ages and grade levels, from infants to adults, and from preschool to college.

In addition to the state-by-state listings of resources, this Guide includes a number of other important features, articles, and sections. Among these are a concise introduction to and overview of learning disabilities, an outline of the rights of children with learning disabilities, definitions of LD terms, and a discussion of educational and vocational alternatives for older students and adults with learning disabilities.

In short, this Guide is a comprehensive and easy-to-use directory of learning disabilities information, programs, materials, and resources.

Following are descriptions of the major sections in this Guide and the information that each contains:

The detailed **Table of Contents** lists section titles and the major topics covered in each section. Use this information to locate specific topics of interest.

Learning Disabilities: The Hidden Handicap offers an introduction to and overview of learning disabilities, including definitions, causes, effects, prevalence, warning signs, and the future outlook for persons with learning disabilities.

The Rights of Children with Learning Disabilities outlines the provisions of Public Law 94-142, the Education for All Handicapped Children Act of 1975, and includes a step-by-step explanation of the development and implementation of an Individualized Education Plan (IEP). Also included is a synopsis of due process and specific suggestions on who to contact for information or complaints related to a federal program.

1

The section **Beyond High School: Alternatives for LD Adults** explores some of the new educational and vocational options and opportunities for persons with learning disabilities. College, vocational training, and entering the work force are discussed and suggestions offered.

The section **Sources of Information and Help** includes:

—Up-to-date addresses for and descriptions of major national organizations in the United States and Canada concerned with learning disabilities.

—U.S. Department of Education officials and other important federal agencies and services.

—Learning disabilities information centers that provide information and publications on learning disabilities and related topics.

—Sources of special materials for the learning disabled, including recorded books and book recording services.

The **State-by-State Listings** of special programs, schools, and services is a comprehensive directory of resources for persons with learning disabilities. Information in this section is in alphabetical order by state to make it easier to locate resources in a particular geographic area. Specifically, the state-by-state listings include:

—Offices of Organizations Concerned with Learning Disabilities. These are the state offices of national organizations concerned with learning disabilities. These offices may be able to provide referrals to private consultants, therapists, and other learning disabilities specialists. These offices may also be able to provide information on recreational and support groups for teenagers and adults and other local or area resources not listed in this Guide.

—State Department of Education Learning Disabilities Personnel. These people can often provide useful information and materials on learning disabilities, student rights, educational programs, and vocational training. They may also be able to act as mediators and intercede with local school districts.

—Private and Day Schools. Use the information in this section to help locate appropriate preschool programs, special educational programs, school-related summer programs, diagnostic or counseling services, and special recreational activities and/or facilities. In some cases, schools that use particular therapies, techniques, or approaches are identified.

—Summer Camps and Programs. Listed here are camps and programs *not* operated by or affiliated with a private or day school. Recreational activities, academic programs, and special programs and services are described. See the heading "Private and Day Schools" for programs that *are* school operated or affiliated.

—College and University Special Programs and Services. The institutions listed provide special services for students with learning disabilities. Many have special learning disabilities centers or clinics.

● These large black dots are used in the college and university listings to highlight a new feature of this edition of the FCLD Guide—descriptions of the growing number of special college and university programs that are designed *specifically* to help students with learning disabilities.

—Hospital Clinics. All of the hospital clinics listed offer services to the learning disabled on an outpatient basis. Many also have inpatient programs. Services offered vary widely and may include testing and diagnosis, school and other educational programs, tutoring, counseling, therapy, and social services.

—Other Services. These include private learning disabilities clinics, educational centers, day and residential treatment centers, rehabilitation centers, and mental health centers.

Books and Other Materials is a bibliography of materials related to learning disabilities. A brief description of each publication is included. Most of the books and materials listed are recent. However, some older materials are included because they are still relevant, important, and helpful. Information on how to order the books and materials is provided.

A Dictionary of LD Terms gives clear and concise definitions of many potentially confusing words and terms used by educators and professionals in the learning disabilities field.

The comprehensive **Index** will help to locate specific schools, colleges, universities, agencies, organizations, and other information. The index can also help identify the resources available in a particular state or area.

A convenient **Order Form** is provided at the back of this Guide if you wish to obtain additional copies.

IMPORTANT NOTE: *The FCLD Learning Disabilities Resource Guide* is published by the Foundation for Children with Learning Disabilities as a service to parents, professionals, educators, and others interested in and concerned about children and adults with learning disabilities. Considerable effort and expense has gone into gathering and verifying the information that it contains. However, the publisher and the Foundation for Children with Learning Disabilities are not responsible for changes, errors, or omissions.

The Foundation for Children with Learning Disabilities does not endorse individual consultants, schools, groups, or organizations, nor does it recommend or endorse any specific treatments, therapies, approaches, or techniques.

Learning Disabilities:
The Hidden Handicap

WHAT ARE LEARNING DISABILITIES?

Learning disabilities are disorders of the mental processes that control how a person uses or understands language. Unlike physical handicaps, learning disabilities are hidden. There are no external indications that there are problems. People with learning disabilities have average or above average intelligence; some are even gifted. Their disabilities are often revealed only after careful testing and evaluation.

The concept of learning disabilities is relatively new. The term was first used in 1962 by Samuel A. Kirk in his textbook *Educating Exceptional Children*. Since then, a number of definitions of learning disabilities have been developed, but so far no single definition is universally accepted. In fact, efforts to identify and help learning disabled children and adults have sometimes been hampered by the inability of the experts to agree on exactly what learning disabilities are.

Learning disability is defined in Public Law 94-142, The Education for all Handicapped Children Act of 1975. Since schools that receive federal funds must use this definition, this definition is probably the most widely used and accepted:

> Specific learning disability means a disorder in one or more of the basic psychological processes involved in understanding or in using language, spoken or written, which may manifest itself in an imperfect ability to listen, think, speak, read, write, spell, or to do mathematical calculations. The term includes such conditions as perceptual handicaps, brain injury, minimal brain dysfunction, dyslexia, and developmental aphasia. The term does not include children who have learning problems that are primarily the result of visual, hearing, or motor handicaps, of mental retardation, of emotional disturbance, or of environmental, cultural, or economic disadvantage.

In September, 1984, the board of directors of ACLD, Inc., the largest organization in the United States concerned with learning disabilities and an important advocacy group for the learning disabled, adopted its own definition of specific learning disabilities.

ACLD's definition is worded so that it does not conflict with the definition in P.L. 94-142. Instead, the ACLD definition emphasizes that the condition persists throughout life and does not "go away" even with special instruction. The ACLD definition is:

> Specific Learning Disabilities is a chronic condition of presumed neurological origin which selectively interferes with the development, integration, and/or demonstration of verbal and/or non-verbal abilities.
>
> Specific Learning Disabilities exists as a distinct handicapping condition in the presence of average to superior intelligence, adequate sensory and motor systems, and adequate learning opportunities. The condition varies in its manifestations and in degree of severity.
>
> Throughout life the condition can affect self-esteem, education, vocation, socialization, and/or daily living activities.

Why is a clear definition of learning disabilities so important? According to ACLD, its new definition was formulated because in schools, underachievement is often equated with learning disabilities, misclassification is too common, and public funds are often being used inappropriately.

In the November 1984 issue of the *Journal of Learning Disabilities*, James J. Gallagher offers three additional reasons why accurate labeling of children and adults with learning disabilities is so important:

1. Accurate labeling makes it possible to provide differentiated treatment.
2. Accurate labeling provides the basis for the search for the cause of learning disabilities.
3. Accurate labeling makes it possible to obtain resources, particularly state and federal funds.

Even though experts disagree on the definition of learning disabilities, there are some assumptions about learning disabilities that are generally accepted. These assumptions include:

—Learning disabilities are caused by internal deficiencies in basic psychological processes, not by poor teaching, emotional problems, poor school attendance, or environmental factors.

—There are significant problems in learning basic skills and these problems persist.

—There is a discrepancy between a person's potential for learning and what that person actually learns.

—The person has average or above average intelligence.

—Some people, including the physically handicapped, emotionally disturbed, or socially disadvantaged, are not classified as learning disabled.

Often adding to the confusion are the specialized terms used in the learning disabilities field. Definitions of some of the most frequently used terms are offered in **A Dictionary of LD Terms** in this Guide.

THE CAUSES OF LEARNING DISABILITIES

Not much is known about the causes of learning disabilities. However, some general observations can be made:

—Some children develop and mature at a slower rate than others in the same age group. As a result, they may not be able to do the school work expected. This kind of learning disability is called "maturational lag."

—Some children with normal vision and hearing may misinterpret everyday sights and sounds because of some unexplained disorder of the nervous system.

—Injuries before birth or in early childhood probably account for some later learning problems.

—Children born prematurely and children who had medical problems soon after birth sometimes have learning disabilities.

—Learning disabilities tend to run in families, so some learning disabilities may be inherited.

—Learning disabilities are five times more common in boys than girls, possibly because boys tend to mature more slowly.

—Some learning disabilities appear to be linked to the irregular spelling, pronunciation, and structure of the English language. The incidence of learning disabilities is lower in Spanish or Italian-speaking countries.

THE EFFECTS OF LEARNING DISABILITIES

Until recently learning disabilities were categorized according to the area of performance they affected. Reading problems were called "dyslexia"; math problems were labeled "dycalculia"; and writing problems were called "dysgraphia." According to Larry Silver and Susan Carleton, two authorities in the field, learning disabilities are currently classified by specialists into four areas corresponding to the four basic steps in the learning process:

Input is the process of perceiving and recording information in the brain. Children and adults with input problems may have trouble seeing and hearing accurately. For example, they may confuse or reverse letters, using 3 for *E*, or *b* for *d*. Reading, writing, or copying designs may be difficult. They may confuse left and right, skip words and lines in reading, and misjudge depth. Eye-hand coordination may be affected, causing problems with catching and hitting a ball, jumping rope, and similar activities. Children and adults with hearing input problems may misunderstand words and respond inappropriately. They may require several repetitions of the same question before they can respond. In a classroom or work situation, sounds may distract them.

Integration involves sequencing—the ability to put things in proper order—and understanding. Problems with sequencing often affect spelling. The child or adult may include all the right letters in a word but put them in the wrong order. Recalling the sequence of events in a story or set of instructions may also be difficult. Children and adults with understanding difficulties may grasp only the literal meaning of words and gestures.

Memory involves storing and retrieving visual and auditory information. Children and adults with short-term memory problems may forget verbal instructions before they can carry them out. Children and adults with long-term memory disabilities forget information that should be stored permanently—their home addresses, for example.

Output is language and motor coordination. Children and adults with language disabilities may grope for words or use the wrong word. They may require several repetitions before responding to a question. A gross motor disability involves the coordination of large groups of muscles like those used in riding a bicycle. A problem with fine motor coordination—the coordination of small movements—often appears as poor, laborious handwriting.

In addition to the learning problems outlined above, children and adults with learning disabilities frequently have behavior problems. These behavior problems are often caused by frustration. Tasks that their peers perform easily are difficult or impossible for them. They may have trouble making friends. Occasionally they seem insensitive because they misinterpret the responses of others. A short attention span and a need to be in constant motion may also accompany learning disabilities.

THE PREVALENCE OF LEARNING DISABILITIES

According to U.S. Department of Education figures, about 1.75 million or about 4.4 percent of the approximately 40 million children enrolled in public schools have learning disabilities. For the 1982-83 school year, more than 40 percent of the nearly 4.3 million children identified by states as handicapped, or more than two out of every five handicapped children, were classified as learning disabled.

The number of children ages 3-21 identified as learning disabled varies widely from state to state because of differences in state laws, definitions, administration, and interpretation. For example, in Maryland, the state with the highest percentage in 1980, approximately 5.7 percent of school children were identified as having specific learning disabilities. In contrast, the figure for Massachusetts was 1.5 percent.

Whatever the figures, many learning disabled children in this country who are eligible for and need special education services are not receiving them. Most of these children are:

—Preschoolers and older teenagers (high school dropouts and 18 to 21-year-olds). Even though they may not be in school, these children are eligible for special services. Check with the state department of education to see what special services are available in your state. State department of education learning disability personnel are included in the **State-by-State Listings** in this Guide.

—Students in regular classrooms. Despite increasing efforts, some learning disabled children have not yet been identified. Research indicates that undetected learning disabilities may be the major problem of many children classified as disciplinary problems, underachievers, dropouts, and delinquents.

Children are not the only group that needs special services and support. Since learning disabilities are permanent, many of the first children diagnosed as learning disabled are now learning disabled adults. Using estimates that approximately 3 percent of the total population of the United States has learning disabilities, approximately 6 million adults in this country are learning disabled. Some of these adults have learned to live with or compensate for their disabilities. However, many still need help. As a result, support groups for learning disabled adults are being formed in many communities across the country, organizations are expanding their services for adults with learning disabilities, and new adult organizations are being created. The names of a number of groups and organizations that provide services to adults with learning disabilities are listed in the section **Beyond High School: Alternatives for Learning Disabled Adults** in this Guide.

LEARNING DISABILITY WARNING SIGNS

Children with learning disabilities exhibit a wide range of symptoms. These include problems with reading comprehension, spoken language, writing, or reasoning ability. Hyperactivity, inattention, and perceptual coordination problems may also be associated with learning disabilities but are not learning disabilities themselves.

Virtually every child exhibits some symptoms of learning disabilities at one time or another. However, if a child consistently lags behind his or her peers in speaking, reading, memory, or coordination, and these problems persist, then the possibility of learning disabilities must be considered.

One of the fundamental characteristics of learning disabilities is a significant difference between a child's achievement in some areas and his or her overall intelligence. Learning disabilities typically show up in five general areas:

1. Spoken language—delays, disorders, and deviations in listening and speaking.

2. Written language—difficulties with reading, writing, and spelling.

3. Arithmetic—difficulty in performing arithmetic operations or in understanding basic concepts.

4. Reasoning—difficulty in organizing and integrating thoughts.

5. Memory—difficulty in remembering information and instructions.

When parents suspect that a child might have a learning disability and feel that the child needs further testing and evaluation, Silver and Carleton offer some suggestions:

—Contact the school and arrange for testing and evaluation. Federal law requires that school districts provide special education and related services to children who need them.

—Take the child to a family physician or pediatrician for a complete physical examination. Check for correctable problems such as hearing loss or poor vision that may cause difficulty in school.

If the tests and examination indicate that the child needs special education services, a school evaluation team will meet to develop an Individualized Education Plan (IEP) geared to the child's needs. The IEP describes in detail an education plan designed to provide the child with the learning resources and skills needed to compensate for his or her disabilities. Silver and Carleton list these examples of strategies that might be employed:

—For children with reading difficulties, prerecorded materials may be used to supplement textbooks and other printed material.
—To help them deal with fine motor coordination problems, children may be encouraged to use a typewriter or tape recorder for writing.
—To compensate for memory disabilities, students may be taught to make outlines and tested immediately after drills.
—For children with hearing problems, written outlines of class presentations may be supplied.

For more information on IEPs and the IEP process, see **The Rights of Children with Learning Disabilities** in this Guide.

THE OUTLOOK FOR PERSONS WITH LEARNING DISABILITIES

Not many years ago, learning disabilities were unknown and unrecognized. Children and adults with these hidden handicaps had to struggle alone to overcome them. Students who could not cope were relegated to classes for slow learners, classified as behavior problems, or simply passed from grade to grade until they ultimately dropped out. Few colleges or universities offered special programs or services. Workers with learning disabilities had to struggle without understanding or support.

Federal and state legislation now guarantee children with learning disabilities the right to a free and appropriate education. Many colleges and universities now offer programs *specifically* designed for students with learning disabilities. A few vocational training programs now accommodate the learning disabled, and spurred by new research, may gain momentum. Employer attitudes are also gradually shifting as they learn more about learning disabilities.

Even the publishing industry is becoming more aware of the special needs of persons with learning disabilities. Since the first edition of this Guide was printed in 1984, at least two commercial companies have published their own guides.

Schools and Learning Disabled Students. According to Madeleine Will, Assistant Secretary for Special Education and Rehabilitative Services in the U.S. Department of Education, the continually increasing number of students counted as learning disabled has stimulated concerted state efforts to:

1) assure the consistent application of eligibility criteria, and
2) strengthen the capacity of regular education programs to deal with learning problems.

The rate of growth of the learning disabled school population appears to be slowing, Assistant Secretary Will says. However, this is a result of increased state efforts to assure that children are accurately classified, not because there are few learning disabled students, she explains.

Preschool (birth-age 5) programs for the handicapped, including children with learning disabilities, are also on the rise. Federal preschool incentive grants now encourage states to begin special education for children as early as possible. According to U.S. Department of Education figures, nearly a quarter of the total increase in the number of children who received special education services in 1982-83 were in the 3 to 5-year-old age group. Thirty-eight states now require that services be provided to at least some portion of the preschool population.

In the elementary and secondary schools, evaluation procedures are constantly being refined and teachers are learning how to recognize and help learning disabled students. Children with learning problems are being identified earlier and special help is started sooner. Experts in special education have developed more effective techniques for helping children overcome their learning problems. The end result is that children with learning disabilities now have an increasingly better chance at a positive school experience.

For students planning to go to a college or university, a growing number of these institutions now offer special programs and support services specifically for students with learning disabilities. For a list of these schools, see the "College and University Special Programs and Services" section of the **State-by-State Listings** in this Guide. Special accommodations are available for taking the achievement tests required by many colleges and universities for admission. For more information on these special tests, see the "College" section of **Beyond High School: Alternatives for Learning Disabled Adults** in this Guide.

Vocational Training and Employment. The vocational training and rehabilitation needs of persons with learning disabilities are becoming the focus of increasing attention. Several research programs and pilot projects are currently under way. An example is a four-year project recently undertaken jointly by the Virginia Department of Rehabilitative Services and the Woodrow Wilson Rehabilitation Center in Fisherville, Virginia. The objectives of the project, which is funded by a grant from the National Institute of Handicapped Research, are to:

1. define and identify vocational rehabilitation needs for adults with severe learning disabilities.
2. define and identify existing and potential barriers to the provision of services to learning disabled adults.
3. identify the factors which result in successful job placement and job maintenance.
4. develop and test appropriate diagnostic instruments.
5. develop and test vocational and education training strategies and materials.

There is a growing trend toward expansion of vocational services and the use of community resources to provide vocational training, Will says. "The Department of Education will assist in the expansion and improvement of transitional services for handicapped children and youth (including the learning disabled) through development of curriculum materials, research on the accessibility of employment training, follow-up studies of secondary-age students, demonstration and dissemination of successful practices, communication among the education and business communities, and development of interagency agreements," she says.

Although much still needs to be done, employer attitudes are also changing as they become more aware of and knowledgeable about learning disabilities. Already, some employers are willing to make accommodations for employees with learning disabilities. For more information on vocational training and entering the work force, see **Beyond High School: Alternatives for Learning Disabled Adults** in this Guide.

The Future. Personal computers—in school and at home—hold promise as educational tools for persons with learning disabilities. Computers are fast, multi-sensory, and give students immediate reinforcement. With computer instruction, the pace, content, and length of time available for response can be adjusted to the needs of individual learners. Unlike human instructors, computers also have infinite patience and allow for virtually infinite repetition of a task without external pressure on the learner.

Computers are not a cure-all, however, cautions Jane Johnston, national coordinator for Time Out to Enjoy, Inc. Based on her experiences, using computers often requires many of the same skills that persons with learning disabilities have trouble with, she notes in the organization's newsletter. Use of a computer keyboard requires eye-hand coordination. Some computer software contains printed information, requiring reading skills. Computer screens are small and letters on the monitor may be in different colors or blurred. Sound effects may be harsh, loud, or hard to adjust.

In the medical field, recent research seems to support the theory that at least some learning disabilities are hereditary. An article in the November/December, 1984 issue of *ACLD Newsbriefs* reports that a team of researchers at the Boys Town Institute for Communication Disorders has linked reading disability with a gene. The researchers tested 84 persons in nine multigeneration families. They found that twelve men, ten women, nineteen boys and nine girls had the disorder. Blood groupings and other genetic markers were then used to pinpoint the chromosome on which the "can't read" gene was located, the article reports.

"Gene mapping, genetic screening techniques and gene splicing technology offer hope that someday disordered genes can be diagnosed and repaired as unemotionally—if not as easily—as getting a shot of penicillin," the article concludes.

Whatever hope new technology and new research hold for the future, learning disabilities are today's reality for many. However, history indicates that persons with learning disabilities often have striking abilities along with their disabilities. With the help and support of informed and caring parents, teachers, employers, and professionals, these children and adults can learn to build on their strengths and minimize their disabilities.

They can succeed—in school and beyond.

Information sources for this article include:

"ACLD: Answering the Crisis in Learning Disabilities," ACLD, Inc., press release dated 10/18/84.

"Annual Report on P.L. 94-142: A Summary," *Programs for the Handicapped*, U.S. Department of Education, Office of Special Education and Rehabilitative Services, September/October, 1984.

"Getting Closer: Genetic Link Found for Reading Disability," *ACLD Newsbriefs*, ACLD Inc., November/December, 1984.

"Learning Disabilities," fact sheet from the National Information Center for Handicapped Children and Youth (NICHCY).

"Learning Disabilities and the Near Future," by James J. Gallagher, *Journal of Learning Disabilities*, Vol. 17, No. 9, November, 1984.

"Learning Disabilities Can Be Helped," by Larry B. Silver and Susan Carleton, *Rx Being Well*, September/October, 1983.

"On Defining Learning Disabilities," by Samuel A. Kirk and Winifred D. Kirk, *Journal of Learning Disabilities*, Vol. 16, No. 1, January, 1983.

"Perceptions: Computers and the LD Person," by Jane Johnston, *Not for Children Only*, the newsletter of Time Out to Enjoy, Inc., April, 1985.

"Rehabilitation of Adults with Learning Disabilities," special issue of the *Journal of Rehabilitation*, National Rehabilitation Association, Vol. 50, No. 2, April/May/June, 1984.

Taking the first step... to solving learning problems, booklet, ACLD, Inc.

The Rights of Children with Learning Disabilities

Children with handicaps—including children with learning disabilities—have a right to a free and appropriate public education. This right is guaranteed by the federal Education for All Handicapped Children Act (Public Law 94-142) of 1975. P.L. 94-142 stipulates that:

—all children with handicaps have a right to receive a free, appropriate education at the public expense.

—every child with handicaps has a right to receive an education based on a full evaluation and assessment of individual needs.

—every child who receives special education services must have an Individualized Education Plan (IEP). The IEP must state what special educational and related services the child will receive.

—parents of children with handicaps have a right to a due process hearing if they disagree with the identification, evaluation, or placement of their child.

—every child with handicaps has a right to be educated with nonhandicapped children to the maximum extent appropriate.

For information on special education programs in the public schools of your state, contact the state department of education. State department of education learning disabilities personnel for every state are in the **State-by-State Listings** in this Guide.

ASSESSMENT

Assessment is the first step in the process of gathering and using information to make decisions about the education of a student. Assessment involves more than just testing. Assessment involves looking at a child and the child's environment, drawing together a variety of information, and using that information to develop a plan of action.

Screening is often the first step in the assessment process. Screening can involve formal measurements or informal observations. Screening identifies children who may have problems. Because screening is quick and inexpensive, schools usually screen everyone.

When a child is identified as one who may have a problem, the school system must inform the child's parents and describe what further evaluation is planned. Before the school proceeds with this evaluation, the parents must agree to it *in writing*. Parents will be told about their rights, including the right to see all records and to get a report of the results that the school will use to make decisions.

A complete assessment may involve others in addition to a child's classroom teacher. When learning disabilities are suspected, specialists such as psychologists, speech and language therapists, occupational therapists, physical education specialists, and others may be involved. Together, these specialists form a multidisciplinary team that assesses all aspects of the suspected handicap.

Many different kinds of information are used in evaluating children suspected of having learning disabilities. Depending on the child and the nature of the suspected handicap, this information might include:

—school records.
—interviews with parents, principal, counselor.
—results of intelligence and other standardized tests.
—informal measures such as checklists, observations, and samples of classwork.

Parents can request that a qualified school staff person explain the results of the assessment to them. If a determination is made that the child needs special education and related services, the school must develop an IEP for the child. Parents have the right to participate in every decision relating to their child. They should be involved in the development of the IEP. Parents should be notified of the meeting and the school must make every attempt to:

1) notify parents of the meeting early enough to ensure that they have the opportunity to attend; and
2) schedule the meeting at a mutually acceptable time and place.

If neither parent can attend, the school must use other methods to insure parent participation, including individual or conference telephone calls. A meeting may be conducted without a parent only if the school is unable to convince the parents that they should attend. In this case, the school must have a record of its attempts to arrange a mutually acceptable time and place.

Parents may request an assessment if they feel that their child needs special education services. The school must answer the parents' request in writing. If the school refuses to provide special education services, it must provide written notice telling why the service was refused. This written notice must also provide a full explanation of all of the rights of parents under P.L. 94-142.

Parents can get an independent assessment from an outside expert if they disagree with the school's assessment results. The parents may have to pay for this outside assessment if the school can prove at a due process hearing that its assessment was appropriate. In any case, the parents have the right to have information from the outside assessment considered when their child's Individualized Education Plan is prepared.

QUESTIONS AND ANSWERS ABOUT IEPs

What is an IEP?

An IEP, or Individualized Education Plan, is a written statement of special education and related services for a child. All children who receive special education services under P.L. 94-142 must have an IEP.

What's included in an IEP?

According to P.L. 94-142, an IEP must include the following:

1. A statement of the child's present level of educational performance, which could include, depending on the nature of the handicap: academic achievement, social adaptation, prevocational and vocational skills, sensory and motor skills, self-help skills, and speech and language skills. This statement must be based on evaluation, and it must be documented.

2. A statement of annual goals.

3. A statement of short term instructional objectives (the intermediate steps that make up the goals).

4. A statement of specific special education and related services to be provided and who will provide them.

5. A statement of the extent to which the child can participate in regular educational programs.

6. A statement of the projected dates for the initiation of special services and the duration of special services.

7. A statement of the appropriate objective criteria and evaluation procedures that will be used to measure progress toward the goals. Progress must be evaluated at least annually.

Is the school responsible for making sure that a child achieves all of the goals stated in the IEP?

No. The school is responsible for providing the services written into an IEP, but it cannot be legally bound if a child does not achieve the goals.

Who develops the IEP?

According to P.L. 94-142, the participants at the meeting to develop the IEP are:

—A representative of the school or public agency other than the child's teacher. This could be a special education teacher, learning disabilities specialist, or the school principal.

—The child's teacher. If the child has more than one teacher, the state may specify which teacher will participate in the meeting.

—One or both of the child's parents.

—The child, where appropriate.

—Other individuals at the discretion of the parents or the state agency.

What is an IEP meeting?

The IEP meeting or conference is usually held in the school with the individuals listed earlier present. The purpose of the meeting is to develop the child's Individualized Education Plan.

What does the school do before an IEP meeting?

When a child is suspected of having a handicap, the school first arranges for an individual evaluation of the child's educational needs. This evaluation must be done by a team of qualified persons and cover all areas related to the handicap. If the evaluation shows or seems to show that the child needs special education and related services, an IEP must be developed.

What can parents do before an IEP meeting?

Parents can prepare for the IEP meeting by looking realistically at their child's strengths and weaknesses, visiting their child's classes, and talking to their child about his or her feelings about school. It is a good idea for parents to write down what they think their child will be able to accomplish during the school year. Also, parents should make notes about what they want to say at the meeting.

What do the parents do at an IEP meeting?

Parents should express their feelings about their child's educational program and ask questions about things they don't understand. Parents can also help the school staff with information and insights about their child.

Can the school make decisions about a child without parental permission?

No. Parental permission must be obtained in writing before a child is initially evaluated to determine if the child has a handicap and to determine the child's special needs. Permission is also required before the child is placed in, transferred to or from, or denied placement in special education.

What if the parents disagree with the school about what is appropriate for their child?

First they should try to settle the disagreement. If the parents cannot reach a satisfactory agreement, they have a right to due process. See the section on "Due Process in Brief" later in this article.

How do parents get a due process hearing?

First, they should contact the school in writing and request a hearing. The parents will be notified of the date of the hearing by a hearing officer or a representative of the hearing officer. The school has a responsibility to inform the parents of any free or low cost legal services available in the area. The parents have a right to legal counsel and to present witnesses at the hearing.

Before the hearing, the parents should review all school reports, files, and records. A record of the hearing will be made. The parents have a right to a word-by-word copy (written or taped) of what is said. The hearing is closed and confidential unless the parents decide that they want the hearing to be public. A decision will be made by an impartial hearing officer and sent to the parents within 45 days of the hearing.

Throughout this process, the child must remain in his or her current placement, unless the parents and the school agree on a different temporary placement.

What can the parents do if they still disagree, even after the due process hearing?

Parents can appeal the decision of the hearing officer to the state department of education. Department personnel will examine the hearing record. They may ask for additional information from either or both sides. They will make an independent decision. If the parents or school still disagree, the case may be appealed in civil courts.

What should parents do if school personnel use unfamiliar words and terms?

Definitions of many of these words and terms are included in **A Dictionary of LD Terms** in this Guide. Also, parents should ask for an explanation when a word or term is unfamiliar. It's important that everyone understand what is being said. Parents need to know that the professionals understand the important things they know about their child. The professionals want the parents to understand what they have found out about the child from the assessment and how they propose to help.

What should parents do after the IEP is developed?

Parents should let teachers know that they are interested in their child's education. If possible, they should visit the classroom, or even volunteer to help. Regular telephone talks with teachers can also be helpful. Parents should ask for suggestions on how they can continue, expand, and reinforce school activities at home. They should let the school know that they would like to be called if they are needed. Also, they should tell the teacher of any activities or significant events that may influence their child's performance in school.

How can parents make sure that the IEP is being implemented?

Parents can ask that samples of the child's work be sent home. If the parents have questions, they should make an appointment to discuss new strategies to meet the child's goals.

When parent want to meet with the teacher, they should take the initiative and call and arrange a visit.

Parents should ask themselves: Is our child reasonably happy? Does he or she feel good about school? Talk to the child about what is going on. Does the child seem to be making progress toward the goals of the IEP? If not, and the parents notice it first, they should contact the school and talk about it.

What about minority children with handicaps?

Sometimes race or cultural background make assessment difficult, especially when children speak another language or do not speak standard English well. These children may appear to have hearing or communications problems, or to be slow learners. They may not understand directions or words on tests, or may be unable to respond correctly.

A child's cultural values may affect behavior in ways that teachers or school psychologists do not understand, even though the behavior is perfectly acceptable in the child's own culture. Assessment instruments or their scoring systems may be biased.

In the past, minority group students were overrepresented in some special education classes. They were sometimes labeled behavior or learning problems on the basis of culturally accepted behavior.

The law stipulates that schools can no longer place children in special programs on the basis of only one test. The evaluation must include several tests and observations and the tests must be given in the child's primary language.

The law also says that the school must use the parents' primary language to communicate with them about their child.

DUE PROCESS IN BRIEF

Following is a summary of the rights of children with handicaps:

Active Participation in the IEP—Parents must give their permission for release of records, preplacement evaluation, and initial placement of their child.

The Parents Must Be Told—before any action regarding identification, evaluation, program, or placement.

Due Process Hearing—If the parents do not agree with the school's plans for their child and they cannot resolve their disagreement informally, the parents are entitled to a free hearing with an impartial hearing officer.

Communication—must be clear and simple and in the parents' native language by a method of communication they can understand. The school must explain everything until the parents understand it.

Information—The parents may review all educational records, request copies of these records (there may be a charge for the copies), and request removal of information that they think is false or misleading.

Independent Educational Evaluation—The parents may obtain an independent educational evaluation at their own expense.

Confidentiality—All information on a handicapped child must be kept confidential.

FILING A DISCRIMINATION COMPLAINT

When anyone feels that discrimination on the basis of physical or mental handicap exists in any education-related program operated by an institution receiving federal funding from the U.S. Department of Education, that person may file a formal complaint with the federal Office of Civil Rights serving his or her state.

The complaint should be filed in writing no later than 180 days after the discrimination occurred. The letter should explain who was discriminated against, how the person was harmed, who to contact for further information, and the name, address, and telephone number of the person filing the complaint. Include as much background information as possible. If necessary, ask regional office personnel for help in writing the complaint.

Below is a list of Office of Civil Rights regional offices and the states served by each office:

Region I—Connecticut, Maine, Massachusetts, New Hampshire, Rhode Island, Vermont: John W. McCormack POCH, Room 222, Post Office Square, Boston, MA 02109. Telephone: (617) 223-4282.

Region II—New Jersey, New York, Puerto Rico, the Virgin Islands: 26 Federal Plaza, Room 33-130, New York, NY 10278. Telephone: (212) 264-5180.

Region III—Delaware, the District of Columbia, Maryland, Pennsylvania, Virginia, West Virginia: Gateway Building, 3535 Market Street, P.O. Box 13716, Philadelphia, PA 19101. Telephone: (215) 596-6772.

Region IV—Alabama, Florida, Georgia, Kentucky, Mississippi, North Carolina, South Carolina, Tennessee: 101 Marietta Street, N.W., 27th Floor, Atlanta, GA 30323. Telephone: (404) 221-2954.

Region V—Illinois, Indiana, Minnesota, Michigan, Ohio, Wisconsin: 300 S. Wacker Drive, Chicago, IL 60606. Telephone: (312) 886-3456.

Region VI—Arkansas, Louisiana, New Mexico, Oklahoma, Texas: 1200 Main Tower Building, Room 1935, Dallas, TX 75202. Telephone: (214) 767-3951.

Region VII—Iowa, Kansas, Missouri, Nebraska: 324 E. 11th Street, 24th Floor, Kansas City, MO 64106. Telephone: (816) 374-2223.

Region VIII—Colorado, Montana, North Dakota, Utah, South Dakota, Wyoming: Federal Office Building, 1961 Stout Street, Room 1185, Denver, CO 80294. Telephone: (303) 844-5695.

Region IX—Arizona, California, Hawaii, Nevada, Guam: 221 Main Street, Tenth Floor, San Francisco, CA 94105. Telephone: (415) 556-9894.

Region X—Alaska, Idaho, Oregon, Washington: Arcade Plaza Building, 2901 Third Avenue, M/S 106, Seattle, WA 98121. Telephone: (206) 442-1635.

Some of the information in this article is adapted from materials developed by the National Information Center for Handicapped Children and Youth (NICHCY), P.O. Box 1492, Washington, DC 20013.

Beyond High School: Alternatives for LD Adults

As public awareness of learning disabilities and the special needs of persons with these hidden handicaps increases, programs and support services for learning disabled adults are also increasing. As a result, persons with learning disabilities have more options than ever before.

After high school, persons with learning disabilities have three major options: attending a college or university, vocational training, or entering the work force. Which of these options is most appropriate depends on the learning disabled person's academic preparation, maturity, financial resources, social skills, motivation, and ability to act independently.

Colleges and universities across the country are developing special programs designed specifically to assist and support students with learning disabilities. Landmark College, exclusively for dyslexics, is scheduled to open in Putney, Vermont, in the fall of 1985.

Vocational training and rehabilitation for persons with learning disabilities is getting increasing attention. In 1984, an entire quarterly issue of the *Journal of Rehabilitation* was devoted to vocational rehabilitation services and methods for training learning disabled adults. In addition, the unique learning styles and special training needs of learning disabled adults are the focus of several current research projects. For persons with learning disabilities entering the work force, a wider range of opportunities is now available. As a result of growing awareness of the special needs of persons with learning disabilities, employers are increasingly willing to make on-the-job accommodations. Job possibilities are opening up that might not even have been considered a few years ago.

Following are discussions of each of the three major options available to the learning disabled after high school.

COLLEGE

For some students with learning disabilities, only minimal services will be necessary for success at college. For others, a strong program of special support services may be crucial.

In the **State-by-State Listings** in this Guide, only those colleges and universities that offer special services for students with learning disabilities are listed. Keep in mind that in many cases these services are also available to other students.

● This symbol highlights a college or university program designed *specifically* for the learning disabled.

A college or university with a program designed specifically for the learning disabled may be the best choice for students who need extensive support services. However, the structure of special programs and the services provided vary widely from college to college. Typically, a special program acts as a support system for a student's regular, full-time college curriculum. This support often includes such services as:

—diagnostic testing.
—special classes in basic skills, study habits, time management, and note taking.
—individual tutoring and counseling.
—special study aids such as taped books.
—a full-time learning disabilities specialist.

Participation in the program may be limited to one or two years. The goal of many of these special programs is to withdraw special services as students progress and no longer need them.

Some special programs limit students with learning disabilities to only a few classes, or require them to take special classes. The goal of these programs is to eventually mainstream learning disabled students into the regular college program.

College and university requirements for admission and for participation in special learning disability programs also vary. The majority require learning disabled students to meet standard admissions requirements and also meet the special requirements of the learning disability program. These special requirements may include verification of learning disability through diagnostic tests, recommendations, a personal writing sample, and an interview.

In some cases, applications from learning disabled students are turned over to the director of the special program for consideration. The director conducts the interview and then makes a recommendation on whether the applicant should be accepted. The college or university then makes the final decision.

When investigating a college or university, ask if there are additional fees for the special program, and if the length of time that students are allowed to participate in the program is limited.

For first-hand evaluations of a program, contact past participants. The director of the program should be able to provide interested applicants with a list of names.

Finally, if there is no special program listed in this Guide for any of the colleges and universities in your area, check with your community college. Many community colleges offer some kind of special program for persons with learning disabilities.

In addition to providing information on specific colleges and universities, the descriptions make it possible to compare the types and extent of services offered at different colleges and universities. Of course, other factors such as size, location, type of school and general academic program should be considered in addition to special programs and services.

Begin the selection process early, suggests Barbara Cordoni, associate professor of special education at Southern Illinois University in an article in the *Journal of Learning Disabilities*. It takes time to investigate special programs and services and to get required information to schools.

Cordoni offers these hints for evaluating college and university special services:

—Look for a director trained in learning disabilities. A trained director usually means a more comprehensive program.

—Look at the range of special services offered. The ideal program has a center or clinic specifically for the learning disabled. Also, look for services such as readers, note takers, taped books, and specialized (untimed or oral) exams. Computers or word processors are also helpful aids.

—Investigate tutorial services. These often cost extra. Be sure to check on the training and/or qualifications of tutors.

—Find out what tests are required for admission. The two most commonly used college placement tests are the Scholastic Aptitude Test (SAT) and the American College Test (ACT). Both can be taken under special conditions. For more information about the special SAT, contact Eleanor Kennedy, Educational Testing Services, Services for Handicapped Students, Princeton, NJ 08541. Telephone: (609) 921-9000. For further information on the special ACT, contact the American College Test Administration and ask for the special testing guide "Taking the ACT Assessment for Special Testing." The mailing address is 2255 N. Dubuque Road, P.O. Box 168, Iowa City, IA 52243. Telephone: (319) 337-1332.

—Find out if the school requires a psycho-educational evaluation. Some schools require an independent evaluation before admission. Others do their own testing. Some do no testing at all. Schools that require testing should be favored, Cordoni says.

Choosing a college or university is only one part of the college planning process. Once a school is chosen, appropriate courses must be selected. It's a good idea to consult advisors or the director of the learning disabilities program for advice when deciding which courses to take, says Susan A. Vogel of Barat College, Lake Forest, Illinois. In an article in the *Journal of Learning Disabilities*, Vogel makes the following suggestions:

Consider the course itself. How does it fit into the departmental sequence of courses? What is the level of difficulty? What are the prerequisites or assumed background knowledge and skills? What is the method of instruction? Speak to the instructor personally about the reading load, course requirements, and frequency and method of evaluation. Ask advisors how to make initial contact with professors.

Be aware of the time frame of a course. For students with long-term memory deficits, shorter grading periods and more frequent evaluations are helpful. Classes that meet three or four times per week often are preferred over classes that meet for an extended class period once a week. How much and how rapidly material is presented can also affect the ability to comprehend information.

Plan a well-balanced work load. Class preparation time is likely to be longer for learning disabled students. At many colleges with special programs for the learning disabled, students are advised to carry the minimum load (usually 12 semester hours). Four to five hours in preparation will probably be required for every hour in class. A 12-hour load could require a minimum of 48 hours of preparation per week. Some students may achieve greater academic success if they enroll as part-time students. This is especially true at the beginning of a college career when students spend a considerable amount of time working on basic skills, study habits, and time management.

Some colleges and universities require learning disabled students to take part in a summer orientation program. During orientation, students become familiar with the school, take courses to sharpen basic skills, and often undergo diagnostic testing by the staff. These programs are sometimes also open to high school students and graduates not enrolled in the college. Check with the college.

Even without a mandatory orientation program, students should not wait until the start of classes to become familiar with the school. It takes time to learn about campus facilities and their locations, to meet with key personnel, and to gather special materials. If students and faculty are familiar with one another by opening day, potential problems can be avoided. Beverly Dexter, associate professor of education at Lynchburg College, Lynchburg, Virginia, in an article in the *Journal of Learning Disabilities*, offers the following suggestions to ease entrance into college life for students with learning disabilities.

The Campus—To avoid confusion, students should familiarize themselves with the campus before classes start. For example, study the layout of the school bookstore and know its payment procedures. Find out how to get a student parking permit. To minimize confusion in the cafeteria, sign up for a meal plan instead of paying cash for each meal.

School Officials—Contact the dean of students and advisors before school begins to discuss specific learning problems. This will help ensure that there are no misunderstandings. If medical history is relevant to learning needs, it should also be discussed.

Special Education Department—If a school has no support program specifically for students with learning disabilities, contact the chairperson of the special education department. The chairperson usually knows what special services are available. There are many resources available on most campuses, Dexter notes, but students must explore to find those best suited to individual needs.

Professors—Talk with individual professors before classes begin to make them aware of special problems and needs. For example, if it is necessary to use a note taker or tape recorder for lectures, get the professor's permission first. A pre-class visit will also give the faculty member a first-hand impression of the student's seriousness, motivational level, and commitment to learning.

Recorded Books—For some learning disabled students it might be worthwhile to contact Recording for the Blind, Inc. This organization records student texts on tape. Also, taped books are available from regional libraries as part of the National Library Service for the Blind and Physically Handicapped. For more information on these organizations and their services, see "Sources of Special Materials for the Learning Disabled" in the section **Sources of Information and Help** in this Guide. Arrangements should be made as far in advance as possible. Try to contact professors early for lists of required texts.

For learning disabled high school graduates not ready for college, a precollege year or post high school program may be an alternative. In a precollege program, strengths and individual learning styles are diagnosed. Reading, study skills, and organization are taught. Classes are small and individualized counseling is usually available. See "Private and Day Schools" and "College and University Special Programs and Services" in the **State-by-State Listings** in this Guide to find out which schools and colleges offer precollege programs.

For additional information on specific colleges, universities, or special programs described in this Guide, write to the contact persons listed.

VOCATIONAL TRAINING

Vocational training programs designed specifically for the learning disabled are increasing, but still considerably less common than special college and university programs. However, vocational education is available through many institutions including technical schools, colleges and universities, vocational centers, and state offices of vocational rehabilitation. Here is an overview of their programs:

Technical Schools. Technical schools offer programs that teach specific trades or skills such as computer science, culinary arts, auto mechanics, photography, and graphic arts. A high school diploma is not always required. A free handbook listing 98 careers that can be learned in two years or less and schools that provide the training is available from the National Association of Trade and Technical Schools. See **Books and Other Materials** in this Guide for ordering information. Contact the individual schools that offer career programs of interest to see what arrangements or accommodations can be made to compensate for learning disabilities.

Colleges and Universities. Many colleges and universities offer vocational programs. Section 504 of the Rehabilitation Act of 1973 requires that these programs serve students with handicaps. Some community colleges don't even require a high school diploma. Contact individual schools for specific information on available programs.

Pilot Projects or Special Employment Programs. A limited number of rehabilitation centers and other organizations operate learning disability research or "pilot" projects. The purpose of these projects is to provide services to the learning disabled, train professionals, and conduct research on the most appropriate techniques and methods for training the learning disabled for work. These programs are usually run in conjunction with the state office of vocational rehabilitation, but it may be difficult to find information on them. Try checking with:

—the state office of vocational rehabilitation.
—the state employment office.
—the state chapter of ACLD.
—state chapters of other disability organizations such as the Easter Seal Society.
—private vocational rehabilitation training centers.
—local offices of Goodwill Industries, Inc. The primary mission of this organization is vocational training and placement of disabled people.

Private consultants and clinics. Some private consultants and clinics offer vocational services for learning disabled adults. Services might include vocational evaluations, counseling, prevocational and vocational training, job placement, job monitoring, and job maintenance. Also, some private employment agencies test and counsel job hunters.

State Offices of Vocational Rehabilitation. Since 1981, state offices of vocational rehabilitation (OVRs) have been authorized to serve the learning disabled. Although titles vary, every state has an OVR charged with helping people overcome or cope successfully with disabilities so that they can be employed. There are local branch OVRs in most cities. They are often listed under the state department of education in the blue pages of the telephone book.

School districts often coordinate services with the OVR for eligible high school students. Services may begin as early as the junior or senior year of high school. The OVR evaluates disabilities and job aptitudes, provides job counseling and training, and helps handicapped individuals find and keep jobs. Many also list available jobs. However, OVRs are required by law to help the most severely handicapped first. Also, in many cases, OVR counselors are not learning disabilities specialists. However, efforts are currently being made to inform vocational rehabilitation professionals of the unique needs and learning styles of the learning disabled.

Other sources. Look for schools that provide services for adults in the "Private and Day Schools" section of the **State-by-State Listings**. Many of these schools offer vocational services. Also, contact your local board of education about adult education programs. Some, like Project ABLE in Connecticut, may offer programs specifically for the learning disabled. See "State and Regional Adult Programs and Services" at the end of this article for a list of adult vocational programs, schools, independent living projects, and other services.

Many organizations offer vocational evaluation and training. However, programs that are not specifically designed for the learning disabled should be checked carefully. Some programs at rehabilitation centers are geared to the mentally retarded or the physically handicapped. Other programs make no provision for persons with learning disabilities. Keep in mind that special services and accommodations for the learning disabled in vocational programs may be as crucial to success as they are in academic programs. Services to look for include an orientation program, tutoring, testing and evaluation, counseling, note takers, tape recorders, special testing, job seeking and job placement assistance, registration assistance, and advocates.

ENTERING THE WORK FORCE

A formal analysis of personal interests, strengths, and weaknesses should be made before beginning any job hunt, personnel experts say. For the learning disabled this strategy may be particularly helpful. Once weaknesses are identified, occupations can be chosen that emphasize strengths and necessary job accommodations can be outlined.

Assistance in making this analysis is available. While still in high school, guidance counselors, vocational education counselors, or work-experience coordinators may be able to help. Individuals eligible for state office of vocational rehabilitation services can work with state vocational counselors in determining strengths and weaknesses. Some of the clinics listed in "Other Services" in the **State-by-State Listings** section of this Guide provide vocational evaluation and counseling services. Private job placement firms will also administer tests and advise job hunters.

Self Analysis/Job Analysis. Learning disabled job seekers should set realistic goals, suggest learning disability consultants Helen Ginandes Weiss and Martin S. Weiss, in their book *The World is a Learning Place: Adults Who Have Made It Against The Odds*. Even entry level jobs give employees an opportunity to prove their value through hard work and reliability.

Begin the job hunt by finding out what skills will be needed on a job and then ask if the job seeker possesses those skills. Typical entry level jobs involve answering the telephone. Answering the phone requires clear, legible handwriting, the ability to remember and write down instructions, and the ability to write while listening on the phone.

Reading, math, spelling, and the ability to meet deadlines and handle stress are important in many occupations. If a job requires writing invoices, sales orders, or reports, adequate handwriting, good addition and multiplication skills, and the ability to use a calculator, computer, or word processor may be necessary.

One way to determine interests, strengths, and weaknesses in an on-the-job setting is to work for an employment contractor or temporary job service. Temporary job services place workers in assignments ranging in length from a day to several months. Most use both skilled and unskilled workers for general office and industrial assignments. Applicants are usually tested to determine the most appropriate placement.

Office duties for temporaries may include addressing envelopes, answering the phone, typing, or word processing. Industrial tasks include quality control inspection and shipping and receiving. Some services even place workers with such specific skills as painting, carpentry, and brick-laying.

For persons with learning disabilities, there are a number of advantages to working for a temporary service. Workers can try several job assignments and discover through on-the-job experience what they do best. They also gain work experience, earn money, and can take time off between assignments if necessary or desirable. However, individuals interested in working for a temporary job service should be open to change and possess good mobility skills. Mobility skills include being able to take public transportation or drive a car and follow road maps and directions.

Social skills on the job are also important but sometimes overlooked. Lloyd W. Tindall, in an article in *Early Adolescence to Early Adulthood: Volume 5, The Best of ACLD*, reports that most learning disabled workers are fired not because they can't do the work, but because they can't deal with authority or can't get along with others. Learning disabled people frequently fail to perceive social situations accurately, or may not pick up subtle social clues or non-verbal communications. On the job, this may result in serious problems, Tindall says.

Finding a Job. Finding a job is a often a difficult task for anyone leaving high school or college. Again, good planning and persistence are among the keys to success. Job hunters should begin by utilizing as many resources available to them as possible. Among these resources are:

—high school or college career center or job placement services.

—high school counselors or college advisors. Ask for leads and job hunting tips.

—state employment office.

—newspaper help wanted ads. Some learning disabled people will need help going through the ads.

—private job placement firms.

—friends and family. Ask if they know anyone who is hiring. If they do, ask for a recommendation.

—trade magazines.

—the state office of vocational rehabilitation.

—the state or local chapter of ACLD.

—local chapters, branches, or offices of other disability organizations such as the Easter Seal Society.

—national organizations for learning disabled adults.

—the local library for information on careers and potential employers.

In her booklet, *Steps to Independence for People with Learning Disabilities*, Dale Brown, who is learning disabled herself, suggests ways for the learning disabled to cope with some specific job-hunting problems:

—The Application. If it is difficult to fill out an application, take it home or have it mailed. If necessary, have someone else fill it out. Be aware of careless errors and illegible writing.

—The Interview. It is essential to be on time. Check the time and place of the interview. Allow enough time to get there. Take extra care in dressing. People with visual perceptual problems should ask someone to check them for neatness and color and clothing coordination. If necessary, a change of clothing can be carried in a briefcase.

Job Accommodations. On the job, rule number one is: "Never, never, never, use LD as an excuse for not trying to do your best, not getting along with others, not trying to control your behavior, or refusing responsibilities that you can live up to!" says Elizabeth Robinson, a learning disabled worker, in an article in the *Journal of Rehabilitation*.

Arranging accommodations requires initiative on the part of the worker, Robinson says. Most employers are reluctant to restructure jobs to the needs of the disabled because they don't know how. Be prepared to show employers what accommodations can be made and how they are reasonable in terms of time, manpower, and cost. It is important to discuss problems in a positive way and to know what to ask for. Accommodations that are necessary for success on the job should be made. However, don't ask for accommodations that are not necessary to meet performance standards.

Avoid jobs where accommodations cannot be made for a disability or where compensation strategies will not help performance, Robinson says. Also, learning disabled workers should discuss their learning disabilities only with those who have a need to know. Even then, avoid discussing the disability in a manner that makes it seem that you are seeking sympathy, making excuses, or trying to be the center of attention, says Robinson. Here are some job accommodation strategies for different learning disability problems suggested and used by Robinson:

Driving—Directional problems can be helped by looking for landmarks along the regular route. These landmarks should be associated with directions, such as right, left, straight.

Dyscalculia—Arrange for someone to help with math and statistics or check work before it is submitted. Use a calculator or adding machine for simple math.

Dysgraphia—Use a typewriter or a dictating machine to draft materials. Have a typist do the final draft. This is especially helpful for people with bad handwriting or those who need to make a lot of revisions.

Hyperactivity— Individuals who are hyperactive, have a short attention span, or are easily distracted should try to get a private or semiprivate office away from busy areas. This is for the benefit of coworkers who may be distracted as well as for the benefit of the learning disabled worker. When necessary, hyperactivity can be worked off by running errands rather than waiting for others. Also, it may be helpful to switch assignments frequently or rotate among several projects in one day.

Short-term memory problems—Write plans for the day or week in a notebook or calendar. List them all and set priorities. Also, keep notes on anything important like assignments and meeting notes. Use a tape recorder if necessary. Weiss and Weiss suggest making checklists of steps to be performed for repetitive tasks.

Social skills—Find a co-worker who will act as a mentor and give honest advice and suggestions about sensitive aspects of work and social behavior. Learn to accept criticism gracefully. Insist that the mentor be honest about such things as personal behavior, remarks that were inappropriate or out of context, or behavior of co-workers that the LD person may have misinterpreted. The mentor can also give advice on when an article of clothing is no longer nice enough, no longer fits properly, or is out of fashion. In exchange, the learning disabled person can offer to help out when the work assignments of the mentor pile up.

Visual perception problems—Have a special place for everything important and always put everything in its proper place. Take care of important transactions right away.

Learning disabled people should also ask for clear, concise directions at work so that they know what is expected of them, Robinson says. Good clerical support can help learning disabled people keep files in order, correct grammar and spelling, and find incomplete or unclear thoughts, words, or sentences in written assignments. However, Robinson advises the learning disabled not to allow themselves to become overly dependent on anyone on or off the job because there is a limit on how much help a person can reasonably ask for.

Continuing Education. Despite problems, people with learning disabilities should strive to do their best at a chosen job, and to reach their full potential, Brown says. If the learning disabled choose jobs based on personal strengths and skills, and study the jobs carefully before accepting them, they have as good a chance for success as anyone else. However, like everyone else in the work force, learning disabled people need to know how to advance in a job, when to change jobs, and when to further their education.

Continuing education is critical for the learning disabled, Tindall emphasizes. High technology occupations, job advancement, and reemployment as a result of a changing economy may depend on continuing education and training.

Because of these uncertainties, like everyone, "learning disabled persons must acquire the philosophy that continuous education is a way of life," Tindall says. Failure to acquire new skills and education may result in lowered earnings or unemployment. Therefore, even after finding a first job, they must be able to identify appropriate future steps. These include seeking out and exploring new educational opportunities, available support services, and new jobs. These abilities will help ensure successful careers for the learning disabled.

NATIONAL ORGANIZATIONS AND SERVICES FOR ADULTS

Listed here in alphabetical order by name are offices of organizations that provide special programs, services, and information for adults with learning disabilities.

ACLD, Inc., Youth and Adult Section, 4156 Library Road, Pittsburgh, PA 15234. Executive Director: Mrs. Jean Peterson. Telephone: (412) 341-1515. ACLD provides resource material for adults and referrals to local facilities and agencies on request. Also, check with your state branch of ACLD for local and area support groups or programs for learning disabled adults.

AFL-CIO Human Resources Development Institute, 815 16th Street, N.W., Room 405, Washington, DC 20006. Coordinator: Mr. Lynn Meyers. Telephone: (202) 638-3912. Places workers with various disabilities, including learning disabilities, in training programs and employment. Operates four local placement demonstration projects located in St. Paul, MN, Houston, TX, St. Louis, MO, and Baltimore, MD.

LAUNCH, Inc., The Coalition of LD Adults. President: Velda Skinner. Executive Director: John Moss. Mailing Address: Special Education Department, East Texas State University, Binnion Hall, Room 221, Commerce, TX 75428-1907. Telephone: (214) 886-5937 or 886-5932. A nonprofit organization for LD adults and their supporters including parents, advocates, businesses, and organizations. Has active local stations in Texas. Runs self-help groups, provides resources, acts as an advocate for civil rights of the learning disabled, and coordinates efforts of other local, state, and national LD organizations. Membership: $4.00 per year; includes monthly newsletter.

Marin Puzzle People, 1368 Lincoln Avenue, Suite 105, San Rafael, CA 94901. Telephone: (415) 453-4006. Executive Director: Jo Ann Haseltine. Organization for learning disabled adults and their supporters dedicated to the social and vocational development of adults with learning disabilities. Operates a drop-in headquarters, information/referral service at the local, state and national levels, and a clearinghouse for information for parents, teachers, and general public. Provides social activities and free minicourses for members on topics such as work, social interaction, driver's education, money management, and health and safety. Membership: $10.00; includes monthly newsletter.

National Network of Learning Disabled Adults, P.O. Box Z, East Texas Station, Commerce, TX 75428-1938. Telephone: (214) 886-5937 or 886-5932. Contact: John Moss. Organization for learning disabled adults and their supporters. Strives to increase communication among learning disabled adults. Acts as an advocate and encourages educational institutions and employers to make accommodations for the learning disabled. Currently raising funds to open an office in Washington, D.C. and establish a toll free information number. Membership: $10.00; includes quarterly newsletter.

Time Out to Enjoy, Inc., 715 Lake Street, Suite 100, Oak Park, IL 60301. National Coordinator: Jane Johnston. Cochairman: Ed Harms. Answering Service: (312) 383-9017. Volunteer organization that provides information on educational and employment services and programs for learning disabled adults. All recommended programs and services are checked out by staff members. The answering service is operated 24 hours a day, 7 days a week. Messages left with the service are usually returned within 24 hours. Membership is not necessary to request information. A guide to postsecondary education is available for $12.00. Membership: $5.00; includes newsletter.

STATE AND REGIONAL ADULT PROGRAMS AND SERVICES

Listed here are schools, vocational training facilities, independent living programs, and demonstration projects that serve learning disabled adults. Organizations are in alphabetical order by state.

Alabama: Sparks Center for Developmental and Learning Disorders, 1720 Seventh Avenue, South, Birmingham, 35294. Telephone: (205) 934-5471. Director: Gary J. Myers. Operates a research and demonstration project to maximize vocational potential for the learning disabled. Ages served: 16 and up. Services: diagnostic and treatment services, vocational training, individual and group tutoring, academic and psychological testing, academic counseling. Notes: Funded by Alabama Vocational Rehabilitation through October 1986. Alabama residents only. Applications taken through Alabama Office of Vocational Rehabilitation.

Alabama: Workshops, Inc., 4244 Third Avenue, South, Birmingham, 35222. Telephone: (205) 592-9683. Executive Director: Jim Crim. Ages served: 16 and up. Grades served: 10 and up. Current enrollment: 150. Maximum enrollment: 180. Scholarships/financial aid available. Services: academic and psychological testing, academic and family counseling, adaptive physical education, vocational training, work-study, job placement, work adjustment training. Notes: All clients must be referred by state office of vocational rehabilitation.

California: Advocates for the Quiet Minority, Project LIFT (Living Independently for Tomorrow), 30 N. Raymond Avenue, Seventh Floor, Pasadena, 91103. Telephone: (818) 449-4705. Director: Marliene Smoker. Independent living program for people with developmental disabilities. Services: residential skills training, vocational training, individual psychosocial development. Notes: Operates programs in Pasadena, San Fernando Valley, and Santa Monica.

California: Goodwill Industries of the Greater East Bay, 1301 30th Avenue, Oakland, 94601. Telephone: (415) 534-6666. Contact: John Holderegger. Three-year vocational rehabilitation demonstration project. Purpose of project is to develop new vocational rehabilitation methods specifically for the learning disabled. Services: vocational evaluation and training, job placement, career development. Notes: Works in cooperation with state department of rehabilitation and school districts.

California: Work Training Program, Inc., 227 N. Nopal Street, Santa Barbara, 93103. Executive Director: Stefen A. Sorsoli. Contact: David Farris. Telephone: (805) 963-1685. Additional location: 5650 Shoup Avenue, Woodland Hills, 91367. Contact: Harriet Rechtman. Telephone: (818) 999-5080. Services: independent living skills training in community-based, supervised apartments; consumer and social survival skills training, prevocational and vocational training; supervised habilitation work crews; supportive services for former residents. Notes: Serves learning disabled, slow learners, and educable mentally retarded.

Connecticut: Chapel Haven, Inc., 1040 Whalley Avenue, New Haven, 06515. Telephone: (203) 397-1714. Executive Director: Jeanne Sargent. Independent living program for the learning disabled. Purpose of program is to prepare residents for independent functioning in vocational, social/emotional, and apartment living activities. Ages served: 18-33. Current enrollment: 39. Maximum enrollment: 39. Services: instruction in social and daily living skills, individual and group tutoring, academic testing, vocational training, work-study, job placement, occupational and recreational therapy.

Connecticut: Project ABLE (Alternatives for a Better Learning Experience), Norwalk Board of Education, Adult Education, 105 Main Street, Norwalk, 06854. Director: Patricia Calise-Giannini. Work telephone: (203) 852-9488 ext. 241. Adult education program for learning disabled adults. Ages served: 16 and up. Services: courses in language arts, basic math, business machines, social studies, and personal development; vocational training, remediation, compensatory learning techniques; resources for diagnosis, prescription, and individual tutoring; high school equivalency test preparation, individualized programs, modification of learning methods. Notes: Emphasis on real life work and social situations rather than traditional textbook learning. Learning disability must be verified through school records.

Delaware: Delaware Elwyn Institute, 321 E. 11th Street, Wilmington, 19801. Telephone: (302) 658-8860. Director: Peter Dakunchak. Training center. Ages served: 18 and up. Current enrollment: 200. Maximum enroll-ment: 250. Services: vocational training, sheltered employment, work activ-ity and adjustment, transitional employment, job placement, individual and group tutoring, academic and psychological testing; physical, speech, and occupational therapy; medical services, audiology services.

Florida: Career Development Institute, 3049 McGregor Boulevard, Fort Myers, 33901. Telephone: (813) 337-5600. President: J. Hamilton Welch. Executive Director: Socrates J. Chaloge. Vocational school with day and residential program. Ages served: 18 and up. Services: one and two-year diploma programs in secretarial and computer sciences and trades such as carpentry and culinary arts; vocational training, work study, job placement, individual and group tutoring, academic and psychological testing, aca-demic and psychological counseling, high school equivalency, precollege year, individual education plans, independent living program, learning dis-ability and gifted divisions. Notes: High school diploma may not be required to enroll.

Florida: Goodwill Industries-Sun Coast, Inc., 10596 Gandy Boulevard, St. Petersburg, 33733. Telephone: (813) 576-3819. Contact: Debbie Passerini. Three-year vocational rehabilitation demonstration project. Purpose of proj-ect is to develop new methods of vocational rehabilitation specifically for the learning disabled. Services: vocational evaluation and training; job place-ment, career development, employer awareness. Notes: Referrals made through state office of vocational rehabilitation.

Georgia: GOALD (The Georgia Organization for Adults with Learning Disabilities), Inc., 475 Burgundy Court, Stone Mountain, 30087. Contact: Richard Kaplan. Home telephone: (404) 498-1606. State organization that helps learning disabled adults achieve personal goals and cope with and compensate for their disabilities. Also promotes public awareness and en-courages postsecondary educators and employers to work with LD adults. Holds monthly meetings and publishes a monthly newsletter.

Illinois: George Halas, Jr. Vocational Center, 8562 S. Vincennes Avenue, Chicago, 60620. Telephone: (312) 651-1100. Director: Stanley Watson. Ages served: 16 and up. Current enrollment: 230. Maximum enrollment: 230. Services: vocational training, job placement, individual and group tutoring, academic and psychological testing, academic and psychological counsel-ing, medical services.

Illinois: Shore Training Center, 7855K Gross Point Road, Skokie, 60077. Telephone: (312) 679-7620. Director: Nancy Baughman. Rehabilitation center. Ages served: 16 and up. Current enrollment: 155. Maximum enrollment: 160. Services: vocational training and counseling, job placement. Notes: Part of North Shore Association for the Retarded. Serves individuals with disabilities that substantially interfere with employment.

Indiana: New Hope Center, 725 Wall Street, Jeffersonville, 47130. Telephone: (812) 288-8248. Executive Director: James A. Bosley. Rehabilitation facility. Current enrollment: 165. Maximum enrollment: 200. Services: vocational training and evaluation, sheltered workshops, job placement, psychological testing and counseling, individual and group counseling, physical therapy, adaptive physical education. Notes: Serves individuals with physical, mental, or emotional disabilities.

Louisiana: Jefferson-Gumbel Vocational Training Centers, 925 Labarre Road, Metairie, 70001. Telephone: (504) 837-0631. Additional location: 5700 Loyola Avenue, New Orleans, 70115. Telephone: (504) 899-0296. Director: Karl Ungeheuer. Vocational training program. Ages served: 16 and up. Current enrollment: 57. Maximum enrollment: 110. Scholarships/financial aid available. Services: vocational evaluation and training, job placement, follow-up services. Notes: Serves individuals with disabilities that are a handicap to employment. State department of vocational rehabilitation determines eligibility.

Maine: Southern Maine Vocational Technical Institute, Two Fort Road, South Portland, 04106. Contact: Gail Christiansen, Learning Disabilities Specialist. Telephone: (207) 799-7303 ext. 264. Vocational school with special services for the learning disabled. Services: individual tutoring, individualized training in study skills, academic counseling, taped books, special examinations, limited diagnostic testing, student resource center, study center, limited readers, computer-assisted instruction.

Massachusetts: Merrimack Valley Rehabilitation Center, 39 First Street, Lowell, 01850. Telephone: (617) 459-0351. Executive Director: Robert F. Vinson. Vocational rehabilitation center. Ages served: 16-22. Services: vocational training, work-study, job placement, transitional employment programs, individual and group tutoring, academic and psychological testing, academic counseling.

Massachusetts: Project Triangle, Inc., 239 Commercial Street, Malden, 02148. Telephone: (617) 322-0400. Executive Director: Joseph P. Churchill.

Vocational rehabilitation facility. Ages served: 16-22. Services: vocational training, job placement, sheltered workshop, counseling and evaluation, group tutoring, academic testing. Notes: Serves individuals with a variety of disabilities, including learning disabilities.

New Hampshire: Day Habilitation Munadnock Workshop, 46 Concord Avenue, Peterborough, 03458. Telephone: (603) 924-3326. Executive Director: Dale Dileo. School with summer program. Ages served: 16 and up. Scholarships/financial aid available. Services: vocational training, job placement, individual and group tutoring, psychological testing and counseling, physical and occupational therapy, adaptive physical education, medical services, daily living skills, community integration, behavioral training.

New Hampshire: New England Trade and Technical Institute, 750 Massabesic Street, Manchester, 03103. Telephone: (613) 669-1231. President: Socrates J. Chaloge. Vocational day and boarding school with special services for the learning disabled. Current enrollment: 75. Maximum enrollment: 125. Ages served: 18 and up. Scholarships/financial aid available. Services: vocational training, job placement, individual tutoring, academic and psychological testing, academic counseling. Notes: Learning disabled students are mainstreamed.

New Jersey: JESPY House, Inc., 65 Academy Street, South Orange, 07079. Telephone: (201) 762-6909. Codirectors: Carol R. Goodman, Stephen R. Goodman. Transitional independent living program for the learning disabled. Ages served: 18-30. Services: supervised apartment settings where residents develop basic independent living and social skills through group living; individual and group counseling, individual goal plans, sex education, vocational evaluation, referral for vocational training, job placement, outclient services for JESPY graduates.

New Jersey: MACLD Apartment Residence/STILE (Success Through Independent Living Experience) Program, 1501 Park Avenue, Asbury Park, 07712. Telephone: (201) 774-4737. Director: John A. Reno. Assistant Director: Carol L. Veizer. Independent living program for the learning disabled. Ages served: 18-31. Services: supervised apartment living, training in independent living skills, food allowance, local transportation, programming and counseling; instruction in job hunting, interviewing skills, and on-the-job behavior; extension program.

New York: Human Resources Center, I.U. Willets Road, Albertson, 11507. Telephone: (516) 747-5400. President: Edwin Martin. Projects focus on transition from school to work for students in grades 11 and 12 with severe disabilities including learning disabilities; assimilation of LD students into college community, and vocational rehabilitation of LD adults. Scholarships/financial aid available. Notes: In vocational rehabilitation project, LD adults are mainstreamed into traditional evaluation training and placement areas with services modified to meet their learning styles.

New York: The PARA-Educator Center for Young Adults, One Washington Place, New York, 10003. Telephone: (212) 598-3906. Director: Judith Kranes. Operates a two-year vocational program to train LD adults to work with children, care for senior citizens, and become teacher aides. Scholarships/financial aid available. Services: individual tutoring, group therapy, vocational training, on-the-job training, work-study. Notes: Full-time course; one day a week at center, rest of week in field.

New York: Summit Travel Camp, 339 N. Broadway, Upper Nyack, NY 10960. Telephone: (914) 358-7772 or (718) 268-6060. Directors: Regina and Gil Skyer. Therapeutic recreation and socialization program for adolescents and young adults with learning and adjustment problems. Uses travel as a medium to encourage the development of social skills, independent living, and interpersonal relationships. Ages served: 18-30. Full-time staff: 15. Maximum enrollment: 100; 40 per tour. Services: psychological counseling. Notes: Two, three, and six-week tours of Israel, Paris, and Amsterdam in 1985.

Pennsyivania: Goodwill Industries of Lancaster County, Inc., 1048 N. Plum Street, Lancaster, 17601. Telephone: (717) 394-0647. Contact: Susan Frankhouser. Three-year vocational rehabilitation demonstration project. Goal is to develop new methods of vocational rehabilitation specifically for the learning disabled. Services: vocational training and evaluation; job placement, career development. Notes: Referrals made through state office of vocational rehabilitation.

Pennsylvania: Vocational Rehabilitation Center, 1323 Forbes Avenue, Pittsburgh, 15219. Telephone: (412) 471-2600. President: Leonard Weitzman. Ages served: 16 and up. Services: vocational training, training in job search and survival skills, diagnostic testing, academic and psychological testing, academic remediation, academic and psychological counseling.

Virginia: Woodrow Wilson Rehabilitation Center, Research and Demonstration Project for Adults with Learning Disabilities, Box 125, Fishersville, 22939. Telephone: (703) 885-9808. In-state toll free number (department of rehabilitative services): (800) 552-5019. Project Director: Kenneth L. Sheldon. Residential vocational rehabilitation project. Ages served: 16 and up. Services: vocational training and evaluation, work-study, job seeking skills, work adjustment and independent living skills programs, academic and psychological testing, academic and psychological counseling, physical and occupational therapy, speech/communication services, medical services.

Washington: Mason/Thurston Community Action Council, 1408 E. State Street, Olympia, 98506-4499. Telephone: (206) 352-9910. Education Coordinator: Nancie Payne. Community agency. Ages served: 16 and up. Scholarships/financial aid available. Services: assessment, individual and group tutoring, academic testing and counseling, vocational and employment counseling, curriculum development, referrals to local agencies, advocacy, individualized approach.

Washington: Morningside, 2611 14th Avenue, N.W., Olympia, 98507. Telephone: (206) 943-0512. Executive Director: Patricia Clifford. School. Ages served: 18 and up. Current enrollment: 180. Maximum enrollment: 200. Services: vocational training, job placement, sheltered workshop, evaluation, work activity center.

Washington: The Wiser Institute, P.O. Box 55223, Seattle, 98155. Telephone: (206) 364-5545. Executive Director: Margo L. Thornley. Adult boarding school with limited services; summer program. Ages served: 16 and up. Current enrollment: 70. Maximum enrollment: 100. Services: special education, academic and psychological testing, physical and occupational therapy, adaptive physical education, vocational training, work-study, job placement. Notes: Serves learning disabled and some developmentally disabled adolescents and young adults.

Information sources used for the text material in this section include:

"A Directory of College LD Services," by Barbara Cordoni, *Journal of Learning Disabilities*, Vol. 15, No. 9, November, 1982.
Early Adolescence to Early Adulthood: Volume 5, The Best of ACLD, edited by William M. Cruickshank and Joanne Marie Kliebhan, Syracuse University Press, 1984.
"Helping Learning Disabled Students Prepare for College," by Beverly L. Dexter, *Journal of Learning Disabilities*, Vol. 15, No. 6, June/July, 1982.
"On Developing LD College Programs," by Susan A. Vogel, *Journal of Learning Disabilities*, Vol. 15, No. 9, November, 1982.

Steps to Independence for People with Learning Disabilities, a booklet by Dale Brown. Copyright 1980 by Closer Look/Parents' Campaign for Handicapped Children and Youth.

"Techniques for Job Hunting," by Elizabeth Robinson, *Journal of Rehabilitation*, Vol. 50, No. 2, April/May/June, 1984.

The World is a Learning Place: Adults Who Have Made it Against the Odds, by Helen Ginandes Weiss and Martin S. Weiss. Copyright 1985 by Treehouse Associates, P.O. Box 1992, Avon, CO 81620.

Sources of Information and Help

Included in this section are national offices of major organizations concerned with learning disabilities and the learning disabled, U.S. government agencies and services (including the U.S. Department of Education), Canadian organizations concerned with learning disabilities, learning disability information centers, and sources of special materials.

NATIONAL ORGANIZATIONS
CONCERNED WITH LEARNING DISABILITIES

The following is an alphabetical list of national offices of organizations concerned with learning disabilities. Brief histories and descriptions of each organization are included. Some of the organizations are primarily for teachers, educators, and professionals in the field. Several act as advocates for the learning disabled. All provide information and help on request. For addresses and telephone numbers of state offices, branches, and chapters, see the **State-by-State Listings** in this Guide.

ACLD, Inc., 4156 Library Road, Pittsburgh, PA 15234. President: Anne Fleming. Executive Director: Mrs. Jean Peterson. Telephone: (412) 341-8077 or 341-1515.

Founded in 1963, ACLD is the oldest and largest volunteer organization specifically concerned with learning disabilities. There are more than 800 state and local chapters throughout the United States and Canada. ACLD works to stimulate the development of early detection programs, develop and promote legislative assistance, and create a climate of public awareness and acceptance. The organization is open to parents, educators, and others concerned about the welfare of learning disabled children and adults. The annual membership fee is $15.00. ACLD publishes a newsletter, holds an annual international conference, and distributes more than 500 publications about learning disabilities.

The Association on Handicapped Student Service Programs in Post-Secondary Education (AHSSPPE), P.O. Box 21192, Columbus, OH 43221. Executive Director: Jane E. Jarrow. Telephone: (614) 488-4972.

For persons involved in providing support services for disabled students in higher education. One association special interest group is specifically concerned with learning disabilities. Membership includes a quarterly bulletin and a newsletter. Professional membership is $40.00. Student membership is $15.00.

CALLED, Inc. (The College Association for Language, Learning, and Educational Disabilities), P.O. Box Z, E.T. Station, Commerce, TX 75428. Executive Director: John Moss. Telephone: (214) 886-5937 or 886-5932. East Coast contact: Richard Cooper. Telephone: (215) 275-7211.

An organization for professionals who work with learning disabled adolescents and adults. CALLED's goal is to help bridge the gap between secondary and postsecondary school teachers, community agencies, and other organizations. Publishes newsletters and a professional journal that provide information on programs, materials, and innovative approaches to the remediation of learning disabilities. Promotes conferences, symposia, and meetings. Membership: $40.00. Newsletters only: $25.00.

Council for Exceptional Children (CEC), 1920 Association Drive, Reston, VA 22091-1589. Executive Director: Mr. Jeptha V. Greer. Telephone: (703) 620-3660.

The council is a professional organization for persons involved in the education of children with special needs. CEC was founded in 1922 and currently has some 1,000 state and local chapters in the United States and Canada and 13 special education divisions. CEC publishes a journal, holds an annual convention, and sponsors conferences on issues of current significance.

CEC's Division for Learning Disabilities (DLD), promotes the development, dissemination, and use of outstanding diagnostic and teaching practices, supports legislation for services to the learning disabled, and encourages research in the area of learning disabilities. Membership in the division is open and costs $15.00 a year in addition to the $43.00 CEC membership fee. Included with membership is a subscription to a quarterly newsletter and two professional journals.

Council for Learning Disabilities (CLD), 9013 W. Brooke Drive, Overland Park, KS 66212. Executive Secretary: Kirsten McBride. Telephone: (913) 492-3840.

CLD is primarily for professionals in the field. However, membership is open to parents and others concerned with learning disabilities. CLD has approximately 20 state and local chapters. The organization holds annual international and regional conferences. The council publishes a journal of research, theory, and opinion on learning disabilities, and a teacher-oriented newsletter. Opinion papers on important topics in the field of learning disabilities are currently being developed. Membership: $25.00 per year. Membership includes the journal and newsletter.

Foundation for Children with Learning Disabilities (FCLD), 99 Park Avenue, New York, NY 10016. President: Mrs. Pete Rozelle. Executive Director: Arlyn Gardner. Telephone: (212) 687-7211.

Organized in 1977, the primary goals of the foundation are to create public awareness of learning disabilities and provide financial support for innovative projects that serve children with learning disabilities. In addition to public service advertising campaigns and other information programs, FCLD funds teacher training and education programs, information and referral services, parent information programs, and projects that directly serve learning disabled children. In addition to this guide, FCLD publishes *Their World*, an annual magazine for parents and others interested in and concerned about learning disabilities. The magazine is $2.00.

International Reading Association (IRA), 800 Barksdale Road, P.O. Box 8139, Newark, DE 19714. President: John C. Manning. Executive Director: Ronald W. Mitchell. Telephone: (302) 731-1600.

IRA is a professional organization for reading teachers and other educators concerned with reading and reading education. The association publishes several professional journals, including *The Reading Teacher* and *The Journal of Reading*. The annual membership fee of $18.00 includes a newsletter about IRA activities. Membership and a subscription to one of the journals is $30.00 a year.

The IRA's Disabled Reader Special Interest Group is specifically concerned with learning disabilities. Contact: Alta Palmer, P.O. Box 940, Covington, LA 70434.

National Easter Seal Society, 2023 W. Ogden Avenue, Chicago, IL 60612. President: Robert B. Coats. Executive Director: John Garrison. Telephone: (312) 243-8400.

The society is the country's oldest and largest nonprofit health care agency providing direct services to people with a wide range of disabilities, including learning disabilities. Services provided vary widely from chapter to chapter, so contact the chapter in your area to find out what services are available. State and local chapters may also make referrals to other local agencies serving people with learning disabilities. A number of publications about learning disabilities are available from the national office.

The Orton Dyslexia Society, 724 York Road, Baltimore, MD 21204. President: Sylvia O. Richardson. Administrative Director: Elinor Hartwig. Telephone: (301) 296-0232.

A nonprofit, educational association, the society promotes the study, treatment, and prevention of dyslexia. Founded in 1949 and named for Dr. Samuel T. Orton, a pioneer in the field of dyslexia, the society includes parents, educators, and other professionals. Annual membership is $35.00 and includes membership in local or regional branches. A quarterly newsletter and an annual scholarly journal, *Annals of Dyslexia*, are free to members. The journal contains articles about teaching reading, research in the area of language disorders, and testing. It is available to nonmembers for $10.45.

UNITED STATES GOVERNMENT AGENCIES

U.S. Department of Education, Office of Special Education and Rehabilitative Services (OSE), 400 Maryland Avenue, S.W., Washington, DC 20202. Assistant Secretary: Madeleine Will. Telephone: (202) 732-1723.

The Office of Special Education and Rehabilitative Services is divided into two main offices: Rehabilitative Services and Special Education Programs. Issues and concerns related to learning disabilities are handled through the Office of Special Education Programs. Acting Director: Patricia J. Guard. Telephone: (202) 732-1012.

The Office of Special Education Programs includes five divisions. Each of these divisions is concerned with specific aspects of education of the handicapped. The person to contact for specific information and help on learning disabilities is Gary Lambour, Research Associate, Division of Educational Services. Telephone: (202) 732-1054.

—The Division of Assistance to States is responsible for the implementation of P.L. 94-142 and the procedures for identifying learning disabled and other handicapped students. Acting Director: William Tyrrell. Telephone: (202) 732-1014.

—The Division of Personnel Preparation is responsible for teacher training programs for special education personnel. Director: Max Mueller. Telephone: (202) 732-1070.

—The Division of Educational Services oversees and provides grants for research in special education. Director: Martin Kaufman. Telephone: (202) 732-1106. Learning disabilities contact: Gary Lambour, Research Associate, Division of Educational Services. Telephone: (202) 732-1054.

—The Division of Innovation and Development funds research and oversees the development of handicapped child model programs. Director: Thomas Behrens. Telephone: (202) 732-1154.

—The Division of Policy Analysis and Planning works with Congress on special education issues and legislation. The division also settles problems of policy and definitions of terms. Director: Shirley Jones. Telephone: (202) 732-1128.

President's Committee on Employment of the Handicapped, 1111 20th Street, N.W., Room 600, Washington, DC 20036. Program Manager: Ms. Dale Brown. Telephone: (202) 653-5010.

Established in 1947, the committee works to promote a positive climate for the acceptance of physically and mentally handicapped people and to eliminate environmental and attitudinal barriers. The committee sponsors an annual meeting, holds seminars and other special meetings, and conducts an ongoing public information program.

CANADIAN ORGANIZATIONS CONCERNED WITH LEARNING DISABILITIES

Canadian Association for Children and Adults with Learning Disabilities (CACLD), Kildare House, 323 Chapel Street, Ottawa, Ontario K1N 7Z2. President: Kathy Smith. Executive Director: June Borgeau. Telephone: (613) 238-5721.

The overall purpose of the association is to advance the education and general well being of children and adults with learning disabilities.

Specifically, CACLD promotes greater public awareness and understanding of learning disabilities; early recognition, diagnosis, treatment, and appropriate educational, social, recreational, and career-oriented programs for the learning disabled. The association also promotes legislation, research, and training of personnel in the field of learning disabilities and provides liaison between its membership, the Canadian government, and other appropriate organizations. Combined membership in CACLD and a provincial chapter ranges from $15.00 to $20.00 per year and includes a subscription to the CACLD's quarterly newsletter. Newsletter subscription only: $8.00.

Atlantic Conference on Learning Disabilities, P.O. Box 2036, D.E.P.S., Dartmouth, N.S. B3W 2X8. Executive Director: Judy Pelletier. Telephone: (902) 469-7282 or 469-8903.

A regional organization dedicated to educating the public on learning disabilities. Acts as a resource center and works to encourage cooperation between health, educational, social, corrections, and family services. Holds an annual conference. No membership fee. Newsletter: $5.00.

LEARNING DISABILITY INFORMATION CENTERS

Some of the organizations and centers listed here have extensive computer databases. Others have informative and useful publications available. Information services are usually free, but in some cases, fees are charged. To request information, contact the information center and describe the information or assistance needed as precisely as possible.

Closer Look/Parents' Campaign for Handicapped Children and Youth, 1201 16th Street, N.W., Washington, DC 20036. Executive Director: Barbara Scheiber. Telephone: (202) 822-7900. LD Teenline toll free number: (800) 522-3458.

The primary purpose of Closer Look is to "help families to help themselves" in raising a child with a handicap. Closer Look provides information about and referrals to services in your area. In addition, the organization publishes a number of booklets, fact sheets, and guides on various aspects of disabilities.

Closer Look also operates LD Teenline, an information and referral service for parents of learning disabled teenagers, educators, and teenagers themselves funded by the Foundation for Children with Learning Disabilities. The information service is available through the toll free number listed above from 10 a.m. to 4 p.m., Monday through Friday.

ERIC Clearinghouse on Handicapped and Gifted Children, CEC Information Center, The Council for Exceptional Children, 1920 Association Drive,

Reston, VA 22091. Associate Director: Mrs. Lynn Smarte. Telephone: (703) 620-3660.

The clearinghouse collects and stores information, articles and research on all types of handicaps, including learning disabilities. The material is indexed by topic and stored in a database. A custom computer search costs $25.00 for CEC members, $35.00 for nonmembers. Information on frequently requested topics costs $10.00. After a search, a list of abstracts available on the topic is sent.

Information Center for Individuals with Disabilities, 20 Park Plaza, Room 330, Boston, MA 02116. Executive Director: Ms. Sandy Bouzoukis. Telephone: (617) 727-5540. In-state toll free number: (800) 462-5015.

The center assists in finding appropriate facilities, services, and programs for persons with all types of disabilities and answers questions about legal rights. Much of the information is about services in Massachusetts. However, the center can provide information on services and programs throughout the country.

HEATH Resource Center, One Dupont Circle, N.W., Suite 670, Washington, DC 20036-1193. Director: Rhona Hartman. Telephone: (202) 833-4707.

The center is a national clearinghouse on postsecondary education for handicapped people, including those with learning disabilities. It maintains a resource file of postsecondary programs, including college, vocational, and other programs, including information on colleges and universities that provide support services for learning disabled students. Fact sheets and information packets are also available. The center is part of the American Council on Education, and is funded by the U.S. Department of Education.

National Association of Private Schools for Exceptional Children (NAP-SEC), 2021 "K" Street, N.W., Suite 315, Washington, DC 20006. Executive Director: Susan B. Nelson. Telephone: (202) 296-1800.

The association provides a free referral service to parents and others seeking educational facilities for children with special needs. The association also publishes a directory of member schools. The directory is $16.00. Schools that belong to NAPSEC must adhere to and practice a code of ethics.

National Information Center for Educational Media (NICEM), Access Innovations, P.O. Box 40130, Albuquerque, NM 87196. Director: James Johnstone. Telephone: (505) 265-3591. Out-of-state toll free number: (800) 421-8711.

NICEM maintains a database called the National Information Center for Special Education Materials (NICSEM). However, no new information has been entered since 1980. This database includes information on all types of special education instructional material including audio recordings, talking books, and filmstrips. Although the service is designed for teachers and other professionals, it may also be useful to parents. The fee for using NICSEM varies according to the information requested. Special education file available on-line through Dialog Information Service.

National Rehabilitation Information Center (NARIC), 4407 Eighth Street, N.E., The Catholic University of America, Washington, DC 20017. Director: Susan Flowers. Telephone: (202) 635-5826 (Voice/TDD).

The center provides information on research, products, and resources in the field of disabilities to professionals, students, and handicapped individuals. NARIC also makes referrals to other organizations and resources. Custom searches of the REHABDATA database for information on many special topics, including learning disabilities, are available. The ABLE-DATA database contains information on more than 11,000 commercially available aids and equipment useful to disabled persons. The fee for a search on either database is $10.00 for the first 100 listings.

National Information Center for Handicapped Children and Youth (NICHCY), P.O. Box 1492, Washington, DC 20013. Project Director: Ms. Toni Haas. Telephone: (703) 522-3332.

NICHCY has developed fact sheets that provide concise definitions and descriptions of various handicaps, including learning disabilities. NICHCY also supplies fact sheets on resources available in individual states and at the national level. In addition, the center sponsors workshops and conferences for parents, educators, and others concerned about learning disabilities.

Resources for Children with Special Needs, Inc., 200 Park Avenue, South, Suite 816, New York, NY 10003. Director: Karen T. Schlesinger. Telephone: (212) 677-4650.

An information, referral, advocacy, and support center primarily for parents and professionals in the New York City area. The organization provides information about and makes referrals to public and private schools, camps and summer programs, medical and therapeutic resources, and other facilities and services. Organizes an annual "special camp" fair primarily for New York City area children. Programs and services are checked by on-site visits and personal contact. When possible, questions are answered by telephone or by letter, but appointments are encouraged. There is a fee for consultations. However, fees are based on a client's ability to pay, and all or part of the fee can be waived.

SpecialNet, National Association of State Directors of Special Education, 2021 "K" Street, N.W., Suite 315, Washington, DC 20006. Director of SpecialNet: Gary Snodgrass. Telephone: (202) 296-1800.

A computer network that allows users to access special education information and to send to and receive information from other users. SpecialNet electronic bulletin boards are updated daily and provide information about legislative activities, advocacy groups, new products and publications, consultants in various areas of education, and other topics. To use SpecialNet, you must have access to a terminal or a microcomputer with telephone communication capability. Annual subscriptions range from $200.00 to $1100.00, depending on the services needed. The cost of access time varies from $4.00 to $13.00 and depends upon the time of day that the system is used.

SPECIAL MATERIALS FOR THE LEARNING DISABLED

Recorded books, magazines, and other special materials are available for persons with learning disabilities that make it difficult or impossible for them to read printed material. Here is information on several such organizations. Some are free, others charge fees for their services.

Recording for the Blind, Inc. (RFB), 20 Roszel Road, Princeton, NJ 08540. Telephone: (609) 452-0606.

Recording for the Blind loans recorded educational books to people who cannot read standard printed materials because of visual, physical, or perceptual handicaps. RFB also provides recording services when a needed book is not already available. Services are free. Applications for the service are available on request. For persons with learning disabilities or dyslexia, a disability statement on the application must by signed by a physician or a learning disabilities specialist.

RFB provides recorded books on special cassettes that contain four hours of recorded text. These cassettes cannot be played on standard cassette tape machines. Special tape players can be purchased from the American Printing House for the Blind, 1839 Frankfort Avenue, Louisville, KY 40206. Telephone: (502) 895-2405. Special machines are also available on a free-loan basis for registered borrowers of the National Library Service for the Blind and Physically Handicapped (see separate listing).

A catalog listing more than 60,000 RFB titles is available for $14.00. Payment must be included with the order. Catalog supplements are sent free with each order. All RFB recorded books are provided on a one-year free loan basis. Loan renewals of up to one additional year are granted on written request. Books are sent with provision for postage-free return.

National Library Service for the Blind and Physically Handicapped, The Library of Congress, 1291 Taylor Street, N.W., Washington, DC 20542. Director: Frank Kurt Cylke. Telephone: (202) 287-5100. Toll free answering service: (800) 424-8567.

Books, magazines, and other publications on records and tapes are available through the National Library Service. More than 38,000 books and 70 magazines are currently available. The service is free for people with reading disabilities caused by an organic dysfunction or a physical handicap. The dysfunction or handicap must be certified by a physician.

Books for the program are selected on the basis of their appeal to a wide range of interests. Included are best sellers, biographies, fiction, and how-to books.

The special materials are distributed through a network of more than 160 libraries across the country. Users select from a catalog issued bimonthly. Materials requested are sent and returned by postage-free mail. Special equipment such as talking book phonographs and cassette tape players may also be borrowed.

For application forms and a list of libraries where special materials are available, contact The Library of Congress or a local library.

Books on Tape, Inc., P.O. Box 7900, Newport Beach, CA 92660. President: Duvall Y. Hecht. Toll free information number: (800) 626-3333.

Provides fiction and non-fiction books on cassette tapes for a fee. The rental period is four weeks. Tapes can be played on standard equipment.

Franklin County Special Education Cooperative, Box 440, Union, MO 63084. Director: Becky Schroeder. Media Coordinator: Angie Donahue. Telephone: (314) 583-8936.

A nonprofit organization that provides textbooks on tape to individuals, schools, and groups for a fee. A catalog listing available titles can be purchased for $2.50 plus postage and handling. A book recording service is also available.

National Information Center for the Association of Radio Reading Services, ARRS, Box 847, Lawrence, KS 66044. President: Rosie Hurwitz. Toll free information number (except Kansas): (800) 255-2777. Kansas telephone: (913) 864-4600.

Radio Reading Services broadcasts educational programming that can be received only on special closed circuit radios. Receivers are provided free of charge to persons who cannot read because of blindness, old age, or learning disability. There is no official application form—each case is judged individually. Contact the association's National Information Center for information on local availability of Radio Reading Services.

State-by-State Listings

This section contains comprehensive state-by-state listings of special programs, schools, and services for children and adults with learning disabilities. Descriptions of specific resources and services available in each state are divided into seven major categories:

1. Offices of organizations concerned with learning disabilities.
2. State department of education learning disabilities personnel.
3. Private and day schools.
4. Summer camps and programs.
5. College and university special programs and services.
6. Hospital clinics.
7. Other services.

Within each state, information on schools, summer camps, hospital clinics, and other services is listed in alphabetical order by *city*. State and national organizations and college and university programs are listed in alphabetical order by *name*.

Following are detailed descriptions of the information contained in each of the seven sections and some suggestions on how the information can be used.

Offices of Organizations Concerned with Learning Disabilities

Listed in this section are state offices and officers of national organizations. Included are state offices, branches, and chapters of ACLD, Inc., the Orton Dyslexia Society, the Council for Exceptional Children, the Easter Seal Society, and other groups concerned with learning disabilities.

The national organizations do not necessarily have offices, branches, or chapters in every state, and specific information and services available through state offices will vary widely. However, state offices and officers may be able to provide valuable information and help. Information and services available may include:

—lists of private learning disabilities diagnosticians, consultants, therapists, tutors, psychologists, and other specialists in your area.
—lists of local and area recreational and support groups for teenagers and adults with learning disabilities at local YMCA's and other community service organizations.
—legal referral services, and in some cases, advocacy and legal support.

State Department of Education Learning Disabilities Personnel

The person who supervises learning disabilities education in each state is listed. Many states now also have consultants or specialists in learning disabilities education. When this is the case, the names of these consultants or specialists are also listed. A state department of education can often provide information and materials on:

—learning disabilities, including teaching and working with learning disabled children at home.
—the rights of children with learning disabilities.
—special schools and school programs, including vocational training and college and university programs.
—due process and due process hearings.

Private and Day Schools

Federal law requires public schools to make special provisions for the education of children with learning disabilities. However, some parents choose to have their children attend private schools. This section lists private preschools, elementary, secondary, and adult schools that have specifically indicated that they offer services to students with learning disabilities. Schools are listed in alphabetical order by *city of location*.

Most of the schools listed in this Guide offer a full range of services to students with learning disabilities. This means that these schools devote a major portion of their resources to serving students with learning disabilities. Typically, a wide range of special programs, services, and facilities are available. Frequently, professional staff members at these schools are specially trained and/or certified in the area of learning disabilities.

Some schools listed have indicated that they provide only *limited* services for students with learning disabilities. This may mean that most of the students attending the school are not learning disabled. Often, these schools accept only a limited number of students with learning disabilities, accept students with mild learning disabilities, or accept students with learning disabilities only under special circumstances.

If a private school that you are interested in is not listed in this Guide, check with the school.

The private and day school listings contain a variety of useful information. The description of each school may include information on:

—preschool programs.
—summer programs offered.
—ages and grade levels served.
—current and maximum student enrollment.
—number of staff (both full and part-time).
—scholarships and financial aid available.
—special diagnostic, counseling, medical, or other services.
—special recreational activities and/or facilities available.
—special techniques, approaches, or therapies used.
—the availability of special precollege or post high school programs for high school graduates who might not be ready for college.
—the availability of special services (tutoring, diagnosis, remediation, etc.) to people not enrolled in the school.

Summer Camps and Programs

Included under this heading are recreational camps, camps with academic programs, and camps with special programs such as diagnostic clinics.

Summer camps and programs are listed in alphabetical order by *city of location*. To make it easier to contact camp personnel during the off-season, a permanent mailing address and telephone number are given for most summer camps and programs.

Some camps and programs listed are specifically for children with learning disabilities. These camps and programs offer a wide range of special programs, services, and facilities.

Many camps and programs indicate that they provide only *limited* services for children with learning disabilities. This may mean that most of the children attending the camp or program are not learning disabled. Often, these camps and programs accept only a limited number of children with learning disabilities, accept only those with mild learning disabilities, or accept children with learning disabilities only under special circumstances.

Summer camp and program descriptions generally include information on:

—camp location.
—ages and grade levels served.

—maximum enrollment.

—special services available.

—academic programs offered.

—recreational activities.

—scholarships and financial aid available.

Important Note: Summer programs run by schools, clinics, and some other organizations are *not* listed here. Check under the headings "Private and Day Schools," "Hospital Clinics," and "Other Services" for additional summer program offerings.

College and University Special Programs and Services

Colleges and universities are in alphabetical order by *name*. Each of the colleges and universities listed offers one or more of the following to students with learning disabilities:

—a special program designed *specifically* for students with learning disabilities.

—special services for handicapped students, including students with learning disabilities.

—a special center or clinic that offers services to the learning disabled.

● **Special Programs.** The symbol at left indicates a special college or university program designed *specifically* for students with learning disabilities. Special program descriptions include information on:

—admissions requirements of the college and/or the special learning disabilities program.

—special program conditions and requirements.

—the focus and content of the special program.

—special services offered.

—the name of the program director, learning disabilities specialist, or other contact person.

Centers/clinics. Some of the college and university centers and clinics listed offer services to the community. These are described as "open to the public" in this Guide. Others limit services to students attending the college or university.

Some centers and clinics specialize in learning disabilities, others are general tutoring or remedial study centers open to all students, including the learning disabled. Services offered, ages and grade levels served, and other important information is included in the description of each center or clinic. Some colleges and universities operate more than one center/clinic. Note: Center and clinic addresses are listed only when that address is different from the college or university address.

Special Services. Special services may include readers, tutoring, ombudsman, special examinations, financial aid, counseling, diagnostic testing, taped books, and other special accommodations. However, these special services are typically available to all handicapped students, not just those with learning disabilities.

When available, the total enrollment of a college or university and the number of students with learning disabilities are given.

Hospital Clinics

Hospital clinics are listed in alphabetical order by *city of location*. All of the hospital clinics listed in this Guide offer services to the learning disabled on an outpatient basis. Some also have inpatient programs. Other special programs and services for the learning disabled that may be available through the hospital clinics listed include:

—preschools.
—elementary and/or secondary schools.
—diagnostic, academic, and psychological testing.
—tutoring.
—counseling.
—speech, language, and occupational therapy.
—social services.
—recommendations for school placement.
—consultation with the child's regular school.

Other Services

A number of organizations offering services to persons with learning disabilities do not fall into any of the six previous categories. Those organizations are listed here in alphabetical order by *city of location*. These organizations include, but are not limited to:

—private clinics.
—educational centers.

—day and residential treatment centers.
—rehabilitation centers.
—mental health centers.

All of the organizations listed offer at least some services to children or adults with learning disabilities. These services may include after school tutoring, diagnostic testing, academic and psychological testing, counseling; speech, language, and occupational therapy; social services, recommendations for school placement, and consultation with a child's regular school.

Some of the organizations listed also hold workshops for parents, educators, and professionals, and in-service training for teachers.

IMPORTANT NOTE: All of the information in the **State-by-State Listings** was furnished by the organizations themselves and is provided here as a service to parents, professionals, educators, and others interested in and concerned about learning disabilities. The Foundation for Children with Learning Disabilities is not responsible for the accuracy or completeness of the information. Also, FCLD does not endorse or recommend any specific programs, schools, organizations, or services. For complete information, contact the individual organizations listed.

ALABAMA

Offices of Organizations Concerned with Learning Disabilities

ACLD, Inc.: P.O. Box 11588, Montgomery, AL 36111. President: Ginger Sewell, 3112 Baldwin Brook Drive, Montgomery, AL 36116. Telephone: (205) 288-0032.

Council for Exceptional Children: President: Thomas A. Wood, 1234 Haley Center, Auburn University, AL 36849. Telephone: (205) 826-5943.

Alabama Easter Seal Society of the Alabama Society for Crippled Children and Adults, Inc.: 2125 E. South Boulevard, P.O. Box 6130, Montgomery, AL 36194-0001. Executive Vice President: Charles T. Higgins. Telephone: (205) 288-8382.

State Department of Education Learning Disabilities Personnel

Anne Ramsey, Coordinator, Program for Exceptional Children and Youth, State Department of Education, 868 State Office Building, Montgomery, AL 36130. Telephone: (205) 261-5099.

Private and Day Schools

Huntsville: Huntsville Achievement School, 600 Governors Drive, S.W., 35801. Telephone: (205) 539-1772. Director: Beverly Branson. Preschool and elementary day school with summer program. Ages served: 2-16. Grades served: ungraded. Current enrollment: 46. Maximum enrollment: 50. Full-time staff: 7. Part-time staff: 2. Limited scholarships/financial aid available. Services: individual and group tutoring, academic testing, occupational therapy, adaptive physical education. Notes: Serves many handicaps including Down's Syndrome, cerebral palsy, autism, and learning disabilities.

Summer Camps and Programs

Montgomery: Camp Ikhananchi, P.O. Box 11588, 36111. Telephone: (205) 272-3184. Camp Director: Peggy H. Dorminey. Day camp with academic program. Ages served: 5-15. Grades served: kindergarten-8. Maximum enrollment: 70. Full-time staff: 10. Scholarships/financial aid available. Services: individual and group tutoring, academic and psychological counseling, adaptive physical education, parenting seminar. Academic programs: math, reading, English, spelling, study skills. Recreation: swimming, field trips, crafts, limited team athletics, individual gross motor programs.

College and University Special Programs and Services

Alabama A & M University: Normal, AL 35762. LD students: 35. Special services: individual tutoring, academic counseling, diagnostic testing; special pro-

ALABAMA

gram scheduled for implementation September, 1985. Contact: A. Grace Robinson, Coordinator of Learning Disabilities. Telephone: (205) 859-7368.

Auburn University: Auburn, AL 36849. Total enrollment: 18,500. LD students: 50. Special services: diagnostic testing, support group, training in study skills, readers, ombudsman. Contact: Debora L. Liddell, Coordinator of Special Programs. Telephone: (205) 826-2353.

Center/clinic: Learning Disabilities Summer Clinic, 1234 Haley Center. Telephone: (205) 826-5943. Director: Craig Darch. Open to public. Grades served: 1-12.

University of Alabama: University, AL 35486. Total enrollment: 16,000. Special services: individual tutoring, academic and career counseling, training in study skills, readers. Contact: Tom Strong, Director of Student Services. Telephone: (205) 348-6794.

University of Alabama-Huntsville: P.O. Box 1247, Huntsville, AL 35899. Total enrollment: 6,000. Special services: individual tutoring, academic counseling, diagnostic testing, training in study skills. Contact: Rhoda E. Wharry, Professor of Developmental Learning. Telephone: (205) 895-6220.

University of Montevallo: Montevallo, AL 35115. Special services: individual and group tutoring, training in study skills, academic counseling, limited taped books. Notes: Serves only enrolled low income college students who have been previously diagnosed. Contact: Elaine Elledge, Project Director, Special Services. Telephone: (205) 665-2521 ext. 308.

Other Services

Montgomery: Montgomery Dyslexia Research Foundation, Inc., 2229 Allendale Road, 36111. Telephone: (205) 265-2840. Director: Joan Barker. Clinic. After school and Saturday morning program; summer session. Ages served: 5 and up. Services: diagnostic testing, academic and psychological testing, individual tutoring, academic and parent counseling.

ALASKA

Offices of Organizations Concerned with Learning Disabilities

ACLD, Inc.: 7030 Dickerson, Anchorage, AK 99504. Contact: Jane Gallant. Telephone: Office (907) 337-1538; Home (907) 333-8139.

The Easter Seal Society of Alaska: 620 E. Tenth Street, Suite 203, Anchorage, AK 99501. Executive Director: Marion Bowles. Telephone: (907) 277-2451.

Orton Dyslexia Society (Puget Sound Branch): 1922 Richmond Beach Drive, N.W., Seattle, WA 98177. President: Lucille Pridemore. Telephone: Office (206) 743-3513; Home (206) 542-1434.

State Department of Education Learning Disabilities Personnel

William Mulnix, Administrator, Office for Special Services, Division of Educational Program Support, Department of Education, Pouch F, Juneau, AK 99811. Telephone: (907) 465-2970. Learning disabilities consultant: Sherman Welch.

College and University Special Programs and Services

Islands Community College: 1101 Sawmill Creek Boulevard, Sitka, AK 99835. Special services: individual and group tutoring, training in study skills, academic and psychological counseling, student resource center, readers, diagnostic testing, ombudsman at the state level. Contact: Burton Augst, Director of Student Services. Telephone: (907) 747-6653.

Center/clinic: Islands Community College Resource Center and Sitka Adult Education Program. Telephone: (907) 747-6542. Adult Education Coordinator: Teresa Holt. Open to public. Ages served: 16 and up. Notes: Must not be enrolled in public school.

University of Alaska-Anchorage: Anchorage, AK 99508. Special services: recommendations for individual tutoring, academic advisement, liaison with faculty. Contact: Marilyn Kay Johnson, Chairperson, Special Education Program. Telephone: (907) 786-1771.

Hospital Clinics

Fort Wainwright: Bassett Army Community Hospital, Pediatric Clinic, 99703. Telephone: (907) 353-5151. Contact: Gregory H. Cain, Chief, Pediatric SVC. Outpatient program. Ages served: birth-18. Services: limited diagnostic testing, basic history and physical examination, referral to appropriate community resources.

ARIZONA

Offices of Organizations Concerned with Learning Disabilities

ACLD, Inc.: P.O. Box 15525, Phoenix, AZ 85060. Telephone: (602) 840-3192. President: Kaaren Morehart.

Council for Exceptional Children: President: Mada Kay Morehead, 221 East Drive, Tempe, AZ 85282. Telephone: (602) 967-7038.

ARIZONA

Easter Seal Society for Disabled Children and Adults of Arizona, Inc.: 903 N. Second Street, Phoenix, AZ 85004. Executive Director: Gene Brantner. Telephone: (602) 252-6061.

State Department of Education Learning Disabilities Personnel

Chuck Essigs, Deputy Associate Superintendent, Special Education, Department of Education, 1535 W. Jefferson, Phoenix, AZ 85007. Telephone: (602) 255-3183.

Private and Day Schools

Casa Grande: Villa-Oasis School, P.O. Box 1218, 85222. Telephone: (602) 466-9226. Associate Director: Jeanette Steinbeck. Secondary boarding school with limited services. Ages served: 12-18. Grades served: 7-12. Current enrollment: 90. Maximum enrollment: 90. Full-time staff: 25. Part-time staff: 4. Scholarships/financial aid available. Services: individual and group tutoring, academic counseling, standard academic program. Recreation: sports, camping, field trips.

Phoenix: ABCS Little Canyon School, 3115 W. Missouri, P.O. Box 27128, 85061. Telephone: (602) 973-8131. Director: Phyllis F. McFarland. Elementary and secondary boarding school with summer program. Ages served: 10-18. Grades served: kindergarten-12. Current enrollment: 24. Maximum enrollment: 24. Full-time staff: 35. Part-time staff: 2. Services: individual and group tutoring, academic and psychological testing; academic, psychological, and family counseling; adaptive physical education, work-study, medical services, psychiatric evaluation. Recreation: softball, soccer, volleyball, basketball, swimming, league football and baseball.

Phoenix: Gompers Rehabilitation Center, 7211 N. Seventh Street, 85201. Telephone: (602) 943-3484. Executive Director: H. Bradley Berkeland. Preschool, elementary, and secondary day school with limited services; summer program. Ages served: 3-22. Grades served: preschool-12. Current enrollment: 60. Maximum enrollment: 80. Full-time staff: 22. Part-time staff: 7. Services: academic and psychological testing, psychological counseling, physical and occupational therapy, adaptive physical education, vocational training, medical services; music, speech, and language therapy. Recreation: bowling, swimming, camping, biking. Notes: Most children enrolled have handicaps other than learning disabilities. Preschool does include developmentally delayed children.

Phoenix: Jane Wayland Center, 2613 W. Campbell Road, 85017. Telephone: (602) 246-4564. Program Director, Residential/Special Education: Richard E. Geasland. Elementary and secondary day and boarding school with limited services; summer program. Ages served: 6-21. Grades served: 1-12. Current enrollment: 32. Maximum enrollment: 36. Full-time staff: 25. Part-time staff: 5. Services: individual and group tutoring, academic and psychological testing; academic, psychological, and family counseling; individual, group, and family therapy; limited work-study, medical services. Recreation: athletic field; city park used for softball, tennis, and other activities. Notes: Primary diagnosis of all students is emotionally handicapped; many are also learning disabled.

Phoenix: The New Foundation School, P.O. Box 8500, 85066. Telephone: (602) 268-3421. Director/Principal: David Hedgcock. Elementary and secondary day school with summer program. Ages served: 13-18. Grades served: ungraded. Current enrollment: 26. Maximum enrollment: 26. Full-time staff: 27. Part-time staff: 1. Services: individual and group tutoring, academic and psychological testing; academic, psychological, and family counseling; adaptive physical education, work-study, medical services, reality group, psychodrama. Recreation: softball, volleyball, football, basketball.

Prescott: Primavera School, 1410 Copper Basin Road, 86301. Telephone: (602) 445-5382. Head of School: William C. Fletcher. Preschool and elementary day school with limited services; summer camp. Ages served: 2½-12. Grades served: preschool-6. Current enrollment: 90. Maximum enrollment: 90. Full-time staff: 8. Part-time staff: 3. Scholarships/financial aid available. Services: individual and group tutoring, academic and psychological testing; academic, psychological, and family counseling; individualized program. Recreation: gymnastics, swimming, creative movement, New Games, sports. Notes: Accepts a limited number of learning disabled students, depending primarily on the school's ability to meet their needs.

Rimrock: Southwestern Academy, Beaver Creek Ranch Campus, 86335. Telephone: (602) 567-4581. Headmaster: Kenneth R. Veronda. Elementary and secondary day and boarding school with limited services. Ages served: 6-18. Grades served: 1-12. Current enrollment: 26. Maximum enrollment: 26. Full-time staff: 7. Part-time staff: 4. Scholarships/financial aid available. Services: individual tutoring, academic and psychological testing, academic and psychological counseling; ability-grouped classes limited to 12 students. Recreation: interscholastic and intramural athletics, outdoor activities. Notes: Geared for the able but lower-achieving student. All admissions handled through California branch: 2800 Monterey Road, San Marino, CA 91108. Telephone: (818) 799-5010.

Scottsdale: New Way School, 4140 N. Miller Road, P.O. Box 1481, 85252. Telephone: (602) 946-9112. Executive Director: Jeanette Bowling. Elementary and secondary day school. Ages served: 5-18. Grades served: kindergarten-12. Current enrollment: 40. Maximum enrollment: 40. Full-time staff: 12. Part-time staff: 2. Scholarships/financial aid available. Services: individual and group tutoring, academic and psychological testing, psychological counseling, adaptive physical education, Orton-Gillingham alphabetic phonics reading program, individualized education plans.

Tucson: Fisher Foundation School, 3499 N. Campbell, Suite 909, 85719. Telephone: (602) 325-5263. Director: Barbara Herman. Elementary day school. Ages served: 7-15. Grades served: 2-8. Current enrollment: 24. Maximum enrollment: 40. Full-time staff: 4. Limited scholarships/financial aid available. Services: individual tutoring, academic testing, emphasis on language arts, classroom adaptation of the Orton-Gillingham multisensory technique, tutoring and testing services for all ages are available to the community. Recreation: daily structured physical activities. Notes: Specifically for children with dyslexia.

West Sedona: Oak Creek Ranch School, P.O. Box NN, 86340. Telephone: (602) 634-5571. Director: David Wick. Elementary and secondary boarding school with limited services; summer program and camp. Ages served: 10-18. Grades served: 5-12. Current enrollment: 100. Maximum enrollment: 125. Full-time staff: 12. Part-time staff: 2. Services: individual and group tutoring, academic and psychological testing, academic and psychological counseling, medical services. Recreation: riding, swimming, fishing, tennis, golf, volleyball, soccer, basketball, field trips.

College and University Special Programs and Services

Arizona State University: Tempe, AZ 85287. Total enrollment: 40,000. LD students: 110. Special services: individual tutoring; training in study, personal, and social skills; academic, psychological, and career counseling; diagnostic testing, special examinations, readers, taped books, computer-assisted instruction, support group, ombudsman, limited scholarships. Contact: Ann Rispoli, Coordinator, Learning Disabilities Services. Telephone: (602) 965-1234.

Mesa Community College: 1833 W. Southern Avenue, Mesa, AZ 85202. Total enrollment: 14,915. Special services: individual tutoring, training in study skills, academic counseling, readers, Kurzweil Reading Machine. Contact: Judith F. Taussig, Director, Student Special Services. Telephone: (602) 833-1261 ext. 333.

Northern Arizona University: Flagstaff, AZ 86011. Total enrollment: 12,000. LD students: 50. Special services: counseling center, individual and group tutoring, academic and psychological counseling, diagnostic testing, training in study skills, student resource center. Contact: Linda Price, Coordinator of Services for the Handicapped. Telephone: (602) 523-2261.

Pima Community College: 2202 W. Anklam Road, Tucson, AZ 85709. Total enrollment: 20,000. LD students: 50. Special services: individual tutoring, training in study skills, academic counseling, taped books, special examinations, student resource center, readers, diagnostic testing, ombudsman. Contact: Lydia Maurer, Special Services Advisor. Telephone: (602) 884-6688. Or Cheryl Cheney-Hipskind, Special Services Advisor. Telephone: (602) 884-6562.

Scottsdale Community College: 9000 E. Chaparral Road, Scottsdale, AZ 85253. Total enrollment: 7,000. LD students: 10. Special services: individual tutoring, training in study skills, academic counseling, taped books, readers, learning assistance center. Contact: Dolores Duggan, Program Advisor, Disabled Student Services. Telephone: (602) 941-0999 ext. 274.

University of Arizona: Old Main 200, Tucson, AZ 85719. Total enrollment: 30,000. LD students: 200. Special services: group tutoring, training in study skills; preadmission, academic, career, and psychological counseling; taped books, special examinations, student resource center, diagnostic testing, ombudsman, support group.

- **Special program:** SALT (Special Academic Learning Techniques). Offers special courses in study and organizational skills, work habits; strategies and compensation techniques, computer learning. Three semesters of English required for all LD students. May take longer than four years to complete degree. Must meet regular and special admissions requirements of the university. Special requirements include: interview, recommendations, psychoeducational evaluation taken in the last five years. Full or part-time students are eligible for the program. Coordinator: Eleanor Harner. Telephone: (602) 621-1171.

Center/clinic: Academic Learning Skills Center, Student Resource Center. Telephone: (602) 621-1171. Director: Eleanor Harner. Not open to public. Ages served: 17 and up. Grades served: freshmen-postgraduate.

Hospital Clinics

Mesa: Mesa Lutheran Hospital, Speech Pathology Department, 525 W. Brown Road, 85204. Telephone: (602) 834-1211. Contact: Sandra M. Row, Manager. Outpatient, inpatient, and after school program. Services: diagnostic testing, parent counseling, speech and language therapy.

Phoenix: Phoenix Children's Hospital, Child Development Center, 1122 E. Culver, 85006. Telephone: (602) 239-4225. Contact: Raun D. Melned. Outpatient and day program. Ages served: newborn-adolescence. Services: School for Learning Disabilities (ages 2-8); Developmental Preschool for children with speech and language problems and/or mild cognitive delays; diagnostic testing, academic and psychological testing, psychological and parent counseling; speech, language, physical, and occupational therapy; diagnostic programs for school-age and preschool youngsters. Notes: Children are seen by individual specialists or a multidisciplinary team.

Other Services

Phoenix: Center for Neurodevelopmental Studies, Inc., 8621 N. Third Street, Suite A, 85020. Telephone: (602) 956-4214. President: Lorna Jean King. Clinic. Day and after school program. Ages served: preschool-young adult. Services: diagnostic testing, parent counseling; speech, language, physical, and occupational therapy; social services, vocational counseling and referral, socialization groups for adolescents and young adults.

ARIZONA

Prescott: Prescott Child Development Center, 710 Whipple Street, 86301. Telephone: (602) 778-1840. Director: Richard A. Parry. Development center. Ages served: all. Services: individual and group tutoring, academic and psychological testing; academic, psychological, and family counseling.

Tucson: Cerebral Palsy Foundation of Southern Arizona, 3825 E. Second Street, 85716. Telephone: (602) 325-1517. Executive Director: Ema Kammeyer. Preschool, adult, and summer program. Ages served: birth-5, adults. Current enrollment: 40 children; 100 adults. Full-time staff: 15. Scholarships/financial aid available. Services: individual and group tutoring, physical and occupational therapy, adaptive physical education, vocational training, job placement, registered nurse on staff; speech, language, and swim therapy. Recreation: bowling and swimming for adults.

Tucson: Computer Learning Resources, 4750 N. Oracle Road, 85705. Telephone: (602) 888-1910. Director: Gerald M. Senf. Clinic. Day and after school program. Services: diagnostic testing, academic and psychological testing, individual and group tutoring; academic, psychological, and parent counseling; cognitive rehabilitation, neurometric evaluation, computer experience including full literacy program, computer-based SAT preparation.

ARKANSAS

Offices of Organizations Concerned with Learning Disabilities

ACLD, Inc.: P.O. Box 7316, Little Rock, AR 72217. Telephone: (501) 666-8777. President: Mrs. Pat Perry. Executive Director: Ms. Maybian Sloan.

Council for Exceptional Children: President: Barbara Semrau, 2905 King Street, Jonesboro, AR 72401. Telephone: (501) 935-2750.

Arkansas Easter Seal Society: 2801 Lee Avenue, P.O. Box 5148, Little Rock, AR 72225. Executive Director: James Butler. Telephone: (501) 663-8331.

State Department of Education Learning Disabilities Personnel

Diane Sydoriak, Coordinator, Special Education Section, State Education Building C, Room 105, Little Rock, AR 72201. Telephone: (501) 371-2161.

Private and Day Schools

Jacksonville: Pathfinder School, P.O. Box 338, 72076. Telephone: (501) 982-0528. Executive Director: Joe Flaherty. Preschool and adult day school. Ages served: 6 weeks-21 years. Grades served: ungraded. Current enrollment: 180. Maximum enrollment: 200. Full-time staff: 55. Part-time staff: 20. Services: individual and group tutoring, psychological testing, psychological and family counseling; physical, speech, and occupational therapy; vocational training, job placement, residential training. Recreation: Special Olympics, park for handicapped.

Little Rock: Archild, Inc., 5312 W. Tenth, 72204. Telephone: (501) 666-2484. Administrator: Dolly Moseley. Preschool. Ages served: 12 months-6. Current enrollment: 30. Maximum enrollment: 30. Full-time staff: 8. Part-time staff: 4. Services: individual and group tutoring, academic and psychological testing, family counseling, physical and speech therapy, limited transportation, before and after school care. Recreation: large playground facilities, adaptive aquatics. Notes: Serves the developmentally delayed.

McGehee: C.B. King Memorial School, S. First Street, P.O. Box 1051, 71654. Telephone: (501) 222-6211. Director: Peggy Hood. Preschool and adult day school with summer program. Ages served: 2-5, 18 and up. Current enrollment: 26 preschool; 26 adults. Maximum enrollment: 52. Full-time staff: 15. Part-time staff: 1. Scholarships/financial aid available. Services: individual and group tutoring, academic and psychological testing, occupational therapy, adaptive physical education, work-study, medical services, transportation, breakfast, hot lunches. Recreation: Special Olympics, music festival, swimming, outings.

North Little Rock: North Hills Services for the Handicapped, Inc., 6900 N. Hills Boulevard, 72116. Telephone: (501) 835-9607. Executive Director: Brian F. Poole. Preschool and adult day school. Ages served: birth-5; 18 and up. Current enrollment: 66. Maximum enrollment: 66. Full-time staff: 17. Part-time staff: 3. Scholarships/financial aid available. Services: individual and group tutoring, academic and psychological testing, psychological and family counseling, occupational therapy, vocational training, job placement. Recreation: weekly field trips including trips to zoo for preschoolers and swimming, movies, arts center for adults.

Salem: Helping Hands School, Box 816, 72576. Telephone: (501) 994-2151. Director: Jennie Lee Stobaugh. Preschool, elementary, secondary, and adult day school with summer program. Ages served: birth-adult. Grades served: ungraded. Current enrollment: 45. Maximum enrollment: 48. Full-time staff: 11. Part-time staff: 1. Scholarships/financial aid available. Services: individual and group tutoring, academic and psychological testing; academic, psychological and family counseling; parent training, physical and occupational therapy, adaptive physical education, vocational training, work-study, job placement, transportation, food service, medical services. Recreation: bowling, swimming.

College and University Special Programs and Services

Arkansas State University: State University, AR 72467. Total enrollment: 8,300. Special services: psychological counseling, diagnostic testing, training in study skills. Contact: Peggy Harrison. Telephone: (501) 972-3106.

Center/clinic: Arkansas State University Clinical Services, P.O. Box 940. Directors: Robert Abbott, psychology; George Herndon, speech pathology; Baron Conaway, reading. Open to public. Telephone: (501) 972-3106. Grades served: kindergarten-adult.

College of the Ozarks: 415 College Avenue, Clarksville, AR 72830. Total enrollment: 700. LD students: 54. Special services: individual and group tutoring; training in reading, writing, and study skills; academic counseling, taped books, special examinations, student resource center, diagnostic testing, scholarships, personal program coordinator.

- **Special program:** Ben B. Caudle Special Learning Center Program. Offers four-phase program of specialized instruction. Number of regular credit hours for which a student is enrolled depends on the specialized skills instruction needed. No minimum number of regular credit hours required to be considered full-time. A complete psychoeducational evaluation by the learning center staff required of all applicants. Director: Betty S. Robinson. Telephone: (501) 754-3839 ext. 421.

University of Arkansas: Fayetteville, AR 72701. Total enrollment: 14,000. LD students: 50. Special services: testing, readers, tutors, academic counseling, vocational counseling and placement, support group. Contact: Jim Hemauer, Program Coordinator, Disabled Student Resource Center. Telephone: (501) 575-5018.

University of Arkansas for Medical Sciences: 4301 W. Markham, Little Rock, AR 72205.

Center/clinic: The Child Study Center. Telephone: (501) 661-5800. Director: John E. Peters. Open to public. Services: diagnostic evaluation, tutoring, treatment, consultations, workshops, lectures, inpatient psychiatric unit, college and vocational planning, adult counseling. Ages served: 3 and up.

University of Central Arkansas: Conway, AR 72032. Special services: training in study skills, academic and psychological counseling. Contact: David Naylor, Chairman, Special Education Department. Telephone: (501) 450-3172.

Center/clinic: UCA Special Education Summer Clinic, Box L. Telephone: (501) 450-3172. Director: Shirley K. Henderson. Open to public. Services: small group teaching for school-age mildly handicapped children. Ages served: 5-16. Grades served: kindergarten-9.

Hospital Clinics

Little Rock: Arkansas Children's Hospital, Developmental Center, 804 Wolfe, 72201. Telephone: (501) 370-1830. Contact: Carolyn Young, Clinic Manager. Outpatient program. Ages served: birth-18. Services: diagnostic testing, academic and psychological testing, psychological and parent counseling, speech and language therapy, social services. Notes: Offers multidisciplinary diagnostic evaluations and therapeutic services for children who have a variety of developmental disabilities including learning disabilities, behavioral and emotional problems, and developmental delays.

CALIFORNIA

Offices of Organizations Concerned with Learning Disabilities

CANHC-ACLD: P.O. Box 61067, Sacramento, CA 95860. Telephone: (415) 234-5669. President: Arlene Davis.

Council for Exceptional Children: President: Harry Schmoll, Jr., 6025 DePalma Street, South Gate, CA 90280. Telephone: Office (213) 742-7565; Home (213) 928-8035.

Easter Seal Society of California: 742 Market Street, Suite 202, San Francisco, CA 94102. Executive Director: William R. Barrett. Telephone: (415) 391-2006.

Orton Dyslexia Society (Inland Empire Branch): Box 56, Blue Jay, CA 92317. President: Gloria DeMent.

Orton Dyslexia Society (Los Angeles County Branch): Box 5358, Sherman Oaks, CA 91413. President: Clarann J. Goldring. Telephone: (818) 784-4380.

Orton Dyslexia Society (Northern California Branch): P.O. Box 370115, Montara, CA 94037. President: Lee Anne King. Telephone: (415) 328-7667.

Orton Dyslexia Society (Orange County Branch): P.O. Box 4263, Irvine, CA 92716. President: Joan McNichols. Telephone: (714) 731-5223.

Orton Dyslexia Society (San Diego Branch): 550 Berland Way, Chula Vista, CA 92010. President: Thomas Mautner. Telephone: (619) 421-3855.

Orton Dyslexia Society (Tri-County Branch): P.O. Box 30484, Santa Barbara, CA 93130. President: Janet Shapiro. Telephone: Branch (805) 687-3711; Office (805) 965-0581 ext. 374.

State Department of Education Learning Disabilities Personnel

Robert Y. Fuchigami, Acting Director, State Department of Education, 721 Capitol Mall, Room 614, Sacramento, CA 95814. Telephone: (916) 445-4036. Director, Personnel Development Unit: Karl Murray. Telephone: (916) 322-3148.

Private and Day Schools

Alameda: Spectrum Center for Educational and Behavioral Development, Inc., 1910 Central Avenue, 94501. Telephone: (415) 522-0445. Agency Director: Robert Pilon. Preschool, elementary, secondary, and adult day school with summer program. Ages served: 3-21. Current enrollment: 50. Full-time staff: 25. Services: individual and group tutoring, academic and psychological testing; academic, psychological, and family counseling; physical and occupational therapy, adaptive physical education, vocational training, work-study, job placement. Notes: School uses behavior management techniques in humanistic setting.

Alhambra: Almansor Education Center, 9½ N. Almansor Street, 91801. Telephone: (818) 282-9131. Executive Director: Nancy Lavelle. Preschool, elementary, secondary, and adult day school with summer program. Ages served: 2-adult. Current enrollment: 72. Maximum enrollment: 72. Full-time staff: 28. Part-time staff: 1. Scholarships/financial aid available. Services: individual and group tutoring, academic and psychological testing; academic, psychological, and family counseling; speech and language therapy, adaptive physical education, vocational training, work-study, job placement. Recreation: after school and adult recreation programs, sports.

Altadena: ESCALON, 536 E. Mendocino Street, 91001. Telephone: (818) 798-0744. Director of Education: Elaine Sleeper. Elementary and secondary day school with summer program. Ages served: 4-22. Grades served: kindergarten-12. Current enrollment: 45. Maximum enrollment: 125. Full-time staff: 13. Scholarships/financial aid available. Services: individual and group tutoring, academic and psychological testing, psychological and family counseling, speech therapy, vocational training. Recreation: swimming, field trips.

Belmont: The Charles Armstrong School, 1405 Solana Drive, 94002. Telephone: (415) 592-7570 or 592-7571. Executive Director: Carol Murray. Elementary and secondary day school with summer program. Ages served: 6-adult. Grades served: 1-12. Current enrollment: 174. Maximum enrollment: 250. Full-time staff: 33. Part-time staff: 10. Scholarships/financial aid available. Services: individual and group tutoring, academic testing and counseling, Slingerland and Malcomesius screening tests for identifying specific language disabilities. Recreation: daily physical education. Notes: Tutoring for individuals of all ages not enrolled in school.

Berkeley: The Growing Mind School, 930 Dwight Way, 94710. Telephone: (415) 548-5670. Director: Hank Tavera. Elementary day school with group homes and summer program. Ages served: 8-17. Grades served: ungraded. Current enrollment: 29. Maximum enrollment: 50. Full-time staff: 15. Part-time staff: 13. Services: individual and group tutoring, academic and psychological testing, vocational training, work-study, job placement; art, group, and occupational therapy; physical education, individual and family counseling, structured behavior management system. Recreation: community facilities, field trips.

Buena Park: Speech and Language Development Center, 8699 Holder Street, 90620. Telephone: (714) 821-3620. Director: Aleen Agranowitz. Preschool, elementary, and secondary day and boarding school with summer program and camp. Ages served: 1½-21. Grades served: preschool-12. Current enrollment: 150. Maximum enrollment: 200. Full-time staff: 63. Part-time staff: 59. Scholarships/financial aid available. Recreation: swimming, roller skating, ice skating, bowling, field trips. Services: individual and group tutoring, academic and psychological testing; academic, psychological, and family counseling; occupational and vision therapy, adaptive physical education, vocational training, medical services, speech/language therapy and testing, audiological and vision screening, auditory training.

Calabasas: The Calabasas Academy, 25000 W. Mureau Road, 91302. Telephone: (818) 703-8383. Executive Director: Richard Kritzer. Elementary and secondary day and boarding school with summer program. Ages served: 10-17. Grades served: 4-12. Current enrollment: 25. Maximum enrollment: 35. Full-time staff: 6. Part-time staff: 20. Services: individual and group tutoring, academic and psychological testing; academic, psychological, and family counseling; computer. Recreation: sports, movies, video games.

Calistoga: The Heritage School, 295 Franz Valley School Road, P.O. Box 528, 94515. Telephone: (707) 942-5133. Headmaster: Ronald H. Whitney. Elementary and secondary boarding school with limited services. Ages served: 8-15. Maximum enrollment: 58. Full-time staff: 12. Part-time staff: 6. Services: individual and group tutoring, academic and psychological testing, academic and psychological counseling, adaptive physical education. Recreation: tennis, skiing, football, softball, basketball, soccer, weight lifting, track and field.

Canoga Park: West Valley Center for Educational Therapy, 7041 Owensmouth Avenue, 91303. Telephone: (818) 883-3500. Executive Director: Claude E. Hill, III. Elementary school with summer program. Ages served: 5-15. Grades served: 1-junior high. Current enrollment: 45. Maximum enrollment: 60. Full-time staff: 16. Part-time staff: 7. Scholarships/financial aid available. Services: individual tutoring, academic and psychological testing, psychological and family counseling, adaptive physical education, speech evaluation and therapy, computer instruction. Recreation: physical education, sports, arts and crafts.

Carmel: Sabin-McEwen Learning Institute, Inc., P.O. Box 22292, 93922. Telephone: (408) 624-0609. Director: Gertrude J. McEwen. Elementary day school with summer program. Ages served: 4 and up. Grades served: 2-8. Current enrollment: 6. Maximum enrollment: 12. Full-time staff: 3. Part-time staff: 5. Scholarships/financial aid available. Services: individual and group tutoring, academic and psychological testing, academic and family counseling, adaptive physical education, work-study; tutoring and educational therapy for individuals not enrolled in school.

Corona: Saint Edward School, 500 Merrill Street, 91720. Telephone: (714) 737-2530. Principal: Sr. Ann McSweeney. Elementary day school with limited services. Ages served: 5-15. Grades served: kindergarten-8. Current enrollment: 396. Maximum enrollment: 420. Full-time staff: 18. Part-time staff: 15. Scholarships/financial aid available. Services: individual tutoring, academic and psychological testing, academic counseling. Recreation: sports.

CALIFORNIA

Costa Mesa: Mardan Center of Educational Therapy, 695 W. 19th Street, 92627. Telephone: (714) 631-6400. Executive Director: David A. Eisenman. Preschool, elementary, secondary, and adult day school with summer program. Ages served: 2-25. Current enrollment: 65. Maximum enrollment: 95. Full-time staff: 22. Part-time staff: 8. Scholarships/financial aid available. Services: individual and group tutoring, academic and psychological testing; academic, psychological, and family counseling; adaptive physical education, vocational training, job placement, independent living skills. Recreation: sports.

Culver City: Cheryl Louise Educational Center, 3841 Motor Avenue, 90232. Telephone: (213) 839-4778. Owner/Principal: Mary Louise Crouch. Preschool and elementary day school with summer program. Ages served: 3-15. Grades served: kindergarten-9. Current enrollment: 75. Maximum enrollment: 101. Full-time staff: 6. Part-time staff: 2. Services: individual tutoring, academic and psychological testing, psychological counseling, physical therapy. Recreation: swimming, dance, singing, arts and crafts.

Culver City: Landmark West School, 11450 Port Road, 90230. Telephone: (213) 390-6282. Headmaster: David R. Drake. Elementary and secondary day school with summer program. Ages served: 8-18. Grades served: 3-12. Current enrollment: 80. Maximum enrollment: 110. Full-time staff: 35. Part-time staff: 2. Scholarships/financial aid available. Services: daily individual tutoring, group tutoring, academic testing and counseling, medical services. Recreation: auditorium, playing field, neighborhood park, field trips to cultural and sports events. Notes: Accepts only average and above average, emotionally sound youngsters having difficulty in regular classrooms.

Encinitas: Rancho Del Mar School, 655 Westlake Drive, 92024. Telephone: (619) 753-5044. Director: Claudia MacDorman. Males only secondary boarding school with summer program. Ages served: 16 and up. Grades served: ungraded. Current enrollment: 12. Maximum enrollment: 14. Full-time staff: 3. Part-time staff: 3. Scholarships/financial aid available. Services: individual and group tutoring, academic and psychological testing, academic and psychological counseling, adaptive physical education, vocational training, work-study, remedial education. Recreation: kickball, baseball games; trips to Disneyland, Universal Studios, Palm Springs, Catalina Island.

Fremont: The Charles Armstrong School, 5301 Curtis Street, 94538. Telephone: (415) 651-2782. Director: Carol Murray. Elementary and secondary day school with summer program. Ages served: 6-14. Grades served: 1-8. Current enrollment: 51. Maximum enrollment: 60. Full-time staff: 6. Part-time staff: 2. Scholarships/financial aid available. Services: individual and group tutoring, academic testing and counseling, adaptive physical education, Slingerland screenings; part-time speech and language pathologist. Notes: Serves children with specific language disabilities.

French Gulch: Pine Meadows School, P.O. Box 5C, 96033. Telephone: (916) 359-2211. Executive Director: David W. Hull. Secondary boarding school with summer program. Ages served: 12-18. Grades served: ungraded. Current enrollment: 24. Maximum enrollment: 31. Full-time staff: 24. Part-time staff: 5. Services: individual tutoring, academic and psychological testing; academic, psychological, group, and family counseling; occupational therapy, adaptive physical education, vocational training, work-study, farming, ranching. Recreation: sports, fishing, swimming, camping, outdoor education and survival, skiing, white water rafting, riding. Notes: Serves learning handicapped students with accompanying behavioral and emotional difficulties.

Fresno: Laboratory School of Natural Sciences, 3774 W. Belmont, 93711. Telephone: (209) 275-3328. Owner/Administrator: Nina Hamm. Elementary and secondary day and boarding school. Ages served: 5-18. Grades served: kindergarten-12. Current enrollment: 70. Full-time staff: 9. Part-time staff: 2. Services: academic and psychological testing, academic and psychological counseling, vocational training.

Garden Grove: Center for Education, 13321 Garden Grove Boulevard, Suite D, 92643. Telephone: (714) 971-5071. Directors: Charlene and Peter Wilhovsky. Elementary and secondary day school with summer program. Ages served: 6-19. Grades served: 1-12. Current enrollment: 30. Maximum enrollment: 49. Full-time staff: 9. Part-time staff: 3. Scholarships/financial aid available. Services: individual and group tutoring, academic and psychological testing; academic, psychological, and family counseling; work-study; tutoring for individuals ages 4 and up not enrolled in school. Recreation: off-campus facilities, YMCA, local parks.

Garden Grove: Rossier Educational and Assessment Center, 11602 Steele Drive, 92640. Telephone: (714) 638-0405. Director: Barbara J. Rossier. Elementary and secondary day school with summer program. Ages served: 6-21. Grades served: 1-12. Current enrollment: 90. Maximum enrollment: 125. Full-time staff: 45. Services: academic and psychological testing; academic, psychological, and family counseling; adaptive physical education, vocational training, work-study, job placement, speech and language therapy. Notes: Serves students with academic, social, and emotional delays.

Garden Grove: Young Horizons, 6202 Cerulean Avenue, 92645. Telephone: (714) 891-0110 or (213) 598-0887. Director: Joseph Mancuso. Elementary and secondary day school with summer program and camp. Ages served: 10-18. Grades served: 6-12. Current enrollment: 35. Maximum enrollment: no limit. Full-time staff: 10. Services: academic and psychological testing; academic, psychological, and family counseling; vocational training, work-study, psychiatric medical services.

Hawthorne: Canyon Verde School, 12501 S. Isis Avenue, 90250. Telephone: (213) 643-8123. Director: Frank H. Langdon. Day school with summer program and camp. Ages served: 6-21. Grades served: ungraded. Current enrollment: 60. Maximum enrollment: 65. Full-time staff: 24. Part-time staff: 5. Services: individual and group tutoring, academic and psychological testing, vocational training; individual, group, and nutrition counseling; educational, speech, and language therapy; adaptive physical education, assertive discipline. Recreation: sports including football, basketball, baseball, swimming. Located next to large park/sports complex.

Hawthorne: Rainbow Bridge Center, 5433 W. 138th Street, 90250. Telephone: (213) 643-5029. Program Director: Patrick J. Croker. Elementary and secondary day school with limited services; summer program. Ages served: 6-21. Current enrollment: 50. Maximum enrollment: 60. Full-time staff: 22. Part-time staff: 3. Services: academic and psychological testing, psychological counseling, adaptive physical education. Recreation: camping, fishing trips, swimming, physical education.

Hillsborough: Nueva Learning Center, 6565 Skyline Boulevard, 94010. Telephone: (415) 348-2272. Director: Anabel L. Jensen. Preschool and elementary day school with summer program. Ages served: 4-12. Grades served: prekindergarten-6. Current enrollment: 232. Maximum enrollment: 238. Full-time staff: 21. Part-time staff: 6. Scholarships/financial aid available. Services: individual and group tutoring, academic and psychological testing, psychological counseling, individualized curriculum. Recreation: physical education.

Kentfield: The CHILD Center, P.O. Box 144, 94914. Telephone: (415) 456-0440. Administrative Director: Winifred Setrakian. Elementary and secondary day school with summer program. Full-time staff: 3. Part-time staff: 12. Current enrollment: 15. Maximum enrollment: 20. Ages served: 8-18. Grades served: ungraded 3-12. Scholarships/financial aid available. Services: individual and group tutoring, academic and psychological testing, psychological and social skills counseling, parent support group; tutoring for individuals ages six and up not enrolled in school. Notes: Emphasizes intensive individual academic remediation and group counseling for peer/adult relationship and self-esteem problems.

La Canada: The Dannen School, 4526 Indianola Way, 91011. Telephone: (818) 952-1122. Executive Director: Robert E. Dannenhold. Elementary and secondary day school with limited services; summer program. Ages served: 6-13. Grades served: 1-8. Maximum enrollment: 36. Full-time staff: 5. Part-time staff: 2. Scholarships/financial aid available. Services: individual and group tutoring, academic and psychological testing; academic, psychological and family counseling; foreign language, art, science, computer education. Recreation: physical education, field trips, noncompetitive sports, travel/learn programs. Notes: Serves students who benefit from small classes and individualized educational programs, but not those with extensive special education needs.

Lafayette: Language Associates, 3408 Deer Hill Road, 94549. Telephone: (415) 283-0200. Director: Violet E. Spraings. Elementary, secondary, and adult day school with summer program. Ages served: 5 and up. Grades served: 1-12. Current enrollment: 100. Maximum enrollment: 150. Full-time staff: 20. Part-time staff: 1. Scholarships/financial aid available. Services: individual and group tutoring, academic and psychological testing; academic, psychological, and family counseling; occupational therapy, adaptive physical education, medical services, prevocational assessment. Recreation: physical education, swimming, art.

Lafayette: Meher Schools, 999 Leland Drive, 94549. Telephone: (415) 938-4826. Principal: Ellen Evans. Preschool and elementary day school with limited services. Grades served: preschool-6. Current enrollment: 310. Full-time staff: 23. Part-time staff: 7. Services: individual and group tutoring, academic testing, psychological and family counseling, physical therapy, medical services.

La Habra: Cleta Harder Developmental School, 981 N. Euclid Avenue, 90631. Telephone: (213) 694-5655. Director: Cleta Harder. Preschool, elementary, and secondary school with summer program. Ages served: 3-21. Grades served: ungraded. Current enrollment: 9. Maximum enrollment: 24. Full-time staff: 6. Part-time staff: 4 plus many volunteers. Scholarships/financial aid available. Services: individual and group tutoring, academic testing, academic and family counseling, physical and speech therapy, vocational training, medical services; extended day program. Recreation: playground, field trips.

Los Angeles: Beverly Center School, 5909 W. Third Street, 90036. Telephone: (213) 938-2828. Executive Director: Ronald Spector. Elementary and secondary day school with summer program. Ages served: 6-18. Grades served: 1-12. Current enrollment: 32. Maximum enrollment: 50. Full-time staff: 13. Part-time staff: 6. Services: individual and group tutoring, academic and psychological testing; academic, psychological and family counseling. Recreation: sports, developmental physical education. Notes: Specializes in learning disabilities combined with attentional and behavioral problems.

Los Angeles: Clearview School, 2000 Stoner Avenue, 90025. Telephone: (213) 478-2586. Executive Director: C. Gilbert Gardner. Secondary day and boarding school with summer program. Ages served: 12-20. Grades served: 7-12. Current enrollment: 60. Maximum enrollment: 70. Full-time staff: 15. Part-time staff: 8. Services: individual and group tutoring, academic and psychological testing; academic, psychological, and family counseling; adaptive physical education, work-study. Recreation: basketball, softball, swimming, flag football, tennis, dance, weight training, volleyball, theater and fine arts, photography.

Los Angeles: Exceptional Children's Foundation, 3750 Martin Luther King Boulevard, 90008. Telephone: (213) 290-2000. Executive Director: Robert D. Shushan. Elementary, secondary, and adult day school with summer program. Ages served: 5-22. Grades served: kindergarten-12. Current enrollment: 12. Maximum enrollment: 24. Full-time staff: 4. Part-time staff: 5. Services: individual and group tutoring, academic and psychological testing; academic, psychological, and family counseling; occupational therapy, vocational training, work-study, job placement, medical services.

CALIFORNIA

Los Angeles: Exceptional Children's Opportunity School, 12204 S. San Pedro Street, 90061. Telephone: (213) 756-9161. Director: Rose M. Mitchell. Elementary day and boarding school with summer program. Ages served: 5-21. Grades served: kindergarten-12. Current enrollment: 4. Maximum enrollment: 12. Services: academic and psychological testing, academic and psychological counseling, physical therapy, adaptive physical education, vocational training, medical services.

Los Angeles: Fernald School, Department of Psychology, UCLA, 405 Hilgard Avenue, 90024. Telephone: (213) 825-3394. Director: Howard S. Adelman. Elementary and secondary day school with summer program. Full-time staff: 12. Part-time staff: 20. Current enrollment: 65. Maximum enrollment: 70. Ages served: 7-21. Grades served: 2-12. Scholarships/financial aid available. Services: individual and group tutoring, academic and psychological testing; academic, psychological, and family counseling; vocational training, adaptive physical education, job placement, work-study; tutoring for preschool children and adults not enrolled in school. Recreation: full program. Notes: UCLA research, training, and demonstration center/laboratory.

Los Angeles: Julia Ann Singer Center, 3321 Edith Avenue, 90064. Telephone: (213) 202-0669. Director: Susan Brown. Preschool and elementary day school. Ages served: 3-8. Grades served: preschool-2. Current enrollment: 12. Maximum enrollment: 12. Full-time staff: 2. Part-time staff: 7. Scholarships/financial aid available. Services: individual and group tutoring, academic and psychological testing, psychological and family counseling, adaptive physical education, speech and movement therapy; after school program offers evaluation and tutoring, family and play therapy, intense behavioral intervention, school consultation, learning disorders and remediation service. Recreation: playground activities.

Los Angeles: The Marianne Frostig Center of Educational Therapy, 2495 E. Mountain Street, 91104. Telephone: (818) 791-1255. Executive Director: H. John van Duyne. Preschool, elementary, and secondary day school with summer program. Ages served: 2½-18. Current enrollment: 55. Maximum enrollment: 100. Full-time staff: 29. Part-time staff: 15. Scholarships/financial aid available. Services: individual and group tutoring, academic and psychological testing, diagnostic/therapeutic preschool, psychotherapy, psychological and family counseling; speech, language, and movement therapy; adaptive physical education, outpatient services. Recreation: movement and physical education, gymnasium, preschool movement facility, nearby park and swimming pool. Notes: Uses interdisciplinary team approach with goal of returning children to regular school setting.

Los Angeles: Park Century School, 2040 Stoner Avenue, 90025. Telephone: (213) 478-5065. Directors: Genny Shain, Gail Tabb. Elementary day school with summer program. Ages served: 6-14. Grades served: kindergarten-9. Current enrollment: 40. Full-time staff: 14. Part-time staff: 8. Scholarships/financial aid available. Services: individual and after school tutoring, academic testing, speech and language therapy, individualized classroom instruction, one-to-one perceptual motor training, student/staff ratio 2:1, therapeutic milieu, multidisciplinary approach. Recreation: physical education.

Los Angeles: Poseidon School, 11811 W. Pico Boulevard, 90064. Telephone: (213) 477-1268. Codirector: Barbara Fryer. Secondary day school with summer program. Ages served: 13-19. Grades served: 7-12. Current enrollment: 33. Maximum enrollment: 50. Full-time staff: 8. Part-time staff: 4. Limited scholarships/financial aid available. Services: individual and group tutoring, academic and psychological testing; academic, psychological, and family counseling; vocational preparation, work-study, job placement, crisis intervention, educational therapy. Recreation: drama, physical education, dance, aerobics.

Los Angeles: Slauson Learning Center, 4000 W. Slauson Avenue, 90043. Telephone: (213) 296-1178. Administrator: Deltha Scutter. Elementary and secondary day school with summer program. Ages served: 7-17. Grades served: ungraded. Current enrollment: 18. Maximum enrollment: 24. Full-time staff: 5. Part-time staff: 3. Services: individual and group tutoring, academic and psychological testing, academic and psychological counseling, adaptive physical education, vocational training; daily hot lunches and transportation. Recreation: bowling, community field trips, annual major trip, tennis, swimming.

Los Olivos: Dunn School, P.O. Box 98, 93441. Telephone: (805) 688-6471. Director of Admissions: Douglas W. Jessup. Secondary day school with limited services; males only boarding school. Ages served: 14-19. Grades served: 9-12. Current enrollment: 25 learning skills program, 153 school. Maximum enrollment: 25 learning skills program, 153 school. Full-time staff: 29. Services: individual tutoring and remediation, group tutoring, academic testing and counseling, limited psychological counseling, college counseling, learning skills center, science center with computer terminals. Recreation: physical education, athletic program, outings. Notes: For students with mild learning difficulties with high motivation and supportive families. Students mainstreamed into a college preparatory curriculum and receive college counseling beginning in sophomore year. Two specialists available to each student for remedial and tutorial assistance.

Mountain Center: Morning Sky Residential School, 29375 Highway 243, 92361. Telephone: (714) 659-4044. Program Director: John Weaver. Elementary and secondary school; males only day and boarding school with summer program. Ages served: 9-19. Grades served: 3-12. Current enrollment: 23. Maximum enrollment: 23. Full-time staff: 10. Part-time staff: 8. Services: individual tutoring, academic and psychological testing; academic, psychological, and family counseling; occupational therapy, adaptive physical education, vocational training. Recreation: hiking and other outdoor pursuits.

Northridge: San Fernando Valley Child Guidance, 9650 Zelzah Avenue, 91325. Telephone: (818) 993-9311. Head, Early Childhood Programs: Carol Falendu.

CALIFORNIA

Therapeutic preschool. Ages served: 2-5. Services: diagnostic testing, psychological testing, individual tutoring, psychological and parent counseling, speech and language therapy, support group, social services.

Oakland: Concordia High School, 6325 Camden Street, 94605. Telephone: (415) 632-4332. Director: Roy Blumhorst. Secondary day school. Grades served: 9-12. Current enrollment: 85. Maximum enrollment: 150. Full-time staff: 6. Part-time staff: 2. Scholarships/financial aid available. Services: individual and group tutoring, academic and psychological testing; academic, psychological, and family counseling. Notes: Has mainstreamed, full service learning disability program for up to 12 students.

Oakland: Raskob Day School, 3520 Mountain Boulevard, 94619. Telephone: (415) 436-1275. Director: Mary Lee Knapp. Elementary day school with summer program. Ages served: 8-14. Grades served: 2-8. Current enrollment: 24. Maximum enrollment: 24. Full-time staff: 4. Part-time staff: 5. Limited scholarships/financial aid available. Services: individual and group tutoring, academic and psychological testing, weekly group counseling, part-time remedial program that is separate from day school. Recreation: field trips, physical education, swimming, music, drama.

Oak Run: Wide Horizons Ranch, Star Route 2, Box 405, 96069. Telephone: (916) 472-3223. Codirectors: George and Jane Summers. Males only elementary boarding school with limited services; summer camp. Ages served: 9-14. Grades served: ungraded. Current enrollment: 14. Maximum enrollment: 14. Full-time staff: 4. Services: individual and group tutoring, academic testing. Recreation: located on cattle ranch, activities include animal care, ranch work, biking, tree forts, hiking, kite flying, sports. Notes: Traditional ranch family style living; emphasis on family atmosphere.

Orange: Providence Speech and Hearing Center, 1301 Providence Avenue, 92668. Telephone: (714) 639-4990. Executive Director: Margaret Anne Inman. Preschool. Ages served: 2-7. Grades served: preschool-kindergarten. Current enrollment: 26. Maximum enrollment: 32. Full-time staff: 5. Part-time staff: 3. Scholarships/financial aid available. Services: individual and group tutoring, academic and psychological testing, psychological and family counseling; physical, occupational, speech, and language therapy; adaptive physical education, medical and audiological services. Recreation: dance.

Oxnard: Assistance League School, 1310 Fremont Way, 93030. Telephone: (805) 485-0068. Executive Director: Frances Merkley. Preschool and elementary day school with summer program. Ages served: 2-8. Grades served: preschool-1. Current enrollment: 34. Maximum enrollment: 40. Full-time staff: 8. Part-time staff: 3. Scholarships/financial aid available. Services: individual and group tutoring, academic and psychological testing, psychological and family counseling; physical, occupational, speech, and language therapy; adaptive physical education.

Palo Alto: Peninsula Children's Center Children and Youth Services, Inc., 3860 Middlefield Road, 94303. Telephone: (415) 494-1200. Executive Director: Gloria F. Leiderman. Preschool, elementary, and secondary day school with summer program. Ages served: 2½-22. Grades served: preschool-12. Current enrollment: 42. Maximum enrollment: 53. Full-time staff: 35. Part-time staff: 5. Scholarships/financial aid available. Services: individual and group tutoring, academic and psychological testing, psychological and family counseling; group, milieu, occupational, speech, and language therapy; adaptive physical education, vocational training. Recreation: sports, community outings, camping, leisure skills training. Notes: Day treatment and special education program for students who cannot be served appropriately in public school.

Pasadena: Pacific Oaks Children's School, 714 W. California Boulevard, 91105. Telephone: (818) 795-9161. Director: Sharon Stine. Preschool and elementary day school with limited services; summer program. Ages served: birth-9. Grades served: preschool-3. Current enrollment: 194. Maximum enrollment: 196. Full-time staff: 20. Part-time staff: 15. Scholarships/financial aid available. Services: family counseling, individual instruction. Notes: Special needs children mainstreamed.

Pasadena: Pasadena Cerebral Palsy Center Pre-School, 355 W. Green Street, 91108. Telephone: (818) 282-9202. Director: Alice G. Crowell. Preschool with limited services. Ages served: 2½-5. Current enrollment: 10. Maximum enrollment: 10. Full-time staff: 4. Part-time staff: 1. Scholarships/financial aid available. Services: individual tutoring; physical, speech, and occupational therapy.

Pasadena: Villa Esperanza, 2116 E. Villa Street, 91107. Telephone: (818) 449-2919. Director: Elene Chaffee. Preschool, elementary, and adult day and boarding school with summer program. Ages served: infant-adult. Grades served: ungraded. Current enrollment: 120. Maximum enrollment: 150. Full-time staff: 21. Part-time staff: 49. Services: family counseling, occupational therapy, vocational training, work-study, job placement. Recreation: park outings, puppet shows, musicals, holiday celebrations, bell games, square dancing.

Piedmont: Circle Preschool, Nine Lake Avenue, 94611. Telephone: (415) 547-6447. Executive Director: Celeste Myers. Preschool with summer program. Ages served: 6 months-6. Grades served: preschool, kindergarten. Current enrollment: 150. Maximum enrollment: 150. Full-time staff: 6. Part-time staff: 30. Scholarships/financial aid available. Services: individual and group tutoring, academic and psychological testing, speech therapy, math, pre-reading; focus on cognitive, language, fine and gross motor, social, and self-help skills. Recreation: music, arts and crafts, nature studies, movement. Notes: Individual attention for special needs children in mainstream setting. Goal is early intervention.

Pleasant Hill: Mt. Diablo Rehabilitation Center, 490 Golf Club Road, 94523. Telephone: (415) 682-6330. Executive Director: Larry Hunn. Elementary, secondary, and adult school with summer program. Ages served: all. Grades served: 1-

college. Current enrollment: 80. Maximum enrollment: 200. Full-time staff: 30. Part-time staff: 10. Scholarships/financial aid available. Services: individual and group tutoring, academic and psychological testing, psychological and family counseling, physical and occupational therapy, vocational training, job placement.

Pomona: First Baptist School, 521 N. Garey Avenue, 91767. Telephone: (714) 622-1053. Principal: Nancy Salverda. Preschool and elementary day school with limited services; summer program. Ages served: 3-14. Grades served: preschool-8. Current enrollment: 580. Maximum enrollment: 600. Full-time staff: 40. Part-time staff: 25. Services: individual and group tutoring, academic testing, academic and family counseling, adaptive physical education. Recreation: gymnastics, track. Notes: 20 learning disabled students currently enrolled; facilities for 25 in grades 1-6.

Riverside: Big Springs School, 190 E. Big Springs Road, 92507. Telephone: (714) 787-0408. Director/Educational Therapist: Regina G. Richards. Elementary day school with summer program. Ages served: 6-10. Grades served: ungraded. Current enrollment: 13. Maximum enrollment: 13. Full-time staff: 5. Part-time staff: 3. Scholarships/financial aid available. Services: individual tutoring, group class, academic testing and counseling; occupational, vision, speech, and language therapy.

Riverside: The Children's Center of Riverside, 7177 Potomac Street, 92504. Telephone: (714) 784-0020. Executive Director: Connie L. Beasley. Preschool with limited services; summer program. Ages served: birth-6 years. Current enrollment: 110. Maximum enrollment: 110. Full-time staff: 18. Part-time staff: 6. Scholarships/financial aid available. Services: individual tutoring, physical and occupational therapy, classroom placement in center based program, home teaching program, parent education and training.

Running Springs: Cedu School, 3500 Seymour Road, P.O. Box 1176, 92382. Telephone: (714) 867-2722. Director of Admissions: Gary Lenkeit. Secondary boarding school with limited services. Ages served: 13-19. Grades served: 7-12. Current enrollment: 75. Maximum enrollment: 112. Full-time staff: 28. Part-time staff: 7. Services: individual and group tutoring, academic testing, academic and psychological counseling, vocational training, work-study, medical services. Recreation: wilderness challenge program; cross country, downhill, and water skiing; studio arts, tennis, basketball, racquetball. Notes: Year-round residential school for adolescents with special emotional and educational needs.

Sacramento: Aldar Academy, 2300 Edison Avenue, 95821. Telephone: (916) 485-9685. Executive Director: A. Nick Noskowski. Secondary day school with summer program. Ages served: 11-21. Grades served: 7-12. Current enrollment: 72. Maximum enrollment: 72. Full-time staff: 9. Scholarships/financial aid available. Services: individual and group tutoring, academic testing, vocational training, work-study, job placement. Recreation: skiing, white water rafting.

Sacramento: Re-Ed West Center for Children, Inc., 1150 Eastern Avenue, 95825. Telephone: (916) 481-8010. Executive Director: Nancy F. Noonan. Elementary day and boarding school with summer program. Ages served: 6-14. Grades served: ungraded. Current enrollment: 55. Maximum enrollment: 60. Full-time staff: 89. Services: individual and group tutoring, academic and psychological testing; academic, psychological, and family counseling; adaptive physical education, medical services.

Sacramento: Sierra School Language Arts Development Center, 2515 Cottage Way, 95825. Telephone: (916) 488-2515. Owner: Louise Bjorgum. Secondary day school with summer program. Ages served: 12-adult. Current enrollment: 15. Maximum enrollment: 50. Full-time staff: 4. Scholarships/financial aid available. Services: individual and group tutoring, academic testing and counseling, vocational training, work-study.

San Diego: Aseltine School, 4027 Normal Street, 92103. Telephone: (619) 296-2135. Executive Director: Marian F. Grant. Elementary and secondary day school with summer program. Ages served: 7-19. Current enrollment: 50. Maximum enrollment: 60. Full-time staff: 25. Part-time staff: 12. Scholarships/financial aid available. Services: individual and group tutoring, academic and psychological testing, psychological and family counseling, physical therapy, adaptive physical education, vocational training. Recreation: art, music, Boy Scouts, Girl Scouts.

San Diego: Bond Street School, 4450 Bond Street, 92109. Telephone: (619) 273-2050. Director: Shirley A. Wilson. Elementary day school with summer program. Ages served: 6-12. Grades served: 1-6. Current enrollment: 10. Full-time staff: 4. Part-time staff: 3. Services: individual tutoring, academic and psychoeducation testing, multisensory learning experiences, sensory motor therapy; after school learning clinic for grades kindergarten-12. Notes: Specializes in one-to-one reading development for dyslexic students.

San Diego: I Am Learning Center/Academy, 6650 Montezuma Road, 92115. Telephone: (714) 697-8499 or 281-0491. Director: Patricia Green Marshall. Elementary and secondary day school with summer program. Ages served: 4-15. Grades served: kindergarten-8. Current enrollment: 23. Maximum enrollment: 60. Full-time staff: 4. Part-time staff: 1-2. Services: individual and group tutoring, academic testing, academic and family counseling.

San Francisco: Edgewood Children's Center, 1801 Vicente Street, 94116. Telephone: (415) 681-3211. Secondary day and boarding school with summer program. Ages served: 6-12. Grades served: 1-6. Current enrollment: 67. Maximum enrollment: 76. Full-time staff: 100. Part-time staff: 25. Services: individual and group tutoring, academic and psychological testing; academic, psychological, and family counseling; occupational and speech therapy, adaptive physical education. Notes: Primary programs are residential and day treatment for emotionally disturbed and educationally handicapped children.

CALIFORNIA

San Francisco: The Laurel School, 901 Balboa Street, 94118. Telephone: (415) 752-3567. Director: Marcia Spitz. Elementary day school with summer program. Ages served: 5-14. Grades served: kindergarten-8. Current enrollment: 50. Maximum enrollment: 50. Full-time staff: 7. Part-time staff: 2. Scholarships/financial aid available. Services: individual tutoring, academic testing. Recreation: sports, drama, music.

San Francisco: Oakes Children's Center, Inc., 1348 Tenth Avenue, 94122. Telephone: (415) 564-2310. Director: Soula Dontchos. Preschool and elementary day school with summer program. Ages served: 2-12. Grades served: ungraded. Current enrollment: 18. Maximum enrollment: 20. Full-time staff: 14. Part-time staff: 8. Services: individual and group tutoring, academic and psychological testing, family counseling, adaptive physical education; movement, art, speech, and play therapy. Recreation: field trips, assemblies, camping.

San Francisco: Open Book School, 320 15th Avenue, 94118. Telephone: (415) 751-6950. Administrative Coordinator: David Whitmore. Elementary day school with summer program. Ages served: 6-13. Grades served: kindergarten-8. Current enrollment: 12. Maximum enrollment: 24. Full-time staff: 4. Part-time staff: 3. Services: individual and group tutoring, academic and psychological testing; academic, psychological, and family counseling; occupational therapy, adaptive physical education, Slingerland screening and language arts approach, perceptual motor services, sensorimotor integration, prevocational training. Recreation: community resources including library, museums, playgrounds, cultural events.

San Francisco: San Francisco Hearing and Speech Center, 1234 Divisadero Street, 94115. Telephone: (415) 921-7658. Director: Rayford Reddell. Preschool and elementary day school. Ages served: 3-12. Grades served: ungraded. Current enrollment: 13. Maximum enrollment: 15. Full-time staff: 4. Part-time staff: 1. Services: individual and group tutoring, academic testing, full-time classes for children with language disorders.

San Francisco: Sterne School, 2690 Jackson Street, 94115. Telephone: (415) 922-6081. Director: Valerie Anthony. Day school with summer program. Ages served: 9-18. Grades served: ungraded. Current enrollment: 60. Maximum enrollment: 60. Full-time staff: 8. Part-time staff: 2. Scholarships/financial aid available. Services: individual and group tutoring, academic testing, work-study.

San Francisco: Sunset Community School, 1811-34th Avenue, 94122. Telephone: (415) 664-7414. Director: Linda L. Chiarucci. Preschool, elementary, and secondary day school with limited services; summer program. Ages served: 5-15. Grades served: preschool-9. Current enrollment: 100. Full-time staff: 12. Part-time staff: 3. Scholarships/financial aid available. Services: individual and group tutoring, academic testing, resource center, computer education. Recreation: physical education, intramural sports. Notes: Extended hours for working parents. Accepts non-English-speaking students.

San Jose: CASOLS: California School of Learning Systems, 5140 Country Lane, 95129. Telephone: (408) 255-9911. Director: Carol Digardi. Secondary and adult day school with summer program. Ages served: 12-19. Grades served: 6-12. Current enrollment: 13. Maximum enrollment: 30. Full-time staff: 4. Part-time staff: 2. Services: individual and group tutoring, academic and psychological testing, academic counseling, adaptive physical education, vocational training, work-study, job placement, music, cooking. Recreation: organized activity period, physical education, field trips.

San Jose: Zonta Children's Center, 4300 Bucknall Road, 95130. Telephone: (408) 374-9050. Executive Director: Carol Zimbelman. Preschool and elementary day school. Ages served: 2-12. Grades served: ungraded. Current enrollment: 35. Maximum enrollment: 42. Full-time staff: 24. Part-time staff: 3. Scholarships/financial aid available. Services: academic testing, psychological and family counseling. Recreation: field trips, gross motor activities, camping. Notes: All students have learning disabilities, but primary diagnosis is emotional or behavioral problems.

San Juan Capistrano: ITOP Center for Learning, 31591 La Novia, 92675. Telephone: (714) 837-8048 or 496-3437. Executive Director: Sr. Paula Jane Tupa. Elementary, secondary, and adult day school with summer program. Grades served: kindergarten-adult. Current enrollment: 70. Full-time staff: 7. Part-time staff: 5. Scholarships/financial aid available. Services: individual and group tutoring, academic testing, vocational training, work-study, perceptual motor therapy, movement education, individualized education programs. Recreation: physical education, after school recreation.

San Marino: Southwestern Academy, 2800 Monterey Road, 91108. Telephone: (818) 799-5010. Headmaster: Kenneth R. Veronda. Elementary and secondary day and boarding school with limited services. Ages served: 6-18. Grades served: 1-12. Current enrollment: 129. Maximum enrollment: 129. Full-time staff: 21. Part-time staff: 10. Scholarships/financial aid available. Services: individual tutoring, academic and psychological testing, academic and psychological counseling; small, ability-grouped classes. Recreation: interscholastic and intramural athletics. Notes: For able but lower-achieving students.

San Mateo: Meridian-Markoff School, 1810 Charing Cross Road, 94402. Telephone: (415) 573-8111. Principal: Elizabeth V.V. Olson. Day school with summer program. Ages served: 6-18. Current enrollment: 45. Maximum enrollment: 100. Full-time staff: 13. Part-time staff: 5. Limited scholarships/financial aid available. Services: individual and group tutoring, academic and psychological testing; individual, group, and family counseling; speech therapy.

San Rafael: LeeBil School and Learning Center, 1411 Lincoln Avenue, 94901. Telephone: (415) 454-6618. Director: William W. Miller. Secondary day school with summer program. Ages served: 14-19. Grades served: 9-12. Current enrollment: 10. Maximum enrollment: 15. Full-time staff: 2. Part-time staff: 2. Services: individual and group tutoring, academic testing, academic and family counseling, adaptive physical education, vocational training, work-study, job placement, sensory integration, development of responsibility, behavior modification, group interaction. Recreation: physical education. Notes: Student government monitors student infractions of school rules. Each person, student and teacher alike, has an equal vote in discipline and correction.

San Rafael: Marin Child Development Center (incorporating Arena School), 2960 Kerner Boulevard, 94901. Telephone: (415) 459-2777. Director: Liz Burns. Program Director: Pat Carmignani. Preschool and elementary day school with summer program. Ages served: 3-12. Grades served: preschool-6. Current enrollment: 26. Maximum enrollment: 28. Full-time staff: 7. Part-time staff: 10. Limited scholarships/financial aid available. Services: individual and group tutoring, academic and psychological testing; academic, psychological, and family counseling; language, sensorimotor, vision, speech, and language therapy; adaptive physical education. Notes: Preschool serves children with developmental delays and emotional/behavioral problems; kindergarten-6 serves children with learning disabilities and maturational lags.

San Rafael: The Marin School for Learning, 160 San Pedro Road, 94903. Telephone: (415) 479-5990. Director: Claire Eckley. Elementary, secondary, and adult day school with summer program. Ages served: 6 and up. Grades served: 1-12. Current enrollment: 13. Maximum enrollment: 36. Full-time staff: 4. Part-time staff: 3. Scholarships/financial aid available. Services: individual and group tutoring, academic and psychological testing, academic and psychological counseling, adaptive physical education, vocational training, work-study, child care.

Santa Ana: Tot Haven Center, 1510 N. Parton, 92706. Telephone: (714) 542-3111. Director: Ellen Franklin. Preschool with summer program. Ages served: 2½-6. Maximum enrollment: 49. Full-time staff: 7. Scholarships/financial aid available. Services: small group instruction, academic testing, academic and family counseling, adaptive physical education, speech and language therapy.

Santa Barbara: Palmer School, 545 N. Patterson, 93111. Telephone: (805) 683-1327. Director/Principal: Carole C. Palmer. Elementary and secondary day school with summer program and camp. Grades served: 1-12. Maximum enrollment: 25. Full-time staff: 3. Scholarships/financial aid available. Services: individual and group tutoring, academic and psychological testing; academic, psychological, and family counseling; adaptive physical education, vocational training, work-study, speech and language therapy. Recreation: farming, gardening, computer science, field trips, camping.

Santa Monica: Wilshire West School, 1516 19th Street, 90404. Telephone: (213) 453-1744. Director: Mark Mitock. Secondary day school with summer program. Ages served: 12-19. Grades served: 7-12. Current enrollment: 35. Maximum enrollment: 45. Full-time staff: 8. Part-time staff: 2. Scholarships/financial aid available. Services: individual tutoring, academic and psychological testing;

academic, psychological, and family counseling; vocational training, work-study, job placement. Recreation: sports, wilderness experiences. Notes: All students attend weekly individual and group counseling sessions.

Santa Rosa: New Horizon School and Learning Center, 804 College Avenue, 95404. Telephone: (707) 542-8463. Directors: M. McCarthy Campbell, Deborah Greene. Elementary, secondary, and adult day school with summer program. Ages served: 8-adult. Grades served: 3-12, postsecondary. Current enrollment: 15 school; 30 learning center. Maximum enrollment: 25 school; 50 learning center. Full-time staff: 2. Part-time staff: 9. Limited scholarships/financial aid available. Services: individual and group tutoring, academic and psychological testing; academic, psychological, and family counseling; occupational therapy, prevocational and vocational training, career and vocational assessment, work-study, consultation, workshops for parents and professionals. Recreation: YMCA.

Sepulveda: Oak Hill School, 9433 Sepulveda Boulevard, 91343. Telephone: (818) 894-8388. Director: Roberta S. Hargis. Elementary and secondary day school with limited services; summer program and camp. Ages served: 4½-19. Grades served: kindergarten-12. Current enrollment: 170. Maximum enrollment: 200. Full-time staff: 20. Part-time staff: 2. Scholarships/financial aid available. Services: individual and group tutoring, academic and psychological testing; academic, psychological, and family counseling; limited vocational training, work-study. Recreation: sports, outings; clubs including computer, photography, yearbook, journalism.

Torrance: Switzer Center, 1110 Sartori Avenue, 90501. Telephone: (213) 328-3611. Executive Director: Janet Switzer. Elementary and secondary day school with summer program. Ages served: 5-21. Grades served: kindergarten-12. Current enrollment: 62. Maximum enrollment: 80. Full-time staff: 40. Part-time staff: 8. Scholarships/financial aid available. Services: individual and group tutoring, academic and psychological testing; academic, psychological, and family counseling; adaptive physical education, vocational training, work-study, job placement, medical services consultation, computer lab, speech and language therapy, special services on an hourly basis to individuals not enrolled in the center. Recreation: sports, theater arts, homemaking skills, dances.

Van Nuys: New School for Child Development, 13130 Burbank Boulevard, 91401. Telephone: (818) 787-1410. Executive Administrator: Barbara Firestone. Elementary and secondary day school. Ages served: 5-19. Grades served: kindergarten-12. Current enrollment: 93. Maximum enrollment: 120. Full-time staff: 56. Part-time staff: 3. Scholarships/financial aid available. Services: individual tutoring, academic and psychological testing, psychological and family counseling, adaptive physical education, speech and language therapy. Recreation: team sports, clubs, arcade room, drama, music, fine arts.

CALIFORNIA

Summer Camps and Programs

Ahwahnee: Skylake Ranch Camp, 45895 Highway 49, 93601. Telephone: (209) 683-7748. Owner/Director: Marian H. Andersen. Day camp. Ages served: 6-17. Grades served: kindergarten-11. Maximum enrollment: 50 girls; 50 boys. Full-time staff: 35. Recreation: camping, hiking, nature study, riding, swimming, waterskiing, archery, team sports, crafts, dance, drama, music, computers, baby farm animals, gardening.

Angelus Oaks: Camp Tautona, 92305. Telephone: (714) 794-4155. Permanent mailing address: San Gorgonio Girl Scout Council, 2233 La Crosse Avenue, Colton, CA 92324. Telephone: (714) 825-8640. Director of Program Services: Marci Mattos. Females only residential camp with limited services. Ages served: 7-18. Grades served: 2-12. Maximum enrollment: 100. Full-time staff: 30. Scholarships/financial aid available. Services: nurse on staff. Recreation: camping, hiking, nature study, swimming, archery, team sports, crafts, dance, music. Notes: Children with disabilities are mainstreamed.

Napa: Wo Kan Da Day Camp, P.O. Box 2775, 94558. Telephone: (707) 226-5606 after 5 p.m. Director: Shirley Roberts. Day camp. Ages served: 6-11. Grades served: kindergarten-4. Maximum enrollment: 100 per session. Scholarships/financial aid available. Recreation: camping, nature study, archery. Notes: No special program for handicapped children. Any child accepted who is able to function in an environment of children and caring adults.

Ojai: Camp Ramah, 385 Fairview, 93023. Telephone: (805) 646-4301. Permanent mailing address: 15600 Mulholland, Los Angeles, CA 90077. Telephone: (213) 476-8571. Director: Rabbi Glenn Karonsky. Residential camp with academic program. Ages served: 10-17. Grades served: ungraded. Maximum enrollment: 32. Full-time staff: 7. Scholarships/financial aid available. Services: adaptive physical education, vocational training, recreation, religious education. Academic programs: computers. Recreation: camping, hiking, field trips, nature study, swimming, archery, crafts, dance, drama, music, photography. Notes: For Jewish children with special learning needs.

Pacific House: Odyssey Academic Camp, 95725. Telephone: (916) 644-1615. Permanent mailing address: 5007 Concord Boulevard, Concord, CA 94521. Telephone: (415) 687-6851. Director: Don C. Smith. Residential camp with academic program. Ages served: 7-17. Grades served: 2-12. Maximum enrollment: 75. Full-time staff: 32. Services: individual tutoring, work-study. Academic programs: math, reading, English, spelling, study skills, college preparatory courses. Recreation: swimming, hiking, riding, field trips, nature study, crafts, team athletics, sailing, canoeing. Notes: Learning disabled children mainstreamed.

College and University Special Programs and Services

Antelope Valley Community College: 3041 W. Avenue "K," Lancaster, CA 93534. Total enrollment: 3,500. LD students: 60. Special services: individual and group tutoring, training in study skills, academic counseling, taped books, special examinations, student resource center, readers, diagnostic testing. Contact: David Greenleaf, Prescriptive Learning Instructor. Telephone: (805) 943-3241 ext. 213.

Center/clinic: Learning Skills Center. Telephone: (805) 943-3241 ext. 213. Director: David Greenleaf. Not open to public. Ages served: adults. Services: tutoring, study skills, basic skills remediation, college survival skills.

Bakersfield College: 1801 Panorama Drive, Bakersfield, CA 93305. Total enrollment: 11,000. LD students: 200. Special services: individual and group tutoring, training in study skills, academic counseling, taped books, special examinations on teacher approval, student resource center, readers, diagnostic testing. Contact: Miss Hoolyse Davijian, Counselor, Handicapped Services. Telephone: (805) 395-4334.

Cabrillo Community College: 6500 Soquel Drive, Aptos, CA 95003. Total enrollment: 10,000. LD students: 117. Special services: diagnostic testing, individual tutoring, small group instruction, academic and vocational counseling, readers, resource center, note takers, interpreters, talking calculators, taped books.

- **Special program:** Learning Skills Program. Must be enrolled in the college full or part-time. Learning disability must be identified through recent records and tests by the college. Division Chairperson: Laura Moyles. Telephone: (408) 425-6478. Learning Disabilities Specialist: Richard Griffiths. Telephone: (408) 425-6220.

California Lutheran College: 60 Olsen Road, Thousand Oaks, CA 91360. Special services: individual and group tutoring, special examinations, academic and psychological counseling, diagnostic testing, student resource center, readers, training in study skills, diagnosis, remediation. Contact: Anne Sapp, Director, Learning Resource Center. Telephone: (805) 492-2411.

California State Polytechnic University: 3801 W. Temple Avenue, 15-110, Pomona, CA 91768. Special services: taped books, special examinations, readers, note takers. Contact: Carol A. Goldstein, Director, Disabled Student Services. Telephone: (714) 598-4810.

California State Polytechnic University: San Luis Obispo, CA 93407. Special services: individual and group tutoring, training in study skills, academic counseling, taped books, cassette recorders, talking calculators, voice synthesized computer, student resource center, readers, note takers, scholarships, ombudsman. Contact: Ana Fryer, Learning Disabilities Specialist. Telephone: (805) 546-1395.

CALIFORNIA

California State University-Chico: Chico, CA 95929. Total enrollment: 14,000. LD students: 65. Special services: individual and group tutoring, special examinations, academic and psychological counseling, support group, diagnostic testing, student resource center, taped books, training in study skills, computer terminals.

- **Special program:** Learning Disabilities Program. Applicants must meet the regular admissions requirements of the university. Learning disability must be verified through recent diagnostic tests. Learning Disabilities Specialist: Patricia G. Stewart. Telephone: (916) 895-5959.

California State University-Dominguez Hills: 1000 E. Victoria Street, Carson, CA 90747. Total enrollment: 8,400. LD students: 12. Special services: readers, individual and group tutoring, ombudsman, academic and psychological counseling, training in study skills, taped books, readers, special examinations, support group, campus and community referrals. Contact: Mark Matsui, Coordinator, Disabled Student Services. Telephone: (213) 516-3660.

California State University-Fresno: Fresno, CA 93740. Total enrollment: 16,000. LD students: 35. Special services: individual tutoring, academic and psychological counseling, student resource center, support group, diagnostic testing, taped books, special examinations, readers, training in study skills. Contact: Weldon Percy, Coordinator, Disabled Student Services. Telephone: (209) 294-2562.

Center/clinic: Interdisciplinary Center for Human Services, Shaw and Maple Avenues, Fresno, CA 93710-9989. Telephone: (209) 294-3909. Codirectors: Joan Fiorello, Robert G. Knudsen. Not open to public.

California State University-Fullerton: 800 State College Boulevard, Fullerton, CA 92634. Total enrollment: 28,000. LD students: 50. Special services: readers, individual tutoring, ombudsman, special examinations, scholarships, academic and psychological counseling, taped books, training in study skills. Contact: Bryan Burdick, Coordinator of Support Services. Telephone: (714) 773-3117.

Center/clinic: Handicapped Student Services Center, L-113. Telephone: (714) 773-3117. Director: Paul Miller. Not open to public. Grades served: college.

California State University-Hayward: Hayward, CA 94542. Special services: readers, note takers, admission and registration assistance; academic, personal, and vocational counseling; campus and community referrals, support group, adaptive equipment. Contact: Paul Preston, Director, Disabled Students Center. Telephone: (415) 881-3868.

Center/clinic: Disabled Students Center. Telephone: (415) 881-3868. Director: Paul Preston. Grades served: university students.

California State University-Long Beach: 1250 Bellflower Boulevard, Long Beach, CA 90840. Special services: assessment, individual tutoring, training in study skills; academic, psychological, career, and group counseling; taped books, special examinations, student resource center, readers, diagnostic testing, scholarships, monitoring.

- **Special program:** Adult Learning Disability Program. Learning disability must be verified through past records and tests, and interviews by the college staff. Each student is assigned a facilitator who arranges for all special needs. Coordinator, Special Student Services: David Sanfilippo. Telephone: (213) 498-5401. Codirector: Helen Irlen. Telephone: (213) 498-4430.

California State University-Los Angeles: 5151 State University Drive, Los Angeles, CA 90032. Special services: individual tutoring, ombudsman, scholarships, academic and psychological counseling, diagnostic testing, training in study skills, note takers, readers.

- **Special program:** Learning Disabilities Program. Program serves students with dyslexia, dysgraphia, dyscalculia, and aphasia. Must meet standard admissions requirements of the university. Learning disability must be identified through diagnostic tests. Director: Carl Ilan. Telephone: (213) 224-3382.

Center/clinic: Disabled Student Services. Telephone: (213) 224-3382. Director: Carl Ilan. Open to public for diagnostic testing. Grades served: university students.

California State University-Northridge: 18111 Nordhoff Street, Northridge, CA 91330. Special services: individual and group tutoring, training in study skills (by referral), academic and psychological counseling, taped books, special examinations, readers, diagnostic testing, scholarships. Contact: Harry J. Murphy, Coordinator, Office of Disabled Student Services. Telephone: (818) 885-2578.

Cañada College: 4200 Farm Hill Boulevard, Redwood City, CA 94061. Special services: individual and group tutoring, academic and psychological counseling, diagnostic testing, training in study skills.

- **Special program:** Learning Disabilities Program. Must be a registered student at the college. Learning disability must be verified through recent diagnostic tests. Director: Ella Turner-Gray. Telephone: (415) 364-1212 ext. 263. Instructor: Glory Bratton. Telephone: (415) 364-1212 ext. 237.

Cerritos Community College: 11110 E. Alondra Boulevard, Norwalk, CA 90650. Total enrollment: 18,000. LD students: 76. Special services: readers, group tutoring, limited individual tutoring, special examinations, scholarships, academic counseling, diagnostic testing, student resource center, support group, taped books, note takers, in-class aides, visual magnifying systems; special remedial instruction in basic skill areas through self-paced, noncredit, open entry classes. Contact: Albert A. Spetrino, Instructor. Telephone: (213) 860-2451 ext. 375. Or Kay Patton, College Specialist. Telephone: (213) 860-2451 ext. 336.

Center/clinic: Special Education Center. Telephone: (213) 860-2451 ext. 375. Director: Albert A. Spetrino. Open to public. Ages served: 18 and up. Grades served: postsecondary.

Cerro Coso Community College: College Heights Boulevard, Ridgecrest, CA 93555. Special services: individual and group tutoring, training in study skills, academic and psychological counseling, taped books, special examinations, student resource center, readers, diagnostic testing, ombudsman, peer counselors, career counseling. Contact: Susan Smith, Special Services Program Coordinator. Telephone: (619) 375-5001 ext. 219. Or Don Mourton, Dean of Student Services. Telephone: (619) 375-5001 ext. 201.

Center/clinic: Learning Assistance Center. Telephone: (619) 375-5001 ext. 219. Codirectors: Susan Smith, Don Mourton. Not open to public. Ages served: 18 and up. Grades served: 13-14.

Chabot College: 25555 Hesperian Boulevard, Hayward, CA 94544. Total enrollment: 17,000. LD students: 328. Special services: individual tutoring, academic and psychological counseling, taped books, special examinations, student resource center, readers, diagnostic testing, scholarships.

- **Special program:** Learning Skills Program. Must fulfill regular admissions requirements of the college. Most students required to verify learning disability through tests administered by college staff. No minimum number of regular college courses required per semester. Contact: Counselor/Coordinator, Programs and Services for Disabled Students. Telephone: (415) 786-6725.

Chaffey Community College: 5885 Haven Avenue, Alta Loma, CA 91701. Special services: individual tutoring, training in study skills, academic counseling, taped books, special examinations, readers, note takers, independent life development, student resource center, diagnostic testing, vocational evaluation, career education and counseling, on-the-job training, job-seeking skills training and assistance. Contact: Zenia K. Loggins, Learning Disabilities Specialist. Telephone: (714) 987-0928 ext. 403.

Center/clinic: Educational Resource Center/Learning Center. Telephone: (714) 987-0928 ext. 370. Director: Inge Pelzer. Open to public. Ages served: 16 and up. Grades served: high school-college.

Chapman College: 333 N. Glassell, Orange, CA 92666. Special services: individual tutoring, training in study skills, academic and psychological counseling, student resource center. Contact: Susan Hunter Hancock, Dean of Students. Telephone: (714) 997-6721.

Citrus College: 18824 E. Foothill Boulevard, Azusa, CA 91702. Special services: individual and group tutoring, training in study skills, academic counseling, taped books, special examinations, readers, diagnostic testing, scholarships, early registration.

- **Special program:** Learning Disabilities Program. Includes special classes in basic skills, study skills, and learning strategies. Participants must be enrolled in the college. Learning Disabilities Specialist: Audrey Abas. Telephone: (818) 335-0521 ext. 2543.

City College of San Francisco: San Francisco, CA 94103. Total enrollment: 15,000. LD students: 225. Special services: individual and group tutoring, training in study skills, academic and psychological counseling, taped books, special examinations, student resource center, readers, diagnostic testing, scholarships. Contact: Rebecca R. Reilly, Department Head, Learning Assistance Programs. Telephone: (415) 239-3238.

Center/clinic: Diagnostic Learning Center, 50 Phelan Avenue C-330, San Francisco, CA 94112. Telephone: (415) 239-3238. Director: Rebecca R. Reilly. Open to public. Ages served: adults.

College of Alameda: 555 Atlantic Avenue, Alameda, CA 94501. Total enrollment: 5,000. LD students: 100. Special services: individual tutoring, training in study skills, academic counseling, limited psychological counseling, taped books, special examinations, student resource center, readers, diagnostic testing; special classes in writing, reading, spelling, math, vocational testing, prevocational writing, and psychology.

- **Special program:** Learning Disabilities Program. Consists of 12 initial hours of diagnostic testing followed by a series of learning skills classes. Each student has an Individual Education Plan. All applicants must be eligible to attend community college and able to profit from instruction leading to, or concurrent with, integration into the regular college or technical/vocational classes. Learning Disabilities Specialist: Pat Kerr. Telephone: (415) 522-7221 ext. 388. Enabler/Coordinator: Marge Maloney. Telephone: (415) 522-7221 ext. 314.

College of the Canyons: 26455 N. Rockwell Canyon Road, Valencia, CA 91355. Total enrollment: 4,000. LD students: 70. Special services: individual and group tutoring, ombudsman, special examinations, academic counseling, diagnostic testing, taped books, note takers, training in study skills, special classes in math and language skills, individualized programs, in-class vocational aides, audiovisual services. Contact: Frances B. Wakefield, Director, Supportive Services. Telephone: (805) 259-7800 ext. 282.

Center/clinic: Supportive Services. Telephone: (805) 259-7800 ext. 282. Director: Frances B. Wakefield. Not open to public.

CALIFORNIA

College of the Desert: 43-500 Monterey Avenue, Palm Desert, CA 92260. Special services: individual and group tutoring, training in study skills, academic counseling, taped books, special examinations, readers, diagnostic testing, scholarships, ombudsman.

- **Special program:** Learning Disabilities Program. Courses in developmental reading and math, independent living skills, language skills, driver education. Must fulfill regular admissions requirements of the college. Learning disability must be certified through records or testing done by college staff. Each student has an educational plan in the form of a learning contract with a special education instructor. Contract must be fulfilled in order to successfully complete the program. Director, Handicap Programs and Services: Diane N. Ramirez. Telephone: (619) 346-8041 ext. 222.

Center/clinic: Special Education Lab. Telephone: (619) 346-8041. Director: Diane N. Ramirez. Open to public. Ages served: 18 and up. Grades served: pre-college, college freshmen and sophomores. Services: diagnostic testing, designs individual education programs, small group activity, individualized instruction.

College of the Redwoods: 7351 Tompkins Hill Road, Eureka, CA 95501. Total enrollment: 780. LD students: 180. Special services: individual and group tutoring, training in study skills, academic counseling, taped books, special examinations, readers, diagnostic testing, support group. Contact: James Harrington, Director, Handicapped Student Services, or Bonita Wilkerson, Learning Disabilities Specialist. Telephone: (707) 443-8411 ext. 570.

Center/clinic: Learning Skills Center. Telephone: (707) 443-8411. Director: James Harrington. Open to public. Ages served: adult. Grades served: college.

College of the Sequoias: 915 S. Mooney Boulevard, Visalia, CA 93277. Special services: readers, individual tutoring, special examinations, academic and psychological counseling, diagnostic testing, student resource center, taped books, training in study skills; courses in learning and study skills, spelling, reading, writing, math. Contact: Don Mast, Director, Enabler Program. Telephone: (209) 733-2050 ext. 295.

Center/clinic: Learning Skills Center. Telephone: (209) 733-2050 ext. 295. Director: Don Mast. Not open to public. Ages served: 18 and up. Grades served: college. Services: courses in spelling, study skills, reading, math, writing.

Columbia Community College: P.O. Box 1849, Columbia, CA 95310. Total enrollment: 2,800. LD students: 20. Special services: individual and group tutoring, training in study skills, academic and psychological counseling, taped books, special examinations, student resource center, readers, diagnostic testing, scholarships, ombudsman. Contact: Patricia Harrelson, Learning Disabilities Specialist. Telephone: (209) 533-5133.

Compton Community College: 1111 E. Artesia Boulevard, Compton, CA 90221. Total enrollment: 3,500. LD students: 100. Special services: individual tutoring, training in study skills, academic counseling, special examinations, readers, diagnostic testing, support group. Contact: Jennell Allen, Counselor. Telephone: (213) 637-2660 ext. 275.

Center/clinic: Learning Development Clinic. Telephone: (213) 637-2660. Director: Roberta West. Not open to public. Ages served: college. Grades served: postsecondary.

Cosumnes River College: 8401 Center Parkway, Sacramento, CA 95823. Total enrollment: 6,000. LD students: 50. Special services: individual tutoring, academic counseling, readers, diagnostic testing, individualized education plan, note takers. Contact: Carol J. Rustigan, Learning Disabilities Specialist. Telephone: (916) 689-1000 ext. 273 or 275.

Center/clinic: Enabling Center/Learning Disabilities Program. Telephone: (916) 689-1000 ext. 273 or 275. Director: Carol J. Rustigan. Not open to public. Ages served: adults. Grades served: 13 and 14.

Crafton Hills College: 11711 Sand Canyon Road, Yucaipa, CA 92399. Total enrollment: 3,800. LD students: 30. Special services: individual tutoring, training in study skills, academic counseling, taped books, special examinations, student resource center, readers, diagnostic testing, support group. Contact: Kirsten S. Colvey, Learning Disabilities Specialist. Telephone: (714) 794-2162 ext. 234.

Cypress College: 9200 Valley View Street, Cypress, CA 90630. Total enrollment: 13,000. LD students: 126. Special services: individual tutoring, training in study skills, academic and psychological counseling, special examinations, student resource center, readers, diagnostic testing, scholarships, ombudsman, support group. Contact: Laurel Best, Director. Telephone: (714) 826-2220 ext. 215.

Center/clinic: Educational Services Center. Telephone: (714) 826-2220 ext. 215. Director: Laurel Best. Not open to public. Grades served: college.

De Anza College: 21250 Stevens Creek Boulevard, Cupertino, CA 95014. Total enrollment: 20,000. LD students: 200. Special services: readers, individual and group tutoring, ombudsman, special examinations, academic and psychological counseling, diagnostic testing, student resource center, support group, taped books, training in study skills, special remedial classes. Contact: Bruce Sturm, Director, Educational Diagnostic Clinic. Telephone: (408) 996-4838.

Center/clinic: Educational Diagnostic Clinic. Telephone: (408) 996-4838. Director: Bruce Sturm. Open to public. Ages served: 18 and up.

Diablo Valley College: 321 Golf Club Road, Pleasant Hill, CA 94523. Special services: individual and group tutoring, training in study skills, academic counseling, taped books, special examinations, readers, diagnostic testing, ombudsman.

CALIFORNIA

Contact: Marianne Goodson, Enabler. Telephone: (415) 685-1230 ext. 3296 or 3276.

Dominican College: San Rafael, CA 94901. Total enrollment: 725. LD students: 15. Special services: individual and group tutoring, academic and psychological counseling, diagnostic assessment, training in study skills, support group, student resource center. Contact: Pamela Wilding, Director, The Learning Center. Telephone: (415) 485-3214 or 457-4440 ext. 214.

Center/clinic: The Learning Center, 1520 Grand Avenue, San Rafael, CA 94901. Telephone: (415) 485-3214 or 457-4440 ext. 214. Director: Pamela Wilding. Open to public. Ages served: children and adults.

El Camino College: 16007 Crenshaw Boulevard, Torrance, CA 90506. Total enrollment: 28,000. LD students: 160. Special services: individual and group tutoring, training in study skills, academic counseling, taped books, special examinations, student resource center, readers, diagnostic testing, ombudsman, support group. Contact: William Hoanzl, Learning Disabilities Specialist. Telephone: (213) 532-3670 ext. 611 or 612.

Center/clinic: Educational Diagnostic Center, 11641 Weatherby, Los Alamitos, CA 90720. Telephone: (213) 532-3670. Director: William Hoanzl. Not open to public. Ages served: 18 and up. Grades served: freshmen, sophomores.

Evergreen Valley College: 3095 Yerba Buena Road, San Jose, CA 95135. Total enrollment: 8,060. LD students: 70. Special services: individual and group tutoring, training in study skills, academic counseling, taped books, special examinations, student resource center, readers, diagnostic testing, support group, tape recorder loans, note takers, diagnostic learning class. Contact: Bonnie Clark, Learning Disabilities Specialist. Telephone: (408) 270-6447.

Feather River College: P.O. Box 1110, Quincy, CA 95971. Total enrollment: 1,300. LD students: 20. Special services: readers, individual and group tutoring, special examinations, academic and psychological counseling, diagnostic testing, student resource center, support group, taped books, training in study skills. Contact: Donald B. Fregulia, Director, Enabler Program. Telephone: (916) 283-0202 ext. 74.

Center/clinic: Enabler Resource Center, P.O. Box 1110. Telephone: (916) 283-0202 ext. 74. Director: Donald B. Fregulia. Open to public. Grades served: college.

Fresno City College: 1101 E. University Avenue, Fresno, CA 93728. Total enrollment: 16,000. LD students: 250. Special services: individual tutoring, training in study skills, academic and psychological counseling, taped books, special examinations, student resource center, diagnostic testing, scholarships, support group, priority registration, vocational counseling and assessment, job training and placement, financial aid assistance.

- **Special program:** Enabler Program: Learning Disabilities Component. Special classes geared to individual needs. Must meet regular admissions requirements of the college. Learning disability must be verified through recent records or diagnostic testing done by the college. Director: Janice M. Emerzian. Telephone: (209) 442-8238.

Fresno Pacific College: 1717 S. Chestnut, Fresno, CA 93702. Special services: individual tutoring, training in study skills, academic and psychological counseling, special examinations, diagnostic testing. Contact: Joan Martens, Counseling Coordinator. Telephone: (209) 251-7194.

Fullerton College: 321 E. Chapman Avenue, Fullerton, CA 92634. Total enrollment: 18,000. LD students: 100. Special services: individual tutoring, academic counseling, taped books, special examinations, student resource center, readers, diagnostic testing, registration assistance. Contact: Thomas M. Cantrell, Learning Disabilities Specialist. Telephone: (714) 871-8000 ext. 374.

Gavilan College: 5055 Santa Teresa Boulevard, Gilroy, CA 95020. Total enrollment: 3,200. LD students: 75. Special services: diagnostic testing and assessment, prescriptive instruction, individual and group tutoring, readers, academic and psychological counseling, training in study skills, special instructional materials, scholarships, student resource center, support group, taped books, special examinations. Contact: Susan Bunch, Instructional Specialist. Telephone: (408) 847-1400.

Center/clinic: Learning Disabilities Center. Telephone: (408) 847-1400. Instructional Specialists: Susan Bunch, Elaine Alster. Open to public. Grades served: postsecondary.

Golden West College: 15744 Golden West Street, Huntington Beach, CA 92647. Total enrollment: 17,000-20,000. LD students: 10. Special services: academic advising, counseling, job placement, note takers, priority registration, readers, taped books, vocational testing, career planning, tutoring. Contact: Lois Shafqat, Director, Disabled Students Program. Telephone: (714) 895-8721.

Hartnell Community College: 156 Homestead Avenue, Salinas, CA 93901. Total enrollment: 4,500. LD students: 75. Special services: individual tutoring, special examinations, scholarships, academic and psychological counseling, student resource center, diagnostic testing, taped books, training in study skills, learning disabilities classes.

- **Special program:** Educational Skills Program. Must be registered at the college but students are not required to enroll in regular college courses to participate. Learning disability must be verified through recent diagnostic tests. Enabler: Wayne Davis. Telephone: (408) 758-8211 ext. 425.

CALIFORNIA

Holy Names College: 3500 Mountain Boulevard, Oakland, CA 94619. Special services: comprehensive assessment, educational and psychological evaluations, small class remediation. Contact: Mary Anne Thatcher, Assistant to the Dean. Telephone: (415) 436-0111.

Center/clinic: Speech and Language Center, Department of Special Education. Telephone: (415) 436-1022. Director: Deborah Shields. Services: clinic for communication disorders; offers speech and language screenings, evaluations, intervention. Open to public. Ages served: all.

Imperial Valley College: Highway 111 and Ira Aten Road, Imperial, CA 92251. Total enrollment: 3,207. LD students: 110. Special services: readers, individual and group tutoring, ombudsman, special examinations, student resource center, support group, diagnostic testing, taped books, training in study skills, career counseling, vocational testing and counseling. Contact: Mel Wendrick, Director. Telephone: (619) 352-8320 ext. 312.

Center/clinic: Physically Limited/Adaptive Learning Center, P.O. Box 158. Telephone: (619) 352-8320 ext. 312. Director: Mel Wendrick. Not open to public. Ages served: 18 and up.

John F. Kennedy University: 12 Altarinda Road, Orinda, CA 94563. Total enrollment: 1,853. LD students: 5. Special services: readers. Contact: David Sanford, Title 504 Coordinator. Telephone: (415) 254-0200 ext. 15.

Kings River Community College: 995 N. Reed Avenue, Reedley, CA 93654. Total enrollment: 3,300. LD students: 110. Special services: individual tutoring, academic and psychological counseling, diagnostic testing, taped books, training in study skills. Contact: Lynn Mancini, Director, Enabler Services. Telephone: (209) 638-3641 ext. 303.

Lake Tahoe Community College: P.O. Box 14445, South Lake Tahoe, CA 95702. LD students: 22. Special services: individual tutoring, training in study skills, academic and psychological counseling, taped books, special examinations, readers, diagnostic testing. Contact: Blair Bolles, Learning Disabilities Specialist. Telephone: (916) 541-4660 ext. 249.

Laney College: 900 Fallon Street, Oakland, CA 94607. Total enrollment: 11,000. LD students: 60. Special services: individual and group tutoring, training in study skills, academic and psychological counseling, taped books, special examinations, readers, diagnostic testing, support group, counseling, financial aid. Contact: Carol Dalessio, Counselor/Enabler. Telephone: (415) 834-5740 ext. 478 or 479.

Center/clinic: Learning Skills Program. Telephone: (415) 834-5740. Not open to public. Director: Sondra Neiman. Ages served: 18 and up. Grades served: college.

Lassen College: P.O. Box 3000, Susanville, CA 96130. Special services: individual and group tutoring, training in study skills, academic and psychological counseling, taped books, special examinations, student resource center, readers, diagnostic testing, scholarships, sensorimotor integration, vision exercises/training. Contact: Christine A. O'Dell, Learning Disabilities Specialist. Telephone: (916) 257-6181 ext. 129 or 186.

Los Angeles City College: 855 N. Vermont Avenue, Los Angeles, CA 90029. Total enrollment: 16,000. LD students: 75. Special services: individual tutoring, training in study skills, academic and psychological counseling, taped books, special examinations, student resource center, limited readers, diagnostic testing, ombudsman, support group.

- **Special program:** Special Learning Program. Strives to provide students with the academic and survival skills necessary to participate in regular college curriculum and become independent, productive citizens. Students spend a minimum of eight hours per week in the program. Hours are individually arranged. An identifiable learning disability must be present. Learning Disabilities Specialist: Susan Ndefo. Telephone: (213) 669-4000 ext. 515.

Los Angeles Mission College: 1212 San Fernando Road, San Fernando, CA 91340. Special services: readers, individual and group tutoring, special examinations, academic and psychological counseling, diagnostic testing, taped books, training in study skills. Contact: Rick Scuderi, Learning Disabilities Specialist. Telephone: (818) 365-8271.

Center/clinic: Special Education Resource Center. Telephone: (213) 365-8271. Director: Jack L. Oliver. Ages served: 18 and up.

Los Angeles Pierce College: 6201 Winnetka Avenue, Woodland Hills, CA 91371. Special services: individual and group tutoring, training in study skills, academic counseling, taped books, special examinations, student resource center, readers, diagnostic testing. Contact: Terrie Reiss Spritzer, Learning Specialist, or Norm Crozer, Director, Special Services Program. Telephone: (818) 347-0551 ext. 425.

Los Medanos College: 2700 Leland Road, Pittsburg, CA 94565. Total enrollment: 5,000. LD students: 100. Special services: individual and group tutoring, training in study skills, academic counseling, taped books, diagnostic testing; specialized instruction in reading, writing, and math. Contact: Nancy Nikhazy, Learning Specialist (Language Arts). Telephone: (415) 439-2181 ext. 3222. Or Jeannine Stein, Learning Specialist (Math). Telephone: (415) 439-2181 ext. 3365.

Loyola Marymount University: Loyola Boulevard at W. 80th Street, Los Angeles, CA 90045. Special services: individual and group tutoring, training in study skills, academic and psychological counseling, diagnostic testing, student resource

CALIFORNIA

center, readers. Contact: Victoria Graf, Director, Department of Education. Telephone: (213) 642-2863.

Center/clinic: Learning Resource Center. Telephone: (213) 642-2847. Director: Lane Bove. Not open to public. Ages served: 17 and up. Grades served: college.

Center/clinic: The Reading Center. Telephone: (213) 642-2863 or 642-2864. Director: Lane Bove. Open to public. Grades served: 2-12. Services: diagnostic testing, individualized instruction, special learning materials.

Merced College: 3600 "M" Street, Merced, CA 95340. Total enrollment: 5,000. LD students: 15. Special services: readers, individual and group tutoring, special examinations, academic counseling, taped books. Contact: Janis Tamberi-Carter, Director, Disabled Student Services. Telephone: (209) 384-6155.

Merritt College: 12500 Campus Drive, Oakland, CA 94619. Total enrollment: 6,900. LD students: 75. Special services: readers, group tutoring, academic and psychological counseling, student resource center, support group, diagnostic testing, taped books, training in study skills, career counseling, classes in basic skills.

- **Special program:** Diagnostic Learning Program. Special courses in basic skills including reading, writing, math, and spelling. Must be enrolled in the college but students not required to take regular college courses. Learning disability must be verified through recent records or diagnostic evaluations by the college. Learning Disabilities Specialists: Anne Long, Ellen Kranz. Telephone: (415) 531-4911 ext. 2579.

Mira Costa Community College: One Barnard Drive, Oceanside, CA 92056. Total enrollment: 6,500. LD students: 40. Special services: readers, individual and group tutoring, ombudsman, special examinations, academic and psychological counseling, diagnostic testing, support group, taped books, training in study skills, remedial classes. Contact: Ronald E. Baker, Coordinator, Handicapped Student Services. Telephone: (619) 757-2121 ext. 296.

Modesto Junior College: 435 College Avenue, Modesto, CA 95350. Total enrollment: 11,041. LD students: 50. Special services: individual and group tutoring, academic counseling, taped books, special examinations, student resource center, readers, diagnostic testing, support group. Contact: Marilyn Stem, Learning Disabilities Specialist. Telephone: (209) 575-6181.

Monterey Peninsula College: 980 Fremont Boulevard, Monterey, CA 93940. Special services: readers, individual and group tutoring, special examinations, academic and psychological counseling, diagnostic testing, student resource center, readers, scholarships, ombudsman, support group, taped books, training in study skills, vocational and career awareness training.

- **Special program:** Learning Disabilities Program. Must be enrolled in the college. Learning disability must be verified through diagnostic testing done by the college. Students not required to enroll in a minimum number of regular college courses. Director: Bill Jones. Telephone: (408) 646-4069.

Moorpark Community College: 7075 Campus Road, Moorpark, CA 93021. Total enrollment: 9,000. LD students: 75. Special services: individual and group tutoring, special examinations, academic counseling, diagnostic testing, student resource center, support group, taped books, training in study skills.

- **Special program:** Learning Disabilities Program. Special courses in basic math, reading, study skills, language development, spelling. Must be enrolled in the college. Learning disability must be verified through recent records or diagnostic evaluation by the college. Students not required to enroll in minimum number of regular college courses. However, program goal is to mainstream learning disabled students into regular college program. Learning Disabilities Specialist: Joanna Dillon. Telephone: (805) 529-2321 ext. 333.

Mt. San Antonio College: 1100 N. Grand Avenue, Walnut, CA 91789. Total enrollment: 20,000. LD students: 40. Special services: individual and group tutoring, special examinations, academic and psychological counseling, diagnostic testing, training in study skills, special classes in reading, writing, math. Contact: Mayme Thornton. Telephone: (714) 594-5611 ext. 290.

Mt. San Jacinto College: San Jacinto, CA 92383. Total enrollment: 3,000. LD students: 30. Special services: readers, individual and group tutoring, special examinations (at instructor's discretion), academic counseling, diagnostic testing, student resource center, taped books, training in study skills, remedial classes.

- **Special program:** Learning Disabilities Program. Support services to enable learning disabled students to succeed in college. Special classes in language arts, math, study skills. Designed for students pursuing a degree or certificate program. Must be registered full or part-time at the college. Learning disability must be verified through recent records or diagnostic testing done by the college. Learning Disabilities Specialist: Marcia Krull. Telephone: (714) 654-8011 ext. 219 or 226.

Napa Valley College: 2277 Napa-Vallejo Highway, Napa, CA 94558. Total enrollment: 6,000-7,000. LD students: 150. Special services: individual and group tutoring, training in study skills, academic counseling, taped books, special examinations, student resource center, readers, diagnostic testing, scholarships, ombudsman, full access to other campus-based student services including financial aid. Contact: JoAnn Busenbark, Director/Enabler, or Gwynne Katz, Learning Disabilities Specialist. Telephone: (707) 255-2100 ext. 395 or 336.

Center/clinic: Diagnostic Learning Center. Telephone: (707) 255-2100 ext. 336. Not open to public. Director: Gwynne Katz. Ages served: 18 and up. Grades served: freshmen, sophomores.

CALIFORNIA

Ohlone College: 43600 Mission Boulevard, Fremont, CA 94539. Total enrollment: 8,000. LD students: 30. Special services: individual tutoring, training in study skills, academic and psychological counseling, taped books, special examinations, student resource center, readers. Contact: Fred R. Hilke, Associate Professor, Counseling. Telephone: (415) 659-6140.

Orange Coast College: 2701 Fairview Road, Costa Mesa, CA 92626. Special services: remediation in reading, spelling, writing, and arithmetic; special examinations (with instructor approval), academic counseling, psychoeducational diagnostic testing. Contact: Kenneth K. Ortiz, Director, Learning Center. Telephone: (714) 432-5042.

Center/clinic: Learning Center. Telephone: (714) 432-5042 or 432-5535. Director: Kenneth K. Ortiz. Ages served: 18 and up.

Oxnard College: 4000 S. Rose Avenue, Oxnard, CA 93033. Total enrollment: 4,800. LD students: 35. Special services: individual tutoring, training in study skills, academic and psychological counseling, special examinations, readers, diagnostic testing, support group. Contact: Carole Frick, Learning Disabilities Specialist, or Joan Jones, Work Evaluator/Counselor. Telephone: (805) 488-0911 ext. 214.

Center/clinic: Special Education Department. Telephone: (805) 488-0911 ext. 214. Director: Carole A. Frick. Not open to public. Ages served: 18 and up. Grades served: college. Services: diagnostic testing, counseling, tutoring, specialized instruction, vocational testing and counseling.

Palomar Community College: 1140 W. Mission Road, San Marcos, CA 92069. Total enrollment: 250. LD students: 40. Special services: individual tutoring, academic and psychological counseling, taped books, student resource center, diagnostic testing. Contact: Gene Zevin, Director. Telephone: (619) 744-1150 ext. 2375.

Pasadena City College: 1570 E. Colorado Boulevard, Pasadena, CA 91106. Total enrollment: 20,000. LD students: 195. Special services: readers, individual and group tutoring, ombudsman, special examinations, academic counseling, diagnostic testing, student resource center, support group, taped books; training in study skills, self-assessment, and self-advocacy.

- **Special program:** Special Services: Learning Disabilities. Special classes to help learning disabled college students enrolled in mainstream classes. Extensive aphasia program. Participants must be able to benefit from the special program and be registered in at least one regular class at the college. Learning disability must be verified through recent records or diagnostic testing done by the college. Teacher Specialist: Emy Lu Weller. Telephone: (818) 578-7127.

Rio Hondo College: 3600 Workman Mill Road, Whittier, CA 90608. Total enrollment: 12,000. LD students: 120. Special services: readers, individual and group tutoring, ombudsman, special examinations, academic and psychological counseling, diagnostic testing, student resource center, support group, taped books, training in study skills, reading machine.

- **Special program:** Disabled Students Program: Learning Disabilities. Support services and special classes. Learning disability must be verified through recent records or diagnostic testing done by the college. Accepts individuals who are not registered at the college. Learning Disabilities Specialist: Judy Shaw. Telephone: (213) 692-0921 ext. 240.

Riverside City College: 4800 Magnolia Avenue, Riverside, CA 92507. Total enrollment: 14,000. LD students: 100. Special services: individual and group tutoring, training in study skills, academic counseling, taped books, special examinations, student resource center, diagnostic testing, support group, personal counseling or referral; reading remediation. Contact: L. Kochenderfer, Learning Disabilities Specialist. Telephone: (714) 684-3240.

Saddleback College: 28000 Marguerite Parkway, Mission Viejo, CA 92692. Total enrollment: 28,000. LD students: 95. Special services: individual and group tutoring, training in study skills, academic and psychological counseling, taped books, special examinations, readers, diagnostic testing. Contact: Paula Jacobs, Learning Specialist. Telephone: (714) 831-4886.

Center/clinic: Learning Development Center. Telephone: (714) 831-4886. Not open to public. Director: Paula Jacobs. Ages served: adults.

St. Mary's College: P.O. Box 316, Moraga, CA 94575. Special services: individual and group tutoring, training in study skills, academic and psychological counseling, taped books, special examinations, readers. Contact: Jeannine Chavez-Parfitt, Director, Tutorial Services Program. Telephone: (415) 376-4411 ext. 358.

San Bernardino Valley College: 701 S. Mount Vernon, San Bernardino, CA 92410. Total enrollment: 611. LD students: 53. Special services: individual and group tutoring, training in study skills, academic and psychological counseling, taped books, special examinations, student resource center, readers, diagnostic testing, scholarships, ombudsman, support group, computer-assisted instruction. Contact: Fritz Hjermstad, Coordinator of Handicapped Services. Telephone: (714) 888-6511 ext. 164.

San Diego Mesa College: 7250 Mesa College Drive, San Diego, CA 92111. Total enrollment: 22,000. LD students: 200. Special services: readers, individual and group tutoring, ombudsman, special examinations, academic and psychological counseling, diagnostic testing, student resource center, support group, taped books, training in study skills, career planning, job placement assistance. Contact: Mary H. Dohrman, Learning Disability Specialist. Telephone: (619) 230-6872.

CALIFORNIA

Center/clinic: The Developmental Learning Lab. Telephone: (619) 230-6872. Contact: Mary H. Dohrman. Not open to public. Grades served: college.

San Diego Miramar College: 10440 Black Mountain Road, San Diego, CA 92126. Total enrollment: 4,911. Special services: individual tutoring, academic and psychological counseling, student resource center, readers. Contact: Ernie L. Williams, Counselor. Telephone: (619) 230-6540.

San Diego State University: San Diego, CA 92182. Special services: individual and group tutoring, academic and psychological counseling, taped books, special examinations, student resource center, readers, note takers, diagnostic testing, ombudsman. Contact: Deirdre Semoff Jordan, Learning Disabilities Specialist. Telephone: (619) 265-6473.

San Joaquin Delta College: 5151 Pacific Avenue, Stockton, CA 95207. Special services: readers, individual and group tutoring, special examinations, scholarships, academic counseling, diagnostic testing, taped books, training in study skills, classes to improve basic skills.

- **Special program:** Learning Disabilities Laboratory. Special classes employ remediation and compensation strategies. Must meet regular admissions requirements of the college. Learning disability must be verified by records no more than a year old or by diagnostic testing done by the college. Full or part-time students eligible. Director: Mary Mendez. Telephone: (209) 474-5259.

San Jose City College: 2100 Moorpark Avenue, San Jose, CA 95128. Total enrollment: 13,000. LD students: 165. Special services: individual and group tutoring, training in study skills, academic counseling, taped books, special examinations, student resource center, readers, diagnostic testing, support group, tape recorder loans, note takers, diagnostic learning class. Contact: M.A. Johnson, Learning Disabilities Specialist. Telephone: (408) 288-3746.

San Jose State University: Washington Square, San Jose, CA 95192. Total enrollment: 25,000. LD students: 30-40. Special services: readers, individual and group tutoring, ombudsman, special examinations, academic and psychological counseling, diagnostic testing, training in study skills, workshops, note takers, adaptive devices including tape recorders and talking calculators, test proctors, special classes for the learning disabled. Contact: Martin Schulter, Director, or Trey Duffy, Support Services Coordinator. Telephone: (408) 277-2971.

Center/clinic: Learning Assistance Lab. Telephone: (408) 277-2658 or 277-2150. Director, Learning Assistance Program: Kathy Carmona. Open to public. Ages served: 5-18. Services: diagnostic testing, bilingual testing available.

Santa Ana College: 17th at Bristol, Santa Ana, CA 90726. Total enrollment: 30,000. LD students: 180-200. Special services: individual and group tutoring, training in study skills, academic and psychological counseling, special examinations, student resource center, readers, diagnostic testing, support group, special classes in job skills, career development, self-adjustment.

- **Special program:** Learning Disability Program. Must be enrolled in the college. Learning disability must be certified through recent records or diagnostic testing done by the college. Students not required to enroll in a minimum number of regular college courses. Learning Disabilities Specialist: Cheryl Dunn-Hoanzl. Telephone: (714) 667-3080.

Santa Barbara City College: 721 Cliff Drive, Santa Barbara, CA 93109. Total enrollment: 10,000. LD students: 150. Special services: individual and group tutoring, training in study skills, academic and psychological counseling, taped books, special examinations, student resource center, readers, diagnostic testing, support group.

- **Special program:** Learning Disabilities Program. Provides educational support for students with learning disabilities enrolled in regular college classes. Offers special classes in reading, writing, math, spelling, study skills, career planning. Learning Disabilities Specialist: Janet Shapiro. Telephone: (805) 965-0581 ext. 374.

Sierra College: 5000 Rocklin Road, Rocklin, CA 95677. Total enrollment: 10,000. LD students: 400. Special services: individual and group tutoring, training in study skills, academic counseling, taped books, special examinations, student resource center, readers, diagnostic testing, scholarships, ombudsman.

- **Special program:** The Learning Disabilities Program of the Learning Opportunity Center. Testing and diagnosis, auditory discrimination and visual perception program, classes in basic reading, writing, and math. Learning disability must be verified through recent records or testing done by college staff. Must be enrolled in the college but students not required to enroll in regular college courses. Learning Disability Specialist: Denise Stone. Telephone: (916) 624-3333 ext. 2378.

Sonoma State University: E. Cotati Avenue, Rhonert Park, CA 94928. Total enrollment: 5,000. LD students: 25-30. Special services: individual tutoring, training in study skills, academic and psychological counseling, taped books, special examinations, student resource center, readers, diagnostic testing, ombudsman, support group, resource and referral network. Contact: Anthony Tusler, Director, Office for Students with Disabilities. Telephone: (707) 664-2677. Or Deborah Greene, Learning Disability Specialist. Telephone: (707) 664-2853.

University of California-Berkeley: Berkeley, CA 94720. Special services: individual and group tutoring, training in study skills, academic and psychological counseling, taped books, special examinations, student resource center, readers, ombudsman, admission assistance, note takers.

CALIFORNIA

- **Special program:** The Learning Disabilities Program. SAT required. Application assistance available through Disabled Students' Program. Learning disability must be verified by educational evaluation not more than two years old. Coordinator of Services for the Learning Disabled: Dorothy Stump. Telephone: (415) 642-0518.

University of California-Los Angeles: Los Angeles, CA 90024. Total enrollment: 33,000. LD students: 2-10. Special services: readers, individual and group tutoring, ombudsman, special examinations, scholarships, academic and psychological counseling, training in study skills, registration assistance. Contact: Michael Butler, Acting Director, Office of Special Services. Telephone: (213) 825-1501.

University of California-Riverside: 900 University Avenue, Riverside, CA 92521. Total enrollment: 5,000. LD students: 5. Special services: individual and group tutoring, ombudsman, special examinations, academic and psychological counseling, diagnostic testing, training in study skills, student resource center, readers, secretarial assistance. Contact: Marcia Theise Schiffer, Coordinator, Disabled Student Services. Telephone: (714) 787-4538.

University of California-San Diego: La Jolla, CA 92093. Total enrollment: 11,700. LD students: 6. Special services: individual and group tutoring, training in study skills, academic counseling, taped books, special examinations, readers, note takers, special equipment loan. Contact: Connie Wilbur, Director, Disabled Student Services. Telephone: (619) 452-4382.

University of San Diego: Alcala Park, San Diego, CA 92110. Special services: training in study skills, academic and psychological counseling. Contact: DeForest L. Strunk, Director of Special and Gifted Education. Telephone: (619) 260-4539.

University of Santa Clara: Santa Clara, CA 95053. Special services: individual tutoring, training in study skills, academic and psychological counseling. Contact: Ruth E. Cook, Acting Director of Special Education. Telephone: (408) 544-4434.

University of Southern California: Los Angeles, CA 90007. Special services: individual tutoring, special examinations (with instructor approval), limited scholarships, academic and psychological counseling, diagnostic testing, taped books, training in study skills. Contact: Janet Eddy, Learning Specialist. Telephone: (213) 743-6544.

Center/clinic: Learning Skills Development Center, University Village, Suite E. Telephone: (213) 743-6544. Director: Dolores Akins. Contact: Janet Eddy, Learning Specialist. Not open to public. Grades served: college. Services: tutoring.

Ventura Community College: 4667 Telegraph Road, Ventura, CA 93003. Special services: readers, individual and group tutoring, ombudsman, special examinations, scholarships, academic and psychological counseling, diagnostic testing, taped books, training in study skills.

- **Special program:** Ventura College Learning Disabilities Program. Eighteen special courses, including classes in memory, math, reading, language, auditory, listening skills. An assessment class a prerequisite for all learning disabled students. Learning disability must be verified through recent diagnostic tests or testing done by the college. Must be enrolled in the college but students not required to take regular college courses. Learning Disabilities Specialists: Jeffrey Barsch, Betty Creson. Telephone: (805) 644-5388.

Victor Valley Community College: P.O. Drawer 00, Victorville, CA 92392. Total enrollment: 4,600. LD students: 28. Special services: individual tutoring, academic counseling, taped books, special examinations, readers, diagnostic testing, note takers, special class for learning disabled. Contact: Cynthia J. Allen, Counselor/Enabler, Handicapped Program. Telephone: (619) 245-4271 ext. 212.

West Hills College: 300 Cherry Lane, Coalinga, CA 93210. Total enrollment: 2,000. LD students: 45. Special services: individual and group tutoring, special examinations, academic and psychological counseling, diagnostic testing, training in study skills, student resource center. Contact: Miss DeMaris, Director. Telephone: (209) 935-0801 ext. 328.

Center/clinic: Learning Resource Center. Telephone: (209) 935-0801. Director: Helen Gladson. Open to public.

West Valley College: 14000 Fruitvale Avenue, Saratoga, CA 95070. Special services: readers, individual and group tutoring, special examinations, scholarships, academic and psychological counseling, diagnostic testing, training in study skills, speech and language development program.

- **Special program:** Instructional Program for the Learning Disabled. Classes in basic skills including math, reading, spelling. Must be enrolled in the college to participate in program. Learning disability must be verified through recent records or testing done by the college. Contact: Jim Peck. Telephone: (408) 867-2200 ext. 463.

Center/clinic: West Valley Learning Services. Telephone: (408) 867-2200 ext. 416 or 511. Ages served: 18 and up.

Yuba College: 2088 N. Beale Road, Marysville, CA 95901. Special services: individual and group tutoring, scholarships, individual and academic counseling, diagnostic testing, taped books, training in study skills, compressed speech tape recorders, print magnifiers, note takers, intervention with mainstream instructors and counselors.

CALIFORNIA

- **Special program:** Learning Disabilities Program. Training in basic skills. Learning disability must be verified through recent records or diagnostic testing done by the college. Must be enrolled in the college but students not required to take regular college courses. Director: Helen David Shaw. Telephone: (916) 741-6758.

Hospital Clinics

Chula Vista: Southwood Psychiatric Hospital, Outpatient Services, 950 Third Avenue, 92011. Telephone: (619) 428-6310. Contact: Rhonda Whitcock. Outpatient, inpatient, and day program. Ages served: 4-17. Services: diagnostic testing, academic and psychological testing, psychological counseling, group and occupational therapy, social services.

Dana Point: Capistrano by the Sea Hospital, 33915 Del Obispo, 92629. Telephone: (714) 496-5702. Contact: L. Stedmitz, Director, Adolescent Services. Outpatient and inpatient program. Ages served: 12-18. Services: diagnostic testing, academic and psychological testing, individual tutoring; academic, psychological, and parent counseling; group and occupational therapy, support group, social services, placement services.

Fresno: Valley Children's Hospital, Department of Developmental and Behavioral Pediatrics, 3151 N. Millbrook, 93703. Telephone: (209) 225-3000. Contact: Carl R. Schneiderman, Director. Outpatient, day, and after school program. Ages served: birth-21. Services: diagnostic testing, psychological testing, individual tutoring; academic, psychological, and parent counseling; group, speech, language, physical, and occupational therapy; social services. Notes: Serves as parent-child advocate on placement issues and continuing education needs.

Los Angeles: Edgemont Hospital, Adolescent Treatment Program, 4841 Hollywood Boulevard, 90027. Telephone: (213) 666-5252. Contact: Al Kubat, Director, Adolescent Services. Outpatient and inpatient program. Ages served: 1-11 outpatient; 11-18 inpatient. Services: diagnostic testing, academic and psychological testing, individual and group tutoring, psychological and parent counseling; group, speech, language, and occupational therapy; social services, behavioral/ social structured program, developmental/medical evaluation, habilitation, special education. Notes: Program serves teens with severe emotional and behavioral difficulties such as depression, truancy, chronic running away, failure to learn, and hostility.

Los Angeles: Pediatric Pavilion, Los Angeles County - University of Southern California Medical Center, School Problems, 1129 N. State Street, 90033. Telephone: (213) 226-3677. Contact: Dora Jorden or Yolanda Moreno. Outpatient program. Ages served: 6-17. Services: diagnostic testing, psychological testing, psychological and parent counseling; group, physical, and occupational therapy; social services.

Oakland: Kaiser Permanente Medical Center, Learning Disabilities Clinic, Department of Pediatrics, 280 W. Macarthur Boulevard, 94611. Telephone: (415) 428-5794. Contact: Joseph H. Rosenthal, Director. Outpatient program. Ages served: young children-adult. Services: diagnostic testing, parent counseling, support group; informational services including pamphlets, lectures, courses, seminars, books, and audiovisuals about learning disabilities.

Oakland: Naval Hospital, Psychology Clinic, 94627. Telephone: (415) 533-5379. Contact: David T. Hargraves, Head, Psychology Department and Outpatient Clinic. Outpatient program. Ages served: adolescent-adult. Services: diagnostic testing, academic and psychological testing. Notes: Services limited to active duty military personnel and their dependents.

Pomona: CPC Horizon Hospital, Adolescent Growth Center, 566 N. Gordon, 91768. Telephone: (714) 629-4011. Contact: Judy Bates, Director of Education. Inpatient program. Ages served: preschool-18. Services: diagnostic testing, academic and psychological testing, individual and group tutoring; academic, psychological, and parent counseling; group and occupational therapy, social services.

Salinas: Natividad Medical Center, Family Practice Clinic, 1330 Natividad Road, P.O. Box 1611, 93902. Telephone: (408) 757-0200. Contact: Director of Family Practice Residency Program. Outpatient and inpatient program. Services: diagnostic testing, academic and psychological testing, psychological and parent counseling; speech, language, physical, and occupational therapy; social services.

San Diego: Children's Hospital and Health Center, Child Guidance Clinic, 8001 Frost Street, 92123. Telephone: (619) 576-5832. Contact: Chris Chase, Learning Disability Coordinator. Outpatient and after school program. Ages served: 4-18. Services: diagnostic testing, academic and psychological testing, individual and group tutoring; academic, psychological, and parent counseling; group therapy, social services, stress management program, school conferencing to help develop programs.

San Diego: UCSD Medical Center, Communicative Disorders Center, 3320 Third Avenue, 92103. Telephone: (619) 294-5700. Contact: Carole Grote, Director. Outpatient and inpatient program. Ages served: 5-adult. Services: diagnostic testing, academic and psychological testing, individual and group tutoring, parent counseling; speech, language, and occupational therapy; social services, pediatric neuropsychological testing.

San Francisco: Children's Hospital of San Francisco, Child Development Center, 3700 California Street, 94118. Telephone: (415) 750-6200. Contact: Joan Taylor Cehn, Administrative Director. Outpatient and after school program. Ages served: birth-16. Services: diagnostic testing, academic and psychological testing, individual tutoring, psychological and parent counseling; speech, language, physical, and occupational therapy; adaptive physical education, social services.

CALIFORNIA

San Francisco: Garden Sullivan Hospital of Pacific Medical Center, Learning and Development Program, 2750 Geary Boulevard, 94118. Telephone: (415) 921-6171 ext. 255. Contact: Antje Shadoan. Outpatient program. Ages served: 3-13. Services: diagnostic testing, academic testing, individual and group tutoring, academic and parent counseling; speech, language, physical, and occupational therapy; support group, social services.

San Francisco: St. Mary's Hospital and Medical Center, Speech and Learning Center, 450 Stanyan, 94117. Telephone: (415) 750-5557. Contact: Doris Rosen, Acting Director. Outpatient, day, and after school program. Ages served: infant-adult. Services: diagnostic testing, academic and psychological testing, individual and group tutoring; academic, psychological, and parent counseling; speech, language, and education therapy; psychoeducational and speech and language evaluations, limited scholarship fund.

Santa Monica: St. John's Hospital, St. John's Child Study Center, 1339 20th Street, 90404. Telephone: (213) 829-8921. Contact: Renee Dubin, Psychologist. Outpatient and after school program. Ages served: 6-adult. Services: diagnostic testing, academic and psychological testing, individual tutoring, psychological and parent counseling; speech, language, physical, and occupational therapy; social services, recommendations for school placement.

Other Services

Albany: Reach for Learning, 902 Curtis Street, 94706. Telephone: (415) 524-6455. Educational Psychologist: Emily Benner. Clinic. Day and after school program. Ages served: all. Services: diagnostic testing, academic and psychological testing, individual and small group tutoring; academic, psychological, and parent counseling; in-service training for teachers, parent groups.

Berkeley: A Learning Place, 1345A Martin Luther King Jr. Way, 94709. Telephone: (415) 527-7323. Associate Director: Susan Hagar. Educational center. After school program. Ages served: 5 and up. Services: diagnostic testing, academic and psychological testing, individual and group tutoring, academic counseling, consulting seminars.

Burlingame: The Reading Research Council, 1799 Old Bayshore Highway, Suite 248, 94010. Telephone: (415) 692-8990. Contact: Ronald Dell Davis. Clinic. Day and after school program. Ages served: 6 and up. Services: diagnostic testing, academic testing; academic, psychological, and parent counseling; support group; in-service training for professionals, counseling services for groups such as schools and other agencies.

Camarillo: Camarillo Reading Clinic, 484 Mobil Avenue, 93010. Telephone: (805) 482-3730. Director: Paula Cornelius-Lopez. Clinic. Day and summer program. Ages served: preschool-adult. Grades served: kindergarten-college. Current enrollment: 96. Full-time staff: 2. Part-time staff: 4. Services: individual and group tutoring, academic and psychological testing, academic and family counseling.

Cathedral City: Desert Occupational Therapy Services, 68-765 First Street, 92234. Telephone: (619) 324-5151. Director: D. Fendley Mount. Clinic. After school program. Ages served: birth-adult. Services: diagnostic testing, parent counseling; speech, language, physical, and occupational therapy; support group, social services, individual and group sensory integration therapy.

Chico: Brislain Learning Center, 14 Williamsburg Lane, 95926. Telephone: (916) 342-2567. Educational Director: Judy Basta-Brislain. Educational center with summer program. Ages served: 4-adult. Current enrollment: 75. Maximum enrollment: no limit. Full-time staff: 3. Part-time staff: 3. Scholarships/financial aid available. Services: individual and group tutoring, academic and psychological testing, counseling, family therapy, neuropsychological rehabilitation.

Covina: Covina Psychological Group, 101 S. Barranca Avenue, Suite 208, 91723. Telephone: (818) 331-9996. Senior Psychologist: Robert H. Oyler. Clinic. Ages served: infant-adult. Services: diagnostic testing, academic and psychological testing, individual tutoring; academic, psychological, and parent counseling; support group, directed reading, parent training. Notes: Spanish spoken.

El Cajon: Rincon Center for Learning, 594 N. Westwind Drive, 92020-2843. Telephone: (619) 442-2722. Director: Lois Dotson. Clinic. After school program. Ages served: 4-adult. Services: diagnostic testing, academic testing, individual tutoring. Notes: Slingerland-trained teacher for dyslexic students.

Elk Grove: Elk Grove Learning Center, 9594 Second Avenue, 95624. Telephone: (916) 685-4033. Contact: Ann Taylor. Clinic. After school program. Ages served: 4-adult. Services: academic testing and counseling, individual tutoring.

Escondido: North County Learning Associates, 142 S. Grape Street, Suite B, 92025. Telephone: (619) 489-6066. Contact: Sally Todd or Victoria Martin. Clinic. Day and after school program. Ages served: preschool-adult. Services: readiness screening, diagnostic testing, academic testing, mental processing and perceptual testing; academic, parent, and career counseling; educational therapy, support group, advocacy, school search.

Fairfield: Solano Learning Center, 1125 Missouri Street, #208, 94533. Telephone: (707) 429-9303. Executive Director: Janet Ose. Clinic. Day and after school program. Ages served: 3-adult. Services: diagnostic testing, academic and psychological testing, individual and group tutoring, academic and parent counseling, adaptive physical education, support group.

CALIFORNIA

Lafayette: Melmed Reading Clinic, Inc., 957 Dewing Avenue, 94549. Telephone: (415) 283-6777. Director: Paul J. Melmed. Clinic. Day and after school program. Ages served: preschool-adult. Services: diagnostic testing, academic and psychological testing, individual and group tutoring; academic, psychological, and parent counseling; speech and language therapy, workshops for parents and professionals.

Los Angeles: Center for Prevention of Learning Difficulties, 1416 Westwood Boulevard, Suite 205, 90024. Telephone: (213) 474-5141. Director: Connie Wright. Clinic. Day, after school, and summer program. Ages served: 4-adult. Services: preschool, diagnostic testing, academic testing and counseling, individual tutoring, school referrals, computer programs.

Los Angeles: child, etc., 2205 Stoner Avenue, Suite 110, 90064. Telephone: (213) 477-5033 or 27-child. Director: Terry Bearman. Clinic. Day, after school, and summer program. Ages served: preschool-adult. Services: diagnostic testing, academic and psychological testing, academic recommendations, parent counseling, speech and language testing, learning style evaluations, in-service training for professionals and parents, placement, consultation with schools and tutors, specific recommendations for learning tactics, follow-up, multidisciplinary team approach. Notes: Designed to help students with unique learning styles realize they can learn.

Los Angeles: The Kelter Center, 12301 Wilshire Avenue, Suite 418, 90025. Telephone: (213) 207-5362. Director: Sasha Borenstein. Clinic. Day and after school program. Ages served: 6-adult. Services: educational therapy, diagnostic testing, academic and psychological testing, individual tutoring, psychological and parent counseling, in-service training for educators, parent education programs.

Novato: Lane's Learning Center, One Gustafson Court, 94947. Telephone: (415) 892-7706. Director: Michele Lane. Clinic. Day and after school program. Ages served: preschool-adult. Services: diagnostic testing, academic testing, individual and group tutoring, adaptive physical education, swimming, computer and vocational education.

Oakland: Easter Seal Rehabilitation Center, 2757 Telegraph Avenue, 94612. Telephone: (415) 835-2131 or 835-2132. Director of Client Services: Cristine Bjork. Rehabilitation center with limited services. Ages served: 2½ and up. Scholarships/financial aid available. Services: psychological testing, family counseling; physical, occupational, speech, and language therapy; medical services.

Oakland: Raskob Learning Institute, 3520 Mountain Boulevard, 94619. Telephone: (415) 436-1275. Director: Mary Lee Knapp. Clinic. Day and after school program. Ages served: 5 and up. Services: diagnostic testing, academic and psychological testing, individual and group tutoring, parent counseling, language therapy; referrals for psychological counseling, speech/articulation and occupational therapy; individualized, specific remediation.

Ojai: Ojai Center for Learning Disabilities, 195 E. El Rublar Drive, 93023. Telephone: (805) 646-3880. Administrator: Frances A. Merkley. Educational center with limited services. Day and summer program. Ages served: infant-adult. Scholarships/financial aid available. Services: individual tutoring, academic and psychological testing; academic, psychological, and family counseling; physical, occupational, speech, and language therapy; workshops for parents and professionals.

Pasadena: Assessment and Resource Center, a division of Pasadena Guidance Clinics, 66 Hurlbut Street, 91106. Telephone: (818) 795-8471 ext. 322. Chief Consultant/Learning Disabilities Specialist: Emy Lu Weller. Clinic. Assessment and referral program. Ages served: all. Services: diagnostic testing, academic and psychological testing, vocational and neuropsychological assessment, referrals.

Pasadena: Georgiana Rodiger Center, 1102 Arden Road, 91106. Telephone: (818) 792-0261. Director: Georgiana Rodiger. Center Coordinator: Leah Kearney. Clinic. Day, after school, and weekend program. Ages served: birth-adult. Services: diagnostic testing, academic and psychological testing, individual and group tutoring; academic, psychological, and parent counseling; group, speech, language, and sensorimotor therapy; limited adaptive physical education, support group.

Pomona: The Attic Reading Center, 939 E. Lincoln Avenue, 91767. Telephone: (714) 622-8361. Director: Jean Boyd Todd. Clinic. Ages served: 7 and up. Services: individual and group tutoring, academic testing. Notes: Diagnoses and remediates difficulties in reading, writing, and spelling.

Riverside: Richards Educational Therapy Center, 190 E. Big Springs Road, 92507. Telephone: (714) 787-0408. Director: Regina G. Richards. Day and after school program. Ages served: preschool-adult. Services: diagnostic testing, academic testing, individual tutoring; speech, language, occupational, and vision therapy; parent training, in-service training for teachers.

Roseville: Sierra Consultants, 4520 Northglen Street, 95678. Telephone: (916) 791-1752. Learning Disabilities Specialist: Denise Stone. Clinic. Ages served: 5 and up. Services: diagnostic and academic testing.

San Dimas: Anastasi Family Counseling, a Professional Corporation, 442-A W. Bonita Avenue, 91773. Telephone: (714) 599-8482. Contact: Maureen Anastasi. After school program. Ages served: 3 and up. Services: diagnostic testing, academic and psychological testing, individual tutoring, psychological and parent counseling. Notes: Can coordinate treatment program with child's school and facilitate placement in special programs.

San Francisco: La Mel Children's Center, 1801 Bush Street, 94109. Telephone: (415) 931-1972. Director: J. LaVonne Lomba. Day treatment facility. Preschool, elementary, secondary, and adult day school. Ages served: 3-21. Grades served:

all. Current enrollment: 65. Maximum enrollment: 75. Full-time staff: 37. Services: individual and group tutoring, academic and psychological testing; academic, psychological, and family counseling; physical, art, and movement therapy; adaptive physical education, vocational training, work-study, job placement, medical services. Recreation: gymnastics, team sports, jogging, other activities. Notes: Serves children and adolescents with adjustment problems because of emotional or neurological handicaps.

San Francisco: Learning Associates, 2465 Union Street, 94123. Telephone: (415) 346-8076 or 459-3249. Coassociates: Vera Obermeyer, Suzanne Warren. Educational service. Ages served: all. Services: diagnostic testing, academic and psychological testing, individual tutoring; academic, psychological, and parent counseling; individual, group, and family therapy; support group.

San Francisco: The Learning Disabilities Center, 1209 Guerrero Street, 94110. Telephone: (415) 821-1082. Codirector: Jane Sprouse. Clinic. After school program. Ages served: 5-adult. Services: diagnostic testing, academic testing, individual tutoring, academic and parent counseling, in-service training for professionals.

San Francisco: Learning Services of Northern California, 2435 Ocean Avenue, 94127. Telephone: (415) 586-1620. Executive Director: Shelley Lobell. Educational center. Day and summer program. Ages served: 3-18. Scholarships/financial aid available. Services: individual and group tutoring, academic and psychological testing; academic, psychological, and family counseling; computer-assisted instruction. Recreation: field trips, camping, art. Notes: Works closely with child's school, teachers, and family.

San Jose: San Jose Children's Health Council, 1671 The Alameda, Suite 217, 95126. Telephone: (408) 293-8288. Director: Iris S. Korol. Mental health clinic. Ages served: 2-17. Services: diagnostic testing, academic and psychological testing, family counseling, medical services, evaluations, referrals. Notes: Interdisciplinary approach to diagnosis and treatment of children with emotional, social, behavioral, and learning disabilities.

San Rafael: Marin Diagnostic and Remedial Center, 1123 Court Street, #8, 94901. Telephone: (415) 459-3249. Director: Suzanne Warren. Clinic. After school program. Ages served: 5-adult. Services: diagnostic testing, academic testing, individual tutoring.

Santa Ana: St. Peter Learning Center, 1510 N. Parton, 92706. Telephone: (714) 542-3111. Director: Ellen Franklin. Clinic. After school and summer program. Ages served: kindergarten-adult. Limited scholarships/financial aid available. Services: diagnostic testing, academic and psychological testing, individual tutoring, academic and parent counseling, gross/sensorimotor training, visual and auditory perception training.

Santa Barbara: The Devereux Foundation-California, P.O. Box 1079, 93102. Telephone: (805) 968-2525. Director: Jacob Azain. Secondary and adult residential treatment facility with summer program. Ages served: 12 and up. Grades served: junior high-adult work activity. Current enrollment: 209. Maximum enrollment: 190 on-campus; 35 community. Full-time staff: 185. Part-time staff: 18. Scholarships/financial aid available. Services: group tutoring, academic and psychological testing; academic, psychological, and family counseling; medical services; physical, occupational, speech, language, art, and music therapy; adaptive physical education, vocational training, job placement. Recreation: gymnasium, swimming pool, tennis courts.

Santa Barbara: The Dubin Learning Center, 22B W. Michelorena Street, 93101. Telephone: (805) 962-7122. Codirectors: Deidre and Barry Dubin. Educational center. Day and after school program. Ages served: kindergarten-12; adults. Services: diagnostic testing, academic and psychological testing, individual and group tutoring, academic and parent counseling, computers, enrichment, individualized approach.

Santa Barbara: Palmer Learning Systems, Inc., 545 N. Patterson Avenue, 93111. Telephone: (805) 683-1327. Contact: Carole C. Palmer. Clinic. Day, after school, and summer program. Ages served: preschool-adult. Services: diagnostic testing, individual and group tutoring, academic and psychological testing; academic, psychological, and parent counseling; speech, group, and language therapy; support group, basic skills for competency tests, consultation, computer programming, in-service education.

Santa Barbara: Santa Barbara Center for Educational Therapy, 2130 Mission Ridge Road, 93103. Telephone: (805) 687-3711. Codirectors: Susan Hamilton, Joyce A. Tolle. Educational center. Day and after school program. Ages served: 7 and up. Services: diagnostic testing, academic testing, individual and group tutoring, one-to-one remediation on an hourly basis. Notes: Specializes in language disabilities.

Santa Clara: Speech-Hearing-Learning Center of Crippled Children's Society, 2851 Park Avenue, 95050. Telephone: (408) 243-7861. Director, Learning Disabilities Programs: Charlotte Bridenbaugh. Clinic. After school and outreach program. Ages served: 6-adult. Services: diagnostic testing, academic testing, individual and group tutoring, speech and language therapy. Notes: Specializes in Orton-Gillingham approach for remediation of specific language disability.

Santa Rosa: California Vision and Learning Institute, 1144 Sonoma Avenue, Suite 106, 95405. Telephone: (707) 527-9131. Director: Hollis Stavn. Educational center. Day program. Full-time staff: 2. Part-time staff: 1. Current enrollment: 10. Ages served: 6-15. Services: individual tutoring, psychological testing, vision training.

CALIFORNIA

Sherman Oaks: The Studio for Academic Achievement, 14008 Ventura Boulevard, 91423. Telephone: (213) 990-6863. Director: Shelby Holley. Educational center. Day and summer program. Ages served: 3-adult. Grades served: kindergarten-adult. Scholarships/financial aid available. Services: individual tutoring, academic and psychological testing; academic, psychological, and family counseling; individualized programs.

Stockton: The Learning and Counseling Center, 1808 Country Club Boulevard, 95204. Telephone: (209) 466-2271. Director: Rhoderick J. Elin. Clinic. Day and after school program. Ages served: 3-adult. Services: diagnostic testing, academic and psychological testing, individual tutoring; academic, psychological, and parent counseling; adaptive physical education.

Walnut Creek: CES Associates, 2020 N. Broadway, #107, 94596. Telephone: (415) 930-6454. Senior Clinician: Judith Tiktinsky. Clinic. Ages served: all. Services: diagnostic testing; academic, psychological, and neuropsychological testing; psychological, parent, and career counseling; speech and language evaluation, coordination, follow-up; psychosocial assessment of individual and family, multidisciplinary team approach.

Walnut Creek: Ygnacio Learning Center, 200 La Casa Via, 94598. Telephone: (415) 937-7323. Directors: Sandra Mitchell, Sue Caputi. Educational center. Day and summer program. Ages served: 6-adult. Grades served: kindergarten-college. Scholarships/financial aid available. Services: individual and group tutoring, academic and psychological testing, academic and psychological counseling, academic therapy.

Woodland Hills: California Center for Educational Therapy, 6016 Fallbrook Avenue, Suite 201, 91367. Telephone: (818) 347-2600. Executive Director: Ken Tabachnick. Adjunctive clinic school. Day, after school, and summer program. Ages served: 3-adult. Grades served: preschool-college. Scholarships/financial aid available. Services: individual educational therapy and tutoring, diagnostic testing, psychological and academic testing, psychological and family counseling, work-study for internships only.

COLORADO

Offices of Organizations Concerned with Learning Disabilities

Council for Exceptional Children: President: Joseph C. Todd, 12313 W. Tufts Avenue, Morrison, CO 80465. Telephone: Office (303) 757-6201; Home (303) 696-7515.

Easter Seal Society for Crippled Children and Adults of Colorado, Inc.: 609 W. Littleton Boulevard, Littleton, CO 80120. Executive Director: Francis Steers. Telephone: (303) 795-2016.

State Department of Education Learning Disabilities Personnel

Brian A. McNulty, Acting Executive Director of Special Education Services Unit, Colorado Department of Education, 303 W. Colfax, Sixth Floor, Denver, CO 80204. Telephone: (303) 573-3230. Learning disabilities consultant: Kay Cessna. Telephone: (303) 573-3232.

Private and Day Schools

Denver: Denver Academy, 1125 S. Race Street, 80210. Telephone: (303) 777-5870. Executive Director: Paul Knott. Elementary and secondary day and boarding school. Ages served: 8-18. Grades served: 3-12. Current enrollment: 200. Maximum enrollment: 200. Full-time staff: 40. Part-time staff: 5. Services: individual and group tutoring, academic and psychological testing, academic and psychological counseling, physical and occupational therapy, work-study. Recreation: photography, foreign study trips; yearbook, computer, drama, and art clubs; Boy Scouts, Girl Scouts, student council, music and band, cheerleading, gymnastics, soccer, basketball, boxing, wrestling, weight lifting, skiing, martial arts. Notes: Usually holds a variety of optional summer programs that vary in scope from year to year.

Littleton: Havern Center, Inc., 4000 S. Wadsworth, 80123. Telephone: (303) 986-4587. Director: Sr. Barbara Schulte. Elementary day school. Ages served: 5-12. Grades served: kindergarten-6. Current enrollment: 75. Maximum enrollment: 75. Full-time staff: 23. Part-time staff: 4. Scholarships/financial aid available. Services: group tutoring, individualized learning programs; speech, language, and occupational therapy. Notes: Student IQs range from 90-150. Most students return to regular schools within two or three years.

Summer Camps and Programs

Almont: Timberline Trails, P.O. Box 397, 81210. Telephone: (303) 641-1562 or 753-0268. President: Art Pliner. Residential camp. Ages served: 8-15. Full-time staff: 15. Maximum enrollment: 30 boys; 10 girls. Limited scholarships/financial aid available. Recreation: hiking, riding, field trips, nature study, crafts, camping, archery, riflery, ropes course, canoeing, fishing. Notes: Children participate in recreational activities stressing community and team work.

College and University Special Programs and Services

Adams State College: Alamosa, CO 81102. Special services: individual and group tutoring, training in study skills, academic counseling, taped books, special examinations, student resource center, readers, scholarships. Contact: Wayne Farley, Dean of Academic Services. Telephone: (303) 589-7321.

Aims Community College: P.O. Box 69, Greeley, CO 80632. Total enrollment: 3,000. LD students: 12. Special services: readers, individual and group tutoring, special examinations, academic counseling, diagnostic testing, taped books, training in study skills, modified equipment. Contact: Virginia Rutledge, Supervisor for Supplemental Services Center. Telephone: (303) 339-2248.

Denver Auraria Community College: Box 600, 1111 W. Colfax Avenue, Denver, CO 80204. Total enrollment: 3,000. LD students: 45. Special services: individual and group tutoring, training in study skills, academic and psychological counseling, taped books, special examinations, student resource center, readers, diagnostic testing, scholarships, support group, faculty consultation. Contact: Betsy Cabell, Coordinator, Special Learning Support Program. Telephone: (303) 629-8456.

Lamar Community College: 2401 S. Main Street, Lamar, CO 81052. Total enrollment: 500. LD students: 25. Special services: individual and group tutoring, training in study skills, academic counseling, special examinations, student resource center. Contact: Dave Leenhouts, Director, Special Services. Telephone: (303) 336-2248.

Loretta Heights College: 3001 S. Federal Boulevard, Denver, CO 80236. Special services: limited individual tutoring, training in study skills, academic and psychological counseling, scholarships. Contact: Office of Student Affairs. Telephone: (303) 936-8441.

Mesa College: P.O. Box 2647, Grand Junction, CO 81502. Total enrollment: 3,150. LD students: 17. Special services: individual and group tutoring, training in study skills, taped books, special examinations, support group. Contact: Gail Youngquist, Coordinator, Tutorial and Learning Center. Telephone: (303) 248-1392.

Northeastern Junior College: Sterling, CO 80751. Total enrollment: 1,504. Special services: individual and group tutoring, training in study skills, academic and psychological counseling, student resource center, diagnostic testing, scholarships, support group. Contact: Gloria Hill, Director, Special Services. Telephone: (303) 522-6600 ext. 670.

Pueblo Community College: 900 W. Orman, Pueblo, CO 81004. Total enrollment: 1,331. LD students: 150. Special services: individual and group tutoring, training in study skills, academic counseling, taped books, readers. Contact: Christopher Campos, Coordinator, Supplemental Services. Telephone: (303) 549-3318.

COLORADO

Red Rocks Community College: 12600 W. Sixth Avenue, Box 15, Golden, CO 80401. Total enrollment: 3,781. LD students: 7. Special services: individual tutoring, training in study skills, academic counseling, taped books, special examinations, student resource center, readers, ombudsman, test writing. Contact: Linda Applegate, Counselor. Telephone: (303) 988-6160 ext. 253.

Regis College: W. 50th Avenue and Lowell Boulevard, Denver, CO 80221. Special services: individual and group tutoring, training in study skills, academic and psychological counseling, special examinations, student resource center, diagnostic testing, reading training; vocabulary, spelling, and writing courses; taped books and readers arranged on a need basis.

Center/clinic: Open Learning Center. Telephone: (303) 458-4148. Director: Carla Clements. Open to public. Ages served: all. Grades served: all. Services: diagnosis, teaching, consultation.

University of Colorado: Boulder, CO 80309. LD students: 65. Special services: individual and group tutoring, academic and educational counseling, diagnostic testing, training in study skills, student resource center, support group, interactive teaching.

- **Special program:** Office of Services to Disabled Students, Learning Disabilities Program. Accepts 12 students who are helped on an individual basis. Must fulfill regular and special admissions requirements. Special requirements include verification of learning disability and a diagnostic interview. Admissions counseling and assistance and special orientation session provided. Learning disabled students usually carry 12 credit hours. Director: Laura Fischer. Telephone: (303) 492-1591.

University of Denver: Denver, CO 80208. Total enrollment: 8,000. LD students: 25. Special services: personal, career, and academic counseling; support group, student resource center, untimed examinations, coordination of tutors, paper editing and library assistance, priority registration, study skills workshops and groups, faculty liaison assistance, readers, access to learning disabilities specialist for diagnostic testing and educational therapy.

- **Special program:** Learning Effectiveness Program (LEP). LEP strives to improve self-esteem and personal effectiveness by reducing anxiety about learning. Offers diagnostic testing, educational therapy, and private tutoring. Director: Maria Armstrong. Telephone: (303) 871-2278.

University of Northern Colorado: Greeley, CO 80639. Total enrollment: 8,500. Special services: readers, individual and group tutoring, ombudsman, special examinations, academic and psychological counseling, diagnostic testing, training in study skills. Contact: Jim Bowen. Telephone: (303) 351-2289.

COLORADO

University of Southern Colorado: 2200 N. Bonforte Boulevard, Pueblo, CO 81001. Special services: individual tutoring, training in study skills, academic counseling. Contact: Joyce E. Azalrath, Coordinator, Student Development Center. Telephone: (303) 549-2833.

Western State College of Colorado: Gunnison, CO 81230. Special services: individual and group tutoring, training in study skills, academic and psychological counseling, taped books, special examinations, student resource center, readers, diagnostic testing, ombudsman.

Center/clinic: School of Education Learning Center. Telephone: (303) 943-3007. Director: Norma Gilmore. Open to public. Grades served: preschool-college.

Hospital Clinics

Denver: Bethesda Hospital Association, 4400 E. Iliff Avenue, 80222. Telephone: (303) 758-1514. Contact: Diane Tucker, Director, Special Education. Outpatient, inpatient, and day program. Ages served: 12 and up. Services: diagnostic testing, academic and psychological testing, individual and group tutoring; academic, psychological, and parent counseling; group and occupational therapy, support group, social services, therapeutic recreation, medical services.

Denver: The Children's Hospital, Audiology/Speech Pathology Department, 1056 E. 19th Avenue, 80218. Telephone: (303) 861-6800. Contact: Ann D. Holmes, Learning Specialist. Outpatient program and summer camp. Ages served: birth-21. Services: diagnostic testing, academic and psychological testing, individual tutoring; academic, psychological, and parent counseling; speech, language, physical, and occupational therapy; support group, social services, school program planning, consultation with classroom teachers, in-service programs for teachers, study skills groups. Two-week summer camp offers learning, speech, language, and occupational therapy.

Denver: Rocky Mountain Child Development Center, University of Colorado Health Sciences Center, 4200 E. Ninth Avenue, 80262. Telephone: (303) 394-7691. Contact: Nancy D. Dixon, Director, Learning Disabilities Clinic. Outpatient program. Ages served: approximately 5-adult. Services: diagnostic testing, academic and psychological testing; academic, psychological, and parent counseling; speech, language, and occupational therapy; support group, social services, assistance in locating tutors, consultation with schools. Notes: Interdisciplinary team evaluates students and meets to discuss findings and make recommendations.

Pueblo: St. Mary-Corwin Hospital, Stepping Stones Pediatric Center, Department of Rehabilitative Services, 1008 Minnequa Avenue, 81004. Telephone: (303) 560-5003. Contact: Kim Megrath, Director of Rehabilitative Services. Outpatient and inpatient program. Ages served: birth-21. Services: diagnostic testing; speech, language, physical, and occupational therapy; adaptive physical education, social services.

Other Services

Denver: Hope Center for the Developmentally Disabled, Inc., 3601 Martin Luther King Boulevard, 80205. Telephone: (303) 388-4801. Executive Director: George Brantley. Preschool and adult day program with limited services. Ages served: 2½-5, adult. Grades served: ungraded. Current enrollment: 165. Maximum enrollment: 180. Full-time staff: 38. Services: group tutoring, academic and psychological testing, occupational therapy, adaptive physical education, vocational training, job placement. Recreation: bowling, swimming, field trips, basketball, football.

CONNECTICUT

Offices of Organizations Concerned with Learning Disabilities

ACLD, Inc.: Boatner Building, 139 N. Main Street, Hartford, CT 06107. Telephone: (203) 236-3953. President: Ruth Tepper.

CACLD (Connecticut Association for Children with Learning Disabilities): 20 N. Main Street, Norwalk, CT 06854. Telephone: (203) 838-5010. Hours: M-W-F 9-12 a.m. Summer: Thursday 9-12 a.m. Executive Director: Beryl Kaufman.

Council for Exceptional Children: President: Marsha A. Bok, 40 California Street B-15, Stratford, CT 06497. Telephone: Office (203) 576-7167; Home (203) 377-4338.

Easter Seal Society of Connecticut: P.O. Box 100, Hebron, CT 06248. Executive Director: John R. Quinn. Telephone: (203) 228-9438.

Orton Dyslexia Society (New England Branch): c/o Rocky Hill School, Ives Road, East Greenwich, RI 02818. President: Emi Flynn. Telephone: (401) 884-3346.

State Department of Education Learning Disabilities Personnel

Tom B. Gillung, Bureau Chief, Bureau of Student Services, State Department of Education, Box 2219, Hartford, CT 06145. Telephone: (203) 566-4383. Learning disabilities consultant: Forest Robert LaValley. Telephone: (203) 566-2492.

Private and Day Schools

Bridgeport: Bridgeport Academy, 115 Highland Avenue, 06608. Telephone: (203) 366-4793. Executive Director: William Jackson. Secondary day and boarding school with summer program. Ages served: 13-21. Grades served: 7-12. Current enrollment: 50. Full-time staff: 20. Part-time staff: 5. Services: individual tutoring, academic and psychological testing; academic, psychological, and family counseling; adaptive physical education, vocational training, work-study, job placement, medical services.

CONNECTICUT

Brooklyn: The Learning Clinic, Inc., P.O. Box 324, 06234. Telephone: (203) 774-7471 or 774-7481. Director: Raymond W. DuCharme. Elementary and secondary day school with summer program and camp. Ages served: 4-18. Grades served: kindergarten-12. Current enrollment: 25. Maximum enrollment: 28. Full-time staff: 7. Part-time staff: 5. Services: individual and group tutoring, academic and psychological testing, readers, ombudsman, scholarships; academic, psychological, and family counseling; diagnostic testing, vocational training, work-study, job placement, training in study skills, computer programming. Recreation: field trips, summer educational camping and wilderness trips.

Darien: Plumfield School, 82 Long Neck Point, 06820. Telephone: (203) 655-1561. Director: Jean Hilton. Elementary day school. Ages served: 5-13. Grades served: kindergarten-8. Current enrollment: 140. Maximum enrollment: 140. Full-time staff: 25. Part-time staff: 15. Services: individual and group tutoring, academic and psychological testing, work-study, speech and language therapy. Recreation: physical education, music, art. Notes: Only one-quarter of school population is learning disabled.

East Haddam: Becket Academy, River Road, 06423. Telephone: (203) 873-8658. Director: Donald R. Hirth. Elementary and secondary boarding school. Ages served: 13-18. Grades served: 6-12. Current enrollment: 124. Maximum enrollment: 124. Full-time staff: 50. Part-time staff: 5. Services: individual and group tutoring, academic and psychological testing; academic, psychological, and family counseling; occupational therapy, vocational training, work-study, job placement, medical services. Recreation: physical education, sports, off-campus wilderness programs, hiking, canoe expeditions.

Greenwich: Eagle Hill School, 45 Glenville Road, 06830. Telephone: (203) 622-9240. Headmaster: Mark J. Griffin. Elementary and secondary boarding and day school with summer program. Ages served: 6-16. Grades served: ungraded. Current enrollment: 154. Maximum enrollment: 154. Full-time staff: 55. Part-time staff: 2. Scholarships/financial aid available. Services: individual and group tutoring, academic and psychological testing, psychological and family counseling, adaptive physical education, speech therapy, full-time remedial program for learning disabled children. Recreation: physical education, motor training, biking, tennis, hiking, camping, swimming instruction, photography and filmmaking, music, drama, woodworking, metal shop, crafts, interscholastic athletic competition. Notes: Educational program is a linguistically-based language arts curriculum. Each student receives 1:1 or 1:3 tutorial instruction once or twice daily, as needed.

Groton: Apple Tree Learning Center, 177 Pleasant Valley Road, South, 06340. Telephone: (203) 446-0441. Director/Head Teacher: Nannette Myers. Preschool and kindergarten with limited services; summer program. Ages served: 3-8. Grades served: preschool-kindergarten. Current enrollment: 44. Maximum enrollment: 44. Full-time staff: 6. Part-time staff: 2. Services: individual tutoring, family counseling, information and referral. Recreation: playground, beach trips.

Litchfield: Forman School, Norfolk Road, 06759. Telephone: (203) 567-8712. Headmaster: Richard G. Peirce. Secondary boarding school with summer program. Ages served: 13-19. Grades served: 9-12. Current enrollment: 219. Maximum enrollment: 219. Full-time staff: 58. Services: individual tutoring, academic and psychological testing, academic and psychological counseling, medical services. Recreation: gymnasium, swimming, baseball, soccer, squash, lakeside camp.

Madison: Grove School, Inc., 175 Copse Road, Box 646, 06443-0646. Telephone: (203) 245-2778. Executive Director: J. Sanford Davis. Elementary and secondary males only boarding school with summer program. Ages served: 10-18. Grades served: 5-12. Current enrollment: 70. Maximum enrollment: 70. Full-time staff: 30. Services: individual and group tutoring, academic and psychological testing; academic, psychological, and family counseling; work-study, individual psychotherapy, medical services. Recreation: hiking, camping, mountain climbing, canoeing, fishing, sailing, water and snow skiing, riding, bowling, camping. Notes: For emotionally disturbed adolescent boys of at least normal intelligence.

Meriden: Student Learning Center, 15 Center Street, 06450. Telephone: (203) 634-8893. Executive Director: Ann Whoolery. Elementary and secondary day school with summer program. Ages served: 7-18. Grades served: ungraded. Current enrollment: 25. Maximum enrollment: 45. Full-time staff: 7. Part-time staff: 3. Scholarships/financial aid available. Services: individual and group tutoring, academic testing, academic and psychological counseling, occupational therapy, adaptive physical education, vocational training, work-study, job placement. Recreation: swimming, hiking, baseball, basketball, school plays. Notes: Major goals are academic success, self-sufficiency, and self-motivation.

New Britain: Elizabeth Brown Day School, 26 Russell Street, 06052. Telephone: (203) 223-2778. Educational Coordinator: Pamela Reardon. Elementary and secondary day school. Ages served: 13-18. Grades served: 6-12. Current enrollment: 11. Maximum enrollment: 14. Full-time staff: 7. Services: academic and psychological testing; individual, group, academic, psychological, and family counseling; one-to-one resource room. Recreation: physical education.

New Haven: Highland Heights, 651 Prospect Street, P.O. Box 1224, 06505. Telephone: (203) 777-5513. Executive Director: Sr. Mary Frances McMahon. Preschool and elementary day and residential school with limited services; summer program. Ages served: 5-13. Grades served: ungraded. Current enrollment: 43. Maximum enrollment: 45. Full-time staff: 14. Services: individual and group tutoring, academic and psychological testing, academic and psychological counseling, adaptive physical education.

CONNECTICUT

New London: Connecticut College Program for Children with Special Needs, Box 1574, 06320. Telephone: (203) 447-7545. Acting Director: Sara Radlinski. Preschool. Ages served: birth-5. Current enrollment: 30. Maximum enrollment: 32. Full-time staff: 6. Part-time staff: 8. Scholarships/financial aid available. Services: psychological testing; physical, speech, and language therapy; group and individual developmental play sessions, parent groups, consultation with parents.

North Stamford: Villa Maria Education Center, 159 Sky Meadow Drive, 06903. Telephone: (203) 322-5886 or 322-5920. Principal: Sr. Carol Ann. Elementary day school. Ages served: 6-14. Grades served: 1-8. Current enrollment: 30. Maximum enrollment: 30. Full-time staff: 8. Part-time staff: 7. Scholarships/financial aid available. Services: individual and group tutoring, academic and psychological testing, academic and psychological counseling; instruction in visual, motor, and auditory perception; guidance program. Recreation: motor perception program, large grounds, multipurpose room. Notes: Staffed by the Bernardine Franciscan Sisters. Students screened to ensure that they are learning disabled and not emotionally disturbed or mentally retarded.

Pomfret: The Rectory School, Routes 44 and 169, 06258. Telephone: (203) 928-7759. Headmaster: John A. Green. Elementary day and males only boarding school with limited services; summer program. Ages served: 11-16. Grades served: 6-9. Current enrollment: 180. Maximum enrollment: 135 boarding; 50-55 day. Full-time staff: 43. Part-time staff: 5. Services: individual tutoring, academic and psychological testing, academic and psychological counseling, medical services. Recreation: interscholastic athletic program; extracurricular programs including many clubs.

Washington: Devereux Glenholme, Two Sabbaday Lane, 06793. Telephone: (203) 868-7377. Director: Gary L. Fitzherbert. Elementary day and boarding school with summer program. Ages served: 5-17. Grades served: kindergarten-8. Current enrollment: 110. Maximum enrollment: 118. Full-time staff: 75. Part-time staff: 24. Scholarships/financial aid available. Services: individual tutoring, academic and psychological testing, psychological and family counseling, adaptive physical education, work-study, medical services, vocational training, social services, therapeutic environment, behaviorally-oriented techniques. Recreation: intramural and interscholastic sports, indoor pool, gymnasium, tennis, game room, hiking trails. Notes: Residential treatment program using an interdisciplinary approach.

West Hartford: The Benny Bronz Academy, 139 N. Main Street, ASD-Boatner Building, 06107. Telephone: (203) 236-5807. Headmaster: Ian Spence. Secondary day school. Ages served: 13-16. Grades served: ungraded 8-10. Maximum enrollment: 60. Full-time staff: teacher/student ratio 5:1. Services: individual and group tutoring, academic testing, academic and family counseling, physical and occupational therapy, adaptive physical education, vocational training, work-study, medical services; emphasis on basic and thinking skills, individual programs tailored to build strengths and remediate weaknesses. Notes: School scheduled to open September, 1985.

West Hartford: Intensive Education Center, Inc., 27 Park Road, 06119. Telephone: (203) 236-2049. Director: Sr. Helen Dowd. Elementary day school. Ages served: 6-16. Current enrollment: 48. Maximum enrollment: 50. Full-time staff: 12. Part-time staff: 11. Scholarships/financial aid available. Services: individual tutoring, academic and psychological testing, psychological counseling, adaptive physical education.

Summer Camps and Programs

Moodus: Shadybrook Language and Learning Center, P.O. Box 365, 06469. Telephone: (203) 873-8800. Director: Les Kershnar. Residential camp with academic program. Ages served: 6-21. Grades served: ungraded. Maximum enrollment: 125. Full-time staff: 68. Limited scholarships/financial aid available. Services: individual tutoring, academic testing, psychological counseling, physical therapy, adaptive physical education, vocational training, medical services. Academic programs: math, reading, spelling. Recreation: swimming, field trips, nature study, crafts, drama, camping, team athletics, woodworking, weekly special events. Notes: All teens work on and off grounds for pay.

Windsor: Camp Shalom, 425 Merriman Road, 06095. Telephone: (203) 688-4202. Permanent mailing address: 335 Bloomfield Avenue, West Hartford, CT 06117. Telephone: (203) 236-4571. Camp Director: David L. Jacobs. Day and residential camp with limited services. Ages served: 4½-14. Grades served: kindergarten-11. Maximum enrollment: 300. Full-time staff: 85. Scholarships/financial aid available. Services: individual and group tutoring. Academic programs: math, reading, English, spelling, study skills. Recreation: swimming, hiking, riding, field trips, nature study, crafts, drama, camping, team athletics, canoeing, waterskiing, tennis, music, archery. Notes: Individual Education Plan from school required.

College and University Special Programs and Services

Eastern Connecticut State University: Willimantic, CT 06226. Special services: individual tutoring, training in study skills, academic and psychological counseling, student resource center. Contact: Shirley Doiron, Coordinator, Disabled Student Services. Telephone: (203) 456-2231 ext. 448.

Housatonic Community College: 510 Barnum Avenue, Bridgeport, CT 06608. Total enrollment: 2,550. LD students: 40. Special services: individual and group tutoring, training in study skills, academic counseling, limited taped books, special examinations, student resource center, readers, diagnostic testing, ombudsman, support group, computer literacy and instruction, cassette players.

CONNECTICUT

- **Special program:** Learning Disabilities Pilot Project. Open to full or part-time students. Learning disability must be verified through recent diagnostic tests. Emphasis on computer assistance and instruction. Director: Natalie Bieber. Telephone: (203) 579-6402.

Center/clinic: Center for Educational Services. Telephone: (203) 579-6402. Director: Barry Curran. Open to public. Ages served: 17 and up. Grades served: 12-postsecondary. Services: CLEP (college level examination program), diagnostic testing, high school equivalency examinations.

Mitchell College: 437 Pequot Avenue, New London, CT 06320. Total enrollment: 500. LD students: 24. Special services: individual and group tutoring, ombudsman, special examinations, academic and psychological counseling, diagnostic testing, taped books, training in study skills, content and skills tutoring.

- **Special program:** The Learning Disabilities Program. Students are mainstreamed into regular college program with special program as support system. Accepts 24 full or part-time students per year. Applicants must go through regular and special admissions procedures. Learning disability must be verified through recent diagnostic tests. Director: Joan M. McGuire. Telephone: (203) 443-2811 ext. 284.

Center/clinic: Learning Resource Center. Telephone: (203) 443-2811 ext. 284. Director: Joan M. McGuire. Not open to public. Grades served: college.

Quinebaug Valley Community College: Box 59, Danielson, CT 06239. Total enrollment: 1,150. LD students: 10. Special services: individual tutoring, academic counseling. Contact: Stephen J. Herman, Dean of Student and Community Services. Telephone: (203) 774-1130.

St. Joseph College: Asylum Avenue, West Hartford, CT 06117.

Center/clinic: Gengras Center, 1678 Asylum Avenue. Telephone: (203) 232-4571 ext. 201. Director: Glenn McGrath. Open to public. Services: speech and language development; individual, group, occupational, and physical therapy; educational and psychological assessment, educational and psychological counseling, vocational evaluation and training, work simulation, exploratory training, cooperative vocational/technical program with A.I. Prince Vocational Technical School. Ages served: 10-21. Grades served: 5-12, postsecondary.

Trinity College: Summitt Street, Hartford, CT 06106. Total enrollment: 1,750. Special services: individual tutoring, training in study skills, academic and psychological counseling, taped books, special examinations, readers, limited diagnostic testing, ombudsman. Contact: David Winer, Dean of Students. Telephone: (203) 527-3151 ext. 433.

CONNECTICUT

University of Connecticut: Storrs, CT 06268. Special services: diagnostic testing, liaison with faculty, computers, word processors, reading machines, tutors, academic and psychological counseling, vocational counseling and placement, remediation, special examinations, training in study skills.

- **Special program:** University of Connecticut Program for the Learning Disabled Student. Must meet regular and special admissions requirements. Special requirements include verification of learning disability through recent diagnostic tests. Open to full or part-time students. Program can be entered at any time during academic year. Director: Stan Shaw. Project Coordinator: Kay Norlander. Telephone: (203) 486-4031.

University of Hartford: West Hartford, CT 06117. Special services: individual tutoring, training in study skills, academic and psychological counseling, taped books, readers, diagnostic testing, scholarships, ombudsman. Contact: Doris B. Coster, Dean of Students. Telephone: (203) 243-4260.

Yale University: New Haven, CT 06520. Total enrollment: 10,920. Special services: on an individual basis.

Center/clinic: Child Study Center, IG82, 230 S. Frontage Road. Telephone: (203) 785-2511. Director: Donald J. Cohen. Contact: Sara Sparrow. Telephone: (203) 785-2548. Open to public. Ages served: 1½-18. Services: diagnostic testing, academic and psychological testing, academic and psychological counseling. Notes: Multidisciplinary team involved in all aspects of assessment and management of children with learning disabilities.

Hospital Clinics

Hartford: Mount Sinai Hospital, Child and Adolescent Psychiatric Service (CAPS), 500 Blue Hills Avenue, 06112. Telephone: (203) 242-4431 ext. 4448. Contact: Daily Intake Worker. Inpatient, day, and after school program. Services: diagnostic testing, academic and psychological testing, individual and group tutoring; academic, psychological, and parent counseling; group, speech, language, physical, and occupational therapy; support group, social services, accredited school program for inpatients, day hospital for adolescents with school and psychiatric services. Notes: A psychiatric service for children and adolescents. Approximately 25-50 percent of the population served have learning disabilities with accompanying emotional problems.

Hartford: St. Francis Hospital and Medical Center, School Problems Program, Section of Developmental and Behavioral Pediatrics, Pediatric Subspecialty Clinic, 06105. Telephone: (203) 548-4355. Contact: Lorraine Scrivano. Outpatient program. Ages served: 3-18. Services: diagnostic testing, academic and psychological testing, limited individual tutoring; academic, psychological, and

CONNECTICUT

parent counseling; speech, language, physical, and occupational therapy; social services.

Newington: Newington Children's Hospital, Program for the Evaluation of Development and Learning (PEDAL), 181 E. Cedar Street, 06111. Telephone: (203) 667-5310. Contact: Patricia Genova, Director. Outpatient and inpatient program. Services: diagnostic testing, academic and psychological testing, individual and group tutoring; academic, psychological, and parent counseling; speech, language, physical, and occupational therapy; support group, social services.

Other Services

Norwalk: Infant and Child Development Services, Box 470, 182 Wolfpit Avenue, 06852. Telephone: (203) 846-9581. Executive Director: Theodore Bergeron. Preschool with limited services. Ages served: birth-6. Current enrollment: 18. Maximum enrollment: 20. Full-time staff: 3. Part-time staff: 5. Scholarships/financial aid available. Services: individual tutoring, family counseling; physical, occupational, and speech therapy; adaptive physical education.

Plainville: Wheeler Clinic, Inc., 91 Northwest Drive, 06062. Telephone: (203) 747-6801 or 527-1644. Education Director: John Mattas. Clinic. Day, after school, residential, and outpatient program. Ages served: 2-14. Services: diagnostic testing, academic and psychological testing, individual and group tutoring; academic, psychological, and parent counseling; group, speech, language, and occupational therapy; support group.

West Hartford: The Learning Incentive, 139 N. Main Street, ASD-Boatner Building, Room 109, 01607. Telephone: (203) 236-5807. Contact: Aileen Stan-Spence, Director. Day, after school, and Saturday program; summer camp. Ages served: 6-adult. Services: diagnostic testing, academic testing, individual and group tutoring, academic counseling, speech and language therapy, study skills remediation, cognitive thinking skills, SSAT/SAT preparation.

DELAWARE

Offices of Organizations Concerned with Learning Disabilities

ACLD, Inc. (Kent/Sussex Chapter): 93 Creek Drive, Millsboro, DE 19966. Telephone: (302) 945-1744. President: Ms. Gay Bowen.

ACLD, Inc. (New Castle County Chapter): P.O. Box 304, Montchanin, DE 19710. Telephone: (302) 478-3353. President: Elizabeth Funer.

Council for Exceptional Children: President: Nancy Campbell, Early Childhood Developmental Center, Lake Forest North Elementary, Main Street, Felton, DE 19943. Telephone: Office (302) 284-9612; Home (302) 422-4454.

Easter Seal Society of Del-Mar: 2705 Baynard Boulevard, Wilmington, DE 19802. Executive Director: Sandra Kother. Telephone: (302) 658-6417.

State Department of Education Learning Disabilities Personnel

Carl M. Haltom, Director, Exceptional Children Special Programs Division, State Department of Public Instruction, Townsend Building, P.O. Box 1402, Dover, DE 19903. Telephone: (302) 736-5471. Learning disabilities consultant: Edward J. Dillon. Telephone: (302) 736-4667.

Private and Day Schools

Newark: Turning Point Academy, 698 Old Baltimore Pike, 19702. Telephone: (302) 731-1137. Executive Director: Wayne P. Dippold. Elementary and secondary day and boarding school with limited services; summer program. Ages served: 12-17. Grades served: 6-12. Current enrollment: 20. Maximum enrollment: 30. Full-time staff: 8. Part-time staff: 5. Scholarships/financial aid available. Services: individual tutoring, academic and psychological testing, academic counseling, adaptive physical education. Recreation: basketball, swimming.

New Castle: John G. Leach School, Landers Lane, 19720. Telephone: (302) 429-4055. Principal: Constance A. Halter. Preschool, elementary, and secondary day school with limited services. Ages served: 2-21. Grades served: preschool-12. Current enrollment: 130. Maximum enrollment: 130. Full-time staff: 60. Part-time staff: 4. Services: individual tutoring, academic and psychological testing, academic and psychological counseling, physical and occupational therapy, adaptive physical education, vocational training, work-study, medical services. Notes: Primarily serves students with physical handicaps; many show characteristics associated with learning disabilities.

Wilmington: Beechwood Individualized Parent-Child Program, Inc., P.O. Box 7235, 19803. Telephone: (302) 658-0429 or 658-3826. Director: Susan K. Gray. Elementary day school with summer program and camp. Ages served: 5-15. Grades served: kindergarten-8. Current enrollment: 45. Maximum enrollment: 48. Full-time staff: 19. Scholarships/financial aid available. Services: individual and group tutoring, academic and psychological testing; speech, language, physical, and occupational therapy. Recreation: swim-gym program at local YMCA, Red Cross instruction, field trips, computers, arts and crafts, choral group.

Wilmington: Centreville School, Delaware Learning Center, 6201 Kennett Pike, 19807. Telephone: (302) 571-0230 or 571-0231. Executive Director: Elfiede Bergmann. Preschool and elementary day school with summer program. Ages served: 2½-12. Current enrollment: 72. Maximum enrollment: 84. Full-time staff: 22. Part-time staff: 9. Scholarships/financial aid available. Services: individ-

DELAWARE

ual and group tutoring, academic and psychological testing; speech, language, occupational, physical, individual, and group therapy; language and sensorimotor testing.

Wilmington: The Pilot School, 100 Garden of Eden Road, 19803. Telephone: (302) 478-1740. Director: Doris Lestourgeon. Elementary and secondary day school with summer program. Ages served: 5-14. Grades served: kindergarten-8. Current enrollment: 149. Maximum enrollment: 150. Full-time staff: 38. Part-time staff: 1. Scholarships/financial aid available. Services: individual and group tutoring, diagnostic testing, academic and psychological testing; academic, psychological, and family counseling; speech and language evaluation/therapy, individualized educational program, adaptive physical education. Recreation: outdoor learning experiences.

Summer Camps and Programs

Lewes: Children's Beach House, Inc., 1800 Bay Avenue, 19958. Telephone: (302) 645-9184. Permanent mailing address: 701 Shipley Street, Wilmington, DE 19801. Telephone: (302) 655-4288. Executive Director: Harold L. Springer, III. Residential camp with limited services. Ages served: 6-12. Maximum enrollment: 23. Full-time staff: 12. Scholarships/financial aid available. Services: family counseling. Recreation: swimming, nature study, crafts. Notes: Limited to Delaware residents.

College and University Special Programs and Services

University of Delaware: Newark, DE 19716. Total enrollment: 18,083. LD students: 40. Special services: individual and group tutoring, training in study skills, support group. Contact: Debbie Bates, Director, Reading Study Center. Telephone: (302) 451-2307. Or Noreen McGuire, Assistant to the Vice President. Telephone: (302) 451-2610.

Center/clinic: Reading Study Center/Psychoeducational Assessment Service, Willard Hall Building, College of Education. Telephone: (302) 451-2307 or 451-8948. Director: Wendy White. Open to public. Ages served: 4-21. Grades served: preschool-high school. Services: child evaluation, parent consultation, individualized reading instruction, summer programs.

Other Services

Wilmington: Educational Service, Inc., 1203 Gilpin Avenue, 19806. Telephone: (302) 655-6283. Executive Director: Tina Maida Masington. Educational center with limited services. Day program. Ages served: 3-adult. Grades served: preschool-college. Current enrollment: 175. Full-time staff: 2. Part-time staff: 30. Services: individual and group tutoring, academic testing and counseling, study skills, SAT preparation, memory, readiness workshops.

DISTRICT OF COLUMBIA

Offices of Organizations Concerned with Learning Disabilities

ACLD, Inc.: P.O. Box 6350, Washington, DC 20015. Telephone: (202) 244-5177. Co-presidents: Ann LaPorta, Cordie Puttkammer.

Council for Exceptional Children: President: Jacquelyn Jackson, 5903 33rd Avenue, Hyattsville, MD 20782. Telephone: Office (202) 724-2141; Home (301) 559-2375.

Easter Seal Society for Disabled Children and Adults, Inc. (District of Columbia Society): 2800 13th Street, N.W., Washington, DC 20009. Executive Director: Nancy Marconi. Telephone: (202) 232-2342.

Orton Dyslexia Society (D.C. Capitol Area Branch): 5606 Gloster Road, Bethesda, MD 20816. President: Carol Gretkowski. Telephone: (301) 320-5589.

District Department of Education Learning Disabilities Personnel

Doris A. Woodson, Assistant Superintendent, Division of Special Education and Pupil Personnel Services, Webster Building, Tenth and "H" Streets, N.W., Washington, DC 20001. Telephone: (202) 724-4018. Learning disabilities consultant: Mattie Cheek. Telephone: (202) 224-2141.

Private and Day Schools

Washington: Easter Seal Society for Disabled Children and Adults, Inc., 2800 13th Street, N.W., 20009. Telephone: (202) 232-2342. Executive Director: Nancy Marconi. Preschool with summer program. Ages served: birth-6. Current enrollment: 60. Maximum enrollment: 60. Full-time staff: 28. Part-time staff: 8. Scholarships/financial aid available. Services: family counseling; physical, occupational, and speech therapy; interdisciplinary program, transportation. Recreation: specially designed playground, field trips, therapeutic swimming program. Notes: Serves children with moderate to severe/profound multiple handicaps, not just the learning disabled.

Washington: FLOC (For Love of Children) Learning Center, 1401 Massachusetts Avenue, N.W., Second Floor, 20005. Telephone: (202) 387-1143. Administrator: Nelson W. Good. Elementary day school. Ages served: 7-14. Grades served: ungraded. Current enrollment: 21. Maximum enrollment: 24. Full-time staff: 6. Part-time staff: 8. Scholarships/financial aid available. Services: individual and group tutoring, academic and psychological testing, psychological and family counseling, art and physical therapy, adaptive physical education, vocational training. Notes: Primarily for emotionally disturbed children.

DISTRICT OF COLUMBIA

Washington: The Lab School of Washington, 4759 Reservoir Road, N.W., 20007. Telephone: (202) 965-6600. Founder/Director: Sally L. Smith. Preschool, elementary, secondary, and adult day school with summer program. Ages served: 4½-adult. Grades served: preschool-9, adult ungraded. Current enrollment: 150. Maximum enrollment: 200. Full-time staff: 26. Part-time staff: 24. Scholarships/financial aid available. Services: individual and group tutoring, academic and psychological testing, academic counseling, occupational and language therapy, diagnostic services, night school for adults. Recreation: after school sailing, gymnastics, canoeing, hiking, puppetry, arts, breakdancing, riding; weekend white water rafting, skiing, and camping trips.

College and University Special Programs and Services

American University: 4400 Massachusetts Avenue, N.W., Washington, DC 20016. Total enrollment: 12,500. LD students: 65. Special services: individual tutoring, training in study skills, academic and psychological counseling, taped books, special examinations, student resource center, diagnostic testing, scholarships, ombudsman, support group. Notes: Required freshman study skills course combined with weekly tutoring sessions. Contact: Faith Leonard, Director of Learning Services. Telephone: (202) 885-3360.

Center/clinic: Center for Psychological and Learning Services, 201 Mary Graydon Center. Telephone: (202) 885-3360. Director: Faith Leonard. Not open to public. Ages served: 17 and up. Grades served: freshmen-graduate.

George Washington University: Washington, DC 20052. Special services: readers, ombudsman, special examinations, scholarships, academic and psychological counseling, diagnostic testing, taped books, training in study skills, note taking assistance, scribes, lab assistance, tape recorders, non-credit minicourse for students with learning disabilities, student resource center, peer and group tutoring, writing lab, reading center. Contact: Linda Donnels, Director of Services for Students with Disabilities, or Christy Willis, Coordinator of Services for Students with Disabilities. Telephone: (202) 676-8250 or 676-8345.

University of the District of Columbia: 2565 Georgia Avenue, N.W., Washington, DC 20001. Special services: individual and group tutoring, training in study skills, limited taped books, special examinations, academic counseling, diagnostic testing, limited scholarships. Contact: Evonne Parker Jones, Director, The Reading Laboratory. Telephone: (202) 673-7150 or 673-7152.

Other Services

Washington: The Kingsbury Center, 2138 Bancroft Place, N.W., 20008. Telephone: (202) 232-5878. Director: Suzanne A. Zunzer. Educational center with diagnostic primary school program. Day and summer program. Ages served: all ages center; 5-7 school. Services: diagnostic and academic testing, individual and group tutoring, psychological and parent counseling, psychological evaluation, school consultation, school/college advisory, family and individual therapy; courses in study skills, creative and expository writing, SAT and SSAT preparation, computer-assisted education. Notes: School serves children with mild developmental lags in perceptual motor integration, language, or social maturity.

FLORIDA

Offices of Organizations Concerned with Learning Disabilities

ACLD, Inc.: 5683 Deerfield Road, Orlando, FL 32808. Telephone: (305) 295-8203. Executive Secretary: Charlotte Love.

Council for Exceptional Children: President: Roxanne Barr, 18 N.E. 107th Street, Miami Shores, FL 33161. Telephone: (305) 685-7923.

The Florida Easter Seal Society, Inc.: 1010 Executive Center Drive, Suite 101, Orlando, FL 32803. Executive Director: Robert J. Griggs. Telephone: (305) 896-7881.

Orton Dyslexia Society: 949 Briarcliff Road, Tallahassee, FL 32308. President: Kay Young. Telephone: Office (904) 488-3718; Home (904) 222-9661.

State Department of Education Learning Disabilities Personnel

Landis Stetler, Interim Chief, Bureau of Education for Exceptional Students, Florida Department of Education, Knott Building, Tallahassee, FL 32301. Telephone: (904) 488-1570. Learning disabilities consultant: Marty Beech. Telephone: (904) 488-1106.

Private and Day Schools

Coconut Grove: The Vanguard School of Coconut Grove, Florida, Inc., 3939 Main Highway, 33133. Telephone: (305) 445-7992. Director/President: John R. Havrilla. Elementary day school with summer program and camp. Ages served: 5-16. Grades served: ungraded. Current enrollment: 94. Maximum enrollment: 99. Full-time staff: 18. Part-time staff: 3. Scholarships/financial aid available. Services: individual and group tutoring, computers, typing.

Daytona Beach: Kalevala School, 233 N. Oleander Avenue, 32108. Telephone: (904) 255-8652. Director/Owner: Ahti Tuomainen. Secondary and adult boarding school with limited services; summer program. Ages served: 10-20. Grades served: 7-12, first year college. Current enrollment: 20. Maximum enrollment: 25. Full-time staff: 8. Part-time staff: 2. Services: individual and group tutoring, academic and psychological testing; academic, psychological, and family counseling; limited vocational training available at nearby college. Recreation: community related activities, travel in United States and overseas. Notes: An international school serving students with special needs.

Fort Lauderdale: Crossroads School, 4650 S.W. 61st Avenue, 33314. Telephone: (305) 584-1100. Administrator: Aubrey Fein. Preschool, elementary, and secondary day school with summer program and camp. Ages served: 6-17. Current enrollment: 60. Maximum enrollment: 90. Full-time staff: 12. Part-time staff: 8. Scholarships/financial aid available. Services: individual and group tutoring, academic and psychological testing, occupational and speech therapy; academic, psychological, and family counseling; work-study. Recreation: basketball, scuba diving, self-defense, wrestling, photography.

Fort Lauderdale: Fort Lauderdale Oral School of Nova University, 3100 S.W. Eighth Avenue, 33315. Telephone: (305) 525-7251. Director: Marya Mavilya. Preschool and elementary day school with limited services. Ages served: birth-16. Grades served: preschool-8. Current enrollment: 27. Full-time staff: 6. Part-time staff: 2. Scholarships/financial aid available. Services: individual and group tutoring, academic testing. Recreation: physical education.

Fort Myers: Hamilton McGregor Technical High School, 3049 McGregor Boulevard, 33901. Telephone: (813) 337-5600. Executive Director: Socrates J. Chaloge. Secondary day and boarding school. Ages served: 14-18. Grades served: 9-12. Current enrollment: 34. Maximum enrollment: 60. Full-time staff: 6. Part-time staff: 8. Limited scholarships/financial aid available. Services: individual and group tutoring, academic and psychological testing, academic and psychological counseling, vocational training, work-study, job placement; exploratory vocational programs in computer science, trades, and culinary arts. Notes: Extension of the J. Hamilton Welch Foundation.

Hollywood: The Banyan School, 1351 S. 14th Avenue, 33020. Telephone: (305) 920-6777. Executive Director: Ellen S. Katzman. Day school. Ages served: 6-16. Grades served: ungraded. Current enrollment: 20. Maximum enrollment: 30. Full-time staff: 8. Part-time staff: 4. Services: individual and group tutoring, academic testing, vocational training.

Hollywood: Developmental Resource Center Day School, 2741 Van Buren Street, 33020. Telephone: (305) 920-2008. Director: Deborah Levy. Preschool, elementary, secondary, and adult day school with summer program and camp. Ages served: 3-adult. Grades served: preschool-high school. Current enrollment: 40. Maximum enrollment: 70. Full-time staff: 9. Part-time staff: 7. Scholarships/financial aid available. Services: individual and group tutoring, academic and psychological testing, academic counseling, individual education plan; after school remedial clinics in math, creative writing, reading, spelling, and study skills. Recreation: karate, physical education.

FLORIDA

Howey-in-the-Hills: DeSisto at Howey, 510 Palm Avenue, 82737. Telephone: (904) 324-2701, 324-2702, or 324-2388. Assistant Executive Director: Sharon Dockter. Secondary boarding school with limited services. Ages served: 13-21. Grades served: 9-college. Current enrollment: 114. Maximum enrollment: 150. Full-time staff: 35. Scholarships/financial aid available. Services: individual and group tutoring, academic and psychological testing; academic, psychological, and family counseling. Recreation: varsity basketball, soccer, baseball, weight training, cheerleading, archery, water sports, dance, tennis, bowling, skating, art, gardening, riding.

Jacksonville: dePaul School of Northeast Florida, 1620 Naldo Avenue, 32207. Telephone: (904) 396-9943. Director: Linda Brookshire. Elementary day school. Ages served: 6-14. Grades served: 1-6. Current enrollment: 50. Maximum enrollment: 62. Full-time staff: 10. Scholarships/financial aid available. Services: individual tutoring; Saturday tutorial program for children and adults not enrolled in school. Recreation: physical education. Notes: School for remediation of dyslexic children.

Jacksonville: Mandarin Learning Center, 3560 Marbon Road, 32223. Telephone: (904) 262-5172. Director: Philip N. Kalfin. Preschool, elementary, and secondary day school. Grades served: preschool-junior high. Current enrollment: 25. Maximum enrollment: 65. Full-time staff: 8. Part-time staff: 1. Scholarships/financial aid available. Services: academic testing, academic and psychological counseling, adaptive physical education, parent training, speech and language therapy. Recreation: soccer, basketball, riding, fishing.

Jacksonville: Morning Star School, 725 Mickler Road, 32211. Telephone: (904) 721-2144. Principal: Teri Aschliman. Elementary day school. Ages served: 4-16. Grades served: preschool-9. Current enrollment: 93. Maximum enrollment: 100. Full-time staff: 14. Part-time staff: 2. Scholarships/financial aid available. Services: academic testing, adaptive physical education, regular academic program.

Lake Wales: The Vanguard School, 2249 Highway 27, North, 33853. Telephone: (813) 676-6091. President: Harry E. Nelson. Elementary and secondary day and boarding school. Full-time staff: 80. Part-time staff: 2. Current enrollment: 143. Maximum enrollment: 144. Ages served: 8-18. Grades served: ungraded. Scholarships/financial aid available. Services: individual and group tutoring, academic and psychological testing, academic and psychological counseling, prevocational training, adaptive physical education. Recreation: gymnasium, swimming pool, tennis courts, basketball, soccer, volleyball, softball, table tennis.

Lighthouse Point: Lighthouse Point Academy, 3701 N.E. 22nd Avenue, 33064. Telephone: (305) 941-3680. Principal: Faye Cameron. Preschool and elementary day school with summer program and camp. Ages served: 6-14. Grades served: 1-9. Current enrollment: 84. Maximum enrollment: 132. Full-time staff: 11. Services: individual tutoring, academic testing. Recreation: basketball, flag football, soccer, band, chorus.

FLORIDA

Longwood: PACE School, 3221 Sand Lake Road, 32779. Telephone: (305) 898-8882. Director: Mary E. Dunn. Elementary and secondary day school with summer program. Ages served: 6-16. Grades served: ungraded. Current enrollment: 105. Full-time staff: 17. Part-time staff: 3. Scholarships/financial aid available. Services: academic and psychological testing, academic and psychological counseling, adaptive physical education, full academic curriculum. Recreation: motor movement, physical education, sailing.

Maitland: Wightwood School, Inc., 200 N. Swoope Avenue, 32751. Telephone: (305) 628-4558. Director: Dorothy R. Wight. Elementary and secondary day school with summer program. Ages served: 6-15. Grades served: 1-9. Current enrollment: 75. Maximum enrollment: 75. Full-time staff: 13. Part-time staff: 3. Limited scholarships/financial aid available. Services: academic curriculum, including math, reading, language arts, science, social studies, is geared to the needs of learning disabled and academically deficient students. Recreation: physical education, art, drama, photography.

Miami: Atlantis Academy, 10780 S.W. 56th Street, 33165 (North Campus), 9600 S.W. 107th Avenue, 33176 (South Campus). Telephone: (North Campus) (305) 279-1148; (South Campus) (305) 271-9771. Directors: Tish Tepper, Zelda Carner. Elementary and secondary day school with summer program and camp. Ages served: 5-18. Grades served: kindergarten-12. Current enrollment: 198. Maximum enrollment: 200. Full-time staff: 30. Part-time staff: 11. Notes: Remediation of diagnosed deficits, sharpening of identified strengths.

Miami: Cantwell Academy, Inc., 8571 S.W. 112th Street, 33156. Telephone: (305) 271-4500. Executive Director: Ronald J. Cantwell. Elementary day school with summer program. Ages served: 5-16. Grades served: kindergarten-8. Current enrollment: 24. Maximum enrollment: 38. Full-time staff: 4. Part-time staff: 2. Scholarships/financial aid available. Services: individual tutoring, academic and psychological testing; academic, psychological, and family counseling; adaptive physical education, work-study, medical services, social skills development.

Miami: Easter Seal Demonstration School, 1475 N.W. 14th Avenue, 33125. Telephone: (305) 325-1626. Director of Education: Joan Bornstein. Preschool and elementary day school with summer program. Ages served: 2½-11. Grades served: ungraded. Current enrollment: 66. Maximum enrollment: 75. Full-time staff: 18. Part-time staff: 1. Scholarships/financial aid available. Services: group tutoring, academic testing, family counseling; physical, occupational, play, and speech therapy; adaptive physical education, individual tutoring in summer.

Miami: Gables Academy, 7700 Miller Drive, 33155. Telephone: (305) 271-9261. Administrator: James O. Meffen. Elementary and secondary day and boarding school with summer program and camp. Ages served: 6-19. Grades served: ungraded. Current enrollment: 82. Maximum enrollment: 120. Full-time staff: 12. Part-time staff: 3. Scholarships/financial aid available. Services: individualized instruction, academic and psychological testing, academic and psychological counseling, work-study. Recreation: athletic program, interscholastic competition, group musical activities, swimming, riding.

Miami: House of Learning, 10545 S.W. 97th Avenue, 33176. Telephone: (305) 274-9259. Director: Mrs. Pat Suiter. Elementary day school. Ages served: 6-12½. Grades served: 1-6. Current enrollment: 106. Maximum enrollment: 115. Full-time staff: 12. Part-time staff: 1. Services: academic and psychological testing.

Naples: Sunrise Academy, 2801 County Barn Road, 33962. Telephone: (813) 775-6777. Principal: Lora M. Cartelli. Elementary and secondary day school with summer program. Ages served: 5-18. Grades served: kindergarten-12. Current enrollment: 39. Maximum enrollment: 80. Full-time staff: 5. Part-time staff: 2. Scholarships/financial aid available. Services: individual and group tutoring, academic and psychological testing, academic counseling. Recreation: after school sports.

Ocala: New Hope School, 2800 S.E. Maricamp Road, 32671. Telephone: (904) 629-4000. Executive Director: Nelle Needham. Preschool, elementary, and secondary day school with limited services; summer program. Ages served: 5-21. Grades served: kindergarten-12. Current enrollment: 38. Full-time staff: 15. Part-time staff: 5. Services: individual tutoring, academic testing; physical, occupational, speech, and communication therapy; adaptive physical education. Recreation: playground activities, Special Olympics.

Orlando: Fairview School, Inc., 4710 Adanson Street, 32804. Telephone: (305) 629-4542. Principal: Aida E. Diaz. Elementary day school with summer program. Ages served: 6-12. Grades served: ungraded. Current enrollment: 45. Full-time staff: 7. Services: individual tutoring, academic testing, work-study, multisensory teaching techniques. Notes: Works only with dyslexic students with average to high IQ.

Pensacola: Children's Resource Center, 6812 Lillian Highway, 32506. Telephone: (904) 456-9095. Educational Director: Viki Bower. Preschool, elementary, secondary, and adult day school with summer program. Ages served: 2-16. Grades served: preschool-8, high school. Current enrollment: 50. Maximum enrollment: 50. Full-time staff: 10. Part-time staff: 3. Scholarships/financial aid available. Services: individual and group tutoring, diagnostic testing, academic and psychological testing; academic, psychological, and family counseling; music and physical therapy, tutoring for individuals not enrolled in school. Recreation: field trips.

Pinellas Park: Center Academy, 6710-86th Avenue, North, 33565. Telephone: (813) 822-6914. Director: Mary J. Fifer. Elementary and secondary day school with summer program and camp. Ages served: 5-18. Grades served: ungraded. Current enrollment: 150. Full-time staff: 30. Part-time staff: 12. Limited scholarships/financial aid available. Services: individual and group tutoring; academic, psychological, neuropsychological, and vocational testing; academic, psychological, and family counseling; psychotherapy. Also provides services on hourly basis.

Recreation: ranch, riding, swimming, nature studies. Notes: School also has residential branch in London, England.

Pinellas Park: Morning Star School of Pinellas Park, 4661 80th Avenue, North, 33565. Telephone: (813) 544-6036. Principal: Sr. Mary Louis. Elementary day school. Ages served: 6-14. Grades served: ungraded. Current enrollment: 46. Maximum enrollment: 50. Full-time staff: 9. Part-time staff: 3. Scholarships/financial aid available. Services: academic and psychological testing, speech and occupational therapy, adaptive physical education, small classes, individual education plans.

St. Petersburg: Center Academy, 105 Fifth Avenue, N.E., 33701. Telephone: (813) 822-6914. Director: Mack R. Hicks. Elementary, secondary, and adult day and boarding school with summer program and camp. Ages served: 6-18. Grades served: 1-12. Current enrollment: 130. Maximum enrollment: 130. Full-time staff: 30. Part-time staff: 10. Scholarships/financial aid available. Services: individual and group tutoring, academic and psychological testing; academic, psychological, and family counseling; adaptive physical education, job placement, medical services. Recreation: riding, pioneering and other country activities. Notes: Exchange program to begin in 1985 with branch in Suffolk, England.

Sarasota: Happiness House Rehabilitation Center, Inc., 401 Braden Avenue, 33580. Telephone: (813) 355-7637. Executive Director: Donald L. Wise. Secondary day school with limited services; summer program. Ages served: 13-22. Grades served: 9-12. Current enrollment: 15. Maximum enrollment: 18. Full-time staff: 2. Part-time staff: 1. Services: individual tutoring, academic testing, physical and occupational therapy, vocational training, work-study, job placement, vocational evaluation, certified Work Activities Center (Department of Labor), speech and audiological services, behavioral counseling and training, medical services.

Seminole: Rivendell Academy, 8894 Seminole Boulevard, Suites 6-8, 33542. Telephone: (813) 393-8841. Preschool, elementary, secondary, and adult day school with summer program. Ages served: all. Grades served: kindergarten-12. Current enrollment: 12. Full-time staff: 3. Part-time staff: 9. Services: individual and group tutoring, academic and psychological testing, academic and college counseling, Orton-Gillingham and Slingerland techniques, study skills, SAT and high school equivalency preparation, multisensory math.

Tallahassee: Woodland Hall Academy, 4745 Centerville Road, 32308. Telephone: (904) 893-2216. Director: Patricia K. Hardman. Elementary, secondary, and adult day school with summer program. Ages served: 6-18. Grades served: kindergarten-12. Current enrollment: 40. Maximum enrollment: 45. Full-time staff: 13. Part-time staff: 1. Limited scholarships/financial aid available. Services: individual and group tutoring, diagnostic testing, academic testing; academic, family, and parent counseling; tutorial support for college students, multisensory approach. Recreation: physical education, skeet club. Notes: Accepts average or above average dyslexic and hyperkinetic students.

Tampa: Academic Achievement Center, 7016 N. Donald Avenue, 33614. Telephone: (813) 932-3731. Educational Director: Arnold L. Stark. Day school with summer program and camp. Ages served: 6-13. Grades served: 2-6. Current enrollment: 7. Maximum enrollment: 12. Full-time staff: 1. Services: individual and group tutoring, academic testing, full curriculum, multisensory reading and math, computer programming. Recreation: nearby community center, swimming, bowling, field trips.

Tampa: Center Academy, 7823 Mushinski Road, 33624. Telephone: (816) 961-0525. Director: Dorothy P. Casolaro. Elementary and secondary day and boarding school with summer program and camp. Ages served: 6-17. Grades served: kindergarten-12. Current enrollment: 40. Maximum enrollment: 60 day; 15 residential. Full-time staff: 12. Part-time staff: 2. Services: individual and group tutoring, academic and psychological testing; academic, psychological, and family counseling; adaptive physical education, medical services. Recreation: ranch, riding, swimming. Notes: School also has residential branch in London, England.

Tampa: Morning Star School, 210 E. Linebaugh Avenue, 33612. Telephone: (813) 935-0232. Principal: Jeanette Friedheim. Day school. Ages served: 6-14. Current enrollment: 88. Full-time staff: 12. Part-time staff: 1. Scholarships/financial aid available. Services: individual and group tutoring, academic testing; full academic program including social skills and motor development.

Tampa: Tampa Reading Clinic and Day School, 3020 Azeele Street, 33609. Telephone: (813) 876-7202. Director: Joan F. Schabacker. Elementary day school with summer program. Ages served: 5-11. Grades served: ungraded. Current enrollment: 48. Maximum enrollment: 48. Full-time staff: 9. Part-time staff: 1. Services: individual tutoring, academic testing and counseling, private instruction for individuals aged 5-adult. Notes: Full-time remedial day school.

Summer Camps and Programs

Tampa: JCC Camp, 2808 Horatio, 33609. Telephone: (813) 872-4451. Program Director: Terry Abrahams. Day camp with limited services. Ages served: 1-16. Grades served: preschool-10. Maximum enrollment: 300. Full-time staff: 30. Scholarships/financial aid available. Recreation: swimming, team sports, crafts, dance. Notes: All children are mainstreamed into the regular program.

College and University Special Programs and Services

Bethune-Cookman College: 640 Second Avenue, Daytona Beach, FL 32015. Special services: readers, individual and group tutoring, special examinations, scholarships, academic and psychological counseling, diagnostic testing, taped books, training in study skills, audiovisual learning aids. Contact: Sigita Ramanauskas, Associate Professor of Exceptional Child Education. Telephone: (904) 255-1401 ext. 414.

Brevard Community College: 1519 Clearlake Road, Cocoa, FL 32926. Special services: individual and group tutoring, training in study skills, academic and psychological counseling, taped books, special examinations, student resource center, readers, diagnostic testing, support group. Contact: Doris Rader, Coordinator of Disabled Student Services. Telephone: (305) 632-1111 ext. 3606.

Center/clinic: Disabled Student Services. Telephone: (305) 632-1111. Director: Doris Rader. Not open to public. Ages served: 18 and up.

Broward Community College: 3501 S.W. Davie Road, Fort Lauderdale, FL 33314. Total enrollment: 19,790. LD students: 13. Special services: individual and group tutoring, training in study skills, academic and psychological counseling, taped books, special examinations, student resource center, readers, scholarships, support group. Contact: Carmella Artale, Coordinator of Handicap Services. Telephone: (305) 475-6527.

Chipola Junior College: College Drive, Marianna, FL 32446. Total enrollment: 1,425. LD students: 5. Special services: individual tutoring, training in study skills, academic and psychological counseling, special examinations, student resource center. Contact: Bob Tanton, Handicapped Student Services Specialist. Telephone: (904) 526-2761 ext. 296.

Daytona Beach Community College: P.O. Box 1111, Daytona Beach, FL 32015. Total enrollment: 8,500. LD students: 4. Special services: individual tutoring, academic counseling, taped books, readers, support group. Contact: M. Sue Hawkins, Coordinator, Learning Support Center. Telephone: (904) 255-8131 ext. 3467.

Embry-Riddle Aeronautical University: Regional Airport, Daytona Beach, FL 32014. Total students: 5,000. LD students: 10. Special services: training in study skills, academic counseling, student resource center, referral to community resources. Contact: Maureen C. Bridger, Director, Health Services. Telephone: (904) 252-5561 ext. 1051.

Center/clinic: Health Services. Telephone: (904) 252-5561 ext. 1051. Director: Maureen C. Bridger. Open to public. Ages served: 17 and up. Grades served: undergraduate and graduate students.

Florida A & M University: Tallahassee, FL 32307. LD students: 9. Special services: individual and group tutoring, training in study skills, academic and psychological counseling, taped books, special examinations, student resource center, readers, diagnostic testing, ombudsman, support group. Contact: Talmadge Frazier, Director of Student Services. Telephone: (904) 599-3313.

Center/clinic: Verbal Communication Center, Special Programs and Services, Room 111. Telephone: (904) 599-3313. Director: Talmadge Frazier. Open to public. Ages served: 14-college. Grades served: 9-college.

Florida Atlantic University: Boca Raton, FL 33431. Total enrollment: 10,200. Special services: readers, individual tutoring, academic and psychological counseling. Contact: Phebe Kerr, Associate Dean of Students. Telephone: (305) 393-3546.

Florida International University: S.C. 260 Bay Vista Campus, Miami, FL 33020. LD students: 3. Special services: readers, note takers, additional course and test time. Contact: Kathryn Trionfo, Associate Director, Student Development. Telephone: (305) 940-5813.

Florida Junior College at Jacksonville: 4501 Capper Road, Jacksonville, FL 32218. Total enrollment: 24,760. LD students: 30. Special services: individual and group tutoring, training in study skills, academic counseling, taped books, student resource center, readers, diagnostic testing. Contact: Glartonnie M. Mayes, Programs for Disabled Students. Telephone: (904) 757-6366.

Center/clinic: Mainstreaming Center. Telephone: (904) 757-6366. Director: Jeffrey G. Oliver. Open to public. Ages served: 18 and up. Grades served: junior college, high school completion.

Lake City Community College: Route 7, Box 378, Lake City, FL 32055. Total enrollment: 1,900. LD students: 8. Special services: individual tutoring, training in study skills, academic and psychological counseling, taped books, student resource center, readers, scholarships, ombudsman. Contact: Dennis King, Director of Student Services. Telephone: (904) 752-1822 ext. 300.

Miami-Dade Community College-North Campus: 11380 N.W. 27th Avenue, Miami, FL 33167. Total enrollment: 20,000. LD students: 300. Special services: academic, social, emotional, and vocational counseling; advisement, intensive program monitoring, special examinations, taped books, career testing.

- **Special program:** Learning Disabilities Lab. Intensive remedial instruction in reading, writing, and math and assistance with college level coursework. Must meet regular admissions requirements of the college. Learning disability must be verified through recent diagnostic tests or tests done by the college. May be enrolled in special program only. Coordinator: Dianne B. Rossman. Telephone: (305) 347-1276 or 347-1272.

Nova University: 3301 College Avenue, Fort Lauderdale, FL 33314.

Center/clinic: The Family Center. Telephone: (305) 475-7670. Associate Director: Susan Talpins. Open to public. Ages served: birth-18. Grades served: kindergarten-high school. Services: individual and group tutoring, speech and language testing and therapy, computer math skills, parent/child interaction classes, developmental nursery, diagnostic testing, academic and psychological testing, individual and family counseling, six-week summer camp.

Seminole Community College: Highway 17-92, Sanford, FL 32771. Special services: individual tutoring, training in study skills, academic counseling, taped books, special examinations, student resource center, diagnostic testing, support group. Contact: David Glaize, Counselor. Telephone: (305) 323-1450 ext. 423.

Stetson University: Deland, FL 32720. Special services: individual tutoring, training in study skills, academic and psychological counseling, diagnostic testing. Contact: Elizabeth Heins, Assistant Professor of Education. Telephone: (904) 734-4121 ext. 280.

University of Miami: University Station, Coral Gables, FL 33124. Special services: individual tutoring, training in study skills, academic and psychological counseling, taped books, special examinations, readers, diagnostic testing, scholarships, ombudsman. Contact: M. Eugene Flipse, Coordinator of Services for the Handicapped. Telephone: (305) 284-5921.

University of North Florida: P.O. Box 17074, Jacksonville, FL 32216. Total enrollment: 600. Special services: individual tutoring, training in study skills, academic and psychological counseling, limited special examinations, student resource center. Contact: Sandra Hansford, Vice President for Student Services. Telephone: (904) 646-2600.

Valencia Community College: P.O. Box 3028, Orlando, FL 32802. Special services: individual tutoring, academic counseling, taped books, special examinations, student resource center, readers. Contact: Margaret F. Edmonds, Handicapped Specialist. Telephone: (305) 299-5000 ext. 523.

Hospital Clinics

Clearwater: Morton Plant Hospital, Department of Communicative Disorders, 905 S. Fort Harrison Street, 33516. Telephone: (813) 462-7074. Contact: Thomas Wekenman, Academic Clinician. Outpatient program. Ages served: 4-adult. Services: diagnostic testing, academic and psychological testing, individual and group tutoring; academic, psychological, and parent counseling; speech, language, and occupational therapy; team consultation, neuropsychological evaluation.

Tampa: Tampa General Hospital, Tampa General Rehabilitation Center, 33606. Telephone: (813) 253-5823. Contact: Dana S. DeBoskey, Chief of Psychological

Services. Outpatient and after school program. Ages served: infant-adult. Services: diagnostic testing, academic and psychological testing, individual tutoring; academic, psychological, and parent counseling; speech, language, physical, and occupational therapy; social services, neuropsychological evaluations. Notes: Group tutoring and therapy are planned but not currently offered.

Other Services

Fort Lauderdale: Educational Center, 3061 N.E. 41st Street, 33308. Telephone: (305) 776-1991. Contact: Suzanne Mellin or Jane Hinman. Clinic. Day and after school program. Ages served: preschool-adult. Services: diagnostic testing, academic testing, individual and group tutoring, academic counseling; liaison between parents, child, school, and other professionals to evaluate and monitor students.

Fort Pierce: Developmental Learning Center, 3546 Okeechobee Road, 33450. Telephone: (305) 465-5405. Clinical Directors: John E. Mauldin, Alexandra T. Pietrewicz. Educational service. Ages served: birth-adult. Grades served: preschool-college. Current enrollment: 30. Maximum enrollment: 50. Full-time staff: 2. Part-time staff: 2. Services: individual tutoring, academic and psychological testing, academic and vocational counseling, behavior management, sensory and perceptual screening, SAT and high school equivalency preparation, computer literacy.

Miami: Educational Guidance Services, Inc., P.O. Box 557251, 33255. Telephone: (305) 264-6700. Contact: Norma Banas. Clinic. Day program. Ages served: 3½ and up. Services: diagnostic testing, academic and psychoeducational testing, individual and group tutoring; academic, psychological, vocational, and parent counseling; speech, language, and occupational therapy; adaptive physical education, career guidance, prescriptive teaching program design.

Naples: Rehab Associates, Inc., 28 Tenth Street, South, 33940. Telephone: (813) 261-4592. Speech and Language Pathologist: Marti Sheff. Clinic. Outpatient program. Ages served: all. Services: diagnostic speech and language testing, parent counseling; speech, language, physical, and occupational therapy; social services, referral to area schools and supplementary programs for learning disabilities.

Seminole: Testing and Remediation Center, 8894 Seminole Boulevard, Suites 6-8, 33542. Telephone: (813) 393-8841. Clinic. Ages served: all. Current enrollment: 12. Full-time staff: 3. Part-time staff: 9. Services: individual and group tutoring, academic and psychological testing, academic counseling, Orton-Gillingham and Slingerland techniques, college counseling, study skills, SAT and high school equivalency preparation, multisensory math.

GEORGIA

Offices of Organizations Concerned with Learning Disabilities

ACLD, Inc.: P.O. Box 29492, Atlanta, GA 30359. Telephone: (404) 633-1236. Co-presidents: Cheri Hoy, Katherine Stalvey. Executive Secretary: Marilyn Principe.

Council for Exceptional Children: President: Gwen Garrison, 339 Peyton Place, S.W., Atlanta, GA 30311. Telephone: Office (404) 755-1618; Home (404) 696-3769.

Georgia Easter Seal Society, Inc.: 1900 Emery Street, N.W., Suite 106, Atlanta, GA 30318. Executive Director: Dennis J. Celorie. Telephone: (404) 351-6551.

State Department of Education Learning Disabilities Personnel

Joan Jordan, Director, Program for Exceptional Children, State Department of Education, 1970 Twin Towers East, Atlanta, GA 30334. Telephone: (404) 656-2425. Learning disabilities consultant: Mary Murphy. Telephone: (404) 656-2426.

Private and Day Schools

Atlanta: Atlanta Speech School, Inc., 3160 Northside Parkway, N.W., 30327. Telephone: (404) 233-5332. Executive Director: Julia W. Hand. Preschool and elementary day school with summer program and camp. Ages served: 3-12. Grades served: preschool-elementary. Current enrollment: 115. Maximum enrollment: 115. Full-time staff: 64. Part-time staff: 21. Scholarships/financial aid available. Services: individual and group tutoring, academic and psychological testing, speech and language therapy; individual instruction in reading, math, language, and fine motor development for children aged 5-14 attending other schools. Recreation: field trips, physical education, music, art. Notes: Facility houses four departments: Audiology/Speech Pathology Clinic (testing and therapy), Oral School for the Hearing Impaired, Regular Preschool/Nursery, Department for Language and Learning Disabilities.

Atlanta: The Barclay School, 385 Mount Paran Road, N.W., 30327. Telephone: (404) 256-2470. Headmaster: Stanley N. Chervin. Elementary and secondary day school with summer program in London, England. Ages served: 7-18. Grades served: elementary-high school. Current enrollment: 100. Maximum enrollment: 125. Full-time staff: 15. Part-time staff: 3. Scholarships/financial aid available. Services: individual tutoring, academic testing, academic and psychological counseling, vocational training, work-study, job placement. Recreation: baseball, volleyball, basketball, track and field, flag football, field day.

Atlanta: Brandon Hall School, 1701 Brandon Hall Drive, 30338. Telephone: (414) 394-8177. President: Harrison W. Kimbrell. Elementary and secondary day school with males only boarding school; summer program. Ages served: 11-18.

Grades served: 5-13. Current enrollment: 180. Maximum enrollment: 180. Full-time staff: 95. Limited scholarships/financial aid available. Services: individual and group tutoring, academic testing and counseling, college preparatory education. Recreation: all sports except football; yearbook, drama, photography.

Atlanta: The Davison School, Inc., 1500 N. Decatur Road, N.E., 30306. Telephone: (404) 373-7288. Director: Lucille M. Pressnell. Preschool, elementary, and secondary day and boarding school with summer program and camp. Ages served: 3-16. Grades served: preschool-10. Current enrollment: 58. Full-time staff: 16. Part-time staff: 2. Limited scholarships/financial aid available. Services: individual tutoring, academic testing, individual speech and language therapy; physical, occupational, and recreational therapy; speech and language testing, adaptive physical education, self-contained classrooms. Recreation: recreational therapist plans off-campus activities including swimming, bowling, roller-skating.

Atlanta: Gables Academy, 1337 Fairview Road, N.E., 30306. Telephone: (404) 377-1721. Director: Bruce L. Kline. Day and boarding school with summer program. Ages served: 11-20. Current enrollment: 25. Full-time staff: 2. Part-time staff: 8. Scholarships/financial aid available. Services: individual and group tutoring, academic and psychological testing, prevocational preparation, group counseling, speech and language therapy. Recreation: physical education including judo, karate, self-defense; photography, computer lab, architectural and mechanical drafting, auto mechanics, electronics, woodshop, carpentry.

Atlanta: The Howard School, Inc., 1246 Ponce de Leon Avenue, N.E., 30306. Telephone: (404) 377-7436. Director: Mary Ben McDorman. Preschool, elementary, and secondary day school with summer program and camp. Ages served: 5-18. Grades served: ungraded. Current enrollment: 122. Full-time staff: 28. Part-time staff: 9. Scholarships/financial aid available. Services: individual tutoring, academic and psychological testing, educational evaluation; academic, individual, and family counseling; occupational therapy, adaptive physical education, limited job placement. Recreation: YMCA for swimming, roller-skating.

Atlanta: The New School in the Lost Forest, 6955 Brandon Mill Road, 30328. Telephone: (404) 255-5951. Executive Director: Tweetie L. Moore. Elementary and secondary day school with summer program and camp. Ages served: 6-18. Grades served: 1-12. Current enrollment: 180. Maximum enrollment: 180. Full-time staff: 36. Part-time staff: 6. Scholarships/financial aid available. Services: individual and group tutoring, academic and psychological testing, academic and family counseling, parent groups, adaptive physical education, college placement services, values groups, goal setting and evaluation. Recreation: therapeutic riding; competitive league for soccer, basketball, baseball, tennis; New Games, swimming, arts and crafts, cooking. Notes: Total treatment program for children with learning disabilities accompanied by mild difficulties with social adjustment and self-esteem.

GEORGIA

Atlanta: St. Francis Day School, 1000 Mt. Vernon Highway, 30327. Telephone: (404) 955-9192. Headmaster: Drew Buccellato. Elementary day school with summer program and camp. Ages served: 5-14. Current enrollment: 90. Full-time staff: 13. Part-time staff: 2. Scholarships/financial aid available. Services: individual tutoring, academic testing and counseling; small group instruction in reading, math, language arts; computer literacy, drama, physical education, art, after school tutoring programs.

Atlanta: The Schenck School, 282 Mt. Paran Road, N.W., 30327. Telephone: (404) 252-2591 or 252-0855. Director: David T. Schenck. Elementary day school with summer program. Ages served: 6-14. Grades served: 1-8. Current enrollment: 82. Maximum enrollment: 82. Full-time staff: 19. Part-time staff: 4. Scholarships/financial aid available. Services: individual and group tutoring, academic and psychological testing; academic, psychological, and family counseling. Recreation: playground.

Macon: The Howard School, Inc., 436 Forest Hill Road, 31210. Telephone: (912) 477-8111. Director: Mary Ben McDorman. Preschool and elementary day school with summer program and camp. Ages served: 5-15. Current enrollment: 25. Maximum enrollment: 36. Full-time staff: 5. Part-time staff: 1. Scholarships/financial aid available. Services: individual tutoring, academic and psychological testing. Notes: There is a branch of The Howard School in Atlanta.

Savannah: Chatham Academy, Inc., P.O. Box 15087, 31416. Telephone: (912) 355-0583. Director: Carolyn M. Hannaford. Elementary and secondary day school with summer program. Ages served: 6-16. Grades served: 1-11. Current enrollment: 42. Maximum enrollment: 60. Full-time staff: 7. Part-time staff: 1. Scholarships/financial aid available. Services: individual and group tutoring, academic testing, academic and family counseling, adaptive physical education, work-study.

Warner Robins: Houston Speech School, 100 Pine Valley Drive, 31093. Telephone: (912) 923-1787. Superintendent: Mrs. Carlieze W. Spencer. Preschool, elementary, and secondary day school with boarding available. Ages served: 4-18. Grades served: kindergarten-12. Current enrollment: 28. Maximum enrollment: 45. Full-time staff: 10. Part-time staff: 2. Scholarships/financial aid available. Services: academic testing and counseling, adaptive physical education, vocational training. Notes: Works closely with state department of vocational rehabilitation and local technical schools to help older students make transition into a career field.

Summer Camps and Programs

College Park: Squirrel Hollow, Inc., 1831 Walker Avenue, 30337. Telephone: (404) 762-7896. Director: Betsy E. Box. Residential camp with academic program. Ages served: 6-19. Grades served: 1-12. Maximum enrollment: 75. Full-time staff: 34. Scholarships/financial aid available. Services: individual and group tutoring, academic and psychological testing, adaptive physical education, parent seminar. Academic programs: math, reading, English, spelling, study skills. Recreation: swimming, hiking, field trips, camping, fishing, canoeing.

Loganville: Camp Bluesprings, P.O. Box 37, 30249. Telephone: (404) 466-2208. Director: Billie Baird. Day camp. Ages served: 3-adult. Maximum enrollment: 75. Full-time staff: 30. Scholarships/financial aid available. Services: adaptive physical education. Recreation: nature study, riding, swimming, team sports, music; reinforcement of academic skills through recreational activities. Notes: Serves all handicaps. Programs individually planned for each camper.

College and University Special Programs and Services

Abraham Baldwin Agricultural College: Box 28, ABAC Station, Tifton, GA 31793-4401. Total enrollment: 1,974. LD students: 15. Special services: individual tutoring, training in study skills, academic and psychological counseling, taped books, special examinations, student resource center. Contact: Rosemary Johnson, Director of Counseling and Testing. Telephone: (912) 386-3233 ext. 8.

Armstrong State College: 11935 Abercorn Street, Savannah, GA 31419-1997. Total enrollment: 2,691. Special services: individual tutoring, training in study skills, academic counseling, special examinations, scholarships. Contact: Lynn Benson, Director of Counseling Services. Telephone: (912) 927-5269.

Atlanta College of Art: 1280 Peachtree Street, N.E., Atlanta, GA 30309. Total enrollment: 245. LD students: 5. Special services: work with students individually, liaison with faculty. Contact: Elizabeth V. Shackelford, Director, Student Services. Telephone: (404) 898-1161.

Brenau College: Washington Street, Gainesville, GA 30501. Total enrollment: 650. LD students: 18. Special services: readers, individual tutoring, special examinations, academic counseling, diagnostic testing, taped books, training in study skills, student resource center, reading therapy, psychological counseling by referral.

- **Special program:** Learning Disability Program. Weekly supplemental individual tutoring, reading therapy, counseling. Must fulfill regular and special admissions requirements. Special requirements include verification of learning disability through recent diagnostic tests and an interview. Students must take 12 credit hours of regular classes. Director: Karen Pfunder. Telephone: (404) 534-6218 or 534-6227.

Clayton Junior College: P.O. Box 285, Morrow, GA 30260. Total enrollment: 3,250. LD students: 10. Special services: individual tutoring, training in study skills, academic and psychological counseling, taped books, special examinations, student resource center, diagnostic testing, scholarships, ombudsman. Contact: D. Jay Feldman, Special Needs Coordinator. Telephone: (404) 961-3515.

Columbus College: Algonquin Drive, Columbus, GA 31993-2399. Special services: individual tutoring, special examinations, academic and psychological counseling, diagnostic testing, training in study skills. Contact: Carol Vander Ghenst, Program Coordinator. Telephone: (404) 568-2412.

Center/clinic: Columbus College Clinical Center. Telephone: (404) 568-2222. Director: Thomas J. Wentland. Open to public. Ages served: preschool-adult. Services: diagnostic testing, speech and language therapy, remediation.

DeKalb Community College-Central Campus: 555 N. Indian Creek Drive, Clarkston, GA 30021. Total enrollment: 6,614. LD students: 15. Special services: individual and group tutoring, training in study skills, academic counseling, student resource center. Contact: Marcia Blanding, Counselor. Telephone: (404) 299-4110 or 299-4112.

Emory University: Atlanta, GA 30322. Special services: individual tutoring, special examinations, diagnostic testing. Contact: Marigene M. Duff, Associate Professor, Language Pathology. Telephone: (404) 329-7790.

Center/clinic: Language-Learning Disabilities Clinic. Telephone: (404) 329-7790. Director: James T. Graham. Ages served: preschool-young adult.

Gainesville Junior College: P.O. Box 1358, Gainesville, GA 30503. Total enrollment: 1,744. LD students: 1. Special services: individual tutoring, training in study skills, academic counseling, student resource center. Contact: Katherine Fuller, Coordinator of Open Learning Lab. Telephone: (404) 535-6271.

Georgia College: Milledgeville, GA 31061. Total enrollment: 3,500. LD students: 5. Special services: individual and group tutoring, special examinations, academic and psychological counseling, diagnostic testing, training in study skills, readers. Contact: Paul Benson, Vice President of Student Affairs. Telephone: (912) 453-5169.

Georgia Southern College: Statesboro, GA 30460-8131. Total enrollment: 6,526. LD students: 15-20. Special services: special examinations, academic and psychological counseling, diagnostic testing, training in study skills. Contact: Robert A. Martin, Head, Education, Psychology and Guidance. Telephone: (912) 681-5301 or 681-5302.

Center/clinic: Learning Analysis Center, L.B. 8131. Telephone: (912) 681-5301 or 681-5302. Codirectors: Robert A. Martin, W. Tucker Anderson. Open to public. Grades served: preschool-college.

Mercer University: 1400 Coleman Avenue, Macon, GA 31201. Special services: individual and group tutoring, academic counseling, taped books, readers. Contact: Mary Jane Polletzer, Coordinator/Counselor, Disabled Student Services. Telephone: (912) 744-2862.

Piedmont College: Demorest, GA 30535. Total enrollment: 388. LD students: 20. Special services: individual and group tutoring, training in study skills, academic and psychological counseling, special examinations, diagnostic testing, support group, special programs unit. Contact: Ellen O'Neal, Director of Special Programs. Telephone: (404) 778-4144.

Reinhardt College: Highway 140, Waleska, GA 30183. Total enrollment: 340. LD students: 12. Special services: individual tutoring, training in study skills, academic and psychological counseling, taped books, readers, diagnostic testing, special examinations. Contact: Connie Cogdell, Director, Academic Support Office. Telephone: (404) 479-1454 ext. 25.

Thomas County Community College: 1501 Millpond Road, Thomasville, GA 31792. Total enrollment: 380. Special services: individual and group tutoring, training in study skills, academic counseling, readers, diagnostic testing. Contact: Gale Whitehurst, Director of Special Services. Telephone: (912) 226-1621 ext. 25.

University of Georgia: Athens, GA 30602. Special services: individual tutoring, group self-help, training in study skills, academic and psychological counseling, taped books, student resource center, readers, diagnostic testing.

- **Special program:** Learning Disabilities Support Service. Provides diagnostic assessment and other services including tutorial and treatment programs to learning disabled students. Students must meet regular admissions requirements of the university. Director: Noel Gregg. Telephone: (404) 542-1685.

Center/clinic: Learning Disabilities Adult Clinic, 570 Aderhold Hall. Telephone: (404) 542-1685. Director: Noel Gregg. Open to public. Ages served: 18-65. Grades served: postsecondary. Services: two-day interdisciplinary psychoeducational evaluations, college learning disabilities program.

Center/clinic: Special Education Children's Clinic, 570 Aderhold Hall. Telephone: (404) 542-1685. Director: Cheri Hoy. Open to public. Ages served: 2-18. Grades served: preschool-12. Services: two-day interdisciplinary psychoeducational evaluations.

Valdosta State College: Valdosta, GA 31698. Total enrollment: 6,095. Special services: individual tutoring, special examinations, academic and psychological counseling, diagnostic testing, taped books, training in study skills. Contact: Malcolm Rainey, Vice President for Academic Affairs. Telephone: (912) 333-5950.

GEORGIA

Center/clinic: The Summer Clinic, Department of Special Education, 101 Education Center. Telephone: (912) 333-5932. Director: Richard Uhlir. Grades served: 1-12. Services: diagnosis, evaluation, remediation, nine-week summer program.

West Georgia College: Carrollton, GA 30118. Total enrollment: 6,000. LD students: 10-15. Special services: readers, individual and group tutoring, ombudsman, special examinations, academic and psychological counseling, diagnostic testing, student resource center, training in study skills.

- **Special program:** Learning Disabilities Program. Study skills course, individual tutoring by graduate assistant specializing in learning disabilities, special college advisor. Learning disability must be verified through diagnostic tests. Program open to full or part-time students. Coordinator of Special Services for Disabled Students: Ann Phillips. Telephone: (404) 834-1416.

Hospital Clinics

Atlanta: Scottish Rite Children's Hospital, Multi-Disciplinary Clinic for Learning Disabilities, 1001 Johnson Ferry Road, 30363. Telephone: (404) 257-2036. Contact: Angie Olsen. Outpatient program. Services: diagnostic testing, psychological testing and counseling; speech, language, physical, and occupational therapy.

Rome: Northwest Georgia Regional Hospital, Adolescent Specialty Treatment Unit, 413 Cooper Drive, 30161. Telephone: (404) 232-5768. Special Education Teacher: Jean V. Anderson. Inpatient and day program. Ages served: 14-17. Services: diagnostic testing, academic and psychological testing, individual and group tutoring; academic, psychological, and parent counseling; group, speech, language, physical, and occupational therapy; adaptive physical education, support group, social services, prevocational and vocational training, rehabilitation services.

Other Services

Atlanta: Child and Family Center of Atlanta, 6135 Barfield Road, Suite 118, 30328. Telephone: (404) 843-0209. Contact: Sunaina Jaim or Carol Fisher. Clinic. After school program. Ages served: birth-adult. Services: diagnostic testing, academic and psychological testing, individual and group tutoring; academic, psychological, and parent counseling; group therapy, support group, social services.

Atlanta: Hillside Treatment Center, 690 Courtenay Drive, N.E., 30306. Telephone: (404) 875-4551. Executive Director: Thomas Corbett. Residential treatment center with elementary and secondary day school. Ages served: 10-18. Grades served: 3-12. Current enrollment: 24. Maximum enrollment: 24. Full-time staff: 20. Part-time staff: 4. Scholarships/financial aid available. Services: individual tutoring, academic and psychological testing, psychological and family counseling, medical services. Recreation: swimming, basketball, softball.

Atlanta: Institute for Child and Family Development and Research, 1601 Clifton Road, 30329. Telephone: (404) 329-1616. Codirector: Melinda Parrill. Multidisciplinary clinic. Ages served: birth-young adult. Services: diagnostic testing, academic and psychological testing, individual remediation; academic, psychological, and parent counseling; language therapy.

Atlanta: Resource Educational Tutoring and Testing, Tuxedo Center, Suite 122, 3580 Piedmont Road, N.E., 30305. Telephone: (404) 237-6342. Contact: Richard Kaplan. Day, after school, and evening program. Ages served: all. Services: diagnostic testing, academic and psychoeducational testing, individual and group tutoring, academic and parent counseling, occupational therapy, support group. Notes: Focuses on remediation of learning disabilities/problems present in social, vocational, and academic environments. Approximately 40 percent of clients are adults.

HAWAII

Offices of Organizations Concerned with Learning Disabilities

ACLD, Inc.: 200 N. Vineyard Boulevard, Room 402, Honolulu, HI 96817. Telephone: (808) 536-9684. President: Marge Kanahele. Executive Director: Ivalee Sinclair.

Council for Exceptional Children: President: Sande Arakaki, 3529 Manoa Road, Honolulu, HI 96822. Telephone: Office (808) 732-7728; Home (808) 988-6021.

Easter Seal Society of Hawaii, Inc.: 710 Green Street, Honolulu, HI 96813. Executive Director: Bill L. Hindman. Telephone: (808) 536-1015.

State Department of Education Learning Disabilities Personnel

Miles S. Kawatachi, Director, Special Needs Branch, State Department of Education, 3430 Leahi Avenue, Honolulu, HI 96815. Telephone: (808) 737-3720.

Private and Day Schools

Honolulu: Academy School, 4819 Kilauea Avenue, 96816. Telephone: (808) 732-6081. Director: Carol Wood. Secondary day school with summer program. Grades served: 7-12. Current enrollment: 16. Maximum enrollment: 16. Full-time staff: 4. Part-time staff: 1. Services: individual and group tutoring, academic and psychological testing, academic counseling, vocational training, work-study, job placement, family consultation and counseling. Recreation: basketball, swimming, exercise room. Notes: Teacher-student ratio is 1:5. Respite school whose goal is to return students to regular school environment.

HAWAII

Honolulu: Fairhaven School, 2062 S. King Street, 96826. Telephone: (808) 944-0173. Director: Jacquelyn N. Sprague. Elementary day school with summer program. Ages served: 7-14. Grades served: 1-8. Current enrollment: 6. Full-time staff: 1. Part-time staff: 2. Scholarships/financial aid available. Services: individual and group tutoring, academic and psychological testing, academic counseling. Recreation: art, music, physical education program including soccer, hiking, yoga, sailing, baseball.

Honolulu: Variety Club School, 710 Palekaua Street, 96816. Telephone: (808) 732-2835. Executive Director: Susan E. Baker. Preschool and elementary day school with summer camp. Ages served: 2½-13. Grades served: ungraded. Current enrollment: 42. Maximum enrollment: 63. Full-time staff: 19. Part-time staff: 2. Scholarships/financial aid available. Services: individual and group tutoring, academic and psychological testing, family counseling, work-study; physical, speech, language, occupational, music, and art therapy; adaptive physical education, computer education, ongoing diagnostics, screening program, developmental preschool, psychiatric consultation, parent/sibling groups. Recreation: camping, Mini-Olympics.

Pearl Harbor: ASSETS School, Box 106, 96860. Telephone: (808) 422-5256. Principal: Barrett B. McCandless. Preschool, elementary, and intermediate day school with summer program. Ages served: 5-14. Grades served: kindergarten-8. Current enrollment: 156. Maximum enrollment: 156. Full-time staff: 26. Part-time staff: 16. Scholarships/financial aid available. Services: individual and group tutoring, academic and psychological testing, vocational training; academic, psychological, and family counseling; physical and speech therapy, adaptive physical education, parent education, gifted enrichment and acceleration. Recreation: physical education including swimming, bowling, organized field sports. Notes: Programs for gifted and learning disabled children.

Summer Camps and Programs

Hilo: Camp Mary Mac, c/o Easter Seals, P.O. Box 715, 96721. Telephone: (808) 961-3081. Day camp with limited services. Ages served: 4-adult. Scholarships/financial aid available. Services: group tutoring, family counseling; physical, occupational, speech, and language therapy. Recreation: camping, hiking, field trips, nature study, riding, swimming, crafts, dance, drama, music, bowling, Special Mini-Olympics.

College and University Special Programs and Services

Chaminade University of Honolulu: 3140 Waialae Avenue, Honolulu, HI 96816. Total enrollment: 1,077. LD students: 3. Special services: individual tutoring, training in study skills, academic and psychological counseling, special examinations, readers, diagnostic testing, support group. Contact: Mary Wilkinson, Director of Special Services. Telephone: (808) 735-4881.

Honolulu Community College: 874 Dillingham Boulevard, Honolulu, HI 96817. Total enrollment: 5,000. LD students: 40. Special services: readers, individual tutoring, academic counseling, taped books, note takers, tape recorders, electronic visual aids, special examinations, training in study skills. Contact: Rona Wong, Counselor. Telephone: (808) 845-9279.

Kapiolani Community College: 620 Pensacola Street, Honolulu, HI 96814. Total enrollment: 5,000. LD students: 16. Special services: individual and group tutoring, academic counseling, taped books, special examinations, readers, ombudsman. Contact: Mary Joan Haverly, Counselor for the Handicapped. Telephone: (808) 531-4654 ext. 215.

Kauai Community College: 3-1901 Kaumualii Highway, Lihue, HI 96766. Total enrollment: 1,200. LD students: 1. Special services: individual tutoring, training in study skills, academic and psychological counseling, student resource center, scholarships, career counseling. Contact: Frances Dinnan, Counselor. Telephone: (808) 245-8286.

Leeward Community College: 96-045 Ala Ike, Pearl City, HI 96782. Special services: individual and group tutoring, academic counseling, diagnostic testing, training in study skills.

- **Special program:** Program for Adult Achievement. Special classes in self-development, reading, writing, math, and study skills. Accepts 15-20 students per semester. Learning disability must be verified through recent records or testing done by college staff. Students may participate in LD program only and eventually be mainstreamed or take special classes and regular classes at the same time. Contact: Michael Gross or Alice Smith. Telephone: (808) 455-0233 or 455-0250.

University of Hawaii-Manoa: 1776 University Avenue, Honolulu, HI 96822. Special services: individual tutoring, psychological counseling, taped books, readers. Contact: James R. Patton, Assistant Professor. Telephone: (808) 948-7956.

Hospital Clinics

Honolulu: Tripler Army Medical Center, Child Development, 96825. Telephone: (808) 433-6696 or 433-6697 or 433-6057. Contact: John T. McCarthy. Outpatient program. Ages served: birth-18. Services: speech, language, physical, and occupational therapy; medical evaluation of learning disabilities including child neurology. Notes: For military families.

IDAHO

Offices of Organizations Concerned with Learning Disabilities

Council for Exceptional Children: President: Marjean Waford, 15351 W. Lacey Road, Pocatello, ID 83202. Telephone: Office (208) 237-2503; Home (208) 237-4367.

Northern Rocky Mountain Easter Seal Society: 4400 Central Avenue, Great Falls, MT 59401. President: William Sirak. Telephone: (406) 761-3680.

Orton Dyslexia Society (Puget Sound Branch): 1922 Richmond Beach Drive, N.W., Seattle, WA 98177. President: Lucille Pridemore. Telephone: Office (206) 743-3513; Home (206) 542-1434.

State Department of Education Learning Disabilities Personnel

Martha Noffsinger, Supervisor of Special Education, Len B. Jordan Building, State Office Building, 650 W. State Street, Boise, ID 83720. Telephone: (208) 334-3940. Learning disabilities consultant: Mike Lowder.

Private and Day Schools

Lewiston: Community Action Agency Lewis-Clark Head Start, 1805 19th Avenue, 83501. Telephone: (208) 743-6573. Head Start Director: Frances Mathison. Preschool. Ages served: 4. Current enrollment: 59. Maximum enrollment: 59. Full-time staff: 2. Part-time staff: 7. Services: individual and group tutoring, academic and psychological testing, psychological and family counseling, physical and occupational therapy, medical services. Recreation: field trips, films, music, painting, cooking, tumbling, holiday parties.

Lewiston: North Idaho Children's Home, Inc., Box 319, 83501. Telephone: (208) 743-9404. Executive Director: Mark A. Hopper. Elementary and secondary day and boarding school with summer program. Ages served: 6-18. Grades served: kindergarten-12. Current enrollment: 72. Maximum enrollment: 72. Full-time staff: 21. Services: individual and group tutoring, academic and psychological testing; academic, psychological, and family counseling; physical and occupational therapy, adaptive physical education, vocational training, work-study, job placement, medical services, arts and crafts program. Recreation: two full-time recreational personnel offering a wide variety of activities.

College and University Special Programs and Services

Boise State University: 1910 University Drive, Boise, ID 83725. Total enrollment: 11,003. LD students: 4. Special services: special examinations, note takers, individual and group tutoring. Notes: Arrangements for special services made on individual basis. Learning disability must be verified through professional evaluation. Contact: Janet Centanni, Special Services Coordinator. Telephone: (208) 385-1583.

College of Idaho: 2112 Cleveland Boulevard, Caldwell, ID 83605. Total enrollment: 700. Special services: individual tutoring, training in study skills, academic and psychological counseling. Contact: Dorothy E. Gerber, Study Skills Coordinator. Telephone: (208) 459-5508.

Idaho State University: Pocatello, ID 83201. Special services: limited special examinations, diagnostic testing. Contact: Director of Special Services. Telephone: (208) 236-3242.

Northwest Nazarene College: 623 Holly, Nampa, ID 83651. Special services: individual and group tutoring, training in study skills, academic and psychological counseling, special examinations, diagnostic testing. Contact: Earl R. Owens, Director of Special Education. Telephone: (208) 467-8256.

Center/clinic: Study Skills Center. Telephone: (208) 467-8256. Director: Evelyn Bennett. Not open to public. Grades served: college.

Center/clinic: Speech, Hearing, and Language Center. Telephone: (208) 467-8666. Director: Earl R. Owens. Open to public. Ages served: 5-adult. Grades served: kindergarten-adult.

Ricks College: Rexburg, ID 83440. Special services: individual and group tutoring, training in study skills, academic and psychological counseling, special examinations, student resource center, readers, diagnostic testing, scholarships, ombudsman. Contact: Richard G. Taylor, Director of Special Services. Telephone: (208) 356-1158.

Center/clinic: Ricks College Learning Assistance Lab. Telephone: (208) 356-1158. Director: Richard G. Taylor. Open to public. Grades served: college freshmen, sophomores. Services: readers, tutors.

University of Idaho: Moscow, ID 83843. Special services: individual and group tutoring, training in study skills, academic and psychological counseling, taped books, special examinations, student resource center, readers, diagnostic testing; developmental classes in reading, writing, spelling, math. Contact: Mary L. Morris, Director, Special Services Project. Telephone: (208) 885-6746. Or Cindy Lou McDonald, Student/Program Consultant. Telephone: (208) 885-6072.

Center/clinic: Special Services Project and Student Advisory Services, Phinney 302. Telephone: (208) 885-6746. Director: Mary L. Morris. Not open to public. Ages served: college. Grades served: undergraduate, graduate.

ILLINOIS

Offices of Organizations Concerned with Learning Disabilities

ACLD, Inc.: P.O. Box A 3239, Chicago, IL 60690. Telephone: (312) 663-9535. Contact: Mary Cotter. President: Sharon Schussler. Telephone: (312) 349-8637.

Coordinating Council for Handicapped Children: 220 S. State Street, Room 412, Chicago, IL 60604. Telephone: (312) 939-3513. Executive Director: Charlotte Des Jardins.

Council for Exceptional Children: President: Lesley P. Graham, 2013 W. Virginia Avenue, Peoria, IL 61604. Telephone: Office (309) 676-7611; Home (309) 685-2317.

Illinois Easter Seal Society, Inc.: P.O. Box 1767, 2715 S. Fourth Street, Springfield, IL 62705. Executive Director: Jim Gray. Telephone: (217) 525-0398.

Orton Dyslexia Society: 9452 Kilbourn, Skokie, IL 60076. President: Beverly Donenberg.

State Department of Education Learning Disabilities Personnel

Joseph E. Fisher, Assistant Superintendent of Specialized Education Services, Illinois State Board of Education, 100 N. First Street, Springfield, IL 62777. Telephone: (217) 782-6601. Learning disabilities consultant: Cindy Terry.

Private and Day Schools

Alton: Catholic Children's Home, Special Education, 1400 State Street, 62002. Telephone: (618) 465-3826. Executive Director: Lawrence P. Drury. Elementary and secondary day school with males only boarding school. Ages served: 5-21. Grades served: kindergarten-12. Current enrollment: 80. Full-time staff: 25. Part-time staff: 8. Limited scholarships/financial aid available. Services: individual tutoring, academic and psychological testing; academic, psychological, and family counseling; art and occupational therapy, adaptive physical education, work-study, job placement, social work. Recreation: intramural sports, arts and crafts.

Assumption: Kemmerer Village School, Route 1, Box 12C, 62557. Telephone: (217) 226-4451. Program Director: Debra McFarling. Elementary and secondary day and boarding school with summer program. Ages served: 10-18. Grades served: junior high-high school. Current enrollment: 31. Maximum enrollment: 40. Full-time staff: 50. Part-time staff: 2. Scholarships/financial aid available. Services: individual and group tutoring, academic and psychological testing; academic, psychological, and family counseling; adaptive physical education, work-study.

Aurora: Aurora Education Center, 441 N. Farnsworth Avenue, 60505. Telephone: (312) 851-6687. Principal: Robert Zanillo. Elementary and secondary day school with limited services; summer program. Ages served: 6-21. Grades served: 1-12. Current enrollment: 90. Maximum enrollment: 150. Full-time staff: 19. Part-time staff: 2. Services: individual and group tutoring, academic and psychological testing; academic, psychological, and family counseling; vocational training, work-study. Recreation: physical education, sports program, games, outdoor education.

Bloomington: Scott Center, P.O. Box 1485, 403 N. State Street, 61701. Telephone: (309) 827-0374. Executive Director: Darrell Torrence. Secondary day school and residential treatment center. Ages served: 11-21. Grades served: 6-12. Current enrollment: 22. Maximum enrollment: 32. Full-time staff: 5. Part-time staff: 2. Services: individual and group tutoring, academic and psychological testing; academic, psychological, group, and family counseling; adaptive physical education, vocational training, work-study, job placement. Recreation: residential program offers girl's athletics including softball, volleyball, basketball; recreation center.

Carbondale: Brehm Preparatory School, 1245 E. Grand Avenue, 62901. Telephone: (618) 457-0371. Administrative Director: Lynne A. Rocklage. Director of Psychological Services: Robert L. Stoneburner. Elementary and secondary day and boarding school. Ages served: 12-21. Grades served: 7-12, postsecondary. Current enrollment: 54. Maximum enrollment: 54; planning expansion. Full-time staff: 23. Part-time staff: 39. Foundation for scholarship assistance being developed. Services: individual and group tutoring, academic and psychological testing; academic, psychological, and group counseling; occupational, speech, and language therapy; adaptive physical education, medical services, individual psychotherapy, intensive learning disabilities programming. Recreation: outdoor, leisure, and recreational activities. Notes: Accepts students who have completed high school and are interested in postsecondary programming prior to college/career/vocational entry.

Chicago: Academy of Our Lady Learning Center, 1309 W. 95th Street, 60642. Telephone: (312) 636-4151 or 445-2300 ext. 34. Director: Sr. Mary Kay Weatherly. Elementary day school with summer program. Ages served: 5-11. Grades served: kindergarten-5. Current enrollment: 32. Maximum enrollment: 36-40. Full-time staff: 4. Part-time staff: 1. Services: individual and group tutoring, academic and psychological testing; visual, motor, and perceptual training; gross and fine motor skills training.

Chicago: Beacon Therapeutic School, 10650 S. Longwood Drive, 60643. Telephone: (312) 881-1005. Executive Director: Margaret M. Morley. Preschool, elementary, and secondary day school with summer program. Ages served: 3-21. Current enrollment: 84. Maximum enrollment: 84. Full-time staff: 38. Services: individual and group tutoring, academic and psychological testing; academic,

ILLINOIS

psychological, and family counseling; occupational therapy, adaptive physical education.

Chicago: Centers for New Horizons Day School, 6423 S. Woodlawn Avenue, 60637. Telephone: (312) 667-4100. Program Director: Judith A. Hunter. Preschool, elementary, and secondary day school with summer program. Ages served: 6-21. Grades served: kindergarten-12. Current enrollment: 26. Maximum enrollment: 35. Full-time staff: 10. Part-time staff: 2. Services: individual and group tutoring, academic and psychological testing; academic, psychological, and family counseling; occupational therapy, adaptive physical education, vocational training, work-study, summer work program. Recreation: gym, student council, bowling, skating.

Chicago: Chase House, Inc., 211 S. Ashland Boulevard, 60607. Telephone: (312) 666-4593. Executive Director: Helen J. Haugsnes. Preschool with limited services; summer program. Ages served: 3-5. Current enrollment: 60. Maximum enrollment: 60. Full-time staff: 15. Part-time staff: 4. Scholarships/financial aid available. Recreation: diversified program with many outdoor activities and field trips.

Chicago: Lawrence Hall School for Boys, 4833 N. Francisco, 60625. Telephone: (312) 769-3500. Executive Director: Gene B. Meirer. Males only elementary and secondary day school with residential treatment program. Ages served: 6-21. Grades served: kindergarten-12. Current enrollment: 70. Maximum enrollment: 80. Full-time staff: 28. Part-time staff: 2. Services: individual and group tutoring, academic and psychological testing; academic, psychological, and family counseling; adaptive physical education, vocational training, work-study, job placement, medical services. Recreation: after school program including basketball, soccer, football, badminton, camping, indoor games, muscle building, biking. Notes: For emotionally disturbed boys. Goal is to provide individualized education and behavior improvement. Students integrated into public school system whenever possible.

Chicago: Potential School for Exceptional Children, 7222 S. Exchange Avenue, 60649. Telephone: (312) 221-9711. Executive Director: Ramona O. Fogerty. Preschool and elementary day school with limited services; summer program. Ages served: 2-16. Grades served: preschool-8. Current enrollment: 80. Maximum enrollment: 104. Full-time staff: 21. Part-time staff: 6. Scholarships/financial aid available. Services: individual and group tutoring, academic and psychological testing; academic, psychological, and family counseling; occupational therapy, adaptive physical education, vocational training. Recreation: weekend farm camp, special competitions in basketball, softball, and soccer.

Chicago: SOL School, 4014 W. Chicago Avenue, 60651. Telephone: (312) 252-3320. School Director: Celia C. Battle. Elementary day school with limited services. Ages served: 3-21. Grades served: ungraded. Current enrollment: 66. Maximum enrollment: 70. Full-time staff: 23. Part-time staff: 4. Services: individual and group tutoring, academic testing; physical, occupational, and music therapy; adaptive physical education, prevocational and vocational training, nursing services, speech pathology, bilingual aides (Spanish/English). Recreation: Special Olympics, scouting.

Chicago: Southern School, 1456 W. Montrose, 60613. Telephone: (312) 769-0185. Executive Director: Jerry Rothman. Elementary and secondary day school with summer program. Ages served: 4-21. Grades served: ungraded. Current enrollment: 40. Maximum enrollment: 50. Full-time staff: 20. Part-time staff: 4. Scholarships/financial aid available. Services: individual and group tutoring, academic testing; academic, psychological, and family counseling; vocational training and workshop, work-study, job placement, computer-assisted instruction; speech, communication, and occupational therapy. Recreation: field trips, recreation room.

Chicago: STEP, Inc., 6740 S. Shore Drive, 60649. Telephone: (312) 667-5566. Executive Director: Elois W. Steward. Elementary day school with limited services; summer program. Ages served: 5-18. Grades served: kindergarten-8. Current enrollment: 45. Maximum enrollment: 50. Full-time staff: 20. Part-time staff: 3. Services: individual tutoring, academic and psychological testing, psychological and family counseling, adaptive physical education. Recreation: gym/swim, track, basketball. Notes: Serves emotionally disturbed children with learning disabilities.

Dundee: Summit School, Inc., 611 E. Main Street, 60118. Telephone: (312) 428-6451. Executive Director: M. Ruth Tofanelli. Preschool, elementary, and secondary day school with summer program. Ages served: 2-21. Grades served: preschool-12. Current enrollment: 198 (100 learning disabled). Maximum enrollment: 213. Full-time staff: 25. Part-time staff: 5. Scholarships/financial aid available. Services: individual tutoring, academic and psychological testing; academic, psychological, and family counseling; occupational therapy, adaptive physical education, medical services, vocational training, Suzuki preschool program, gifted program. Recreation: field trips.

Evanston: Cove School, Inc., 1100 Forest Avenue, 60202. Telephone: (312) 475-6646. Executive Director: Susan A. Vogel. Elementary and secondary day school with summer program and camp. Ages served: 6-20. Grades served: 1-12. Current enrollment: 81. Scholarships/financial aid available. Services: academic testing, individual and group counseling, parent support group, work-study; speech, language, art and visual motor therapy; adaptive physical education. Recreation: field trips, physical education, ice-skating, swimming, intramurals.

Hoyleton: Hoyleton Children's Home, P.O. Box 218, 325 N. Main, 62803. Telephone: (618) 493-7382. Executive Director: Paul Schippel. Elementary and secondary day school with summer program. Ages served: 9-17. Grades served: elementary-high school. Current enrollment: 30. Full-time staff: 9. Services: individual tutoring, academic and psychological testing; academic, psychological, and family counseling; adaptive physical education, vocational training, job placement, medical services. Recreation: formal therapeutic recreational program.

Joliet: Guardian Angel Home, Plainfield at Theodore, 60435. Telephone: (815) 741-6600. Director of Day Treatment Center: Daniel J. Malloy. Elementary day school. Ages served: 5-18. Grades served: kindergarten-12. Current enrollment: 40. Maximum enrollment: 40. Full-time staff: 19. Services: academic and psychological testing, psychological and family counseling, adaptive physical education, limited work-study, medical services. Recreation: physical education.

Lake Forest: Woodlands Academy, 760 E. Westleigh Road, 60045. Telephone: (312) 234-4300. Principal: Sr. Francis de la Chapelle. Females only secondary day and boarding school with limited services. Grades served: 9-12. Current enrollment: 200. Maximum enrollment: 250. Full-time staff: 35. Part-time staff: 4. Scholarships/financial aid available. Services: individual and group tutoring, academic testing, academic and psychological counseling, work-study, medical services. Recreation: volleyball, basketball, tennis, softball, clubs, literary magazine, yearbook.

Lake Villa: Allendale School, P.O. Box 277, 60046. Telephone: (312) 356-2351. Executive Director: Robert Holway. Elementary and secondary day school and males only boarding school with summer program; residential treatment center; community group home. Ages served: 8-18. Grades served: kindergarten-12. Current enrollment: 55. Maximum enrollment: 60. Full-time staff: 120. Part-time staff: 16. Scholarships/financial aid available. Services: individual and group tutoring; group, academic, psychological, and family counseling; academic and psychological testing, therapeutic recreation, vocational training, work-study, job placement; individual, physical, speech, language, and family therapy; medical and psychiatric services. Recreation: 120-acre campus with lake, sports, arts and crafts, individually designed programming. Notes: Psychiatric treatment facility for educationally maladjusted, emotionally disturbed, and conduct-disordered youth.

Lockport: Lockport Education Center, Reed School Building, 143rd Street, 60441. Telephone: (815) 838-4900. Executive Director: Robert Neubeck. Elementary and secondary day school with summer program. Ages served: 5-21. Grades served: 1-12. Current enrollment: 100. Maximum enrollment: 150. Full-time staff: 20. Services: individual tutoring; academic, psychological, and family counseling; adaptive physical education, vocational training, medical services. Recreation: physical education.

Naperville: Little Friends School, 619 E. Franklin, 60540. Telephone: (312) 355-6870. Director: Dottee Krejci. Preschool, elementary, and secondary day school with summer program. Ages served: birth-21. Grades served: preschool-12. Current enrollment: 107. Maximum enrollment: 120. Full-time staff: 70. Part-time staff: 2. Services: individual and group tutoring, academic testing; academic, psychological, and family counseling; physical, occupational, music, speech, and family therapy; adaptive physical education, vocational training, early intervention program. Recreation: ice-skating, riding, swimming, adaptive physical education, recreational therapy. Notes: Most students referred by school districts for emotional and behavioral disorders. Many are severely learning disabled.

Palos Heights: Elim Christian School, 13020 S. Central, 60462. Telephone: (312) 389-0555. Superintendent: John Kamp. Preschool, elementary, and secondary day and boarding school with limited services. Ages served: 3-21. Grades served: preschool-12. Current enrollment: 120. Maximum enrollment: 120. Full-time staff: 75. Part-time staff: 25. Limited scholarships/financial aid available. Services: academic and psychological testing, academic and psychological counseling, physical and occupational therapy, adaptive physical education, vocational training, medical services, day and residential school placement, self-contained classes for severely learning disabled. Recreation: swimming, sports, field trips.

Paris: Edgar County Children's Home On Site/Treatment and Learning Center, 300 Eads Avenue, 61944. Telephone: (217) 465-6451. Executive Director: Richard A. Nelson. Elementary and secondary day and boarding school. Ages served: 10-18. Grades served: 4-12. Current enrollment: 22. Maximum enrollment: 22-25. Full-time staff: 5. Part-time staff: 6. Services: individual tutoring, academic and psychological testing; academic, psychological, and family counseling; vocational training, work-study, job placement.

Park Ridge: Jeanine Schultz Memorial School, 2101 W. Oakton Street, 60068. Telephone: (312) 696-3315. Executive Director: Joseph C. Zummo. Preschool, elementary, and secondary day school with summer program; residential treatment facility. Ages served: 3-21. Grades served: kindergarten-12. Current enrollment: 52. Maximum enrollment: 60. Full-time staff: 15. Part-time staff: 3. Services: individual and group tutoring, academic testing, psychological counseling, adaptive physical education, vocational training, milieu therapy, individual psychotherapy, prevocational training, art instruction. Notes: Serves emotionally disturbed children; learning disabilities are common.

Springfield: Family Service Center Daycare, 1308 S. Seventh Street, 62703. Telephone: (217) 528-8409. Day Care Director: Mary Jane Forney. Preschool and day care center with limited services. Ages served: 1½ months-6 years. Current enrollment: 122. Maximum enrollment: 141. Full-time staff: 30. Services: full social service agency providing counseling, adoption, foster care, teen-parents program. Recreation: playground.

Summer Camps and Programs

Algonquin: Camp Algonquin, Cary Road, 60102. Telephone: (312) 658-8212. Permanent mailing address: United Charities of Chicago, 14 E. Jackson Boulevard, Chicago, IL 60604. Telephone: (312) 461-0800. Director, Camping Services: Jane T. Pirsig. Residential camp with limited services. Ages served: 1 and up.

ILLINOIS

Grades served: 1-10. Maximum enrollment: 200. Full-time staff: 12. Part-time staff: 84. Scholarships/financial aid available. Services: family counseling, follow-up, referrals. Recreation: camping, hiking, nature study, swimming, team sports, crafts. Notes: All families interviewed prior to acceptance.

Gilman: Camp Wahanaha, Route 1, 60938. Telephone: (815) 683-2381. Permanent mailing address: Green Meadows Girl Scout Council, 1405 N. Lincoln, Urbana, IL 61801. Telephone: (217) 328-5112. Director of Camping Services: Delaine Deal. Females only camp with limited services. Ages served: 6-18. Grades served: 2-12. Full-time staff: 30-35. Limited scholarships/financial aid available. Recreation: camping, hiking, nature study, riding, swimming, team sports, crafts, canoeing. Notes: Handicapped campers mainstreamed.

College and University Special Programs and Services

Barat College: Lake Forest, IL 60045. Total enrollment: 700. LD students: 30. Special services: individual and group tutoring, ombudsman, special examinations, scholarships, academic counseling and remediation, diagnostic testing, student resource center, support group, taped books, training in study skills.

- **Special program:** Learning Opportunities Program. Students mainstreamed in regular classes. Diagnostic testing to determine learning strengths and weaknesses, individual tutoring with LD specialist; language, math, and learning labs; word processors. Learning disability must be verified through recent records or testing done by the college. Program accepts students enrolled full or part-time at the college. Acting Director: Pamela Adelman. Telephone: (312) 234-3000 ext. 331.

Bradley University: Peoria, IL 61625. Special services: individual tutoring, training in study skills, academic and psychological counseling, taped books, special examinations, student resource center, readers, diagnostic testing, ombudsman. Contact: Joan L. Sattler, Associate Professor and Chairperson. Telephone: (309) 676-7611 ext. 265.

Chicago City-Wide College, City Colleges of Chicago: 30 E. Lake Street, Chicago, IL 60601. Total enrollment: 17,741. LD students: 63. Special services: group tutoring, training in study skills, academic counseling, taped books, readers, adaptive equipment, examination modifications. Contact: JoAnn Roderfeld, Coordinator of Student Support Services. Telephone: (312) 781-9430 ext. 2705.

College of Lake County: 19351 W. Washington Street, Grayslake, IL 60030. Total enrollment: 10,000. LD students: 25. Special services: individual and group tutoring, training in study skills, academic and psychological counseling, taped books, special examinations, student resource center, readers, ombudsman, computer-assisted study, vocational counseling. Contact: Carole Bulakowski, Director of Learning Assistance Center. Telephone: (312) 223-6601 ext. 446.

DePaul University: 25 E. Jackson Boulevard, Chicago, IL 60614. Total enrollment: 12,000. Special services: readers, individual tutoring, ombudsman, special examinations, scholarships, academic and psychological counseling, diagnostic testing, training in study skills, support group.

- **Special program:** Project Learning Strategies (PLuS). Accepts 10 students per year. Must meet regular and special admissions requirements of the college. Special requirements include verification of learning disability through recent diagnostic tests or tests done by the university and an interview. Full or part-time, degree-seeking students are eligible for the program. Project Director: Carol T. Wren. Telephone: (312) 341-6750.

Center/clinic: Center for Reading and Learning, 2323 N. Seminary, Room 220. Telephone: (312) 341-8362. Director: Chris Carger. Open to public. Ages served: 5-adult. Services: individual and group tutoring, academic testing.

Greenville College: 315 E. College, Greenville, IL 62246. Total enrollment: 650. LD students: 8. Special services: readers, individual and group tutoring, special examinations, academic and psychological counseling, student resource center, diagnostic testing, training in study skills. Contact: Kimberly A. Ellis, Director, Academic Enrichment Center. Telephone: (618) 664-1840 ext. 360.

Center/clinic: Academic Enrichment Center. Telephone: (618) 664-1840 ext. 360. Director: Kimberly A. Ellis. Not open to public. Grades served: college.

Illinois Central College: East Peoria, IL 61635. Total enrollment: 14,000. LD students: 15. Special services: individual tutoring, training in study skills, academic counseling, taped books, student resource center, readers. Contact: Vickie Draksler, Coordinator of Handicapped Services. Telephone: (309) 694-5131.

Illinois State University: Normal, IL 61761. Total enrollment: 20,000. LD students: 150. Special services: readers, individual and group tutoring, academic and psychological counseling, training in study and writing skills, taped books, readers, ombudsman, untimed tests, writers, proofreaders. Contact: Judy Smithson, Coordinator for Services for the Handicapped. Telephone: (309) 438-5853.

Kankakee Community College: Box 888, River Road, Kankakee, IL 60901. Total enrollment: 3,000. Special services: individual tutoring, training in study skills, academic counseling, special examinations, student resource center, scholarships. Contact: Maurice M. Manuel, Acting Dean of Student Services. Telephone: (815) 933-0226.

Lake Land Community College: S. Route 45, Mattoon, IL 61938. Special services: individual and group tutoring, training in study skills, academic and psychological counseling, taped books and lectures, student resource center, readers, note takers, support group, pencil holders, high school equivalency classes, special test taking situations, career development seminars. Contact: Beverly J.

ILLINOIS

Voris, Special Needs Counselor. Telephone: (217) 235-3131 ext. 259. In-state toll free number: (800) 252-4121 ext. 259.

Lincoln College: 300 Keokuk, Lincoln, IL 62656. Total enrollment: 320. Special services: individual and group tutoring, training in study skills, academic counseling, student resource center. Contact: Mary S. McLaughlin, Director of Admissions. Telephone: (217) 732-3155 ext. 239.

Lincoln Trail College: Route 3, Robinson, IL 62454. Total enrollment: 888. LD students: 12. Special services: individual tutoring, training in study skills, academic and psychological counseling, readers, individualized instruction. Contact: Searoba Mascher, Director of Study Skill Center. Telephone: (618) 544-8657 ext. 41.

Morton College: 3801 S. Central Avenue, Cicero, IL 60650. Total enrollment: 4,500. LD students: 10. Special services: training in study skills, academic counseling, diagnostic testing. Contact: Patricia Valente, Counselor. Telephone: (312) 656-8000 ext. 250.

Northern Illinois University: DeKalb, IL 60115. Special services: training in study skills, academic and psychological counseling, taped books, special examinations, readers. Contact: Michael H. Epstein, Chairperson, Faculty of Special Education. Telephone: (815) 753-0657.

Northwestern University: 2003 Sheridan Road, Evanston, IL 60201.

Center/clinic: Learning Disabilities Center, 2299 Sheridan Road. Telephone: (312) 491-3183. Director: Doris Johnson. Open to public. Ages served: all. Services: two-day diagnostic evaluations.

Oakton Community College: 1600 E. Golf Road, Des Plaines, IL 60016. Total enrollment: 10,777. LD students: 90. Special services: individual and group tutoring, training in study skills, academic and psychological counseling, taped books, special examinations, readers, limited diagnostic testing, scholarships. Contact: Kathy Appleby-Knoll, Special Needs Coordinator. Telephone: (312) 635-1759.

- Special program: ASSIST (Additional Student Services Instructional Support Team). Personal, academic, and career counseling; noncredit remedial courses in math, reading, and writing; basic skills assessment. Learning disability must be verified through recent records or tests done by the college. Can enroll in noncredit remedial courses only. Assistant Professor: Jill Mawhinney. Telephone: (312) 635-1845. Assistant Professor: Sally Witt. Telephone: (312) 635-1923.

Parkland College: 2400 W. Bradley Avenue, Champaign, IL 61821. Total enrollment: 9,000. Special services: readers, ombudsman, academic counseling, taped books, training in study skills. Contact: Jane Moore, Coordinator for Handicapped Services. Telephone: (217) 351-2200 ext. 247.

Rockford College: 5050 E. State Street, Rockford, IL 61101. Special services: individual and group tutoring, special examinations, diagnostic testing, training in study skills. Contact: Mary Ann Wham, Director, Learning Resources Center. Telephone: (815) 226-4087 or 226-4088.

Center/clinic: Learning Resources Center. Telephone: (815) 226-4087 or 226-4088. Director: Mary Ann Wham.

Rosary College: 7900 W. Division Street, River Forest, IL 60305.

Center/clinic: Educational Evaluation Center. Telephone: (312) 366-2490 ext. 347. Director: Sr. Marie Grant. Open to public. Ages served: preschool-adult. Services: testing, educational evaluation.

Saint Xavier College: 3700 W. 103rd Street, Chicago, IL 60655. Special services: individual and group tutoring, academic counseling, diagnostic testing, training in study skills, special examinations, student resource center, support group. Contact: Carol Condron, Educational Diagnostician. Telephone: (312) 779-3300 ext. 361.

Center/clinic: Saint Xavier College Learning Disabilities Clinic. Telephone: (312) 779-3300 ext. 357. Director: Joan Kardatzke. Open to public. Ages served: 3-adult. Services: diagnosis and remediation.

Southern Illinois University: Carbondale, IL 62901. Total enrollment: 23,000-24,000. LD students: 97. Special services: readers, individual tutoring, ombudsman, academic and psychological counseling, diagnostic testing, taped books, training in study skills, proctored testing, student resource center, support group, microcomputer lab, remedial help.

- **Special program:** The Achieve Program. Students are mainstreamed and must be enrolled full-time in regular university courses. Must fulfill regular and special admissions requirements. Special requirements include verification of learning disability through recent records and diagnostic tests by the Achieve staff. Director: Barbara Cordoni. Assistant Program Coordinator: Sally DeDecker. Telephone: (618) 453-2595 ext. 41.

Truman College: 1145 W. Wilson, Chicago, IL 60640. Total enrollment: 6,000. LD students: 5. Special services: group tutoring, academic counseling, taped books, readers. Contact: Joseph A. Kalista, Counselor, or Bruce Rose, Special Needs Advisor. Telephone: (312) 878-1700 ext. 2354.

University of Illinois: 1310 S. Sixth, Champaign, IL 61820. Special services: group tutoring, training in study skills, academic and psychological counseling, taped books, special examinations, student resource center, readers, diagnostic testing, scholarships, ombudsman, assistantships. Contact: R. Henderson, Professor and Chairman, Department of Special Education. Telephone: (217) 333-0260.

ILLINOIS

Center/clinic: Division of Rehabilitation-Education Services, 1207 S. Oak. Telephone: (217) 333-4600. Director: Timothy J. Nugent. Open to public.

University of Illinois-Chicago: P.O. Box 4348, Chicago, IL 60680. Total enrollment: 17,000. LD students: 200. Special services: individual and group tutoring, academic and psychological counseling, taped books, diagnostic testing, training in study skills. Contact: Arthur Neyhus, Director of Child Study Facility. Telephone: (312) 996-8137.

Center/clinic: Child Study Facility, College of Education. Telephone: (312) 996-5650. Director: Arthur Neyhus. Open to public. Ages served: birth and up. Grades served: all. Services: diagnostic testing; remediation of reading, writing, and study skills.

Western Illinois University: Adams Street, Macomb, IL 61455. Total enrollment: 10,400. LD students: 8. Special services: tutoring, training in study skills, academic and psychological counseling, taped books, readers, student advocate, support group, special examinations; writing, reading, and math labs. Note: Learning disability must be documented prior to enrollment. Contact: Candace McLaughlin, Advisor to the Handicapped. Telephone: (309) 298-1846.

William Rainey Harper College: Algonquin and Roselle Roads, Palatine, IL 60067. Total enrollment: 22,000. LD students: 100. Special services: readers, individual and group tutoring, special examinations, academic and psychological counseling, student resource center, diagnostic testing, taped books, training in study skills; educational assistance and remediation by LD specialists. Contact: Tom Thompson, Coordinator, Disabled Student Services. Telephone: (312) 397-3000 ext. 266.

Hospital Clinics

Chicago: Children's Memorial Hospital, Child Psychiatry, 2300 Children's Plaza, 60614. Telephone: (312) 880-4855. Contact: Intake Worker. Outpatient and inpatient program. Ages served: birth-16. Services: diagnostic testing, academic and psychological testing, individual and group tutoring; academic, psychological, and parent counseling; group, speech, and language therapy.

Chicago: Michael Reese Hospital and Medical Center, Dysfunctioning Child Center, 2915 S. Ellis, 60616. Telephone: (312) 791-3848. Associate Director: William J. White. Outpatient and after school program. Ages served: all. Services: diagnostic testing, academic and psychological testing, limited psychological counseling, parent counseling, group and occupational therapy, limited speech and language therapy, social services. Notes: Multidisciplinary center.

Evanston: St. Francis Hospital of Evanston, Adult and Child Guidance Center, 355 Ridge Avenue, 60202. Telephone: (312) 492-6250. Contact: Intake Worker. Outpatient program. Ages served: all. Services: psychological and parent counseling, psychotherapy and family therapy, psychological and psychoeducational learning disabilities testing for patients in therapy at the center. Notes: Does not accept clients for testing only. Serves Evanston residents and patients of St. Francis Hospital physicians.

Oak Lawn: Christ Hospital, Developmental Pediatrics, 4440 W. 95th Street, 60453. Telephone: (312) 857-5352. Contact: Colleen Schmitt. Outpatient and inpatient program. Ages served: birth-21. Services: diagnostic testing, academic and psychological testing, individual and group tutoring; academic, psychological, and parent counseling; group, speech, language, physical, and occupational therapy; adaptive physical education, support group, social services.

Urbana: Mercy Hospital, Learning Abilities Program, 1400 W. Park Avenue, 61801. Telephone: (217) 337-4518. Educational Consultant: Wendy McCaughrin. Outpatient, inpatient, day, and after school program. Ages served: 6 and up. Services: diagnostic testing, academic and psychological testing, individual tutoring; academic, psychological, and parent counseling; speech, language, physical, and occupational therapy; social services.

Other Services

Arlington Heights: Northwest Suburban Child Development Clinic, Inc., 3365 N. Arlington Heights Road, Suite K, 60004. Telephone: (312) 398-2945. Clinical Director: Richard Malter. Clinic. After school program. Ages served: 2 and up. Services: diagnostic testing, academic and psychological testing, individual tutoring; academic, psychological, and parent counseling; group, speech, language, auditory, and occupational therapy; support group, nutrition consultation, distributes research papers, presentations for parent and professional groups.

Chicago: Chicago Clinic for Child Development, 1525 E. 53rd Street, 60615. Telephone: (312) 241-5771. Contact: Jean Fisk or Esther Washington. Clinic. After school program. Ages served: birth-21. Services: diagnostic testing, academic and psychological testing, individual and group tutoring; academic, psychological, and parent counseling; group, speech, language, physical, family, and occupational therapy; functional visual evaluation and therapy, social services, medical services.

Chicago: The David T. Siegel Institute for Communicative Disorders, 3033 S. Cottage Grove, 60616. Telephone: (312) 791-2936 or 791-2900. Contact: Myra Goldberg-Hier or Frederic Curry. Day and after school program. Ages served: school-age and up. Services: diagnostic testing, academic and psychological testing, individual and group tutoring; academic, psychological, and family counseling; speech, language, physical, and occupational therapy; social services, audiological services, neurological and psychiatric evaluations, electroencephalogram testing. Notes: Multidisciplinary approach to diagnosis and remediation.

ILLINOIS

Chicago: Englewood Learning Center, 6201 S. Sangamon Street, 60621. Telephone: (312) 487-1700. Acting Executive Director: Travis Baldwin. Elementary day school with summer program. Ages served: 6-18. Grades served: ungraded. Current enrollment: 60. Maximum enrollment: 60. Full-time staff: 20. Services: academic and psychological testing, psychological and family counseling, adaptive physical education.

Elgin: Larkin Home for Children - Special Education, 1212 Larkin Avenue, 60120. Telephone: (312) 695-5656. Executive Director: Michael R. Horwitz. Elementary and secondary day and residential treatment facility with limited services. Ages served: 5-21. Grades served: 1-12. Current enrollment: 90. Maximum enrollment: 94. Full-time staff: 120. Part-time staff: 2. Services: psychological testing, psychological and family counseling, adaptive physical education, vocational training, job placement, medical services, individual and group therapy, recreational services, psychiatric consultation. Recreation: group sports, individual programs.

Peoria: Easter Seal Center: Alternative Beginnings for Children (ABC) Program, 320 E. Armstrong Avenue, 61603. Telephone: (309) 672-6330. Executive Director: John Pavek. Preschool with summer program. Ages served: birth-3. Current enrollment: 11. Maximum enrollment: 40. Scholarships/financial aid available. Services: counseling; physical, speech, language, and occupational therapy; developmental stimulation, special education, medical consultancy, client advocacy. Recreation: field trips.

Urbana: The Reading Group, 607 W. Nevada, 61801. Telephone: (217) 367-0914. Director: Marilyn Kay. Clinic. Day program. Ages served: all. Services: diagnostic testing, academic and psychological testing, individual and group tutoring; academic, psychological, and parent counseling; demonstrations and workshops for parents and teachers.

Villa Park: Du Page Easter Seal Treatment Center, 706 E. Park, 60148. Telephone: (312) 620-4433. Executive Director: James W. Errant. Cooperative day care center with outpatient treatment program. Ages served: birth-13. Current enrollment: 220. Maximum enrollment: 220. Full-time staff: 22. Part-time staff: 3. Scholarships/financial aid available. Services: family counseling; physical, occupational, and speech therapy; audiological services. Recreation: riding, swimming.

Wilmette: The One-to-One Learning Center, Highcrest Community Center, Illinois and Hunter Roads, 60091. Telephone: (312) 256-3400. Executive Director: Phyllis C. Myers. Clinic. After school program. Ages served: 3 and up. Services: diagnostic testing, academic and psychological testing, individual tutoring; academic, psychological, and parent counseling; speech and language therapy, school advocacy, college placement.

INDIANA

Offices of Organizations Concerned with Learning Disabilities

ACLD, Inc.: IACLD, P.O. Box 20584, Indianapolis, IN 46226. President: Laura Doeden. Telephone: (317) 339-4736.

Council for Exceptional Children: President: Michael Livovich, c/o Westlake Special Education Cooperative, 8616 Columbia Avenue, Munster, IN 46321. Telephone: Office (219) 836-5251; Home (219) 763-2330.

Indiana Easter Seal Society, Inc.: 3816 E. 96th Street, Indianapolis, IN 46240. Executive Director: James A. Carter. Telephone: (317) 844-7919.

Orton Dyslexia Society: 7801 N. College Avenue, Indianapolis, IN 46240. Telephone: (317) 253-2906. President: Carolyn S. Connors.

State Department of Education Learning Disabilities Personnel

Gilbert Bliton, Director of Special Education, Department of Public Instruction, 229 State House, Indianapolis, IN 46204. Telephone: (317) 927-0216.

Private and Day Schools

Canton: Shipley Day Treatment Center, Child and Adolescent Service Center, 919 Second Street, N.E., 44704. Telephone: (216) 456-2244. Day Treatment Program Coordinator: Sandra Dragomire. Preschool and elementary day school with limited services; summer program. Ages served: 2-12. Grades served: ungraded. Current enrollment: 48. Maximum enrollment: 48. Full-time staff: 12. Services: individual and group tutoring, academic and psychological testing; academic, psychological, and family counseling; physical therapy consultation, nursing services, language therapy, out-client services for children and their families. Recreation: field trips, gymnasium, playground. Notes: For children with social/emotional/behavioral problems. Most have a developmental disability.

Indianapolis: Crossroads Rehabilitation Center, 3242 Sutherland Avenue, 46205. Telephone: (317) 924-3251. President: James J. Vento. Preschool and adult day school with limited services; summer program. Ages served: birth-5, adult. Grades served: preschool, postschool. Current enrollment: 100 preschool, 40 adult. Maximum enrollment: 100 preschool, adult open. Full-time staff: 8. Scholarships/financial aid available. Services: group tutoring, academic and psychological testing, psychological and family counseling, physical and occupational therapy, vocational training, work-study, job placement, medical services, speech pathology, audiology, sheltered employment, vocational evaluation, adult basic education. Notes: A comprehensive outpatient rehabilitation center.

INDIANA

Logansport: Woodlawn Center, 1416 Woodlawn Avenue, 46947. Telephone: (219) 753-4104. Executive Director: Carolyn D. Moore. Preschool and adult day school with limited services; children's summer program. Ages served: birth-5, 18 and up. Grades served: ungraded. Current enrollment: 125. Maximum enrollment: 140. Full-time staff: 38. Part-time staff: 11. Services: psychological testing, family counseling; physical, speech, and occupational therapy; vocational training, job placement, sheltered work, vocational evaluation and adjustment, transportation, adult community living program. Recreation: gross motor skills, bowling, field trips, skating. Notes: Serves the developmentally and vocationally disabled.

Michigan City: Laporte Therapy Center, 3200 S. Cleveland Avenue, 46360. Telephone: (219) 872-6996. Executive Director: Robert J. St. Germaine. Preschool. Ages served: birth-5. Current enrollment: 66. Maximum enrollment: 68. Full-time staff: 18. Part-time staff: 3. Services: academic and psychological testing, psychological and family counseling; physical, speech, and language therapy; transportation, school lunch. Recreation: field trips, play therapy.

Summer Camps and Programs

Indianapolis: Midwest Computer Camp, Inc., 9392 Lafayette Road, 46278. Telephone: (317) 297-2700. President: Lynn Crawford. Residential camp with limited services; academic program. Ages served: 8-18. Grades served: 3-12. Maximum enrollment: 104. Full-time staff: 40 summer; 6 winter. Part-time staff: 14. Scholarships/financial aid available. Services: individual and group tutoring. Academic programs: math, reading, computers. Recreation: swimming, hiking, nature study, arts and crafts, camping, photography, team athletics, astronomy, forestry. Notes: Special emphasis on computers and their applications.

College and University Special Programs and Services

Anderson College: Anderson, IN 46012-3462. Special services: individual tutoring, psychological counseling, training in study skills. Contact: Karen Nelson, Learning Resources Center. Telephone: (317) 649-9071 ext. 2315.

Center/clinic: Learning Resources Center. Telephone: (317) 649-9071 ext. 2315. Director: Karen Nelson. Not open to public. Grades served: college. Services: tutoring, audiovisual and independent study materials, group workshops.

Ball State University: 2000 University Avenue, Muncie, IN 47306. Special services: readers, diagnostic testing, academic and psychological counseling, special examinations, taped books, training in study skills, ombudsman. Contact: Joseph Maumcheff, Director of Admissions. Telephone: (317) 285-8287.

Center/clinic: Diagnostic Learning Center, 621 N. Calvert Street. Telephone: (317) 285-5728. Director: Linda Hargrove. Open to public. Ages served: preschool-high school. Services: diagnosis and prescription.

Franklin College of Indiana: Monroe Street, Franklin, IN 46131. Special services: individual tutoring, taped books, special examinations, readers. Contact: Barbara L. Howald, Registrar. Telephone: (317) 736-8441 ext. 115. Or Nolan Cooper, Vice President for Admissions. Telephone: (317) 736-8441 ext. 200.

Indiana Central University: 1400 E. Hanna Avenue, Indianapolis, IN 46227. Total enrollment: 1,700. LD students: 10. Special services: training in study skills, student resource center, readers, individual and group tutoring, special examinations, academic and psychological counseling; diagnostic testing can be arranged. Contact: Nancy O'Dell, Associate Professor of Education. Telephone: (317) 788-3369.

Center/clinic: Miriam Bender Diagnostic Center. Telephone: (317) 788-3285 or 788-3369. Codirectors: Nancy O'Dell, Patricia Cook. Open to public. Ages served: all. Grades served: all. Services: diagnostic testing, nutrition counseling, remediation of neck reflex problems which directors believe contribute to learning difficulties. Notes: financial aid available.

Indiana State University: Terre Haute, IN 47809. Total enrollment: 12,000. LD students: 40. Special services: individual and group tutoring, training in study skills, academic and psychological counseling, taped books, limited readers, diagnostic testing. Contact: Catherine A. Baker, Reading Specialist, Special Services Program. Telephone: (812) 232-6311 ext. 2592.

Center/clinic: Learning Resource Center, 526 N. Sixth Street. Director: Charles Hedrick. Telephone: (812) 232-6311 ext. 2874. Not open to public. Grades served: college. Services: personal and specialized counseling, academic advisement, tutoring, writing lab, limited readers, taped textbooks, study skills classes.

Indiana University: Bloomington, IN 47401. Total enrollment: 33,000. LD students: 50. Special services: individual and group tutoring, training in study skills, academic and psychological counseling, taped books, special examinations, readers, diagnostic testing, ombudsman, support group, special advising, library help; resource center for the print handicapped (open to public). Contact: Sam Goodin, Coordinator. Telephone: (812) 335-0826.

Center/clinic: Indiana University Speech and Hearing Center. Telephone: (812) 335-6251. Coordinator: Dorothy Saltzman. Open to public. Ages served: 3 and up. Grades served: preschool-adult. Services: preschool, summer program and camp, individual and group tutoring, academic and psychological testing, family counseling; speech, language, and group therapy; audiological assessment, auditory training and aural rehabilitation.

Indiana University East: 2325 Chester Boulevard, Richmond, IN 47374. Total enrollment: 1,410. LD students: 2. Special services: individual tutoring, training in study skills, academic counseling, taped books, readers, test proctoring, taped or oral exams. Contact: Carolyn S. Smith, Project Director. Telephone: (317) 966-8261 ext. 302.

INDIANA

Indiana University-Purdue University at Indianapolis: Indianapolis, IN 46202. Total enrollment: 23,000. LD students: 9. Special services: individual tutoring, academic counseling, taped books, special examinations, readers, scholarships, ombudsman. Contact: Donald P. Wakefield, Director, Disabled Student Services and Counseling/Testing Center. Telephone: (317) 264-2540.

Marion College: 4201 S. Washington Street, Marion, IN 46952. Total enrollment: 1,400. LD students: 6-12. Special services: individual and group tutoring, limited training in study skills, academic and psychological counseling, student resource center, readers, psychological testing. Contact: Sharon Plew, Coordinator. Telephone: (317) 674-6901 ext. 257.

Center/clinic: The Writing Center. Telephone: (317) 674-6901 ext. 188. Director: Linda Bush. Grades served: college. Services: oral testing, tapes, diagnostic testing.

Center/clinic: The Counseling and Career Center. Telephone: (317) 674-6901 ext. 257. Coordinator: Sharon Plew. Services: tutoring, note taking; personal, academic, and career counseling.

Purdue University: West Lafayette, IN 47907. Total enrollment: 31,500. LD students: 20-25. Special services: training in study skills, taped books, diagnostic testing. Contact: Betty M. Nelson, Associate Dean of Students. Telephone: (317) 494-1252.

Center/clinic: Purdue Achievement Center, Education Building 99B. Telephone: (317) 494-9750. Coordinator: Anne Dwyer. Grades served: kindergarten-12. Services: diagnostic evaluation.

Purdue University-Calumet: Hammond, IN 46323. Total enrollment: 336. LD students: 6. Special services: readers, individual tutoring, untimed special examinations, academic counseling, training in study skills. Contact: Ms. Berry Fitzner, Counselor. Telephone: (219) 844-0520 ext. 454.

Taylor University: Upland, IN 46989. Special services: individual tutoring, training in study skills, academic counseling, student resource center, readers; IEP model used. Contact: Billie Manor, Director, Learning Skills Center. Telephone: (317) 998-5391.

University of Notre Dame: Notre Dame, IN 46556. Special services: readers, individual tutoring, ombudsman, special examinations, psychological counseling, taped books. Contact: Sr. Jean Lenz, Assistant Vice President for Student Affairs. Telephone: (219) 239-5550.

Valparaiso University: Valparaiso, IN 46383. Special services: individual and group tutoring, academic and psychological counseling, training in study skills. Contact: Dorothy P. Smith, Vice President for Admissions and Financial Aid.

Telephone: (219) 464-5015. Or Daryll Hersemann, Vice President for Student Services. Telephone: (219) 464-5411.

Hospital Clinics

Indianapolis: James Whitcomb Riley Hospital for Children, Indiana University Medical Center, Riley Child Development Program, 702 Barnhill Drive, 46223. Telephone: (317) 264-8167. Outpatient and inpatient program. Ages served: birth-18. Services: diagnostic testing, academic and psychological testing; academic, psychological, and parent counseling; speech, language, physical, and occupational therapy; social services, neuropsychological examination, audiological testing, vision screening.

Terre Haute: Hamilton Center, Inc., 615 Eighth Avenue, 47804. Telephone: (812) 231-8376. Contact: Peggy S. Byrer, Coordinator. Outpatient and after school program. Ages served: birth-18. Services: diagnostic testing, academic and psychological testing, psychological and parent counseling, group therapy, support group, social services.

Other Services

Indianapolis: Strauss Learning Center, 6214 Morenci Trail, Suite 130, 46268. Telephone: (317) 299-4331. Director: Phillip B. Strauss. Clinic. After school program. Ages served: 5 and up. Services: diagnostic testing, academic testing, individual and group tutoring. Notes: Specialized personnel for the learning disabled.

IOWA

Offices of Organizations Concerned with Learning Disabilities

ACLD, Inc.: P.O. Box 116, Garner, IA 50438. Telephone: State office (515) 923-2229. President: Arlene Greiman. Telephone: (515) 923-2518.

Council for Exceptional Children: President: Ron Anderson, Department of Special Education, University of Northern Iowa, Cedar Falls, IA 50614. Telephone: (319) 273-3291.

The Easter Seal Society of Iowa, Inc.: P.O. Box 4002, Highland Park Station, Des Moines, IA 50333. Executive Director: Rolfe B. Karlsson. Telephone: (515) 289-1933.

State Department of Education Learning Disabilities Personnel

J. Frank Vance, Director of Special Education, Iowa Department of Public Instruction, Grimes State Office Building, Des Moines, IA 50319. Telephone: (515) 281-3176. Learning disabilities consultant: James Reese.

IOWA

Private and Day Schools

Burt: Exceptional Opportunities, Inc., Box 197, 50522. Telephone: (515) 924-3251. Administrator: Cecil Wattermann. Preschool, elementary, secondary, and adult day school. Ages served: birth-21. Grades served: preschool-12. Current enrollment: 45. Maximum enrollment: 50. Full-time staff: 13. Part-time staff: 7. Services: individual tutoring, psychological testing, family counseling, physical and occupational therapy, adaptive physical education, vocational training, medical services. Recreation: skating, swimming, camping, dance, aerobics, Special Olympics.

Waterloo: Columbus High School, 3231 W. Ninth Street, 50701. Telephone: (319) 233-3358. Principal: Rev. Walter Brunkan. Secondary day school with limited services. Ages served: 14-18. Grades served: 9-12. Current enrollment: 38. Maximum enrollment: 38. Full-time staff: 49. Part-time staff: 5. Scholarships/financial aid available. Services: individual and group tutoring, academic and psychological testing, academic and psychological counseling, vocational training, speech and language tutoring, developmental reading program. Recreation: volleyball, football, basketball, track, hockey, cross country, gymnastics, tennis, softball, baseball, weight lifting.

Summer Camps and Programs

Des Moines: Camp Sacajawea and Camp Stuther, Moingona Girl Scouts Council, 10715 Hickman Boulevard, 50322. Telephone: (515) 278-2881. Camping Services Director: Jo Hecht. Females only day and residential camps with limited services. Ages served: 7-17. Grades served: 1-12. Maximum enrollment: 200. Total full-time staff: 55. Scholarships/financial aid available to registered Girl Scouts. Services: adaptive physical education, medical services. Recreation: camping, hiking, field trips, nature study, riding, swimming, sailing, archery, team sports, crafts, dance, drama, music.

Des Moines: Day Camp Shakoda, 948 73rd Street, 50312. Telephone: (515) 224-1888. Director: Paul Blythe. Day camp with limited services. Ages served: 5-13. Grades served: 1-6. Maximum enrollment: 150 per session. Full-time staff: 18. Part-time staff: 8-12. Scholarships/financial aid available. Recreation: camping, hiking, nature study, swimming, archery, team sports, crafts, music.

Woodward: Camp Mitigwa, Route 4, Box 39, 50276. Telephone: (515) 438-2351. Permanent mailing address: Mid-Iowa Council, Inc., Boy Scouts of America, 1659 E. Euclid Avenue, Des Moines, IA 50313. Telephone: (515) 266-2135. Camp Director: Donald J. Suedmeier. Males only day and residential camp with limited services. Ages served: 8-18. Grades served: 2-12. Maximum enrollment: 250. Full-time staff: 37. Limited scholarships/financial aid available. Academic programs: computers, merit badge subjects. Recreation: camping, hiking, field trips, nature study, swimming, sailing, archery, team sports, crafts, challenge course.

College and University Special Programs and Services

Buena Vista College: Storm Lake, IA 50588. Special services: individual and group tutoring, training in study skills, academic and psychological counseling, taped books, special examinations, student resource center, readers, on-campus learning center, programmed texts, individual counseling. Contact: Gary Musgrave, Dean of Student Affairs. Telephone: (712) 749-2123.

Center/clinic: Learning Center. Telephone: (712) 749-2145. Director: Mary Slagle. Not open to public. Grades served: college. Services: self-improvement courses including speed-reading, vocabulary building, spelling, term papers; individual tutoring for any subject, English as a second language.

Coe College: 1220 First Avenue, N.E., Cedar Rapids, IA 52402. Total enrollment: 1,167. LD students: 4. Special services: individual and group tutoring, training in study skills, academic and psychological counseling, student resource center. Contact: Niambi Webster, Director, Special Services. Telephone: (319) 399-8546.

Dordt College: Sioux Center, IA 51250. Special services: individual tutoring, training in study skills, academic and psychological counseling, taped books, student resource center, readers, ombudsman, special living arrangements. Contact: M.D. Van Soelen, Dean of Students. Telephone: (712) 722-6070.

Drake University: 25th Street and University Avenue, Des Moines, IA 50311. Special services: individual and group tutoring, ombudsman, special examinations, academic and psychological counseling, diagnostic testing, taped books arranged, training in study skills. Contact: Joseph A. Fisher, Director, Reading and Study Skills Clinic. Telephone: (515) 271-3125.

Center/clinic: Reading and Study Skills Clinic. Telephone: (515) 271-3125. Director: Joseph A. Fisher. Services: family relationship and motivation counseling, diagnostic testing, training in study skills, time management, organization and environmental control, test preparation and test taking, concept development, note taking, reading and comprehension skills, compressed speech tapes.

Graceland College: Lamoni, IA 50140. Special services: individual and group tutoring, training in study skills, academic and psychological counseling, student resource center, readers, ombudsman. Contact: Di Smith, Director, Special Services. Telephone: (515) 784-6473.

Grand View College: 1200 Grand View Avenue, Des Moines, IA 50316. Total enrollment: 1,400. LD students: 1. Special services: individual tutoring, academic and psychological counseling. Contact: A. Jane Molden, Academic Support Counselor. Telephone: (515) 263-2887.

IOWA

Iowa Lakes Community College: 300 S. 18th, Estherville, IA 51334. Total enrollment: 1,500. LD students: 40. Special services: individual tutoring, training in study skills, academic counseling, special examinations, diagnostic testing. Contact: Roy H. Wiegert, Department Chairman, Learning Resource Center. Telephone: (712) 362-2604 ext. 18.

Iowa Western Community College: 2700 College Road, Box 4C, Council Bluffs, IA 51502. Total enrollment: 3,142. LD students: 12. Special services: individual tutoring, training in study skills, academic counseling, taped books, special examinations, student resource center, readers, diagnostic testing. Contact: Fred Stoye, Jr., Coordinator of Developmental Studies Programs of Special Needs, or Ray Olson, Director. Telephone: (712) 325-3209 or 325-3252.

Center/clinic: Developmental Learning Center. Telephone: (712) 325-3209 or 325-3252. Assistant Coordinator: Fred Stoye, Jr. Open to public. Ages served: 17 and up. Grades served: freshman-sophomore vocational/technical programs. Services: diagnostic testing, individualized educational planning, multisensory training, career counseling.

Northeast Iowa Technical Institute: Route 1, Peosta, IA 52068. Special services: individual tutoring, training in study skills, academic counseling, special examinations, student resource center, diagnostic testing. Contact: Jim Arneson, Learning Resources Coordinator. Telephone: (319) 556-5110 ext. 215.

North Iowa Area Community College: 500 College Drive, Mason City, IA 50401. Special services: individual tutoring, training in study skills, special examinations, readers, diagnostic testing, taped books, student resource center. Contact: Homer Bienfang, Director of Special Needs. Telephone: (515) 421-4361.

Center/clinic: Independent Study Lab. Telephone: (515) 421-4266. Director: Linda J. Schmidt. Open to public. Ages served: 16 and up. Grades served: 12-14. Services: individual assessment, tutoring, and class instruction.

Southeastern Community College: P.O. Drawer F, West Burlington, IA 52655. Total enrollment: 2,800. LD students: 12. Special services: individual and group tutoring, training in study skills; academic, social work, and psychological counseling; special examinations, student resource center, readers, diagnostic testing, ombudsman, support group, living skills.

- **Special program:** STEP (Secondary Transitional Education Program). Career education program that provides special support services for the learning disabled. Only accepts residents of the community college district. Arrangements must be made while still in high school. Learning disability must be verified through recent records. Accepts full or part-time students. Director: Dennis Morgan. Telephone: (319) 752-2731 ext. 178. Special Needs Coordinator: Mr. Jan Galbraith. Telephone: (319) 752-2731 ext. 128.

University of Northern Iowa: Cedar Falls, IA 50614. Total enrollment: 11,000. LD students: 10-12. Special services: academic and psychological counseling, training in study skills. Contact: Wayne King, Director, Learning Skills Center. Telephone: (319) 273-2346. Or Larry Steinhauser, Handicapped Student Services Coordinator. Telephone: (319) 273-2676.

Center/clinic: Learning Skills Center. Telephone: (319) 273-2346. Director: Wayne King. Grades served: college.

Hospital Clinics

Davenport: Mercy Hospital, W. Central Park at Marquette, 52804. Telephone: (319) 383-1466. Contact: Michele Budd, Coordinator, Rehabilitation Medicine Program. Outpatient program. Ages served: all. Services: speech, language, physical, and occupational therapy; social services, auditory diagnostic testing, summer clinic for speech and language impaired children.

Iowa City: University of Iowa Hospitals and Clinics, Child Development Clinic, Learning Disorder Pediatric Clinic, Department of Pediatrics, 52242. Telephone: (319) 356-1616. Contact: Jan White, Director, or Lynn Richman, Professor of Pediatrics. Outpatient and summer residential program. Services: diagnostic testing, academic and psychological testing, individual and group tutoring; academic, psychological, and parent counseling; speech and language therapy, social services.

Sioux City: Marian Health Center, 801 Fifth Street, 51101. Telephone: (712) 279-2146. Contact: Verna Welte. Outpatient and inpatient program. Ages served: all. Services: diagnostic testing, academic and psychological testing, individual and group tutoring, psychological and parent counseling; speech, language, physical, and occupational therapy; social services, Adolescent Psychiatric Unit for children 12-17 who need special attention in academics.

Other Services

Decorah: Keystone Area Education Agency, Regional Office, Claiborne Drive, 52101. Telephone: (319) 382-2870. Contact: Richard Guilgot, Instructional Consultant. School support service. Grades served: kindergarten-12. Services: diagnostic testing, academic and psychological testing; academic, psychological, and parent counseling; speech, language, physical, and occupational therapy; social services, curriculum lab, school consultation services, work-study and work experience placements, audiological services.

KANSAS

Offices of Organizations Concerned with Learning Disabilities

ACLD, Inc.: P.O. Box 4424, Topeka, KS 66604. President: Norma Dyck.

Council for Exceptional Children: President: Narnie Woolley, 1110 Charlotte Street, Wichita, KS 67208. Telephone: Office (316) 943-4871; Home (316) 683-8824. Executive Secretary: Kate Schmidtberger, P.O. Box 831, Hays, KS 67601.

Kansas Easter Seal Society, Inc.: 3709 Plaza Drive, White Lakes Plaza West, Topeka, KS 66609. Executive Director: Don F. Clement. Telephone: (913) 267-4590.

State Department of Education Learning Disabilities Personnel

James E. Marshall, Director of Special Education, Special Education Administration, 120 E. Tenth Street, Topeka, KS 66612. Telephone: (913) 296-4945. Learning disabilities consultant: Sid Cooley.

Private and Day Schools

Wichita: Institute of Logopedics, 2400 Jardine Drive, 67219. Telephone: (316) 262-8271; out-of-state toll free number: (800) 835-1043. President: Frank R. Kleffner. Preschool, elementary, and secondary day and boarding school with limited services; summer program and camp. Full-time staff: 150. Part-time staff: 10. Current enrollment: 140. Ages served: birth-21. Grades served: ungraded. Scholarships/financial aid available. Services: individual tutoring, academic testing, psychological testing and counseling, vocational and life skills training, adaptive physical education, medical services; physical, occupational, speech, and oral-muscular therapy; audiology, evaluation, diagnosis. Recreation: Special Olympics, after school sports, group activities, art, music. Notes: Requirement for enrollment is a communication disorder. Disorder may be in conjunction with physical and/or mental handicaps.

College and University Special Programs and Services

Barton County Community College: Great Bend, KS 67530. Total enrollment: 1,000. Special services: individual tutoring, training in study skills, academic counseling, taped books, diagnostic testing. Contact: Jeanne Gotsche, Instructor. Telephone: (316) 792-2701 ext. 163.

Johnson County Community College: 12345 College Boulevard at Quivera, Overland Park, KS 66210. Total enrollment: 8,000. LD students: 50. Special services: individual tutoring, training in study skills, academic and psychological counseling, taped books, special examinations, student resource center, diagnostic testing, ombudsman.

- **Special program:** Strategies to Improve Learning Efficiency. Offers ten courses for credit in eight learning strategies including writing, reading, memory, listening, and note taking. Learning disability must be verified through recent records or testing done by the college. Students can participate in LD program only. Director: Ed Franklin. Telephone: (913) 888-8500 ext. 3830. Program Specialists: Pegi H. Denton, ext. 3335 and Joanne Bodner, ext. 3226.

Kansas City Kansas Community College: 7250 State Avenue, Kansas City, KS 66112. Total enrollment: 3,696. LD students: 12. Special services: individual tutoring, training in study skills, academic counseling, taped books, special examinations, student resource center, readers, job placement. Contact: Linda DeMarais, Coordinator, Disabled Student Services. Telephone: (913) 334-1100 ext. 170.

Kansas State University: 101 Holton Hall, Manhattan, KS 66506. Special services: individual and group tutoring, training in study skills, academic and psychological counseling, taped books, special examinations, readers, ombudsman. Contact: Gretchen Holden, Coordinator. Telephone: (913) 532-6441.

Pittsburg State University: Pittsburg, KS 66762. Special services: academic and psychological counseling. Contact: Nick A. Henry, Coordinator of Learning Disabilities. Telephone: (316) 231-8464.

University of Kansas: Lawrence, KS 66045. Total enrollment: 25,000. LD students: 22. Special services: diagnostic testing, classroom accommodation in regular courses, Kurzweil Reading Machine. Contact: Lorraine Michel, Assistant Director, Student Assistance Center. Telephone: (913) 864-4064. Notes: Educational history required for special student services.

Hospital Clinics

Hutchinson: Horizon Mental Health Center, 1715 E. 23rd, 67502. Telephone: (316) 665-2240. Contact: Steve Reiner. Outpatient program. Services: diagnostic testing, academic and psychological testing, psychological and parent counseling.

Topeka: Children's Hospital, The Menninger Foundation, Box 829, 66601. Telephone: (913) 273-7500 ext. 800. Contact: Children's Admissions Office. Outpatient, inpatient, and day program. Ages served: infants-adults. Services: diagnostic testing, academic and psychological testing, individual and group tutoring; academic, psychological, and parent counseling; group, speech, and language therapy; social services, comprehensive outpatient evaluation with psychoeducational testing, multidisciplinary approach; inpatient treatment for emotionally disturbed/learning disabled children; preschool day treatment center.

KANSAS

Other Services

Dodge City: Arrowhead West, Inc., 1100 E. Wyatt Earp Boulevard, P.O. Box 1353, 67801. Telephone: (316) 227-8803. President: Don Pendergast. Preschool (home-based service); sheltered adult workshop with residential services. Ages served: birth-5; 18 and up. Grades served: ungraded. Current enrollment: 50 children; 48 adults. Maximum enrollment: 53 children; 55 adults. Full-time staff: 44. Services: family counseling; physical, occupational, speech, and language therapy; adaptive physical education, vocational training, work-study, job placement, life skills training, hearing and vision screenings, help with social and behavior problems.

Manhattan: Big Lakes Developmental Center, Inc., 1500 Hayes Drive, 66502. Telephone: (913) 776-9201. Executive Director: James K. Shaver. Preschool and adult agency with limited services. Day school, sheltered workshop, residential services for adults. Ages served: birth-6, 16 and up. Current enrollment: 45 preschool; 91 adults. Maximum enrollment: 45 preschool; 91 adults. Scholarships/financial aid available. Services: individual and group tutoring, academic and psychological testing, psychological and family counseling, parent counseling, speech and occupational therapy, adaptive physical education, vocational training, job placement, comprehensive evaluations, preschool activities, residential and community living programs. Recreation: Special Olympics, planned activities.

Olathe: The Classworks, P.O. Box 2061, 101 S. Cherry, 66061. Telephone: (913) 764-6940. Director: Suzanne K. Reuber. Clinic. Ages served: kindergarten-adult. Services: diagnostic testing, academic and psychological testing, individual and group tutoring, academic and parent counseling, speech and language therapy referrals. Notes: Tries to coordinate services with those available through public and private schools and avoid duplication.

KENTUCKY

Offices of Organizations Concerned with Learning Disabilities

ACLD, Inc.: 403 Caple Avenue, Fairdale, KY 40118. Telephone: (502) 361-9527. President: Carol Larkin. Secretary: Marilyn Kreisle.

Council for Exceptional Children: President: Laura Thomson, Education Department, Northern Kentucky University, Highland Heights, KY 41076. Telephone: Office (606) 572-5599; Home (606) 356-3476.

Kentucky Easter Seal Society: 233 E. Broadway, Louisville, KY 40202. Executive Director: Mr. Guion Miller. Telephone: (502) 584-9781.

KENTUCKY

State Department of Education Learning Disabilities Personnel

Lois Adams, Associate Assistant Superintendent, Office of Education for Exceptional Children, Capitol Plaza Tower, Eighth Floor, Frankfort, KY 40601. Telephone: (502) 564-4970. Learning disabilities consultant: Nancy LaCount.

Private and Day Schools

Lexington: Lexington Hearing and Speech Center, 158 N. Ashland Avenue, 40502. Telephone: (606) 268-4545. Executive Director: Jane Midkiff Polk. Preschool with limited services. Ages served: birth-6. Current enrollment: 30. Maximum enrollment: 50. Full-time staff: 7. Part-time staff: 4. Scholarships/financial aid available. Services: individual tutoring, academic testing, audiological and speech diagnosis, evaluation and therapy. Notes: Serves hearing and speech impaired children; some have learning disabilities.

Louisville: The de Paul School, 1925 Duker Avenue, 40205. Telephone: (502) 459-6131. Executive Director: Sr. Anne Rita Mauck. Principal: Lillie Roberts. Preschool and elementary day school with summer program. Ages served: 5-13. Grades served: kindergarten-8. Current enrollment: 292. Maximum enrollment: 310. Full-time staff: 44. Scholarships/financial aid available. Services: individual and group tutoring, academic testing and counseling, full curriculum. Notes: Specifically for children who have been diagnosed as dyslexic. Teacher/student ratio 1:7.

Louisville: Ursuline-Pitt School, 2117 Payne Street, 40206. Telephone: (502) 895-7488. Administrator: Sr. Regina Marie Bevelacqua. Preschool, elementary, and secondary day school with summer program. Full-time staff: 14. Part-time staff: 1. Current enrollment: 74. Maximum enrollment: 85. Ages served: 3-26. Grades served: preschool-12. Scholarships/financial aid available. Services: individual and group tutoring, academic counseling, adaptive physical education, work-study, physical and speech therapy, vocational training, job placement. Recreation: gymnasium, auditorium, Special Olympics; student-run business.

Mayfield: The Charles L. Shedd APSL Research Academy, 1023 W. Broadway, 42066-2040. Telephone: (502) 247-8007. Director: Katherine C. Cole. Preschool, elementary, secondary, and adult day and boarding school; summer program. Ages served: 7-adult. Grades served: preschool-12, precollege year. Current enrollment: 39. Maximum enrollment: 40. Full-time staff: 11. Part-time staff: 4. Services: individual and group tutoring, academic and psychological testing; academic, psychological, and family counseling; adaptive physical education, medical services. Recreation: local facilities for boating, skiing, swimming, canoeing, nature studies, archaeological digs. Notes: Precollege year offers a college environment for gifted students with specific learning disabilities.

KENTUCKY

Summer Camps and Programs

Lexington: Life Adventure Camp, 180 E. Maxwell Street, 40508. Telephone: (606) 252-4733. Camp Director: Elizabeth Ivey. Residential camp with limited services. Ages served: 8-18. Services: individual and group tutoring, group living and problem solving, follow-up program. Recreation: camping, hiking, nature study, swimming, team sports, crafts, music. Notes: Serves children and youth with emotional and behavior problems.

Louisville: Camp Green Shores and Camp Kysoc, Kentucky Easter Seal Society, Inc., 233 E. Broadway, 40202. Telephone: (502) 584-9781. Residential camp with limited services. Twelve-day sessions. Ages served: 7 and up. Maximum enrollment: 72. Full-time staff: 4. Part-time staff: 50-60. Scholarships/financial aid available. Services: socialization. Recreation: swimming, riding, nature study, crafts, camping, cookouts, dances and skits, boating, fishing, campfire stories, sports, games.

College and University Special Programs and Services

Asbury College: Wilmore, KY 40390. Special services: individual tutoring, training in study skills, academic and psychological counseling, readers, diagnostic testing. Contact: Ed Blue, Dean of Student Development. Telephone: (606) 858-3511 ext. 108.

Bellarmine College: 2001 Newburg Road, Louisville, KY 40205. Special services: individual tutoring, academic counseling, training in study skills, student resource center. Contact: J. Alan Burke, Dean of Admissions and Educational Services. Telephone: (502) 452-8131.

Brescia College: 120 W. Seventh Street, Owensboro, KY 42301. Total enrollment: 851. LD students: 2. Special services: individual tutoring, special examinations, psychological counseling, training in study skills. Contact: Ellen Dugan-Barrette, Director of Special Services. Telephone: (502) 685-3131 ext. 259.

Center/clinic: Special Services English and Math Tutoring Lab. Telephone: (502) 685-3131. Director: Ellen Dugan-Barrette. Not open to public. Grades served: college. Services: developmental courses, individual tutoring, counseling.

Lexington Community College: Cooper Drive, Oswald Building, Lexington, KY 40506-0235. Total enrollment: 2,456. LD students: 15. Special services: individual tutoring, training in study skills, academic and psychological counseling, taped books, special examinations, readers; developmental program in English, math, and accounting. Contact: Frances Hunter, Coordinator, Handicapped Student Services. Telephone: (606) 257-6068.

Madisonville Community College: University Drive, Madisonville, KY 42431. Special services: individual tutoring, training in study skills, academic counseling, student resource center, diagnostic testing. Contact: Carl Barnett, Associate Director of Student Services. Telephone: (502) 821-2250 ext. 102.

Center/clinic: Learning Center. Telephone: (502) 821-2250 ext. 149 or 150. Instructor: Joan Smith. Lab Supervisor: Ronna Love. Not open to public. Grades served: college. Services: developmental and basic skills classes, reading and refresher courses, tutoring, study skills workshops.

Morehead State University: 401 Ginger Hall, Morehead, KY 40351. Special services: individual tutoring, training in study skills, academic and psychological counseling, student resource center. Contact: Betty Moran, Coordinator, or Janet Bignon, Learning Specialist. Telephone: (606) 783-2005.

Center/clinic: Learning Lab, UPO 1238. Telephone: (606) 783-2005. Coordinator: Betty Moran. Not open to public. Grades served: college. Services: academic and personal counseling, remediation, computers, individual tutoring, advocacy.

Murray State University: Murray, KY 42071. Total enrollment: 6,500. Special services: diagnostic testing, tutors, taped books, note takers, training in study skills, liaison with faculty, academic counseling, support group. Contact: Peggy Phelan, Coordinator, Learning Center. Telephone: (502) 762-2666.

Northern Kentucky University: College Station, Highland Heights, KY 41076. Total enrollment: 8,000. LD students: 30. Special services: special orientation, readers, individual and group tutoring, ombudsman, test proctoring; academic, career, and psychological counseling; diagnostic testing, referrals, taped books, training in study skills, Kurzweil reading machine, self-tutoring computer. Contact: David Cover, Counselor for Students with Disabilities. Telephone: (606) 572-5189.

Center/clinic: Center for Exceptional Children, BEP 264. Telephone: (606) 572-5236. Director: Janet M. Johnson. Open to public. Services: diagnostic testing, classroom unit. Grades served: kindergarten-12.

University of Kentucky: Lexington, KY 40506. Total enrollment: 21,237. LD students: 5-10. Special services: special examinations, diagnostic testing, speech and hearing clinic offering speech therapy and diagnostic services. Contact: Jake Karnes, Director, Handicapped Student Services. Telephone: (606) 257-2754.

Center/clinic: Educational Assessment Clinic, 229 TEB 0001. Telephone: (606) 257-4713. Director: Donald P. Cross.

University of Louisville: Third and Eastern Parkway, Louisville, KY 40292. Special services: individual tutoring, training in study skills, taped books, special examinations, student resource center, diagnostic testing. Contact: Bill Cox, Director, Special Student Services. Telephone: (502) 588-6927.

KENTUCKY

Center/clinic: The Resource Center, Strickler Hall. Telephone: (502) 588-6703. Director: Chris Hall. Not open to public. Grades served: college. Services: study skills, tutoring, note taking, remediation.

Western Kentucky University: Bowling Green, KY 42101. Special services: individual and group tutoring, training in study skills, academic and psychological counseling, peer tutoring program. Contact: Judy Rust, Director of Special Services. Telephone: (502) 745-4308.

Center/clinic: The Reading Clinic. Telephone: (502) 745-4541. Director: Robert Panchyshyn. Open to public. Ages served: all. Services: diagnostic and instructional testing, reading evaluations, remedial reading.

Center/clinic: Communication Disorders Clinic. Telephone: (502) 745-4541. Director: Frank Kersting. Open to public. Ages served: preschool and up. Services: diagnosis, speech and language therapy.

Other Services

Lexington: Multidisciplinary Institute, 2459 Nicholasville Road, 40503. Telephone: (606) 278-7462. Contact: James R. Watkins. Clinic. After school program. Ages served: birth-30. Services: diagnostic testing, academic and psychological testing, parent counseling; developmental, visual, and educational therapy; parent orientation and training.

LOUISIANA

Offices of Organizations Concerned with Learning Disabilities

ACLD, Inc.: Route 4, Box 110, Arnaudville, LA 70512. President: Karen La-Grange. Telephone: (318) 754-5287.

Council for Exceptional Children: President: Douglas Granier, 108 E. Oaklawn Drive, Thibodeaux, LA 70301. Telephone: (504) 446-1306.

Easter Seal Society for Crippled Children and Adults of Louisiana, Inc.: 4631 W. Napoleon Avenue, Metairie, LA 70001. Mailing address: P.O. Box 8425, Metairie, LA 70011. Executive Director: Daniel H. Underwood. Telephone: (504) 885-9960.

State Department of Education Learning Disabilities Personnel

Irene M. Newby, Assistant Superintendent, Office of Special Educational Services, Louisiana Department of Education, P.O. Box 94064, Baton Rouge, LA 70804-9064. Telephone: (504) 342-3631. Learning disabilities consultant: Nancy Hicks.

LOUISIANA

Private and Day Schools

Baton Rouge: dePaul Dyslexia Association, Inc., 9150 Bereford Drive, 70809. Telephone: (504) 923-2068. Principal: Sophie Gibson. Elementary, secondary, and adult day school with summer program. Ages served: 6-14 school; 6-adult summer/Saturday. Grades served: 1-8 school; ungraded summer/Saturday. Current enrollment: 140 school; 45 Saturday. Full-time staff: 21. Part-time staff: 5. Limited scholarships/financial aid available. Services: individual and group tutoring, academic testing and counseling, Saturday morning individual tutorial services.

Baton Rouge: Gables Academy, 11809 Jefferson Highway, 70816. Telephone: (504) 292-9231. Director: Susan C. Kramer. Elementary and secondary day school with summer program. Ages served: 6-20. Grades served: 1-12. Current enrollment: 60. Maximum enrollment: 90. Full-time staff: 8. Part-time staff: 1. Services: individual tutoring, academic testing, psychological counseling, speech therapy, small classes. Notes: For students who have not been successful in a conventional setting.

Lafayette: Reading Research Foundation, P.O. Box 30185, 70503. Telephone: (318) 984-7485. Executive Vice President: Sylvia O. Fitzgerald. Elementary day school with summer program. Ages served: 7-14. Grades served: 1-8. Current enrollment: 20. Maximum enrollment: 32. Full-time staff: 4. Part-time staff: 4. Services: individual tutoring, academic and family counseling. Recreation: swimming, tennis.

Lake Charles: Regina Caeli Center, 3903 Kingston Street, 70605. Telephone: (318) 478-1970. Principal: Sr. Helen Mary Gieb. Elementary day school. Ages served: 6-16. Grades served: 1-6. Current enrollment: 44. Maximum enrollment: 50. Full-time staff: 4. Part-time staff: 1. Scholarships/financial aid available. Services: group tutoring, full academic curriculum; speech therapy, academic and psychological testing provided by public school system.

New Orleans: Crescent Academy, 926 Milan Street, 70115. Telephone: (504) 895-3952. Director: Laura H. Burchfield. Elementary day school with summer program and camp. Ages served: 6-14. Grades served: ungraded 1-8. Current enrollment: 50. Maximum enrollment: 55. Full-time staff: 11. Part-time staff: 2. Services: individual tutoring, academic and psychological testing, art and language therapy, visual and auditory perception training, psychotherapy. Recreation: gymnasium, playgrounds.

New Orleans: Gables Academy/New Orleans, 3900 General Taylor Street, 70125. Telephone: (504) 822-7844. Regional Director: R. Wm. Hottenstein. Elementary and secondary day school with summer program. Ages served: 6-21. Grades served: 1-12. Current enrollment: 50. Maximum enrollment: 60. Full-time staff: 7. Scholarships/financial aid available. Services: individual and group tutoring, academic and psychological testing; academic, psychological, and family counseling; work-study.

LOUISIANA

New Orleans: Walters Developmental School, 206-210 Midway Drive, 70123. Telephone: (504) 737-9430. Director: Marjorie Walters. Elementary and adult day and boarding school with summer program. Ages served: 5-adult. Grades served: 1-8. Current enrollment: 35 boarding; 26 day. Maximum enrollment: 50 boarding; 60 day. Full-time staff: 11. Part-time staff: 25. Limited scholarships/financial aid available. Services: group tutoring, academic testing and counseling, adaptive physical education, visual-motor exercises. Recreation: games, sports.

College and University Special Programs and Services

Louisiana State University-Baton Rouge: Baton Rouge, LA 70803. Special services: noncredit remedial courses in reading, math, English. Contact: Kaylene Long, Director of Special Services. Telephone: (504) 388-2873.

Louisiana Technical University: College of Education, Ruston, LA 71272. Special services: psychological counseling, individual consultation with special education staff. Contact: Don Wells, Assistant Professor. Telephone: (318) 257-4088.

McNeese State University: Ryan Street, Lake Charles, LA 70609. Special services: individual and group tutoring, training in study skills, academic and psychological counseling, student resource center, readers, diagnostic testing and evaluations, ombudsman. Contact: Brenda Ball, Director of Special Projects, or Sena Theall, Coordinator of Tutorial Lab. Telephone: (318) 474-9127.

Northeast Louisiana University: 700 University Avenue, Monroe, LA 71209. Special services: individual tutoring, academic and psychological counseling, special examinations, student resource center, readers, diagnostic testing, training in study skills. Contact: Mr. Lamoine S. Miller, Professor of Education. Telephone: (318) 342-4151.

Center/clinic: Summer Clinic, 224 Strauss Hall. Telephone: (318) 342-4151. Director: Mr. Lamoine S. Miller. Open to public. Grades served: kindergarten-12. Services: individual tutoring, academic testing; limited tutorial services during academic year.

Northwestern State University: Natchitoches, LA 71457. Special services: individual tutoring, ombudsman, special examinations, academic and psychological counseling, diagnostic testing, training in study skills. Contact: Francis Watkins, Director of Special Services. Telephone: (318) 357-5435.

Southeastern Louisiana University: University Station, Hammond, LA 70402. Special services: academic and psychological counseling, special examinations, diagnostic testing. Contact: Thomas Terrell, Director, Comprehensive Counseling Center. Telephone: (504) 549-2239.

Center/clinic: Comprehensive Counseling Center, P.O. Box 387. Telephone: (504) 549-2239. Director: Thomas Terrell. Not open to public. Ages served: college.

University of New Orleans: Lakefront, New Orleans, LA 70122.

Center/clinic: Special Education Center. Telephone: (504) 286-6620. Director: Donald A. Pekarek. Open to public. Ages served: infants-21. Grades served: kindergarten-college. Services: evaluation.

Other Services

Baton Rouge: Cerebral Palsy Center of Greater Baton Rouge, 1805 College Drive, 70815. Telephone: (504) 923-3420. Executive Director: Alice McCracken. Day treatment center with limited services. Ages served: all. Grades served: all. Current enrollment: 125. Maximum enrollment: 135. Full-time staff: 8. Part-time staff: 8. Scholarships/financial aid available. Services: individual tutoring, academic and psychological testing; academic, psychological, and family counseling; speech, language, physical, and occupational therapy; medical services. Notes: Serves children with cerebral palsy, learning disabilities, or developmental delays.

New Orleans: Ochsner Clinic, Child Development Center, 1514 Jefferson Highway, 70121. Telephone: (504) 838-3900. Director: Andrea L. Starrett. Coordinator: Jamie Hill. Clinic. Outpatient program. Ages served: birth-adolescence. Services: diagnostic testing; academic, psychological, and neuropsychological testing; academic, psychological, and parent counseling; speech, language, and occupational therapy; social services, medical evaluation with specialists in child neurology and developmental pediatrics; school consultations, comprehensive neurodiagnostic studies.

MAINE

Offices of Organizations Concerned with Learning Disabilities

Council for Exceptional Children: President: Sanford J. Prince, Gorham School Department, Gorham High School, 41 Morrill Avenue, Gorham, ME 04038. Telephone: (207) 839-3533.

Pine Tree Society for Handicapped Children and Adults, Inc.: 84 Front Street, P.O. Box 518, Bath, ME 04530. Executive Director: William F. Haney. Telephone: (207) 443-3341.

Orton Dyslexia Society (New England Branch): c/o Rocky Hill School, Ives Road, East Greenwich, RI 02818. President: Emi Flynn. Telephone: (401) 884-3346.

State Department of Education Learning Disabilities Personnel

David Stockford, Director, Division of Special Education, Department of Educational and Cultural Services, State House Station #23, Augusta, ME 04333. Telephone: (207) 289-3451. Learning disabilities consultant: Marjorie Scott Fallon.

MAINE

Private and Day Schools

Augusta: Mid-State United Cerebral Palsy, Inc., 273 Capital Street Extension, 04330. Telephone: (207) 587-2461. Executive Director: Kathleen F. Saufl. Preschool, elementary, secondary, and adult day school. Ages served: birth-20. Grades served: preschool-12. Current enrollment: 18. Maximum enrollment: 20. Full-time staff: 7. Part-time staff: 5. Services: individual and group tutoring, academic testing; physical, occupational, and speech therapy. Recreation: weekly swim program, field trips.

Bangor: Children's Garden, c/o Community Health and Counseling Service, 43 Illinois Avenue, 04401. Telephone: (207) 947-0366. Coordinator of Early Childhood Education: Gail A. Wagner. Preschool and elementary day school. Ages served: 3-7. Grades served: preschool-kindergarten. Current enrollment: 15. Maximum enrollment: 15. Full-time staff: 5. Part-time staff: 2. Scholarships/financial aid available. Services: psychological testing, psychological and family counseling, physical and occupational therapy, adaptive physical education, preschool consultation within Penobscot County, training workshops.

Poland Spring: The Pinehenge School at Elan, Route Box 370, 04274. Telephone: (207) 774-2269. Headmaster/Director of Special Education: Jack J. McCarthy III. Secondary boarding school with limited services; summer program and camp. Ages served: 13-18. Grades served: 7-12. Current enrollment: 130. Maximum enrollment: 150. Full-time staff: 45. Part-time staff: 20. Scholarships/financial aid available. Services: individual and group tutoring, academic and psychological testing; academic, psychological, group, and family counseling; medical services. Recreation: swimming, volleyball, basketball, softball, riding, skiing, deep sea fishing, hiking. Notes: Highly structured therapeutic program for nonpsychotic emotionally disturbed youths. Special education certified for grades 7-12.

Summer Camps and Programs

Harrison: Camp Bendito, 04040. Telephone: (207) 583-2544. Codirectors: George and Joan Vandemark. Females only residential camp with academic program and limited services. Ages served: 7-15. Grades served: 1-10. Maximum enrollment: 60. Full-time staff: 15. Services: individual tutoring, academic testing, medical services. Academic programs: math, reading, English, spelling, study skills. Recreation: camping, hiking, field trips, nature study, riding, swimming, sailing, archery, team sports, crafts, drama, music.

Scarborough: Camp Ketcha Day Camp, 336 Black Point Road, 04074. Telephone: (207) 883-4353. Executive Director: Elizabeth K. Berry. Day camp. Ages served: 4-15. Grades served: prekindergarten-9. Maximum enrollment: 140. Full-time staff: 25. Scholarships/financial aid available. Recreation: camping, hiking, field trips, nature study, riding, swimming, archery, crafts, drama.

College and University Special Programs and Services

Bates College: Lewiston, ME 04240. Total enrollment: 1,435. Special services: individual tutoring, training in study skills, academic and psychological counseling, taped books, scholarships, extra exam time. Contact: James W. Carignan, Dean of the College. Telephone: (207) 786-6223.

Husson College: One College Circle, Bangor, ME 04401. LD students: 6. Special services: readers, individual and group tutoring, special examinations, academic and psychological counseling, diagnostic testing, taped books, training in study skills, individual education plans.

- **Special Program:** ACHIEVE. A one-year college preparatory program. Includes special courses in math, English composition, and reading. Students can take two three-credit college courses in addition to ACHIEVE courses. Admissions requirements include an interview, specialized test results, and teacher recommendations. Director: Suzanne Comins. Telephone: (207) 947-1121.

Unity College: Quaker Hill Road, Unity, ME 04988. Total enrollment: 300. LD students: 15. Special services: precollege summer program, developmental courses in basic skills, specialized academic advising; academic, psychological, and personal counseling; study skills workshops, tutoring by faculty and trained peer tutors, reduced course load options, untimed exams, student resource center, diagnostic testing, limited taped textbooks. Contact: James J. Horan, Director, Learning Resource Center. Telephone: (207) 948-3131 ext. 241 or 236.

University of Maine: Farmington, ME 04938. Special services: university students provide tutoring and limited assessment for school-aged children.

University of Maine-Augusta: Augusta, ME 04330. Special services: readers, individual and group tutoring, academic and psychological counseling, taped books, training in study skills, developmental courses, student resource center, diagnostic testing. Contact: Sally Grande, Special Services Counselor. Telephone: (207) 622-7131 ext. 228.

University of Southern Maine: Gorham, ME 04038. Special services: as needed on an individual basis. Contact: Dexter Huntoon, Coordinator, Career Planning and Handicapped Services. Telephone: (207) 780-4050.

Hospital Clinics

Bangor: Eastern Maine Medical Center, Behavioral and Developmental Pediatrics, 489 State Street, 04401. Telephone: (207) 945-7572. Contact: Sherry Faulkner. Outpatient program. Ages served: birth-21. Services: diagnostic testing, academic and psychological testing, individual tutoring; academic, psychological, and parent counseling; group, speech, language, physical, and occupational

MAINE

therapy; multidisciplinary team approach. Notes: Approximately 60 percent of clients are learning disabled.

Caribou: Cary Medical Center, Van Buren Road, 04736. Telephone: (207) 498-3111 ext. 170. Contact: Laura McBey. Outpatient program. Ages served: pre-school-adult. Services: diagnostic testing; speech, language, physical, and occupational therapy; audiological testing.

Other Services

Bangor: United Cerebral Palsy of Northeastern Maine, 103 Texas Avenue, 04401. Telephone: (207) 947-6771. Executive Director: Ruth P. Shook. Infant development program and preschool. Ages served: birth-5. Current enrollment: 65. Maximum enrollment: 65. Full-time staff: 7. Part-time staff: 2. Scholarships/financial aid available. Services: physical and occupational therapy, medical and child development services, home teaching, family support. Notes: Serves children with developmental disabilities and delays.

Ellsworth: Hancock County Children's Center, Community Health and Counseling Services, 78 Union Street, 04605. Telephone: (207) 667-5357. Program Director: Donna Salisbury. Preschool with limited services. Ages served: infant-6. Current enrollment: 60. Maximum enrollment: 75. Full-time staff: 5. Part-time staff: 6. Scholarships/financial aid available. Services: individual and group tutoring, academic and psychological testing, family counseling, physical and occupational therapy, work-study, home teaching.

MARYLAND

Offices of Organizations Concerned with Learning Disabilities

ACLD, Inc.: 320 Maryland National Bank Building, Baltimore, MD 21202. Telephone: (301) 665-3309. President: Ann Vinup.

Council for Exceptional Children: President: Catherine Giovannoni, General Delivery, Leonardtown, MD 20650. Telephone: Office (301) 475-5655; Home (301) 475-3991.

Central Maryland Chapter of the National Easter Seal Society: 3700 Fourth Street, Baltimore, MD 21225. Executive Director: Letitia Simmons. Telephone: (301) 355-0100.

Orton Dyslexia Society: 300 W. Lanvale Street, Baltimore, MD 21217. President: Fran Levin Bowman. Telephone: (301) 260-6167.

MARYLAND

State Department of Education Learning Disabilities Personnel

Martha Irvin, Assistant State Superintendent, Division of Special Education, State Department of Education, 200 W. Baltimore Street, Baltimore, MD 21201-2595. Telephone: (301) 659-2489. Learning disabilities consultant: Richard Mainzer. Telephone: (301) 659-2496.

Private and Day Schools

Baltimore: The John F. Kennedy Institute School, 707 N. Broadway, Room 216, 21205. Telephone: (301) 522-5417. Director: Michael Bender. Elementary day school. Ages served: 6-13. Grades served: 1-6. Current enrollment: 44. Maximum enrollment: 44. Full-time staff: 9. Part-time staff: 7. Services: individual tutoring, academic and psychological testing; parent, psychological, and family counseling; psychiatric and medical services; occupational, physical, speech, and language therapy; nutrition, social work. Recreation: games, sports.

Baltimore: Woodbourne School, 1301 Woodbourne Avenue, 21239. Telephone: (301) 433-1000. Executive Director: John Hodge-Williams. Secondary day and boarding school with summer program. Ages served: 12-16. Grades served: 7-9. Current enrollment: 61. Maximum enrollment: 61. Full-time staff: 18. Part-time staff: 6. Services: individual and group tutoring, academic and psychological testing, psychological and family counseling, occupational therapy, adaptive physical education, vocational training, work-study, medical services, summer work program. Recreation: intramural basketball, soccer, volleyball, softball.

Bethesda: Christ Church Child Center, 8011 Old Georgetown Road, 20814. Telephone: (301) 986-1635. Director: Shari Gelman. Preschool and elementary day school with summer program and camp. Ages served: birth-12. Grades served: ungraded. Current enrollment: 116. Maximum enrollment: 120. Full-time staff: 52. Part-time staff: 30. Scholarships/financial aid available. Services: individual and group tutoring, academic testing, psychotherapy; physical, occupational, speech, music, and recreation therapy; psychological, family, speech, language, and group counseling; parent training, behavior management consultations, referrals to community resources, adaptive physical education.

Bowie: Bowie Therapeutic Nursery Center, 3120 Belair Drive, 20715. Telephone: (301) 262-9167. Administrative Director: Mary W. Hitch. Preschool with limited services. Ages served: 2½-5½. Current enrollment: 16. Maximum enrollment: 20. Full-time staff: 2. Part-time staff: 7. Scholarships/financial aid available. Services: academic and psychological testing, psychological and family counseling, adaptive physical education, recreational therapy. Notes: Serves emotionally disturbed children; some are also learning disabled.

Centreville: The Gunston School, P.O. Box 200, 21617. Telephone: (301) 758-0620. Headmaster: Paul M. Long. Females only secondary day and boarding school with limited services. Ages served: 14-19. Grades served: 9-12. Current enrollment: 80. Maximum enrollment: 80. Full-time staff: 16. Part-time staff: 1. Scholarships/financial aid available. Services: individual tutoring, academic counseling. Recreation: riding, sailing, tennis, hockey, softball, basketball.

Chevy Chase: The Center School, 3200 Woodbine Street, 20815. Telephone: (301) 652-1370. Director: Ruth B. Spodak. Elementary day school with summer program and camp. Ages served: 6-14. Grades served: ungraded. Current enrollment: 100. Full-time staff: 30. Part-time staff: 4. Scholarships/financial aid available. Services: individual and group tutoring, academic and psychological testing, academic and psychological counseling, adaptive physical education, speech and language therapy, parent group, program for gifted learning disabled students. Recreation: riding, swimming, computers, archaeology, drama, music, art, sports.

Chevy Chase: Cottleston Hall Montessori, 3200 Woodbine Street, 20815. Telephone: (301) 652-1370. Codirectors: Ruth B. Spodak, Betty S. Levinson. Preschool and elementary day school. Ages served: 3-6. Grades served: ungraded. Current enrollment: 10. Maximum enrollment: 16. Full-time staff: 1. Part-time staff: 3. Scholarships/financial aid available. Services: individual and group tutoring, academic and psychological testing, adaptive physical education, speech and language therapy, motor development, art instruction. Notes: Serves children without special needs as well as children with developmental delays in speech/language areas and motor development.

Frostburg: Long Stretch Learning Center, Star Route Box 28, 21532. Telephone: (301) 689-6197. Educational Coordinator: Robert De Vore. Males only elementary and secondary day and boarding school with summer program. Ages served: 13 and up. Current enrollment: 36. Maximum enrollment: 42. Full-time staff: 5. Part-time staff: 1. Services: individual and group tutoring, academic and psychological testing, academic and psychological counseling, vocational training, medical services, independent living skills, family life education. Recreation: basketball, softball. Notes: Strives to help students return to public school, get a high school equivalency, or function independently.

Nanjemoy: Melwood Farm, Route 1, Box 50-A, 20662. Telephone: (301) 870-3215. Director: Daniel D. Pearce. Secondary and adult day and boarding school with limited services; summer program and camp. Ages served: 16 and up. Current enrollment: 70. Maximum enrollment: 80. Full-time staff: 30. Part-time staff: 10. Services: individual and group tutoring, psychological and family counseling, vocational training, job placement.

Owings Mills: The Jemicy School, 11 Celadon Road, 21210. Telephone: (301) 653-2700. Director: David Malin. Elementary day school with summer camp. Ages served: 6-14. Grades served: 1-8. Current enrollment: 113. Maximum enrollment: 113. Full-time staff: 35. Scholarships/financial aid available. Services: individual and group tutoring, academic testing and counseling, adaptive physical education. Recreation: all seasonal sports including swimming; computer and science clubs. Notes: Specifically for children with dyslexia.

Rockville: The Frost School, 4915 Aspen Hill Road, 20853. Telephone: (301) 933-3451. Director: Richard A. Miller. Secondary day school with limited services; summer program. Ages served: 13-19. Grades served: 7-12. Current enrollment: 36. Maximum enrollment: 36. Full-time staff: 10. Part-time staff: 5. Scholarships/financial aid available. Services: individual and group tutoring, academic and psychological testing; academic, psychological, and family counseling; occupational therapy, vocational training, work-study, career planning, job placement. Recreation: physical education, weight lifting; wilderness challenge program including rock climbing, caving, camping, canoeing. Notes: Also serves emotionally troubled adolescents.

Rockville: The Treatment Centers, 1000 Twinbrook Parkway, 20851. Telephone: (301) 424-5200. Preschool Coordinator: Jean Thayer. Preschool with summer camp. Ages served: 2-6. Grades served: preschool-kindergarten. Current enrollment: 85. Maximum enrollment: 120. Full-time staff: 35. Part-time staff: 14. Services: psychological testing, psychological and family counseling; physical, occupational, and speech therapy; audiological screening.

Silver Spring: The Chelsea School, 900 Jesup Blair Drive, 20910. Telephone: (301) 585-1430. Headmaster: William O'Flanagan. Secondary day school with summer program. Ages served: 14-19. Grades served: 9-12. Current enrollment: 61. Maximum enrollment: 61. Full-time staff: 14. Part-time staff: 8. Scholarships/financial aid available. Services: individual and group tutoring, academic and psychological testing, academic and psychological counseling, adaptive physical education. Recreation: softball, soccer, basketball, tennis club, art and pottery studios. Notes: Goal of school is to help students remediate and compensate for learning disabilities.

Silver Spring: Montgomery Preschool Achievement Center, 10611 Tenbrook Drive, 20901. Telephone: (301) 593-3797. Director: Helen Rubin. Preschool with limited services. Ages served: 2-5. Current enrollment: 49. Maximum enrollment: 75. Full-time staff: 16. Part-time staff: 6. Services: physical, occupational, and speech therapy; behavior management.

Silver Spring: Pathways Center, 1200 University Boulevard, West, 20902. Telephone: (301) 593-8680. Program Director: Kevin A. Sawyer. Secondary day school with limited services. Ages served: 14-18. Current enrollment: 12. Maximum enrollment: 21. Full-time staff: 6. Part-time staff: 2. Services: individual tutoring, academic testing, psychological and family counseling, adaptive physical education, vocational training, work-study, job placement. Recreation: outings including cycling, canoeing, fishing, ice-skating, swimming. Notes: Primarily serves emotionally impaired adolescents.

MARYLAND

Summer Camps and Programs

Chestertown: Easter Seal Society of Del-Mar, Camp Fairlee Manor, Route 2, Box 319, 21620. Telephone: (301) 778-0566. Director of Camping and Recreation: Nancy M. Jones. Residential camp with limited services. Ages served: 5 and up. Maximum enrollment: 50 per 2-week session (5 sessions). Full-time staff: 30. Scholarships/financial aid available. Services: adaptive physical education, introduction to computers. Recreation: swimming, hiking, riding, field trips, nature study, crafts, drama, camping, camp fires, hayrides, canoeing, special events. Notes: Serves individuals with cerebral palsy, muscular dystrophy, spina bifida, visual impairments, and mental handicaps.

College and University Special Programs and Services

Catonsville Community College: 800 S. Rolling Road, Baltimore, MD 21228. Total enrollment: 9,793. LD students: 40. Special services: individual tutoring, training in study skills and test taking, academic and psychological counseling, taped books, special examinations, student resource center, readers, diagnostic testing, individual education plan, follow-up, scholarships, ombudsman, career counseling. Contact: Marjorie Zensky, Learning Specialist. Telephone: (301) 455-4356.

Center/clinic: The Learning Lab. Telephone: (301) 455-4744. Director: Claudia Chiesi. Not open to public. Grades served: college. Services: individual and small group tutoring; remedial, corrective, and developmental instructional aids and materials.

Coppin State College: 2500 W. North Avenue, Baltimore, MD 21216. Total enrollment: 1,976. Special services: individual tutoring, academic and psychological counseling, student resource center, scholarships, diagnostic testing, training in study skills. Contact: Charles Woodward, Dean, Student Services. Telephone: (301) 383-5955.

Dundalk Community College: 7200 Sollers Point Road, Baltimore, MD 21222. Special services: individual tutoring, training in study skills, academic counseling, taped books, special examinations; reading, writing, and math centers; readers, diagnostic testing. Contact: Nancy Boozer, Coordinator, Developmental Education. Telephone: (301) 522-5776.

Essex Community College: Rossville Road, Baltimore, MD 21237. Total enrollment: 10,000. LD students: 75. Special services: individual tutoring, training in study skills, academic and psychological counseling, taped books, special examinations, student resource center, readers, diagnostic testing, scholarships, support group. Contact: Peggy Hayeslip, Learning Disabilities Specialist, or Kathy McSweeney, Coordinator of Services for Students with Disabilities. Telephone: (301) 522-1641.

Frostburg State College: Frostburg, MD 21532. Special services: individual and group tutoring, training in study skills, academic and psychological counseling, taped books, special examinations, readers, limited diagnostic testing, ombudsman, support group, individualized instruction in freshman composition, training on word processor, evaluation team, individual education plans. Contact: Todd Hutton, Director, Office of Disabled Student Services. Telephone: (301) 689-4481.

- **Special program:** Looking into the Future: A Model College Experience. Precollege summer residential program for LD high school juniors and seniors. Designed to create a bridge between high school and college. Six weeks. Accepts 30 students. Addresses academic and social skills. All students take courses in composition, critical reading, math, and career exploration. Admissions requirements: demonstrated potential to do college level work, formal diagnosis of a specific learning disability, personal interview. Director: Joseph F. Malak. Telephone: (301) 689-4214.

Howard Community College: Little Patuxent Parkway, Columbia, MD 21044. LD students: 30. Special services: individual and group tutoring, training in study skills, academic and career counseling, taped books, special examinations, readers, scholarships, test writers, large print materials, liaison between student and faculty, advocacy, helps locate resources. Contact: Barbara C. Greenfeld, Director, Special Services for the Disadvantaged. Telephone: (301) 992-4822.

Johns Hopkins University: Charles and 34th Streets, Baltimore, MD 21218.

Center/clinic: Interdisciplinary Program for the Exceptional. Telephone: (301) 338-8273. Coordinator: Linda J. Schuerholz. Open to public. Ages served: 5-adult. Grades served: kindergarten and up. Services: diagnosis, remediation, counseling, career and vocational guidance.

Loyola University: 4501 N. Charles Street, Baltimore, MD 21210. LD students: 50. Special services: student resource center, diagnostic testing. Contact: William Amoriell, Chairman, Education Department. Telephone: (301) 323-1010 ext. 304.

Center/clinic: Clinic for Students with Special Needs. Telephone: (301) 323-1010 ext. 304. Director: William Amoriell. Open to public. Ages served: 7-16. Grades served: 1-12. Services: assessment and programming.

Montgomery College: 51 Mannakee Street, Rockville, MD 20850. Total enrollment: 19,890. LD students: 150. Special services: individual and group tutoring, training in study skills, academic and psychological counseling, special examinations, student resource center, readers, diagnostic testing, support group, advisory committee. Contact: Lynne Imamshah, Coordinator of Special Student Services. Telephone: (301) 279-5058.

MARYLAND

Center/clinic: Learning Center. Telephone: (301) 279-5058. Director: Lynne Imamshah. Not open to public. Ages served: 18 and up. Grades served: postsecondary. Services: prescriptive/tutorial support for developmental English and reading classes at center, workshops, support for freshman English, faculty liaison, counseling.

Towson State University: Towson, MD 21204. Special services: individual tutoring, training in study skills, academic and psychological counseling, taped books, special examinations, readers, diagnostic testing, ombudsman, note taking, transcribing. Contact: Margaret Warrington, Director, Office of Special Needs. Telephone: (301) 321-2638.

University of Maryland-College Park: College Park, MD 20742. Total enrollment: 38,000. Special services: individual tutoring, training in study skills, academic and psychological counseling, taped books, special examinations, readers, ombudsman. Contact: William Scales, Director, Disabled Student Services. Telephone: (301) 454-6460.

Hospital Clinics

Baltimore: Mt. Washington Pediatric Hospital, Inc., 1708 W. Rogers Avenue, 21209. Telephone: (301) 578-8600. Contact: Nancy J. Bell, Director of Psychological Services. Outpatient program. Ages served: 4-21. Services: academic and psychological testing, psychological and parent counseling; speech, language, physical, and occupational therapy; liaison with schools and referring agencies.

Other Services

Rockville: Center for Unique Learners, 12220 Wilkins Avenue, 20852. Telephone: (301) 231-0115. Director: Nancy Dworkin. Educational center with summer program. Ages served: 6-adult. Grades served: 1-postgraduate. Current enrollment: 65-100. Full-time staff: 15. Part-time staff: 5. Limited scholarships/financial aid available. Services: individual and group tutoring, academic and psychological testing; academic, psychological, and family counseling; individual and family therapy, vocational training, work-study, job placement, transition skills.

Rockville: Specific Diagnostic Studies, Inc., 11600 Nebel Street, Suite 130, 20852. Telephone: (301) 468-6616. Director: Lynn Martin O'Brien. Educational testing and tutoring center. Day, after school, and summer program. Ages served: 5-adult. Services: diagnostic testing, individual and group tutoring, parent counseling, remedial programs; speech, language, and learning services; courses in learning strategies, SAT preparation. Notes: Specializes in learning differences.

Silver Spring: Endeavor Learning Center, 12518 Littleton Street, 20906. Telephone: (301) 933-8546. Director: Matthew J. Kamins. Clinic. After school program. Ages served: 4-young adult. Services: diagnostic testing, academic testing, individual and group tutoring, academic and parent counseling, advocacy, vocational assessment and counseling, compensatory strategies training.

MASSACHUSETTS

Offices of Organizations Concerned with Learning Disabilities

ACLD, Inc.: P.O. Box 28, West Newton, MA 02165. Telephone: (617) 254-3800 ext. 244; Answering service (617) 891-5009. President: Ruth Smith.

Council for Exceptional Children: President: Mr. Tracy Baldrate, 29 Filmore Street, Plymouth, MA 02360. Telephone: Office (617) 697-1200 ext. 2229; Home (617) 746-2352.

Massachusetts Easter Seal Society: Denholm Building, 484 Main Street, Worcester, MA 01608. President: Richard A. LaPierre. Telephone: (617) 757-2756.

Orton Dyslexia Society (New England Branch): c/o Rocky Hill School, Ives Road, East Greenwich, RI 02818. President: Emi Flynn. Telephone: (401) 884-3346.

State Department of Education Learning Disabilities Personnel

Roger W. Brown, Associate Commissioner of Special Education, Division of Special Education, State Department of Education, 1385 Hancock Street, Quincy, MA 02169. Telephone: (617) 770-7468.

Private and Day Schools

Arlington: Dearborn Elementary School and Carroll-Hall School, 34 Winter Street, 02174. Telephone: (617) 641-2424. Director: Eric M. Gordon. Elementary and secondary day school. Ages served: 5-18. Grades served: kindergarten-12. Current enrollment: 67. Maximum enrollment: 70. Full-time staff: 28. Part-time staff: 8. Services: individual and group tutoring, academic and psychological testing; academic, psychological, and family counseling; adaptive physical education, prevocational and vocational training, work-study, speech and language therapy, parent outreach. Recreation: swimming, field trips.

Barre: Stetson School, Inc., South Street, 01005. Telephone: (617) 355-4541. Executive Director: Richard J. Robinson. Males only boarding school with summer program. Ages served: 10-15 at intake. Current enrollment: 30. Maximum enrollment: 34. Full-time staff: 42. Part-time staff: 6. Services: individual and group tutoring, academic and psychological testing, vocational training, work-study, group and individual therapy; academic, psychological, and family counseling; adaptive physical education, vocational training, work-study, behavior modification. Recreation: sports, hobbies, clubs, alternative noncompetitive games, weight training.

MASSACHUSETTS

Boston: Bay Cove Adolescent Programs, 125 Lincoln Street, 02111. Telephone: (617) 426-6193. Director: Ms. Jan Storm. Elementary and secondary day school with limited services; summer program, camp, and after school center. Ages served: 12-21. Current enrollment: 24 high school; 18 after school center. Maximum enrollment: 24 high school; 18 after school center. Full-time staff: 25. Part-time staff: 2. Services: individual and group tutoring, academic and psychological testing; academic, psychological, and family counseling; occupational therapy, adaptive physical education, vocational training, work-study, job placement, medical services. Notes: Serves inner city adolescents with educational and/or emotional dysfunctions.

Boston: Center for Alternative Education, 650 Beacon Street, 02215. Telephone: (617) 437-1418. Director: David W. Zuckerman. Day school with summer program. Ages served: 14-21. Current enrollment: 35. Full-time staff: 16. Part-time staff: 11. Scholarships/financial aid available. Services: individual and group tutoring, academic testing, prevocational training, work-study, individualized psychotherapy, group counseling, family and art therapy, outreach services, college preparation, psychoeducational services.

Boston: COMPASS, 115 Warren Street, 02119. Telephone: (617) 442-2181. Executive Director: David W. Manzo. Secondary day school with summer program. Ages served: 11-19. Current enrollment: 28. Maximum enrollment: 28. Full-time staff: 14. Part-time staff: 2. Services: individual and group tutoring, academic and psychological testing, academic and psychological counseling, vocational training, work-study, job placement, medical services, computer-assisted education. Recreation: sports, use of Boston area recreational facilities, camping.

Boston: The Kingsley School, 30 Fairfield Street, 02116. Telephone: (617) 536-5984. Director: Lowell V. Kingsley. Elementary day school with limited services. Ages served: 6-14. Grades served: 1-8. Current enrollment: 70. Maximum enrollment: 80. Full-time staff: 11. Part-time staff: 2. Scholarships/financial aid available. Services: group tutoring, academic testing and counseling. Recreation: games, sports, after school program for grades 1-5, YMCA gym-and-swim. Notes: For academically capable children with mild learning difficulties.

Brockton: Mathoms Program, 165 Quincy Street, 02402. Telephone: (617) 580-0800 ext. 158 or 159. Director: Beverly Elliott. Elementary and secondary day school with summer program. Ages served: 9-21. Grades served: ungraded. Current enrollment: 24. Maximum enrollment: 30. Full-time staff: 11. Services: individual and group tutoring, academic and psychological testing, academic and psychological counseling, medical services, adaptive physical education, vocational training, work-study, job placement. Recreation: Outward Bound-type physical education program, ropes course, camping, sports, field trips.

Brookline: Community Preschool Therapeutic Nursery, 16 Hurd Road, 02146. Telephone: (617) 731-5020. Director: Nancy Fuller. Preschool and elementary day school with summer program. Full-time staff: 10. Part-time staff: 5. Current enrollment: 22. Maximum enrollment: 25. Ages served: 3-10. Services: individual and group tutoring, academic and psychological testing; academic, psychological, and family counseling; individual, group, occupational, speech, and language therapy; individual psychotherapy, adaptive physical education, medical services, parent group, special education program.

Cambridge: Cambridge Montessori School, 161 Garden Street, 02138. Telephone: (617) 492-3410. Director: Jacqueline Melton Scott. Preschool and elementary day school with limited services; summer camp. Ages served: 1½-14. Grades served: preschool-8. Current enrollment: 140. Maximum enrollment: 140. Full-time staff: 10. Part-time staff: 13 including 7 foster grandparents. Scholarships/financial aid available. Services: individual and group tutoring, academic testing, psychological counseling; physical and occupational therapy. Recreation: gym, swimming, playground. Notes: Special department for learning disabilities.

Cambridge: Castle School, 298 Harvard Street, 02139. Telephone: (617) 354-5410. Director: Linda Corwin. Residential secondary school with limited services; summer program. Ages served: 13-17. Current enrollment: 7. Maximum enrollment: 12. Full-time staff: 14. Part-time staff: 4-6. Services: individual tutoring, academic testing; academic, individual, group, and family counseling; adaptive physical education, prevocational training, work-study, job placement, medical services. Recreation: community and inhouse activities, field and camping trips, sports. Notes: Serves emotionally disturbed adolescents with behavior problems. Priority given to Cambridge/Somerville area children.

Cambridge: Charles River Academy, Five Clinton Street, 02139. Telephone: (617) 868-5380. Director of Residence: Byron Martin. Twelve-month day and residential secondary school. Ages served: 14-21. Grades served: 9-12. Current enrollment: 30. Maximum enrollment: 40. Full-time staff: 14. Part-time staff: 2. Services: individual and group tutoring, academic testing, psychological and family counseling, vocational training, work-study, job placement, computer studies. Recreation: sports, skiing, camping, hiking, arts and crafts, bowling, school newspaper.

Charlestown: Oliver Holden Academy, Eight Pearl Street, 02129. Telephone: (617) 242-3940. Director: Janice I. Brenner. Elementary and secondary day school with limited services. Ages served: 12-18. Grades served: 6-12. Current enrollment: 36. Maximum enrollment: 80. Full-time staff: 5. Part-time staff: 3. Services: individual and group tutoring, academic testing, academic and psychological counseling, work-study, vocational training, computer and resource classes. Recreation: game room, field trips, physical education, woodworking.

Concord: Concord-Assabet School, Inc., P.O. Box 114, 01742. Telephone: (617) 263-1750. Executive Director: Stephen A. Joffe. Females only secondary boarding school with limited services; summer program. Ages served: 13-18. Grades served: 9-12. Current enrollment: 16. Maximum enrollment: 16. Full-time staff: 18. Part-time staff: 4. Services: individual and group tutoring, academic testing, work-study, family and milieu therapy; group, individual, and family counseling; psychological testing and medical facilities available in community. Recreation: biking, swimming, museums, whale watching. Notes: Serves emotionally disturbed adolescents.

East Sandwich: Riverview School, 587 Route 6A, 02537. Telephone: (617) 888-0489. Executive Director: Joanne Brooks. Day and boarding school. Ages served: 12-17. Current enrollment: 109 residential; 10 day. Full-time staff: 75. Part-time staff: 8. Limited scholarships/financial aid available. Services: individual and group tutoring, academic and psychological testing, prevocational training, work-study, limited job placement. Recreation: gymnasium, soccer, softball, tennis, golf, swimming, roller-skating. Notes: All students have learning disabilities or language disorders.

Framingham: Reed Academy, One Winch Street, 01701. Telephone: (617) 877-1222. Executive Director: Edward Cohen. Elementary and secondary boarding school with summer camp. Ages served: at enrollment 7-14; may attend until 21. Grades served: ungraded. Current enrollment: 15. Maximum enrollment: 15. Full-time staff: 16. Part-time staff: 10. Services: individual and group tutoring, academic and psychological testing; academic, psychological, and family counseling; physical and occupational therapy, adaptive physical education, vocational training, work-study, medical services, basic living skills. Notes: Serves children with moderate to extreme emotional difficulties. Goal is to promote developmental and academic growth as well as behavioral change.

Hardwick: Eagle Hill School, Old Petersham Road, 01037. Telephone: (413) 477-6000. Headmaster: George O. Thomson. Elementary and secondary boarding school with summer program and camp. Ages served: 8-18. Grades served: 3-12. Current enrollment: 88. Maximum enrollment: 88. Full-time staff: 39. Services: individual and group tutoring, academic and psychological testing, academic and psychological counseling, medical facilities, adaptive physical education, prevocational training, remedial program. Recreation: sports, gymnasium, playing fields, pool, tennis court, ski slope, ropes course, darkroom, student lounge, arts/crafts center, island in Maine for wilderness program. Notes: Many students return to traditional schools. Ninety-five percent of graduates attend college or technical school.

Lenox: Valleyhead, Inc., P.O. Box 714, Reservoir Road, 01240. Telephone: (413) 637-3635. Director: Matthew J. Merritt, Jr. Females only elementary and secondary boarding school with summer program and camp. Ages served: 10 and up. Grades served: ungraded. Current enrollment: 66. Maximum enrollment: 66. Full-time staff: 60. Part-time staff: 2. Services: individual and group tutoring, academic and psychological testing; academic, psychological, individual, group, and family counseling; physical and occupational therapy, adaptive physical education, vocational training, work-study, job placement, medical services. Recreation: tennis, pool, athletic fields.

Lexington: Krebs School Foundation, 453 Concord Avenue, 02173. Telephone: (617) 862-7323. Director: Ida G. Krebs. Elementary and secondary day school with summer program. Ages served: 5-20. Grades served: ungraded. Current enrollment: 42. Maximum enrollment: 54. Full-time staff: 11. Part-time staff: 7. Services: individual and group tutoring, academic and psychological testing, academic and family counseling, vocational training, speech and occupational therapy, adaptive physical education, motor development; computer, science, and music programs. Recreation: gymnasium, intramural sports, summer swim program, organized recess activities, drama, field trips.

Lincoln: The Carroll School, P.O. Box 280, Baker Bridge Road, 01773. Telephone: (617) 259-8342. Head: Margaret Logue. Elementary and secondary day school with summer program and camp. Ages served: 6-19. Grades served: readiness-12. Current enrollment: 190. Maximum enrollment: 190. Full-time staff: 65. Part-time staff: 6. Scholarships/financial aid available. Services: individual and group tutoring, academic testing, academic and psychological counseling, adaptive physical education, work-study, medical services, speech and language therapy. Recreation: sports, Outward Bound, arts, film, video, drama. Notes: For dyslexic and language disabled students with average or above average intelligence.

Ludlow: Children's Language Institute, Inc., Box 211, 01056. Telephone: (413) 589-9161. Executive Director: Kathleen K. Mullins. Preschool and elementary day school. Ages served: 3-14. Grades served: ungraded. Current enrollment: 24. Maximum enrollment: 36. Full-time staff: 17. Part-time staff: 5. Services: individual and group tutoring, academic and psychological testing, psychological and family counseling, physical and occupational therapy, adaptive physical education, speech and language therapy and evaluations. Recreation: swimming. Notes: Serves language disabled children who also have other learning and physical problems. Teachers are speech language pathologists.

Methuen: St. Ann's Home, Inc., 100A Haverhill Street, 01844. Telephone: (617) 682-5276. Executive Director: Patrick T. Villani. Elementary and secondary day and boarding school with limited services. Ages served: 6-17. Grades served: ungraded. Current enrollment: 105. Maximum enrollment: 110. Full-time staff: 125. Part-time staff: 5. Services: individual and group tutoring, academic and psychological testing; academic, psychological, and family counseling; adaptive physical education, medical services. Recreation: arts and crafts, athletics, riding, swimming, field trips. Notes: Serves children with learning disabilities but primarily for emotionally disturbed children.

Needham: Walker Home and School, 1968 Central Avenue, 02192. Telephone: (617) 449-4500. Associate Director: Floyd J. Alwon. Males only elementary and secondary day and boarding school with summer program. Ages served: 6-14. Grades served: ungraded. Current enrollment: 52. Maximum enrollment: 53. Full-time staff: 65. Scholarships/financial aid available. Services: individual and group tutoring, academic and psychological testing, psychological and family counseling, medical services. Recreation: after school clubs, community activities. Notes: Serves the emotionally disturbed and learning disabled.

New Marlborough: The Kolburne Schools, Inc., Southfield Road, 01230. Telephone: (413) 229-8787. Executive Director: Jeane K. Weinstein. Elementary and secondary boarding school with summer program. Ages served: 7-22. Grades served: kindergarten-12. Current enrollment: 130. Maximum enrollment: 136. Full-time staff: 165. Part-time staff: 10. Scholarships/financial aid available. Services: individual and group tutoring, academic and psychological testing; academic, psychological, and family counseling; physical, speech, and occupational therapy; adaptive physical education, vocational training, work-study, medical services. Recreation: gymnasiums, pool, ball fields, tennis courts, lakes, 1,500-acre campus.

Norfolk: Leland Hall, 27 Leland Road, 02056. Telephone: (617) 528-0882. Headmaster: Robert A. O'Meara. Director of Programs/Admissions: Arlene O'Meara. Elementary and secondary day and boarding school. Ages served: 6-22. Grades served: 1-12, post high school program. Current enrollment: 75. Maximum enrollment: 100. Full-time staff: 17. Part-time staff: 5. Services: individual and group tutoring, psychological testing, vocational training, work-study, job placement, speech and language therapy, college preparatory program, cooperative college courses at Dean Junior College, art courses, music, physical education. Recreation: racquetball, soccer, karate, basketball, swimming, skiing, biking.

North Brookfield: Valley View School, Oakham Road, Box 338, 01535. Telephone: (617) 867-6505. Director: Philip G. Spiva. Males only elementary and secondary boarding school with limited services. Ages served: 12-16. Grades served: 7-12. Current enrollment: 34. Maximum enrollment: 34. Full-time staff: 28. Part-time staff: 6. Services: individual and group tutoring, academic and psychological testing, academic and psychological counseling, medical services. Recreation: computer center, woodworking shop, gym, athletic field, camping, scuba, biking, hang gliding, rock climbing. Notes: Provides a therapeutic educational environment for boys functioning below their academic and social potential.

North Chelmsford: Lighthouse School, P.O. Box 99, 01863. Telephone: (617) 256-9300. Executive Director: Michael Pappafagos. Day school. Ages served: 3-22. Grades served: ungraded. Current enrollment: 100. Maximum enrollment: 100. Full-time staff: 30. Part-time staff: 35. Services: individual and group tutoring, academic and psychological testing; academic, psychological, and family counseling; physical, occupational, and speech therapy; adaptive physical education, vocational training, work-study, job placement, medical services. Recreation: intramural sports, camping.

Northfield: Linden Hill School, S. Mountain Road, 01360. Telephone: (413) 498-2906. Headmaster: William F. Patterson. Males only elementary boarding school.

Ages served: 10-14. Grades served: ungraded. Current enrollment: 30. Maximum enrollment: 30. Full-time staff: 10. Services: individual and group tutoring, academic and psychological testing, adaptive physical education, remediation of developmental dyslexia, Orton-Gillingham teaching method. Recreation: soccer, gymnastics, skiing, hockey, swimming, tennis, running.

Pittsfield: Berkshire Learning Center, 823 North Street, P.O. Box 1224, 01202. Telephone: (413) 442-5531. Executive Director: Marianne E. Rud. Males only secondary and adult boarding school with summer program. Ages served: 13-29. Grades served: ungraded. Current enrollment: 30. Maximum enrollment: 30. Full-time staff: 40. Part-time staff: 1. Services: individual and group tutoring, academic and psychological testing; academic, psychological, and family counseling; medical services, prevocational and vocational training, work-study, job placement, psychotherapy; physical, occupational, and family therapy; group reality training. Recreation: Outward Bound, physical education, basketball, swimming, skiing, fishing, bowling, roller-skating, weight lifting.

Prides Crossing: Landmark School, 412 Hale Street, 01965-0417. Telephone: (617) 927-4440. Headmaster: Charles Drake. Elementary and secondary day and boarding school with summer program, camp, and precollege year. Ages served: 8-21. Grades served: ungraded. Current enrollment: 375. Maximum enrollment: 395. Full-time staff: 260. Part-time staff: 5. Scholarships/financial aid available. Services: individual tutoring, academic and psychological testing, academic and psychological counseling, adaptive physical education, vocational training, limited work-study, job placement, medical services. Notes: Exclusively for the learning disabled. Student/teacher ratio 2½:1.

Randolph: Boston School Serving Deaf and Aphasic Students, 800 N. Main Street, 02368. Telephone: (617) 963-8150. Principal: Sr. Bernadette Kenney. Preschool, elementary, and secondary four-day boarding school. Ages served: 3½-21. Grades served: preschool-high school. Current enrollment: 212. Maximum enrollment: 225. Full-time staff: 79. Part-time staff: 4. Services: individual and group tutoring, academic and psychological testing, psychological counseling, adaptive physical education, vocational training, work-study. Recreation: basketball, track, softball, volleyball, bowling.

Rutland: Devereux School, Miles Road, 01543. Telephone: (617) 886-4746. Director: Frederic A. Hervey. Preschool and elementary boarding school with summer program. Ages served: 6-16. Grades served: kindergarten-8. Current enrollment: 106. Full-time staff: 115. Part-time staff: 30. Services: group tutoring, academic and psychological testing, psychological counseling, medical services, adaptive physical education, prevocational training. Recreation: tennis, pool, riding, basketball, soccer.

South Walpole: Massasoit School, Inc., 1852 Washington Street, 02071. Telephone: (617) 668-8200. Director of Education: Paul Stanish. Elementary, secondary, and adult day school. Ages served: 13-22. Grades served: 6-12. Current enrollment: 40. Maximum enrollment: 50. Full-time staff: 21. Part-time staff: 3. Services: individual and group tutoring, academic and psychological testing; academic, psychological, and family counseling; physical therapy, adaptive physical education, vocational training, work-study, job placement, medical services. Recreation: arts and crafts, team sports, outings.

Springfield: The EWT School of Experiment With Travel, Inc., 281 Franklin Street, Box 2452, 01101. Telephone: (413) 788-0973. Director: Pamela Holliday. Secondary day school. Ages served: 12-18. Grades served: 1-13. Current enrollment: 18. Maximum enrollment: 25. Full-time staff: 8. Part-time staff: 3. Services: individual and group tutoring, academic and psychological testing; academic, psychological, and family counseling; adaptive physical education, vocational training, work-study, job placement, education program that integrates wilderness adventures into academic and clinical programs. Recreation: caving, rock climbing, scuba, white water rafting, canoeing, kayaking, hiking, pioneering, rescue training. Notes: Serves primarily socially and emotionally maladaptive adolescents.

Sudbury: Willow Hill School, 98 Haynes Road, 01776. Telephone: (617) 443-2581. Director: Jane-Elisabeth Jakuc. Secondary day school. Ages served: 10-19. Grades served: 5-12. Current enrollment: 30. Maximum enrollment: 35. Full-time staff: 10. Part-time staff: 2. Scholarships/financial aid available. Services: individual tutoring, academic and psychological testing; academic, psychological, and family counseling; adaptive physical education, work-study, job placement, medical services, career education, drama and fine arts program, individual foreign language instruction, parent support group, college placement service, SAT administration, class size 6-8. Recreation: sports, adapted Outward Bound program, musical productions, silversmithing, painting, pottery, enameling. Notes: Offers small, supportive environment for students of average to superior intelligence who cannot succeed in "regular" school environment.

Waltham: Chapel Hill-Chauncy Hall School, 785 Beaver Street, 02254. Telephone: (617) 894-2644. Headmaster: Sean O'Neil. Secondary day and boarding school with limited services; summer drama program. Ages served: 14-19. Grades served: 9-12. Current enrollment: 172. Maximum enrollment: 180. Full-time staff: 33. Scholarships/financial aid available. Services: Individually Guided Studies program, individual and group tutoring, academic testing and counseling, college counseling, untimed SAT, nurse. Recreation: athletic program including basketball, soccer, lacrosse, tennis, racquetball, squash; weight training, dance, theater. Notes: Individually Guided Studies program limited to 24 learning disabled students in ninth and tenth grade.

Wendell: Maple Valley School, P.O. Box 248, 01379. Telephone: (617) 544-6913. Executive Director: Mitchell Kosh. Secondary boarding school with summer program. Ages served: 13-18. Current enrollment: 24. Maximum enrollment: 24. Services: individual and group tutoring, academic and psychological testing; academic, psychological, and family counseling; vocational training, medical services.

Westfield: East Mountain Center, 91 E. Mountain Road, 01085. Telephone: (413) 568-0152. Executive Director: V. Pauline Curry. Preschool. Ages served: 3-7. Current enrollment: 40. Maximum enrollment: 50. Full-time staff: 20. Part-time staff: 2. Scholarships/financial aid available. Services: individual and group tutoring, academic testing, family counseling; speech, language, physical, and occupational therapy; adaptive physical education, medical services.

West Newton: Clearway School, 61 Chestnut Street, 02165. Telephone: (617) 964-6186. Administrator: Victoria Neeson. Secondary school. Ages served: 10-18. Grades served: ungraded. Current enrollment: 21. Maximum enrollment: 24. Full-time staff: 6. Part-time staff: 4. Services: individual and group tutoring, academic testing, family counseling, vocational training. Recreation: art, music, gymnastics, karate, aerobic dancing, video taping, camping, woodworking, power and motorcycle mechanics, computers.

West Newton: Little People's/Learning Prep School, 1507 Washington Street, 02165. Telephone: (617) 965-0764. Director: Nancy Rosoff. Elementary and secondary day school. Ages served: 6-22. Grades served: kindergarten-high school. Current enrollment: 200. Maximum enrollment: 300. Full-time staff: 80. Part-time staff: 10. Services: individual and group tutoring, academic and psychological testing; academic, psychological, and family counseling; physical, occupational, and speech therapy; adaptive physical education, vocational training, work-study, job placement, medical services, career education.

West Springfield: Our Lady of Providence Children's Center, Inc., 2112 Riverdale Street, 01089. Telephone: (413) 788-7366. Principal: Tom Philpott. Elementary and secondary day and boarding school with summer program and camp. Ages served: 6-15. Grades served: kindergarten-9. Current enrollment: 44. Maximum enrollment: 60. Full-time staff: 20. Part-time staff: 25. Services: individual and group tutoring, academic and psychological testing; academic, psychological, and family counseling; adaptive physical education, medical services; physical, individual, group, speech, and family therapy. Recreation: pool, gymnasium, basketball, baseball, tennis, playing fields, Project Adventure course, field trips.

Williamstown: The HighCroft School, 163 Gale Road, 01267. Telephone: (413) 458-8136. Headmaster: David Wilson Milne. Elementary and secondary boarding school with limited services; summer program. Ages served: 9-19. Grades served: 4-12, post high school program. Current enrollment: 84. Maximum enrollment: 84. Full-time staff: teacher/student ratio 1:2. Limited scholarships/financial aid available to returning students. Services: individual and group tutoring, small classes, academic testing and counseling, college placement, English as a second language, Orton-Gillingham reading correction program. Recreation: soccer, basketball, baseball, volleyball, running, skiing, swimming, tennis. Notes: Serves the student of average or above average ability not reaching full potential.

MASSACHUSETTS

Summer Camps and Programs

Brewster: Favorite, Box 1018, 02631. Telephone: (617) 896-3831. Permanent mailing address: Patriots' Trail Girl Scout Council, Six St. James Avenue, Boston, MA 02116. Telephone: (617) 482-1078. Director: Peggy Mellors. Females only residential camp with limited services. Ages served: 11-17. Grades served: 6-12. Maximum enrollment: 100. Scholarships/financial aid available. Medical services. Recreation: swimming, sailing, crafts.

Great Barrington: Half Moon Camps, Inc., P.O. Box 188, 01230. Telephone: (413) 528-0940. Director: Edward Mann. Males only residential camp with academic program and limited services. Ages served: 6-15. Grades served: kindergarten-10. Maximum enrollment: 125; 20 learning disabled. Full-time staff: 30. Services: individual and group tutoring, academic testing, adaptive physical education, medical services. Academic programs: math, reading, English, spelling, study skills. Recreation: swimming, hiking, riding, field trips, nature study, crafts, drama, camping, photography, team athletics, computers. Notes: Individual sports instruction.

Springfield: Springfield College Day Camp, Box 1720, Springfield College, 01107. Telephone: (413) 782-0461. Director: Paul Katz. Day camp with limited services. Ages served: 6-12. Grades served: kindergarten-6. Scholarships/financial aid available. Recreation: camping, nature study, swimming, archery, crafts, drama, music, adventure programs. Notes: All children must be mainstreamed in school to be accepted by camp.

West Stockbridge: Camp Kingsmont, Route 2, 01266. Telephone: (413) 232-8518. Directors: Lloyd O. Appleton, Janet Rohrbacher, Richard Rohrbacher. Residential camp with academic program and limited services. Ages served: 7-19. Grades served: all. Maximum enrollment: 350. Full-time staff: 90. Part-time staff: 10. Scholarships/financial aid available. Services: individual tutoring, psychological counseling, adaptive physical education. Academic programs: math, reading, English, spelling, study skills, college prep courses. Recreation: swimming, hiking, riding, field trips, nature study, crafts, drama, camping, photography, team athletics, bicycling.

College and University Special Programs and Services

American International College: 1000 State Street, Springfield, MA 01109. Total enrollment: 1,200-1,500. LD students: 100. Special services: readers, individual tutoring, academic and psychological counseling, pass/fail option, special English course, special examinations, ombudsman, taped books, training in study skills, student resource center.

- **Special program:** Supportive Services Program for Undergraduates with Learning Disabilities. Must fulfill regular and special admissions requirements. Special requirements include verification of learning disability through recent diagnostic tests and an interview. Students may take a reduced load of four instead of five regular courses. Coordinator of Supportive Learning Services: Mary M. Saltus. Telephone: (413) 737-7000 ext. 430.

Center/clinic: Curtis Blake Center. Telephone: (413) 737-7000 ext. 430. Director: Mary M. Saltus. Not open to public. Ages served: college.

Bentley College: Beaver and Forest Streets, Waltham, MA 02254. Total enrollment: 7,000. LD students: 15. Special services: limited individual tutoring, training in study skills, academic and psychological counseling, taped books, untimed examinations. Contact: Donna Melillo, Counseling Psychologist. Telephone: (617) 891-2274.

Boston College: Chestnut Hill, MA 02167. Total enrollment: 11,700. Total LD students: 50. Special services: limited subject tutoring, academic and psychological counseling. Contact: David John Smith, Associate Director, University Counseling Services. Telephone: (617) 552-3310.

Bradford College: S. Main Street, Haverhill, MA 01830. Total enrollment: 400. LD students: 25-28. Special services: individual and group tutoring, training in study skills, academic and psychological counseling, taped books, untimed or modified examinations with instructor approval, student resource center, support group, ombudsman, writing center.

- **Special program:** College Learning Program. Focuses on reading, writing, and study skills. Offers workshops in time management, organizational skills, concentration and memory, and note taking. Students participate in program while they pursue regular college courses and are gradually phased out as they progress. Must meet regular and special admissions requirements. Special requirements include verification of learning disability through diagnostic tests, writing sample, recommendations, and interview. Director: Diane D. Waldron. Telephone: (617) 372-7161 ext. 318 or 319.

Brandeis University: Waltham, MA 02154. Total enrollment: 2,600. LD students: 10-20. Special services: individual tutoring, training in study skills, academic and psychological counseling, taped books, special examinations, diagnostic testing, medical support. Contact: Jana Nidiffer, Assistant Dean. Telephone: (617) 647-2111.

Clark University: 950 Main Street, Worcester, MA 01610. Special services: individual tutoring, training in study skills, academic and psychological counseling, taped books from Recording for the Blind, special examinations, student resource center, readers by individual arrangement, diagnostic testing, scholarships, ombudsman, assistance in transition to college. Contact: Renee L. Goldberg, Coordinator, Services for Learning Disabled Students. Telephone: (617) 793-7468.

MASSACHUSETTS

Center/clinic: Academic Advising Center. Telephone: (617) 793-7468. Coordinator: Renee L. Goldberg. Not open to public. Grades served: college.

Curry College: Blue Hill Avenue, Milton, MA 02186. Special services: individual and group tutoring, training in study skills, academic counseling, taped books, special examinations, student resource center, diagnostic testing.

- **Special program:** Program for Advancement of Learning (PAL). Individually designed programs for LD students, in conjunction with regular full-time college curriculum. Goal of program is to help students become independent learners within one year. Must meet regular and special admissions requirements. Special requirements include verification of learning disability through diagnostic tests and a conference with LD staff. Director: Gertrude M. Webb. Telephone: (617) 333-0500 ext. 250 or 270.

Center/clinic: Learning Center. Telephone: (617) 333-0500 ext. 250 or 270. Director: Gertrude M. Webb. Open to public for diagnostic testing. Ages served: college students; all ages diagnostic testing.

Labouré College: 2124 Dorchester Avenue, Boston, MA 02124. Total enrollment: 681. Special services: group tutoring, academic counseling. Contact: Joann Nelson, Financial Aid Officer. Telephone: (617) 296-8300 ext. 4014.

Lesley College: 29 Everett Street, Cambridge, MA 02238. Special services: group tutoring, training in study skills, academic and psychological counseling, student resource center, ombudsman. Contact: Kathryn Morgenthau, Advisor, Students with Special Needs. Telephone: (617) 868-9600.

Middlesex Community College: Springs Road, Bedford, MA 01730. Total enrollment: 2,100. LD students: 50. Special services: individual and group tutoring, training in study skills, academic and psychological counseling, taped books, special examinations, readers, diagnostic testing, scholarships, support group, part-time learning specialist. Contact: Stanley Hitron, Director of Special Services. Telephone: (617) 275-8910 ext. 341.

- **Special program:** MCC Transition Program. Self-contained, two-year certificate program. Offers a core curriculum of specially designed courses in consumer life, personal and social development, and occupational exploration and preparation. Includes internships in business and industry two days per week. Must be a Massachusetts resident. Learning disability must be verified through recent diagnostic tests. Director: Pat Seppanen. Telephone: (617) 272-7342.

Mount Wachusett Community College: 444 Green Street, Gardner, MA 01440. Special services: individual and group tutoring, training in study skills, academic and psychological counseling, taped books, special examinations, student resource center, readers, diagnostic testing, ombudsman, developmental courses. Contact: Stephen A. Zona, Learning Disabilities Specialist. Telephone: (617) 632-6600.

Center/clinic: Learning Center. Telephone: (617) 632-6600 ext. 209. Director: Stuart Shuman. Not open to public. Services: oral/untimed exams, note takers, taped lectures, readers, tutoring, counseling, learning disabilities specialist.

North Shore Community College: Essex Street, Beverly, MA 01915. Special services: individual and group tutoring, training in study skills, academic and psychological counseling, study and counseling centers, untimed testing with faculty approval. Contact: Jean Keith, Assistant Coordinator, Academic Assistance Department. Telephone: (617) 927-4850 ext. 555.

Regis College: 235 Wellesley Street, Weston, MA 02193. Special services: individual tutoring, training in study skills, academic and psychological counseling, special examinations, diagnostic testing, scholarships. Contact: S. Loretto Hegarty, Director. Telephone: (617) 893-1820 ext. 240.

Salem State College: 352 Lafayette Street, Salem, MA 01970. Special services: individual and group tutoring, academic and psychological counseling, taped books, student resource center, readers, diagnostic testing, ombudsman; training in study, reading, writing, and math skills. Contact: Joanne Allen, Coordinator of Community Relations, Learning Center. Telephone: (617) 745-0556 ext. 2636.

Center/clinic: Learning Center. Telephone: (617) 745-0556 ext. 2629. Director: Jeffrey Bright. Not open to public. Services: diagnostic testing, tutorial services.

Simmons College: 300 The Fenway, Boston, MA 02115. Special services: individual and group tutoring, training in study skills, academic and psychological counseling, special examinations, student resource center, readers, ombudsman. Contact: Helen Boulware Moore, Director, Supportive Instructional Services. Telephone: (617) 738-2137.

Center/clinic: Supportive Instructional Services. Telephone: (617) 738-2137. Director: Helen Boulware Moore. Not open to public. Grades served: college.

Southeastern Massachusetts University: North Dartmouth, MA 02743. Total enrollment: 5,500. Special services: individual and group tutoring, academic counseling, taped books. Contact: Carole Johnson, Director, Disabled Student Services. Telephone: (617) 999-8711.

University of Massachusetts: Boston, MA 02125. Special services: individual tutoring, training in study skills, academic and psychological counseling, taped books, readers. Contact: Andrea Schein, Director, Student Disabled Center. Telephone: (617) 929-8000.

MASSACHUSETTS

Hospital Clinics

Boston: Boston University Medical Center-University Hospital, Daniels Speech and Language Clinic, 75 E. Newton Street, 02118. Telephone: (617) 437-1027. Contact: Appointment Secretary. Outpatient and inpatient program. Ages served: birth-adult. Services: diagnostic testing, academic testing, parent counseling, speech and language therapy.

Brighton: Kennedy Memorial Hospital for Children, 30 Warren Street, 02135. Telephone: (617) 254-2800. Contact: Appointment Desk. Outpatient and day school program. Ages served: birth-22 hospital; 3-16 day school. Services: diagnostic testing, academic and psychological testing, individual and group tutoring; academic, psychological, and parent counseling; speech, language, physical, and occupational therapy; adaptive physical education, social services.

Fitchburg: Burbank Hospital, Speech, Language, and Hearing Center, Nichols Road, 01420. Telephone: (617) 343-5005. Contact: Joan E. Lada, Clinical Director. Outpatient and inpatient program. Ages served: all. Services: diagnostic testing, parent counseling; group, speech, language, physical, and occupational therapy.

Gardner: Henry Heywood Memorial Hospital, 242 Green Street, 01440. Telephone: (617) 632-3420. Contacts: Cheryl Ethier, Loretta DeCrow. Outpatient and inpatient program. Ages served: all. Services: speech, language, and occupational therapy.

Holyoke: Holyoke Hospital, Inc., Speech and Hearing Center, 575 Beech Street, 01040. Telephone: (413) 536-5221 ext. 341. Contact: Mrs. Esmat Ezzat, Director. Outpatient, inpatient, and after school program. Ages served: all. Services: diagnostic testing, individual tutoring, speech and language therapy, audiological testing, central auditory processing.

Stoneham: New England Memorial Hospital, Human Services Department, Five Woodland Road, 02180. Telephone: (617) 665-1740 ext. 755. Contact: Felton Pervier, Assistant Director. Outpatient and inpatient program. Ages served: all. Services: diagnostic testing, psychological testing, psychological and parent counseling; group, speech, language, physical, and occupational therapy; social services.

Worcester: University of Massachusetts Medical Center, Learning Problems Clinic, Department of Pediatrics, 55 Lake Avenue, North, 01605. Telephone: (617) 856-3951. Contact: Martha C. Starr. Outpatient program. Ages served: 5-18. Services: diagnostic testing, academic and psychological testing; occupational and physical therapy evaluations; evaluations in all medical specialities arranged within the institution. Notes: All children evaluated by a physician, a psychologist, and a learning disabilities specialist.

Other Services

New Bedford: I.H. Schwartz Children's Rehabilitation Center, 374 Rockdale Avenue, 02740. Telephone: (617) 996-3391. Executive Director: Agnes I. Raposa. Day and summer program with limited services. Ages served: birth-16. Current enrollment: 189. Maximum enrollment: 200. Full-time staff: 32. Part-time staff: 25. Scholarships/financial aid available. Services: physical, occupational, speech, and language therapy; medical services, audiological evaluations.

Wellesley: Center for Teaching/Learning of Mathematics, 11 River Street, 02181. Telephone: (617) 235-7200 or 877-7895. Director: Mahesh C. Sharma. Clinic. After school and summer program. Ages served: 6 and up. Full-time staff: 2. Services: individual and group tutoring, diagnostic testing, parent counseling, correspondence course.

MICHIGAN

Offices of Organizations Concerned with Learning Disabilities

ACLD, Inc.: 20777 Randall, Farmington, MI 48024. Telephone: (313) 471-0790. President: Sylvia Perttunen.

Council for Exceptional Children: President: Mary Campbell, 3161 Lewis Avenue, Ida, MI 48140. Telephone: Office (313) 269-3875; Home (313) 269-6225.

Easter Seal Society of Michigan, Inc.: 4065 Saladin Drive, S.E., Grand Rapids, MI 49506. Acting Director: Susan Quinn. Telephone: (616) 942-2081.

Orton Dyslexia Society: P.O. Box 1612, Kalamazoo, MI 49005. President: Betty Hartmann. Telephone: (616) 345-2661.

State Department of Education Learning Disabilities Personnel

Edward L. Birch, Director, Special Education Services, Michigan Department of Education, P.O. Box 30008, Lansing, MI 48909. Telephone: (517) 373-9433. Learning disabilities consultant: Deborah Livingston-White. Telephone: (517) 373-6325.

Private and Day Schools

Detroit: Lutheran School for the Deaf, 6861 E. Nevada Avenue, 48234. Telephone: (313) 368-1220. Executive Director: Rev. Rodney R. Rynearson. Elementary and secondary day and boarding school. Ages served: 6-18. Current enrollment: 151. Maximum enrollment: 600. Full-time staff: 43. Part-time staff: 4. Scholarships/financial aid available. Services: individual and group tutoring, academic and psychological testing, psychological and family counseling, adap-

MICHIGAN

tive physical education. Recreation: YMCA program, interscholastic sports. Notes: Serves hearing as well as deaf children.

Detroit: Precious Blood, 13436 Grove, 48235. Telephone: (313) 864-6087. Principal: Catherine Myszka. Elementary day school with limited services. Ages served: 6-13. Grades served: kindergarten-8. Current enrollment: 30. Maximum enrollment: 30. Full-time staff: 2. Services: academic and psychological testing, adaptive physical education, individualized classes, two classrooms for students with learning disabilities.

Grand Rapids: Christian Learning Center, 2520 Eastern Avenue, S.E., 49507. Telephone: (616) 245-8388. Director of Services: Richard H. Berends. Elementary and secondary day school. Ages served: 5-18. Grades served: kindergarten-12. Current enrollment: 80. Full-time staff: 5. Part-time staff: 2. Scholarships/financial aid available. Services: individual tutoring, academic and psychological testing, psychological and family counseling.

Harper Woods: Our Lady Queen of Peace, 21101 Bournemouth, 48225. Telephone: (313) 881-3629. Principal: Sr. John Ann Mulvern. Elementary day school with summer program. Ages served: 6-15. Grades served: 1-8. Current enrollment: 30. Maximum enrollment: 30. Full-time staff: 2. Part-time staff: 5. Services: individual and group tutoring, academic and psychological testing, academic counseling, adaptive physical education.

Summer Camps and Programs

Delton: Circle Pines Center, 8650 Mullen Road, 49046. Telephone: (616) 623-5555. Program Coordinator: Mark Ottenad. Day and residential camp with limited services. Ages served: 8-18. Grades served: 3-12. Maximum enrollment: 100. Full-time staff: 30. Scholarships/financial aid available. Services: medical services. Recreation: camping, hiking, field trips, nature study, swimming, team sports, crafts, dance, drama, music, photography. Notes: Daily schedule of cooperative work-projects.

Dryden: Camp Niobe, 4580 Mill Road, 48428. Telephone: (313) 796-2018. Permanent mailing address: 18443 Muirland, Detroit, MI 48221. Telephone: (313) 864-0717. Director: Joanne Mandel. Residential camp with limited services. Ages served: 6-14. Grades served: 1-8. Maximum enrollment: 25-30. Full-time staff: 12. Part-time staff: 3-4. Scholarships/financial aid available. Services: occupational, recreation, art, and music therapy; adaptive physical education, medical services. Recreation: camping, hiking, field trips, nature study, swimming, sailing, team sports, crafts, dance, drama, music, newspaper, cooking, animal care. Notes: For children with learning problems who need a structured and supportive environment.

Frankfort: Crystalaire, 1327 S. Shore, 49635. Telephone: (616) 352-7589. Director: David Reid. Residential camp with limited services. Ages served: 8-17. Maximum enrollment: 88. Full-time staff: 24. Limited scholarships/financial aid available. Recreation: camping, hiking, riding, swimming, sailing, team sports, crafts, informal drama, photography. Notes: Learning disabled campers mainstreamed into general camp population.

Greenville: Camp Anna Behrens, 9841 Colby Road, 48838. Telephone: (616) 949-4475. Permanent mailing address: Michigan Trails Girl Scouts, 2915 Hall Street, S.E., Grand Rapids, MI 49506. Director: Diane Jolliffe. Females only residential camp. Ages served: 13-21. Grades served: 7-12. Maximum enrollment: 10. Full-time staff: 2. Part-time staff: 6. Scholarships/financial aid available. Medical services. Recreation: camping, hiking, nature study, riding, swimming, sailing, archery, team sports, crafts, dance, drama, music, photography.

Hersey: Eagle Village Camp, Route 1, Box 300, 49639. Telephone: (616) 832-4614. Permanent telephone: (616) 832-2234. Director, Alternative Programs: Jean Hainley. Camp Director: Cathey Prudhomme. Residential camp with limited services. Ages served: 7-17. Maximum enrollment: 100. Full-time staff: 4. Part-time staff: 30. Limited scholarships/financial aid available. Services: family counseling. Recreation: camping, hiking, nature study, riding, swimming, archery, team sports, crafts.

Linden: Camp Linden, 5285 Hogan Road, 48451. Telephone: (313) 735-5427. Permanent mailing address: Huron Valley Girl Scout Council, P.O. Box 539, 19 N. Hamilton, Ypsilanti, MI 48197. Telephone: (313) 483-2370. Camp Administrator: Kathy Treiber. Females only residential camp with limited services. Ages served: 9-17. Grades served: 4-12. Maximum enrollment: 160. Full-time staff: 1. Part-time staff: 36. Scholarships/financial aid available for registered Girl Scouts. Recreation: camping, hiking, nature study, riding, swimming, sailing, archery, team sports, crafts, dance, drama, music, photography, computers.

Mayville: Camp Happy Hollow, Inc., 2315 Harmon Lake Road, 48744. Telephone: (517) 673-3666. Permanent mailing address: P.O. Box 131, Plymouth, MI 48170. Telephone: (313) 459-1774. Executive Director: Peter D. Schweitzer. Residential camp with limited services. Ages served: 8 and up. Maximum enrollment: 64. Full-time staff: 30. Scholarships/financial aid available. Recreation: swimming, hiking, field trips, nature study, crafts, camping, confidence course.

Northport: Shady Trails Camp, 49670. Telephone: (616) 386-5111. Permanent mailing address: 1111 E. Catherine, Ann Arbor, MI 48109. Telephone: (313) 764-4493. Director: Gary J. Rentschler. Residential camp with limited services. Ages served: 8-18. Maximum enrollment: 100. Full-time staff: 2. Part-time staff: 60. Scholarships/financial aid available. Services: adaptive physical education, speech and language therapy. Recreation: swimming, hiking, field trips, nature study, crafts, team athletics.

MICHIGAN

College and University Special Programs and Services

Bay de Noc Community College: College Avenue, Escanaba, MI 49829. Total enrollment: 1,800. LD students: 5. Special services: individual and group tutoring, training in study skills, academic counseling, taped books, readers, ombudsman. Contact: Mary Joy Johnson, Special Needs Coordinator. Telephone: (906) 786-5802 ext. 128.

Calvin College: Grand Rapids, MI 49506. Special services: individual tutoring, academic and psychological counseling, diagnostic testing, training in study skills. Contact: Corrine E. Kass, Dean for Academic Administration. Telephone: (616) 957-6112.

Center/clinic: Academic Support Program. Telephone: (616) 957-6122. Director: Evelyn Diephouse. Grades served: college.

Central Michigan University: Mount Pleasant, MI 48859. Total enrollment: 15-16,000. Special services: readers, individual and group tutoring, diagnostic testing, ombudsman, special examinations, academic and psychological counseling, taped books, training in study skills. Contact: Shawmut Christensen, Assistant Director, Office of Student Life. Telephone: (517) 774-3016 or 774-3018.

Center/clinic: Mid-Michigan Learning Center, Ronan Hall. Telephone: (517) 774-3975. Directors: Sherrel Lee Haight, Susan Day. Open to public. Ages served: 4-adult. Services: educational diagnosis and programming. Notes: Summer only.

Center/clinic: CMU Summer Remedial Clinics, Moore Hall, 444. Telephone: (517) 774-7290. Director: Bradford L. Swartz. Open to public. Ages served: 6 and up. Grades served: 1-adult. Services: six-week residential clinic offering speech and language development, social interaction and use of communication skills; swimming, field trips, crafts, team athletics. Notes: Serves people with communication disorders; some may also have learning disabilities.

Grand Rapids Junior College: 143 Bostwick, N.E., Grand Rapids, MI 49503. Special services: individual and group tutoring, training in study skills, academic and psychological counseling, taped books, special examinations, student resource center, readers, note takers, diagnostic testing, scholarships, ombudsman, typing, library assistance, prescheduling, student organization. Contact: Doris Parsons, Coordinator. Telephone: (616) 456-3798.

Center/clinic: Handicapped Student Program, Counseling and Academic Support Center. Telephone: (616) 456-3798. Coordinator: Doris Parsons. Open to public. Grades served: high school diploma and up.

Grand Valley State College: Allendale, MI 49401. Total enrollment: 7,000. LD students: 10. Special services: individual tutoring, academic and psychological counseling, training in study skills. Contact: Al Walczak, Counselor, Special Services. Telephone: (616) 895-3498.

Center/clinic: Academic Resource Center, Commons Building. Telephone: (616) 895-6611. Director: Mary Seeger. Grades served: college. Services: tutoring; math, reading, and writing centers.

Henry Ford Community College: 5101 Evergreen, Dearborn, MI 48128. Special services: readers, individual and group tutoring, ombudsman, special examinations, academic and psychological counseling, diagnostic testing, taped books, training in study skills. Contact: Theodore Hunt, Jr., Special Needs Program Manager. Telephone: (313) 845-9617 ext. 326.

Kellogg Community College: 450 North Avenue, Battle Creek, MI 49016. Total enrollment: 4,500. LD students: 2. Special services: readers, individual and group tutoring, ombudsman, special examinations, scholarships, academic and psychological counseling, diagnostic testing, taped books, training in study skills; basic skills clinics in reading, writing, and math; career testing and counseling, student resource center, Literacy Council. Contact: John M. Rinke, Special Needs Coordinator/Counselor. Telephone: (616) 965-3931 ext. 386.

Center/clinic: Special Needs. Telephone: (616) 965-3931 ext. 386. Coordinator/Counselor: John M. Rinke. Open to public. Grades served: 7-college.

Lansing Community College: 419 N. Capitol, Lansing, MI 48901. Total enrollment: 22,000. Special services: readers, individual and group tutoring, special examinations, academic and personal counseling, taped books, training in study skills, student resource center. Contact: Lynnae M. Ruttledge, Coordinator, Handicapper Student Services. Telephone: (517) 483-1207.

Macomb Community College: 14500 Twelve Mile Road, Warren, MI 48093. Total enrollment: 31,152. Special services: individual and group tutoring, training in study skills, academic and psychological counseling, taped books, special examinations, student resource center, readers, diagnostic testing, scholarships, ombudsman. Contact: Diane Steil, Secretary, Special Services Unit. Telephone: (313) 445-7420.

Michigan State University: East Lansing, MI 48824. Special services: individual and group tutoring, training in study skills, academic and psychological counseling, taped books, special examinations, student resource center, readers, ombudsman. Contact: Mary E. Fuller, Instructor, Learning Disabilities Program. Telephone: (517) 355-1835 or 355-1755.

Center/clinic: Learning Resources Center, 204 Bessey Hall. Telephone: (517) 355-2363. Director: Elaine Cherney. Not open to public. Grades served: university students.

Center/clinic: The Learning Clinic, 250 Erickson Hall. Telephone: (517) 355-1755. Director: Norman R. Stewart. Open to public. Grades served: 1-12. Services: learning disability program, counseling, gifted assessment, math

MICHIGAN

assessment, parent groups, reading diagnostic testing, reading tutorial. Notes: teaching/training clinic serving the community.

Michigan Technological University: Houghton, MI 49931. Total enrollment: 7,000. Special services: individual tutoring, academic and psychological counseling, diagnostic testing, training in study skills, support group. Contact: William Parker, Clinical Psychologist/Counselor. Telephone: (906) 487-2692.

Center/clinic: Counseling Services, 118 Administration Building. Telephone: (906) 487-2538. Director: Jeanine D. Sewell. Not open to public. Grades served: college.

Mid-Michigan Community College: 1375 S. Clare Avenue, Harrison, MI 48625. LD students: 13. Special services: readers, individual tutoring, ombudsman, scholarships, academic and psychological counseling, diagnostic testing, taped books, training in study skills, note takers. Contact: Donna L. Gilmet, Special Needs Coordinator. Telephone: (517) 386-7792 ext. 268.

Center/clinic: Special Needs Program. Telephone: (517) 386-7792 ext. 268. Director: Donna L. Gilmet. Not open to public. Ages served: 18 and up.

Mott Community College: 1401 E. Court Street, Flint, MI 48502. Special services: individual and group tutoring, training in study skills, academic counseling, taped books, special examinations, readers, diagnostic testing. Contact: Marguerite L. Fordyce, Director, Handicapped Student Services. Telephone: (313) 762-0399.

Northern Michigan University: Marquette, MI 49855. Total enrollment: 7,600. Special services: individual tutoring, academic and psychological counseling, training in study skills. Contact: Norman Hefke, Vice President, Student Services. Telephone: (906) 227-2000.

Northwestern Michigan College: Traverse City, MI 49684. Total enrollment: 3,250. Special services: individual and group tutoring, academic counseling, diagnostic testing, taped books, training in study skills, note takers. Contact: Connie Jason, Advocate Coordinator for Special Needs. Telephone: (616) 922-1038.

Oakland Community College: 2480 Opdyke Road, Bloomfield Hills, MI 48013. Total enrollment: 28,000. LD students: 70. Special services: readers, individual tutoring, ombudsman, academic counseling, training in study skills, taped books, special examinations, diagnostic testing, learning assistance center at each campus. Contact: Lawrence J. Gage, Professor, Counseling Department, Orchard Ridge Campus. Telephone: (313) 471-7588 or 471-7616.

Schoolcraft College: 18600 Haggerty, Livonia, MI 48152. Special services: readers, individual and group tutoring, special examinations, scholarships, academic and psychological counseling, diagnostic testing, taped books, training in study skills, faculty liaison. Contact: Mrs. Sirkka Gudan. Telephone: (313) 591-6400 ext. 494.

Center/clinic: Learning Assistance Center. Telephone: (313) 591-6400 ext. 494. Director: Mrs. Sirkka Gudan. Grades served: college.

Suomi College: Quincy Street, Hancock, MI 49930. Total enrollment: 648. Special services: individual and group tutoring, special examinations, academic counseling, diagnostic testing, training in study skills, computer-assisted learning opportunities. Contact: Barbara Leary, Director, Teaching/Learning Center. Telephone: (906) 482-5300 ext. 255.

University of Michigan: Ann Arbor, MI 48109. Total enrollment: 34,000. LD students: 7. Special services: scholarships, readers, alternative testing procedures, academic support services, training in study skills, taped books, student resource center. Contact: James Kubaiko, Director, Disabled Student Services. Telephone: (313) 763-3000.

Hospital Clinics

Bay City: Bay Medical Center, 1900 Columbus Avenue, 48708. Telephone: (517) 894-3144. Contact: Frank Presty. Outpatient and day program. Ages served: all. Services: speech, language, physical, and occupational therapy; social services.

Royal Oak: William Beaumont Hospital System, Neuro-Education Center, 3203 Coolidge Highway, 48072. Telephone: (313) 288-2332. Contact: Richard R. Galpin, Director. Outpatient, day, and after school program. Ages served: preschool-adult. Services: diagnostic testing, academic and psychological testing, individual and group tutoring; academic, psychological, and parent counseling.

Westland: Westland Medical Center, Pediatric Primary Care, 48185. Telephone: (313) 467-2677. Contact: John Paul Board, Jr., Staff Pediatrician. Outpatient program. Ages served: birth-18. Services: speech, language, physical, and occupational therapy; medical and clinical neurological examinations, speech pathology evaluations.

Other Services

Flint: Mott Children's Health Center, Educational Services Department, 806 W. Sixth Avenue, 48504. Telephone: (313) 767-5750 ext. 230. President: Arthur L. Tuuri. Outpatient, preschool, and summer program. Ages served: 5-25. Services: individual and group tutoring, academic testing, family counseling, multidisciplinary care. Notes: Limited to Genesee County children. Parent involvement stressed. Bulk of work is diagnostic.

MICHIGAN

Grand Haven: Creative Education, 234½ Washington, 49417. Telephone: (616) 728-7321. Contact: Bari S. Johnson. Diagnostic center. Ages served: 4-adult. Services: diagnostic testing, academic testing and counseling, staff development seminars.

Kalamazoo: Specific Language Disability Center, P.O. Box 1404, 49005. Telephone: (616) 345-2661. Executive Director: Jack Gilman. Elementary, secondary, and adult tutoring service. Day and after school service. Ages served: 6 and up. Grades served: kindergarten-12. Limited scholarships/financial aid available. Services: diagnostic testing, academic testing, parent counseling, individual tutoring.

Kalamazoo: Westside Family Mental Health Clinic, P.C., 4025 W. Main Street, Suite 101, 49007. Telephone: (616) 381-2626. Contact: Michael Ryan. Clinic. Ages served: 3 and up. Services: diagnostic testing, academic and psychological testing; academic, psychological, and parent counseling; group therapy, consultation for schools and universities. Notes: Services by appointment.

MINNESOTA

Offices of Organizations Concerned with Learning Disabilities

ACLD, Inc.: 1821 University Avenue, Suite 494 North, St. Paul, MN 55104. Telephone: (612) 646-6136. President: F. Alexandra Klas. Executive Director: Gary Berg.

Council for Exceptional Children: President: Ron Sandness, 244 W. Main Street, Marshall, MN 56258. Telephone: Office (507) 532-2221; Home (507) 537-1911.

Orton Dyslexia Society (Upper Midwest Branch): 10000 32nd Avenue, North, Minneapolis, MN 55441. President: C. Wilson Anderson, Jr. Telephone: Office (612) 546-3266; Home (612) 545-5515.

State Department of Education Learning Disabilities Personnel

Norena Hale, Acting Manager of Special Education, 818 Capitol Square Building, 550 Cedar Street, St. Paul, MN 55101. Telephone: (612) 296-1793. Learning disabilities consultant: Carolyn Elliott. Telephone: (612) 296-2548.

Private and Day Schools

Duluth: United Cerebral Palsy Preschool for Children with Learning Differences, 105 Ordean Building, 424 W. Superior Street, 55802. Telephone: (218) 726-4724. Project Director: Helmi Lammi. Preschool. Ages served: 3-5. Current enrollment: 16. Maximum enrollment: 16. Part-time staff: 4. Scholarships/financial aid available. Services: individual and group tutoring, academic and psychological testing in cooperation with other agencies, family counseling. Notes: For children with learning differences; need not be cerebral palsied.

Minneapolis: Fraser School (Division of Louise Whitbeck Fraser Community Services, Inc.), 2400 W. 64th Street, 55423. Telephone: (612) 861-1688. Executive Director: Robert J. Kowalczyk. Preschool and elementary day school. Ages served: 6 weeks-8 years. Grades served: ungraded. Current enrollment: 100. Maximum enrollment: 100. Full-time staff: 35. Scholarships/financial aid available. Services: individual and group tutoring, family counseling; corrective, physical, occupational, and music therapy; activities of daily living.

St. Louis Park: The Groves Learning Center, 3200 Highway 100 South, 55416. Telephone: (612) 920-6377. Executive Director: Raleigh J. Huizinga. Preschool, elementary, and secondary day school with summer program. Ages served: 2-17. Grades served: preschool-12. Current enrollment: 165. Full-time staff: 24. Part-time staff: 5. Scholarships/financial aid available. Services: individual and group tutoring, academic and psychological testing, nursery school; academic, psychological, and family counseling; adaptive physical education, vocational training.

Summer Camps and Programs

Annandale: Chi Rho Camp for Learning Disabled Children, 55302. Telephone: (612) 274-8307. Permanent mailing address: St. John's Lutheran Church-Chi Rho, Minneapolis, MN 55409. Telephone: (612) 827-4406. Director: Karen Hart. Residential camp with academic program. Ages served: 9-12. Grades served: 4-6. Maximum enrollment: 75. Full-time staff: 26. Part-time staff: 8. Scholarships/financial aid available. Services: individual and group tutoring, academic testing and counseling, adaptive physical education, registered nurse on duty. Academic programs: math, reading, spelling, study skills. Recreation: swimming, hiking, field trips, nature study, crafts, drama, camping, team athletics, basketball, softball, volleyball, soccer, boating.

Ely: Camp Buckskin, Box 389, 55731. Telephone: (218) 365-2121. Permanent mailing address: 3811 W. Broadway, Robbinsdale, MN 55422. Telephone: (612) 533-9674. Camp Director: Ralston S. Bauer. Residential camp with academic program. Ages served: 6-17. Grades served: 1-10. Maximum enrollment: 320. Full-time staff: 52. Services: individual and group tutoring, academic testing. Academic programs: reading, study skills. Recreation: swimming, canoeing, field trips, nature study, camping, crafts.

Golden Valley: Camp Courage, Courage Center, 3915 Golden Valley Road, 55422. Telephone: (612) 588-0811. Director of Camping Services: Bob Polland. Residential camp. Ages served: 7-13. Maximum enrollment: 72. Full-time staff: 50. Scholarships/financial aid available. Services: speech and language therapy, audiology services. Recreation: swimming, riding, field trips, nature study, crafts, camping, photography, team athletics.

MINNESOTA

Lake Crystal: I Can Do Camp, Route 2, 56055. Telephone: (507) 726-2742. Directors: Mark and Jane Schuck. Residential camp with academic program. Ages served: 6-13. Grades served: kindergarten-6. Maximum enrollment: 25. Full-time staff: 5. Part-time staff: 5. Scholarships/financial aid available. Services: individual and group tutoring, adaptive physical education. Academic programs: math, reading, spelling, study skills. Recreation: swimming, hiking, riding, field trips, nature study, crafts, drama, camping.

College and University Special Programs and Services

Augsburg College: 731 21st Avenue, South, Minneapolis, MN 55454. Total enrollment: 1,200. LD students: 15. Special services: individual and group tutoring, training in study skills, academic and psychological counseling, taped books, special examinations, student resource center, readers, diagnostic testing, ombudsman, support group, preadmission advising, peer tours of campus.

- **Special program:** Learning Disabilities Program. Provides individual education plans; one-year course covering study and living skills, time management, career planning, and strategies to improve reading rate and comprehension; one semester orientation course, computer lab. Learning disability must be verified through recent records or testing done by the college. Program open to full or part-time students. Learning Disabilities Specialist: Kathleen Heikkila. Telephone: (612) 330-1167.

Center/clinic: Center for Student Development, Academic Skills Center. Telephone: (612) 330-1160. Director: Don Warren. Not open to public. Ages served: 18 and up. Grades served: college.

Austin Community College: 1600 Eighth Avenue, N.W., Austin, MN 55912. Total enrollment: 987. Special services: individual tutoring, training in study skills, academic and psychological counseling, special examinations. Contact: Patrick M. Johns, Dean. Telephone: (507) 433-0516.

Bethel College: 3900 Bethel Drive, St. Paul, MN 55112. Total enrollment: 1,870. LD students: 20. Special services: individual and group tutoring, training in study skills, academic and psychological counseling, diagnostic testing, support group, advocacy. Contact: Lucie Johnson, Professor of Psychology. Telephone: (612) 638-6353.

The College of St. Scholastica: 1200 Kenwood Avenue, Duluth, MN 55811. Total enrollment: 1,500. LD students: 10. Special services: individual and group tutoring, training in study skills, academic and psychological counseling, taped books, student resource center, readers, diagnostic testing, ombudsman. Contact: Robert Quackenbush, Academic Counselor. Telephone: (218) 723-6552.

College of Saint Thomas: 2115 Summit Avenue, St. Paul, MN 55105. Total enrollment: 6,000. Special services: individual tutoring, special examinations, academic and psychological counseling, training in study skills, student resource center. Contact: Ann G. Ryan, Associate Professor. Telephone: (612) 647-5820 ext. 5174.

Center/clinic: Study Skills Center. Telephone: (612) 647-5820. Director: Joyce Pederson. Not open to public. Grades served: college.

Concordia College: Moorhead, MN 56560. Total enrollment: 2,464. LD students: 5. Special services: individual tutoring, training in study skills, academic counseling, taped books, special examinations, student resource center, scholarships. Contact: Donald E. Dale, Registrar. Telephone: (218) 299-3949.

Macalester College: 1600 Grand Avenue, St. Paul, MN 55105. Total enrollment: 1,600. LD students: 40. Special services: individual tutoring, training in study skills, academic and psychological counseling, taped books, special examinations, readers. Contact: Charles Norman, Director, Learning Skills Center. Telephone: (612) 696-6146.

Mankato State University: Mankato, MN 56001. Total enrollment: 14,000. Special services: academic counseling. Contact: Daniel Beebe, Director, Handicapped Student Services. Telephone: (507) 389-2825.

Normandale Community College: 9700 France Avenue, South, Bloomington, MN 55431. Total enrollment: 6,200. LD students: 40. Special services: individual tutoring, training in study skills, academic and psychological counseling, taped books, note taking, proofreading of assignments, special examinations, student resource center, ombudsman, support group.

- **Special program:** DEEDS (Designing Educational Experiences for Disabled Students Program). A three-quarter sequence of classes covering techniques for accommodating a learning disability at the college level, grammar, language, and composition skills. Must apply to the college as a regular student and complete a special application for DEEDS services. Learning disability must be verified through recent records. DEEDS Coordinator: Mary Jibben. Telephone: (612) 830-9372. Director: Karen Hanson. Telephone: (612) 830-9377.

Rochester Community College: Highway 14 East, Rochester, MN 55901. Total enrollment: 3,000. LD students: 40. Special services: individual and group tutoring, training in study skills, academic and psychological counseling, special examinations, student resource center, readers, diagnostic testing, taped books, scholarships, support groups, special orientation, course planning; credit classes in developmental reading, math, and English. Contact: Joyce A. Hackett, Director, Developmental Learning Center. Telephone: (507) 285-7230.

MINNESOTA

Center/clinic: Developmental Learning Center. Telephone: (507) 285-7230. Director: Joyce A. Hackett. Not open to public. Grades served: postsecondary.

St. Cloud State University: St. Cloud, MN 56301. Total enrollment: 12,000. LD students: 20. Special services: readers, group tutoring, special examinations, academic and psychological counseling, taped books, training in study skills. Contact: Patricia Potter, Director of Handicapped Student Services. Telephone: (612) 255-3111.

St. Olaf College: Northfield, MN 55057. Total enrollment: 3,000. LD students: 15-20. Special services: individual tutoring, training in study skills, academic and psychological counseling, taped books, readers. Contact: Linda Hunter, Director, Academic Support Center. Telephone: (507) 663-3288.

Southwest State University: E. College Drive, Marshall, MN 56258. Total enrollment: 2,000. LD students: 40. Special services: individual and group tutoring, training in study skills, academic and psychological counseling, taped books, special examinations, student resource center, readers, diagnostic testing, support group; developmental courses in study, reading, writing, and thinking skills. Contact: Mary Jo Carrow, Academic Accommodations Coordinator. Telephone: (507) 537-6169.

Center/clinic: Learning Resources, Bellows 109. Telephone: (507) 537-6169. Director: Marilyn M. Leach. Not open to public. Ages served: adult. Services: developmental courses, academic tutoring, resource library, speech evaluations and therapy, workshops.

University of Minnesota: Minneapolis, MN 55455. Total enrollment: 47,000. LD students: 70. Special services: prescreening and referral for diagnosis, assistance with obtaining accommodations, study skills seminars, support groups, peer tutors, taped textbooks; personal, career, academic, and psychological counseling; extra time to complete coursework, library assistance. Contact: Kaia Svien or Lynda Price, Learning Disabilities Counselors, Student Counseling Bureau. Telephone: (612) 373-4193.

Center/clinic: Office for Students with Disabilities, 12 Johnston Hall, 101 Pleasant Street, S.E. Telephone: (612) 373-3714. Grades served: college.

University of Minnesota-Crookston: Crookston, MN 56716. Total enrollment: 1,400. LD students: 30. Special services: individual and group tutoring, training in study skills, academic and psychological counseling, taped books, special examinations, student resource center, diagnostic testing, ombudsman. Contact: Angela Fox, Disabled Students Program. Telephone: (218) 281-6510 ext. 391.

University of Minnesota-Morris: Morris, MN 56267. Total enrollment: 1,665. LD students: 4. Special services: individual tutoring, training in study skills, academic and psychological counseling, special examinations, readers, diagnostic

MINNESOTA

testing, ombudsman. Contact: Stephen Granger, Assistant Provost for Student Affairs. Telephone: (612) 589-2211 ext. 6025.

University of Minnesota Technical College-Waseca: Waseca, MN 56093. Total enrollment: 1,012. LD students: 20. Special services: individual and group tutoring, training in study skills, academic and psychological counseling, taped books, special examinations, readers, scholarships, ombudsman. Contact: Allan Ward, Director, Student Support Services. Telephone: (507) 835-1000 ext. 256.

Hospital Clinics

Alexandria: Douglas County Hospital, 111-17th Avenue, East, 56308. Telephone: (612) 762-1511 ext. 225. Contact: Verna Pauley, Director of Nursing. Outpatient, inpatient, and after school program. Ages served: all. Services: psychological testing, psychological and parent counseling; group, speech, language, physical, and occupational therapy; audiological services, support group.

Minneapolis: Fairview Hospital, 2312 S. Sixth Street, 55454. Telephone: (612) 371-6512. Contact: Susan Meneghel, Chief Speech and Language Pathologist. Outpatient, inpatient, day, and after school program. Ages served: 3 and up. Services: diagnostic testing, academic testing and counseling; speech, language, and physical therapy.

Minneapolis: Minneapolis Children's Medical Center, Learning Disorders Clinic, Department of Speech Pathology and Audiology, 2525 Chicago Avenue, South, 55404. Telephone: (612) 874-6254. Contact: Nancy Pflager, Director, Special Services. Outpatient program. Ages served: 3-16. Services: preschool, diagnostic testing, academic and psychological testing, psychological and parent counseling; group, speech, language, physical, and occupational therapy; social services.

Minneapolis: University of Minnesota Hospitals and Clinics, Division of Child and Adolescent Psychiatry, Box 95, Mayo Building, 55455. Telephone: (612) 373-8871. Contact: Ann Voelker, Nurse Clinician. Outpatient and inpatient program. Ages served: 5-18. Services: diagnostic testing, academic and psychological testing, individual tutoring, psychological and parent counseling, group therapy, adaptive physical education, support group, social services; testing and treatment for individuals with Attention Deficit Disorder.

St. Cloud: St. Cloud Hospital, St. Cloud Rehabilitation Center, 1406 Sixth Avenue, North, 56301. Telephone: (612) 251-2700. Contact: Earl E. Pederson, Rehabilitation Director. Outpatient and inpatient program. Ages served: birth-15. Services: diagnostic testing, academic and psychological testing, psychological and parent counseling; speech, language, physical, and occupational therapy; social services.

MINNESOTA

Other Services

Chisholm: Range Center, Inc., 1001 Eighth Avenue, N.W., P.O. Box 629, 55719. Telephone: (218) 254-3347. Executive Director: James N. Mickelson. Preschool and adult day facility. Ages served: 1-4, 18 and up. Current enrollment: 8 preschool; 47 adult. Maximum enrollment: 10 preschool; 50 adult. Full-time staff: 18. Services: individual and group instruction, physical and occupational therapy, adaptive physical education, vocational training, language and speech remediation, training for functional skills for community living. Notes: Serves mentally and physically handicapped as well as the learning disabled.

Duluth: Harbour North Clinic, Ltd., 1722 London Road, 55812. Telephone: (218) 728-6464. Director: Angelo S. Bolea. Clinic. Day program. Ages served: school age, adults. Services: diagnostic testing, academic and psychological testing, psychological and parent counseling, group therapy, specific neuropsychological assessment, art psychotherapy for treatment of visual learning disorders.

Duluth: Northwood Children's Home, 714 College Street, 55811. Telephone: (218) 724-8815. Executive Director: James Yeager. Residential treatment center. Day and boarding school with summer program. Ages served: 5-15 at admission. Grades served: preschool-9. Current enrollment: 60. Maximum enrollment: 60. Full-time staff: 88. Services: individual tutoring, academic and psychological testing; academic, psychological, and family counseling; physical and occupational therapy, adaptive physical education, vocational training, work-study, medical services. Recreation: sports teams, tumbling, skiing, lake cabin. Notes: Serves emotionally disturbed and learning disabled.

Minneapolis: eLDA Reading and Math Clinic, Learning Disabilities Association, 2344 Nicollet Avenue, Suite 300, 55404. Telephone: (612) 871-9011. Executive Director: Peter Pearson. Clinic. Day and after school program. Ages served: 7 and up. Services: diagnostic testing, individual tutoring; VO-PREP program designed to prepare learning disabled students for college or technical school; liaison and consultation, outreach and information, in-service training for professionals, individually designed programs for special needs.

Minneapolis: Learning and Language Specialists, 6155 Duluth Street, 55422. Telephone: (612) 545-7708. Contact: Susan Storti. Clinic. Day and after school program. Ages served: 2-adult. Services: diagnostic testing, academic and psychological testing, individual and group tutoring; academic, psychological, and parent counseling; group, speech, and language therapy; support group.

Minnetonka: Neuropsychology Services, 13544 McGinty Road, East, 55343. Telephone: (612) 938-1214. Contact: Cris W. Johnston. Clinic. Outpatient program. Ages served: all. Services: diagnostic testing, academic and psychological testing, psychological and parent counseling, computer-assisted perceptual-cognitive retraining, outpatient evaluation.

St. Cloud: St. Cloud Children's Home Program, 1726 Seventh Avenue, South, 56301. Telephone: (612) 251-8811. Coordinator: William Nelson. Secondary residential treatment center with summer program. Ages served: 9-18. Grades served: 5-12. Maximum enrollment: 72. Services: individual and group tutoring, academic and psychological testing; academic, psychological, individual, group, and family counseling; occupational therapy, adaptive physical education, work-study, medical services.

MISSISSIPPI

Offices of Organizations Concerned with Learning Disabilities

ACLD, Inc.: P.O. Box 9387, Jackson, MS 39206. President: Rita Nordan. Telephone: (601) 982-6767.

Council for Exceptional Children: President: John Schwenn, 209 Marler Street, Cleveland, MS 38732. Telephone: Office (601) 843-8955; Home (601) 846-7966.

Mississippi Easter Seal Society: P.O. Box 4958, 3226 N. State Street, Jackson, MS 39216. Executive Director: Lee O. Dees. Telephone: (601) 982-7051.

State Department of Education Learning Disabilities Personnel

Karen B. Hexton, Director, Division for Programs for Exceptional Children, P.O. Box 771, Jackson, MS 39205-0771. Telephone: (601) 359-3490. Learning disabilities consultant: Debra Burris-Montgomery.

Private and Day Schools

Gulfport: Gulf Coast Education Center, 01025 Pass Road, Handsboro, 39501-3599. Telephone: (601) 896-5526. Director/Owner: Mary Grace Carruth. Elementary and secondary day school. Grades served: upper elementary-12. Current enrollment: 21. Maximum enrollment: 40. Full-time staff: 4. Scholarships/financial aid available. Services: individual and group tutoring, academic testing. Recreation: limited outside activities, table games.

Jackson: Developmental Achievement Center, 4909 Ridgewood Road, 39211. Telephone: (601) 362-9793. Director: Deborah B. Johnson. Preschool and elementary day school with summer program. Ages served: 2-15. Grades served: kindergarten-8. Current enrollment: 25. Maximum enrollment: 30. Services: individual and group tutoring, academic testing, developmental preschool program. Notes: Director and teacher for each group of five students.

Jackson: Early Education Center, P.O. Box 10356, 39209. Telephone: (601) 353-1664. Director: Martha Coppinger. Preschool with limited services. Ages served: 6 months-5. Current enrollment: 55. Maximum enrollment: 55. Full-time staff: 19.

MISSISSIPPI

Part-time staff: 6. Services: individual and group tutoring, family counseling, physical therapy, adaptive physical education, individualized programming in small classroom setting.

Jackson: The Education Center, 4080 Old Canton Road, Box 9387, 39206. Telephone: (601) 982-2812. Director: Martha T. Kabbes. Elementary and secondary day school with summer program. Grades served: 1-12. Current enrollment: 299. Maximum enrollment: 360. Full-time staff: 16. Part-time staff: 3. Services: individual tutoring, small classes, individualized programs, diagnosis of specific learning and academic deficiencies; individual tutoring and diagnostic testing on an hourly basis for students attending other schools.

Jackson: Heritage School, P.O. Box 20434 Westland Station, 39209. Telephone: (601) 969-0603. Director: Jeanie Muirhead. Elementary day school with remedial summer program. Ages served: 6-15. Grades served: 1-8. Current enrollment: 32. Maximum enrollment: 40. Full-time staff: 9. Part-time staff: 4. Services: small, ungraded, self-contained classes; academic testing, adaptive physical education. Special program provides intensive training in auditory and visual perception. Recreation: city parks and recreational facilities.

Picayune: St. Michael's Farm and School for Boys, Inc., P.O. Drawer 640, 39466. Telephone: (601) 798-2418. Director: Robert Escudero. Males only secondary boarding school with limited services. Ages served: 13-18. Grades served: ungraded. Current enrollment: 12. Maximum enrollment: 15-18. Full-time staff: 9. Part-time staff: 2. Services: individual and group tutoring, academic testing and counseling, vocational training, medical services. Recreation: riding, swimming, fishing, camping and other outdoor activities. Notes: Episcopal Church-related home and school for boys whose problems or environment have made them the concern of juvenile courts and officials.

College and University Special Programs and Services

Alcorn State University: Lorman, MS 39096. Special services: readers, individual and group tutoring, special examinations, scholarships, academic and psychological counseling, diagnostic testing, training in study skills. Contact: Danella Murphy, Assistant Professor of Special Education. Telephone: (601) 877-6205.

Delta State University: Box 3111, Cleveland, MS 38733. Special services: individual tutoring, academic and psychological counseling, special examinations, student resource center, diagnostic testing. Contact: John Schwenn, Director of Special Education. Telephone: (601) 843-8955.

Mississippi State University: Mississippi State, MS 39762.

Center/clinic: Child Service Demonstration Center, P.O. Box 5365. Telephone: (601) 325-3158. Directors: Eugene F. Martin, Nancy K. Wallner. Grades served: kindergarten-12. Services: diagnostic testing, training in study skills, individual and group tutoring, diagnostic/prescriptive teaching in all subject areas, consultations with parents and school districts. Notes: Center provides teacher training for university students.

Mississippi University for Women: Columbus, MS 39701. Total enrollment: 2,400. Special services: individual and group tutoring, special examinations, academic counseling, diagnostic testing, training in study skills, student resource center. Contact: James W. Hunt, Director, Center for Special Children. Telephone: (601) 329-4750 ext. 439.

Center/clinic: Center for Special Children, W-Box 280. Telephone: (601) 329-4750 ext. 439. Director: James W. Hunt. Open to public. Ages served: 6-18.

MISSOURI

Offices of Organizations Concerned with Learning Disabilities

ACLD, Inc.: P.O. Box 3303, Glenstone Station, Springfield, MO 65808. Telephone: (417) 831-6291. President: Marianne Toombs. Office Coordinator: Eleanor Scherff.

Council for Exceptional Children: President: Sharon Adams, 211 St. Marys Boulevard, Apt. E, Jefferson City, MO 65101. Telephone: Office (314) 636-7171 ext. 241; Home (314) 635-6306.

Missouri Easter Seal Society: 10000 Watson Road, Suite 18, St. Louis, MO 63126. Executive Director: Barbara Robinson. Telephone: (314) 821-6001.

State Department of Education Learning Disabilities Personnel

Delores John, Director of Special Education, Department of Elementary and Secondary Education, Section of Special Education, P.O. Box 480, Jefferson City, MO 65102. Telephone: (314) 751-2965 or 751-4909.

Private and Day Schools

Blue Springs: Rainbow Center for Communicative Disorders, P.O. Box 352, 701 N. 15th Street, 64015. Telephone: (816) 229-3869. Director: Marilu W. Blake. Preschool and elementary day school with summer program. Ages served: 2-15. Grades served: ungraded. Current enrollment: 17. Maximum enrollment: 25. Full-time staff: 3. Part-time staff: 6. Services: individual and group tutoring, academic testing; speech, language, physical, and occupational therapy; adaptive physical education, behavior management.

MISSOURI

Kansas City: Joan Davis School for Special Education, 10515 Grandview Road, 64137. Telephone: (816) 761-3157. Executive Director: Judith L. Estes. Elementary and secondary day school. Ages served: 8-18. Grades served: 1-12. Current enrollment: 42. Maximum enrollment: 50. Full-time staff: 12. Part-time staff: 4. Services: individual and group tutoring, academic and psychological testing; academic, psychological, and family counseling; occupational therapy, adaptive physical education.

Kansas City: Operation Discovery School, 3929 Pennsylvania, 64111. Telephone: (816) 931-7210. Director: Coisela Jumara. Preschool and elementary day school with summer program. Ages served: 2-12. Grades served: preschool-6. Current enrollment: 110. Maximum enrollment: 140. Full-time staff: 13. Part-time staff: 9. Services: academic and psychological testing, occupational therapy. Recreation: physical education. Notes: Mainstreamed program.

St. Joseph: Children Rehabilitation Unit, 1802 Union, 64501. Telephone: (816) 364-1501. Director: Linda Leftwich. Preschool with limited services; summer program. Ages served: birth-7. Current enrollment: 80-90. Maximum enrollment: 90. Full-time staff: 13. Part-time staff: 2. Services: academic and psychological testing, psychological and family counseling, adaptive physical education, day treatment; occupational, play, and speech therapy; speech evaluation, infant stimulation, adaptive behavior treatment, parent groups. Recreation: swimming, ice-skating. Notes: Also serves clients of all ages on an individual basis.

St. Louis: Childhaven, 9333 Clayton Road, 63124. Telephone: (314) 991-4111. Executive Director: Estelle McDoniel. Preschool and elementary day school with summer program. Ages served: 2-11. Current enrollment: 5. Maximum enrollment: 5. Full-time staff: 12. Part-time staff: 3. Services: individual programming; occupational, communication, behavioral, developmental, and educational therapy.

St. Louis: The Churchill School, 1035 Price School Lane, 63124. Telephone: (314) 997-4343. Director: Sandra K. Gilligan. Elementary and secondary day school with summer program. Ages served: 8-16. Grades served: ungraded. Current enrollment: 91. Maximum enrollment: 102. Full-time staff: 31. Part-time staff: 3. Scholarships/financial aid available. Services: individual and group tutoring, academic testing, parent support groups, teacher workshops. Notes: Teacher/student ratio 1:4.

St. Louis: Edgewood Children's Center, 330 N. Gore, 63119. Telephone: (314) 968-2060. Executive Director: Ralph S. Lehman. Elementary and secondary day and boarding school with summer program. Ages served: 5-17. Grades served: kindergarten-12. Current enrollment: 67. Maximum enrollment: 70. Services: individual and group tutoring, academic and psychological testing; academic, psychological, and family counseling; art, music, occupational, and recreational therapy; adaptive physical education, vocational training, work-study, medical services, outdoor education. Recreation: team sports, balance activities, gymnastics, trampoline, rope, camping, canoeing, swimming, aerobics, jogging.

St. Louis: Good Shepherd School for Children, 13157 Olive Spur Road, North, 63141. Telephone: (314) 878-4845. Director: Thomas Mihail. Preschool and elementary day school with summer program. Ages served: 2-10. Grades served: ungraded. Current enrollment: 40. Maximum enrollment: 40. Full-time staff: 16. Part-time staff: 1. Volunteers: 50. Scholarships/financial aid available. Services: individual and group tutoring, academic testing, family counseling; occupational, speech, and language therapy; child advocacy, referrals. Notes: Serves developmentally disabled children, including the learning disabled.

St. Louis: New Hope Learning Center, 1200 S. Grand, 63104. Telephone: (314) 776-2414. Director: Betty Graves. Preschool. Ages served: 1½-5. Current enrollment: 30. Maximum enrollment: 30. Full-time staff: 8-10. Scholarships/financial aid available. Services: academic testing, family counseling; speech, language, and physical therapy.

St. Louis: Special Lutheran Classes, 3558 S. Jefferson, 63118. Telephone: (314) 776-0500. Executive Director: Lloyd W. Haertling. Elementary school with limited services. Ages served: 5-15. Grades served: kindergarten-8. Current enrollment: 66. Maximum enrollment: 75. Full-time staff: 11. Scholarships/financial aid available. Services: academic testing and counseling.

Springfield: Bellwether School, 430 South Avenue, 65806. Telephone: (417) 831-4108. Director: Carole R. Stone. Headmistress: Rebecca Standley. Elementary day school with summer program. Grades served: preschool-8. Current enrollment: 6. Maximum enrollment: 6 children per teacher. Full-time staff: 1. Part-time staff: 3. Services: individual and group tutoring, academic and psychological testing; academic, psychological, and family counseling; physical and occupational therapy, adaptive physical education, medical services for admission requirements, speech and language services, sensory integration activities. Recreation: swimming, weight lifting, bowling, roller-skating, group play.

Springfield: United Cerebral Palsy of Southwest Missouri, 1545 E. Pythian, 65802. Telephone: (417) 831-1545. Director: Ron Mitchum. Preschool with limited services. Ages served: birth-5. Current enrollment: 48. Maximum enrollment: 50. Full-time staff: 14. Part-time staff: 3. Scholarships/financial aid available. Services: psychological testing, family counseling, physical and occupational therapy.

Webster Groves: The Miriam School, 524 Bismark, 63119. Telephone: (314) 968-5225. Acting Director: Rita Holmes Shaughnessy. Preschool and elementary day school with summer camp. Ages served: 3-9. Grades served: ungraded. Current enrollment: 80. Maximum enrollment: 83. Full-time staff: 13. Part-time staff: 3. Scholarships/financial aid available. Services: individual tutoring; occupational,

MISSOURI

speech, and language therapy; behavior management training for parents. Notes: Also serves behavior disordered students.

College and University Special Programs and Services

Avila College: 11901 Wornall Road, Kansas City, MO 64145. Special services: individual tutoring, training in study skills, academic counseling, student resource center, readers. Contact: Kathleen Meagher, Chairperson, Education and Psychology Department. Telephone: (816) 942-8400 ext. 269.

Central Missouri State University: Warrensburg, MO 64093. Total enrollment: 8,500. Special services: readers, individual and group tutoring, special examinations, academic and psychological counseling, taped books, training in study skills, student resource center, ombudsman, diagnostic testing. Contact: Alice Gower, Director of Special Student Services. Telephone: (816) 429-4421.

Center/clinic: Reading Clinic, Lovinger 209. Telephone: (816) 429-4023. Director: Glen Anderson. Open to public. Grades served: kindergarten-12.

Center/clinic: Educational Development Center, Humphreys Building. Telephone: (816) 429-4061. Director: David DeFrain. Not open to public. Grades served: college. Services: individual tutoring for reading, math, and composition.

Center/clinic: Learning Center, Humphreys Building. Telephone: (816) 429-4061. Director: David DeFrain. Not open to public. Grades served: college.

Lindenwood College: Kingshighway and Watson, St. Charles, MO 63301. Special services: individual and group tutoring, training in study skills, academic and psychological counseling, student resource center, readers. Contact: Ann Canale, Faculty Coordinator, Academic Assistance Program. Telephone: (314) 946-6912 ext. 316 or 334.

Mineral Area College: Flat River, MO 63601. Total enrollment: 1800. LD students: 12. Special services: individual and group tutoring, training in study skills, academic counseling, taped books, special examinations, student resource center, readers, scholarships, ombudsman, support group, vocational evaluation, job placement. Contact: Margaret M. Scobee, Vocational Resource Educator, Special Needs Services. Telephone: (314) 431-4593 ext. 54.

Northwest Missouri State University: Maryville, MO 64468. Total enrollment: 4,500. LD students: 75. Special services: individual and group tutoring, special examinations, academic and psychological counseling, diagnostic testing, taped books, training in study skills, support group, readers. Contact: Bill Dizney, Head of Student Specialized Services. Telephone: (816) 562-1219.

Center/clinic: Summer Learning Institute, 216 Horace Mann. Telephone: (816) 562-1236. Director: Ann Laing. Open to public. Grades served: preschool-6.

MISSOURI

Rockhurst College: 5225 Troost Avenue, Kansas City, MO 64110. Total enrollment: 2,860. LD students: 12. Services: individual and group tutoring, training in study skills, academic counseling, diagnostic testing. Contact: Debi Spickelmier, Learning Center Teacher. Telephone: (816) 926-4052.

Center/clinic: The Learning Center. Telephone: (816) 926-4052. Director: Calvin W. Evans. Not open to public. Grades served: college.

St. Louis Community College at Forest Park: 5600 Oakland, St. Louis, MO 63110. Total enrollment: 9,000. LD students: 23. Special services: individual and group tutoring, training in study skills, academic and psychological counseling, taped books, special examinations, student resource center, readers, diagnostic testing, scholarships, support group. Contact: Bard Irwin Schatzman, Vocational Resource Educator. Telephone: (314) 644-9243.

St. Louis Community College at Meramec: 11333 Big Bend, Kirkwood, MO 63122. Total enrollment: 12,668. LD students: 121. Special services: individual tutoring, training in study skills, academic and psychological counseling, special examinations, student resource center, support group, interpersonal skill development, planning for success. Contact: Margaret A. Glad, Counselor/Coordinator, Enabler Program. Telephone: (314) 966-7568.

St. Louis University: 221 N. Grand Boulevard, St. Louis, MO 63103. Special services: individual and group tutoring, training in study skills, academic and psychological counseling, special examinations, student resource center, readers, diagnostic testing, scholarships, ombudsman, support group. Contact: Joseph L. Meindl, Chair, Department of Education. Telephone: (314) 658-2510.

Center/clinic: Special Learning Center, Department of Education. Telephone: (314) 658-2510. Director: Mary O. Dasovich. Open to public. Grades served: preschool-high school. Services: diagnostic and habilitative teaching.

Southwest Missouri State University: Springfield, MO 65804. Special services: limited readers, individual tutoring, special examinations, academic and psychological counseling, diagnostic testing, taped books, training in study skills. Contact: James R. Layton, Dean, College of Education and Psychology. Telephone: (417) 836-5255.

Center/clinic: Learning Diagnostic Clinic, Hill Hall, 901 S. National Avenue. Telephone: (417) 836-5833. Director: Virgil McCall. Open to public. Grades served: kindergarten-adult. Services: diagnostic testing, tutoring.

Tarkio College: Tarkio, MO 64491. Special services: individual and group tutoring, training in study skills, academic and psychological counseling, special examinations, student resource center, diagnostic testing, scholarships. Contact: James Dunsmore, Director, Educational Resource Center. Telephone: (816) 736-4131 ext. 438.

MISSOURI

Center/clinic: Educational Resource Center, 808 Chestnut Street. Telephone: (816) 736-5843. Director: James Dunsmore. Not open to public. Grades served: undergraduate.

University of Missouri-Columbia: Columbia, MO 65211. Special services: readers, ombudsman, special examinations, academic and psychological counseling, taped books, training in study skills. Contact: Donna Hetrick, Coordinator of Access Office. Telephone: (314) 882-3839.

Center/clinic: Child Study Clinic, 217 Education Building. Telephone: (314) 882-3677 or 882-3863. Director: Veralee B. Hardin. Open to residents of Missouri on referral basis. Grades served: preschool-college. Services: psychoeducational assessment.

University of Missouri-Kansas City: 5100 Rockhill Road, Kansas City, MO 64110. Special services: group tutoring, ombudsman, academic and psychological counseling, training in study skills. Contact: Linda O'Donnell, Coordinator of Special Education Program. Telephone: (816) 276-2254.

Center/clinic: Student Learning Center, Student Services Building. Telephone: (816) 276-1174. Director: Deanna Martin. Open to public. Grades served: college. Services: courses in reading and writing, training in study skills.

Center/clinic: Counseling Center, Student Services Building. Telephone: (816) 276-1174. Director: Dan Schemmel. Open to public. Grades served: college.

Center/clinic: Learning Disabilities Clinic, Education Building, Room 365. Telephone: (816) 276-2254. Director: Linda O'Donnell. Open to public. Grades served: preschool-adult. Services: full diagnostic evaluation and follow-up. Notes: Summer clinic only.

Washington University-St. Louis: St. Louis, MO 63130. Total enrollment: 10,000. Special services: readers, individual and group tutoring, ombudsman, special examinations, scholarships, academic and psychological counseling, diagnostic testing, taped books, training in study skills. Contact: Richard Young, Registrar. Telephone: (314) 889-5959. Or Don Sander, Counselor. Telephone: (314) 889-5970.

Webster University: 470 E. Lockwood, St. Louis, MO 63119. Special services: training in study skills, student resource center, career and personal counseling, special examinations. Contact: Karin Niemeyer. Telephone: (314) 968-7495.

Westminster College: Fulton, MO 65201. Special services: readers, individual tutoring, special examinations, academic and psychological counseling, diagnostic testing, taped books, training in study skills, word processors.

- **Special program:** Learning Disability Program. Must meet regular and special admissions requirements. Special requirements include verification of learning disability through recent records or tests by the college.

Most students enroll in four regular college courses, but a reduced course load option is available first semester. Director: Henry F. Ottinger. Telephone: (314) 642-3361 ext. 304.

Hospital Clinics

Kansas City: St. Luke's Hospital, 44th and Wornall, 64111. Telephone: (816) 561-1703. Contact: Lisa Bingham, Assistant Director of Developmental Preschool. Outpatient, inpatient, day, and after school program. Ages served: 1 and up. Services: developmental preschool, outpatient individual therapy, diagnostic testing; group, speech, language, physical, and occupational therapy; social services. Notes: Preschool program for children 1-6 with various handicaps. Classes team taught by speech pathologist and occupational therapist.

North Kansas City: North Kansas City Memorial Hospital, Tri-County Community Health Center, 2900 Hospital Drive, 64116-3281. Telephone: (816) 474-5747. Contact: James Dugan. Outpatient program. Ages served: 2-adult. Services: diagnostic testing, psychological testing, psychological and parent counseling, occupational therapy, social services.

St. Louis: Cardinal Glennon Memorial Hospital for Children, Knights of Columbus Developmental Center, 1465 S. Grand, 63104. Telephone: (314) 577-5609. Contact: Pasquale Accardo, Director. Outpatient program. Ages served: birth-17. Services: diagnostic testing, academic and psychological testing; extensive multidisciplinary evaluation including neurodevelopmental, psychological, educational, and family assessments; follow-up services, family and individual counseling, group training sessions for parents or teachers.

St. Louis: Children's Hospital at the Washington University Medical Center, 400 S. Kingshighway Boulevard, P.O. Box 14871, 63110. Telephone: (314) 454-6000 or 454-6103. Contact: Greg Echele, Manager of Social Service. Outpatient and inpatient program. Ages served: birth-21. Services: diagnostic testing, academic and psychological testing, psychological and parent counseling; group, speech, language, physical, and occupational therapy; adaptive physical education, tutoring referrals, support group, social services.

St. Louis: De Paul Community Health Center, 12303 De Paul Drive, 63044. Telephone: (314) 344-6000. Contact: M.H. Burgdorf, Chairman, Department of Pediatrics. Outpatient, inpatient, day, and after school program. Ages served: all. Services: diagnostic testing, academic and psychological testing, individual tutoring, psychological and parent counseling; group, speech, language, physical, and occupational therapy; adaptive physical education, social services.

Other Services

Clayton: Learning Consultants, Inc., 222 S. Bemiston, Suite 200, 63105. Telephone: (314) 863-0232. Contact: William Ferzacca. Clinic. After school program.

MISSOURI

Ages served: 4-30. Services: diagnostic testing, academic and psychological testing, individual tutoring; academic, psychological, and parent counseling; group and occupational therapy, support group, social services.

Kansas City: Diagnosis and Intervention, 4101 Oak, 64111. Telephone: (816) 561-3285. Director: Nancy K. Lowrey. Clinic. After school program. Ages served: preschool-adult. Services: diagnostic testing, academic testing, individual tutoring, academic and parent counseling, support group.

Kirkwood: Robert J. Mosby and Associates, Inc., Family Psychological Services, 315 N. Dickson, 63122. Telephone: (314) 965-0642. Contact: Robert J. Mosby. Clinic. Day and after school program. Ages served: school age and up. Services: diagnostic testing, academic and psychological testing, individual and group tutoring; academic, psychological, life management, and parent counseling; group therapy, support group, school program intervention and advocacy.

St. Louis: Programs for Learning, 1251 E. Clayton Road, 63011. Telephone: (314) 227-0555. Director: Lucy F. Burcke. Clinic. After school program. Ages served: 4-adult. Services: diagnostic testing, academic testing and counseling, individual and group tutoring, study and academic organizational skills program.

Springfield: Rapid Learning Systems, Suite 309, Plaza Towers, 1736 E. Sunshine, 65804. Telephone: (417) 882-7501. Director: Carole R. Stone. Clinic. Day and after school program. Ages served: all. Services: diagnostic testing, academic and psychological testing, individual and group tutoring, academic counseling, speech and language therapy, preschool evaluations, language development and preschool readiness programs, advocacy, individualized learning program. Notes: Clients typically seen for one hour twice a week.

MONTANA

Offices of Organizations Concerned with Learning Disabilities

ACLD, Inc.: 3024 Macona Lane, Billings, MT 59102. President: Ellen Alweis. Telephone: (406) 252-4845.

Council for Exceptional Children: President: Christine Y. Mason, Institute for Habilitative Services, Eastern Montana College, 1500 N. 30th Street, Billings, MT 59101-0298. Telephone: (406) 657-2081.

Northern Rocky Mountain Easter Seal Society: 4400 Central Avenue, Great Falls, MT 59405. President: William Sirak. Telephone: (406) 761-3680.

State Department of Education Learning Disabilities Personnel

Judith A. Johnson, Assistant Superintendent, Department of Special Services, Office of Public Instruction, State Capitol, Helena, MT 59620. Telephone: (406) 444-3693. Learning disabilities consultant: Robert Runkel. Telephone: (406) 444-2423.

College and University Special Programs and Services

College of Great Falls: 1301-20th Street, South, Great Falls, MT 59404. Special services: readers, individual tutoring, academic and psychological counseling, training in study skills. Contact: Bob Haddock, Director of Special Services. Telephone: (406) 761-8210 ext. 211.

Eastern Montana College: 1500 N. 30th, Billings, MT 54901-0298.

Center/clinic: Montana Center for Handicapped Children. Telephone: (406) 657-2312. Director: Michael Hagen. Open to public. Ages served: birth-21. Services: diagnostic testing, academic and psychological testing, family counseling; speech, language, nutritional, audiological, and physical evaluations; summer program.

Montana State University: Bozeman, MT 59717. Total enrollment: 11,400. LD students: 73. Special services: individual and group tutoring, training in study skills, academic and psychological counseling, taped books, special examinations, student resource center, readers, diagnostic testing, scholarships. Contact: Robert Frazier, Director, Disabled Student Services. Telephone: (406) 994-2824.

Northern Montana College: Havre, MT 59501. Total enrollment: 1,811. LD students: 16. Special services: individual and group tutoring, training in study skills, academic counseling, student resource center, diagnostic testing, scholarships. Contact: Don Lyon, Director, Center for Individualized Instruction. Telephone: (406) 265-7821 ext. 3283.

Center/clinic: Center for Individualized Instruction. Telephone: (406) 265-7821 ext. 3283. Director: Don Lyon. Open to public. Ages served: all. Grades served: all. Services: diagnostic testing, tutoring, individualized lab programs; personal, academic, and career counseling.

University of Montana: Missoula, MT 59812. Special services: individual tutoring, training in study skills, academic and psychological counseling, recorders, taped books, note takers, supplemental lecture notes, special examinations, readers, scholarships; classes in math, English, composition, and reading; assessment and treatment of speech, hearing, and language problems. Contact: Mary Ann Powers, Counselor/Advisor, Disabled Students. Telephone: (406) 243-4711.

MONTANA

Other Services

Billings: The Child Study Center, 1230 N. 28th Street, Box 2000, 59103. Telephone: (406) 252-6601. Contact: Paul Crellin. Clinic. Diagnostic program. Ages served: birth-22. Services: diagnostic testing, academic and psychological testing; academic, psychological, and parent counseling; group therapy, support group.

NEBRASKA

Offices of Organizations Concerned with Learning Disabilities

ACLD, Inc.: 1808 N. 58th Street, Omaha, NE 68104. President: Marianne Wessling. Telephone: (402) 551-2380.

Council for Exceptional Children: President: Linda Stocks, 2635 Ryons Street, Lincoln, NE 68502.

Easter Seal Society of Nebraska, Inc.: 12177 Pacific Street, Omaha, NE 68154. Acting Executive Director: Doris Levine. Telephone: (402) 333-9306.

Orton Dyslexia Society: 6301 Roca Road, Roca, NE 68430. President: Joan C. Stoner. Telephone: (402) 792-2194.

State Department of Education Learning Disabilities Personnel

Gary Sherman, Director, Special Education Division, 301 Centennial Mall, South, P.O. Box 94987, Lincoln, NE 68509. Telephone: (402) 471-2471. Learning disabilities consultant: Pete Biaggio.

Private and Day Schools

York: Epworth Village Educational Therapy Program, P.O. Box 503, 68467-0503. Telephone: (402) 362-3353. Executive Director: Dean W. Pulliam. Elementary and secondary day and boarding school with limited services; summer program. Ages served: 8-21. Grades served: kindergarten-12. Current enrollment: 16. Maximum enrollment: 36. Full-time staff: 13. Part-time staff: 8. Services: individual and group tutoring, academic and psychological testing; academic, psychological, and family counseling; adaptive physical education, work-study, medical services, psychiatric evaluations and consultations. Recreation: camping, hiking, bowling, swimming, field games, ceramics, pottery.

Summer Camps and Programs

Gretna: Eastern Nebraska 4-H Center, Route 1, Box 164, 68028. Telephone: (402) 332-4496. Camp Director: Jim Bell. Day and residential camp with limited services. Ages served: all. Grades served: all. Maximum enrollment: 200. Full-time staff: 2. Part-time staff: 8. Services: work-study, computers. Recreation: camping, hiking, field trips, nature study, team sports, crafts, dance, drama, music, rope challenge course, shooting, canoeing. Notes: Staff trained to work with learning disabled youth.

College and University Special Programs and Services

Concordia College: 800 N. Columbia Avenue, Seward, NE 68434. Special services: individual and group tutoring, training in study skills, academic and psychological counseling, taped books, special examinations, student resource center, readers. Contact: Judy Preuss, Director of Special Education. Telephone: (402) 643-3651 ext. 7475.

Center/clinic: Concordia Learning Center. Telephone: (402) 643-3651. Director: Dian Viesselmeyer. Not open to public. Grades served: college.

Creighton University: California Street, Omaha, NE 68178.

Center/clinic: Learning Disabilities Clinic, Department of Special Education. Telephone: (402) 280-2820 or 280-2562. Director: Beverly A. Doyle. Open to public. Services: diagnostic testing, remediation in reading and math, individual tutoring, training in study skills. Ages served: all. Grades served: all.

Hastings College: Seventh at Turner, Hastings, NE 68901. Special services: individual and group tutoring, training in study skills, academic counseling, student resource center. Contact: Jan Watkins, Associate Professor, Special Education. Telephone: (402) 463-2402 ext. 204.

Metropolitan Technical Community College: P.O. Box 3777, Omaha, NE 68103. Total enrollment: 6,100. LD students: 150. Special services: individual tutoring, training in study skills, academic and psychological counseling, taped books, student resource center, readers. Contact: Mark A. Carta, Director, Special Needs Programs. Telephone: (402) 449-8504.

Peru State College: Peru, NE 68421. Special services: individual and group tutoring, training in study skills, academic counseling, taped books, special examinations, student resource center, readers, diagnostic testing, scholarships. Contact: Linda Warren, Director, Communication Skills Center. Telephone: (402) 872-3815 ext. 203.

Center/clinic: Communications Skills Center. Telephone: (402) 872-3815 ext. 203. Director: Linda Warren. Ages served: college.

Southeast Community College-Lincoln: 8800 "O" Street, Lincoln, NE 68520-1299. Total enrollment: 3,200. Special services: training in study skills, academic counseling, student resource center, diagnostic testing. Contact: Ron Snyder, Counseling Supervisor. Telephone: (402) 471-3333 ext. 223.

NEBRASKA

Hospital Clinics

Omaha: University of Nebraska Medical Center, Meyer Rehabilitation Institute, Learning Disabilities Department, 444 S. 44th Street, 68131. Telephone: (402) 559-4393. Coordinator of Learning Disabilities: John W. Hill. Outpatient and after school program. Ages served: preschool-adult. Services: diagnostic testing, academic and psychological testing, diagnostic teaching; academic, psychological, and parent counseling; group, speech, language, physical, and occupational therapy; social services. Notes: Not a tutoring program; uses assigned work to develop individual strategies for learning.

NEVADA

Offices of Organizations Concerned with Learning Disabilities

ACLD, Inc.: P.O. Box 188, Alamo, NV 89001. Telephone: (702) 725-3552. President: Kristin Thomas.

Council for Exceptional Children: President: Don McHenry, Clark County School District, 2832 E. Flamingo Road, Las Vegas, NV 89121. Telephone: (702) 736-5471.

Nevada Easter Seal Society: 1455 E. Tropicana Avenue, Suite 660, Las Vegas, NV 89119. Executive Director: Nancy Kosik. Telephone: (702) 739-7771.

State Department of Education Learning Disabilities Personnel

Jane Early, Director of Special Education, 400 W. King Street, Carson City, NV 89710. Telephone: (702) 885-3140.

Private and Day Schools

Las Vegas: New Horizons Center for Learning, 401 Campbell Drive, 89107. Telephone: (702) 870-5353. Executive Director: Theresa C. Smith. Elementary and secondary day school with summer program. Ages served: 5-18. Grades served: kindergarten-12. Current enrollment: 58. Maximum enrollment: 58. Full-time staff: 9. Volunteers: 8. Scholarships/financial aid available. Services: individual tutoring, academic and psychological testing, adaptive physical education.

College and University Special Programs and Services

University of Nevada-Las Vegas: 4505 Maryland Parkway, Las Vegas, NV 89154. Total enrollment: 11,000. LD students: 35. Special services: individual and group tutoring, training in study skills, special examinations, taped books, diagnostic testing, readers, academic and psychological counseling, vocational counseling and placement, student resource center, support group, mentor, proofreading, typing services; computer-assisted instruction for math, visual perception, and memory.

- **Special program:** Learning Abilities Program (LAP). Goal is to develop gradual academic independence. First semester consists of one-half abilities and skill development courses and one-half required courses. Number of credits and required courses taken per semester increases with student progress. A degree usually takes more than four years to complete. All applicants must take an evaluation battery with LAP staff. Director: Judith H. Dettre. Telephone: (702) 739-3781.

Center/clinic: Reading Center and Clinic. Telephone: (702) 739-3781. Director: Judith H. Dettre. Open to public. Ages served: 7-adult. Grades served: 2-college. Services: testing, remediation/tutoring, advisement, mentors, proofreading, typing services, untimed and/or oral examinations.

Center/clinic: Exceptional Children Services, Department of Special Education. Telephone: (702) 739-3205. Director: John C. Van Vactor. Open to public. Ages served: all.

University of Nevada-Reno: Reno, NV 89557. Special services: individual tutoring in math and reading, academic counseling, readers, note takers, vocational counseling and placement. Contact: Ada Cook, Director, Special Programs and Academic Skills Center. Telephone: (702) 784-6801.

Center/clinic: Reading and Learning Disabilities Center, College of Education. Telephone: (702) 784-4961. Director: Paul M. Hollingsworth. Open to public. Grades served: 2-10, first grade repeaters. Services: diagnostic testing, curriculum-based assessment, vision survey, auditory discrimination and perception survey, individual and group tutoring.

Center/clinic: Special Programs/Academic Skills Center, TSSC Room 107. Telephone: (702) 784-6801. Director: Ada Cook. Open to public. Services: tutoring, writing clinic, vocational counseling and placement, academic counseling.

Hospital Clinics

Las Vegas: Southern Nevada Memorial Hospital, Claude I. Howard Rehabilitation Center, 1800 W. Charleston Boulevard, 89102. Telephone: (702) 383-2313. Contact: Lynn Cremen, Supervisor, Speech Pathology/Audiology. Outpatient, inpatient, day, and after school program. Ages served: all. Services: diagnostic testing, psychological testing, individual tutoring, parent counseling; group, speech, language, physical, and occupational therapy; support group, social services, computer-assisted training.

NEW HAMPSHIRE

Offices of Organizations Concerned with Learning Disabilities

Council for Exceptional Children: President: Jean Richards, Southwest Road, Canterbury, NH 03224. Telephone: (603) 783-9932.

Easter Seal Society-Goodwill Industries of Vermont/New Hampshire: 555 Auburn Street, Manchester, NH 03103. Executive Director: Robert G. Cholette. Telephone: (603) 623-8863.

Orton Dyslexia Society (New England Branch): c/o Rocky Hill School, Ives Road, East Greenwich, RI 02818. President: Emi Flynn. Telephone: (401) 884-3346.

State Department of Education Learning Disabilities Personnel

Robert T. Kennedy, Director of Special Education, State Department of Education, 101 Pleasant Street, Concord, NH 03301. Telephone: (603) 271-3741. Learning disabilities consultant: Jane Weissmann.

Private and Day Schools

Concord: Alternative High School Program, Project Second Start, 450 N. State, 03301. Telephone: (603) 225-3318. Program Coordinator: Karl T. Bergeron. Secondary day school. Ages served: 14-18. Grades served: 8-12. Current enrollment: 50. Maximum enrollment: 60. Full-time staff: 8. Part-time staff: 1. Services: individual and group tutoring, academic testing and counseling, adaptive physical education, computers, vocational training, work-study, job placement. Recreation: cross-country skiing, volleyball, softball, soccer, hiking, backpacking. Notes: Individualized academic program with primary emphasis on math, reading, and writing.

Greenfield: Crotched Mountain Rehabilitation Center School, 03047. Telephone: (603) 547-3311. Director of Educational Services: Kenneth Mann. Elementary and secondary day and residential school with summer program and camp. Ages served: 7-21. Grades served: ungraded kindergarten-12. Current enrollment: 106. Maximum enrollment: 126. Full-time staff: 60. Services: individual and group tutoring, academic and psychological testing; academic, psychological, and family counseling; physical and occupational therapy, adaptive physical education, vocational training, medical services; specialized instruction in visual motor integration, perceptual, fine, and gross motor skills, visual and auditory perception, computer education. Recreation: arts and crafts, music, driver education. Notes: Behavior modification program.

Suncook: Pine Haven Boys Center, P.O. Box 162, 03275. Telephone: (603) 485-7141. Director: Rev. Albert Zanatta. Males only elementary boarding school. Ages served: 9-15. Grades served: 1-8. Current enrollment: 16. Maximum enrollment:

24. Full-time staff: 20. Part-time staff: 4. Services: individual and group tutoring, psychological testing; psychological, individual, and family counseling; vocational training. Recreation: baseball, football, basketball, soccer, skiing, swimming, ice-skating, biking.

Summer Camps and Programs

Bedford: Camp Allen, Inc., Route 5, 03102. Telephone: (603) 622-8471. Director: Stephen P. Sullivan. Residential camp. Ages served: 6-adult. Maximum enrollment: 60. Full-time staff: 50. Volunteers: 2-4. Scholarships/financial aid available. Services: adaptive physical education, vocational training, medical services, environmental education. Recreation: swimming, hiking, riding, field trips, nature study, crafts, drama, camping. Notes: Serves physically and developmentally disabled.

Bradford: Wabasso, Box 430, 03221. Telephone: (603) 938-2240. Permanent mailing address: Patriots' Trail Girl Scout Council, Six St. James Avenue, Boston, MA 02116. Telephone: (617) 482-1078. Director: Cindy Nugent. Females only residential camp with limited services. Ages served: 6-17. Grades served: 2-12. Maximum enrollment: 140. Full-time staff: 35. Scholarships/financial aid available. Medical services. Recreation: camping, nature study, riding, swimming, team sports, crafts, drama, canoeing.

Canaan: War Bonnet for Boys, Inc., Route 1, Box 29, 03741. Telephone: (603) 523-4276. Director: Richard E. Vandall. Males only day and residential camp. Maximum enrollment: 75. Grades served: 7-12. Full-time staff: 23. Part-time staff: 22. Scholarships/financial aid available. Services: individual tutoring, psychological testing, psychological and family counseling, work-study, job placement, therapeutic milieu. Recreation: swimming, hiking, field trips, nature study, crafts, camping, photography, scuba, mini bikes, cycling, sailing, jetski, gliding, hang gliding, extensive travel. Notes: Operates an alternative living project during the school year that serves adolescent boys with school, social, behavioral, and family problems. The boys attend the local high school, but their education is supplemented by the project's in-house tutorial study and enrichment program.

Meredith: Menotomy, Meredith Neck Road, 03253. Telephone: (603) 279-6022. Permanent mailing address: Patriots' Trail Girl Scout Council, Six St. James Avenue, Boston, MA 02116. Telephone: (617) 482-1078. Director: Marty Elkins. Females only residential camp with limited services. Ages served: 8-15. Grades served: 4-10. Maximum enrollment: 100. Full-time staff: 30. Scholarships/financial aid available. Medical services. Recreation: hiking, nature study, swimming, sailing, crafts, canoeing.

College and University Special Programs and Services

Keene State College: 229 Main Street, Keene, NH 03431. Special services: individual, group, and peer tutoring; training in study skills; academic, financial aid, and psychological counseling; limited taped books and readers, ombudsman, academic skills workshops, academic advising and support. Contact: Chrystal Montgomery, Director, Special Academic Services. Telephone: (603) 352-1909 ext. 559.

New Hampshire College: 2500 N. River Road, Manchester, NH 03104. Total enrollment: 1,766. Special services: individual and group tutoring, training in study skills, academic and psychological counseling, student resource center, diagnostic testing. Contact: F.G. Doucette, Director, Learning Center. Telephone: (603) 623-1423.

Notre Dame College: 2321 Elm Street, Manchester, NH 03104. Total enrollment: 750. LD students: 10. Special services: student resource center, support group.

- **Special program:** SNAP (Special Needs and Assistance Program). Must meet regular and special admissions requirements. Special requirements include verification of learning disability through recent diagnostic tests and an interview. Full or part-time students eligible for the program. Director: Robert Cray-Andrews. Telephone: (603) 669-4298 ext. 151.

Rivier College: S. Main Street, Nashua, NH 03060. Total enrollment: 2,257. Special services: special examinations, support group, diagnostic testing, individual tutoring, training in study skills, academic and psychological counseling. Contact: Bonnie Sunstein, Director, Learning Center. Telephone: (603) 888-1311 ext. 240.

Center/clinic: The Learning Center. Telephone: (603) 888-1311 ext. 240. Director: Bonnie Sunstein. Grades served: college.

University of New Hampshire: Durham, NH 03824. Total enrollment: 10,600. LD students: 30. Special services: readers, individual and group tutoring, special examinations, academic and psychological counseling, diagnostic testing, taped books, training in study skills, support group. Contact: Sharon Kraft-Lund, Coordinator, Handicapped Services. Telephone: (603) 862-2607.

NEW JERSEY

Offices of Organizations Concerned with Learning Disabilities

ACLD, Inc.: P.O. Box 215, Eatontown, NJ 07724. President: Allan Goldberg. Telephone: (201) 431-0986.

Easter Seal Society for Crippled Children and Adults of New Jersey: 32 Ford Avenue, P.O. Box 155, Milltown, NJ 08850. President: Clark J. Paradise. Telephone: (201) 247-8353.

Orton Dyslexia Society: 236 Millbrook Avenue, Randolph, NJ 07836. President: Lois H. Rothschild. Telephone: (201) 328-1512.

State Department of Education Learning Disabilities Personnel

Jeffrey V. Osowski, Director, Division of Special Education, CN 500, 225 W. State Street, Trenton, NJ 08625. Telephone: (609) 292-0147 or 633-6833.

Private and Day Schools

Alloway: Ranch Hope/Strang School, Box 325, 08001. Telephone: (609) 935-1555. School Administrator: Colleen G. Cary. Males only secondary boarding school with limited services. Ages served: 11-16. Grades served: ungraded. Current enrollment: 30. Maximum enrollment: 40. Full-time staff: 44. Part-time staff: 5. Scholarships/financial aid available. Services: individual and group tutoring, academic and psychological testing; academic, psychological, and family counseling; vocational training, limited work-study, medical services. Recreation: basketball, football, running club, swimming, riding, softball.

Atco: Archway School, 197 Jackson Road, 08004. Telephone: (609) 767-5757. Executive Director: Chester M. Whittaker. Preschool, elementary, secondary, and adult day and boarding school with summer program and camp. Ages served: 2-22. Grades served: preschool-12. Current enrollment: 200. Maximum enrollment: 200. Full-time staff: 65. Part-time staff: 12. Services: individual and group tutoring, academic and psychological testing; academic, psychological, and family counseling; physical and occupational therapy, adaptive physical education, vocational training, work-study, job placement, medical services. Recreation: swimming, boating, fishing, ponies, petting zoo, nature studies.

Basking Ridge: Jerry Davis Early Childhood Center, Hamilton Lane, 07920. Telephone: (201) 658-4359. Executive Director: Joan Sapienza. Preschool with summer program. Ages served: birth-6. Current enrollment: 35. Maximum enrollment: 50. Full-time staff: 11. Part-time staff: 2. Services: academic testing, family counseling; physical, occupational, and speech therapy; adaptive physical education, medical services, developmental daycare, parent training, center and home-based program model.

Basking Ridge: Lord Stirling School, Lord Stirling Road, 07920. Telephone: (201) 766-1786. Director: Joseph Gorga. Elementary and secondary day school. Ages served: 13-20. Grades served: 7-12. Current enrollment: 41. Maximum enrollment: 55. Full-time staff: 14. Part-time staff: 5. Services: individual and group tutoring, academic and psychological testing; academic, psychological, and family counseling; adaptive physical education, vocational training, work-study, job placement. Recreation: swimming, soccer, track and field, baseball, basketball, cooking, photography, sewing, art, weight lifting, computer games.

NEW JERSEY

Blawenbury: The Rock Brook School, Box 297, 08504. Telephone: (609) 466-2989. Director: Claireanne Ganssle. Preschool and elementary day school. Ages served: 3-9. Grades served: preschool-3. Current enrollment: 26. Maximum enrollment: 26. Full-time staff: 11. Part-time staff: 3. Limited scholarships/financial aid available. Services: individual and group tutoring, academic testing; occupational, speech, and language therapy. Notes: For children with language, speech, and learning disabilities.

Demarest: Community High School, 15 Columbus Road, 07627. Telephone: (201) 767-6016. Director of Education: Toby Braunstein. Director of Program: Dennis Cohen. Secondary day school. Ages served: 14-21. Grades served: 9-12, post high school program. Current enrollment: 100. Maximum enrollment: 100. Full-time staff: 32. Part-time staff: 5. Scholarships/financial aid available. Services: individual and group tutoring, academic and psychological testing, academic counseling, adaptive physical education, work-study, medical facilities, computer skills, SAT preparation, vocational orientation and training. Recreation: gym, weight room, intramural sports. Notes: Students in post high school program attend college part-time.

East Orange: United Cerebral Palsy of North Jersey, Inc., 91 S. Harrison Street, 07018. Telephone: (201) 674-1150. Executive Director: Steven Proctor. Preschool and elementary day school. Ages served: birth-15. Current enrollment: 130. Maximum enrollment: 200. Full-time staff: 30. Part-time staff: 20. Scholarships/financial aid available. Services: psychological and family counseling, physical and occupational therapy, adaptive physical education, vocational training.

Eatontown: Harbor School, 240 Broad Street, 07724. Telephone: (201) 544-9394. Educational Director: Rochelle Borsky. Elementary and secondary day school. Ages served: 5-16. Current enrollment: 82. Maximum enrollment: 90. Full-time staff: 25. Part-time staff: 4. Services: individual and group tutoring, academic testing, family counseling, adaptive physical education, occupational and speech therapy.

Edison: Cerebral Palsy Association of Middlesex County, Oak Drive, Roosevelt Park, 08837. Telephone: (201) 549-5580. Executive Director: Dominic Ursino. Preschool, elementary, secondary, and adult day school with summer program. Ages served: 3-21. Grades served: preschool-adult. Current enrollment: 112. Maximum enrollment: 112. Full-time staff: 40-45. Part-time staff: 30. Scholarships/financial aid available. Services: individual instruction, limited psychological testing; physical, occupational, and speech therapy; adaptive physical education, prevocational training, work-study in sheltered workshop, medical services, parent support groups, nonvocal communication and therapy evaluations.

Englewood Cliffs: The Learning Center for Exceptional Children, c/o South Cliff School, Bayview Avenue, 07632. Telephone: (201) 944-5423. Executive Director: Linda J. Buonauro. Preschool and elementary day school with summer camp. Ages served: 2½-18. Current enrollment: 85. Maximum enrollment: 125.

Full-time staff: 24. Part-time staff: 1. Scholarships/financial aid available. Services: individual and group tutoring, academic and psychological testing, psychological and family counseling, physical and occupational therapy, adaptive physical education, vocational training, work-study. Recreation: field trips, athletics.

Haddonfield: The Bancroft School, Hopkins Lane, 08033. Telephone: (609) 429-0010. Acting President: George Nieman. Contact: Ms. Yolanda Katona, Director of Admissions. Preschool and adult day and boarding school with summer camp. Ages served: 5 and up. Grades served: ungraded. Current enrollment: 252 children; 149 adults. Full-time staff: 258. Part-time staff: 133. Scholarships/financial aid available. Services: academic and psychological testing, psychological and family counseling, physical therapy, adaptive physical education, vocational training, work-study, job placement, medical services. Recreation: swimming, bicycling, roller-skating, bowling, tennis, hiking, camping, boating, riding, skiing. Notes: Serves mildly to moderately mentally retarded, neurologically and communication handicapped, and multiply handicapped.

Haddonfield: Kingsway Learning Center, 144 Kings Highway, West, 08033. Telephone: (609) 428-8108. Executive Director: David J. Panner. Preschool and elementary day school with summer program. Ages served: birth-14. Current enrollment: 187. Maximum enrollment: 187. Full-time staff: 53. Part-time staff: 18. Services: individual and group tutoring, academic and psychological testing; academic, psychological, and family counseling; physical and occupational therapy, vocational training, work-study, medical services, therapeutic education program for ages 3-14.

Haworth: Bergen Center for Child Development, Inc., 140 Park Street, 07641. Telephone: (201) 385-4857. Director: Adrienne Lefebvre. Elementary and secondary day school. Ages served: 5-21. Current enrollment: 75. Maximum enrollment: 80. Full-time staff: 34. Part-time staff: 6. Services: individual tutoring, academic and psychological testing, psychological and family counseling, art and occupational therapy, adaptive physical education, vocational training, work-study, small group instruction. Recreation: physical education, field trips, camping.

Kendall Park: The Newgrange School, 30 Roberts Street, 08824. Telephone: (201) 821-5180. Administrative Director: Lois Young. Elementary and secondary day school. Ages served: 8-18. Grades served: ungraded. Current enrollment: 50. Maximum enrollment: 50. Full-time staff: 18. Services: individual tutoring, academic counseling; speech, language, physical, and occupational therapy; adaptive physical education, work-study, medical services, computers, video workshops. Recreation: after school swimming, bowling, hiking, canoeing, karate.

Lakewood: Alpha School, Forest Avenue and 11th Street, 08701. Telephone: (201) 370-1150. Administrative Director: Ruth Reinhard. Elementary day school. Ages served: 5-16. Current enrollment: 97. Maximum enrollment: 110. Full-time

NEW JERSEY

staff: 30. Part-time staff: 6. Services: individual and group tutoring, academic testing, psychological counseling, adaptive physical education, vocational training; occupational, speech, and language therapy.

Livingston: The Gramon School, 346 E. Mt. Pleasant Avenue, 07039. Telephone: (201) 533-1313. Director: David F. Weeks. Elementary and secondary day school with limited services. Ages served: 6-21. Grades served: 1-12. Current enrollment: 71. Maximum enrollment: 80. Full-time staff: 24. Part-time staff: 4. Services: individual and group tutoring, academic testing; academic, psychological, group, individual, and family counseling; adaptive physical education, medical services, prevocational training, art therapy. Recreation: basketball, volleyball, softball, swimming, riding, roller-skating. Notes: Reality therapy and logical consequences therapeutic milieu.

Lodi: The Felician School for Exceptional Children, 260 S. Main Street, Box 530, 07644. Telephone: (201) 777-5355. Director: Sr. Mary Ramona Borkowski. Preschool and elementary day school. Ages served: 1-20. Current enrollment: 125. Maximum enrollment: 130. Full-time staff: 48. Part-time staff: 9. Services: psychological testing, physical therapy, adaptive physical education, vocational training, work-study.

Lumberton: Midway School, P.O. Box 216, Newbold's Corner Road, 08048. Telephone: (609) 267-5366. Director: Barbara C. Fahrenbruch. Elementary and secondary day school with summer camp. Ages served: 5-19. Grades served: 1-12. Current enrollment: 53. Maximum enrollment: 80. Full-time staff: 20. Part-time staff: 4. Services: group tutoring, academic testing, psychological and family counseling, adaptive physical education, vocational training, work-study, medical services, speech and language therapy; family living center. Recreation: intramurals, art, music, assemblies, field trips, physical education. Notes: Strictly for the learning disabled. Emphasis on functional academics.

Morristown: Early Childhood Learning Centers of New Jersey, 186 Morris Street, 07960. Telephone: (201) 267-4508. Executive Director: Dulcie Ann Freeman. Elementary day school with summer program. Ages served: 5-16. Grades served: preschool-junior high. Current enrollment: 190. Maximum enrollment: 200. Full-time staff: 42. Part-time staff: 15. Scholarships/financial aid available. Services: individual and group tutoring, academic and psychological testing, psychological and family counseling, physical and occupational therapy, adaptive physical education, prevocational training, medical services. Recreation: scouting, clubs, sports, music, art. Notes: Emphasis on social development.

Mountain Lakes: The Wilson School Supplementary Department, 271 Boulevard, 07046. Telephone: (201) 334-0181. Director: Louise A. Garzinsky. Elementary and secondary day school with summer program. Ages served: 6-13. Grades served: 1-6. Current enrollment: 25. Maximum enrollment: 28. Full-time staff: 8. Part-time staff: 3. Services: individual and group tutoring, academic testing and counseling. Recreation: swimming, art. Notes: Students mainstreamed in art, music, library, physical education, swimming, computers.

Mount Freedom: Kingsbrook Academy, 20 Brookside Road, 07960. Telephone: (201) 895-3063. Coordinator: Judith Oehler. Secondary day school. Ages served: 13-20. Current enrollment: 50. Maximum enrollment: 80. Full-time staff: 10. Part-time staff: 4. Scholarships/financial aid available. Services: individual and group tutoring, academic and psychological testing; academic, psychological, and family counseling; vocational training, work-study, medical services. Recreation: gym, pool, park, community resources.

North Branch: The Midland School, Readington Road, P.O. Box 5026, 08876. Telephone: (201) 722-8222. Executive Director: Edward G. Scagliotta. Elementary day school with summer program and camp. Ages served: 5-21. Grades served: ungraded. Current enrollment: 187. Maximum enrollment: 189. Full-time staff: 65. Services: individual and group tutoring, academic testing; academic, psychological, and family counseling; adaptive physical education, medical services.

Orange: Community School, 395 S. Center Street, 07050. Telephone: (201) 675-3817. Director: L. Jane Smith. Elementary day school with limited services; summer camp. Ages served: 5-12. Grades served: ungraded. Current enrollment: 21. Maximum enrollment: 24. Full-time staff: 6. Part-time staff: 7. Services: individual and group tutoring, psychological testing; academic, psychological, and family counseling; speech and movement therapy. Recreation: swimming, art, cooking. Notes: Primary diagnosis of students is emotionally disturbed. Learning disability is a secondary diagnosis.

Phillipsburg: Stepping Stone School, Second and Aurora Streets, 08865. Telephone: (201) 859-3900. Executive Director: Lana Asmund. Elementary day school. Ages served: 5-14. Grades served: kindergarten-9. Current enrollment: 37. Maximum enrollment: 45. Full-time staff: 14. Part-time staff: 3. Services: individual, group, psychological, and family counseling; adaptive physical education, individualized instruction, speech therapy. Notes: Serves emotionally disturbed.

Pompton Plains: Chancellor Academy, 93 W. End Avenue, 07444. Telephone: (201) 835-4989. Director: Richard A. Sheridan. Secondary day school. Ages served: 13-21. Grades served: 7-12. Current enrollment: 56. Maximum enrollment: 64. Full-time staff: 11. Part-time staff: 3. Services: individual and group tutoring, academic and psychological testing; individual, group, academic, psychological, and family counseling; adaptive physical education, vocational training, work-study, job placement. Recreation: arts and crafts, bowling, sports, physical fitness, Nautilus. Notes: Entire facility is maintained by students to teach responsibility.

NEW JERSEY

Princeton: Princeton School for Exceptional Children, Box 50, 08540. Mailing address: Four Willowood Drive, West Trenton, NJ 08628. Telephone: (609) 924-8555 or 924-8559. Executive Director: Stephen P. Hritz. Elementary and secondary day school. Ages served: 7-18. Grades served: 1-12. Current enrollment: 56. Maximum enrollment: 58. Full-time staff: 21. Part-time staff: 3. Services: individual and group tutoring, academic testing, psychological and family counseling, adaptive physical education. Recreation: physical education.

Ridgefield: Early Childhood Learning Centers of New Jersey, 455 Shaler Boulevard, 07657. Telephone: (201) 941-4011. Principal: Vicki Lindorff. Day school with summer program. Ages served: 4-13. Grades served: ungraded. Current enrollment: 50. Maximum enrollment: 60. Full-time staff: 17. Part-time staff: 7. Services: group tutoring, academic and psychological testing; academic, psychological, and family counseling; occupational therapy, adaptive physical education, vocational training, nurse. Notes: Serves communication and neurologically impaired.

Ridgewood: The Holmstead School, 14 Hope Street, 07451. Telephone: (201) 447-1696. Director: Patricia G. Whitehead. Secondary day school with limited services. Ages served: 13-18. Grades served: 9-12. Current enrollment: 43. Maximum enrollment: 46. Full-time staff: 12. Part-time staff: 3. Scholarships/financial aid available. Services: psychological testing, psychological and family counseling. Recreation: daily sports and recreation program including volleyball, basketball, yearbook, art, cooking.

South River: Gateway School, 80 David Street, 08882. Telephone: (201) 238-6877. Administrative Director: Loretta A. Kennedy. Educational Director: Ellyn Learner. Elementary day school. Ages served: 5-16. Current enrollment: 49. Full-time staff: 14. Part-time staff: 4. Services: adaptive physical education; occupational, speech, and art therapy; music. Recreation: gymnasium.

Summit: The Winston School, 275 Morris Avenue, 07901. Telephone: (201) 277-6350. Director: R.J. Dewey. Elementary day school. Ages served: 6-14. Grades served: ungraded. Current enrollment: 36. Maximum enrollment: 44. Full-time staff: 10. Part-time staff: 7. Scholarships/financial aid available. Services: individual and group tutoring, academic testing, academic and family counseling, adaptive physical education, art, music. Recreation: playground, playing fields, swimming, physical and outdoor education, three-day camping trip.

Teaneck: The Community School of Bergen County, Inc. (Lower School), 11 W. Forest Avenue, 07666. Telephone: (201) 837-8070. Executive Director: Rita Rowan. Elementary day school. Ages served: 6-14. Grades served: 1-8. Current enrollment: 104. Maximum enrollment: 110. Full-time staff: 33. Part-time staff: 4. Services: individual and group tutoring, academic testing, academic and psychological counseling, adaptive physical education, speech and language remediation.

Union: United Cerebral Palsy League of Union County, 373 Clermont Terrace, 07083-9990. Telephone: (201) 354-5800. Executive Director: David Spelkoman. Preschool, elementary, and secondary day school with summer camp; adult workshop. Ages served: 3 months-adult. Grades served: preschool-6, adult. Current enrollment: 60. Maximum enrollment: 75. Full-time staff: 33. Part-time staff: 1. Scholarships/financial aid available for Camp Summershine. Services: group tutoring, academic testing, psychological and family counseling; physical, occupational, and speech therapy; adaptive physical education, vocational training, medical clinic, transportation. Recreation: Camp Summershine, weekend respite program.

Warren: The Center School, 46 Washington Valley Road, 07060. Telephone: (201) 356-5196. Director: Helen Goldberg. Elementary and secondary day school. Full-time staff: 42. Part-time staff: 10. Current enrollment: 108. Maximum enrollment: 114. Ages served: 5-18. Grades served: kindergarten-12. Services: individual and group instruction, academic testing, counseling, adaptive physical education, prevocational training; occupational, speech, and language therapy; computers. Recreation: playing field. Notes: For neurologically impaired or emotionally disturbed children of average or above average intelligence.

Wayne: Clearview School, 45 Urban Club Road, 07470. Telephone: (201) 694-5900. Director: Richard S. Arilotta. Elementary and secondary day school. Ages served: 5-21. Grades served: kindergarten-12. Current enrollment: 50. Maximum enrollment: 66. Full-time staff: 17. Services: individual and group tutoring; academic, speech, and language testing; academic and family counseling, speech and language therapy. Notes: For emotionally disturbed, neurologically impaired, and communication handicapped.

Winfield Park: Kohler Child Development Center, 39½ Wavecrest Avenue, 07036. Telephone: (201) 925-2390. Principal: Pam Venckus. Preschool. Ages served: birth-7. Current enrollment: 60. Maximum enrollment: 68. Full-time staff: 21. Part-time staff: 2. Scholarships/financial aid available. Services: academic and psychological testing, physical and occupational therapy.

College and University Special Programs and Services

Caldwell College: Ryerson Avenue, Caldwell, NJ 07006. Total enrollment: 307. LD students: 4. Special services: individual and group tutoring, training in study skills, academic counseling, taped books, special examinations. Contact: Harriet Schenk, Learning Center Director. Telephone: (201) 228-4424 ext. 271.

Fairleigh Dickinson University: Teaneck, NJ 07666.

Center/clinic: Center for Clinical Teaching. Telephone: (201) 692-2808 or 692-2837. Director: Mary L. Farrell. Open to public. Ages served: 7-18. Grades served: 2-12. Services: individualized instruction in remedial reading, writing, and math; computer instruction, learning evaluations.

NEW JERSEY

Jersey City State College: 2039 Kennedy Boulevard, Jersey City, NJ 07305.

Center/clinic: Learning Disabilities Clinic. Telephone: (201) 547-3023. Director: George Voller. Open to public. Grades served: preschool-adult. Services: individual and group tutoring, training in study skills, academic and psychological counseling, taped books, special examinations, readers, diagnostic testing.

Kean College of New Jersey: Morris Avenue, Union, NJ 07083. Special services: individual tutoring, training in study skills, academic and psychological counseling, special examinations, diagnostic testing, ombudsman. Contact: Marie Segal, Acting Director, Institute of Child Study. Telephone: (201) 527-2380.

Center/clinic: Institute of Child Study. Telephone: (201) 527-2380. Director: Marie Segal. Open to public. Ages served: all. Grades served: all.

Middlesex County College: Woodbridge Avenue, Edison, NJ 08818. Special services: individual and group tutoring, training in study skills, academic and psychological counseling, taped books, special examinations, student resource center, readers, diagnostic testing, ombudsman.

- **Special program:** Project Connections. Must fulfill regular and special admissions requirements. Special requirements include an interview and verification of learning disability through recent diagnostic tests. Director: Judith Kuperstein. Telephone: (201) 548-6000 ext. 377. Counselor for Disabled Students: Elaine Weir. Telephone: (201) 548-6000 ext. 373.

Montclair State College: Upper Montclair, NJ 07043. Total enrollment: 15,800. LD students: 20. Special services: individual tutoring, ombudsman, special examinations, academic counseling, diagnostic testing, taped books, training in study skills. Contact: Edward Martin, Dean of Students. Telephone: (201) 893-4118.

Center/clinic: Psychoeducational Center. Telephone: (201) 893-4255. Director: Antoinette Spiotta. Open to public. Ages served: all.

Rutgers University: New Brunswick, NJ 08903. Special services: training in study skills, academic and psychological counseling, ombudsman. Notes: Learning disabilities clinic currently being planned. Contact: Steven A. Carlson, Assistant Professor. Telephone: (201) 932-7567.

Seton Hall University: S. Orange Avenue, South Orange, NJ 07079. Special services: group tutoring, training in study skills, academic and psychological counseling, student resource center. Contact: Marietta Esposito Peskin, Director, Learning Disabilities Graduate Program. Telephone: (201) 761-9450.

Trenton State College: CN 550 Hillwood Lakes, Trenton, NJ 08625. Total enrollment: 10,000. LD students: 12. Special services: individual tutoring, training in study skills, academic and psychological counseling, taped books, special examinations, readers, diagnostic testing. Contact: Betty Cohen, Program Assistant. Telephone: (609) 771-2272.

Hospital Clinics

Camden: Cooper Hospital/University Medical Center, Speech Pathology and Audiology, or Child Evaluation Center, One Cooper Plaza, 08103. Telephone: (609) 342-3060. Contact: Beth Kaplan, Administrative Director, Clinical Services. Outpatient and after school program. Ages served: birth-18. Services: diagnostic testing, psychological testing, individual tutoring; speech, language, physical, and occupational therapy; social services, coordination with community agencies and school systems to develop individual care plans.

Edison: John F. Kennedy Medical Center, The Johnson Institute, Pediatric Rehabilitation Department, 2050 Oak Tree Road, 08820. Telephone: (201) 321-7515. Contact: Thomas Kennedy III, Executive Director. Day program. Ages served: birth-adolescence. Services: early intervention and preschool program, individual tutoring, academic and psychological testing, psychological and family counseling, physical and occupational therapy, adaptive physical education, medical services, speech and language evaluation and therapy.

Hackensack: Hackensack Medical Center, Institute for Child Development, Johnson Hall, 30 Prospect Avenue, 07601. Telephone: (201) 441-2371. Contact: Marvin I. Gottlieb or Dorothy Kletzkin. Outpatient, day, after school, and summer program. Ages served: birth-18. Services: school for children with communication-based learning disabilities; diagnostic testing, academic and psychological testing, individual tutoring; academic, psychological, and parent counseling; speech, language, physical, and occupational therapy; adaptive physical education, support group, social services, interdisciplinary evaluations.

Long Branch: Monmouth Medical Center, Child Evaluation Center, 307 Third Avenue, 07740. Telephone: (201) 870-5211. Contact: Ed Mc Hugh. Outpatient and inpatient program. Ages served: birth-21. Services: diagnostic testing, academic and psychological testing, academic and psychological counseling; speech, language, physical, and occupational therapy; social services referrals.

Mt. Holly: Memorial Hospital of Burlington County, Speech and Hearing/Pediatric Rehabilitation Program, Tiffany Square Office Building, Suite 102, 2615 Route 38, 08060. Telephone: (609) 261-7040 or 261-7030. Contact: Beth Kocher, Manager. Outpatient, inpatient, day, and after school program. Ages served: all. Services: diagnostic testing, academic and psychological testing, individual tutoring, parent counseling; speech, language, physical, and occupational therapy; social services, audiological and central auditory testing.

Neptune: Jersey Shore Medical Center, Fitkin Hospital, Child Evaluation and Learning Disabilities Center, 1945 Corlies Avenue, 07753. Telephone: (201) 775-5500. Contact: Janice Grebler, Clinical Supervisor. Outpatient program. Ages

NEW JERSEY

served: birth-18. Services: diagnostic testing, academic and psychological testing, social services.

Princeton: The Medical Center at Princeton, Merwick Unit, Bayard Lane, 08540. Telephone: (609) 734-4616. Contact: Patricia B. Henry, Chief, Communication Disorders Unit. Outpatient, inpatient, day, and after school program. Ages served: all. Services: diagnostic testing by multidisciplinary team, psychological testing, referrals; speech, language, physical, and occupational therapy.

Somerville: Somerset Medical Center, Speech and Hearing Department-Child Study Team, Rehill Avenue, 08876. Telephone: (201) 685-2946. Contact: Irwin Blake, Director of Speech and Hearing. Outpatient, inpatient, and after school program. Ages served: preschool-adult. Services: diagnostic testing, academic and psychological testing, individual and group tutoring, parent counseling; group, speech, language, physical, and occupational therapy; social services, computer-assisted learning.

Trenton: St. Francis Medical Center, 601 Hamilton Avenue, 08629. Contact: Jane M. Malkiewicz, Speech and Hearing Center. Telephone: (609) 599-5220. Or Mike Esmond, Physical Medicine and Rehabilitation. Telephone: (609) 599-5225. Outpatient and inpatient program. Ages served: all. Services: speech, language, physical, and occupational therapy.

Other Services

Ho Ho Kus: Northeast Consultants Group, P.O. Box 344, 07423. Telephone: (201) 652-6951. Codirector: Marijanet Doonan. Organization serving learning disabled adolescents. Services: individual and group tutoring, training in study skills, academic and psychological counseling, readers, diagnostic testing, ombudsman, support group, SAT preparation, evaluations, college support program, presentations to parent and professional groups.

Margate: Atlantic County Association for Children and Adults with Learning Disabilities, P.O. Box 3241, 08402. Telephone: (609) 822-4082. Director: Ann Carlino. Clinic. Day, after school, and summer program. Ages served: 2-adult. Parent Information Hotline: (609) 822-2443 or 822-4082. Services: diagnostic testing, academic and psychological testing, individual and group tutoring, academic and parent counseling, speech and language therapy, support group, evaluation of the gifted, remediation in all academic areas, referrals.

New Brunswick: Educational Services Center, Three Voorhees Road, 08901. Telephone: (201) 545-5328. Director: Sally Hindes. Clinic. Day and after school program. Ages served: 3-25. Services: diagnostic testing, academic testing, individual tutoring; academic, psychological, and parent counseling; speech and language therapy.

NEW MEXICO

Offices of Organizations Concerned with Learning Disabilities

ACLD, Inc.: 824 Vassar Drive, N.E., Albuquerque, NM 87106. Contact: Marjorie S. McCament. Telephone: (505) 842-3741.

Council for Exceptional Children: President: Gary Adamson, 10521 Toltec Road, N.E., Albuquerque, NM 87111. Telephone: Office (505) 277-5018; Home (505) 299-2040.

Easter Seal Society of New Mexico: 4805 Menaul, N.E., Albuquerque, NM 87110. Executive Director: Timothy Taschwer. Telephone: (505) 888-3811.

Orton Dyslexia Society: 450 Branding Iron Road, Rio Rancho, NM 87124. President: Patricia S. Tomlan.

State Department of Education Learning Disabilities Personnel

Mr. Elie Gutierrez, Director of Special Education, State Department of Education, State Education Building, 300 Don Gaspar Street, Santa Fe, NM 85701-2786. Telephone: (505) 827-6541.

Private and Day Schools

Santa Fe: Brush Ranch School, P.O. Box 2450, 87501. Telephone: (505) 757-6114. Director: Newcomb Rice. Elementary and secondary boarding school. Ages served: 10-17. Grades served: ungraded. Current enrollment: 64. Maximum enrollment: 64. Full-time staff: 37. Part-time staff: 3. Services: individual and group tutoring, academic testing, academic and social counseling, adaptive physical education, prevocational training, full academic program, individual education plans. Recreation: 283-acre site in Santa Fe National Forest; basketball, softball, soccer, swimming, tennis, volleyball, ice-skating, hiking, riding. Notes: For children with learning problems who are unable to achieve their maximum potential in a normal classroom situation.

Summer Camps and Programs

Chimayo: Camp Frank Rand, P.O. Box 478, 87522. Permanent mailing address: Great Southwest Council, Boy Scouts of America, 4600 Montgomery Boulevard, N.E., Suite 4, Albuquerque, NM 87109-1218. Telephone: (505) 881-5322. District Executive/Camp Director: Michael L. McHugh. Males only residential camp. Ages served: 11-17. Grades served: 6-12. Maximum enrollment: 240. Full-time staff: 2. Part-time staff: 35. Scholarships/financial aid available. Services: limited medical services. Academic program: computers. Recreation: camping, hiking, nature study, riding, swimming, archery, crafts, rifle and shotgun, camp fires, songs, llamas, pioneering, basic life skills in the wilderness. Notes: Learning disabled children are mainstreamed.

Rincon: Camp Tonuco, 87940. Permanent mailing address: 1900 Telshore, Suite A, Las Cruces, NM 88001. Telephone: (505) 522-2073. Director: Leslie W. Dalton, Jr. Day and residential camp with academic program. Ages served: 8-18. Grades served: 1-12. Maximum enrollment: 90. Full-time staff: 8. Part-time staff: staff/student ratio 1:5. Scholarships/financial aid available. Services: individual and group tutoring, academic and psychological testing; academic, psychological, and family counseling; occupational therapy, vocational training, work-study, job placement, medical services. Academic programs: math, reading, English, spelling, study skills, college preparatory courses, computers, home study computer tutorials. Recreation: camping, hiking, field trips, nature study, riding, swimming, team sports, crafts, dance, drama, music, photography, fishing, TV script writing and directing, construction skills. Notes: Programs are year-round.

College and University Special Programs and Services

Eastern New Mexico University: Portales, NM 88130. Special services: individual and group tutoring, training in study skills, academic and psychological counseling, limited taped books, student resource center. Contact: Joyce F. Blasi, Coordinator of Special Education. Telephone: (505) 562-2169.

University of New Mexico: Albuquerque, NM 87131. Special services: readers, individual tutoring, special examinations, academic and psychological counseling, diagnostic testing, training in study skills, note takers, transcribers, photocopying, manual/oral interpreters. Contact: Marsha Alarid, Administrative Secretary, Special Services Program. Telephone: (505) 277-3506.

Center/clinic: Special Services Program, 2013 Mesa Vista Hall. Telephone: (505) 277-3506. Director: Juan J. Candelaria. Grades served: undergraduate, graduate.

Hospital Clinics

Albuquerque: University of New Mexico Mental Health Center, Bernalillo County Mental Health/Mental Retardation Center, Developmental Disabilities Division, 2600 Marble, N.E., 87106. Telephone: (505) 843-2952 or 843-2943. Contact: Maryanne O'Meara or Virginia Archuleta. Outpatient program. Ages served: birth-21. Services: diagnostic testing, academic and psychological testing.

NEW YORK

Offices of Organizations Concerned with Learning Disabilities

ACLD, Inc.: NYALD, Inc., 155 Washington Avenue, Third Floor, Albany, NY 12210. Telephone: (518) 436-4633. President: Rose Marie Raccioppi. Executive Director: Patricia Lilac.

Advocates for Children of New York, Inc.: 24-16 Bridge Plaza, South, Long Island City, NY 11101. Telephone: (718) 729-8866. Executive Director: Jane Stern.

Association for the Learning Disabled of the Genesee Valley (ALD): 973 East Avenue, Rochester, NY 14607. Telephone: (716) 271-3540. President: Dorinda Goggin. Program Director: Shirley A. Cass.

Council for Exceptional Children: President: Sally Quinby, 2679 Blakely Road, South Wales, NY 14139. Telephone: Office (716) 999-3413; Home (716) 652-1528.

Foundation for Children with Learning Disabilities: 99 Park Avenue, New York, NY 10016. Telephone: (212) 687-7211. President: Mrs. Pete Rozelle. Executive Director: Arlyn Gardner.

LD Hotline: (212) 677-3838. A New York metropolitan area information and referral service operated by the New York Association for the Learning Disabled, 817 Broadway, Sixth Floor, New York, NY 10003. Executive Director: Beth Reiman.

New York Easter Seal Society: 194 Washington Avenue, Albany, NY 12210. Executive Director: David Timko. Telephone: (518) 434-4103.

Orton Dyslexia Society (Buffalo Branch): The Gow School, Emery Road, South Wales, NY 14139. President: Mark D. Kimball. Telephone: (716) 652-3450.

Orton Dyslexia Society (New York Branch): 80 Fifth Avenue, Room 903, New York, NY 10011. Telephone: (212) 691-1930. President: Catherine Angle.

Orton Dyslexia Society (Suffolk Branch): P.O. Box 433, Lake Grove, NY 11755. President: Joyce Leo. Telephone: (516) 698-7579.

Resources for Children with Special Needs, Inc.: 200 Park Avenue, South, Suite 816, New York, NY 10003. Telephone: (212) 677-4650. Director: Karen T. Schlesinger.

Westchester Association for Children with Learning Disabilities: 470 Mamaroneck Avenue, Room 206, White Plains, NY 10605. Telephone: (914) 949-0085. Executive Director: Michele Winograd.

NEW YORK

State Department of Education Learning Disabilities Personnel

Lawrence Gloeckler, Assistant Commissioner, Office for Education of Children with Handicapping Conditions, State Education Department, Room 1073 EBA, Albany, NY 12234. Telephone: (518) 474-5548.

Private and Day Schools

Albany: SUNY Albany Prekindergarten Program, SUNY Albany, Department of Educational Psychology, ED231, 12222. Telephone: (518) 457-4654. Director: Edward Welch. Preschool with summer program. Ages served: 2-5. Current enrollment: 50. Maximum enrollment: 60. Full-time staff: 20. Part-time staff: 5. Scholarships/financial aid available. Services: individual and group tutoring, academic and psychological testing; physical, occupational, speech, and language therapy; transition services. Recreation: field trips.

Allegany: Rehabilitation Center of Cattaraugus County, Route 1, Box 149, S. Nine Mile Road, 14706. Telephone: (716) 372-8909. Executive Director: Patrick Carroll. Preschool and elementary day school with limited services; summer program. Ages served: birth-18. Grades served: ungraded. Current enrollment: 110. Maximum enrollment: 125. Full-time staff: 30. Part-time staff: 5. Scholarships/financial aid available. Services: individual tutoring, psychological and audiological testing; academic, psychological, and family counseling; physical, occupational, and speech therapy; medical services, educational programming. Recreation: field trips, gross motor activities.

Amenia: Kildonan School, Morse Hill Road, 12501. Telephone: (914) 373-8111. Headmaster: George B. Vosburgh. Males only elementary and secondary boarding school with coeducational summer program and camp. Ages served: 9-19. Grades served: ungraded. Current enrollment: 120. Maximum enrollment: 120. Full-time staff: 44. Scholarships/financial aid available after first year. Services: individual and group tutoring, academic testing; academic, psychological, and family counseling; medical services. Recreation: sports.

Amenia: Maplebrook School, Inc., North Road, 12501. Telephone: (914) 373-8191. Headmaster: Mr. Lonnie L. Adams. Elementary boarding school with summer program and camp. Ages served: 11-19. Grades served: ungraded. Current enrollment: 47. Maximum enrollment: 55. Full-time staff: 30. Part-time staff: 4. Services: group tutoring, academic and psychological testing, psychological counseling, adaptive physical education, medical services, prevocational training, work-study, special education. Recreation: sports, swimming pool, skiing, social activities.

Barneveld: United Cerebral Palsy Center, Route 2, N. Gage Road, 13304. Telephone: (315) 896-2654. Executive Director: Louis B. Tehan. Preschool with limited services; summer program. Ages served: 2½-8. Current enrollment: 96. Maximum enrollment: 110. Full-time staff: 24. Part-time staff: 6. Scholarships/

financial aid available. Services: individual and group tutoring, psychological testing, psychological and family counseling, physical and occupational therapy, adaptive physical education, medical services.

Bayside: Lowell School, 203-05 32nd Avenue, 11361. Telephone: (718) 352-2100. Director: Harriet Blau. Secondary day school. Ages served: 13-16. Grades served: ungraded. Current enrollment: 93. Maximum enrollment: 132. Full-time staff: 15. Part-time staff: 17. Services: individual and group tutoring, academic and psychological testing; individual, group, college, academic, psychological, and family counseling; physical, occupational, speech, language, music, and art therapy; adaptive physical education, medical services, life skills and language-based classes, vocational training, work-study, job placement. Recreation: intramural sports, driver's education, clubs.

Brewster: Green Chimneys School, Putnam Lake Road, 10509. Telephone: (914) 279-2996. Executive Director: Samuel B. Ross, Jr. Preschool, elementary, and junior high day and boarding school with summer program and camp. Ages served: 2-15. Current enrollment: 30 day; 88 residential. Maximum enrollment: 30 day; 88 residential. Full-time staff: 103. Services: individual and group tutoring, academic and psychological testing; academic, psychological, and family counseling; adaptive physical education, vocational training, job placement, medical services; horticultural, equestrian, and animal-facilitated therapy; outdoor education, computers. Recreation: sports, swimming pool, riding, adventure programs including ropes course. Notes: Beginning in July, 1985, will offer residential summer school/camp program for 30 mild to moderate learning disabled youngsters.

Brooklyn: Alternative School, 555 Remsen Avenue, 11236. Telephone: (718) 495-2100. Principal: George Bouklas. Secondary day school. Ages served: 13-21. Grades served: 8-12. Current enrollment: 68. Maximum enrollment: 90. Full-time staff: 25. Part-time staff: 3. Services: individual tutoring, psychological counseling, occupational therapy, adaptive physical education, academic testing, vocational training, work-study, job placement.

Brooklyn: Mary McDowell Center for Learning, 110 Schermerhorn Street, 11201. Telephone: (718) 625-3939. Acting Director: Susan L. Weiner. Elementary day school. Ages served: 5-9. Grades served: ungraded. Current enrollment: 4. Maximum enrollment: 20. Full-time staff: 3. Part-time staff: 1. Scholarships/financial aid available. Services: individual and group tutoring, academic and psychological testing, language therapy.

Brooklyn: York Day School, 212 Hicks Street, 11201. Telephone: (718) 855-5010. Headmaster: Samuel W. Hedrick. Secondary day school with summer program. Ages served: 10-18. Grades served: 6-12. Current enrollment: 58. Maximum enrollment: 85. Full-time staff: 7. Part-time staff: 3. Services: individual and group tutoring, academic and psychological testing; academic, psychological, and family counseling; occupational therapy, adaptive physical education, vocational training, work-study, job placement, computer-assisted instruction, adapted typing; remedial reading, writing, and math. Recreation: basketball, gymnastics, martial arts, boxing, cheerleading, aerobic dance.

Clinton Corners: High Valley, Sunset Trail, 12514. Telephone: (914) 266-3621. Director: Olga Smyth. Preschool, elementary day and five-day boarding school. Ages served: 3-21. Grades served: ungraded. Current enrollment: 26. Maximum enrollment: 40. Full-time staff: 12. Part-time staff: 3. Services: psychological testing and counseling, occupational therapy. Recreation: lake, tennis, riding. Notes: Primary diagnosis of students is emotionally disturbed.

Commack: United Cerebral Palsy Association of Greater Suffolk, Inc., 159 Indian Head Road, 11725. Telephone: (516) 543-5100. Executive Director: Ira E. Jacobs. Preschool, elementary, and secondary day school with summer program. Ages served: birth-21. Current enrollment: 300. Full-time staff: 130. Scholarships/financial aid available. Services: individual and group tutoring, academic and psychological testing, psychological and family counseling; physical, occupational, speech, language, music, and art therapy; adaptive physical education, prevocational and vocational training, medical services, audiology, augmentative and total communications programs. Recreation: field trips, adapted aquatics, arts and crafts.

Flushing: Lowell Upper School, 24-20 Parsons Boulevard, 11357. Telephone: (718) 445-4222. Principal: Mary Ellen McCann. Secondary day school. Ages served: 16-21. Grades served: ungraded. Current enrollment: 95. Maximum enrollment: 108. Full-time staff: 31. Part-time staff: 10. Services: individual and group tutoring, academic and psychological testing, academic and psychological counseling; art, music, speech, language, and occupational therapy; remedial reading, vocational training and counseling, work-study, job placement, driver's education, career development center. Recreation: clubs, after school sports.

Freeport: Woodward Mental Health Center, 201 W. Merrick Road, 11520. Telephone: (516) 379-0900. Executive Director: Nina L. Sloan. Preschool, elementary, and secondary day school with summer program and camp. Ages served: 3-21. Grades served: preschool-12. Current enrollment: 62. Maximum enrollment: 85. Full-time staff: 30. Part-time staff: 3. Services: individual and group tutoring, academic and psychological testing; academic, psychological, and family counseling; adaptive physical education, vocational training, work-study, job placement, medical services.

Fresh Meadows: Lowell School, 67-25 188th Street, 11365. Telephone: (718) 454-6460. Director: Harriet Blau. Elementary day school. Ages served: 6-14. Grades served: ungraded. Current enrollment: 60. Maximum enrollment: 68. Full-time staff: 9. Part-time staff: 14. Services: individual and group tutoring; individual, group, academic, and psychological testing; academic, psychological, and family counseling; speech, language, physical, occupational, music, and art therapy;

adaptive physical education, vocational training, job placement. Recreation: playground.

Garden City: Little Village School, Bayberry Avenue, 11530. Telephone: (516) 746-5575. Administrative Director: Barbara Feingold. Preschool and elementary day school with summer program. Ages served: birth-11. Grades served: ungraded. Current enrollment: 120. Full-time staff: 60. Part-time staff: 20. Services: psychological testing, psychological and family counseling, adaptive physical education, medical services; speech, language, physical, occupational, movement, and play therapy.

Hoosick: Hoosac School, Box 8, 12089. Telephone: (518) 686-7331. Headmaster: Donn Wright. Secondary boarding school with limited services. Ages served: 13-19. Grades served: 8-post high school program. Current enrollment: 75. Maximum enrollment: 85. Full-time staff: 17. Scholarships/financial aid available. Services: individual and group tutoring, academic and psychological counseling, adaptive physical education, medical services. Recreation: team and individual sports.

Huntington: Madonna Heights Services, Burrs Lane, 11743-0677. Telephone: (516) 643-8800. Executive Director: Sr. Mary James. Females only elementary and secondary day and boarding school with limited services; summer program and camp. Ages served: 11-18. Grades served: 7-12. Current enrollment: 75. Maximum enrollment: 95. Full-time staff: 60. Part-time staff: 30. Services: individual and group tutoring, academic and psychological testing; academic, psychological, and family counseling; medical services, vocational training, psychiatric evaluations, psychological and casework services for students and families, individual and group therapy. Recreation: swimming, tennis, softball, volleyball, badminton, glee club, drama.

Lake Grove: Lake Grove School, Moriches Road, P.O. Box L, 11755. Telephone: (516) 585-8776. Executive Director: Albert A. Brayson II. Secondary boarding school with summer program. Ages served: 13-21. Grades served: 8-12. Current enrollment: 70. Full-time staff: 100. Services: individual and group tutoring, academic and psychological testing; academic, psychological and family counseling; adaptive physical education, vocational training, work-study, job placement, medical services. Recreation: intermural sports, swimming.

Lockport: Wyndham Lawn Campus School, 6395 Old Niagara Road, 14094. Telephone: (716) 433-4487. Principal: Raymond P. Gebhard. Elementary and secondary day and boarding school with summer program. Ages served: 8-16. Grades served: 1-10. Current enrollment: 54. Maximum enrollment: 55. Full-time staff: 14. Part-time staff: 2. Services: individual and group tutoring, academic and psychological testing; academic, psychological and family counseling; adaptive physical education, medical services, speech therapy, job placement. Recreation: gym, tennis, basketball, swimming pool, baseball, weight room, woodshop, ceramics, photography.

NEW YORK

Mamaroneck: The Hallen School, 1310 Harrison Avenue, 10543. Telephone: (914) 381-2006. Educational Director: Irma L. Levine. Elementary and secondary day school. Ages served: 6-21. Grades served: kindergarten-12. Current enrollment: 185. Maximum enrollment: 210. Full-time staff: 96. Part-time staff: 2. Scholarships/financial aid available. Services: individual and group tutoring, academic and psychological testing; academic, psychological, and family counseling; individual, occupational, speech, language, group, family, and art therapy; medical services, vocational training, work-study, job placement. Recreation: physical education, arts and crafts, music.

Mount Kisco: The Karafin School, P.O. Box 277, 40 Radio Circle, 10549. Telephone: (914) 666-9211. Director: John E. Greenfieldt. Elementary, secondary, and adult day school with summer program. Ages served: 7-19. Grades served: ungraded. Current enrollment: 65. Maximum enrollment: 80. Full-time staff: 23. Part-time staff: 2. Scholarships/financial aid available. Services: individual and group tutoring, academic and psychological testing; academic, psychological, and family counseling; physical, occupational, speech, language, music, and art therapy; wood shop, vocational training, work-study, job placement, regular and adaptive physical education. Notes: Always call for appointment.

New Lebanon: Darrow School, Shaker Road, 12125. Telephone: (518) 794-7700. Director of Admissions: Mr. Macauley B. Nash. Secondary boarding school with limited services. Ages served: 15-18. Grades served: 9-12. Current enrollment: 130 including 26 in LD Program. Maximum enrollment: 151. Full-time staff: 35. Part-time staff: 4. Scholarships/financial aid available. Services: individual tutoring, academic counseling, small classes. Recreation: gym, playing fields, tennis, interscholastic and noncompetitive sports. Notes: LD program students mainstreamed into regular college preparatory program within two years.

New York City: The Children's House, a division of Spence-Chapin Services to Families and Children, Three E. 94th Street, 10562. Telephone: (212) 369-0300. Director: Ms. Andronike C. Tsamas. Twelve-month preschool day treatment program. Ages served: 2-5. Current enrollment: 25. Maximum enrollment: 28. Services: individual tutoring, psychological testing, family counseling, physical therapy, adaptive physical education, medical services.

New York City: The Child School, 112 E. 75th Street, 10021. Telephone: (212) 744-1990. Director: Maari de Souza. Elementary day school. Ages served: 5-15. Grades served: ungraded. Current enrollment: 41. Maximum enrollment: 48. Full-time staff: 17. Part-time staff: 2. Services: individual and group tutoring, academic and psychological testing; academic, psychological, and family counseling; speech, language, and music therapy; computer science, life skills, adaptive physical education. Recreation: art, drama, gymnastics.

New York City: The Churchill School and Center for Learning Disabilities, 22 E. 95th Street, 10028. Telephone: (212) 722-0610. Director: Mary Newmann. Elementary day school. Ages served: 6-13. Grades served: ungraded. Current enrollment: 82. Maximum enrollment: 82. Full-time staff: 32. Part-time staff: 14. Scholarships/financial aid available. Services: individual and group tutoring, academic and psychological testing; academic, psychological, and family counseling; individual, group, occupational, and language therapy; adaptive physical education; Project Heroes, a study of famous learning disabled people; referrals, workshops and conferences for parents and professionals, school advisory service. Recreation: physical education. Publishes the Churchill Forum, a free, quarterly newsletter on learning disabilities.

New York City: The Gateway School of New York, 921 Madison Avenue, 10021. Telephone: (212) 628-3560. Director: Davida Fischbein. Preschool and elementary day school. Ages served: 5-10. Grades served: ungraded. Current enrollment: 31. Maximum enrollment: 31. Full-time staff: 10. Part-time staff: 7. Services: academic and psychological testing, family counseling; speech, language, and occupational therapy; adaptive physical education, music, dance, social skills development program, small classes. Recreation: after school swimming, sports. Notes: Intensive three to four-year program to prepare children to return to mainstreamed classrooms.

New York City: The Lorge Lower School, 353 W. 17th Street, 10011. Telephone: (212) 929-8660. Director: Ruth G. Benov. Elementary day school. Ages served: 5-12. Grades served: kindergarten-6. Current enrollment: 38. Maximum enrollment: 65. Services: individual and group tutoring, academic and psychological testing, academic and psychological counseling, art therapy, adaptive physical education, career education and counseling, vocational training, work-study, job placement, woodworking and electrical shops. Recreation: basketball team, music, dance.

New York City: The Lorge Upper School, 320 W. 31st Street, 10001. Telephone: (212) 594-8945. Director: Ruth G. Benov. Secondary day school. Ages served: 13-21. Grades served: 7-12. Current enrollment: 83. Maximum enrollment: 120. Services: individual and group tutoring, academic and psychological testing, academic and psychological counseling, art therapy, adaptive physical education, career education and counseling, vocational training, work-study, job placement, woodworking and electrical shops. Recreation: basketball team, music, dance.

New York City: Manhattan Day School, 310 W. 75th Street, 10023. Telephone: (212) 595-6800. Director of Learning Disabilities Program: David B. Lazerson. Elementary day school. Ages served: 6-13. Grades served: 1-8. Current enrollment: 24. Maximum enrollment: 25. Full-time staff: 8. Part-time staff: 1. Limited scholarships/financial aid available. Services: individual and group tutoring, academic testing, speech and language therapy, computers. Recreation: sports, dance, computers, Hebrew, choir.

New York City: Northside Day School, 1301 Fifth Avenue, 10029. Telephone: (212) 860-1606. Principal: John King. Elementary day school with summer program. Ages served: 6-12. Grades served: ungraded. Current enrollment: 42. Maximum enrollment: 42. Full-time staff: 14. Part-time staff: 5. Services: individual and group tutoring, academic and psychological testing; academic, psychological, and family counseling; occupational, speech, language, music, and drama therapy; adaptive physical education, vocational training, medical services. Recreation: drama, Special Olympics.

New York City: Reece School, 180 E. 93rd Street, 10028. Telephone: (212) 289-4872. Director: Alice M. Childs. Elementary day school. Ages served: 5-13. Grades served: ungraded. Current enrollment: 38. Maximum enrollment: 42. Full-time staff: 23. Part-time staff: 4. Services: individual and group tutoring, academic testing; teacher/student ratio 1:3; academic, psychological, and family counseling; physical and occupational therapy, adaptive physical education, vocational training; speech, language, and learning disabilities diagnosis and remediation, exercises for hand/eye coordination and gross and small motor deficits. Recreation: gym, swimming. Notes: Serves children of average to above average intelligence who are emotionally handicapped, neurologically impaired, language delayed, and/or learning disabled.

New York City: Robert Louis Stevenson School, 24 W. 74th Street, 10023. Telephone: (212) 787-6400. Director: Lucille Rhodes. Secondary school. Ages served: 12-18. Current enrollment: 110. Full-time staff: 22. Part-time staff: 7. Scholarships/financial aid available. Services: group tutoring. Recreation: sports, performing and visual arts. Notes: College preparatory program for gifted, underachieving adolescents; many have learning disabilities. Admission based on full battery of psychological and educational tests.

New York City: Stephen Gaynor School, 22 W. 74th Street, 10023. Telephone: (212) 787-7070. Director: Miriam Michael. Elementary day school. Ages served: 6-13. Grades served: ungraded. Current enrollment: 100. Maximum enrollment: 100. Full-time staff: 30. Part-time staff: 6. Limited scholarships/financial aid available. Services: individual tutoring, academic testing, psychological counseling, adaptive physical education, occupational therapy, sensory motor training, computer lab, typing. Recreation: music, art, shop, physical education. Notes: Remedial education stresses highly sequential instructional approaches, methods, and materials.

New York City: The Winston Preparatory School, Four W. 76th Street, 10710. Telephone: (212) 496-8400. Director: Roberta S. Michaels. Secondary day school. Ages served: 12½-18. Grades served: 7-12. Current enrollment: 63. Full-time staff: 17. Part-time staff: 5. Scholarships/financial aid available. Services: academic and psychological testing, academic and psychological counseling, group tutoring; individual tutoring in reading, math, speech, and language. Recreation: gym, seasonal sports.

New York City: The Yoder Day School, 250 E. 79th Street, 10021. Telephone: (212) 535-8124. Director: Elizabeth Ferraro. Preschool, elementary, and secondary day school with summer program. Ages served: 5½-21. Grades served: kindergarten-12. Current enrollment: 40. Maximum enrollment: 80. Full-time staff: 11. Part-time staff: 8. Services: individual and group tutoring, academic and psychological testing; academic, psychological, and family counseling; adaptive physical education. Recreation: karate, swimming. Notes: Serves only the learning disabled.

Pawling: Trinity Pawling School, 161 Route 22, 12564. Telephone: (914) 855-3100. Headmaster: Phillip Smith. Males only secondary boarding school with limited services. Ages served: 14-16. Grades served: 9 and 10. Current enrollment: 292 including 52 in Language Retraining Program. Full-time staff: 33. Part-time staff: 3. Scholarships/financial aid available. Services: individual and group tutoring, academic testing. Recreation: athletic program. Notes: Two-year Language Retraining Program for mildly dyslexic boys of average to above average intelligence; can enter in ninth or tenth grade only; designed to prepare students to enter school's regular college preparatory program.

Poughkeepsie: The Astor Day Treatment Center, 400 Church Street, 12601. Telephone: (914) 452-1630. Assistant Executive Director: John B. Mordock. Preschool and elementary day school with summer program. Ages served: 3-12. Grades served: ungraded. Current enrollment: 32. Maximum enrollment: 40. Full-time staff: 18. Part-time staff: 3. Services: academic and psychological testing, psychological and family counseling, adaptive physical education, milieu therapy. Recreation: swimming, field trips, arts and crafts. Notes: For the emotionally disturbed.

Purdys: Westchester Exceptional Children's School, Route 1, Box 1, 10578. Telephone: (914) 277-5533. Director: Linda Murphy. Elementary and secondary day school. Ages served: 5-21. Grades served: ungraded. Current enrollment: 56. Maximum enrollment: 60. Full-time staff: 25. Part-time staff: 3. Services: individual tutoring, academic and psychological testing, vocational training, speech therapy; sibling, psychological, and family counseling; adaptive physical education, parent group. Recreation: gym, playground. Notes: Serves emotionally handicapped, other health impaired, and learning disabled children referred by local school districts.

Rochester: Day Treatment Unit Services/Rochester Mental Health Center, 1425 Portland Avenue, 14621. Telephone: (716) 544-5220 ext. 5159. Director: Joseph Gold. Elementary and secondary school with limited services; summer program. Ages served: 5-16. Grades served: ungraded. Current enrollment: 65. Maximum enrollment: 65. Full-time staff: 20. Part-time staff: 6. Services: individual tutoring, academic and psychological testing; academic, psychological, and family counseling; vocational training, work-study, medical services. Recreation: physical education. Notes: Majority of student population classified as emotionally disturbed; many have secondary learning disability problems.

Rochester: The Norman Howard School, 220 Helendale Road, 14609. Telephone: (716) 288-3080. Director: Betsy C. McIsaac. Secondary day school. Ages served:

12-18. Grades served: 7-12. Current enrollment: 38. Maximum enrollment: 50. Full-time staff: 8. Part-time staff: 2. Scholarships/financial aid available. Services: individual and group tutoring, academic and psychological testing; academic, psychological, and family counseling. Recreation: sports, skiing. Notes: Structured to serve learning disabled students.

Rochester: United Cerebral Palsy Association, 1000 Elmwood Avenue, 14610. Telephone: (716) 271-6423. Acting Director of Children's Services: Margaret M. Kintz. Preschool and summer program. Ages served: birth-6 preschool; 3-16 summer program. Current enrollment: 73. Maximum enrollment: no limit. Full-time staff: 31. Part-time staff: 3. Services: individual and group tutoring, academic and psychological testing, psychological and family counseling; speech, physical, and occupational therapy; adaptive physical education, medical services. Recreation: swimming, gym-swim, therapeutic riding.

Sayville: Leeway School, 335 Johnson Avenue, 11782. Telephone: (516) 589-8060. Director: Deborah A. Jackson. Preschool and elementary day school. Ages served: 2½-14. Grades served: ungraded. Current enrollment: 32. Full time staff: 20. Services: individual and group tutoring, academic and psychological testing; academic, psychological, and family counseling; horticultural therapy, vision training, adaptive physical education and therapy, speech pathology. Recreation: roller-skating, bowling. Notes: One special education teacher and one assistant for every six students.

Schenectady: Northeast Parent and Child Society, 122 Park Avenue, 12304. Telephone: (518) 346-2387. Director: Lance Jackson. Elementary and secondary day and boarding school with summer program. Ages served: 12-16. Grades served: special education, 6-12. Current enrollment: 70-80. Full-time staff: 27. Services: individual and group tutoring, academic and psychological testing; academic, psychological, and family counseling; occupational therapy/exploration, work-study, medical services, vocational training, job placement, psychotherapy. Recreation: field trips, sports. Notes: School serves children with emotional handicaps or learning disabilities. Also runs day treatment, males only residential, and temporary in-residence diagnostic programs.

Schenectady: Wildwood School, Birchwood Lane, 12309. Telephone: (518) 783-1644. Director: Virginia Rossuck. Preschool, elementary, secondary, and adult day school with summer program and camp. Full-time staff: 63. Part-time staff: 15. Current enrollment: 98. Maximum enrollment: 120. Ages served: 3-21. Grades served: ungraded. Services: individual and group tutoring, academic testing, family counseling; language, music, and occupational therapy; adaptive physical education, prevocational and vocational training, work-study, job placement, medical consultation. Recreation: adolescent community center. Notes: Serves the emotionally disturbed and learning disabled.

Scotia: Oak Hill School, 39 Charlton Road, 12302. Telephone: (518) 399-5048. Director: Jon Tobiessen. Elementary school with limited services. Ages served: 8-

14. Grades served: 3-8. Current enrollment: 19. Maximum enrollment: 20. Full-time staff: 6. Part-time staff: 7. Scholarships/financial aid available. Services: individual and group tutoring, academic and psychological testing, psychological and family counseling. Recreation: hiking, camping, skiing, skating.

Silver Creek: Silver Creek Montessori School, 87 Main, 14136. Telephone: (716) 934-4274. Director: Susan Newman. Preschool. Ages served: birth-6. Current enrollment: 50. Part-time staff: 15. Scholarships/financial aid available. Services: academic and psychological testing, psychological and family counseling, physical and occupational therapy; speech, language, and auditory training.

Smithtown: Suffolk Child Development Center, Hollywood Drive, 11706. Telephone: (516) 724-1717. Executive Director: Martin D. Hamburg. Preschool, elementary, secondary, and adult day school with limited services; summer program. Ages served: birth-adult. Grades served: ungraded. Current enrollment: 200. Maximum enrollment: no limit. Full-time staff: 175. Part-time staff: 10. Services: academic and psychological testing, family counseling, physical therapy, adaptive physical education, vocational training, summer work-study, medical services. Recreation: playground.

South Wales: The Gow School, Emery Road, 14139. Telephone: (716) 652-3450. Headmaster: David W. Gow. Males only secondary boarding school. Ages served: 12-19. Grades served: 7-12. Current enrollment: 133. Maximum enrollment: 150. Full-time staff: 26. Part-time staff: 3. Scholarships/financial aid available. Services: individual and group tutoring, academic testing and counseling. Recreation: daily athletics and interscholastic competition, basketball, lacrosse, soccer, skiing, riding, camping, yearbook, newspaper, choir, drama, cultural outings. Notes: College preparatory program exclusively for dyslexic boys.

Springfield Gardens: Martin de Porres School, 136-25 218th Street, 11413. Telephone: (212) 525-3414. Executive Director: Br. Paul Fantetti. Elementary and secondary day school. Ages served: 8-20. Grades served: ungraded. Current enrollment: 128. Maximum enrollment: 130. Full-time staff: 42. Services: individual and group tutoring, academic and psychological testing; academic, psychological, and family counseling; adaptive physical education; vocational training including construction, automotive, and culinary programs; work-study, job placement. Recreation: weekend swimming and basketball teams, cross-country, indoor and outdoor track, touch football league.

Staatsburg-on-Hudson: The Anderson School, Route 9, 12580. Telephone: (914) 889-4034. Administrator: Dominic Giambona. Elementary and secondary day and boarding school with limited services; summer program. Ages served: 6-21. Grades served: 8-12. Current enrollment: 88 residential; 6 day. Maximum enrollment: 111 residential; 8 day. Full-time staff: 180. Part-time staff: 5. Scholarships/financial aid available. Services: individual tutoring, academic and psychological testing, academic and psychological counseling, adaptive physical education, work-study, prevocational training, medical and psychiatric services. Recreation:

hiking, woodcutting, farming, fishing, canoeing; competitive sports including basketball and football.

Syosset: Variety Pre-Schooler's Workshop, 47 Humphrey Drive, 11791. Telephone: (516) 921-7171. Director: Judith Bloch. Preschool with summer program. Ages served: infants-7. Grades served: infants-kindergarten. Current enrollment: 140. Maximum enrollment: 140. Full-time staff: 49. Part-time staff: 28. Scholarships/financial aid available. Services: individual and group tutoring, academic and psychological testing; academic, psychological, and family counseling; physical and occupational therapy, adaptive physical education, nurse on staff, after school program, Sunday respite program, sibling groups, family support services.

Tonawanda: Language Development Program of Western New York, 300 Fries Road, 14150. Telephone: (716) 837-2441. Executive Director: Nancy Harris. Preschool and elementary school with summer program. Ages served: birth-12. Grades served: ungraded. Current enrollment: 260. Maximum enrollment: 320. Full-time staff: 90. Part-time staff: 8. Scholarships/financial aid available. Services: individual and group tutoring, academic and psychological testing; academic, psychological, and family counseling; physical, occupational, speech, and language therapy; adaptive physical education, auditory training, medical and social services, home training. Recreation: field trips, classroom activities. Notes: Serves children with severe communication disorders.

Upper Nyack: Summit School, 339 N. Broadway, 10960. Telephone: (914) 358-7772. Director: Bruce Goldsmith. Elementary and secondary day and boarding school with summer program. Ages served: 8-21. Grades served: 1-12. Current enrollment: 100. Maximum enrollment: 100. Full-time staff: 70. Part-time staff: 45. Scholarships/financial aid available. Services: individual tutoring, academic and psychological testing; academic, psychological, and family counseling; adaptive physical education, vocational training, work-study, job placement, medical services, psychotherapy. Recreation: sports, swimming, art, wood shop, cooking, computers, music, photography, video.

White Plains: Windward School, Windward Avenue, 10605. Telephone: (914) 949-6968. Executive Director: Thomas J. Bamrick III. Elementary and secondary day school with summer program and camp. Ages served: 5-18. Grades served: kindergarten-12. Current enrollment: 125. Maximum enrollment: 150. Full-time staff: 25. Part-time staff: 26. Scholarships/financial aid available. Services: individual and group tutoring, academic and psychological testing, academic and psychological counseling, physical therapy, adaptive physical education, vocational training, work-study. Recreation: athletic fields, basketball court, playground, gym, exercise room; competitive teams including soccer and baseball; after school social programs.

Wynantskill: Vanderheyden Hall School, Box 218, 12065. Telephone: (518) 371-1904. Executive Director: Leonard Yaffe. Elementary and secondary day school with limited services. Ages served: 12-16. Grades served: 7-12. Current enrollment: 65. Maximum enrollment: 75. Full-time staff: 15. Services: academic and psychological testing, family counseling, adaptive physical education, prevocational training, work-study, medical and social services.

Summer Camps and Programs

Canandaigua: YWCA Camp Onanda, 4965 W. Lake Road, 14424. Telephone: (716) 396-2752. Permanent mailing address: YWCA of Rochester and Monroe County, 175 N. Clinton Avenue, Rochester, NY 14604. Telephone: (716) 546-5820. Camp Director: Wanda Terhaar. Females only residential camp. Ages served: 7-16. Grades served: 2-11. Maximum enrollment: 120. Full-time staff: 35. Scholarships/financial aid available. Recreation: camping, hiking, field trips, nature study, riding, swimming, sailing, waterskiing, archery, team sports, crafts, dance, drama, singing. Notes: Accepts campers with learning disabilities.

Dix Hills: Summer Education Extension Program, Camp NYABIC, 645 Half Hollow Road, 11746. Telephone: (516) 586-3332. Director: David Finklestein. Camp. Ages served: 3-17. Grades served: preschool-high school. Maximum enrollment: 100. Full-time staff: 50. Scholarships/financial aid available. Services: individual and group tutoring, adaptive physical education, medical services, speech and language therapy. Recreation: swimming, gymnastics, softball, basketball.

Franklinville: Camp Lakeland, Route 2, 14737. Telephone: (716) 676-9942. Permanent mailing address: Jewish Center of Greater Buffalo, Inc., 2640 N. Forest Road, Getzville, NY 14068. Telephone: (716) 688-4033. Camp Director: Michael Hyman. Residential camp. Ages served: 7-16. Grades served: 3-10. Maximum enrollment: 200. Full-time staff: 55. Scholarships/financial aid available. Services: individual tutoring, psychological testing, medical services. Recreation: camping, hiking, field trips, nature study, riding, swimming, sailing, waterskiing, archery, team sports, crafts, dance, drama, music, photography.

Gainesville: Camp Twin Pines, Route 1, 14006. Telephone: (716) 786-2940. Permanent mailing address: Western New York Association for the Learning Disabled, 190 Franklin Street, Third Floor, 14202. Telephone: (716) 855-1135. Program Coordinator: Barb Beecher. Camp. Ages served: 6-18. Maximum enrollment: 70. Part-time staff: 15. Scholarships/financial aid available. Recreation: swimming, hiking, riding, crafts, camping, team athletics, canoeing, archery, outdoor education, self-defense. Notes: For learning disabled children.

Hancock: Camp Radalbek, Inc., Route 1, Box 28K, 13783. Telephone: (607) 467-2159. Director: Grace Kinzer. Residential camp with academic program and limited services. Ages served: all ages summer; adults winter. Maximum enrollment: 100. Full-time staff: 8. Part-time staff: 16. Services: group tutoring, psychological counseling, physical and occupational therapy, vocational training, work-study, medical services, respite care. Academic programs: math, reading, spelling, study skills. Recreation: camping, hiking, field trips, nature study, swimming, crafts, drama, team athletics, music, dance, gardening, food preparation. Notes: A farm camp training program with animals and gardening.

High Falls: Camp Huntington, Bruceville Road, 12440. Telephone: (914) 687-7840. Permanent mailing address: 49 Pleasant Ridge Drive, Poughkeepsie, NY 12603. Telephone: (914) 462-0991. Director: Bruria K. Falik. Residential camp with academic program. Ages served: 7-21. Grades served: all. Maximum enrollment: 150. Full-time staff: 50. Services: individual and group tutoring, psychological testing, academic and psychological counseling; physical, occupational, and speech therapy; adaptive physical education, vocational training, medical services, therapeutic horseback riding, adaptive aquatics. Academic programs: math, reading, English, spelling, study skills, perceptual training. Recreation: camping, hiking, field trips, nature study, riding, swimming, team sports, crafts, dance, drama, music, photography, cooking, sewing, gardening, mini golf, woodworking, tennis, field and court games. Notes: Program geared to the needs of individual camper.

Lake Clear: Camp Triangle, P.O. Box 5, 12945. Telephone: (518) 891-3311. Permanent mailing address: 2575 Troy Road, Schenectady, NY 12309. Telephone: (518) 783-1233. Camp Administrator: Shirley A. Schofield. Residential camp with academic program. Ages served: 7-adult. Maximum enrollment: 72. Services: group tutoring, academic testing, psychological counseling, occupational therapy, adaptive physical education, vocational training, medical services, speech and language development. Academic programs: math, reading, spelling, study skills, activities of daily living skills. Recreation: swimming, hiking, nature study, crafts, drama, camping, team athletics, boating, canoeing, music, art, special events.

Remsen: Camp Northwood, Route 1, 13438. Telephone: (315) 831-3621. Permanent mailing address: Ten W. 66th Street, New York, NY 10023. Telephone: (212) 799-4089. Directors: Jim and Kristy Rein. Residential camp with academic program. Ages served: 7-17. Maximum enrollment: 135. Full-time staff: 75. Scholarships/financial aid available. Services: individual and group tutoring, occupational therapy, adaptive physical education, work-study, medical services. Academic programs: math, reading, English, spelling, study skills. Recreation: swimming, hiking, field trips, nature study, crafts, drama, camping, photography, team athletics, rocketry, video, radio station, TV studio, music, waterskiing. Notes: For children with learning disabilities and those classified as underachievers.

Remsen: Northwood Sports Camp, Route 1, 13438. Telephone: (315) 831-3621. Permanent mailing address: Ten W. 66th Street, New York, NY 10023. Telephone: (212) 799-4089. Director: Jim Rein. Day and residential camp. Ages served: 7-17. Maximum enrollment: 85. Full-time staff: 30. Scholarships/financial aid available. Services: adaptive physical education, medical services. Recreation: swimming, team athletics, sports-oriented program.

Rhinebeck: Ramapo Anchorage Camp, Box 266, 12572. Telephone: (914) 876-4273. Director: Don Thomases. Residential camp with academic program and limited services. Ages served: 4½-16. Grades served: preschool-9. Maximum enrollment: 154. Full-time staff: 160. Scholarships/financial aid available. Services: individual tutoring, adaptive physical education, vocational training, work-study. Academic programs: math, reading, English, spelling, study skills. Recreation: swimming, hiking, field trips, nature study, crafts, drama, camping, photography, team athletics.

Roslyn: North Shore YM and YWHA Day Camp, P.O. Box 393, 11576. Telephone: (516) 484-1545. Special Services Director: Jonathan Berent. Day camp with limited services. Ages served: 6-13. Grades served: 1-7. Maximum enrollment: 350 including 25 learning disabled. Full-time staff: 80. Services: social therapy. Recreation: swimming, field trips, nature study, crafts, drama, camping, team athletics. Notes: Mainstreamed social therapy program for high functioning learning disabled children.

Skaneateles: Lourdes Camp, Ten Mile Point, Skaneateles Lake, 13152. Telephone: (315) 673-2888. Permanent mailing address: 1654 W. Onondaga Street, Syracuse, NY 13204. Telephone: (315) 424-1812. Director: Michael Preston. Residential camp with limited services. Ages served: 7-14. Maximum enrollment: 240. Full-time staff: 50. Scholarships/financial aid available. Services: individual tutoring, reading, medical services. Recreation: camping, hiking, riding, swimming, archery, team sports, crafts, drama, photography.

Staten Island: Young Peoples Day Camp of Staten Island, 77 Lincoln Avenue, 10306. Telephone: (718) 979-7550. Director: Peter Dowd. Day camp. Ages served: 6-14. Full-time staff: teacher/student ratio 1:10. Services: adaptive physical education. Recreation: camping, hiking, field trips, swimming, team sports, crafts, music.

College and University Special Programs and Services

Adelphi University: Garden City, NY 11530. Total enrollment: 1,100. LD students: 70. Special services: readers, individual and group tutoring, ombudsman, untimed special examinations, academic and psychological counseling, taped books, training in study skills, summer diagnostic and experiential program, student resource center, support group.

- **Special program:** Program for Learning Disabled College Students. Applicants must fulfill regular and special admissions requirements. Special requirements include verification of learning disability through diagnostic tests no more than one year old and an interview. Students must be enrolled full time in regular college courses. Incoming students must attend five-week diagnostic session. Special courses in communication and critical thinking, expository writing, and rhetoric are required. Director: Fred Barbaro. Telephone: (516) 663-1006.

NEW YORK

Adirondack Community College: Bay Road, Glens Falls, NY 12801. Total enrollment: 3,100. LD students: 40. Special services: individual and group tutoring, training in study skills, academic and psychological counseling, special examinations, student resource center, college learning center, readers, diagnostic testing, support group. Contact: Robert L. Hutchinson, Dean of Students. Telephone: (518) 793-4491 ext. 273.

Brooklyn College of the City University of New York: Bedford Avenue and Avenue "H," Brooklyn, NY 11210. Special services: individual tutoring, training in study skills, academic and psychological counseling, taped books, special examinations, student resource center, readers, scholarships, ombudsman. Contact: Nathaniel A. Jones, Associate Dean of Students. Telephone: (718) 780-5352.

Canisius College: 2001 Main Street, Buffalo, NY 14208. Special services: individual tutoring, training in study skills, academic and psychological counseling, taped books, student resource center, readers, ombudsman. Contact: Lillian M. Levy, Vice President for Student Affairs. Telephone: (716) 883-7000 ext. 232.

City College of New York: 138th Street and Convent Avenue, New York, NY 10031. Special services: individual tutoring, training in study skills, academic and psychological counseling, taped books, special examinations, readers, diagnostic testing, scholarships. Contact: Frances Geteles, Coordinator, Services for Disabled Students. Telephone: (212) 690-4264.

Center/clinic: Neurocognition Program, CCNY Psychology Department, NAC - Room 7/120. Telephone: (212) 690-8330. Director: J. Rosen. Open to public. Ages served: all. Grades served: all. Services: diagnostic testing, referrals, limited remediation.

College of New Rochelle: Castle Place, New Rochelle, NY 10801. LD students: 150. Special services: readers, individual and group tutoring, diagnostic testing, training in study skills, student resource center. Contact: Jonathan L. Zager, Coordinator, Education Center. Telephone: (914) 632-5300 ext. 333.

Center/clinic: Education Center. Telephone: (914) 632-5300 ext. 333. Coordinator: Jonathan L. Zager. Open to public. Grades served: elementary and secondary. Notes: Program designed to teach and/or strengthen learning skills.

The College of Staten Island (Sunnyside Campus): 715 Ocean Terrace, Staten Island, NY 10301. Special services: individual tutoring, academic and psychological counseling, special examinations, student resource center, readers. Contact: Jed Luchow, Program Coordinator of Special Education. Telephone: (718) 390-7980.

Columbia University, Barnard College: 3009 Broadway, New York, NY 10027. Total enrollment: 2,400. LD students: 10. Special services: individual tutoring, training in study skills, academic and psychological counseling, taped books, special examinations, student resource center, readers, scholarships, peer support.

Contact: Susan Quinby, Associate Director, or Julie V. Marsteller, Dean for Disabled Students. Telephone: (212) 280-4634 (Voice/TDD).

Columbia University, Columbia College: New York, NY 10027. Special services: training in study skills, academic and psychological counseling, student resource center, diagnostic testing, scholarships, screening evaluations, referrals to clinics or private practitioners. Contact: Jonathan Cohen, Clinical Psychologist, College Counseling Services. Telephone: (212) 280-2468.

Columbia University, Teachers College: New York, NY 10027. Special services: individual tutoring, training in study skills, academic and psychological counseling, taped books, special examinations, readers, diagnostic testing. Contact: Barbara Rivlin, Director, Office for Handicapped Students. Telephone: (212) 678-3157.

Center/clinic: Child Study Center, Department of Special Education, Box 223. Telephone: (212) 678-3881. Director: Jeannette Fleischner. Open to public. Ages served: 2-adult. Services: diagnostic testing, limited tutoring.

Center/clinic: Reading Center, Division of Psychology. Telephone: (212) 678-3906. Director: Mr. Dale Bryant. Open to public. Ages served: 8-16. Services: reading remediation.

Cornell University: Ithaca, NY 14853. Total enrollment: 17,500. Special services: individual tutoring, training in study skills, academic and psychological counseling, taped books, readers, ombudsman. Contact: Kathleen Donovan, Coordinator for the Disabled. Telephone: (607) 256-5298.

Dutchess Community College: Pendell Road, Poughkeepsie, NY 12601. Total enrollment: 7,084. LD students: 20. Special services: individual tutoring, training in study skills, academic and psychological counseling, taped books, special examinations, student resource center, ombudsman. Contact: Kathleen Sortino, Coordinator of Special Services for the Disabled. Telephone: (914) 471-4500 ext. 418.

Elizabeth Seton College: 1061 N. Broadway, Yonkers, NY 10701. Total enrollment: 1,500. LD students: 24. Special services: individual and group tutoring, training in study skills, academic and psychological counseling, taped books, special examinations, student resource center.

- **Special program:** College Assistance Program (CAP). Designed to help learning disabled students strengthen self-confidence and develop individual abilities. Candidates must be socially mature, emotionally stable, and motivated to work hard toward success in college. Admissions requirements include submission of complete psychological evaluation, two recommendations, and an interview with dean of admissions and CAP coordinator. Students enroll full time in regular college curriculum. Amount of time spent in support services depends on individual needs, nature of disability, and major. Program begins with special three-week summer session. Acting Coordinator: Sandi Galst. Telephone: (914) 969-4000 ext. 306.

Herkimer County Community College: Reservoir Road, Herkimer, NY 13350. Total enrollment: 1,574. LD students: 5. Special services: writing lab, career services, talking calculators, Apollo Portareader, speech compressing cassette recorders. Contact: Robert M. Ichihana. Telephone: (315) 866-0300 ext. 285.

Hudson Valley Community College: Vandenburgh Avenue, Troy, NY 12180. Total enrollment: 8,500. LD students: 25. Special services: individual tutoring, training in study skills, academic and psychological counseling, taped books, special examinations, student resource center, readers, scholarships, support group; reading, writing, and math labs. Contact: Pablo E. Negron, Jr., Coordinator, Disabled Student Services. Telephone: (518) 283-1100 ext. 746.

Hunter College: City University of New York, 695 Park Avenue, New York, NY 10021. Special services: academic counseling, support group. Contact: Sandra LaPorta, Coordinator for Disabled Students. Telephone: (212) 772-4888.
Note: Individualized tutoring for children available as part of teacher training program.

John Jay College of Criminal Justice, City University of New York: 445 W. 59th Street, New York, NY 10019. Total enrollment: 6,618. LD students: 3. Special services: individual tutoring, academic and psychological counseling, taped books, special examinations, support group. Note: Currently developing diagnostic testing center. Contact: Farris Forsythe, Coordinator, Disabled Student Services. Telephone: (212) 489-5110.

Kingsborough Community College: 2001 Oriental Boulevard, Manhattan Beach, Brooklyn, NY 11235. Total enrollment: 9,000. LD students: 60. Special services: individual and group tutoring, training in study skills, academic and psychological counseling, taped books, special examinations, student resource center, readers, diagnostic testing, ombudsman, support group. Contact: Irwin Rosenthal, Director of Services for Learning Disabled. Telephone: (718) 934-5175.

Center/clinic: Special Needs Career Development Program. Telephone: (718) 934-5280. Director: Irwin Rosenthal. Not open to public. Ages served: 17 and up. Grades served: college. Services: tutoring, faculty intervention, individual and group counseling, special testing.

Manhattan College: Bronx, NY 10471. Total enrollment: 4,800. Special services: individual and group tutoring, academic and psychological counseling, diagnostic testing, training in study skills, student resource center. Contact: Estelle Fryburg, Director, Institute for Cognitive Development. Telephone: (212) 920-0106.

Center/clinic: Institute for Cognitive Development. Telephone: (212) 920-0416 or 920-0106. Director: Estelle Fryburg. Open to public. Ages served: all.

Manhattanville College: Purchase, NY 10577. Special services: testing, tutors, academic and psychological counseling, vocational counseling and placement, word processing, resource center.

- **Special program:** Learning Disabilities Program. One-year program with reduced course load of four instead of five classes and weekly tutoring and counseling sessions. Introductory five-week summer program mandatory. Applicants must meet regular and special admissions requirements. Special requirements include verification of learning disability through recent diagnostic tests, interview, and recommendations. Admissions Counselor: Jennifer Brockelman. Telephone: (914) 694-2200 ext. 464.

Marist College: 82 North Road, Poughkeepsie, NY 12601. Special services: individual and group tutoring, training in study skills; academic, psychological, and career counseling; taped books, special examinations, student resource center, readers, limited scholarships, ombudsman, note takers. Contact: Diane C. Perreira, Director, Special Services. Telephone: (914) 471-3240 ext. 274.

New York University: New York, NY 10003. Special services: diagnostic testing, individual and small group tutoring and counseling, taped books, computer-assisted instruction, specialized materials, special examinations, summer skills program.

- **Special program:** Project CLASS (Career and Learning Assistance and Support Services) for Learning Disabled Students. For full or part-time students. Must fulfill regular admissions requirements. Learning disability must be verified through recent diagnostic tests. Codirectors: Barnard Katz, Irwin Rosenthal. Coordinator: Patricia Stockinger. Telephone: (212) 598-7841 or 598-7849.

New York State University College-Oneonta: Oneonta, NY 13820. Total enrollment: 6,000. LD students: 50. Special services: individual tutoring, academic counseling, taped books, readers. Contact: Shirley Kendall, 504 Coordinator. Telephone: (607) 431-2451.

Niagara County Community College: 3111 Saunders Settlement Road, Sanborn, NY 14132. Total enrollment: 4,000. LD students: 80-100. Special services: individual and group tutoring, training in study skills, academic counseling, taped books, special examinations, ombudsman. Contact: Monica R. Pullano, Counselor/Coordinator, Services for Disabled Students. Telephone: (716) 731-3271 ext. 386.

Queensborough Community College: 56th Avenue and Springfield Boulevard, Bayside, NY 11357. Total enrollment: 13,400. LD students: 50. Special services: group tutoring, academic and psychological counseling, taped books, special examinations, student resource center, readers, ombudsman, support group. Contact: Elliot L. Rosman, Director, Office of Disabled Student Services. Telephone: (718) 631-6257.

Russell Sage College: Troy, NY 12180. Special services: individual tutoring, training in study skills, academic and psychological counseling, scholarships. Contact: Sheila Murphy, Vice President for Student Affairs. Telephone: (518) 270-2212.

St. Thomas Aquinas College: Route 340, Sparkill, NY 10976. Total enrollment: 1,800. LD students: 42. Special services: mentors, group study sessions, training in study skills, academic and psychological counseling, taped books, special examinations, student resource center, readers, diagnostic testing, ombudsman, support group, summer program for LD high school graduates and college students, seminars, internships.

- **Special program:** The STAC Exchange. Teaches learning disabled students to utilize strengths and compensate for weaknesses. Focuses on development of critical thinking, abstract reasoning, and independent learning skills. Students must attend special summer program. Must be enrolled in four regular college courses. Learning disability must be verified through recent diagnostic tests. Director: Marijanet Doonan. Telephone: (914) 359-9500 ext. 275.

Schenectady County Community College: 78 Washington Avenue, Schenectady, NY 12305. Total enrollment: 3,000. LD students: 16. Special services: individual and group tutoring, training in study skills, academic counseling, taped books for culinary arts program, special examinations. Contact: Gary A. Messina, Coordinator. Telephone: (518) 346-6211 ext. 145.

Southampton College of Long Island University: Southampton, NY 11968. Total enrollment: 1,150. Special services: individual and group tutoring, special examinations, academic counseling, diagnostic testing, training in study skills, interdisciplinary program of developmental courses. Contact: Pamela L. Topping, Director, The Study Center. Telephone: (516) 283-4000 ext. 136.

Center/clinic: The Study Center. Telephone: (516) 283-4000 ext. 136. Director: Pamela C. Topping. Grades served: college.

State University College-Geneseo: Geneseo, NY 14454. Total enrollment: 5,000. Special services: academic and psychological counseling, diagnostic testing; taped books, and other aids for the visually handicapped. Contact: William Caron, Assistant Vice President. Telephone: (716) 245-5619.

State University of New York Agricultural and Technical College: Alfred, NY 14802. Total enrollment: 3,838. LD students: 30-50. Special services: individual and group tutoring, training in study skills, academic and psychological counseling, taped books, special examinations. Contact: Grace Barton, Director, Center for Developmental Studies. Telephone: (607) 871-6122.

State University of New York-Albany: 1400 Washington Avenue, Albany, NY 12222. Total enrollment: 15,000. LD students: 25. Special services: individual tutoring, academic and psychological counseling, taped books, special examinations, readers, diagnostic testing, ombudsman, introductory letter to faculty, pre-registration. Contact: Nancy Belowich, Director, Disabled Student Services. Telephone: (518) 457-3094.

Center/clinic: Child Research and Study Center, Husted Hall 160B. Telephone: (518) 455-6267. Director: Frank Vellutino. Open to public. Ages served: 2-adult. Grades served: preschool-12. Services: psychoeducational evaluation including math, reading, and oral and written language; psychosocial evaluation, school consultation, limited therapy and referrals.

State University of New York Canton Agricultural and Technical College: Cornel Drive, Canton, NY 13617. LD students: 10-15. Special services: individual and group tutoring, training in study skills, academic counseling, student resource center. Contact: Debora L. Camp, Coordinator of Accommodative Services. Telephone: (315) 386-7121.

State University of New York Cobbleskill Agricultural and Technical College: Cobbleskill, NY 12043. Total enrollment: 2,700. LD students: 15. Special services: training in study skills, academic and psychological counseling, taped books, extended test time and tutoring may be available depending on individual circumstances. Contact: Wayne Morris, Counselor. Telephone: (518) 234-5211.

State University of New York-Cortland: Box 2000, Cortland, NY 13045. Special services: individual tutoring on paid peer basis, training in study skills, psychological counseling. Contact: Sheila Dai, Counselor, Rehabilitation Services. Telephone: (607) 753-4728.

State University of New York-Farmingdale: Farmingdale, NY 11735. Total enrollment: 12,900. LD students: 65. Special services: individual and group tutoring, training in study skills, academic and psychological counseling, taped books, special examinations, readers, diagnostic testing, scholarships, support group. Contact: Anita Tritell, Coordinator, Services for Students with Special Needs. Telephone: (516) 420-2450.

State University of New York-New Paltz: New Paltz, NY 12561. Total enrollment: 7,500. LD students: 50. Special services: individual and group tutoring, academic and psychological counseling, special examinations, student resource center. Contact: Alice L. Matzdorf, Director, Special Student Programs. Telephone: (914) 257-2467.

State University of New York-Oswego: Oswego, NY 13126. Total enrollment: 7,600. LD students: 16. Special services: limited individual tutoring, training in study skills, academic and psychological counseling, taped books, limited readers.

NEW YORK

Contact: Barry W. Atkinson, Coordinator, Disabled Student Services. Telephone: (315) 341-2240.

State University of New York-Stony Brook: Stony Brook, NY 11794. Total enrollment: 16,000. LD students: 15. Special services: individual and group tutoring, academic and psychological counseling, taped books, student resource center, readers, diagnostic testing, ombudsman, support group. Contact: Monica Roth, Coordinator, Office of the Disabled. Telephone: (516) 246-6051.

Suffolk County Community College-Ammerman Campus: 533 College Road, Selden, NY 11784. Total enrollment: 12,683. LD students: 25. Special services: individual tutoring, training in study skills, academic and psychological counseling, taped books, untimed tests, student resource center, readers, computer-assisted instruction, audiovisual materials; reading, math, and writing centers; Kurzweil Reading Machine. Contact: Elmira L. Johnson, Director, Special Services. Telephone: (516) 451-4045.

Syracuse University: Syracuse, NY 13210. Special services: individual and group tutoring, training in study skills, academic and psychological counseling, taped books, special examinations, student resource center, readers, diagnostic testing, support group. Contact: Ms. Terry M. MacDonald, Diagnostician/LD Specialist. Telephone: (315) 423-4498 or 423-2005.

Center/clinic: Academic Support Center, 804 University Avenue, Room 005. Telephone: (315) 423-2005. Director: John D. Radigan. Not open to public. Ages served: all. Grades served: college.

Center/clinic: Syracuse University Psychoeducational Teaching Laboratory, 805 S. Crouse Avenue, 13210. Telephone: (315) 423-4485 or 423-4486. Director: Corinne R. Smith. Open to public. Ages served: preschool-adult. Services: diagnostic testing, academic and psychological testing; consultation with school regarding modification in school programming.

Hospital Clinics

Bronx: Children's Evaluation and Rehabilitation Center, Rose F. Kennedy Center for Research in Mental Retardation and Human Development, Albert Einstein College of Medicine of Yeshiva University, 1410 Pelham Parkway, South, 10461. Telephone: (212) 430-2434. Contact: Ruth L. Gottesman. Outpatient and after school program. Ages served: birth-21. Services: diagnostic testing, academic and psychological testing, individual and group tutoring; academic, psychological, and parent counseling; group, speech, language, physical, and occupational therapy; social services. Notes: Psychological counseling and group therapy for individuals aged 13 and up.

Brooklyn: Kings County Hospital Center, Developmental Evaluation Clinic, "N" Building, Box 26, 451 Clarkson Avenue, 11203. Telephone: (718) 270-2918, 270-2919, 270-1438, 735-3917. Contact: Robert Carberry. Outpatient program. Ages served: 3-16. Services: diagnostic testing, academic and psychological testing, psychological and parent counseling, speech and language therapy, social services.

Brooklyn: Long Island College Hospital, Stanley S. Lamm Institute for Developmental Disabilities and Children's Circle Preschool, 110 Amity Street, 11201. Contact for Institute: Cristobal Amador, Intake Worker. Telephone: (718) 780-1549. Contact for Preschool: MaryAnn O'Brien, Director. Telephone: (718) 780-4646. Outpatient program and preschool. Ages served: infant-21. Services: diagnostic testing, psychological testing, psychological and parent counseling; group, speech, language, physical, and occupational therapy; social services, pediatric neurologic evaluation and follow-up, orthopedic pediatrics, referral services. Notes: Developing a computer-assisted learning program utilizing digitized speech feedback. Preschool located at 75 Hicks Street, Brooklyn, NY 11201.

Brooklyn: Maimonides Medical Center, Child and Adolescent Services of the Community Mental Health Center, 20-48th Street, 11219. Telephone: (718) 270-8128. Contact: Antonio Giancotti, Director. Outpatient program. Ages served: birth-adult. Services: diagnostic testing, psychological testing, individual tutoring, perceptual clinic, psychological and parent counseling, social services.

Buffalo: Children's Hospital of Buffalo, Department of Child Psychiatry, 219 Bryant Street, 14221. Telephone: (716) 878-7611. Contact: Mitchell Parker, Coordinator. Outpatient and summer after school program. Ages served: 5-18. Services: diagnostic testing, academic and psychological testing, summer individual and group tutoring; academic, psychological, and parent counseling; group, speech, and language therapy; summer academic and socialization program.

Jamaica: Queens Hospital Center, Children's Rehabilitation Service, Building "J," 82-68 164th Street, 11432. Telephone: (212) 990-2282. Contact: Phyllis Bonder, Social Worker. Outpatient and after school program. Ages served: 3-12. Services: diagnostic testing, psychological testing, psychological and parent counseling; speech, language, physical, and occupational therapy; adaptive physical education, support group, social services.

Melville: Sagamore Psychiatric Center for Children and Youth, Box 755, 11747. Telephone: (516) 673-7700. Contact: Richard Willson, Director of Outpatient Services. Outpatient and day program. Ages served: 6-17. Services: diagnostic testing, academic and psychological testing, psychological and parent counseling, group therapy, support group.

New York City: Beth Israel Medical Center, Beth Israel Learning Disabilities Center, Nathan Perlman Place, 10003. Telephone: (212) 420-4135. Contact: Michael Osborn, Director. Outpatient program. Ages served: all. Services: diagnostic testing, academic and psychological testing, individual tutoring, psychological and parent counseling; group, speech, language, and occupational therapy; social services. Notes: Program currently being reorganized to include treatment and management.

NEW YORK

New York City: Lenox Hill Hospital, Center for Learning Disorders, 100 E. 77th Street, 10021. Telephone: (212) 794-4873. Contact: David M. Kaufman or Richard C. Sullivan, Codirectors. Outpatient program. Ages served: birth-21. Services: diagnostic testing, academic and psychological testing; academic, psychological, and parent counseling.

New York City: Mt. Sinai Hospital, Communications Disorder Center-Learning Disabilities Clinic, One Gustave Levy Plaza, 10029. Telephone: (212) 650-6153. Contact: Asher Bar or Mary Ellen Isaacs. Outpatient, inpatient, and day program. Ages served: all. Services: diagnostic testing, academic and psychological testing, individual tutoring; academic, psychological, and parent counseling; group, speech, and language therapy; occupational therapy evaluations, parent support group, social services.

New York City: New York University Medical Center, Rusk Institute for Rehabilitation, Pre-school and Infant Development Program, 400 E. 34th Street, 10012. Telephone: (212) 340-6045. Contact: Ronnie Gordon or Helen Hochburg. Outpatient, inpatient, day, and after school program. Ages served: 2-18. Services: diagnostic testing, psychological testing; academic, psychological, and parent counseling; physical and occupational therapy, social services.

New York City: St. Luke's/Roosevelt Hospital Center, St. Luke's Therapeutic Nursery, 411 W. 114th Street, 10025. Telephone: (212) 870-6351. Contact: Sally Arroyo. Outpatient and day program. Ages served: 2-5. Services: diagnostic testing, psychological testing, psychological and parent counseling; group, speech, and language therapy; social services. Notes: Nursery located in Riverside Church at 120th Street and Riverside Drive.

New York City: St. Vincent's Hospital and Medical Center of New York, Pediatric Rehabilitation, 130 W. 12th Street, 10011. Telephone: (212) 790-7881. Contact: Gabriel A. Nigrin. Outpatient and inpatient program. Ages served: birth-19. Services: diagnostic testing, academic and psychological testing, psychological and parent counseling; speech, language, physical, and occupational therapy; social services, child and adolescent psychiatry.

Poughkeepsie: St. Francis Hospital, Department of Communication Disorders, North Road, 12601. Telephone: (914) 431-8800. Contact: Frederick G. Attanasio. Outpatient and after school program. Ages served: preschool-adult. Services: diagnostic testing, academic testing, individual tutoring, parent counseling, speech and language therapy.

Rochester: University of Rochester Medical Center, Strong Memorial Hospital, University Affiliated Program for Developmental Disabilities, Box 671, 601 Elmwood Avenue, 14642. Telephone: (716) 275-2986. Contact: Philip W. Davidson, Director. Outpatient and inpatient program. Ages served: all. Services: diagnostic testing, academic and psychological testing, individual and group tutoring; academic, psychological, and parent counseling; group, speech, language, physical, and occupational therapy; social services, hyperactivity and behavior disorders clinics.

Suffern: Good Samaritan Hospital, Speech and Hearing Department, Route 59, 10901. Telephone: (914) 357-3300. Contact: Dennis Hampton. Outpatient and inpatient program. Ages served: all. Services: diagnostic testing; speech, language, physical, and occupational therapy; social services.

Watertown: Mercy Hospital of Watertown, 218 Stone Street, 13601. Telephone: (315) 782-7400. Contact: Sr. Rose Curtin, Speech and Hearing Department; Dorris Powers, Occupational Therapy Department; Leon Schilling, Community Mental Health Center. Outpatient program. Ages served: 3 and up. Services: psychological testing, psychological and parent counseling; speech, language, and occupational therapy.

Other Services

Albany: Parsons Child Family Center: The Neil Hellman School, 60 Academy Road, 12208. Telephone: (518) 447-5211. Executive Director: John W. Carswell. Residential treatment and child care facility. Elementary and secondary school with summer program. Ages served: 5-21. Current enrollment: 140. Full-time staff: 63. Part-time staff: 1. Services: individual and group tutoring, academic and psychological testing; academic, psychological, and family counseling; adaptive physical education, vocational training, work study, job placement, medical services; speech, language, and art therapy. Recreation: physical education, Special Olympics, gym. Notes: For young people with emotional, behavioral, and developmental disabilities with autistic features.

Albertson: Carl M. Walton Center for Independent Living, Nine Albertson Avenue, 11507. Telephone: (516) 625-0419. Director of Community Support Systems: Helaine Raskin. Clinic. Day and after school program. Ages served: all. Services: diagnostic testing, individual tutoring; psychological, parent, and couple counseling; group and individual therapy, adaptive physical education, support group, social services, vocational assessment and counseling, travel training, recreation, employability and job placement programs, supportive living facilities.

Bayside: Association for Neurologically Impaired Brain Injured Children (ANIBIC), 212-12 26th Avenue, 11360. Telephone: (718) 423-9550. Executive Director: Bernadette Claps. Clinic. After school, weekend, and summer day camp program. Ages served: 4½-adult. Services: individual tutoring, psychological and parent counseling, group therapy, support group, social services; scouts, information and referral, job development, socialization, and recreation programs; advocate in education, vocational training, legislation, and professional development.

Bronx: Montefiore Medical Center Speech and Hearing Center, 111 E. 210th Street, 10467. Telephone: (212) 920-5445. Contact: Karin S. Riordan or William Dolan. Clinic. Day and after school program. Ages served: all. Services: diagnos-

NEW YORK

tic testing, psychological testing, parent counseling, speech and language therapy, audiological assessment.

Brooklyn: Bailin - Mann Associates, 603 E. 23rd Street, 11210. Telephone: (718) 859-3367 or 338-2675. Contact: Marcia Mann or Amy Bailin. Clinic. After school program. Ages served: all. Services: academic testing, individual tutoring; academic, psychological, and parent counseling; group, speech, and language therapy; support group. Notes: Educational therapists trained in Orton-Gillingham, multisensory teaching techniques.

Brooklyn: Brooklyn Community Counseling Center, 1683 Flatbush Avenue, 11210. Telephone: (718) 338-4622. Contact: Connie Peters. Clinic. Day program. Ages served: all. Services: diagnostic testing, psychological testing, individual tutoring, psychological and parent counseling, group therapy.

Brooklyn: Kennedy Learning Clinic, 1877 Ocean Avenue, 11230. Telephone: (718) 252-6900 or 258-2222. Director: Richard A. Schere. Clinic. Day, after school, and weekend program. Ages served: all. Services: diagnostic testing, academic and psychological testing, individual and group tutoring; academic, psychological, and parent counseling; group, speech, and language therapy; support group.

Brooklyn: New Hope Guild Centers, 1777 E. 21st Street, 11229. Telephone: (718) 252-4200. Director: Ellen Sheldon. Clinic. Day and after school program. Ages served: 5 and up. Services: diagnostic testing, academic and psychological testing, individual and group tutoring; academic, psychological, and parent counseling; group and language therapy, support group, workshops. Notes: Three other sites besides main center: Bay Ridge Center, 9543 Ridge Boulevard, Brooklyn, NY 11209, telephone: (718) 238-6444; Howard Beach Center, 151-20 88th Street, Howard Beach, NY 11414, telephone: (718) 738-6800; Flatlands Center, 971 Jerome Street, Brooklyn, NY 11207, telephone: (718) 272-3300. All sites provide listed services.

Buffalo: Western New York Association for the Learning Disabled, 190 Franklin Street, 14202. Telephone: (716) 855-1135. Executive Director: Donald N. Policella. Clinic. After school program and summer residential camp. Ages served: 6-adult. Services: diagnostic testing, academic testing, psychological and parent counseling, group therapy, adaptive physical education, support group, social services, therapeutic recreation; vocational evaluation, counseling, training, and placement services; educational consultation, information and referral.

Dix Hills: Learning Foundations, 270 Deer Park Avenue, 11746. Telephone: (516) 499-2557. Director: Charles M. Richardson. Clinic. After school program. Ages served: 6-adult. Services: diagnostic testing, academic testing, individual tutoring, academic and parent counseling; computer programming, word processing; counseling and referral for vision, nutrition, or applied kinesiology therapy; preparation for SAT, ACT, GRE, civil service and high school equivalency exams.

Flushing: New York Testing and Guidance Center, 140-15 Sanford Avenue, 11355. Telephone: (718) 762-1313. Director: Daniel Cohen. Clinic. After school and Saturday program. Ages served: all. Services: diagnostic testing, academic and psychological testing, individual and group tutoring; academic, psychological, and parent counseling; group, speech, language, and art therapy.

Glens Falls: Diagnostic Learning Center, 416 Ridge Road, 12801. Telephone: (518) 793-0668. Director: Jan Bishop. Clinic. After school program. Ages served: prekindergarten-adult. Services: diagnostic testing, individual and group tutoring, parent counseling referrals.

Mineola: North Shore Learning Center, Nine Shortridge Drive, 11501. Telephone: (516) 248-7356. Contact: Howard Boll, Learning Disabilities Specialist. Clinic. Day and after school program. Ages served: 2½ to adult. Services: diagnostic testing, academic and psychological testing, individual tutoring; academic, psychological, and parent counseling; speech and language therapy, school evaluation and placement recommendations.

New York City: 92nd Street YM-YWHA, 1395 Lexington Avenue, 10128. Telephone: (212) 427-6000 ext. 179. Director, Special Services: Yvonne Pisacane. Art and recreation center. After school program with summer day camp. Ages served: 6-18 day program; 6-15 camp. Services: classes including art, modern dance and movement, drama, sports, games, and basic Jewish studies; social club, teen volunteer program; teen workshops covering topics such as grooming and dating; Cub Scouts, Brownies. Notes: All programs designed specifically for the learning disabled.

New York City: Up The Ladder, 30 Rockefeller Plaza, 10020. Telephone: (212) 582-9549. Director: Claudette Blumenson. Educational service. After school program. Ages served: 4 and up. Grades served: nursery-college. Part-time staff: 10. Services: diagnostic testing, individual tutoring, academic and psychological testing; academic, psychological, and parent counseling.

Rhinebeck: The Astor Learning Center, 36 Mill Street, 12572. Telephone: (914) 876-4081. Director of Education/Principal: Steve Throne. Residential treatment center. Ages served: 5-13. Grades served: prekindergarten-8. Current enrollment: 75. Maximum enrollment: 75. Full-time staff: 28. Part-time staff: 1. Services: individual and group tutoring, academic and psychological testing, psychological and family counseling, adaptive physical education, medical services.

Spring Valley: Rockland Psychological and Educational Center, 21 Alturas Road, 10977. Telephone: (914) 356-7250. Program Director: Neil Garofano. Clinic. Day and after school program. Ages served: 4 and up. Full-time staff: 7. Part-time staff: 12. Scholarships/financial aid available. Services: diagnostic testing, individual tutoring, academic and psychological testing; academic, psychological, and family counseling; speech, language, sensory integration, group, physical, and occupational therapy; adaptive physical education, vocational training, work-

NEW YORK

study, job placement, support group, social worker, biofeedback vocational testing and counseling, college and career planning.

Staten Island: Elizabeth W. Pouch Center for Special People, Staten Island Mental Health Society, Inc., 657 Castleton Avenue, 10301. Telephone: (718) 448-9775. Director: Gerald M. Spielman. Clinic. Outpatient services. Ages served: birth-adult. Services: diagnostic testing, psychological testing, psychological and parent counseling; group, speech, language, physical, and occupational therapy; social services, early childhood educational programs.

Yonkers: The Orchard School, Andrus Children's Home, 1156 N. Broadway, 10701. Telephone: (914) 965-8786. Director of Education: Bernard Kosberg. Day and residential treatment center with summer program. Ages served: 7-18. Grades served: 1-10. Current enrollment: 45. Maximum enrollment: 60. Full-time staff: 11. Part-time staff: 2. Scholarships/financial aid available. Services: individual and group tutoring, academic and psychological testing; academic, psychological, and family counseling; physical and occupational therapy, adaptive physical education, vocational training, job placement, work-study, medical services. Recreation: swimming pool, baseball field, basketball court, gym, weight training, football, field hockey, soccer, tennis, volleyball.

NORTH CAROLINA

Offices of Organizations Concerned with Learning Disabilities

ACLD, Inc.: 1703 Emerson Road, Kinston, NC 28501. President: Judy Rochelle. Telephone: Office (919) 527-4166; Home (919) 522-3579.

Council for Exceptional Children: President: J. Michael Ortiz, Department of Special Education, Appalachian State University, Boone, NC 28608. Telephone: (704) 262-2182.

The Easter Seal Society of North Carolina, Inc.: 832 Wake Forest Road, Raleigh, NC 27604. Executive Director: Edward Kershaw. Telephone: (919) 834-1191.

Orton Dyslexia Society (Carolinas Branch): 28 Montrose Drive, Greenville, SC 29607. President: Grace L. Hill. Telephone: (803) 288-8629.

State Department of Education Learning Disabilities Personnel

E. Lowell Harris, Director, Division for Exceptional Children, State Department of Public Instruction, Education Building, 114 E. Edenton Street, Raleigh, NC 27611. Telephone: (919) 733-3921. Learning disabilities consultant: Mary Anne Tharin. Telephone: (919) 733-3004.

Private and Day Schools

Charlotte: Mary Dore Private School, 108 Bradford Drive, 28208. Telephone: (704) 394-2341. Administrator: Mary D. Dore. Elementary and secondary day school with summer program. Ages served: 6-18. Grades served: 1-12. Current enrollment: 65. Maximum enrollment: 75. Full-time staff: 13. Part-time staff: 5. Services: individual and group tutoring, academic and psychological testing; academic, psychological, vocational, and family counseling; college preparatory high school program.

Durham: Hill Learning Development Center, 3130 Pickett Road, 27705. Telephone: (919) 489-7464 or 929-1008. Director: Margaret Sigmon. Preschool, elementary, and secondary day school with summer program. Ages served: 5 and up. Grades served: kindergarten-12. Current enrollment: 77. Maximum enrollment: 77. Full-time staff: 15. Part-time staff: 3. Scholarships/financial aid available. Services: individual and group tutoring, academic testing, small group instruction, individualized programs in language arts and math, 1:3 teacher/student ratio. Notes: Half-day program; students return to regular classrooms in local schools for remainder of day. High school credit offered in English, Spanish, algebra, geometry.

Gastonia: Crestwood Hall, Inc.- The Dyslexia School of North Carolina, 941 S. New Hope Road, 28052. Telephone: (704) 866-8251. Director: Cecilia M. Feemster. Elementary and secondary day school with summer program. Ages served: 6-15. Current enrollment: 20. Full-time staff: 5. Part-time staff: 1. Scholarships/financial aid available. Services: individual tutoring, academic and psychological testing; academic, psychological, and family counseling; tutoring for adults.

Hickory: The Learning Center of Catawba County, Inc., 16 First Avenue, N.E., 28601. Mailing address: P.O. Box 1521, 28603. Telephone: (704) 328-5326. Executive Director: Patricia Benfield. Elementary, secondary, and adult day school with summer program. Ages served: preschool-adult. Grades served: kindergarten-college. Current enrollment: 100. Maximum enrollment: 125. Full-time staff: 5. Part-time staff: 7. Limited scholarships/financial aid available. Services: individual and group tutoring, academic and psychological testing; academic, psychological, and family counseling; educational therapy, medical services, work-study.

Lenoir: The Patterson School, Route 5, Box 170, 28645. Telephone: (704) 758-2374. Headmaster: William H. Woodbury, Jr. Secondary day and boarding school with limited services. Ages served: 12-18. Grades served: 7-12. Current enrollment: 130. Maximum enrollment: 130. Full-time staff: 16. Part-time staff: 2. Scholarships/financial aid available. Services: individual tutoring, academic testing and counseling. Recreation: interscholastic and intramural sports, skiing.

NORTH CAROLINA

Raleigh: The Achievement School, Inc., 6700 Old Wake Forest Road, 27604. Telephone: (919) 872-0853. Director: Leon D. Silber. Elementary and secondary day school with summer program. Ages served: 6-adult. Grades served: 1-12. Current enrollment: 56. Maximum enrollment: 100. Full-time staff: 13. Part-time staff: 4. Services: individual and group tutoring, academic and psychological testing, academic and psychological counseling, job placement, work-study, half day and full day programs, 1:3 teacher/student ratio, adaptive physical education. Notes: Serves learning disabled, educable mentally retarded, and students with behavior problems.

Winston-Salem: The Jefferson Academy, 1360 Lyndale Drive, 27106. Telephone: (919) 924-4908. Director: Vea L. Snyder. Elementary and secondary day school. Ages served: 5-14. Grades served: kindergarten-8. Current enrollment: 59. Full-time staff: 9. Part-time staff: 2. Services: individual tutoring, academic and psychological testing, individualized classroom instruction. Recreation: physical education.

Summer Camps and Programs

Bat Cave: Camp Mishemokwa, P.O. Box 40, 28710. Telephone: (704) 625-9051. Permanent mailing address: Camp Mishemokwa, P.O. Box 516, Gulf Breeze, FL 32561. Telephone: (904) 932-9465. Directors: Seaton E. and Lucille Smith, Jr. Residential camp with limited services and academic program. Ages served: 6-16. Grades served: 1-10. Maximum enrollment: 200. Full-time staff: 60. Services: individual and group tutoring, academic testing. Academic programs: math, reading, computers. Recreation: camping, hiking, field trips, nature study, riding, swimming, sailing, archery, team sports, crafts, music, karate, soccer, tennis, canoeing, tubing, white water rafting, pottery, ceramics, arts and crafts, watersliding, miniature golf, rock climbing.

Jefferson: 4H Wilderness Experience, Ashe County 4H, Box 338, Jefferson, NC 28640. Telephone: (919) 246-3021. Program Coordinator: Lisa S. Perry. Day and residential camp. Ages served: 8-17. Grades served: 2-12. Maximum enrollment: 10. Full-time staff: 1. Part-time staff: 6. Recreation: camping, hiking, field trips, nature study, swimming, rock climbing, rappelling, canoeing, caving, cross country skiing, urban adventure trips, backpacking. Notes: Therapeutic delinquency prevention program for high risk youth.

College and University Special Programs and Services

Anson Technical College: P.O. Box 68, Ansonville, NC 28007. Total enrollment: 500. LD students: 15-20. Special services: individual tutoring, academic counseling. Contact: Pennington Mills, Learning Lab Coordinator. Telephone: (704) 272-7635.

Appalachian State University: Boone, NC 28608. Total enrollment: 10,000. Special services: individual tutoring, special examinations, academic and psychological counseling, taped books, training in study skills; developmental courses in reading, math, and English.

- **Special program:** Learning Disabilities Program. Provides registration counseling and assistance, liaison with faculty, tutoring, and alternative methods and materials. Must meet regular admissions requirements of the college. Verification of learning disability through recent diagnostic tests is requested. Coordinator: Arlene J. Lundquist. Telephone: (704) 262-2291 ext. 12.

Carteret Technical College: 3505 Arendell Street, Morehead City, NC 28557. Total enrollment: 1,057. Special services: individual tutoring, training in study skills, academic counseling, taped books, special examinations, student resource center, readers, diagnostic testing. Contact: Gail Strand, Instructor, Guided Studies. Telephone: (919) 247-3134 ext. 218.

Central Piedmont Community College: Charlotte, NC 28235-5009. Total enrollment: 22,000. LD students: 47. Special services: readers, individual tutoring, special examinations, academic counseling, diagnostic testing, taped books, training in study skills, note takers, student resource center, support group. Contact: Pat Goings, Learning Disabilities Specialist. Telephone: (704) 373-6621.

Center/clinic: Special Services, P.O. Box 35009. Telephone: (704) 373-6621. Director: Costas Boukouvalas. Not open to public. Ages served: 17 and up.

Duke University: Durham, NC 27708. Special services: psychological counseling, student resource center. Contact: Suzanne Wasiolek, Dean for Student Life. Telephone: (919) 684-6488.

Center/clinic: Duke Reading/Academic Skills Center, Nine W. Duke Building. Telephone: (919) 684-5917. Acting Director: Mary H. Peete. Open to public on a limited basis. Ages served: 5-adult. Services: academic counseling, training in study skills, individual tutoring, diagnostic testing.

East Carolina University: Greenville, NC 27834. Total enrollment: 13,800. LD students: 25. Special services: individual tutoring, academic and psychological counseling, readers, ombudsman, special examinations, diagnostic testing, training in study skills, support group. Contact: C.C. Rowe, Coordinator, Office of Handicapped Student Services. Telephone: (919) 757-6799.

Center/clinic: Learning Disabilities Clinic, Speight Building. Telephone: (919) 757-6846. Director: Betty A. Levey. Open to public. Ages served: 6-22.

Center/clinic: Learning Disabilities Summer Clinic, Speight 135. Telephone: (919) 757-6846. Director: Betty A. Levey. Open to public. Ages served: 7-14. Grades served: 2-9. Services: diagnostic/prescriptive teaching, metacognitive approach, diagnostic evaluation for ages 6-adult. Notes: Four-week program.

NORTH CAROLINA

Forsyth Technical Institute: 2100 Silas Creek Parkway, Winston-Salem, NC 27103. Total enrollment: 2,800. LD students: 15. Special services: individual and group tutoring, training in study skills, academic counseling, diagnostic testing. Contact: Marilyn Stowers, Chairperson, PreTechnical Department. Telephone: (919) 723-0371 ext. 311.

North Carolina State University: Box 7801, Raleigh, NC 27695-7801. Special services: individual tutoring, training in study skills, academic and psychological counseling, taped books, readers, diagnostic testing. Contact: Cathy L. Crossland, Director of Diagnostic Teaching Clinic. Telephone: (919) 737-3221.

Center/clinic: Diagnostic Teaching Clinic, 402 Poe Hall. Telephone: (919) 737-3221. Director: Cathy L. Crossland. Open to public through referrals. Ages served: 2-adult. Grades served: prekindergarten-college.

Pembroke State University: College Street, Pembroke, NC 28372. Special services: individual tutoring, academic and psychological counseling, special examinations, readers. Contact: Jesse M. Lomm, Coordinator of Special Education. Telephone: (919) 521-4214 ext. 221.

Southwestern Technical College: 275 Webster Road, Sylva, NC 28779. Total enrollment: 1,207. Special services: individual tutoring, training in study skills, academic counseling. Contact: Richard O. Wilson, Dean of Student Services. Telephone: (704) 586-4091 ext. 216.

University of North Carolina-Charlotte: UNCC Station, Charlotte, NC 28223. Special services: individual and group tutoring, training in study skills, academic and psychological counseling, taped books, special examinations, student resource center, readers, diagnostic testing, ombudsman, awareness meetings for faculty. Contact: Janet D. Daniel, Coordinator, Disabled Student Services. Telephone: (704) 597-2162.

Center/clinic: Learning Assistance Services/Disabled Student Services. Telephone: (704) 597-2162. Director: Janet D. Daniel. Not open to public. Grades served: college. Services: transcribing and typing reports, individualized education plans, individual and support services.

University of North Carolina-Wilmington: 601 S. College Road, Wilmington, NC 28403. Special services: readers, individual tutoring, special examinations, academic and psychological counseling, diagnostic testing, taped books, training in study skills. Contact: Marcee J. Meyers, Associate Professor. Telephone: (919) 395-3365.

Western Carolina University: Cullowhee, NC 28723. Total enrollment: 6,135. LD students: 36. Special services: readers, individual tutoring, special examinations, academic and psychological counseling, diagnostic testing, taped books, training in study skills. Contact: Barbara A. Mann, Coordinator of Handicap Student Services. Telephone: (704) 227-7234.

NORTH CAROLINA

Hospital Clinics

Asheville: Thoms Rehabilitation Hospital, Pediatric Department, One Rotary Drive, 28803. Telephone: (704) 274-2400 ext. 4143 or 4144. Contact: Ariane S. Piercy, Pediatric O.T. Supervisor. Outpatient and inpatient program. Ages served: birth-19. Services: diagnostic testing, psychological testing and counseling; group, speech, language, physical, and occupational therapy; social services.

Charlotte: Charlotte Rehabilitation Hospital, Inc., Speech and Audiology Department, Occupational Therapy Department, 1100 Blythe Boulevard, 28203. Telephone: (704) 333-6634. Contact: Peggy Treacy, Director of Speech and Audiology, or Carol Talley George, Occupational Therapist. Outpatient and after school program. Ages served: 3 and up. Services: diagnostic testing, speech and occupational therapy, language evaluations, gross and fine motor tasks and training, perceptual and preacademic skills, computer-assisted training.

Durham: Lenox Baker Children's Hospital, L.E.A. Division Human Resources, State of North Carolina, 3000 Erwin Road, 27705. Telephone: (919) 683-6890. Contact: J. Robert Gray, Administrator. Outpatient, inpatient, and day program. Ages served: birth-21. Services: diagnostic testing, academic and psychological testing, individual and group tutoring; academic, psychological, and parent counseling; group, speech, language, physical, and occupational therapy; social services, adaptive recreation.

Other Services

Greensboro: Julian Psychological Associates, 912 N. Elm Street, 27401. Telephone: (919) 275-0828. Director: Betty Julian. Clinic. Ages served: all. Services: diagnostic testing, academic and psychological testing, individual and group tutoring; academic, psychological, and parent counseling; psychotherapy.

Raleigh: Counseling and School Psychological Services, 1322 Dogwood Lane, 27607. Telephone: (919) 782-9506. Contact: Gloria H. Blanton. Clinic. Ages served: 2-adult. Services: diagnostic testing, academic and psychological testing; academic, psychological, and parent counseling; courses for parents and teachers.

Winston-Salem: Day Treatment and Tutorial Programs of the Child Guidance Clinic, Inc., 1200 Glade Street, 27101. Telephone: (919) 723-3571. Executive Director: Clyde Benedict. Therapeutic preschool and tutoring program with limited services. Day school with summer program. Ages served: 2½-7 preschool; all ages for tutoring. Full-time staff: 4. Part-time staff: 1. Services: individual and group tutoring, psychological testing, psychological and family counseling, in-service training and consultation for professionals.

NORTH CAROLINA

Winston-Salem: Forsyth Psychological Associates, 1396 Old Mill Circle, 27103. Telephone: (919) 765-3030. Contact: C. Drew Edwards. Clinic. Day program. Ages served: preschool-adult. Services: diagnostic testing, academic and psychological testing, psychological and parent counseling.

NORTH DAKOTA

Offices of Organizations Concerned with Learning Disabilities

ACLD, Inc.: 2025 Ida Mae Court, Minot, ND 58701. President: Doralyn Brown. Telephone: (701) 839-6877.

Council for Exceptional Children: President: Mary Jean Burkhart, Box 477, Cooperstown, ND 58425. Telephone: Office (701) 797-2831; Home (701) 733-2315.

Easter Seal Society of North Dakota, Inc.: Box 490, Bismarck, ND 58502. Executive Director: Wilbur L. Ashworth. Telephone: (701) 663-6828.

Orton Dyslexia Society (Upper Midwest Branch): 10000 32nd Avenue, North, Minneapolis, MN 55441. President: C. Wilson Anderson, Jr. Telephone: Office (612) 546-3266; Home (612) 545-5515.

State Department of Education Learning Disabilities Personnel

Gary Gronberg, Director of Special Education, Department of Public Instruction, Special Education Division, Bismarck, ND 58505. Telephone: (701) 224-2277. Learning disabilities consultant: Brenda Oas.

College and University Special Programs and Services

Mayville State College: Mayville, ND 58257. Total enrollment: 728. Special services: individual tutoring, training in study skills, academic and psychological counseling. Contact: Ray Gerszewski, Director, Counseling/Career Center. Telephone: (701) 786-2301 ext. 167.

Minot State College: Minot, ND 58701. Total enrollment: 3,000. Special services: individual tutoring and diagnostic testing. Contact: Daryl Wilcox, Director, Learning Disabilities Clinic. Telephone: (701) 857-3020.

Center/clinic: Learning Disabilities Clinic, Special Education Division. Telephone: (701) 857-3020. Director: Daryl Wilcox. Open to public. Ages served: all. Services: diagnostic testing.

North Dakota State School of Science: Wahpeton, ND 58075. Total enrollment: 3,000. LD students: 30. Special services: individual and group tutoring, training in study skills; academic, psychological, pre-enrollment, and vocational counseling; taped books, special examinations, student resource center, readers, note takers. Contact: Paula Ahles, Special Needs Counselor. Telephone: (701) 671-2327. Or Marcia Schutt, Director, Resource Program for the Handicapped. Telephone: (701) 671-2132.

Center/clinic: Learning Skills Center. Telephone: (701) 671-2622. Director: Rene Moen. Not open to public. Grades served: college. Services: special courses in basic English, math, reading, composition, effective listening and memory development, spelling, vocabulary.

North Dakota State University: Fargo, ND 58105. Total enrollment: 9,500-10,000. LD students: 30. Special services: individual and group tutoring, training in study skills, academic and psychological counseling, taped books, special examinations, readers, limited diagnostic testing, limited scholarships, ombudsman, support group, note takers, special orientation for disabled students. Contact: Liz Sepe, Learning Disabilities Specialist. Telephone: (701) 237-7671 or 237-7714. Or Bruce Bower, Director, Disabled Student Services. Telephone: (701) 237-7198.

North Dakota State University-Bottineau: First and Simrall Boulevard, Bottineau, ND 58318. Special services: individual and group tutoring, training in study skills, diagnostic testing. Contact: Ken Grodz, Director, Student Services. Telephone: (701) 228-2277.

Center/clinic: Student Opportunity Program. Telephone: (701) 228-2277. Director: Faye Bernstein. Not open to public. Grades served: freshmen and sophomores. Services: tutoring in study skills, reading, math, science, English.

Trinity Bible College: 50 Sixth Avenue, South, Ellendale, ND 58436. Total enrollment: 424. Special services: training in study skills, academic counseling, diagnostic testing. Contact: David C. Zink, Registrar. Telephone: (701) 349-3495.

OHIO

Offices of Organizations Concerned with Learning Disabilities

ACLD, Inc.: Ohio ACLD, P.O. Box 14931, Columbus, OH 43214. President: Robert Gast. Telephone: (614) 891-1167.

Council for Exceptional Children: President: Julie Holton Todd, 470 Glenmont Avenue, Columbus, OH 43214. Telephone: (614) 262-6131.

Ohio Easter Seal Society, Inc.: 2204 S. Hamilton Road, P.O. Box 32462, Columbus, OH 43232. Executive Director: Prentis M. Wilson. Telephone: (614) 868-9126.

OHIO

Orton Dyslexia Society (Ohio Valley Branch): 6401 Grand Vista Avenue, Cincinnati, OH 45213. President: Catherine F. Wagner. Telephone: (513) 631-4096 after 5 p.m.

State Department of Education Learning Disabilities Personnel

Frank E. New, Director of Special Education, Ohio Division of Special Education, 933 High Street, Worthington, OH 43085. Telephone: (614) 466-2650. Learning disabilities consultant: Karen Sanders.

Private and Day Schools

Akron: Our Lady of the Elms Special Education School, 1230 W. Market Street, 44313. Telephone: (216) 836-3734. Principal: Sr. Shirley Ann Nugent. Elementary day school. Ages served: 5-15. Grades served: kindergarten-8. Maximum enrollment: 74. Full-time staff: 10. Part-time staff: 6. Scholarships/financial aid available. Services: individual and group tutoring, academic and psychological testing; academic, psychological, and family counseling; physical, speech, and language therapy; adaptive physical education, vocational training, art and music. Recreation: scout troops, theater.

Canton: Day Treatment Center, 919 Second Street, N.E., 44704. Telephone: (216) 456-2244. Day Treatment Program Coordinator: Sandra Dragomire. Preschool and elementary day school with limited services; summer camp. Ages served: 2-12. Grades served: kindergarten-6. Current enrollment: 35. Maximum enrollment: 38. Full-time staff: 15. Services: individual and group tutoring, academic and psychological testing; individual, psychological, and family counseling; language therapy. Recreation: field trips, gymnasium, playground. Notes: Serves children with social/emotional/behavioral problems. Most children also have a developmental disability.

Cincinnati: Springer Educational Foundation, 2121 Madison Road, 45208. Telephone: (513) 871-6080. Executive Director: Sr. Marianne Van Vurst. Principal: Norita Aplin. Elementary day school. Ages served: 6-14. Grades served: 1-8. Current enrollment: 110. Maximum enrollment: 115. Full-time staff: 22. Services: individual and group tutoring, academic and psychological testing; academic, psychological, and family counseling; adaptive physical education, speech and language therapy. Recreation: intramural basketball, soccer, track; volleyball, cheerleading, after school art classes.

Cleveland: Our Lady of Angels Special School, 3570 Rocky River Drive, 44111. Telephone: (216) 251-4711. Principal: John Shipacasse. Elementary day school with limited services. Ages served: 6-18. Grades served: 1-8. Current enrollment: 28. Maximum enrollment: 32. Full-time staff: 4. Part-time staff: 2. Scholarships/financial aid available. Services: individual and group tutoring, academic and psychological testing, psychological and family counseling.

OHIO

Columbus: The Childhood League Center, 850 S. 18th Street, 43206. Telephone: (614) 443-9425. Director: Dave A. Proctor. Preschool and elementary day school with limited services. Ages served: 3-7. Grades served: preschool-kindergarten. Current enrollment: 57. Maximum enrollment: 57. Full-time staff: 12. Scholarships/financial aid available. Services: individual and group tutoring, academic testing, family counseling; speech, language, and occupational therapy; adaptive physical education.

Columbus: Marburn Academy, 1680 Becket Avenue, 43220. Telephone: (614) 457-8835. Headmaster: Allan L. Forsythe. Program Director: Norma Leclair. Elementary and secondary day school with summer program. Ages served: 7-17. Grades served: 1-12. Current enrollment: 66. Maximum enrollment: 100. Full-time staff: 11. Part-time staff: 6. Scholarships/financial aid available. Services: individual and group tutoring, academic and psychological counseling, vocational training, work-study, job placement. Recreation: gym, stage.

Dayton: Alpha School, 2701 S. Smithville, 45459. Telephone: (513) 254-1316. Director: Ann Claypoole. Elementary day school with summer program. Ages served: 7-16. Grades served: 1-10. Current enrollment: 46. Maximum enrollment: 55. Full-time staff: 14. Part-time staff: 2. Scholarships/financial aid available. Services: individual and group tutoring, academic and psychological testing; academic, psychological, and family counseling; adaptive physical education, vocational training. Notes: Emphasis on remedial reading and math.

Lyndhurst: Julie Billiart School, 4982 Clubside Road, 44124. Telephone: (216) 381-1191. Principal: Sr. Agnesmarie. Elementary day school. Ages served: 6-13. Grades served: 1-8. Current enrollment: 125. Maximum enrollment: 130. Full-time staff: 13. Part-time staff: 2. Notes: For children with learning disabilities and problems succeeding in regular classrooms. Children with mild cerebral palsy may be accepted.

Tiffin: Betty Jane Nursery School, 65 St. Francis Avenue, 44883. Telephone: (419) 447-8824. Director: Carol A. Campbell. Preschool with limited services. Ages served: 2½-5. Current enrollment: 150. Maximum enrollment: 160. Full-time staff: 3. Part-time staff: 3. Scholarships/financial aid available. Services: family counseling; physical, speech, and occupational therapy; medical services. Notes: Serves both handicapped and nonhandicapped children.

Warren: Children's Rehabilitation Center, 885 Howland-Wilson Road, 44446. Telephone: (216) 856-5617. Executive Director: Barbara Anderson. Director of Preschool/Day Care: Donna Alcorn. Preschool with limited services. Ages served: 3-5. Current enrollment: 60. Maximum enrollment: 60. Full-time staff: 4. Part-time staff: 3. Scholarships/financial aid available. Services: psychological testing, psychological and family counseling; physical, occupational, and speech therapy; medical services.

OHIO

West Liberty: Adriel School, Box 188, 43357. Telephone: (513) 465-5010. Executive Director: James Burkett. Elementary and secondary day and boarding school with summer program. Ages served: 6-18. Grades served: kindergarten-12. Current enrollment: 70. Maximum enrollment: 70. Full-time staff: 65. Part-time staff: 2. Services: individual tutoring, psychological and family counseling, work-study, special education classrooms, individual and activity therapy. Recreation: sports, individual and small group games.

Summer Camps and Programs

Clarksville: Joy Education Center, P.O. Box 157, 45113. Telephone: (513) 381-8689. Executive Director: Lee Snooks. Residential camp. Ages served: 10-13. Grades served: 5-7. Maximum enrollment: 40. Full-time staff: 1. Scholarships/financial aid available. Services: adaptive physical education. Recreation: camping, hiking, field trips, nature study, swimming, archery.

Cleveland: Beech Brook, 3737 Lander Road, 44124. Telephone: (216) 831-2255. Associate Program Director: Myrtle Astrachan. Day and residential camp with academic program. Ages served: 5-12. Grades served: kindergarten-6. Maximum enrollment: 75. Full-time staff: 1:2 staff/child ratio. Services: individual and group tutoring, academic and psychological testing; academic, psychological, and family counseling; medical services. Academic programs: math, reading, English, spelling, study skills. Recreation: swimming, hiking, field trips, nature study, crafts, drama, team athletics. Notes: For children with emotional problems and associated learning difficulties.

Pepper Pike: Frontier Day Camp for Children with Learning Disabilities, 2550 Lander Road, 44124. Telephone: (216) 449-4200. Executive Director: Gary Polster. Day camp. Ages served: 6-12. Full-time staff: 2:1 camper/staff ratio. Scholarships/financial aid available. Services: individual tutoring, small discussion groups; nurse, help in reading, writing, math, study skills. Recreation: singing, hiking, field trips, riding, swimming, sports, crafts, drama; noncompetitive outdoor and indoor social activities to improve motor, verbal, and social skills.

Perrysville: Camp Nuhop, Inc., "The Warm Fuzzy Camp", Camp Wesley, Route 2, 44864. Telephone: (419) 938-7151. Permanent mailing address: 1271 Center Street, Ashland, OH 44805. Telephone: (419) 289-2048. Director: Jerry Dunlap. Residential camp. Ages served: 6-16. Grades served: kindergarten-12. Maximum enrollment: 55. Full-time staff: 22. Scholarships/financial aid available. Recreation: swimming, hiking, nature study, crafts, camping, biking, canoeing, backpacking. Notes: For children with learning disabilities and/or behavior disorders. Offers nine camper programs.

College and University Special Programs and Services

Art Academy of Cincinnati: Eden Park, Cincinnati, OH 45202. Total enrollment: 240. LD students: 2. Special services: individual tutoring, academic counseling. Contact: Jane T. Stanton, Academic Dean. Telephone: (513) 721-5205 ext. 263.

Bowling Green State University: Bowling Green, OH 43403. Special services: individual tutoring, training in study skills, academic and psychological counseling, taped books, special examinations, readers. Contact: Jan ScottBey, Director, Handicapped Services. Telephone: (419) 372-0495.

The Cleveland Institute of Art: 11141 East Boulevard, Cleveland, OH 44106. Total enrollment: 525. LD students: 50. Special services: individual tutoring, academic and psychological counseling. Contact: Ann Roulet, Dean of Students. Telephone: (216) 229-0940.

Cleveland State University: E. 24th and Euclid Avenue, Cleveland, OH 44115. Total enrollment: 65. LD students: 6. Special services: individual tutoring, training in study skills, academic and psychological counseling, taped books, special examinations, student resource center, readers, diagnostic testing, ombudsman. Contact: Michael J. Zuccaro, Coordinator, Handicapped Services. Telephone: (216) 687-2015.

College of Mount Saint Joseph: Mount St. Joseph, OH 45051. Total enrollment: 1,942. LD students: 7. Special services: individual and group tutoring, training in study skills, academic and psychological counseling, taped books, special examinations, readers, diagnostic testing, scholarships, support group, paper typing service, liaison with professors, study group workshops.

- **Special program:** Project EXCEL. Goal is to give learning disabled students the special attention they need to succeed in college. Includes one-to-one instruction in reading, writing, study skills. All applicants must undergo psychoeducational evaluation and interview at the college. Contact: Carletta Claxton, Learning Disabilities Consultant. Telephone: (513) 244-4812 ext. 4210.

Center/clinic: Community Services. Telephone: (513) 244-4812. Director: Sr. Jacqueline Kowalski. Open to public. Grades served: preschool-adult. Services: diagnostic testing.

Columbus Technical Institute: 550 E. Spring Street, Columbus, OH 43215. Special services: individual tutoring, training in study skills, academic counseling, taped books, special examinations, student resource center, readers, scribes, note takers. Contact: Wayne Cocchi, Adaptive Education Specialist. Telephone: (614) 227-2571.

Hocking Technical College: Nelsonville, OH 45764. Special services: readers, peer tutoring, academic counseling, training in study skills. Contact: John F. Locker, Counselor. Telephone: (614) 753-3591 ext. 279.

OHIO

Jefferson Technical College: 4000 Sunset Boulevard, Steubenville, OH 43952. Total enrollment: 1,449. Special services: individual and group tutoring, academic and psychological counseling, diagnostic testing, training in study skills. Contact: Michael P. Joyce, Dean of Student Affairs. Telephone (614) 264-5591 ext. 208.

Kent State University: Kent, OH 44242. Total enrollment: 20,066. Total LD students: 20-30. Special services: reader/writer referral, test proctoring, academic and personal counseling, assistance ordering taped materials, preferred registration; tutoring in basic math, reading, English, and study skills. Contact: Joanna M. Gartner, Coordinator. Telephone: (216) 672-3391. Notes: Must be registered student with documented learning disability to receive special services.

Mount Vernon Nazarene College: 800 Martinsburg Road, Mount Vernon, OH 43050. Special services: individual tutoring, training in study skills, academic and psychological counseling, diagnostic testing. Contact: Randie L. Timpe, Assistant Academic Dean. Telephone: (614) 397-1244 ext. 220.

Notre Dame College of Ohio: 4545 College Road, South Euclid, OH 44121. Special services: individual and group tutoring, training in study skills, academic counseling, student resource center, diagnostic testing, taped lectures, oral examinations. Contact: Sr. Helene Marie Gregos, Coordinator of Special Education. Telephone: (216) 381-1680.

Center/clinic: Notre Dame College Diagnostic Clinic. Telephone: (216) 381-1680 ext. 282. Director: Linda B. Killea-Malik. Open to public. Ages served: 6-adult. Grades served: 1-13. Services: psychoeducational assessment, classroom observation, teacher conference, interpretation and comparison of test results and social/emotional factors, recommendations for classroom adjustments and remediation techniques.

Ohio University: Athens, OH 45701. Special services: individual tutoring, training in study skills, academic and psychological counseling, tape recorders, taped books, speech and hearing clinic. Contact: Mary Ann Henry, Assistant Director, Affirmative Action. Telephone: (614) 594-5246.

Ohio University-Zanesville: 1425 Newark Road, Zanesville, OH 43701. Total enrollment: 1,100. Special services: individual tutoring, academic counseling, taped books, special examinations, responds to requested needs. Contact: Debbie Kladivko, Director of Student Services. Telephone: (614) 453-0762 ext. 371.

Center/clinic: The Learning Team, 58 Sunnyside Drive. Telephone: (614) 594-6529. Director: Larry Jageman. Open to public. Ages served: 7-13. Services: summer academic program for learning disabled students, special educators, regular classroom teachers, and psychologists.

Sinclair Community College: 444 W. Third Street, Dayton, OH 45402. Total enrollment: 18,000. LD students: 100-200. Special services: individual tutoring, special examinations, academic counseling, training in study skills. Contact: Dennis Lettman, Director of Counseling and Student Development. Telephone: (513) 226-2748.

Stark Technical College: 6200 Frank Avenue, N.W., Canton, OH 44720. Total enrollment: 4,083. LD students: 1-5. Special services: individual and group tutoring, training in study skills, academic counseling, student resource center. Contact: John Herring, Coordinator of Developmental Education. Telephone: (216) 494-6170.

University of Dayton: 300 College Park, Dayton, OH 45469. Special services: individual tutoring, training in study skills, academic and psychological counseling, readers, limited diagnostic testing. Contact: Susan M. Iwinski, Coordinator of Handicapped Student Services. Telephone: (513) 229-3141.

Ursuline College: 2550 Lander Road, Cleveland, OH 44124. Special services: individual and group tutoring, academic and psychological counseling, diagnostic testing, training in study skills. Contact: Sr. M. Petra, Director of Support Services. Telephone: (216) 449-4200.

Wright State University: Colonel Glenn Highway, Dayton, OH 45435. Special services: academic and psychological counseling, diagnostic testing, training in study skills, taped books, special examinations, readers, scholarships, ombudsman, resource center. Contact: Stephen H. Simon, Director of Handicapped Student Services. Telephone: (513) 873-2141.

Center/clinic: Learning Disabilities Clinic. Telephone: (513) 873-2679. Director: Fran Landers. Open to public. Ages served: 6-16.

Xavier University: 3800 Victory Parkway, Cincinnati, OH 45207. Total enrollment: 7,000. LD students: 10. Special services: readers, individual and group tutoring, special examinations, academic and psychological counseling, diagnostic testing, training in study skills, taped books, ombudsman, handbook for special students assistance program. Contact: Sally W. Pruden, Director of Special Education and Special Students Assistance Program. Telephone: (513) 745-3655.

Hospital Clinics

Cincinnati: Children's Hospital, Cincinnati Center for Developmental Disorders, 3300 Elland Avenue, 45229. Telephone: (513) 559-4321. Contact: Dorothyann Feldis, Director of Special Education. Outpatient program. Ages served: 3-18. Services: interdisciplinary diagnostic evaluations, treatment, training, and education; professional training.

OHIO

Cincinnati: The Jewish Hospital of Cincinnati, Department of Physical Medicine and Rehabilitation, 3200 Burnet Avenue, 45229. Telephone: (513) 569-2370. Contact: Merritt S. Oleski, Clinical Neuropsychologist. Outpatient program. Ages served: 10 and up. Services: diagnostic testing, psychological testing, individual tutoring, psychological and parent counseling.

Columbus: Doctors Hospital, 1087 Dennison Avenue, 43201. Telephone: (614) 297-4190. Contact: Mari Kay Dono. Outpatient and inpatient program. Ages served: 5 and up. Services: diagnostic testing, parent counseling; group, speech, and language therapy.

Dayton: Children's Medical Center, Learning Disabilities Clinic, One Children's Plaza, 45404. Telephone: (513) 226-8410 or 226-8401. Contact: Jim Huebner or Gregory Ramey. Outpatient and inpatient program. Ages served: birth-18. Services: diagnostic testing, academic and psychological testing, psychological and parent counseling, social services.

Other Services

Akron: Akron Reading and Speech Center, 700 Ghent Road, 44313. Telephone: (216) 666-1161. Director: Ms. Ardath Franck. Clinic. Ages served: all. Grades served: all. Current enrollment: 200-250. Full-time staff: 2. Part-time staff: 6. Services: individual tutoring, academic and psychological testing, academic and psychological counseling, remedial and developmental reading, study skills, speech therapy, courses for high school credit.

Athens: Tri-County Mental Health and Counseling, Inc., 28 W. Stimson, 45701. Telephone: (614) 592-3091. Executive Director: George Weigly. Mental health center. Services: psychological testing, psychological and family counseling.

Chagrin Falls: Townsend Reading and Learning Center, 210 Bell Street, 44022. Telephone: (216) 247-8300. Executive Director: Sarah T. Littlefield. Clinic. Day and summer program with camp. Ages served: all. Current enrollment: 100. Full-time staff: 3. Part-time staff: 10. Scholarships/financial aid available. Services: diagnostic testing, academic and psychological testing, individual and group tutoring, academic and psychological counseling; occupational, speech, and language therapy.

Cincinnati: The Children's Home Therapeutic Treatment Center, 5050 Madison Road, 45227. Telephone: (513) 272-2800 ext. 215. Director of Education: Christina M. Russo. Therapeutic treatment center with elementary and secondary day and boarding school with limited services; summer program. Ages served: 11-18. Grades served: 1-12. Current enrollment: 36. Maximum enrollment: 36. Full-time staff: 9. Scholarships/financial aid available. Services: individual tutoring, academic and psychological testing; academic, psychological, and family counseling; adaptive physical education, medical services. Notes: To attend school, students must first be admitted to residential or day treatment program.

Cincinnati: The Olympus Center, 38 E. Hollister Street, 45219. Telephone: (513) 621-4606. Contact: Jane Pohlman. Clinic. Ages served: 5-adult. Services: diagnostic testing, individualized psychological and educational testing, multidisciplinary staff.

Columbus: The Educational Clinic, Inc., 867 S. James Road, 43227-1099. Telephone: (614) 236-1604. Director: Gerald J. Pruzan. Clinic. Day and after school program. Ages served: all. Services: diagnostic testing, academic and psychological testing, individual and group tutoring; individual, academic, psychological, family, marriage, and vocational counseling; group, speech, and language therapy; study and test taking skills, high school equivalency, biofeedback training, hypnotherapy.

Columbus: Hannah Neil Center for Children, 301 Obetz Road, 43207. Telephone: (614) 491-5784. Director: JoAnne F. Milburn. Day and residential treatment center with summer program. Elementary school with limited services. Ages served: 6-13. Grades served: 1-6. Current enrollment: 44 residential; 20 day. Maximum enrollment: 44 residential; 20 day. Full-time staff: 52. Part-time staff: 13. Services: individual and group tutoring, academic and psychological testing, psychological and family counseling, occupational and group therapy, social skills training. Recreation: swimming, motor development activities, sports skill building activities, camping, hiking. Notes: For children with behavior and emotional problems; many also have learning difficulties.

Smithville: Boys' Village School - Boys' Village Inc., P.O. Box 518, 44677. Telephone: (216) 264-3232. Administrator: William R. Schultz. Residential treatment center with limited services. Elementary and secondary school. Ages served: 12-17. Grades served: 4-12. Current enrollment: 64. Maximum enrollment: 68 treatment center; 55 school. Full-time staff: 62. Part-time staff: 3. Volunteers: 125. Services: individual and group tutoring, academic and psychological testing; academic, psychological, and family counseling; occupational, individual, and group therapy; adaptive physical education, vocational training, work-study. Recreation: small group and leisure activities, intramural and interscholastic sports.

Springfield: Oesterlen Services for Youth, 1918 Mechanicsburg Road, 45503. Telephone: (513) 399-6101. Executive Director: Walter R. Brooker. Residential treatment center. On-grounds secondary school staffed by public school teachers. Ages served: 13-18. Grades served: 8-12. Current enrollment: 45. Maximum enrollment: 48. Full-time staff: 70. Part-time staff: 10. Services: individual tutoring, academic and psychoeducational testing; academic, psychological, and family counseling; vocational training, medical services, individual and group therapy, prevocational work experience. Recreation: camping, athletics.

Youngstown: ACLD Learning Center, 201 Wick Avenue, 44503. Telephone: (216) 746-0604. Director: Mollie Kessler. Tutorial service with limited services. Ages served: 5 and up. Current enrollment: 67. Maximum enrollment: 183. Full-time staff: 10. Part-time staff: 3. Services: individual and group tutoring, academic testing, adaptive physical education; auditory, visual, and motor remediation.

OKLAHOMA

Offices of Organizations Concerned with Learning Disabilities

ACLD, Inc.: 3701 N.W. 62nd Street, Oklahoma City, OK 73112. Telephone: (405) 943-9434.

Council for Exceptional Children: President: Pam Sparks, 12601 N. Pennsylvania, Apt. 298, Oklahoma City, OK 73120. Telephone: Office (405) 521-3351; Home (405) 755-8169.

Oklahoma Society for Crippled Children, Inc.: 2100 N.W. 63rd Street, Oklahoma City, OK 73116. Executive Director: Wallace P. Bonifield. Telephone: (405) 848-7603.

State Department of Education Learning Disabilities Personnel

Jimmie L.V. Prickett, Administrator of Special Education, Special Education Section, 2500 N. Lincoln, Oklahoma City, OK 73105. Telephone: (405) 521-3351. Learning disabilities consultant: Evelyn Llewellyn.

Private and Day Schools

Edmond: Crescent Academy, 123 N. University, 73034. Telephone: (405) 348-5573. Headmistresses: Minette Kelson, Judee Koch. Elementary day school with summer program. Ages served: 6-13. Grades served: 1-8. Current enrollment: 25. Maximum enrollment: 40. Full-time staff: 3. Part-time staff: 9. Scholarships/financial aid available. Services: individual tutoring, academic testing and counseling, multisensory teaching in all academic areas, adaptive physical education. Recreation: swimming, gymnastics. Notes: Teacher/student ratio 1:10. Specifically for children with average or above average intelligence not meeting their potential in traditional school settings.

Oklahoma City: Timberridge Institute, 6001 N. Classen, 73118. Telephone: (405) 848-3518. Directors: Richard E. Sternlof, Ellen R. Oakes. Elementary and secondary day school with summer program. Ages served: 5-16. Grades served: kindergarten-12. Current enrollment: 20. Maximum enrollment: 30. Full-time staff: 3. Part-time staff: 3. Scholarships/financial aid available. Services: individual and group tutoring, academic and psychological testing; academic, psychological, and family counseling; adaptive physical education.

Oklahoma City: Trinity School, 6400 N. Pennsylvania, 73116. Telephone: (405) 843-5231. Headmaster: Bill Haddock. Preschool and elementary day school with limited services. Ages served: 3-13. Grades served: preschool-8. Current enrollment: 143. Maximum enrollment: 180. Full-time staff: 18. Part-time staff: 5. Scholarships/financial aid available. Services: individual tutoring, academic testing and counseling. Recreation: physical education.

Tulsa: Town and Country School, 2931 E. 31st Street, 74105. Telephone: (918) 747-3679. Director: Jo Ellen Beard. Preschool and elementary day school. Ages served: 4-14. Grades served: preschool-8. Current enrollment: 74. Maximum enrollment: 88. Full-time staff: 17. Part-time staff: 3. Scholarships/financial aid available. Services: individual and group tutoring, academic and psychological testing; academic, psychological, and family counseling; adaptive physical education. Recreation: bowling, ice-skating, swimming lessons, field trips.

College and University Special Programs and Services

Bacone College: Muskogee, OK 74401. Total enrollment: 464. Special services: individual tutoring, academic counseling, diagnostic testing, training in study skills, special examinations, readers, scholarships. Contact: Betty Gore. Telephone: (918) 683-4581.

Center/clinic: College Skills Center. Telephone: (918) 683-4581 ext. 240. Director: Charles Ballard. Not open to public. Grades served: freshmen, sophomores. Services: peer tutoring and counseling.

Cameron University: 2800 W. Gore Boulevard, Lawton, OK 73505. Total enrollment: 5,030. Special services: training in study skills, diagnostic testing, reading skills assistance, developmental labs. Contact: Charles Elkins, Dean of Student Services. Telephone: (405) 248-2200 ext. 280.

Carl Albert Junior College: P.O. Box 606, Poteau, OK 74953. Special services: individual tutoring, training in study skills, academic and psychological counseling, student resource center. Contact: Jim A. James, Dean of Students. Telephone: (918) 647-2124 ext. 276.

Central State University: 100 N. University Drive, Edmond, OK 73034. Special services: academic and psychological counseling, diagnostic testing, training in study skills. Contact: Darryll Gilliland, Counseling Center. Telephone: (405) 341-2980 ext. 2725.

Center/clinic: Special School Services. Telephone: (405) 341-2980 ext. 707. Director: Ruth Taylor. Ages served: 6-17. Services: diagnostic testing and evaluations.

East Central Oklahoma State University: Ada, OK 74820. Total enrollment: 4,000. LD students: 12. Special services: individual tutoring, training in study skills, academic and psychological counseling, taped books, special examinations, readers. Contact: Jim Caruthers, Director, Learning Resource Center. Telephone: (405) 332-8000 ext. 292.

Northeastern State University: Tahlequah, OK 74464. Special services: psychological counseling, student resource center, diagnostic testing. Contact: Robert Smallwood, Acting Dean of Student Affairs. Telephone: (918) 456-5511 ext. 394.

Center/clinic: Speech and Hearing Clinic. Telephone: (918) 456-5511 ext. 364. Director: William Riddle. Open to public. Ages served: all. Grades served: kindergarten-12. Services: hearing and speech evaluation, speech therapy.

Oklahoma State University: Stillwater, OK 74078. Special services: individual tutoring, training in study skills, academic and psychological counseling, diagnostic testing. Contact: Barbara Wilkinson, Associate Professor. Telephone: (405) 624-6036.

Center/clinic: Applied Behavioral Studies Summer LD Learning Program, 304 N. Murray Hall. Telephone: (405) 624-6036. Director: Barbara Wilkinson. Open to public. Ages served: 6-18. Grades served: 1-12. Services: tutoring, study skills.

Oral Roberts University: 7777 S. Lewis, Tulsa, OK 74171. Special services: individual and group tutoring, training in study skills, academic counseling, taped books, special examinations, readers, diagnostic testing, note takers, modified degree plans. Contact: Wanda Lee Hartman, Associate Dean, School of Education. Telephone: (918) 495-7015.

St. Gregory's College: 1900 W. MacArthur, Shawnee, OK 74801. Total enrollment: 296. Special services: individual and group tutoring, training in study skills, academic and psychological counseling, student resource center, readers. Contact: Judy Cawthon, Director, Resource Center, or Ira DasGupta, Director, Counseling Services. Telephone: (405) 273-9870.

Southwestern Oklahoma State University: Weatherford, OK 73096.

Center/clinic: Child Service Clinic, School of Education, 100 Campus Drive. Telephone: (405) 772-6611. Director: Ms. Pat Morrison. Open to public. Grades served: kindergarten.

Tulsa Junior College: Tulsa, OK 74119. Total enrollment: 13,148. LD students: 96. Special services: individual tutoring, training in study skills, academic and psychological counseling, note takers, taped books, special examinations, student resource center, readers, diagnostic testing. Contact: Maureen Bigson, Learning Specialist. Telephone: (918) 587-6561 ext. 427.

Center/clinic: Diagnostic Prescriptive Learning Center, 909 S. Boston. Telephone: (918) 587-6561 ext. 305. Not open to public. Ages served: 17 and up. Grades served: junior college. Services: academic testing.

Center/clinic: Counseling Center, 909 S. Boston. Telephone: (918) 587-6561 ext. 300. Director: Peggy Martin. Not open to public. Ages served: 17 and up. Grades served: junior college. Services: academic counseling.

University of Oklahoma: 660 Parrington Oval, Norman, OK 73019. Total enrollment: 20,000. LD students: 12. Special services: readers, individual and group tutoring, special examinations, academic and psychological counseling, diagnostic testing, taped books, training in study skills, other services based on individual student needs. Contact: Linda Zinner, Coordinator of Handicapped Student Services. Telephone: (405) 325-4006.

University of Oklahoma Health Science Center: 1000 Stanton L. Young Boulevard, Oklahoma City, OK 73190. Special services: individual and group tutoring, training in study skills, academic and psychological counseling, student resource center, ombudsman. Contact: Willie V. Bryan, Vice Provost and Registrar. Telephone: (405) 271-2655.

University of Science and Arts of Oklahoma: 17th and Grand, Chickasha, OK 73018. Special services: individual tutoring, academic and psychological counseling. Contact: Steve Siera, Director, Student Services. Telephone: (405) 224-3140 ext. 278.

University of Tulsa: 600 S. College, Tulsa, OK 74104. Special services: diagnostic testing. Contact: Penny Brunner, Assistant to the Provost. Telephone: (918) 592-6000.

Center/clinic: Chapman Center. Telephone: (918) 592-6000. Director: Jack Anderson. Open to public. Ages served: all. Grades served: all. Services: treats hearing and speech impairments.

Hospital Clinics

Oklahoma City: Oklahoma Children's Memorial Hospital, Child Study Center, 1100 N.E. 13th Street, 73117. Telephone: (405) 271-5700. Contact: Ellidee D. Thomas, Clinical and Program Director. Outpatient, day, and limited after school program. Ages served: birth-21. Services: diagnostic testing, academic and psychological testing, individual and group tutoring; academic, psychological, and parent counseling; group, speech, language, physical, and occupational therapy; social services.

Other Services

Oklahoma City: Jordan Diagnostic Center, 5700 N. Portland, Suite 211, 73112. Telephone: (405) 946-3033. Director: Dale R. Jordan. Clinic. Day and after school program. Ages served: 5-adult. Current enrollment: 25. Maximum enrollment: 40. Full-time staff: 4. Scholarships/financial aid available. Services: diagnostic testing, individual tutoring, academic testing; academic, psychological, and family counseling.

OREGON

Offices of Organizations Concerned with Learning Disabilities

ACLD, Inc.: OACLD, Portland State University, PSU Box 751, Portland, OR 97207. Telephone: (503) 229-4439. President: David Carboneau. Executive Director: Evelyn Murphy.

Council for Exceptional Children: President: Nancy Golden, 1970 Van Buren Street, Eugene, OR 97405. Telephone: Office (503) 686-3530; Home (503) 342-4025.

Easter Seal Society for Crippled Children and Adults of Oregon: 5757 S.W. Macadam, Portland, OR 97201. President: Bruce Whitaker. Telephone: (503) 228-5108.

Orton Dyslexia Society: P.O. Box 3677, Portland, OR 97208. President: Gloria Z. Davis.

State Department of Education Learning Disabilities Personnel

Patricia A. Ellis, Associate Superintendent for Special Education and Student Services, Oregon Department of Education, 700 Pringle Parkway, S.E., Salem, OR 97310. Telephone: (503) 378-2265. Learning disabilities consultant: Howard Smith. Telephone: (503) 378-3567.

Private and Day Schools

Bend: Tamarack Learning Center, Inc., 1560 N.W. Newport, 97701. Telephone: (503) 382-8646. Executive Director: Thomas M. Del Nero. Elementary, secondary, and adult day school with summer program. Ages served: 5 and up. Grades served: 1-12. Current enrollment: 40. Maximum enrollment: 40. Full-time staff: 6. Part-time staff: 4. Scholarships/financial aid available. Services: individual and group tutoring, academic and psychological testing; academic, psychological, and family counseling; vocational training, work-study, job placement.

McMinnville: Rainbow Lodge Youth Care Center, Route 2, Box 381, 97128. Telephone: (503) 472-3432. Director: John DeMay. Males only secondary boarding school with limited services; summer program and camp. Ages served: 14-18. Grades served: 7-12. Current enrollment: 11. Maximum enrollment: 12. Full-time staff 10. Part-time staff: 3. Services: individual and group tutoring, academic and psychological testing; academic, psychological, and family counseling; prevocational training, work-study, group and family therapy, psychotherapy. Recreation: seasonal sports, swimming, weight lifting, fishing, running, annual backpacking trip. Notes: Residential program for adjudicated youth; many have learning disabilities.

Portland: Open Meadow Learning Center, 7602 N. Emerald, 97217. Telephone: (503) 285-0508. Administrative Coordinator: Carole Smith. Elementary and secondary day school with limited services; summer program. Ages served: 13-18. Grades served: ungraded. Current enrollment: 35. Maximum enrollment: 35. Full-time staff: 5. Services: individual and group tutoring, academic testing, academic and limited family counseling, work-study, limited job placement.

Portland: Serendipity Academy, 2400 S.E. 148th Street, 97233. Telephone: (503) 761-7139. Executive Director: Susan Schriver. Elementary and secondary day school with summer program. Ages served: 6-21. Grades served: 1-12. Current enrollment: 110. Maximum enrollment: 125. Full-time staff: 14. Part-time staff: 4. Services: individual, group, and peer tutoring; academic testing; academic, psychological, group, and family counseling; adaptive physical education, small classes, work-study, vocational training. Recreation: physical education, outings. Notes: All students have failed repeatedly at other facilities.

College and University Special Programs and Services

Chemeketa Community College: P.O. Box 14007, Salem, OR 97309. Total enrollment: 10,945. LD students: 30. Special services: individual and group tutoring, training in study skills, academic and psychological counseling, taped books, special examinations, student resource center, readers, diagnostic testing, scholarships, support group. Contact: Nancy Barnes, Diagnostician. Telephone: (503) 399-5120. Or Connie Judd, Learning Disabilities Instructor. Telephone: (503) 399-5093.

- **Special program:** Learning Disabilities Program. Special tutoring, test interpretation, class restructuring, counseling, agency referrals, individualized education plans. Must be diagnosed learning disabled. Also provides awareness workshops for faculty and liaison with vocational and college transfer programs. Open to public but priority given to registered students. Ages served: 16-adult. Director: Donna Lane. Telephone: (503) 399-5136.

Clackamas Community College: 19600 S. Molalla Avenue, Oregon City, OR 97222. Total enrollment: 3,500. Special services: individual and group tutoring, training in study skills, academic counseling, taped textbooks, student resource center, readers, scholarships. Notes: Learning disabilities center to open fall, 1985. Contact: Cynthia R. Pucci, Department Chairperson, Educational Support Services. Telephone: (503) 657-8400 ext. 315.

OREGON

Lane Community College: 4000 E. 30th Avenue, Eugene, OR 97405. Total enrollment: 8,000. Special services: individual and group tutoring, training in study skills, academic and psychological counseling, special examinations, student resource center, diagnostic testing, remediation. Contact: Patricia John, Department Head, Study Skills Learning Center. Telephone: (503) 747-4501 ext. 2439.

Center/clinic: Study Skills Learning Center. Telephone: (503) 747-4501 ext. 2439. Director: Patricia John. Open to public. Ages served: 17 and up. Grades served: 12 and up. Services: diagnosis, remediation, individual tutoring, counseling.

Portland State University: P.O. Box 751, Portland, OR 97207. Special services: volunteer readers, scholarships, academic and psychological testing, taped textbooks, training in study skills, note taking information and referral, disabled students organization. Contact: Cindy Callis Oberg. Telephone: (503) 229-4446.

Southern Oregon State College: Ashland, OR 97520. Special services: individual tutoring, training in study skills, academic and psychological counseling, special examinations, student resource center, readers, diagnostic testing, ombudsman. Contact: Judy Lonergan, Coordinator, Handicapped Services. Telephone: (503) 482-6213.

Center/clinic: Omnibus Learning Disabilities Clinic, EdPsych 012. Telephone: (503) 482-5664. Directors: Doug Smith, Neil McDowell. Open to public. Ages served: 4-18. Grades served: kindergarten-12. Services: diagnostic testing.

Umpqua Community College: P.O. Box 967, Roseburg, OR 97470. Total enrollment: 500. LD students: 75. Special services: individual and group tutoring, training in study skills, academic and psychological counseling, taped books, special examinations, student resource center, readers, diagnostic testing, scholarships, ombudsman, support group. Contact: Sandy Swanson, Coordinator Educational Services, Special Needs Students. Telephone: (503) 440-4600 ext. 714.

University of Oregon: Eugene, OR 97403. Total enrollment: 15,840. LD students: 10-15. Special services: readers, individual and group tutoring, special examinations, academic and psychological counseling, training in study skills, taped books, support group, writing and math labs. Contact: Larry Bridges, Associate Director, Educational Opportunities. Telephone: (503) 686-3232.

University of Portland: 5000 N. Willamette, Portland, OR 97203. Special services: individual tutoring, training in study skills, academic and psychological counseling, diagnostic testing. Contact: Dvenna A. Duncan, Coordinator, Special Education. Telephone: (503) 283-7344.

Western Oregon State College: Monmouth, OR 97361. Special services: diagnostic testing, tutors, ombudsman, academic and psychological counseling, vocational counseling and placement. Contact: Julia Smith, Counselor/Coordinator of Services to Handicapped Students. Telephone: (503) 838-1220 ext. 396.

Center/clinic: Education Evaluation Center. Telephone: (503) 838-1220 ext. 322. Director: Thomas Roland. Open to public. Ages served: 3-21. Services: diagnostic testing and evaluation.

PENNSYLVANIA

Offices of Organizations Concerned with Learning Disabilities

ACLD, Inc.: PACLD, Toomey Building, Suite 7, Box 208, Uwchland, PA 19480. Telephone: (215) 458-8391. In-state toll free number: (800) 692-6200. Executive Director: Mary Rita Hanley. President: Donald Girouard. Telephone: (814) 237-6323.

Council for Exceptional Children: President: Richard E. Brown, 504 Hummel Avenue, Lemoyne, PA 17043. Telephone: (717) 763-8511.

The Pennsylvania Easter Seal Society: P.O. Box 497, Middletown, PA 17057-0497. Executive Director: William E. Graffius. Telephone: (717) 939-7801.

Orton Dyslexia Society (Greater Philadelphia Branch): Box 251, Bryn Mawr, PA 19010. President: Mary Lee Young.

State Department of Education Learning Disabilities Personnel

Gary J. Makuch, Director, Bureau of Special Education, 333 Market Street, Harrisburg, PA 17126-0333. Telephone: (717) 783-6913. Learning disabilities consultant: Bernie Manning.

Private and Day Schools

Dresher: Temple University Laboratory School, 530 Twining Road, 19025. Telephone: (215) 887-5150. Director: Herbert Wartenberg. Elementary and secondary day school with summer program. Ages served: 7-18. Grades served: 1-12. Current enrollment: 100. Maximum enrollment: 100. Full-time staff: 12. Part-time staff: 11. Scholarships/financial aid available. Services: individual and group tutoring, academic and psychological testing; academic, psychological, and family counseling.

Emmaus: The Hillside School, P.O. Box 216, Route 29 and Township Road, 18049. Telephone: (215) 967-5449 or 967-3701. Director: Roselyn M. Knapp. Assistant Director: Linda L. Whitney. Elementary day school with summer program. Ages served: 6-13. Grades served: ungraded kindergarten-6. Current enrollment: 27. Maximum enrollment: 32. Full-time staff: 7. Part-time staff: 1. Scholarships/financial aid available. Services: individual and group tutoring, academic and psychological testing; academic, psychological, and family counseling; adaptive physical education. Recreation: physical education.

PENNSYLVANIA

Erie: Dr. Gertrude A. Barber Center, 136 East Avenue, 16507. Telephone: (814) 453-7661. Founder/President: Gertrude A. Barber. Preschool, elementary, and secondary school; adult vocational training center. Ages served: birth-21. Grades served: ungraded. Current enrollment: 260. Full-time staff: 50. Part-time staff: 10. Services: academic and psychological testing, psychological and family counseling, physical and occupational therapy, adaptive physical education, medical services.

Fort Washington: Wordsworth Academy, Pennsylvania Avenue and Camp Hill Road, 19034. Telephone: (215) 643-5400. Director: Bernard Cooper. Preschool, elementary, and secondary day and boarding school with summer program and camp. Ages served: 3-21. Grades served: preschool-12. Current enrollment: 300. Maximum enrollment: 300. Scholarships/financial aid available. Services: individual tutoring, academic and psychological testing, psychological and family counseling, adaptive physical education, vocational training, work-study, medical services, partial hospital and outpatient psychiatric services. Recreation: sports, swimming, movies, roller-skating.

Jeffersonville: The Pathway School, 162 Egypt Road, 19403. Telephone: (215) 277-0660. Executive Director: B.H. Newill. Administrative Director: Stephen Vitali. Elementary and secondary day and boarding school. Ages served: 5-16 at admission. Grades served: ungraded. Current enrollment: 126. Maximum enrollment: 140. Full-time staff: 76. Part-time staff: 10. Services: individual tutoring, academic testing, psychological testing, medical facilities, physical therapy, prevocational training, speech therapy, adaptive physical education, art, music; clinical support including individual and group psychotherapy. Recreation: intramural sports, trips to Philadelphia, Valley Forge area.

Lancaster: The Easter Seal Rehabilitation Center, 625 Community Way, 17603. Telephone: (717) 393-0425. Executive Director: F. Timothy Muri. Preschool with limited services. Ages served: 18 months-kindergarten. Current enrollment: 45. Maximum enrollment: 50. Full-time staff: 4. Scholarships/financial aid available. Services: individual therapy, psychological testing, family counseling; physical, occupational, and speech therapy; adaptive physical education, medical services.

Lansdowne: Stratford Friends School, 82 N. Lansdowne Avenue, 19050. Telephone: (215) 259-5211. Codirectors: Dorothy Flanagan, Sandra Howze. Elementary day school. Ages served: 6-12. Grades served: ungraded. Current enrollment: 25. Maximum enrollment: 25. Full-time staff: 5. Part-time staff: 6. Scholarships/financial aid available. Services: individual tutoring, academic testing and counseling.

Malvern: The Phelps School, Sugartown Road, 19355. Telephone: (215) 644-1754. Headmaster: Norman T. Phelps, Jr. Males only secondary boarding school with summer program and camp. Ages served: 12-18. Grades served: 7-post high school program. Current enrollment: 145. Maximum enrollment: 145. Full-time staff: 21. Part-time staff: 6. Scholarships/financial aid available. Services: individual and group tutoring, academic and psychological testing, academic and psychological counseling, vocational training. Recreation: sports, riding, computers, woodworking, farming, bowling, art, auto mechanics.

Media: Benchmark School, 2107 N. Providence Road, 19063. Telephone: (215) 565-3741. Director: Irene W. Gaskins. Elementary day school with summer program. Ages served: 6-14. Grades served: 1-8. Current enrollment: 160. Maximum enrollment: 161. Full-time staff: 38. Part-time staff: 23. Scholarships/financial aid available. Services: individual and group tutoring, academic and psychological testing; academic, psychological, and family counseling; adaptive physical education. Recreation: gym, Outward Bound, soccer, hockey, baseball, swimming. Notes: Summer school provides remedial instruction in reading, study skills.

Newtown Square: Community School, 32 Media Line Road, 19073. Telephone: (215) 359-1990. Principal: Catherine Johnson. Elementary and secondary day school with summer camp. Ages served: 6-21. Grades served: kindergarten-12. Current enrollment: 115. Maximum enrollment: 125. Full-time staff: 35. Services: group tutoring, academic and psychological testing; academic, psychological, individual, group, and family counseling; adaptive physical education, vocational training, work-study, medical services, family therapy. Recreation: arts and crafts, cooking, living skills classes.

Newtown Square: Dynamic Springs Prep School, 3951 Providence Road, 19073. Telephone: (215) 353-6333. Headmaster: Nicholas L. Zouras. Elementary and secondary day school with limited services; summer program and camp. Ages served: 6-19. Grades served: 1-12. Current enrollment: 25. Maximum enrollment: 40. Full-time staff: 5. Part-time staff: 5. Scholarships/financial aid available. Services: individual and group tutoring, academic and psychological testing; academic, psychological, and family counseling; psychiatric evaluations, marital therapy for parents. Recreation: tennis, canoeing, biking, riding, track and field, cross country running, camping, basketball, music, arts, singing, outdoor barbecues.

Paoli: The Crossroads School, N. Valley Road, P.O. Box 730, 19301. Telephone: (215) 296-6765. Director: Donald G. Ross, Jr. Elementary day school with summer program. Ages served: 5-12. Grades served: ungraded kindergarten-8. Current enrollment: 70. Maximum enrollment: 80. Full-time staff: 15. Part-time staff: 3. Scholarships/financial aid available. Services: individual and group tutoring, academic testing, adaptive physical education, remedial services, Orton-Gillingham-based tutorial program for dyslexic children, language training, organization and study skills. Recreation: physical education, sports, playground, swimming. Notes: Exclusively for children with mild learning disabilities; does not accept children with behavior problems.

Philadelphia: The Delta School, 3515 Woodhaven Road, 19154. Telephone: (215) 632-5904. Director of Education: Robert W. Long. Elementary and secondary day school. Ages served: 4-21. Current enrollment: 160. Maximum enrollment:

300. Full-time staff: 30. Part-time staff: 3. Scholarships/financial aid available. Services: group tutoring, psychological counseling, adaptive physical education, work-study, speech therapy. Recreation: shows, dances, sports.

Philadelphia: New Path Montessori School and Center, Old York and Stenton, 19141. Telephone: (215) 924-6144. Director: Ilona Shafer. Preschool and elementary day school with summer camp. Ages served: 3-14. Grades served: preschool-8. Current enrollment: 206 school; 26 center. Maximum enrollment: 206 school; 26 center. Full-time staff: 20 school; 4 center. Part-time staff: 2 school; 2 center. Scholarships/financial aid available. Services: individual tutoring, academic and psychological testing; academic, psychological, and family counseling; occupational and speech therapy. Notes: The Center, two special classrooms within school, is specifically for the learning disabled. School offers limited services.

Pittsburgh: Activity and Development Center, 5244 Clarwin Avenue, 15229. Telephone: (412) 931-7404. Executive Director: Thomas W. Fogarty. Elementary and secondary day school with summer program. Ages served: 6-20. Grades served: ungraded. Current enrollment: 125. Maximum enrollment: 130. Full-time staff: 30. Part-time staff: 7. Services: group tutoring, academic and psychological testing; academic, psychological, and family counseling; adaptive physical education, vocational training. Notes: Serves learning disabled children and adolescents from 33 school districts in Allegheny, Butler, Washington, and Westmoreland Counties.

Pittsburgh: The Easter Seal Society of Allegheny County, 110 Seventh Street, 15222. Telephone: (412) 281-7244. Executive Director: Andrew J. Wasko. Director of Education: Beulah C. Moody. Preschool and elementary day school. Ages served: 2-8. Grades served: preschool-2. Current enrollment: 75. Maximum enrollment: 100. Scholarships/financial aid available. Services: individual and group tutoring, academic testing, family counseling; physical, speech, and occupational therapy; adaptive physical education, medical services.

Pittsburgh: Pace School, 200 S. Beatty Street at Baum, 15206. Telephone: (412) 441-1111. Executive Director: Barbara J. Bazron. Elementary day school. Ages served: 6-15. Grades served: 1-8. Current enrollment: 134. Maximum enrollment: 150. Full-time staff: 48. Part-time staff: 3. Services: individual and group tutoring, academic and psychological testing; academic, psychological, and family counseling; adaptive physical education, vocational training, speech and language training, medical services. Recreation: art, music, physical education.

Pittsburgh: St. Peter's Child Development Center, 4127 Brownsville Road, 15227. Telephone: (412) 882-6330. Director: Shirley A. Small. Preschool with limited services; summer program and camp. Ages served: 2-5. Current enrollment: 130. Maximum enrollment: 140. Full-time staff: 55. Services: individual and group tutoring, academic testing, family counseling, physical therapy. Recreation: music, art, creative play, field trips.

Rosemont: The Hill Top Preparatory School, S. Ithan Avenue and Clyde Road, 19010. Telephone: (215) 527-3230. Director: Elissa L. Fisher. Director of Admissions: Mary Jane Nelson. Secondary day school. Ages served: 12-21. Grades served: 7-12, precollege year. Current enrollment: 102. Maximum enrollment: 105. Full-time staff: 36. Part-time staff: 4. Scholarships/financial aid available. Services: individual tutoring, academic and psychological testing; academic, psychological, and family counseling; adaptive physical education, college placement, mandatory group therapy. Recreation: soccer, basketball, floor hockey, softball.

Saint Marys: Pre-School at Elk County Society for Crippled Children and Adults, Johnsonburgh Road, P.O. Box 422, 15857. Telephone: (814) 834-2535. Director: Joan Smith. Preschool with limited services; summer program. Ages served: 2-6. Current enrollment: 28. Maximum enrollment: 32. Full-time staff: 1. Part-time staff: 4. Scholarships/financial aid available. Services: speech therapy, visual perceptual activities. Speech therapy also offered privately for school-aged children and adults.

Scranton: The de Paul School, 1627 N. Main Avenue, 18508. Telephone: (717) 346-5855. Director of Education: Joan E. Gigantino. Elementary day school. Ages served: 6-13. Grades served: 1-8. Current enrollment: 25. Maximum enrollment: 35. Full-time staff: 7. Services: academic and psychological testing, parent self-help group, individual and group tutoring, counseling. Notes: Exclusively for dyslexic students.

Scranton: Friendship House Children's Center, 1615 E. Elm Street, 18505. Telephone: (717) 342-8305. President: James M. Thomas. Preschool and elementary day and boarding school with limited services; summer program and camp. Ages served: 3-15. Grades served: kindergarten-8. Current enrollment: 108. Maximum enrollment: 120. Full-time staff: 120. Part-time staff: 14. Services: individual and group tutoring, academic and psychological testing; academic, psychological, and family counseling; adaptive physical education, medical services, art and music therapy, psychiatric services. Recreation: swimming, bowling, nature hikes, field trips, bicycling.

Scranton: United Cerebral Palsy of Northeast Pennsylvania, 230 Lackawanna Avenue, 18503. Telephone: (717) 347-3357. School address: 423 Center Street, Clarks Summit, 18411. School telephone: (717) 587-5892. Executive Director: Lydia Ann Coulter. Preschool with limited services; summer program. Ages served: birth-5. Current enrollment: 63. Maximum enrollment: 65. Full-time staff: 26. Part-time staff: 4. Services: academic and psychological testing, physical and occupational therapy, adaptive physical education, medical services; early intervention program provides integrated therapeutic and educational services.

Williamsport: Hope Consolidated Services, Inc., P.O. Box 1837, 17703-1837. Telephone: (717) 326-7413. President: Paul Daniels. Preschool with limited services. Ages served: birth-5. Current enrollment: 50. Maximum enrollment: 50.

PENNSYLVANIA

Full-time staff: 5. Part-time staff: 2. Scholarships/financial aid available. Services: individual and group tutoring, psychological testing, family counseling, physical and occupational therapy. Notes: Serves children with various disabilities.

Williamsport: Lycoming County Crippled Children's Society, Inc., 625 W. Edwin Street, 17701. Telephone: (717) 326-0565. Executive Director: Lawrence Savitsky. Preschool with limited services. Ages served: 3-6. Current enrollment: 22. Maximum enrollment: 22. Full-time staff: 5. Scholarships/financial aid available. Services: group tutoring, academic testing, physical and speech therapy, adaptive physical education, medical services, bimonthly pediatric neurology clinic. Recreation: swim/gym, music therapy. Notes: Serves children with speech and hearing, emotional/social, physical, perceptual, and other handicaps.

Summer Camps and Programs

Bechtelsville: Helping Hands, Inc., Route 1, Box 360, 19505. Telephone: (215) 754-6491. Recreation/Support and Referral Director: Nancy J. Daniels. Day residential camps with academic programs. Ages served: 5 and up. Academic programs: math, reading, spelling. Recreation: camping, hiking, field trips, nature study, swimming, team sports, crafts, music. Notes: Camp sites change yearly.

Broomall: Camp Betashire, 16 Rittenhouse Road, 19008. Telephone: (215) 356-8714. Director: Sara Jane Cronin. Day camp. Ages served: 6-12. Grades served: kindergarten-6. Maximum enrollment: 50. Full-time staff: 20. Part-time staff: 1. Scholarships/financial aid available. Recreation: swimming, hiking, field trips, crafts, drama, camping, academic enrichment, decision-making program.

Friendsville: Camp Choconut, 18818. Telephone: (717) 553-2233. Permanent mailing address: 1436 Rose Glen Road, Box 33, Gladwyne, PA 19035. Telephone: (215) 649-3548. Director: S. Hamill Horne. Males only residential camp with limited services. Ages served: 9-14. Maximum enrollment: 75. Full-time staff: 15. Recreation: camping, hiking, nature study, swimming, sailing, archery, crafts, music, carpentry, work projects.

Honesdale: Summit Camp Program, Route 3, 18431. Telephone: (717) 253-4381. Permanent mailing address: 339 N. Broadway, Upper Nyack, NY 10960. Telephone: (914) 358-7772 or (718) 268-6060. Director: Mayer A. Stiskin. Residential camp with academic program. Ages served: 7-18. Full-time staff: 130. Maximum enrollment: 200. Services: individual and group tutoring, adaptive physical education, work-study, prevocational education, medical services. Academic programs: math, reading, computer lab. Recreation: swimming, hiking, field trips, nature study, crafts, drama, camping, team athletics, industrial arts, ceramics, dance, creative movement, trampoline, boating, canoeing. Notes: Therapeutic camping for children with learning disabilities.

Kulpsville: Camp Can Do, Box 333, Sumneytown Pike, 19443. Telephone: (215) 256-4211. Director: Paul Goldenberg. Day camp. Ages served: 3-21. Maximum enrollment: 70. Full-time staff: 25. Scholarships/financial aid available. Services: group tutoring, family counseling, physical and occupational therapy, adaptive physical education. Recreation: field trips, nature study, swimming, team sports, crafts, dance, music.

Lackawaxen: Camp Lee Mar, Route 590, 18435. Telephone: (717) 685-7188. Permanent mailing address: 985 E. 24th Street, Brooklyn, NY 11210. Telephone: (718) 338-0064. Director: Ms. Lee Morrone. Residential camp with academic program. Ages served: 5-16. Grades served: ungraded. Full-time staff: 65. Part-time staff: 5. Maximum enrollment: 175. Services: group tutoring, psychological and family counseling, adaptive physical education, vocational training, medical services, speech therapy. Academic programs: math, reading, spelling. Recreation: swimming, hiking, nature study, crafts, camping, team athletics. Notes: Serves educable retarded, brain injured, and learning disabled children.

Lake Como: Round Lake Camp, Route 247, 18437. Telephone: (717) 798-2551. Permanent mailing address: 21 Plymouth Street, Fairfield, NJ 07006. Telephone: (201) 575-3333. Assistant Executive Director: Eugene Bell. Residential camp with academic program. Ages served: 7-16. Full-time staff: 65. Maximum enrollment: 100. Scholarships/financial aid available. Services: individual and group tutoring, psychological counseling, occupational therapy, adaptive physical education, vocational training, medical services, therapeutic recreation. Academic programs: math, reading, study skills, computers. Recreation: swimming, hiking, riding, field trips, nature study, crafts, drama, camping, photography, team athletics, archery, music, dance. Notes: Serves children with mild learning disabilities.

Thompson: Rock Creek Farm, Route 1, Box 53, 18465. Telephone: (717) 756-2706. Directors: Bernard and Joanne Wray. Residential camp with academic program. Ages served: 6-17. Full-time staff: 55. Maximum enrollment: 96. Services: individual tutoring, medical services. Recreation: swimming, hiking, field trips, nature study, crafts, drama, camping, team athletics, industrial arts, auto mechanics, forestry, teen work program, boating, fishing, sports. Notes: Serves emotionally handicapped and learning disabled.

College and University Special Programs and Services

Antioch University: 1811 Spring Garden Street, Philadelphia, PA 19130. Special services: training in study skills, special examinations, readers. Contact: Louisa D. Groce, Program Administrator, Master of Education Program. Telephone: (215) 665-0445 ext. 215.

Beaver College: Glenside, PA 19038. Special services: individual and group tutoring, training in study skills, academic and psychological counseling, student resource center. Contact: Barbara Nodine, Associate Professor, Psychology. Telephone: (215) 572-2181.

PENNSYLVANIA

Bloomsburg University of Pennsylvania: Bloomsburg, PA 17815. Total enrollment: 6,200. LD students: 80-100. Special services: readers, individual and group tutoring, academic and psychological counseling, special examinations, diagnostic testing, taped books, training in study skills, ombudsman, support group. Contact: Colleen Marks, Professor. Telephone: (717) 389-4080 or 389-4119. Or Peter B. Walters, Director of Special Services. Telephone: (717) 389-4275.

California University of Pennsylvania: California, PA 15419. Special services: individual and group tutoring, training in study skills, academic and psychological counseling, special examinations, diagnostic testing, ombudsman. Contact: Arthur L. Bakewell, 504 Coordinator. Telephone: (412) 938-4076.

Community College of Allegheny County-Allegheny Campus: 808 Ridge Avenue, Pittsburgh, PA 15212. Total enrollment: 7,645. LD students: 56. Special services: individual and group tutoring, training in study skills, academic and psychological counseling, taped books, talking calculators, tape recorders, special examinations, student resource center, readers, diagnostic testing, ombudsman, support group, note takers, developmental classes, test anxiety workshops, precollege program. Contact: Mary Beth Doyle, Director, Handicapped Services. Telephone: (412) 237-4612.

Community College of Allegheny County-Boyce Campus: 595 Beatty Road, Monroeville, PA 15146. Total enrollment: 5,300. LD students: 10. Special services: individual tutoring, training in study skills, academic and psychological counseling, taped books, student resource center, ombudsman. Contact: Renee Clark, Director, Supportive Services. Telephone: (412) 733-4220.

Community College of Philadelphia: 1700 Spring Garden Street, Philadelphia, PA 19130. Total enrollment: 16,000. LD students: 150. Special services: academic and psychological counseling, taped books, tape recorders, sound-proof study booths, talking calculators, special examinations, student resource center, readers, note takers, support group.

- **Special program:** Learning Disabilities Project. Diagnostic testing and evaluation, individual and group tutoring, training in study skills, precollege summer workshops, special remedial coursework, community education and sensitization to learning disabilities. Coordinator: Jay Segal. Telephone: (215) 751-8289.

Duquesne University: 600 Forbes Avenue, Pittsburgh, PA 15282. Special services: readers, individual and group tutoring, ombudsman, special examinations, academic and psychological counseling, diagnostic testing, training in study skills. Contact: Joseph T. Brennan, Director of Reading Clinic. Telephone: (412) 434-6088.

Center/clinic: Duquesne University Reading Clinic, School of Education, Canevin Hall. Telephone: (412) 434-6088. Director: Joseph T. Brennan. Open to public.

Keystone Junior College: La Plume, PA 18411. Total enrollment: 750. Special services: individual and group tutoring, training in study skills, developmental courses in language skills and math, learning center, individualized learning programs, small classes, academic counseling, special examinations. Notes: Also sponsors Nokomis, a precollege experience for high school and college-bound students. The five-week residential summer program is designed to stimulate students into becoming motivated learners by combining academics, physical work, and group learning. Contact: Ms. Jan Kaskey, Tutor Coordinator. Telephone: (717) 945-5141 ext. 244.

Lycoming College: College Place, Williamsport, PA 17701. Total enrollment: 1286. LD students: 7. Special services: individual tutoring, training in study skills, academic and psychological counseling, taped books, ombudsman. Contact: Jack C. Buckle, Dean of Student Services. Telephone: (717) 326-1951 ext. 236.

Northampton County Area Community College: 3835 Green Pond Road, Bethlehem, PA 18017. Total enrollment: 4,300. LD students: 40. Special services: individual and group tutoring, training in study skills, academic and psychological counseling, taped books, readers, diagnostic testing, ombudsman. Contact: Wendy P. Cole, Learning Disabilities Specialist. Telephone: (215) 861-5347.

Pennsylvania State University: University Park, PA 16802. Total enrollment: 38,000. LD students: 90. Special services: individual tutoring, training in study skills; individual, academic, and psychological counseling; taped books, diagnostic testing, scholarships.

- **Special program:** Comprehensive Service Program. Identification and diagnosis, individualized education plans, individual tutoring and counseling, course substitutions, special examinations, compensating strategies, library assistance. Must be matriculated in university degree program. Services on first come, first served basis. Director: Anna Gajar. Telephone: (814) 863-2438.

Shippensburg University: Shippensburg, PA 17257. Special services: individual and group tutoring, training in study skills, academic and psychological counseling, taped books, diagnostic testing. Contact: Bradley Little, Professor, Special Education. Telephone: (717) 532-1724.

Slippery Rock University of Pennsylvania: Slippery Rock, PA 16057. Special services: individual and group tutoring, training in study skills, academic counseling, special examinations, readers, diagnostic testing, ombudsman, preadmission conference. Contact: Champ R. Storch, Chairperson, Academic Support Services Program. Telephone: (412) 794-7571.

University of Pennsylvania: Philadelphia, PA 19104. Total enrollment: 16,000. LD students: 10. Special services: individual and group tutoring, training in study skills, academic and psychological counseling, taped books, student resource cen-

PENNSYLVANIA

ter, readers, scholarships, ombudsman, support group, extended time on examinations. Contact: Alice Nagle, Coordinator, Programs for the Handicapped. Telephone: (215) 898-6993.

University of Pittsburgh: Pittsburgh, PA 15260. Total enrollment: 29,000. LD students: 5. Special services: readers, individual tutoring, ombudsman, special examinations, academic and psychological counseling, taped books, training in study skills, referral for diagnostic testing, learning skills center. Contact: Tom Galante, Coordinator, Disabled Student Services. Telephone: (412) 624-6738.

Williamsport Area Community College: 1005 W. Third Street, Williamsport, PA 17701. Total enrollment: 4,000. LD students: 20. Special services: individual tutoring, training in study skills, academic and psychological counseling, taped books, special examinations, support group. Contact: Kathryn A. Ferrence, Counselor for Special Needs Students. Telephone: (717) 326-3761 ext. 398.

Hospital Clinics

Hershey: Milton S. Hershey Medical Center, Learning Disabilities Clinic, Department of Pediatrics, 17033. Telephone: (717) 534-8603 or 534-8006. Contact: Angelica Brennan or Jeanette Ramer. Outpatient program. Ages served: 4-18. Services: diagnostic testing, psychological testing, psychological and parent counseling.

Philadelphia: The Children's Hospital of Philadelphia, School-Aged Evaluation Program, Division of Child Development and Rehabilitation, 19104. Telephone: (215) 596-9876. Contact: Marion Carr. Outpatient program. Ages served: 5-18. Services: diagnostic testing, academic and psychological testing; speech, language, physical, and occupational therapy; social services, developmental pediatric evaluation, neuropsychological evaluation, child-family psychiatric assessment, multidisciplinary team.

Philadelphia: Thomas Jefferson University Hospital, Pediatric Neurology and Child Psychiatry, 111 S. 11th Street, Suite 8050, 19107. Telephone: (215) 928-6940 or 928-6822. Contact: Jeanette Mason or Leonard Graziani. Outpatient program. Ages served: all. Services: diagnostic testing, academic and psychological testing; academic, psychological, and parent counseling; speech, language, physical, and occupational therapy; psychiatric evaluation and treatment, neurodevelopmental evaluation, biomedical testing.

Philadelphia: The Medical College of Pennsylvania Hospital, Neurodevelopmental Program, 3300 Henry Avenue, 19129. Telephone: (215) 842-6684. Contact: Lawrence W. Brown. Outpatient, inpatient, and day program. Ages served: birth-18. Services: diagnostic testing, academic and psychological testing, psychological and parent counseling; group, speech, and language therapy; social services.

Philadelphia: Shriners Hospital for Crippled Children, 8400 Roosevelt Boulevard, 19152. Telephone: (215) 332-4500 ext. 227. Contact: Roberta Ciocco. Outpatient, inpatient, day, and after school program. Ages served: birth-21. Services: diagnostic testing, psychological testing and counseling; speech, language, physical, and occupational therapy; social services.

Pittsburgh: Children's Hospital of Pittsburgh, Child Development Unit, 125 DeSoto Street, 15213. Telephone: (412) 647-5560. Intake Coordinator: Joyce Welsh. Day and after school program. Ages served: birth-18. Services: diagnostic testing, academic and psychological testing; academic, psychological, and parent counseling; support group, developmental and functional assessments, behavioral evaluation and therapy.

Pittsburgh: St. Francis Medical Center, 45th Street off Penn Avenue, 15201. Developmental Evaluative Services for Children (DESC), telephone: (412) 622-4135. Contact: Holly Dick. Community Mental Health/Mental Retardation (MH/MR), telephone: (412) 622-4590. Contact: Jane Lockwood. Outpatient and inpatient program. Ages served: birth-6 (DESC); 6-17 (MH/MR). Services: diagnostic testing, psychological testing, psychological and parent counseling; group, speech, and language therapy; social services.

Sewickley: D.T. Watson Rehabilitation Hospital, Camp Meeting Road, 15143. Telephone: (412) 741-9500. Contact: Jean L. Becker, Director of Education. Outpatient and day school program. Ages served: 3-21 day school; school-age and up outpatient services. Services: diagnostic testing, academic and psychological testing, individual tutoring, academic and parent counseling; speech, language, physical, and occupational therapy; adaptive physical education, social services, remediation of specific deficit areas, compensatory strategies.

Sewickley: Sewickley Valley Hospital, Staunton Clinic, Blackburn Road, 15143. Telephone: (412) 741-6600 ext. 1493. Contact: Lee Fisher or John H. Dwyer. Outpatient program. Services: diagnostic testing, psychological and parent counseling, group therapy.

Other Services

Aliquippa: Vista Learning and Diagnostic Center, 1500 Brodhead Road, 15001. Telephone: (412) 375-7030. Director: Michelle Gernat. Clinic. Day, after school, and summer program. Ages served: 4 and up. Current enrollment: 30. Full-time staff: 1. Part-time staff: 1. Scholarships/financial aid available. Services: individual tutoring, visual perceptual training.

Bryn Mawr: Learning Disabilities Consultants, P.O. Box 716, 19010. Telephone: (215) 275-7211. Director of Educational and Vocational Services: Richard

PENNSYLVANIA

Cooper. Clinic. Day and after school program. Ages served: 12 and up. Services: diagnostic testing, academic testing, individual and group tutoring; academic, psychological, parent, family, and career counseling; group therapy, support group, job placement and maintenance, vocational evaluation, hypnotherapy, word processing training; workshops and training to schools, colleges, parent groups, and professionals.

Bryn Mawr: Main Line Speech Consultants, 950 County Line Road, 19010. Telephone: (215) 527-2688. Contact: Shelly E. Hahn, Meryl A. Joblin. Clinic. After school program. Ages served: preschool-adult. Services: diagnostic testing, individual tutoring, parent counseling, speech and language therapy, communication effectiveness for learning disabled adolescents and adults, group and individual programs.

Devon: The Devereux Foundation, 19 S. Waterloo Road, P.O. Box 400, 19333-0418. Telephone: (215) 964-3100. Admissions Director: Ellwood M. Smith. Residential treatment center and day school. Ages served: 5-adult. Services: diagnostic testing, academic and psychological testing, individual and group tutoring; academic, psychological, and parent counseling; group, speech, language, physical, and occupational therapy; adaptive physical education, support group, social services, therapeutic recreation, cultural enrichment and social skills development program; individualized treatment and education plans designed by multidisciplinary team. Notes: Serves the learning disabled, emotionally disturbed, and mentally handicapped.

Lancaster: Assessments Unlimited, 2895 Kissel Hill Road, P.O. Box 5038, 17601. Telephone: (717) 569-6223. Contact: Margaret J. Humphrey-Kay. Clinic. Ages served: 3 and up. Services: diagnostic testing, academic and psychological testing; academic, psychological, and parent counseling; tutor referral service.

Paoli: Adventure Challenges, Community Council for the Exceptional Person, 1700 Russell Road, 19301. Telephone: (215) 296-4524 or 296-4523. Executive Director: Larry P. Isaacson. Year-round therapeutic recreation program. Ages served: 15 and up. Full-time staff: 6. Part-time staff: 10-20. Scholarships/financial aid available. Recreation: camping, hiking, swimming, sailing, canoeing, backpacking, cross country skiing tours. Notes: Provides challenging outdoor wilderness experiences to the disabled.

State College: The Learning Center, 444 E. College Avenue, Suite 500, 16801. Telephone: (814) 234-3450. Director: Cynthia A. Minter. Clinic. Day and after school program. Ages served: 6-15. Services: diagnostic testing, academic testing, individual tutoring, parent counseling, individual learning program.

RHODE ISLAND

Offices of Organizations Concerned with Learning Disabilities

ACLD, Inc.: P.O. Box 6685, Providence, RI 02904. Co-presidents: Cynthia Braca, telephone (401) 274-7026; Mrs. Garilyn Wilson, telephone (401) 885-1883.

Council for Exceptional Children: President: Daniel MacGregor, North Kingstown School Department, 100 Fairway Drive, North Kingstown, RI 02852. Telephone: (401) 294-4581.

The Easter Seal Society of Rhode Island, Inc.: 667 Waterman Avenue, East Providence, RI 02914. Executive Director: Nancy D'Wolf. Telephone: (401) 438-9500.

Orton Dyslexia Society (New England Branch): c/o Rocky Hill School, Ives Road, East Greenwich, RI 02818. President: Emi Flynn. Telephone: (401) 884-3346.

State Department of Education Learning Disabilities Personnel

Charles J. Harrington, Coordinator of Special Education, Special Education Program Services Unit, 22 Hayes Street, Providence, RI 02908. Telephone: (401) 277-3505. Learning disabilities consultant: Robert Pryhoda.

Private and Day Schools

East Providence: Governor Center School, 29 Carlton Avenue, 02914. Telephone: (401) 438-8980. Director: Dolores M. Neville. Ages served: 5-15. Grades served: kindergarten-6. Current enrollment: 13. Maximum enrollment: 50. Full-time staff: 5. Part-time staff: 6. Services: individual and group tutoring, academic testing, adaptive physical education, individual and small group language therapy. Recreation: swimming, cooking.

Providence: Center for Individualized Training and Education, Inc., 345 Blackstone Boulevard, 02906. Telephone: (401) 351-0610. Executive Director: Robert E. Fricklas. Preschool, elementary, and secondary day school with limited services; summer program. Ages served: 3-21. Grades served: preschool-12. Current enrollment: 23. Maximum enrollment: 30. Full-time staff: 10. Part-time staff: 8. Services: individual and group tutoring, academic and psychological testing; academic, psychological, and family counseling; physical therapy, adaptive physical education, medical services, career exploration. Recreation: swimming, bowling, field trips.

Providence: Sargent Rehabilitation Center, 229 Waterman Street, 02906. Telephone: (401) 751-3113. Program Director: Marilyn Serra. Preschool, elementary, and secondary day school with summer program; adult vocational program. Ages served: 3-21. Grades served: ungraded. Current enrollment: 27. Full-time staff: 25. Services: individual and group tutoring, academic and psychological testing, psychological and family counseling, physical and occupational therapy, adaptive physical education, outside placements for vocational training, job placement, medical services.

College and University Special Programs and Services

Brown University: Providence, RI 02912. Total enrollment: 5,150. LD students: 30. Special services: individual tutoring, training in study skills, academic and psychological counseling, taped books, special examinations, student resource center, diagnostic testing, support group, on-campus chapter of Orton Dyslexia Society. Contact: Robert A. Shaw, Assistant Dean. Telephone: (401) 863-2315.

Providence College: River Avenue, Providence, RI 02918. Total enrollment: 4,000. LD students: 40. Special services: readers, tutors, academic and psychological counseling, training in study skills, taped books, support group. Contact: Frances Musco Shipps, Director for Learning Assistance. Telephone: (401) 865-2494.

Rhode Island College: 600 Mount Pleasant Avenue, Providence, RI 02908. Total enrollment: 5,900. Special services: diagnostic testing, academic and psychological testing, tutoring, counseling. Contact: Barbara S. Goldstein, Social Work Coordinator for the Learning Center. Telephone: (401) 456-8287.

Center/clinic: Learning Center, Mann Hall. Telephone: (401) 456-8068. Director: John Laffey. Open to public. Ages served: 5-adult.

University of Rhode Island: Kingston, RI 02881-0801.

Center/clinic: Practicum in Reading/Summer Laboratory School, Chafee Building, Room 251. Telephone: (401) 792-5835. Director: Marion McGuire. Open to public. Ages served: 8-18. Services: diagnosis and planning of special education program; reading, composition, spelling, vocabulary development, and study skills instruction. Notes: Total language arts program for students with serious reading problems. Most preregister in spring. Two students per teacher.

Hospital Clinics

East Providence: Emma Pendleton Bradley Hospital, 1011 Veterans Memorial Parkway, 02915. Telephone: (401) 434-3400. Contact: Kevin P. Myers, Director of Education. Outpatient, inpatient, and day program. Ages served: 3-18. Services: diagnostic testing, academic and psychological testing; academic, psychological, and parent counseling; group, speech, language, physical, and occupational therapy; adaptive physical education, support group, social services.

Providence: Rhode Island Hospital, Child Development Center, 593 Eddy Street, 02902. Telephone: (401) 277-5071. Contact: Siegfried Pueschel. Outpatient program. Ages served: 3-21. Services: diagnostic testing; academic, neurological, and psychological testing; speech, language, physical, and occupational therapy; social services, speech and language evaluation, audiological and central auditory testing.

SOUTH CAROLINA

Offices of Organizations Concerned with Learning Disabilities

ACLD, Inc.: 2357 Brevard Road, Charleston, SC 29407. President: Bonnie Koontz. Telephone: Office (803) 723-0232; Home (803) 556-4502.

Council for Exceptional Children: President: Laura Mohr, P.O. Box 981, Easley, SC 29640. Telephone: (803) 295-2610.

Easter Seal Society of South Carolina, Inc.: 3020 Farrow Road, Columbia, SC 29203. Executive Director: Herman L. Shealy, Jr. Telephone: (803) 256-0735.

Orton Dyslexia Society (Carolinas Branch): 28 Montrose Drive, Greenville, SC 29607. President: Grace L. Hill. Telephone: (803) 288-8629.

State Department of Education Learning Disabilities Personnel

Robert S. Black, Director, Office of Programs for the Handicapped, State Department of Education, Koger Executive Center, 100 Executive Center Drive, Santee Building, Suite A-24, Columbia, SC 29210. Telephone: (803) 758-6122.

Private and Day Schools

Camden: Springdale School, 50 Springdale Drive, 29020. Telephone: (803) 432-3251. Executive Director: Richard W. Mears. Preschool, elementary, and secondary day and boarding school with summer program. Ages served: 6-21. Grades served: kindergarten-13. Current enrollment: 55. Maximum enrollment: 65. Full-time staff: 22. Part-time staff: 8. Scholarships/financial aid available. Services: individual tutoring, academic and psychological testing; academic, psychological, and family counseling; adaptive physical education, vocational training, medical services, speech and language therapy. Recreation: sports including swimming, soccer, softball, basketball, tennis; hiking, camping, riding.

Charleston: Learn and Play Preschool, Charles Webb Center, 325 Calhoun Street, 29400. Telephone: (803) 723-7224. Executive Director: Wilbur Cook. Program Director: Cathie Diggs. Preschool with limited services. Ages served: 2-5. Grades served: preschool-kindergarten. Current enrollment: 11. Maximum enrollment: 60. Full-time staff: 3. Part-time staff: 2. Scholarships/financial aid available. Services: preacademic testing/educational assessment, family counseling, physical therapy, afternoon extended child care program. Recreation: art. Notes: For both developmentally delayed and normally developing children.

SOUTH CAROLINA

Columbia: Sandhills Academy, 4335 Timberlane Drive, 29205. Telephone: (803) 787-2441. Director: Joan B. Hathaway. Elementary day and boarding school with summer program. Ages served: 6-15. Grades served: 1-8. Current enrollment: 31. Maximum enrollment: 40. Full-time staff: 10. Part-time staff: 1. Scholarships/financial aid available. Services: individual and group tutoring, academic and psychological testing, academic and family counseling. Recreation: soccer, student council, yearbook, basketball, animal club.

Mount Pleasant: Trident Academy, P.O. Box 804, 29464. Telephone: (803) 884-7046. Headmaster: Dan H. Balcome. Elementary and secondary day and boarding school with summer program. Ages served: 6-18. Grades served: 1-12. Current enrollment: 137. Maximum enrollment: 145. Full-time staff: 42. Part-time staff: 6. Scholarships/financial aid available. Services: individual and group tutoring, academic testing and counseling, adaptive physical education, work-study, vocational training. Recreation: art, gym, soccer, basketball, volleyball, hiking, softball.

College and University Special Programs and Services

Aiken Technical College: P.O. Drawer 696, Aiken, SC 29801. Total enrollment: 1,100. Special services: academic counseling, diagnostic testing. Contact: Gloria Busch-Johnson, Dean of Student Services. Telephone: (803) 593-9231 ext. 240.

Clemson University: 201 Sikes Hall, Clemson, SC 29631. Total enrollment: 10,000. LD students: 5. Special services: academic and psychological counseling, taped books, training in study skills. Contact: Mickey Lewis, Assistant Dean of Student Life. Telephone: (803) 656-2153.

College of Charleston: 66 George Street, Charleston, SC 29424. Total enrollment: 6,500. LD students: 40. Special services: individual tutoring, ombudsman, special examinations, academic and psychological counseling, diagnostic testing. Contact: Susan J. Schenck, Coordinator of Learning Disability Services. Telephone: (803) 792-5613.

Converse College: 580 E. Main Street, Spartanburg, SC 29301. Total enrollment: 800. LD students: 2. Special services: individual and group tutoring, academic and psychological counseling, taped books, training in study skills, readers, modified examinations. Contact: John P. Martin, Director of Special Education. Telephone: (803) 596-9081.

Erskine College: Due West, SC 29639. Special services: readers, daily individual tutoring, special examinations, academic and psychological counseling, taped books, language therapist, training in study skills, tape recorders.

- **Special program:** Specific Learning Disability Program. Accepts 10 students per year. Must fulfill regular and special admissions requirements. Special requirements include an interview and verification of learning disability through recent diagnostic tests. Director: Molly Ruble. Telephone: (803) 379-8878.

Furman University: Poinsett Highway, Greenville, SC 29613. Total enrollment: 2,500. LD students: 3-10. Special services: individual and group tutoring, special examinations, academic and psychological counseling, diagnostic testing, training in study skills. Contact: Thomas Cloer, Jr., Director of Special Services. Telephone: (803) 294-2110.

Center/clinic: Special Services. Telephone: (803) 294-2110. Director: Thomas Cloer, Jr. Not open to public. Grades served: college.

Center/clinic: Summer Institute for Children with Learning/Behavior Disorders. Telephone: (803) 294-3087. Director: Lesley Ann Wheatley. Open to public. Ages served: 6-18. Notes: Five-week program run by graduate students. Children are pre- and post-tested.

Greenville Technical College: P.O. Box 5616, Station "B," Greenville, SC 29606. Total enrollment: 12,000. LD students: 15-20. Special services: individual tutoring, training in study skills, academic counseling, diagnostic testing, scholarships. Contact: Hazel P. Hall, Vice President for Student Affairs. Telephone: (803) 239-3000.

University of South Carolina: Columbia, SC 29208. Special services: individual and group tutoring, special examinations, diagnostic testing. Contact: Dean K. McIntosh, Associate Professor of Special Education. Telephone: (803) 777-7138.

Center/clinic: Educational Services Clinic, College of Education, Box 57. Telephone: (803) 777-7138. Ages served: 3-21. Director: Gail I. Raymond. Open to public.

Winthrop College: Rock Hill, SC 29733. Special services: individual tutoring, training in study skills, academic and psychological counseling. Contact: John Gallien. Telephone: (803) 323-2151.

Center/clinic: Human Development Center. Telephone: (803) 323-2244. Director: Fran Travis. Open to public. Services: tutoring, diagnostic testing, training in study skills, medical and neurological examinations.

SOUTH DAKOTA

Offices of Organizations Concerned with Learning Disabilities

ACLD, Inc.: 1605 S. Tenth Avenue, Sioux Falls, SD 57105. President: Jan Van Veen. Telephone: (605) 339-9640.

SOUTH DAKOTA

Council for Exceptional Children: President: Jack Kreitzer, 181 Cliff, Deadwood, SD 57732. Telephone: (605) 578-1914.

Easter Seal Society of South Dakota, Inc.: 106 W. Capitol, Pierre, SD 57501. Executive Director: Bart Bailey. Telephone: (605) 224-5879.

Orton Dyslexia Society (Upper Midwest Branch): 10000 32nd Avenue, North, Minneapolis, MN 55441. President: C. Wilson Anderson, Jr. Telephone: Office (612) 546-3266; Home (612) 545-5515.

State Department of Education Learning Disabilities Personnel

George R. Levin, State Director, Section for Special Education, Kneip Building, 700 N. Illinois Street, Pierre, SD 57501. Telephone: (605) 773-3678. Learning disabilities consultant: Charmaine Rickard.

Private and Day Schools

Sioux Falls: Children's Home Society of South Dakota, East River School, 1000 W. 28th Street, 57105. Telephone: (605) 335-8925. Director, Special Education Services: James C. Streedbeck. Preschool, elementary, and secondary day school with summer program. Ages served: 5-17. Grades served: preschool-9. Current enrollment: 41. Maximum enrollment: 51. Full-time staff: 19. Services: individual and group tutoring, academic and psychological testing; academic, psychological, and family counseling; psychological/psychiatric treatment; play, music, individual, group, and family therapy.

Sky Ranch: Sky Ranch for Boys, Sky Ranch Lane, 57724. Telephone: (605) 797-4422. Director: Scott Louks. Director of Special Education: Sandra Grey Eagle. Males only elementary and secondary boarding school. Ages served: 10-18. Grades served: 3-12. Current enrollment: 32. Maximum enrollment: 40. Full-time staff: 35. Part-time staff: 2. Limited scholarships/financial aid available. Services: individual and group tutoring, academic and psychological testing; academic, psychological, and family counseling; vocational training, work-study, flight training for boys 16 and older, high school equivalency option. Recreation: sports, riding, fishing, hiking, seasonal ranch work, camping, sauna, whirlpool, ceramics, pottery. Notes: Therapeutic treatment program for delinquent or pre-delinquent youth; not strictly for learning disabled boys.

College and University Special Programs and Services

Black Hills State College: Spearfish, SD 57783. Special services: readers, individual tutoring, academic and psychological counseling, diagnostic testing, taped books, training in study skills. Contact: Walter Higbee, Professor of Special Education. Telephone: (605) 642-6329.

Center/clinic: Development Center. Telephone: (605) 642-6329. Director: Betty Anderson.

Dakota Wesleyan University: Mitchell, SD 57301. Total enrollment: 550. Special services: readers, individual and group tutoring, basic skills classes, special examinations; academic, personal, and career counseling; training in study skills; psychological and diagnostic testing available in community; referrals. Contact: Mary Kingsbury, Director of Student Assistance Center. Telephone: (605) 996-6511 ext. 304.

University of South Dakota: Vermillion, SD 57069. Total enrollment: 5,700. LD students: 10. Special services: individual tutoring, academic counseling, diagnostic testing. Contact: W.R. Donahue, Vice President for Student Life. Telephone: (605) 677-5331.

TENNESSEE

Offices of Organizations Concerned with Learning Disabilities

ACLD, Inc.: TACLD, P.O. Box 281028, Memphis, TN 38128. Telephone: (901) 323-1430. President: Fred Wimmer. Executive Director: Shera Bie.

Council for Exceptional Children: President: Mr. S.C. Ashcroft, Box 328, Peabody College, Vanderbilt University, Nashville, TN 37203. Telephone: (615) 322-8165.

State Department of Education Learning Disabilities Personnel

Joleta Reynolds, Assistant Commissioner, Tennessee Department of Education, Division of Special Programs, 132 Cordell Hull Building, Nashville, TN 37219. Telephone: (615) 741-2851.

Private and Day Schools

Chattanooga: Scenic Land School, 3319 Hixson Pike, 37415. Telephone: (615) 877-4002. Director: Marcia Carter. Elementary day school with summer program. Ages served: 5-14. Grades served: kindergarten-8. Current enrollment: 48. Maximum enrollment: 48. Full-time staff: 6. Part-time staff: 1. Scholarships/financial aid available. Services: individual tutoring, academic testing.

Chattanooga: Siskin Preschool Center, Siskin Rehabilitation Center, 529 Oak Street, 37403. Telephone: (615) 265-3491 ext. 32. Executive Director, Rehabilitation Center: Mr. Terry Wallace. Preschool with summer program. Ages served: birth-7. Grades served: preschool-kindergarten. Maximum enrollment: 92. Scholarships/financial aid available. Services: academic and psychological testing, psychological and family counseling, physical and occupational therapy, adaptive physical education, infant stimulation. Notes: Serves a limited number of learning disabled children.

TENNESSEE

Germantown: The Bodine School, 2432 Yester Oaks Drive, 38138. Telephone: (901) 754-1800. Program Administrator: John W. Schifani. Secondary day school with summer program. Ages served: 10-18. Grades served: 5-12. Current enrollment: 36. Maximum enrollment: 45. Full-time staff: 5. Part-time staff: 3. Scholarships/financial aid available. Services: individual and group tutoring, academic and psychological testing, academic counseling, computer-assisted instruction, individualized curriculum.

Memphis: De Neuville Heights School for Girls, 3060 Baskin, 38127. Telephone: (901) 357-7316. Administrator: Sr. Mary Rosa Linda. Females only secondary boarding school with limited services. Ages served: 12-17. Grades served: 7-12. Current enrollment: 45. Maximum enrollment: 52. Full-time staff: 20. Part-time staff: 5. Services: individual tutoring, academic and psychological testing; academic, psychological, and family counseling; job placement. Recreation: softball, volleyball, swimming, Jazzercize, soccer, basketball.

Memphis: Memphis Academy for Learning Disabilities, 837 Craft Road, 38116. Telephone: (901) 398-4813. Codirectors: Bob Boehm, Patricia Webb. Elementary day school. Ages served: 6-21. Grades served: kindergarten-8. Current enrollment: 8. Maximum enrollment: 12. Full-time staff: 2. Part-time staff: 1. Services: individual and group tutoring, academic testing, adaptive physical education.

Morristown: Aveyron Day Care Center, Morristown-Hamblen Day Care Centers, Inc., P.O. Box 1936, 37814. Telephone: (615) 587-3001 or 581-4980. Executive Director: James M. Tingle. Preschool with limited services. Ages served: 6 months-4. Grades served: preschool. Current enrollment: 9. Maximum enrollment: 10. Full-time staff: 2. Part-time staff: 5. Scholarships/financial aid available. Services: group tutoring, academic testing, family counseling, physical therapy, developmental program, individual habilitation plans.

Nashville: Institute of Learning Research, 3710 N. Natchez Court, 37211. Telephone: (615) 834-7832. Executive Director: Renald C. Eichler. Secondary day school with summer program and camp. Ages served: 12-22. Grades served: 9-12. Current enrollment: 52. Maximum enrollment: 55. Full-time staff: 29. Services: individual tutoring, academic and psychological testing; individual, group, academic, psychological, and family counseling; family and occupational therapy, adaptive physical education, vocational training, work-study, job placement.

Nashville: Westminster School, 3900 West End Avenue, 37205. Telephone: (615) 269-0020. Director: Elizabeth Macklin. Elementary day school with summer program. Ages served: 5-14. Grades served: kindergarten-8. Current enrollment: 200. Maximum enrollment: 200. Full-time staff: 42. Part-time staff: 1. Scholarships/financial aid available. Services: individual tutoring, academic testing, transition recommendations, follow-up visits for students moving out of Westminster into mainstreamed or special education placements. Recreation: basketball, soccer, dance troupe, physical education. Notes: Serves only learning disabled students.

Sunbright: Plateau Home School, Route 1, Box 118, 37872. Telephone: (615) 628-2289. Director: Sr. Julia Jacomet. Elementary day school with limited services. Ages served: 5-16. Grades served: 1-8. Current enrollment: 12. Maximum enrollment: 18. Full-time staff: 2. Part-time staff: 2. Scholarships/financial aid available. Services: individual and group tutoring, academic and psychological testing; academic, psychological, and family counseling; vocational training. Recreation: weekly field trips, daily physical education, basketball team.

College and University Special Programs and Services

Austin Peay State University: Clarksville, TN 37040. Total enrollment: 5,000. LD students: 6-10. Special services: academic and psychological counseling; developmental studies program provides remedial instruction in English, mathematics, and study skills. Contact: Gary N. Morrison, Assistant Professor. Telephone: (615) 648-7511 or 648-7512.

Lambuth College: Jackson, TN 38301. Special services: readers, individual and group tutoring, special examinations, academic and psychological counseling, diagnostic testing, training in study skills. Contact: Bridgie Ford, Professor of Education. Telephone: (901) 427-1500 ext. 267.

Center/clinic: Learning Enrichment Center, Lambuth Boulevard. Telephone: (901) 427-1500. Director: Evelyn Whybrew. Open to public. Grades served: kindergarten-adult. Services: diagnostic testing and tutoring.

Memphis Academy of Arts: Overton Park, Memphis, TN 38112. Total enrollment: 242. LD students: 2. Special services: academic counseling. Contact: Billy C. Boyd, Assistant to the Dean/Registrar. Telephone: (901) 726-4085.

Memphis State University: Memphis, TN 38152. Total enrollment: 20,000. LD students: 32. Special services: readers, individual and group tutoring, taped books, special examinations, academic and psychological counseling, diagnostic testing, training in study skills, scholarships, ombudsman. Contact: Dona Sparger, Director, Handicapped Student Services. Telephone: (901) 454-2880.

Center/clinic: Handicapped Student Services, 215 Scates Hall. Telephone: (901) 454-2880. Director: Dona Sparger. Not open to public. Grades served: college.

The University of Tennessee-Chattanooga: 615 McCallie Avenue, Chattanooga, TN 37402. Special services: individual and group tutoring, training in study skills, academic and psychological counseling, taped books, special examinations, readers, diagnostic testing, job awareness training, job interest evaluation.

- **Special program:** CAP (College Access Program). Demonstration project for learning disabled students. Must meet regular admissions requirements. Learning disability must be verified through recent diagnostic tests or tests done by the university staff. Full or part-time students may participate in the program. Coordinator: Pat Snowden. Telephone: (615) 755-4006.

Center/clinic: Youth Evaluation, Assessment, and Research (YEAR). Telephone: (615) 755-4175. Director: Janice Davis. Open to public. Ages served: 3-adult. Grades served: all.

University of Tennessee-Knoxville: Cumberland Avenue, Knoxville, TN 37996-3400. Total enrollment: 26,000. LD students: 22. Special services: readers, individual and group tutoring, special examinations, academic and psychological counseling, taped books, training in study skills, large-print typewriter. Contact: Martha R. Bryan, Director. Telephone: (615) 974-6087 ext. 7905.

Center/clinic: Learning Intervention Services. Telephone: (615) 974-4133 or 974-2321. Director: Robert Frey. Open to public. Ages served: 5-19. Services: tutoring for children with special needs, training for graduate students. Also serves university students.

Hospital Clinics

Knoxville: East Tennessee Children's Hospital, P.O. Box 15010, 37901. Telephone: (615) 544-3138. Contact: Rebecca C. Thomas, Assistant Administrator for Patient Services. Outpatient program. Ages served: birth-21. Services: diagnostic testing.

Memphis: Methodist Hospitals of Memphis, Rehabilitation Services Department, 1265 Union Avenue, 38104. Telephone: (901) 726-7684. Contact: Beverly McKinney or Ms. Jeri Saper. Outpatient, after school, and summer program. Ages served: 3-14. Services: diagnostic testing, academic testing, individual and group tutoring, parent counseling; group, speech, language, physical, and occupational therapy; social services.

Other Services

Memphis: University of Tennessee Center for the Health Sciences, Child Development Center, 711 Jefferson Avenue, 38105. Telephone: (901) 528-6586. Chief of Special Education: Carolyn P. McKellar. Outpatient diagnostic and habilitation center; preschool and elementary day school with summer program. Ages served: 6 weeks-10 years school; adults. Current enrollment: 52. Maximum enrollment: 60. Full-time staff: 12. Services: individual tutoring, academic and psychological testing, psychological and family counseling, physical and occupational therapy, diagnostic services, childhood aphasia program.

Nashville: Vanderbilt Child and Adolescent Psychiatry School, Medical Center South, 2100 Pierce Avenue, 37212. Telephone: (615) 322-7588. Director: Susan M. Smartt. Preschool, elementary, and secondary school; residential treatment center with summer program. Ages served: 4-16. Grades served: preschool-10. Current enrollment: 16. Maximum enrollment: 18. Full-time staff: 7. Services: group tutoring, academic and psychological testing; academic, psychological, and family counseling; occupational therapy, adaptive physical education, medical services. Recreation: swimming, daily recreational therapy in gym or outdoors; fall camp-out, bowling. Notes: Serves children with emotional disorders and learning disabilities.

TEXAS

Offices of Organizations Concerned with Learning Disabilities

ACLD, Inc.: TACLD, 1011 W. 31st Street, Austin, TX 78705. Telephone: (512) 458-8234. President: Jean Kueker. Office Coordinator: Dorothy Strance.

Council for Exceptional Children: President: Linda Brown, 2425 Ashdale Drive #75, Austin, TX 78758. Telephone: (512) 454-9850.

Texas Easter Seal Society: 4300 Beltway, Dallas, TX 75244. Executive Director: Adele Foschia. Telephone: (214) 934-9104.

Orton Dyslexia Society (Dallas Branch): 9235 Whitehurst, Dallas, TX 75243. President: Faye Handlogten. Telephone: Office (214) 340-2440; Home (214) 349-2647.

Orton Dyslexia Society (Houston Branch): P.O. Box 771961, Houston, TX 77215-1961. President: Nancy E. LaFevers. Telephone: (713) 529-1975.

State Department of Education Learning Disabilities Personnel

Donna Livingston, Associate Commissioner of Special Education, Division of Special Education, Texas Education Agency, 201 E. 11th Street, Austin, TX 78701. Telephone: (512) 834-4495. Learning disabilities consultant: Mary Cole. Telephone: (512) 834-4418. In-state toll free number: (800) 252-9668.

Private and Day Schools

Arlington: Adaptive Learning Center, 1608 N. Davis Drive, 76012. Telephone: (817) 261-7089. Director: Elwyn Carl Hulett. Elementary day school with summer program. Ages served: 6-15. Grades served: 1-8. Current enrollment: 36. Maximum enrollment: 56. Full-time staff: 8. Part-time staff: 1. Limited scholarships/financial aid available. Services: individual tutoring, academic testing, adaptive physical education, small classes. Notes: Accepts only students of average or above average intelligence with diagnosed learning disabilities.

Dallas: Dallas Academy, 950 Tiffany Way, 75218. Telephone: (214) 324-1481. Director: Jim Richardson. Secondary boarding school. Ages served: 13-19. Grades served: 7-12. Current enrollment: 75. Maximum enrollment: 75. Full-time staff: 13. Part-time staff: 2. Scholarships/financial aid available. Services: individual and group tutoring, academic testing and counseling, adaptive physical education, vocational training, work-study. Recreation: competitive sports; trips to state parks, museums, and ski areas. Notes: Learning disability must be verified through academic, psychological, and neurological records in order to be considered for placement.

Dallas: Fairhill School, 6039 Churchill Way, 75230. Telephone: (214) 233-1026. Executive Director: Jane Sego. Elementary and secondary day school. Ages served: 6-18. Grades served: 1-12. Current enrollment: 165. Maximum enrollment: 170. Full-time staff: 25. Part-time staff: 2. Services: academic and psychological testing, psychological and family counseling, adaptive physical education. Recreation: after school sports.

Dallas: Preston Hollow Presbyterian Week Day School, 9800 Preston Road, 75230. Telephone: (214) 363-9593. Director: Sheila Phaneuf. Day school with summer program. Ages served: 6-12. Grades served: 1-6. Current enrollment: 66. Maximum enrollment: 67. Full-time staff: 12. Part-time staff: 3. Scholarships/financial aid available. Services: speech, occupational, and music therapy; individual tutoring, adaptive physical education. Recreation: after school sports.

Dallas: Winston School, 5707 Royal Lane, 75229. Telephone: (214) 691-6950. Headmaster: Paul R. Erwin. Elementary and secondary day school. Ages served: 6-18. Grades served: 1-12. Current enrollment: 240. Maximum enrollment: 240. Full-time staff: 45. Scholarships/financial aid available. Services: group tutoring, academic and psychological testing; academic, psychological, and family counseling; adaptive physical education, work-study, computers. Recreation: sports, outdoor education, summer trips, art, drama.

Euless: Treetops, Mid-Cities Learning Center, 12500 S. Pipeline, Route 1, Box 257, 76040. Telephone: (817) 283-1771. Director: Chris Kallstrom. Preschool, elementary, and secondary day school with limited services; summer program and camp. Ages served: birth-18. Grades served: ungraded. Current enrollment: 150. Maximum enrollment: 150. Full-time staff: 15. Part-time staff: 10. Services: individual and group tutoring, academic and psychological testing; academic, psychological, and family counseling; adaptive physical education, perceptual-motor therapy, environmental skills, therapeutic arts, programs for the gifted learning disabled; preschool learning disabilities screening. Recreation: fencing, archery, trails, museum, play areas, festivals, drama, travel, camping.

Fort Worth: Dean School, Inc., 3563 Manderly Place, 76109. Telephone: (817) 921-3777. Director: Margaret Dean. Elementary and secondary day school with summer program. Ages served: 3-21. Grades served: kindergarten-12. Current enrollment: 60. Full-time staff: 8. Part-time staff: 2. Scholarships/financial aid available. Services: individual and group tutoring, academic testing and counseling, vocational training, speech therapy, work-study. Recreation: gym, physical development program.

Fort Worth: Starpoint School, Texas Christian Universary, P.O. Box 32918, 76129. Telephone: (817) 921-7141. Principal: Laura Lee Crane. Day school with summer program. Ages served: 6-9. Grades served: ungraded. Current enrollment: 38. Maximum enrollment: 40. Full-time staff: 7. Part-time staff: 7 student assistants. Scholarships/financial aid available. Services: individual and group tutoring, academic and psychological testing.

Granbury: Happy Hill Farm Children's Home, Inc., Star Route, Box 56, 76048. Telephone: (817) 897-4822. Director: C. Edward Shipman. Males only year-round boarding school. Ages served: 7-18. Grades served: kindergarten-12. Current enrollment: 40. Full-time staff: 10. Scholarships/financial aid available. Services: individual and group tutoring, academic and psychological testing; academic, psychological, and family counseling; occupational therapy, adaptive physical education, vocational training, work-study, job placement, medical services. Recreation: sports. Notes: Working farm.

Houston: The Cliffwood School, P.O. Box 35386, 77235. Telephone: (713) 667-4649. Director: Donna Weinberg. Elementary, secondary, and adult day school with summer program. Ages served: 6-20. Grades served: 1-12. Current enrollment: 90. Maximum enrollment: 100. Full-time staff: 17. Part-time staff: 3. Services: individual and group tutoring, academic testing and counseling, work-study. Recreation: physical education, field trips.

Houston: The Parish School, 11059 Timberline Street, 77043. Telephone: (713) 467-4696. Director: Robbin Parish. Preschool and elementary day school with summer camp. Grades served: preschool-2. Current enrollment: 40. Maximum enrollment: 50. Full-time staff: 14. Part-time staff: 4. Services: individual and group tutoring, academic testing and counseling; occupational, speech, and language therapy. Notes: Language-based program for early identification of learning disabilities.

Laredo: Ruthe B. Cowl Rehabilitation Center, 1220 Malinche Avenue, 78040. Telephone: (512) 722-2431. Director: Ruthe B. Cowl. Day school with summer program. Ages served: 3-21. Grades served: ungraded. Current enrollment: 41. Maximum enrollment: 55. Full-time staff: 14. Services: individual and group tutoring, family counseling, physical and occupational therapy, medical services, adaptive physical education.

Longview: Crisman Preparatory School, 2455 N. Eastman Road, 75601. Telephone: (214) 758-9741. Director: Gloria Keller. Elementary day school. Ages served: 5-12. Grades served: kindergarten-6. Current enrollment: 40. Maximum enrollment: 50. Full-time staff: 8. Part-time staff: 1. Scholarships/financial aid available. Services: academic and psychological testing, small classes, alphabetic phonics reading program; perceptual, motor, art, and speech programs; learning disability parent and professional resource center. Notes: Specifically for children with learning disabilities.

TEXAS

Mesquite: Meadowview School, 1424 Barnes Bridge, 75150. Telephone: (214) 681-2913. Director: Beverly Presley. Elementary day school. Ages served: 6-14. Grades served: 1-8. Current enrollment: 31. Maximum enrollment: 31. Full-time staff: 6. Services: diagnostic testing, academic testing and counseling, adaptive physical education, multisensory teaching techniques.

San Antonio: St. Martin's Hall, Resource Unit, Our Lady of the Lake University, 411 S.W. 24th, 78285. Telephone: (512) 434-6711 ext. 413. Director, Special Education Program: Jacquelyn Alexander. Elementary day school. Ages served: 7-12. Grades served: 2-6. Current enrollment: 11. Maximum enrollment: 12. Full-time staff: 1. Part-time staff: 2. Scholarships/financial aid available. Services: academic and psychological testing, psychological and family counseling. Recreation: physical education, soccer team. Notes: Campus demonstration school.

Victoria: The Devereux Foundation, Box 2666, 77902. Telephone: (512) 575-8271. Branch Director: Thomas K. Porter. Preschool, elementary, secondary, and adult boarding school with summer program and camp. Ages served: 6-24. Grades served: kindergarten-12, adults. Current enrollment: 135. Maximum enrollment: 164. Full-time staff: 140. Part-time staff: 25. Limited scholarships/financial aid available. Services: individual and group tutoring, academic and psychological testing, psychological and family counseling, adaptive physical education, vocational training, job placement, medical and psychiatric services. Recreation: competitive swimming, softball, basketball; therapeutic recreation program. Notes: 12-month program with admission any time.

Summer Camps and Programs

Caldwell: Camp Wagon Wheel, P.O. Box 422, 77836. Telephone: (409) 535-7590. Winter telephone: (601) 266-5236. Camp Director and Owner: Basil L. Gaar. Residential camp with academic program. Ages served: 6-13. Grades served: 1-6. Maximum enrollment: 60. Full-time staff: 20. Services: group tutoring, academic testing, family counseling. Academic programs: math, reading, spelling, perceptual and gross motor training. Recreation: swimming, hiking, riding, field trips, crafts, team athletics, aerobics.

College and University Special Programs and Services

Amarillo College: 2200 S. Washington, P.O. Box 447, Amarillo, TX 79178. Total enrollment: 6,151. LD students: 12. Special services: individual and group tutoring, training in study skills, academic counseling, taped books, special examinations, readers, diagnostic testing, scholarships, support group, talking computer, tape recorders, note takers. Contact: Marshall Mitchell, Coordinator of Handicap Services. Telephone: (806) 376-5111 ext. 2440.

Bee County College: 3800 Charco Road, Beeville, TX 78102. Total enrollment: 2,200. LD students: 12. Special services: individual and group tutoring, training in study skills, taped books, special examinations, student resource center, readers. Contact: Patricia Myers, Special Needs Counselor. Telephone: (512) 358-6988.

Cedar Valley College: 3030 N. Dallas Avenue, Lancaster, TX 75134. Total enrollment: 2,200. LD students: 30. Special services: individual and group tutoring, training in study skills, academic and psychological counseling, taped books, readers, diagnostic testing, scholarships, special classes. Contact: Margie P. Fenton, Coordinator of Special Services. Telephone: (214) 372-8182.

Del Mar College: Baldwin and Ayers Streets, Corpus Christi, TX 78404. Total enrollment: 8,403. Special services: individual tutoring, limited training in study skills, academic counseling, student resource center, readers, note takers. Contact: Pete Rivera, Jr., Coordinator, Special Projects. Telephone: (512) 881-6297.

Eastfield College: Mesquite, TX 75150. Total enrollment: 9,000. LD students: 35. Special services: individual tutoring, training in study skills, academic and psychological counseling, taped books, talking calculator, modified examinations, student resource center, readers. Contact: Reva O. Rattan, Coordinator, Services for Handicapped Students. Telephone: (214) 324-7032.

East Texas State University: East Texas Station, Commerce, TX 75428. Special services: individual tutoring, training in study skills, academic and psychological counseling, taped books, special examinations, student resource center, readers, diagnostic testing, ombudsman, learning disabled student organization; socialization, writing, reading, and math skills; speech and hearing center; biofeedback, hypnosis, student development center. Contact: John R. Moss, Launch Faculty Advisor. Telephone: (214) 886-5932 or 886-5937.

- **Special program:** Launch Inc., The Coalition of Learning Disabled Adults. Self-help group. Provides a forum for student discussion and action, counseling for students; consultation for faculty on specific student needs, instructional questions, and requested support services. Contact: Mrs. Jerry Ferguson, Launch Office Manager. Telephone: (214) 886-5937 or 886-5932 or 886-5940.

Center/clinic: Mach III, Special Services. Telephone: (214) 886-5934. Director: Frank Perez. Not open to public. Ages served: 16 and up. Grades served: undergraduate-graduate. Services: counseling, consultation, treatment, evaluation, assessment.

El Centro College: Main and Lamar, Dallas, TX 75202. Total enrollment: 5,800. LD students: 50-100. Special services: individual tutoring, training in study skills, academic and psychological counseling, taped books, special examinations, student resource center, readers, support group. Contact: Jim Handy, Counselor/Coordinator, Special Services. Telephone: (214) 746-2073.

TEXAS

El Paso Community College: P.O. Box 20500, El Paso, TX 79998. Total enrollment: 1,400. LD students: 20. Special services: individual and group tutoring, training in study skills, academic and psychological counseling, taped books, special examinations, student resource center, readers, ombudsman, note takers. Contact: Ann Lemke, Coordinator, Handicapped Services. Telephone: (915) 594-2426.

Laredo Junior College: West End Washington Street, Laredo, TX 78040. Total enrollment: 4,000. Special services: group tutoring, training in study skills, academic counseling. Contact: Jesse Porras, Counselor. Telephone: (512) 722-0521 ext. 130.

Lon Morris College: 800 College Avenue, Jacksonville, TX 75766. Total enrollment: 301. Special services: individual and group tutoring, training in study skills, academic and psychological counseling, diagnostic testing, scholarships. Contact: Virgil Matthews, Academic Dean. Telephone: (214) 586-2471 ext. 25. Or Gerry Draper, Learning Services. Telephone: (214) 586-2471 ext. 51.

Mountain View College: 4849 W. Illinois, Dallas, TX 75211. Total enrollment: 5,000. Special services: individual tutoring, training in study skills, academic and psychological counseling, taped books, readers, diagnostic testing. Contact: Donna Richards, Director, Health/Disabled Student Services. Telephone: (214) 333-8699.

North Lake College: 5001 N. MacArthur, Irving, TX 75038. Total enrollment: 5,000. LD students: 37. Special services: individual and group tutoring, training in study skills, academic counseling, taped books, special examinations, student resource center, readers, diagnostic testing, scholarships. Contact: Mary G. Ciminelli, Coordinator/Counselor, Services to Students with Special Needs. Telephone: (214) 659-5237.

Pan American University: 1201 W. University, Edinburg, TX 78539. Special services: individual and group tutoring, training in study skills, academic and psychological counseling, special examinations, readers, diagnostic testing. Contact: Arturo Ramos, Assistant Director, Learning Assistance Center. Telephone: (512) 381-2585.

Richland College: 12800 Abrams, Dallas, TX 75243. Total enrollment: 13,500. LD students: 125. Special services: individual and group tutoring, training in study skills, academic and psychological counseling, taped books, special examinations, readers, diagnostic testing, scholarships, support group.

- **Special program:** Learning Disabilities Program. Small group classes in multisensory reading, spelling, and math. Night and high school programs also available. Learning disability must be verified through recent records or tests done by the college. Full or part-time students may participate in program. Director: Jeanne Brewer. Telephone: (214) 238-6353.

Sam Houston State University: Huntsville, TX 77341. Special services: academic and psychological counseling; counseling center acts as liaison for learning disabled students. Contact: Carl Harris, Dean of College of Education and Applied Sciences. Telephone: (409) 294-1100.

Schreiner College: Highway 27, Kerrville, TX 78028. Total enrollment: 500. LD students: 50. Special services: individual and group tutoring, training in study skills, academic counseling, taped books, special examinations. Contact: Karen K. Dooley, Director of the Learning Support Services Program. Telephone: (512) 896-5411 ext. 272.

Southern Methodist University: Dallas, TX 75275. Total enrollment: 9,000. LD students: 35. Special services: training in study skills, academic and psychological counseling, taped books, special examinations, student resource center, diagnostic testing. Contact: William C. McIntyre, Assistant Dean of Student Life. Telephone: (214) 692-2780.

Tarrant County Junior College-Northeast Campus: 828 Harwood Road, Hurst, TX 76054. LD students: 15. Special services: readers, individual tutoring, academic counseling, taped books, special testing accommodations. Contact: Joyce Brewer, Coordinator. Telephone: (817) 281-7860 ext. 333.

Center/clinic: SCOOP (Service Center for Opportunities to Overcome Problems). Telephone: (817) 281-7860 ext. 333. Director: Joyce Brewer. Not open to public. Grades served: college.

Tarrant County Junior College-Northwest Campus: 4801 Marine Creek Parkway, Fort Worth, TX 76179. Total enrollment: 4,800. LD students: 4. Special services: individual tutoring, training in study skills, academic and psychological counseling, special examinations, student resource center, readers, support group. Contact: Kim Dunaway, Coordinator of SCOOP, (Service Center for Opportunities to Overcome Problems). Telephone: (817) 232-7733.

Tarrant County Junior College-South Campus: 5301 Campus Drive, Fort Worth, TX 76119. LD students: 6. Special services: individual and group tutoring, training in study skills, academic and psychological counseling, taped books, special examinations, readers. Contact: Elizabeth Davis, Coordinator of SCOOP, (Service Center for Opportunities to Overcome Problems). Telephone: (817) 531-0454.

Texas A & M University: College Station, TX 77843. Total enrollment: 36,000. Special services: readers, individual and group tutoring, academic and psychological counseling, training in study skills, special examinations. Contact: Jan N. Hughes, Director, Counseling and Assessment Clinic. Telephone: (409) 845-2324.

TEXAS

Center/clinic: Texas A & M Reading Clinic, College of Education, Department EDCI. Telephone: (409) 845-7140. Director: William Rupley. Grades served: all. Services: diagnosis and remediation. Notes: Summer only.

Texas Southern University: 3100 Cleburne, Houston, TX 77004. Special services: individual and group tutoring, training in study skills, academic and psychological counseling, special examinations, student resource center, diagnostic testing, scholarships, vocational counseling, reading clinic. Contact: Deanna Burrell, Coordinator, Counseling Services. Telephone: (713) 527-7370 or 527-7101.

Center/clinic: Texas Southern University Psychological Clinic, 3112 Wheeler. Telephone: (713) 527-7344. Director: Lendell Braud. Open to public. Ages served: 2-adult. Grades served: 1-college. Services: diagnostic testing, remediation treatment; identification of perception and neurological disabilities and reading dysfunctions; various therapies including behavioral, relaxation, Rogerian, group, individual, transactional, conventional, biofeedback, and hypnosis.

University of Texas-Austin: Austin, TX 78712. Special services: individual tutoring, ombudsman, academic and psychological counseling, taped books, note taking, mentoring program, speech and hearing evaluations and therapy, special examinations, student resource center, readers, support group, early registration and assistance. Contact: John Jones, Peer Advisor II. Telephone: (512) 471-1201.

Center/clinic: Learning Abilities Center, 252 Education Building. Telephone: (512) 471-1963. Director: William Harmer. Open to public. Grades served: kindergarten-12. Services: diagnostic testing.

University of Texas-Dallas: P.O. Box 688, Richardson, TX 75080. Special services: group tutoring, training in study skills, academic and psychological counseling, taped books, special examinations, student resource center, readers, note takers. Contact: Gloria Williams, Advisor, Office of Special Services. Telephone: (214) 690-2098.

Center/clinic: Callier Center for Communication Disorders, 1966 Inwood Road, Dallas, TX 75235. Telephone: (214) 783-3034. Acting Director: Thomas Tigthe. Open to public. Ages served: infants-adult. Services: diagnostic testing and referrals.

West Texas State University: West Texas Station, Canyon, TX 79016. Special services: individual and group tutoring, training in study skills, academic and psychological counseling, student resource center, diagnostic testing, scholarships. Contact: Lloyd Kinnison, Chairman, Department of Curriculum and Instruction. Telephone: (806) 656-3259.

Hospital Clinics

Abilene: Woods Psychiatric Institute, 1115 Industrial Boulevard, Box 5749, 79608. Telephone: (915) 698-2320; in-state toll free number (800) 592-4441. Outpatient and inpatient program. Ages served: 3-21 outpatient; 6-17 inpatient. Services: diagnostic testing, academic and psychological testing, individual and group tutoring; academic, psychological, and parent counseling; occupational therapy.

Dallas: Texas Scottish Rite Hospital for Crippled Children, Child Development Division, 2222 Welborn, 75219. Telephone: (214) 521-3168 ext. 208 or 213. Contact: Anna Ramey, Assistant Director. Outpatient program. Ages served: birth-15. Services: diagnostic testing.

Houston: West Oaks Psychiatric Institute of Houston, 6500 Hornwood, 77074. Telephone: (713) 995-0909 ext. 116. Contact: Margo Bishop, Director of Program Services. Outpatient, day, and after school program. Services: diagnostic testing, academic and psychological testing, individual tutoring; academic, psychological, parent, and vocational counseling; speech, language, and occupational therapy. Notes: Focus on learning disabled students who have developed emotional problems as a result of their disability. Private school on hospital grounds.

San Antonio: Wilford Hall Medical Center, SGHP Pediatrics Clinic, 78236-5300. Telephone: (512) 670-7515. Contact: Chris Johnson, Coordinator. Outpatient and after school program. Ages served: 5-15. Services: diagnostic testing, psychological testing, central auditory processing evaluation.

Other Services

Amarillo: Killgore Children's Psychiatric Center, 1200 Wallace Boulevard, 79106. Telephone: (806) 358-9031. Executive Director: Joel Allison. Psychiatric center with day and boarding school. Ages served: 3-17. Grades served: preschool-12. Current enrollment: 11. Maximum enrollment: 34. Full-time staff: 45. Part-time staff: 1. Services: individual and group tutoring, academic and psychological testing; academic, psychological, and family counseling; physical, occupational, music, speech, and recreation therapy; adaptive physical education, medical services. Recreation: swimming, fishing, bowling, hiking, movies, skating, volleyball, softball.

Corpus Christi: Learning, Inc., 1118 Third Street, 78404. Telephone: (512) 883-6801. Chief Administrators: Ann Nickerson, Jacki Etheridge. Clinic. Tutoring and resource room for private schools. Ages served: 5-adult. Grades served: all. Full-time staff: 2. Part-time staff: 3. Services: individual tutoring, academic testing; Special Perceptual Development Program includes right and left hand orientation, coordination, gross and fine motor training, development of visual and auditory perceptual skills, listening and handwriting skills.

Dallas: Psychoeducational Diagnostic Services, 7233 Brentfield, 75248. Telephone: (214) 931-5299. Contact: Harrian B. Stern. Clinic. Day and after school

TEXAS

program. Ages served: 3-adult. Services: diagnostic testing, academic and psychological testing, referrals.

Fort Worth: Child Study Center, 1300 W. Lancaster, 76102. Telephone: (817) 336-8611. Executive Director: Larry Eason. Evaluation and treatment center with preschool. Ages served: birth-14. Current enrollment: 100 school. Maximum enrollment: 100 school. Full-time staff: 13 school; 100 entire facility. Scholarships/ financial aid available. Services: individual and group tutoring, academic and psychological testing; academic, psychological, genetic, and family counseling; physical, occupational, and speech therapy; medical services; dental, audiological, and neuropsychological testing.

Houston: Houston Child Guidance Center, 3214 Austin Street, 77004. Telephone: (713) 526-3232. Associate Director: Walter H. Delange. Clinic. Day and after school program. Ages served: 5-18. Services: diagnostic testing, psychological testing, psychological and parent counseling, group therapy, support group, social services, psychiatric consultation/evaluation.

Lubbock: Scottish Rite Learning Center of Western Texas, P.O. Box 10135, 79408. Telephone: (806) 765-9150. Director: Betty J. Roy. Clinic. Day program. Ages served: 6-21. Services: language retraining for dyslexics, diagnostic testing, academic and psychological testing, individual and group tutoring, academic and parent counseling, teacher training.

Mesquite: Presley Clinic, Inc., 1424 Barnes Bridge Road, 75150. Telephone: (214) 270-1184. Director: Beverly Presley. Clinic. Day and after school program. Ages served: 5-18. Services: diagnostic testing, academic testing, individual tutoring.

San Antonio: Diagnostic and Remedial Reading Clinic, 7310 Blanco Road, Suite 110, 78216. Telephone: (512) 341-7417. Director: Lola H. Austin. Clinic. After school and summer program. Ages served: 5-adult. Services: diagnostic testing, academic and psychological testing, individual tutoring; academic, psychological, and parent counseling; group therapy, support group, visual-motor perceptual training, auditory discrimination training.

San Antonio: Easter Seal Rehabilitation Center, 2203 Babcock Road, 78229. Telephone: (512) 699-3911. Executive Director: Randel W. Aaron. Rehabilitation center. Outpatient program. Ages served: all. Current enrollment: 324. Full-time staff: 26. Part-time staff: 3. Scholarships/financial aid available. Services: preschool with limited services, physical and occupational therapy, vocational training, medical services, language training (speech pathology), early intervention program.

UTAH

Offices of Organizations Concerned with Learning Disabilities

ACLD, Inc.: 2754 E. 4510 South, Salt Lake City, UT 84117. President: Gladys Tucker. Telephone: (801) 272-5509.

Council for Exceptional Children: President: Stevan Kukic, 2344 Catalina Drive, Salt Lake City, UT 84121. Telephone: Office (801) 263-3915; Home (801) 943-6280.

Utah Easter Seal Society, Inc.: 331 S. Rio Grande, Suite 206, Salt Lake City, UT 84101. Executive Director: Mark Whitley. Telephone: (801) 531-0522.

State Department of Education Learning Disabilities Personnel

R. Elwood Pace, Coordinator of Special Education, Utah State Office of Education, 250 E. Fifth, South, Salt Lake City, UT 84111. Telephone: (801) 533-5982. Learning disabilities consultant: Cy W. Freston.

Private and Day Schools

Provo: Provo Canyon School, P.O. Box 1441, 84603. Telephone: (801) 227-2088. Director: Joyce Petersen. Males only year-round boarding school. Ages served: 11-17. Grades served: 6-12. Current enrollment: 210. Maximum enrollment: 220. Full-time staff: 130. Part-time staff: 77. Services: individual tutoring, individual and physical therapy, academic and psychological testing, medical facilities (infirmary), adaptive physical education, vocational training, work-study. Recreation: football, basketball, baseball, bowling, tennis, swimming pool, boats, water and snow skiing.

Summer Camps and Programs

Salt Lake City: Utah Easter Seals Day and Residential Camp, 331 S. Rio Grande, Suite 206, 84101. Telephone: (801) 531-0522. Therapeutic Recreation Director: Connie Malitor. Day and residential camp. Ages served: 8 and up. Grades served: 3 and up. Maximum enrollment: 6-9 day; 10 residential. Full-time staff: 3 day; 6 residential. Scholarships/financial aid available. Services: family counseling, adaptive physical education, nurse. Recreation: camping, hiking, field trips, nature study, riding, swimming, archery, team sports, crafts, dance, drama, music. Notes: Camps are held in different locations throughout the state.

College and University Special Programs and Services

Brigham Young University: Provo, UT 84602. Total enrollment: 25,000. LD students: 50. Special services: readers, individual tutoring, ombudsman, special examinations, academic and psychological counseling, diagnostic testing, taped books, training in study skills, student resource center, scholarships. Contact: Kelly R. Fielding, Administrative Aide, Handicapped Student Services. Telephone: (801) 378-2767.

Center/clinic: Educational Psychology Comprehensive Clinic, 332-E, MCKB. Telephone: (801) 378-5055 or 378-2658. Director: Cregg Ingram. Open to public. Ages served: all. Grades served: all.

Snow College: 150 E. College Avenue, Ephraim, UT 84627. Total enrollment: 1,400. LD students: 60. Special services: individual tutoring, training in study skills, academic and psychological counseling, taped books, special examinations, readers, diagnostic testing, career counseling. Contact: DeMont C. Wiser, Director, Student Development. Telephone: (801) 283-4021 ext. 314.

University of Utah: Salt Lake City, UT 84112. Total enrollment: 23,000. LD students: 40. Special services: academic and psychological counseling, special examinations, tutors, readers, taped textbooks, tape recorders, early registration, ombudsman, support group, scholarships, substitute for English 101. Contact: Olga Nadeau, Director of Handicapped Services. Telephone: (802) 581-5020.

Utah State University: Logan, UT 84322. Total enrollment: 11,000. Special services: individual tutoring, academic and psychological counseling, workshops, taped books, special examinations, readers, diagnostic testing, skills assessment. Contact: Diane Baum, Assistant Director, or Karen Dolid, Coordinator. Telephone: (801) 750-1923.

Center/clinic: Developmental Center for Handicapped Persons, UMC 68. Telephone: (801) 750-1923. Coordinator: John Killoran. Assistant Director: Diane Baum. Open to public. Ages served: birth-21. Services: individualized curriculum; parent, speech, and language training; physical, occupational, and music therapy; nutritional consultation, recreation programming, taped textbook program, tutoring, academic and personal counseling.

Hospital Clinics

Salt Lake City: Primary Children's Medical Center, Learning Problems Clinic, 401 12th Avenue, 84103. Telephone: (801) 521-1693. Contact: Helen Bigelow or Cheryl Kuehne. Outpatient program. Ages served: 4-16. Services: diagnostic testing, academic and psychological testing; academic, psychological, and parent counseling; group, speech, language, physical, and occupational therapy; medication management for youngsters with attention deficit disorders; study skills group, tutoring referrals, multidisciplinary approach.

Other Services

Orem: Mountain West Clinic for Neuro-therapy, 1544 S. 325, West, 84058. Telephone: (801) 226-8111. Contact: Mariellen Staley. Clinic. Ages served: preschool-adult. Services: diagnostic testing, academic testing, academic and parent counseling; speech, language, physical, and occupational therapy; adaptive physical education.

VERMONT

Offices of Organizations Concerned with Learning Disabilities

ACLD, Inc.: VALD, Nine Heaton Street, Montpelier, VT 05602. Telephone: (802) 223-5480. President: Iris Gardner, P.O. Box 23, Riverton, VT 05668. Telephone: (802) 485-8880.

Council for Exceptional Children: President: Virginia Tomasi, E-14 Stonehenge Drive, South Burlington, VT 05401. Telephone: Office (802) 372-6921; Home (802) 658-0595.

Easter Seal Society-Goodwill Industries of Vermont/New Hampshire: 555 Auburn Street, Manchester, NH 03103. Executive Director: Robert G. Cholette. Telephone: (603) 623-8863.

Orton Dyslexia Society (New England Branch): c/o Rocky Hill School, Ives Road, East Greenwich, RI 02818. President: Emi Flynn. Telephone: (401) 884-3346.

State Department of Education Learning Disabilities Personnel

Theodore Riggen, Director, Division of Special and Compensatory Education, State Department of Education, State Office Building, 120 State Street, Montpelier, VT 05602. Telephone: (802) 828-3141. Learning disabilities consultant: Ms. Garet Allen-Malley.

Private and Day Schools

Burlington: Rock Point School, Institute Road, 05401. Telephone: (802) 863-1104. Headmaster: Russell R. Ellis. Secondary boarding school with limited services. Ages served: 14-17. Grades served: 9-12. Current enrollment: 25. Maximum enrollment: 25. Full-time staff: 12. Part-time staff: 3. Scholarships/financial aid available. Services: individual and group tutoring, academic testing and counseling; psychological testing, medical facilities, vocational training available in area. Recreation: cross country skiing and running trails, beaches, tennis courts; local gymnasiums and swimming pools. Notes: Program for underachievers and children with poor self-images or difficulty coping with adolescence.

Putney: The Greenwood School, Box 58-A, Route 2, 05346. Telephone: (802) 387-4545. Director: Thomas D. Scheidler. Males only elementary boarding school. Ages served: 8-14. Grades served: ungraded. Current enrollment: 35. Maximum enrollment: 40. Full-time staff: 14. Part-time staff: 4. Scholarships/financial aid available. Services: individual and group tutoring, academic testing and counseling. Recreation: soccer, skiing, baseball, swimming, running, farm program. Notes: Art, music, and leadership training are part of school program.

Williston: Pine Ridge School, Inc., 1075 Williston Road, 05495. Telephone: (802) 434-2161. Headmaster: Gardner Hopwood. Secondary boarding school with summer program and camp. Ages served: 13-18. Grades served: ungraded. Current enrollment: 88. Maximum enrollment: 88. Full-time staff: 67. Part-time staff: 4. Services: individual tutoring, academic testing; daily remedial language tutorial with emphasis on Orton-Gillingham method; small classes; individualized English, science, social studies, and math programs. Recreation: camping, hiking, cross country and downhill skiing, snowshoeing, backpacking, wilderness survival, newspaper, yearbook, clubs, weekend trips.

Woodstock: Woodstock Learning Clinic, 32 Pleasant Street, 05091. Telephone: (802) 457-1176. Director: Mr. Terry Brown. Preschool. Ages served: birth-6. Current enrollment: 20. Maximum enrollment: no limit. Full-time staff: 10. Part-time staff: 6. Services: academic testing, psychological and family counseling, physical and occupational therapy, sensorimotor development, speech and language therapy, sensory integration and stimulation; developmental activities in communication, self-care, and socialization. Notes: Serves children with mild to severe developmental delays.

Summer Camps and Programs

Fairlee: Aloha Camps, Route 1, Box 91A, 05045. Telephone: (802) 333-9113. Managing Director: Paul S. Pilcher. Residential camp with academic program and limited services. Ages served: 7-17. Grades served: 1-11. Maximum enrollment: 350. Full-time staff: 150. Scholarships/financial aid available. Services: individual tutoring, medical services. Academic programs: math, reading, English, spelling, study skills, college preparatory program. Recreation: camping, hiking, field trips, nature study, riding, swimming, sailing, archery, team sports, crafts, dance, drama, music, photography, riflery, gymnastics, ropes course, woodshop, tennis.

College and University Special Programs and Services

Castleton State College: Castleton, VT 05735. Total enrollment: 1,300. LD students: 5. Special services: individual and group tutoring, academic counseling, training in study skills, taped books, readers, vocational counseling and placement, student resource center; reading, study, math, and English skills. Contact: Robert Rummel, Director of Special Programs. Telephone: (802) 468-5611 ext. 321.

Johnson State College: Johnson, VT 05656. Total enrollment: 900. LD students: 30. Special services: individual and group tutoring, special examinations, academic counseling, diagnostic testing, taped books, training in study skills, student resource center. Contact: Susan Davidson, Director of Special Services. Telephone: (802) 635-2356 ext. 342.

Landmark College: Putney, VT 05346. (Scheduled to open September, 1985.) Special services: individual and group tutoring, training in study skills, academic and psychological counseling, special examinations, student resource center, diagnostic testing, word processing, clinic, precollege program to develop language and literacy skills.

- **Special program:** Landmark College is exclusively for students with language disabilities/dyslexia. Emphasis is on remediation, not compensation. All students required to take computer classes. Must be of average intelligence and have no primary emotional disorders. Admissions requirements include an interview, submission of all recent records that verify the learning disability, and testing done by the college staff. Contact: James Baucom, Director of Education, 412 Hale Street, Prides Crossing, MA 01965-0417. Telephone: (617) 927-2802.

Norwich University-Military College of Vermont: Northfield, VT 05663. Total enrollment: 2,300. LD students: 50. Special services: individual and group tutoring, training in study skills, academic and psychological counseling, taped books, readers, diagnostic testing, support group. Contact: Beverly E. Bozsik, Director, Learning Skills Center. Telephone: (802) 485-5011 ext. 259.

Southern Vermont College: Bennington, VT 05201. Total enrollment: 500. LD students: 25. Special services: individual and group tutoring, training in study skills, academic and psychological counseling, taped books, special examinations, student resource center, diagnostic testing, scholarships, ombudsman, support group.

- **Special program:** Learning Disabilities Program. Learning disabilities specialist works with students individually and in small groups. Offers word processing workshops and proctored study sessions. Coordinator: Lisa Nissenbaum Schell. Telephone: (802) 442-5427 ext. 53.

University of Vermont: 146 S. Williams Street, Burlington, VT 05405. Total enrollment: 8,000. LD students: 45. Special services: readers, individual and group tutoring, ombudsman, special examinations, academic counseling, diagnostic testing, taped books, training in study skills, note takers, reading and writing skill development, auditory/information processing programs, priority registration, faculty consultation, library services, personal and career counseling, talking computer, student resource center. Contact: Nancy Oliker, Coordinator. Telephone: (802) 656-3340.

Center/clinic: University of Vermont Reading Center. Telephone: (802) 656-3838. Director: Lyman C. Hunt. Open to public. Services: evaluation. Notes: Serves children from area public schools.

VERMONT

Vermont College of Norwich University: Montpelier, VT 05602. Total enrollment: 2,300. LD students: 10. Special services: individual and group tutoring, training in study skills, academic and psychological counseling, taped books, readers, diagnostic testing, support group. Contact: Beverly E. Bozsik, Director, Learning Skills Center. Telephone: (802) 229-0522 ext. 226.

Other Services

Marshfield: The Clearing, Route 1, Box 1600, 05658. Telephone: (802) 426-3810. Director: Robert Belenky. Counseling center and all-season camp with limited services. Residential program. Ages served: 12-20. Grades served: 6-15. Current enrollment: 2-5. Maximum enrollment: 5. Full-time staff: 2. Part-time staff: 3. Scholarships/financial aid available. Services: individual tutoring, academic and psychological testing, academic and family counseling, wilderness experience. Recreation: skiing, swimming, hiking, crafts, canoeing. Notes: Rustic setting with no electricity or telephone. Camp accessible only by boat or canoe.

VIRGINIA

Offices of Organizations Concerned with Learning Disabilities

ACLD, Inc.: 103 Sabre Drive, Williamsburg, VA 23185. President: Bill Hawthorne. Telephone: (804) 220-3137.

Council for Exceptional Children: President: Ms. Pat Strang Jones, Henrico County Schools, P.O. Box 40, Highland Springs, VA 23075. Telephone: (804) 644-1201.

Easter Seal Society of Virginia, Inc.: 4841 Williamson Road, P.O. Box 5496, Roanoke, VA 24012. Executive Director: F. Robert Knight. Telephone: (703) 362-1656.

Orton Dyslexia Society: 1255 Keffield Street, Roanoke, VA 24019. President: Barbara Ann Whitwell. Telephone: (703) 982-0128.

State Department of Education Learning Disabilities Personnel

James T. Micklem, Sr., Director of Special Education, Programs and Pupil Personnel Services, Virginia Department of Education, P.O. Box 6Q, Richmond, VA 23216. Telephone: (804) 225-2861. Learning disabilities consultant: Mary Louise Trusdell. Telephone: (804) 225-2880.

Private and Day Schools

Alexandria: Leary School, Inc., 6349 Lincolnia Road, 22312. Telephone: (703) 941-8150. Director: Eugene F. Meale. Elementary and secondary day school with summer program. Ages served: 7-21. Grades served: ungraded. Current enrollment: 55. Maximum enrollment: 60. Full-time staff: 14. Part-time staff: 8. Services: individual and group tutoring, academic and psychological testing, psychological and family counseling, adaptive physical education, vocational training, work-study, computer programming; art, occupational, and speech therapy. Recreation: physical education, field trips, basketball, camping and fishing trips, small gym, use of public recreational facilities.

Alexandria: Resurrection Children's Center, 2280 N. Beauregard Street, 22311. Telephone: (703) 578-1314. Director: Mary Ellen Hoy. Preschool with limited services. Ages served: 2-5. Current enrollment: 50. Maximum enrollment: 55. Part-time staff: 14. Scholarships/financial aid available. Services: family counseling, speech and occupational therapy, parent education, support groups. Notes: Mainstream setting. Twenty percent of children have special needs.

Annandale: Oakwood School, 7210 Braddock Road, 22003. Telephone: (703) 941-5788. Executive Director: Robert C. McIntyre. Elementary and secondary day school with summer program and camp. Ages served: 6-15. Grades served: kindergarten-9. Current enrollment: 71. Maximum enrollment: 90. Full-time staff: 21. Part-time staff: 2. Scholarships/financial aid available. Services: individual and group tutoring, academic and psychological testing; academic, psychological, and family counseling; occupational, speech, and language therapy; adaptive physical education, individual programming, small classes. Recreation: playground. Notes: Highly structured program for children with specific learning and mild emotional disorders.

Boyd Tavern: Oakland School, Oakland Farm, 22947. Telephone: (804) 293-8965 or 293-9059. Director: Joanne Dondero. Elementary and secondary day and boarding school with summer program and camp. Ages served: 8-16. Grades served: 1-9. Current enrollment: 84. Maximum enrollment: 84. Full-time staff: 34. Part-time staff: 2. Services: individual and group tutoring, speech therapy, academic testing, academic and psychological counseling, psychotherapy. Recreation: gym and recreation building, structured recreation program, daily physical education, riding instruction. Notes: Family-operated school.

Charlottesville: Adventure Bound School, P.O. Box 574, 22902. Telephone: (804) 971-3525. Executive Director: G.W. Duncan. Males only secondary boarding school. Ages served: 8-18. Grades served: 4-12. Current enrollment: 26. Maximum enrollment: 26. Full-time staff: 26. Part-time staff: 5. Services: individual tutoring, academic and psychological testing; academic, psychological, and family counseling; adaptive physical education, work-study. Recreation: hiking, camping, Outward Bound-type activities.

Charlottesville: Lafayette Academy, 1924 Arlington Boulevard, Suite 210, 22903. Telephone: (804) 295-8005. Director: William R. Keyser. Secondary day school. Ages served: 13-19. Grades served: 6-12. Current enrollment: 12. Maximum enrollment: 18. Full-time staff: 3. Part-time staff: 1. Services: individual and group tutoring, academic and psychological testing; academic, psychological, and family counseling; adaptive physical education, medical services.

Dillwyn: New Dominion School, Inc., P.O. Box 540, 23936. Telephone: (804) 983-2051. Administrator: James M. O'Connor. Males only secondary boarding school. Ages served: 11-18. Current enrollment: 60. Maximum enrollment: 60. Full-time staff: 38. Part-time staff: 4. Scholarships/financial aid available. Services: individual and group tutoring, academic testing; academic, group, and family counseling; medical facilities, adaptive physical education, vocational training, work-study, remedial academics, occupational and milieu therapy, job placement. Recreation: year-round wilderness program for emotionally disturbed and learning disabled youths; hiking and canoeing trips last up to 30 days.

Keswick: Little Keswick School, Inc., P.O. Box 24, 22947. Telephone: (804) 295-0457. Director: Mrs. Terry Columbus. Males only elementary and secondary boarding school with summer program and camp. Ages served: 7-16. Grades served: all. Current enrollment: 26. Maximum enrollment: 26. Full-time staff: 22. Part-time staff: 4. Services: individual and group tutoring, academic and psychological testing; academic, psychological, and family counseling; adaptive physical education, occupational and speech therapy, prevocational and vocational training.

Manakin-Sabot: Buford Academy, Route 250, 23103. Mailing address: P.O. Box 29498, Richmond, VA 23229. Telephone: (804) 784-3325. Headmistress: Elizabeth Stephenson. Elementary day school. Ages served: 5-17. Grades served: ungraded kindergarten-9. Current enrollment: 30. Maximum enrollment: 40. Full-time staff: 7. Part-time staff: 3. Services: individual and group tutoring, academic testing and counseling, adaptive physical education. Recreation: daily physical education, swimming, art.

McLean: Northern Virginia Developmental Preschool, 888 Dolley Madison Boulevard, 22101. Telephone: (703) 356-2833. Director: Laura Rubinoff. Preschool with camp. Ages served: 2½-5. Current enrollment: 10. Maximum enrollment: 10. Full-time staff: 3. Part-time staff: 7. Scholarships/financial aid available. Services: individual and group tutoring, psychological testing and counseling, speech and language testing and therapy. Recreation: playground. Notes: Program for children who have difficulty understanding or using spoken language.

Richmond: Educational Development Center of Psychiatric Institute of Richmond, 3001 Fifth Avenue, 23222. Telephone: (804) 329-4392. Administrator: Don Hansen. Elementary and secondary day school. Ages served: 5-18. Grades served: kindergarten-12. Current enrollment: 100. Maximum enrollment: 120. Full-time staff: 22. Services: individual and group tutoring, academic and psychological testing; academic, psychological, and family counseling; occupational therapy, job placement.

Richmond: The New Community School, 4211 Hermitage Road, 23227. Telephone: (804) 266-2494. Head of the School: Julia Ann Greenwood. Secondary day school. Ages served: 12-19. Grades served: 7-12. Current enrollment: 62. Maximum enrollment: 62. Full-time staff: 17. Part-time staff: 6. Scholarships/financial aid available. Services: individual tutoring, academic testing and counseling, college preparatory program, remediation of language skills. Recreation: elective courses in practical and fine arts, interscholastic athletics, special programs and events.

Richmond: Riverside School, Inc., 2110 McRae Road, P.O. Box 2933, 23235. Telephone: (804) 320-3465. Director: Patricia W. DeOrio. Elementary day school. Ages served: 6-14. Grades served: 1-8. Current enrollment: 50. Maximum enrollment: 50. Full-time staff: 9. Part-time staff: 8. Services: individual tutoring, academic and psychological testing, academic and psychological counseling. Recreation: gymnastics.

Richmond: Vocational Center, Virginia Home for Boys, 8716 W. Broad Street, 23229. Telephone: (804) 270-6566. Executive Director: Martin E. Balsbaugh. Males only secondary day and boarding school. Ages served: 14-19. Grades served: ungraded. Current enrollment: 20. Maximum enrollment: 24. Full-time staff: 6. Part-time staff: 2. Scholarships/financial aid available for boarding school. Services: individual and group tutoring, academic testing, academic and psychological counseling, adaptive physical education, vocational training, job placement, medical services. Recreation: team sports, weight room, tennis, swimming, weekly field trips. Notes: Serves the learning disabled and emotionally disturbed.

Roanoke: The Achievement Center, 615 N. Jefferson Street, 24016. Telephone: (703) 982-0128. Administrator: David J. Prestipino. Principal: Barbara A. Whitwell. Elementary and secondary day school with summer program. Ages served: 6-15. Grades served: ungraded. Current enrollment: 60. Maximum enrollment: 80. Full-time staff: 30. Scholarships/financial aid available. Services: individual and group tutoring, academic testing, psychological counseling, adaptive physical education, speech and language therapy, individualized educational programs available.

Roanoke: Early Learning Center, 3637 Colonial Avenue, S.W., 24014. Telephone: (703) 989-3739. Director: Mary Jo Shannon. Preschool and elementary day school with limited services. Ages served: 2½-8. Grades served: preschool-3. Current enrollment: 41. Maximum enrollment: 50. Full-time staff: 6. Part-time staff: 1. Scholarships/financial aid available. Services: individual tutoring, academic counseling, academic and psychological testing; Saturday and summer programs for grades 1-12 offering one-to-one tutoring in language and math, small group instruction in auditory discrimination, perceptual motor skills, and social values are sometimes available.

VIRGINIA

Springfield: Accotink Academy, 8519 Tuttle Road, 22152. Telephone: (703) 451-8041. Director: Elaine McConnell. Elementary and secondary day school. Ages served: 5-21. Grades served: kindergarten-12. Current enrollment: 114. Maximum enrollment: 120. Full-time staff: 46. Part-time staff: 8. Scholarships/financial aid available. Services: individual and group tutoring, academic and psychological testing; academic, psychological, and family counseling; adaptive physical education, vocational training, work-study, job placement; physical, occupational, speech, language, and art therapy; art education, special reading classes. Recreation: daily physical education.

Springfield: School for Contemporary Education, 7203 Wimsatt Road, 22151. Telephone: (703) 941-8810. Administrative Director: Sally A. Sibley. Preschool, elementary, and secondary day school. Ages served: 2-21. Grades served: kindergarten-12. Current enrollment: 96. Maximum enrollment: 117. Full-time staff: 65. Part-time staff: 16. Services: individual tutoring, academic testing; academic, psychological, and family counseling; physical, occupational, speech, and language therapy; adaptive physical education, prevocational and vocational training, work-study, job placement, family services. Recreation: physical education. Notes: Special foster care program for emotionally disturbed children available.

Winchester: Timber Ridge, P.O. Box 3160, 22601. Telephone: (703) 888-3456 or 667-6303. Executive Director: John M. Markwood. Males only secondary boarding school with limited services; summer program and camp. Ages served: 11-21. Current enrollment: 56. Maximum enrollment: 60. Full-time staff: 56. Part-time staff: 8. Services: group tutoring, academic and psychological testing, psychological counseling, prevocational and vocational training, work-study, medical services. Recreation: gym, recreation hall, ball fields, fishing, lake, art room; area facilities include park, bowling, skating rink, theaters. Notes: Behavior management program encourages student self-control.

College and University Special Programs and Services

Blue Ridge Community College: P.O. Box 80, Weyers Cave, VA 24486. Total enrollment: 2,000. LD students: 7. Special services: training in study skills, academic counseling, taped books, special examinations, student resource center, ombudsman. Contact: E.B. Cox, Coordinator of Counseling Services. Telephone: (703) 234-9261 ext. 218.

George Mason University: 4400 University Drive, Fairfax, VA 22030. Total enrollment: 15,000. LD students: 35. Special services: readers in library, alternative forms and extended time for examinations, note takers, option to tape record lectures, individual counseling. Contact: Paul Bousel, Advisor to Disabled Students. Telephone: (703) 323-2523.

Hampton University: Hampton, VA 23668. Special services: individual and group tutoring, training in study skills, academic and psychological counseling, taped books, student resource center, readers, diagnostic testing, scholarships.

Contact: William T. Harper, III, Director, Student Special Services. Telephone: (804) 727-5705.

James Madison University: Harrisonburg, VA 22807. Special services: individual tutoring, training in study skills, academic and psychological counseling, taped books, special examinations, readers, ombudsman. Contact: Elizabeth L. Ihle, Coordinator, Services for the Handicapped. Telephone: (703) 568-6830 or 568-6705.

Lynchburg College: Lynchburg, VA 24501. Total enrollment: 1,500. LD students: 15. Special services: accepts untimed SAT, academic and psychological counseling, placement testing, merit and need-based scholarships, writing skills center, peer tutoring program. Contact: Mr. Shelley Blumenthal, Director of Admissions. Telephone: (804) 522-8300. In-state toll free number: (800) 542-1222. Out-of-state toll free number: (800) 426-8101.

New River Community College: Dublin, VA 24084. LD students: 7. Special services: individual and group tutoring, training in study skills, academic and psychological counseling, taped books, special examinations, student resource center, readers, diagnostic testing, financial aid, ombudsman, support group, summer orientation for LD students for credit, human development courses.

- **Special program:** The Learning Achievement Program. Learning disability must be verified through recent diagnostic tests. Full or part-time students are eligible for the program. Coordinator: Jeananne Dixon. Telephone: (703) 674-4121 ext. 358. Counselor: Marlene Herakovich. Telephone: (703) 674-4121 ext. 357.

Radford University: Radford, VA 24142. Total enrollment: 6,800. LD students: 20. Special services: readers, individual tutoring, special examinations, academic and psychological counseling, taped books, training in study skills, reading and writing lab. Contact: Michael Walsh, Assistant Director for Residential Life. Telephone: (703) 731-5375.

Center/clinic: Project TAP (Technical Assistance to Parents of Learning Disabled Children) Resource Center, Box 5820. Telephone: (703) 731-5196. Codirectors: Nancy Eiss, Deborah Callan. Open to public. Services: provides literature on learning disabilities to parents of learning disabled children in grades kindergarten-12.

Southern Seminary Junior College: Buena Vista, VA 24416. Special services: individual and group tutoring, training in study skills, psychological counseling. Contact: Joseph L. Carter, Academic Dean. Telephone: (703) 261-6181.

University of Richmond: Richmond, VA 23173. Special services: diagnostic testing. Contact: Warren Hopkins, Center for Psychological Services. Telephone: (804) 285-6270.

VIRGINIA

University of Virginia: Charlottesville, VA 22903. Total enrollment: 16,500. LD students: 80. Special services: testing, readers, tutors, academic and psychological counseling, vocational counseling and placement.

Center/clinic: Learning Needs and Evaluation Center, Student Affairs-The Rotunda. Telephone: (804) 924-3139. Director: Eleanore Westhead. Open to public on limited basis. Grades served: college. Services: diagnostic testing, tutors, special examinations, academic and psychological counseling, word processing, scribes, taped books, vocational counseling and placement, readers, editing service, limited outside assessments.

Virginia Commonwealth University: 901 W. Franklin Street, Richmond, VA 23284. Total enrollment: 20,000. Special services: individual and group tutoring, taped books, special examinations, readers, academic and psychological counseling, diagnostic testing, training in study skills, student resource center, scholarships, ombudsman. Contact: Earl Wheatfall, Director of Educational Support Programs. Telephone: (804) 257-1651.

Center/clinic: Reading and Child Study Center, 109 N. Harrison Street. Telephone: (804) 257-1139 or 257-1140. Coordinator: Shyla M. Ipsen. Open to public. Ages served: 2 and up. Grades served: all. Services: tutoring in reading and math, psychological and educational testing, social evaluation.

Virginia Polytechnic Institute and State University: Blacksburg, VA 24061. Total enrollment: 21,000. LD students: 14. Special services: individual tutoring, training in study skills, academic and psychological counseling, taped books, special examinations. Contact: Wayne E. Speer, Handicap Concerns Officer. Telephone: (703) 961-7500.

Virginia Western Community College: 3095 Colonial Avenue, S.W., Roanoke, VA 24038. Total enrollment: 5,500. LD students: 15. Special services: training in study skills, academic counseling, taped books, readers, tutorial assistance, writing and math centers, career/personal testing and assessment, cultural enrichment seminars, workshops, field trips, financial aid information and referral, math and writing/English specialists. Contact: William A. Salyers, Jr., Director, Special Services Project. Telephone: (703) 982-7286.

Wytheville Community College: 1000 E. Main Street, Wytheville, VA 24382. Special services: individual tutoring, academic counseling, taped books, limited special examinations, readers, limited diagnostic testing, ombudsman, student special services project, faculty awareness. Contact: James S. Presgraves, Director, Special Services Project. Telephone: (703) 228-5541.

Hospital Clinics

Charlottesville: University of Virginia Children's Rehabilitation Center, Neurodevelopmental Clinic, 2270 Ivy Road, 22901. Telephone: (804) 924-8184. Contact: Sharon Helt. Outpatient program. Ages served: 2-18. Services: diagnostic testing, academic and psychological testing; academic, psychological, and parent counseling; speech, language, physical, and occupational therapy; adaptive physical education, social services, socialization skills.

Norfolk: Virginia Center for Psychiatry, 100 Kingsley Lane, 23505. Telephone: (804) 489-1072. Contact: T. Jack Baker, Director of Educational Therapy. Outpatient and inpatient program. Ages served: 13-18. Services: diagnostic testing, academic and psychological testing, individual tutoring; academic, psychological, and parent counseling; group, speech, language, physical, and occupational therapy; adaptive physical education, support group, social services.

Other Services

Charlottesville: Center for Dyslexia, 170 Rugby Road, 22903. Telephone: (804) 977-2010. Contact: Rebecca B. Richardson or Cynthia A. Cleveland. Clinic. Day and after school program. Ages served: 5-adult. Services: diagnostic testing, academic and psychological testing, individual tutoring; academic, psychological, and parent counseling; support group.

Goochland: Elk Hill Farm, Inc., P.O. Box 99, 23063. Telephone: (804) 457-4866 or 784-4392. Executive Director: Richard C. David. Males only residential treatment center; secondary school with limited services. Ages served: 13-17. Grades served: 7-12. Current enrollment: 19. Maximum enrollment: 22. Full-time staff: 16. Part-time staff: 1. Limited scholarships/financial aid available. Services: individual and group tutoring, academic testing; academic, group, and family counseling; prevocational training, work-study. Recreation: backpacking, white water canoeing, rock climbing, jogging, basketball, football, baseball, Ping Pong, board games. Notes: Serves teenagers from Virginia with educational, legal, or emotional problems.

McLean: Speech and Language Center of Northern Virginia, 888 Dolley Madison Boulevard, 22101. Telephone: (703) 356-2833. Director: Laura Rubinoff. Clinic. Day and after school program. Ages served: 2½-18. Services: diagnostic testing, psychological testing, individual and group tutoring, psychological and parent counseling, speech and language therapy.

WASHINGTON

Offices of Organizations Concerned with Learning Disabilities

ACLD, Inc.: 300 120th Avenue, N.E., Building 1, Suite 217, Bellevue, WA 98005. Telephone: (206) 451-9171. President: Nancy Goldberg. Executive Director: Joann Brammer.

WASHINGTON

Council for Exceptional Children: President: Dick Christensen, 3726 N. 33rd Street, Tacoma, WA 98407. Telephone: Office (206) 593-6965; Home (206) 752-8153.

Easter Seal Society of Washington, Inc.: 521 Second Avenue, West, Seattle, WA 98119. Executive Director: William E. Unti. Telephone: (206) 284-5700.

Orton Dyslexia Society (Puget Sound Branch): 1922 Richmond Beach Drive, N.W., Seattle, WA 98177. President: Lucille Pridemore. Telephone: Office (206) 743-3513; Home (206) 542-1434.

State Department of Education Learning Disabilities Personnel

Greg Kirsch, Director of Special Education, Superintendent of Public Instruction, Special Education Section, Old Capitol Building, FG-11, Olympia, WA 98504. Telephone: (206) 753-6733. Learning disabilities consultant: Jane Dailey. Telephone: (206) 753-2563.

Private and Day Schools

Bellingham: Karum School, 5602 Mission Road, 98226. Telephone: (206) 592-5664. Educational Administrator: Julia L. Katz. Secondary day and boarding school with summer program. Ages served: 12-18. Grades served: 7-12. Current enrollment: 18. Maximum enrollment: 25. Full-time staff: 8. Services: individual and group tutoring, academic testing; academic, psychological, and family counseling; adaptive physical education, vocational training, work-study. Recreation: jogging, baseball, volleyball, basketball, swimming.

Kent: Pediatric Therapy Center: First Steps, 11420 S.E. 248th, 98031. Telephone: (206) 854-7025. Executive Director: Elizabeth A. Hannley. Preschool with summer program. Ages served: birth-5. Current enrollment: 58. Maximum enrollment: 70. Full-time staff: 7. Part-time staff: 3. Scholarships/financial aid available. Services: individual and group tutoring, academic testing, physical and occupational therapy, speech and language pathology, parent education. Notes: For neuromuscularly and neurologically impaired children; medical referral required.

Redmond: The Stanford Schools, 19315 N.E. 95th Street, 98053. Telephone: (206) 883-7555. Executive Director: Theodore J. Hope. Elementary and secondary day school with summer program. Ages served: 9-20. Grades served: 3-12. Current enrollment: 105. Maximum enrollment: 120. Full-time staff: 20. Part-time staff: 4. Scholarships/financial aid available. Services: individual and group tutoring, academic testing; academic, psychological, and family counseling; adaptive physical education, vocational training, work-study, job placement; accelerated or remedial curriculum tailored to individual needs of each student; faculty/student ratio 1:7. Recreation: outdoor education program including rock climbing and canoeing; travel. Notes: Emphasis on basic academic skills and social and personal growth.

Seattle: Experimental Education Unit, WJ-10, CDMRC, University of Washington, 98195. Telephone: (206) 543-4011. Director: Joseph Jenkins. Preschool, elementary, and secondary day school with summer program. Ages served: birth-21. Grades served: preschool-12. Current enrollment: 142. Services: academic and psychological testing, physical and occupational therapy, adaptive physical education, work-study. Notes: Participates in university research and student training.

Seattle: Morningside Learning Center, 144 N.E. 54th Street, 98105. Telephone: (206) 522-0031. Director and Psychologist: Kent R. Johnson. Elementary day school with summer program. Ages served: 7-16. Grades served: 1-8. Current enrollment: 40. Maximum enrollment: 60. Full-time staff: 10. Part-time staff: 4. Scholarships/financial aid available. Services: individual and group tutoring, academic testing and counseling. Recreation: art, field trips. Notes: Highly structured program with ungraded format specifically designed for individuals with learning disabilities.

Seattle: Seattle Learning Center, 4649 Sunnyside, North, 98103. Telephone: (206) 634-3500. Codirectors: Peggy Gloth, Mary Johnson. Elementary day school with summer program. Ages served: 8-12. Grades served: 2-6. Current enrollment: 21. Maximum enrollment: 21. Full-time staff: 3. Part-time staff: 2. Services: individual and group tutoring, academic testing and counseling. Recreation: field trips, adjacent to city park. Notes: Provides intensive remediation so students can return to home schools.

Seattle: The Seattle Seguin School, 12515 Greenwood, North, 98133. Telephone: (206) 367-2220. Director: Margo Engdahl. Secondary day school. Ages served: 11-18. Grades served: 6-12. Current enrollment: 17. Maximum enrollment: 25. Full-time staff: 4. Scholarships/financial aid available. Services: academic testing and counseling, vocational training, work-study. Recreation: physical education program including swimming and soccer.

Spokane: Northeast Child Development Center, N. 4001 Cook, 99205. Telephone: (509) 484-3470. Director: Patricia A. Mougey. Preschool. Ages served: birth-6. Current enrollment: 45. Maximum enrollment: 50. Full-time staff: 3. Part-time staff: 4. Scholarships/financial aid available. Services: individual and group tutoring, academic and psychological testing, psychological and family counseling; physical, occupational, speech, and language therapy; work-study. Recreation: summer field trips. Notes: Special education program serves children birth-3.

Summer Camps and Programs

Port Orchard: Camp Niwana, 5290 S.W. Lake Helena Road, 98366. Telephone: (206) 377-5513. Permanent mailing address: Kit-No-Ma Council of Camp Fire, 1109 Warren Avenue, Bremerton, WA 98366. Camp Director: Sharon George. Females only and coeducational day and residential camp with limited services.

WASHINGTON

Ages served: 6-18. Grades served: 1-12. Maximum enrollment: 70 per week. Full-time staff: 25. Scholarships/financial aid available. Services: nurse on site. Recreation: camping, hiking, nature study, riding, swimming, archery, crafts, dance, music, horsemanship, singing, canoeing, rowing. Notes: Children with learning disabilities mainstreamed into regular camp programs. Works with children in small groups to develop camaraderie and self-esteem.

College and University Special Programs and Services

Central Washington University: Ellensburg, WA 98926. Special services: individual and group tutoring, training in study skills, academic counseling, taped books, special examinations, note takers. Contact: Ann Thompson, Director, Handicapped Student Service. Telephone: (509) 963-2171.

The Evergreen State College: Olympia, WA 98505. Total enrollment: 2,300. LD students: 3. Special services: individual tutoring, training in study skills, academic and psychological counseling, taped books, readers, diagnostic testing, support group. Contact: Cathy Turner, Handicapped Access Coordinator. Telephone: (206) 866-6000 ext. 6364.

Center/clinic: Learning Resource Center. Telephone: (206) 866-6000 ext. 6420. Director: Stella Jordan. Not open to public. Services: tutoring, evaluation.

Olympic Community College: 16th and Chester Avenue, Bremerton, WA 98310. Total enrollment: 11,000. LD students: 25. Special services: individual and group tutoring, training in study skills, academic and psychological counseling, taped books, special examinations, student resource center, readers, diagnostic testing, scholarships, career counseling, cooperative education program, community referral. Contact: Anna Hoey, Program Manager, Supportive Services. Telephone: (206) 478-4607.

Pacific Lutheran University: Tacoma, WA 98447. Special services: individual tutoring, training in study skills, academic and psychological counseling. Contact: Kathy Olson Mannelly, Associate Dean for Student Life. Telephone: (206) 535-7191.

Seattle Central Community College: 1801 Broadway, Seattle, WA 98122. Total enrollment: 8,128. Special services: individual and group tutoring, training in study skills, academic counseling, special examinations, student resource center, readers. Contact: Kathern J. Carlstrom, Disabled Student Services Coordinator. Telephone: (206) 587-4183.

Seattle University: Broadway and Madison, Seattle, WA 98122. Total enrollment: 4,700. LD students: 35. Special services: readers, individual and group tutoring, taped books, special examinations, academic and psychological counseling, diagnostic testing, training in study skills, student resource center. Contact: Marie Hudgins, Director, Disabled Student Resources. Telephone: (206) 626-5310.

Center/clinic: Seattle University Testing Center. Telephone: (206) 626-5416. Contact: Bonnie Denoon. Open to public. Grades served: kindergarten-adult. Services: diagnostic testing.

Shoreline Community College: 16101 Greenwood Avenue, North, Seattle, WA 98133. Total enrollment: 7,000. Special services: individual tutoring, training in study skills, academic and psychological counseling, limited taped books, special examinations, referral for diagnostic testing. Contact: Nancy Field, Counselor. Telephone: (206) 546-4596.

Spokane Falls Community College: W3410 Fort George Wright Drive, Spokane, WA 99204. Total enrollment: 3,000-4,000. LD students: 15-20. Special services: limited individual tutoring, training in study skills, academic counseling, taped books, student resource center, diagnostic testing, communications learning center. Contact: Ben Webinger, Director/Counselor, Disabled Student Services. Telephone: (509) 459-3543.

University of Washington: Seattle, WA 98195. Special services: academic counseling, taped books, special examinations, student resource center, readers, note takers, student support group. Contact: Roxanne L. Baker, Program Coordinator, Disabled Student Services. Telephone: (206) 543-8924.

Washington State University: Pullman, WA 99164.

Center/clinic: Communication Disorders Clinic, Daggy Hall. Telephone: (509) 335-1500. Coordinator of Clinical Services: Charles L. Madison. Open to public. Ages served: all. Services: diagnostic testing, psychological counseling, speech and language therapy.

Western Washington University: 516 High Street, Bellingham, WA 98225. Total enrollment: 9,500. LD students: 50. Special services: academic and psychological counseling, diagnostic testing, student resource center, support group, training in study skills, individual arrangements. Contact: Dorothy Crow, Learning Disabilities Coordinator. Telephone: (206) 676-3187 or 676-3855.

Center/clinic: Educational Counseling/Reading Skills Counseling Center, Miller Hall 262. Telephone: (206) 676-3164. Director: Saundra Taylor. Not open to public. Grades served: college.

Yakima Valley Community College: 16th Avenue and Nob Hill Boulevard, P.O. Box 1647, Yakima, WA 98907. LD students: 30. Special services: readers, individual and group tutoring, academic and psychological counseling, ombudsman, training in study skills, student resource center, support group, taped books, readers. Contact: Mark Cornett, Handicapped Services and Affirmative Action. Telephone: (509) 575-2473.

WASHINGTON

Other Services

Seattle: Easter Seal Children's Clinic and Preschool, 1850 Boyer Avenue, East, 98112. Telephone: (206) 325-8477. Deputy Executive Director: Judith A. Moore. Summer program. Ages served: birth-adolescence. Current enrollment: 70. Maximum enrollment: 120. Full-time staff: 12. Part-time staff: 11. Scholarships/financial aid available. Services: preschool, academic testing, family counseling, physical and occupational therapy, adaptive physical education, medical services.

WEST VIRGINIA

Offices of Organizations Concerned with Learning Disabilities

ACLD, Inc.: 1725 Crestmont Drive, Huntington, WV 25701. President: Mrs. Litz Jarvis. Telephone: (304) 529-4985. Also contact: Kenneth E. Guyer, treasurer and past president. Telephone: (304) 525-6565.

Council for Exceptional Children: President: James Freeland, 30 Greentree Road, Wheeling, WV 26003. Telephone: Office (304) 242-3430; Home (304) 242-0841.

Easter Seal Society for Crippled Children and Adults of West Virginia, Inc.: 1210 Virginia Street, East, Charleston, WV 25301. Executive Director: John C. Stepp. Telephone: (304) 346-3508.

State Department of Education Learning Disabilities Personnel

William Capehart, Director, Office of Special Education Administration, West Virginia Department of Education, Capitol Complex, Building 6, Room 309, Charleston, WV 25305. Telephone: (304) 348-8830. Learning disabilities consultant: Frank Andrews.

Private and Day Schools

St. Albans: The Swain Learning Center, 55 Olde Main Plaza, 25177. Telephone: (304) 727-0610. Director: Emma Halstead Swain. Preschool, elementary, and secondary day school with limited services. Ages served: 5-18. Grades served: kindergarten-12. Current enrollment: 65. Maximum enrollment: 90. Full-time staff: 2. Part-time staff: 10. Services: individual tutoring, educational testing.

College and University Special Programs and Services

Bluefield State College: Bluefield, WV 24701. Special services: individual and group tutoring, training in study skills, academic and psychological counseling, taped books, special examinations, student resource center, readers, diagnostic testing, scholarships. Contact: Claudius Oni, Counselor/Assistant Director. Telephone: (304) 325-7102 ext. 352.

Glenville State College: 200 High Street, Glenville, WV 26351. Total enrollment: 1,800. LD students: 10. Special services: special examinations arranged by individual instructors, training in study skills; support group, individual tutoring and diagnostic assistance on request. Contact: Annette C. Roberts, Assistant Professor. Telephone: (304) 462-7361 ext. 301.

Marshall University: Huntington, WV 25701. Total enrollment: 13,000. LD students: 38. Special services: readers, individual tutoring in reading and spelling, group tutoring, special examinations, academic and psychological counseling, diagnostic testing, taped books, training in study and test taking skills, support group, liaison with professors.

- **Special program:** Learning Disabilities Tutorial Program. Learning disability must be verified through recent records. Full or part-time students may participate in the program. Director: Barbara Guyer. Telephone: (304) 696-2340.

Potomac State College of West Virginia University: Keyser, WV 26726. Total enrollment: 1,062. LD students: 20-25. Special services: individual and group tutoring, training in study skills, academic and psychological counseling, taped books, student resource center, diagnostic testing. Contact: Hunter J. Conrad, Assistant Dean for Admissions and Records. Telephone: (304) 788-3011 ext. 226 or 227.

Salem College: Salem, WV 26426. Special services: individual tutoring, training in study skills, academic and psychological counseling, taped books, special examinations, student resource center, readers, word processors. Contact: James Giesey, Director of Counseling, Development. Telephone: (304) 782-5243.

West Virginia State College: Institute, WV 25112. Special services: individual tutoring, training in study skills, academic counseling, taped books, special examinations, student resource center, readers, diagnostic testing, disability services counselor. Contact: C. Whyte, Director, Collegiate Support Services. Telephone: (304) 766-3110.

West Virginia University: Morgantown, WV 26506. Special services: individual and group tutoring, academic and psychological counseling, diagnostic testing, taped books, readers, ombudsman. Contact: Gordon Kent, Director, Center for Disabled Student Services. Telephone: (304) 293-5313.

Center/clinic: Reading Center, 506 Allen Hall. Telephone: (304) 293-4769. Coordinator: Marilyn Fairbanks. Open to public. Grades served: elementary and secondary.

Center/clinic: Reading Lab, 139 Stansburg Hall. Telephone: (304) 293-4997. Director: John Van Wert. Not open to public. Grades served: university students. Services: academic counseling, basic skills study groups.

WEST VIRGINIA

Center/clinic: Interdisciplinary Diagnostic Clinic, 509 Allen Hall, P.O. Box 6122. Telephone: (304) 293-4692 or 293-6220 or 293-3350. Coordinator: Charles A. Thatcher. Open to public. Ages served: 5-adult. Services: diagnostic testing, academic and psychological testing; academic, psychological, and parent counseling.

West Virginia Wesleyan College: Buckhannon, WV 26201. Total enrollment: 1,300. LD students: 50. Special services: individual and group tutoring, untimed examinations, academic counseling, diagnostic testing, taped books, training in study and writing skills, support group. Contact: Phyllis Coston, Director, Learning Center. Telephone: (304) 473-8498.

Center/clinic: Learning Center. Telephone: (304) 473-8498. Director: Phyllis Coston. Not open to public. Grades served: college.

WISCONSIN

Offices of Organizations Concerned with Learning Disabilities

ACLD, Inc.: 2114 Doemel Street, Oshkosh, WI 54901. President: John R. Burr. Telephone: (414) 233-1977.

Council for Exceptional Children: President: Phyllis Ollie, 4105 W. Portage Street, Milwaukee, WI 53209. Telephone: Office (414) 475-8131; Home (414) 351-5883.

The Easter Seal Society of Wisconsin, Inc.: 2702 Monroe Street, Madison, WI 53711. Executive Director: Roy Campbell. Telephone: (608) 231-3411.

Orton Dyslexia Society: P.O. Box 4, Butte Des Morts, WI 54927. President: Robert Nash. Telephone: Office (414) 424-1033; Home (414) 582-4315.

State Department of Education Learning Disabilities Personnel

Victor J. Contrucci, Director of Special Education, Division for Handicapped Children and Pupil Services, P.O. Box 7481, Madison, WI 53707. Telephone: (608) 266-1649. Learning disabilities consultant: Harold Schmidt. Telephone: (608) 266-5583.

Private and Day Schools

Brookfield: Brookfield Learning Center, 4340 Meadow View, East, 53005. Telephone: (414) 781-3634. Director: Thomas A. Zaborske. Elementary and secondary day school with summer program and camp. Ages served: 6-17. Grades served: kindergarten-11. Current enrollment: 93. Full-time staff: 7. Part-time staff: 28. Services: individual and group tutoring, academic and psychological testing; academic, psychological, and family counseling.

Dousman: Lad Lake, Inc./Lakewood School, P.O. Box 158, 53118. Telephone: (414) 965-2131 ext. 12. Executive Director: Gary L. Erdmann. Males only elementary and secondary day and boarding school with limited services; summer program. Ages served: 7-18. Grades served: 4-12. Current enrollment: 50. Maximum enrollment: 65. Full-time staff: 61. Part-time staff: 5. Scholarships/financial aid available. Services: individual and group tutoring, academic and psychological testing; academic, psychological, and family counseling; vocational training, work-study, job placement, recreational and art therapy. Recreation: water sports including fishing, boating; riding, minibikes, arts, crafts, cross country skiing, camping.

Eagle River: Pinewood Academy, 1800 Silver Forest Lane, 54521. Telephone: (715) 479-4114. Administrator-Director of Admissions: Edward R. Soroosh. Males only secondary boarding school with summer program and camp. Ages served: 12-19. Grades served: 7-12. Current enrollment: 25. Maximum enrollment: 25. Full-time staff: 10. Part-time staff: 2. Services: individual and group tutoring, academic testing and counseling, study-travel. Recreation: skiing, backpacking. Notes: Serves learning disabled, dyslexic boys of average or above average intelligence. Full college preparatory curriculum.

Menomonee Falls: Children's Community Center, Inc., P.O. Box 371, 53051. Telephone: (414) 251-1212. Director: Phyllis Waters. Preschool with summer program. Ages served: 1 month-6 years. Current enrollment: 150. Maximum enrollment: 200. Full-time staff: 3. Part-time staff: 20. Scholarships/financial aid available. Services: physical, speech, and occupational therapy; adaptive physical education, child rearing counseling. Recreation: art, music, field trips, drama.

Milwaukee: St. Francis Children's Activity and Achievement Center, 6700 N. Port Washington Road, 53217. Telephone: (414) 351-0450. Executive Director: Sr. Joanne Marie Kliebhan. Preschool and elementary day school. Ages served: birth-10. Current enrollment: 165. Maximum enrollment: 165. Full-time staff: 37. Part-time staff: 30. Limited scholarships/financial aid available. Services: individual tutoring, academic and psychological testing, psychological and family counseling; physical, occupational, and aqua therapy; vision and speech evaluation and therapy, adaptive physical education, audiological testing, special education. Recreation: gym activities, swimming, outdoor play.

Milwaukee: St. Rose Residence and Day Education, 3801 N. 88th Street, 53222. Telephone: (414) 466-9450. Executive Director: Kenneth Czaplewski. Females only secondary day and boarding school with limited services; summer program. Ages served: 8-18. Grades served: 7-12. Current enrollment: 28 residential; 6 day. Maximum enrollment: 30 residential; 6 day. Full-time staff: 5. Part-time staff: 4. Services: individual and group tutoring, academic testing; academic, psychological, and family counseling; occupational and group therapy, work-study. Recreation: swimming, gym, movies, sports, cultural events. Notes: Primary problems emotional disturbance and/or learning disabilities.

WISCONSIN

Wittenberg: Homme Home for Boys, P.O. Box G, 54499. Telephone: (715) 253-2116. Supervisor of Education: Patricia LesStrang. Males only elementary and secondary day school with limited services; summer program. Ages served: 12-18. Grades served: 7-12. Current enrollment: 25. Maximum enrollment: 27. Full-time staff: 4. Part-time staff: 2. Services: individual and group tutoring, academic and psychological testing, academic and family counseling, vocational training, job placement, high school equivalency preparation, medical services. Recreation: NYPUM (National Youth Project Using Minibikes), softball, basketball, canoeing, horseshoes.

Summer Camps and Programs

Conover: The Tikvah Program at Camp Ramah, 54519. Telephone: (715) 479-4400. Permanent mailing address: 59 E. Van Buren Street, Suite 1610, Chicago, IL 60605. Telephone: (312) 939-2393. Director: Rabbi David Soloff. Residential camp. Ages served: 13-17. Maximum enrollment: 14. Full-time staff: 7. Scholarships/financial aid available. Services: individual and group tutoring, vocational training, Jewish education. Recreation: camping, hiking, field trips, nature study, swimming, sailing, team sports, crafts, dance, drama, music, photography. Notes: Combines Jewish study with a full recreational program for teenagers with learning disabilities.

Rhinelander: Algonquin Reading Camp, Route 3, 54501. Telephone: (715) 369-1277. Permanent mailing address: 8402 E. Sage Drive, Scottsdale, AZ 85253. Telephone: (602) 994-0169. Owner/Director: Jim Doran. Males only residential camp with academic program. Maximum enrollment: 140. Ages served: 7-17. Grades served: 1-12. Full-time staff: 60. Services: occupational therapy. Academic programs: math, reading, English, spelling, study skills, mental processing instruction, college preparatory courses. Recreation: swimming, hiking, team athletics, tennis, sailing, canoeing, waterskiing.

College and University Special Programs and Services

Beloit College: Beloit, WI 53511. Special services: test readers, individual tutoring, academic counseling, training in study skills, ombudsman. Contact: Elissa GoldbergBelle, Director, Educational Development Program. Telephone: (608) 365-3391 ext. 620.

Center/clinic: Educational Development Program. Telephone: (608) 365-3391 ext. 620. Director: Elissa GoldbergBelle. Grades served: college. Services: academic advising, study skills, tutoring assistance, personal support.

Cardinal Stritch College: 6801 N. Yates Road, Milwaukee, WI 53217. Total enrollment: 2,010. LD students: 100. Special services: individual and group tutoring, academic counseling, special examinations, diagnostic testing, training in study skills, scholarships. Contact: Robert A. Pavlik, Director, Reading and Learning Center Programs. Telephone: (414) 351-7511.

Center/clinic: Reading and Learning Center. Telephone: (414) 351-7511. Director: Robert Pavlik. Open to public. Grades served: kindergarten-college. Services: individual tutoring, small classes, remedial classes, vision and hearing screening, individual reading tests and interest inventories, language developmental and intelligence tests, study skills assessment, information sessions.

District One Technical Institute: 620 W. Clairemont Avenue, Eau Claire, WI 54701. Total enrollment: 3,500. LD students: 38. Special services: individual and group tutoring, training in study skills, academic counseling, taped books, special examinations, student resource center, readers, diagnostic testing, ombudsman. Contact: Robert Benedict, Special Needs Supervisor. Telephone: (715) 836-4941.

Fox Valley Technical Institute: 1825 N. Bluemound Drive, Appleton, WI 54913-2277. Total enrollment: 8,000. LD students: 40. Special services: individual tutoring, training in study skills, academic counseling, taped books, special examinations, student resource center, readers, diagnostic testing, scholarships, support group. Contact: Shary Schwabenlender, Special Needs Instructor/Coordinator. Telephone: (414) 735-5679.

Center/clinic: Learning Evaluation Center. Telephone: (414) 735-5682. Director: Lori Weyers. Open to public. Ages served: 18 and up. Grades served: 13-14. Services: instructional support, tutoring, note takers, counseling, evaluation of learning difficulties.

Gateway Technical Institute: 1001 S. Main Street, Racine, WI 53403. Total enrollment: 5,600. LD students: 138. Special services: individual and group tutoring, training in study skills, academic and psychological counseling, taped books, special examinations, student resource center, readers, diagnostic testing, scholarships/grants, ombudsman. Contact: Jo Krohn-Bailey, Learning Skills Specialist. Telephone: (414) 631-7379.

Center/clinic: Career Assessment Planning, 3520 30th Avenue, Kenosha, WI 53141. Telephone: (414) 631-7393. Manager: Doris Myers. Open to public. Ages served: 16 and up. Grades served: 13 and up.

Marquette University: Milwaukee, WI 53233. Special services: psychological, educational, and social assessment; individual, group, and family counseling; play therapy, reading diagnosis and remedial instruction, behavior management, training in study skills, individual tutoring. Contact: Bernard M. Raiche, Director, Education Clinic. Telephone: (414) 224-1433.

Center/clinic: Education Clinic, School of Education, Schroeder Complex. Telephone: (414) 224-7235. Director: Bernard M. Raiche. Open to public. Grades served: kindergarten-12. Ages served: 4-18. Services: individual tutoring, training in study skills; academic, psychological, group, and family counseling; special examinations, diagnostic testing, remedial reading diagnosis and treatment, behavior management.

WISCONSIN

Northland College: Ashland, WI 54806. Total enrollment: 600. LD students: 14. Special services: readers, individual and group tutoring, ombudsman, special examinations, academic and psychological counseling, taped books, training in study skills. Notes: Enrolls a maximum of five students with learning disabilities each year. Contact: Jim Miller, Dean of Admissions. Telephone: (715) 682-4531 ext. 224.

Center/clinic: Learning Center. Telephone: (715) 682-4531 ext. 237. Director: Irene H. Blakely. Open to public. Grades served: college.

University of Wisconsin-Green Bay: Green Bay, WI 54301. Total enrollment: 5,000. Special services: individual and group tutoring, training in study skills, support group. Contact: Jerry Olson, Dean of Students. Telephone: (414) 465-2615.

Center/clinic: Academic Support Program Tutoring Lab, SS1930. Telephone: (414) 465-2710. Director: Evalyn Rozek. Grades served: college.

University of Wisconsin-La Crosse: 1725 State Street, La Crosse, WI 54601. Special services: readers, individual and group tutoring, special examinations, academic counseling, psychological counseling and referrals, diagnostic testing, taped books, training in study skills, support group, preregistration.

Center/clinic: Academic Skills Center, Wilder Hall. Telephone: (608) 785-8535. Director: H. Laury LePage. Grades served: college.

University of Wisconsin-Madison: Madison, WI 53715. Special services: training in study skills, academic counseling, taped books, special examinations, student resource center, diagnostic testing, ombudsman. Contact: Nancy Smith, Director, McBurney Resource Center. Telephone: (608) 263-2741.

Center/clinic: Waisman Center, 1500 Highland Avenue, 53705. Telephone: (608) 263-6467. Contact: Linda Tuchman, Special Education Clinician. Ages served: birth-adult. Services: diagnostic testing, academic and psychological testing; academic, psychological, and parent counseling; group therapy, support group, social services, consultation with schools.

University of Wisconsin-Milwaukee: Box 413, Milwaukee, WI 53201. Special services: individual and group tutoring, training in study skills, academic and psychological counseling, taped books, special examinations, student resource center, readers. Contact: Jeantz Martin, Coordinator, Disabled Student Services. Telephone: (414) 963-5822.

University of Wisconsin-Oshkosh: Oshkosh, WI 54901. Total enrollment: 11,200. LD students: 114. Special services: readers, individual and group tutoring, academic counseling, diagnostic testing, support group.

- **Special program:** Project Success. Serves students with dyslexia enrolled full time in regular college courses. Dyslexia must be diagnosed through recent diagnostic tests or tests by the college. Director: Robert Nash. Telephone: (414) 424-1033.

University of Wisconsin-Platteville: 725 W. Main Street, Platteville, WI 53818. Total enrollment: 5,400. LD students: 30. Special services: individual and group tutoring, training in study skills, academic and psychological counseling, taped books, special examinations, student resource center, readers, diagnostic testing, scholarships, ombudsman, support group. Contact: Dale Bernhardt, Director, Special Services Program. Telephone: (608) 342-1816.

University of Wisconsin-River Falls: River Falls, WI 54022. Total enrollment: 5,000. Special services: group tutoring, academic and psychological counseling, special examinations with instructor approval, diagnostic testing, training in study skills. Contact: John Hamann, Director, Counseling Center. Telephone: (715) 425-3884.

Center/clinic: Reading Clinic. Telephone: (715) 425-3509. Director: Kathleen Daly.

University of Wisconsin-Stevens Point: Stevens Point, WI 54481. Special services: academic and psychological counseling, training in study skills. Contact: John Timcak, Director, New Student Programs. Telephone: (715) 346-3361.

Center/clinic: Student Assistance Center, Room 103, Student Services Building. Telephone: (715) 346-3361. Director: John Timcak. Grades served: college.

Western Wisconsin Technical Institute: Sixth and Vine Streets, La Crosse, WI 54632. Total enrollment: 3,500. LD students: 6. Special services: individual tutoring, academic counseling, taped books, readers. Contact: Philip Malin, Special Needs Counselor. Telephone: (608) 785-9144.

Hospital Clinics

Menomonee Falls: Community Memorial Hospital, W180N8085 Town Hall Road, 53051. Telephone: (414) 251-1000 ext. 3080. Contact: Sally Soper-Cotter, Speech Pathologist. Outpatient and inpatient program. Ages served: all. Services: speech and language therapy.

Other Services

Eau Claire: Northwest Reading Clinic, Box 746, 54701. Telephone: (715) 834-4684. Director: Ruth E. Harris. Clinic. Day and after school program. Ages served: all. Services: diagnostic testing, academic and psychological testing, individual and small group tutoring; academic, psychological, and parent counseling; preparation for high school equivalency test, ACT, SAT; consultation with job training programs, visual perceptual and study skills training. Notes: Works

WISCONSIN

closely with schools, universities, department of vocational rehabilitation, and social service agencies.

La Crosse: Gundersen Clinic, Ltd., 1836 South Avenue, 54601. Telephone: (608) 782-7300. Coordinator: Donna Myer. Medical clinic. Ages served: infant-adult. Services: diagnostic testing, academic and psychological testing; academic, psychological, and parent counseling; group, speech, language, physical, and occupational therapy; social services, outreach consultation to schools and agencies, vocational assessment and counseling; symposiums on topics of interest to learning disabilities practitioners and parents.

Neillsville: Riverview School of Sunburst Youth Homes, 1210 W. Fifth Street, 54456. Telephone: (715) 743-3154. Director of Education/Recreation Therapy: Gladys Bartelt. Day and residential treatment center; elementary and secondary school with summer program. Ages served: 7-18. Grades served: 1-12. Current enrollment: 61. Maximum enrollment: 80. Full-time staff: 23. Scholarships/financial aid available. Services: individual and group tutoring, academic and psychological testing; academic, psychological, and family counseling; adaptive physical education, medical services, recreation therapy. Recreation: swimming, skiing, riding, adventure program, canoeing. Notes: For the emotionally disturbed; many students have learning disabilities as their primary problems.

Prairie Du Chien: Wyalusing Academy, 601 S. Beaumont Road, Box 269, 53821. Telephone: (608) 326-6481. Director of Education: Robert Pickett. Residential treatment center with secondary school and summer program. Ages served: 13-18. Current enrollment: 62. Maximum enrollment: 70. Full-time staff: 75. Part-time staff: 3. Services: individual and group tutoring, academic testing and counseling; occupational, recreational, speech, and language therapy; vocational training, work-study, job placement, medical services, high school equivalency class, social work therapy, body awareness (stress) therapy. Recreation: swimming, camping, roller-skating, intramural athletics, hiking, fishing, movies, field trips. Notes: For emotionally disturbed, learning disabled, and low functioning adolescents.

WYOMING

Offices of Organizations Concerned with Learning Disabilities

Council for Exceptional Children: President: Loxi Calmes, 804 Walnut Street, Rock Springs, WY 82901. Telephone: Office (307) 382-2474; Home (307) 382-4011.

Northern Rocky Mountain Easter Seal Society: 4400 Central Avenue, Great Falls, MT 59405. President: William Sirak. Telephone: (406) 761-3680.

WYOMING

State Department of Education Learning Disabilities Personnel

Carol Nantkes, Director, Special Programs Unit, Wyoming Department of Education, Hathaway Building, Cheyenne, WY 82002. Telephone: (307) 777-7417.

College and University Special Programs and Services

Sheridan College: P.O. Box 1500, Sheridan, WY 82801. Special services: individual tutoring, training in study skills, academic and psychological counseling, taped books, special examinations, student resource center, readers, diagnostic testing, ombudsman. Contact: Tena Hanes, Director, Learning Skills Center. Telephone: (307) 674-6446 ext. 194.

Center/clinic: Learning Skills Center. Telephone: (307) 674-6446 ext. 194. Director: Tena Hanes. Open to public. Ages served: 16 and up. Services: skills development courses, tutors.

University of Wyoming: P.O. Box 3808, University Station, Laramie, WY 82071. Total enrollment: 10,500. LD students: 300. Special services: readers, tutors; academic, career, and personal counseling; special examinations, taped books, vocational counseling and placement, student advocacy with faculty and administration. Contact: Bonnie Helm, Assistant Director, Student Educational Opportunities. Telephone: (307) 766-6189 ext. 27.

Hospital Clinics

Evanston: Wyoming State Hospital, Box 177, 82930. Telephone: (307) 789-3464. Director of Education: Charles D. Bright. Outpatient, inpatient, and day program. Ages served: 12-20. Services: diagnostic testing, academic and psychological testing, individual and group tutoring; academic, psychological, and parent counseling; group, speech, language, physical, and occupational therapy; adaptive physical education.

Books and Other Materials

This section describes important books, magazines, and other materials related to learning disabilities. Within categories, materials are listed in alphabetical order by title. Materials for this section were selected for their timeliness, usefulness, and relevance. Most are recent—1980 or later. However, some older books and other materials are included because they are still important, relevant, and helpful. Price and ordering information is provided. However, many of the books and other materials may be available at local libraries at no cost. Also, librarians may be able to supply names and addresses of local learning disabilities organizations, agencies, and support groups.

BOOKS

Academics and Beyond: Volume 4, The Best of ACLD, edited by William Cruickshank and Eli Tash, 1983, 193 pages. Syracuse University Press, 1600 Jamesville Avenue, Syracuse, NY 13210, $13.95. For professionals. Contains selected papers from the 1982 ACLD International Conference. Topics covered include communication, administration and postschool years, early education and activity programs.

The Basic Language Kit: A Teaching-Tutoring Aid for Adolescents and Young Adults, by Martin S. Weiss and Helen Ginandes Weiss, 1979, 134 pages. Treehouse Associates, P.O. Box 1992, Avon, CO 81620, $11.75. Designed to give classroom teachers basic tools to teach LD adolescents reading, writing, spelling, and study skills. Suggests materials, educational games, and assessment methods. Includes a chart of LD symptoms, associated learning problems and teaching techniques. Also offers methods for training students in note taking, report writing, outlining, and proofreading. Appendixes include the McMahon List of 300 High Utility Words.

College and the Learning Disabled Student: A Guide to Program Selection, Development, and Implementation, by Charles T. Mangrum, II, and Stephen S. Strichart, 1984, 209 pages. Grune and Stratton, Inc., 6277 Sea Harbor Drive, Orlando, FL 32887, $24.50 prepaid. For professionals, but also a good resource for parents and learning disabled adults. Offers plans for developing special college programs for the learning disabled, explains the impact of state and federal laws on post-secondary education for the learning disabled and gives suggestions to counselors for preparing the LD high school student for college. Describes special aids and services offered by colleges and suggests guidelines for selecting programs.

Due Process in Special Education, by James A. Shrybman, 1982, 516 pages. Aspen Systems Corporation, P.O. Box 6018, Gaithersburg, MD 20877, $39.00 prepaid. For parents and others interested in the legal aspects of P.L. 94-142, the Education for All Handicapped Children Act. Detailed explanations of due process, legal standards for identification, evaluation, placement, and the rights and responsibilities of those involved. Also included is a suggested timeline for the tasks and procedures required for due process.

Early Adolescence to Early Adulthood: Volume 5, The Best of ACLD, edited by William M. Cruickshank and Joanne Marie Kliebhan, 1984, 189 pages. Syracuse University Press, 1600 Jamesville Avenue, Syracuse, NY 13210, $12.95. For professionals. Contains selected papers from the 1983 ACLD International Conference. Includes overviews of such topics as the link between learning disabilities and juvenile delinquency, educational and social techniques, steps to employment, and programs for adolescents.

Families of Children with Special Needs: Early Intervention Techniques for the Practitioner, by Allen A. Mori, 1983, 288 pages. Aspen Systems Corporation, P.O. Box 6018, Gaithersburg, MD 20877, $30.50 prepaid. Primarily for professionals, but may be useful to parents who want information about programs for disabled infants and preschoolers. Focuses on helping families cope with the problems of raising children with special needs. A few sections are devoted to learning disabilities. Model family support services and programs for developing skills and attitude changes in families are also described.

Helping Children with Specific Learning Disabilities: A Practical Guide for Parents and Teachers, by Donald H. Painting, 1983, 196 pages. Prentice-Hall, Inc., Englewood Cliffs, NJ 07632, $6.95. For parents and professionals. Examines behavioral traits and underlying reasons for such specific learning disabilities as hyperactivity, inattention, and poor coordination. Suggestions for behavior management and a description of a model behavior management program are included. This model program is currently being used at a private school that provides special education and clinical services for children with learning disabilities.

How to Get Services by Being Assertive, by Charlotte Des Jardins, 1980, approximately 100 pages. Coordinating Council For Handicapped Children, 407 S. Dearborn, Room 680, Chicago, IL 60605, $5.00 plus $1.00 postage and handling. Advises parents on how to get services for their handicapped children. Contains assertiveness training exercises. Offers suggestions for avoiding the runaround, dealing with intimidation, being effective at IEP (Individualized Education Plan) meetings, gaining access to school records, preparing for a due process hearing, public speaking, and using politicians and the press to obtain services.

How to Organize an Effective Parent/Advocacy Group and Move Bureaucracies, by Charlotte Des Jardins, 1980, approximately 130 pages. Coordinating Council for Handicapped Children, 407 S. Dearborn, Room 680, Chicago, IL 60605, $5.00 plus $1.00 postage and handling. A handbook for parents that covers the basics in organizing a parent/advocacy group including suggestions for choosing effective leaders, recruiting volunteers, lobbying, and getting public funds. A chapter on press coverage explains how to write press releases, hold news conferences, and gain publicity for your cause.

How to Raise Your Child to Be A Winner, by Gene R. Hawes, Helen Ginandes Weiss, and Martin S. Weiss, 1980, 317 pages. Published by Rawson, Wade Publishers, Inc. Distributed by Treehouse Associates, P.O. Box 1992, Avon, CO 81620, $8.30. A parent's guide to preparing children to be successful, self-reliant adults. The chapter devoted to children with learning disabilities includes a list of learning skills that may be delayed in children with dyslexia, a checklist of learning disability symptoms, and explanations of terms frequently used in Individualized Education Plans (IEPs). Other relevant chapters cover testing, school readiness activities, proper programming and placement, alternative learning methods, secondary programs that prepare students for top colleges and careers, and alternatives to college.

How to Write an I.E.P., by John Arena, 1978, 95 pages. Academic Therapy Publications, 20 Commercial Boulevard, Novato, CA 94947, $4.00 plus $1.50 postage and handling. An easy to understand resource for parents who want to be involved in the development of their child's IEP (Individualized Education Plan). The educator and parent are taken through the process of writing, implementing, and evaluating an IEP. One chapter is devoted specifically to learning disabilities. Contains a checklist of the required parts of the IEP, sample forms, and worksheets for IEP preparation. Outlines the educational rights of handicapped children and their parents.

Learning Disabilities: A Family Affair, by Betty B. Osman, 1979, 224 pages. Warner Books, Inc., Box 690, New York, NY 10019, $3.50 plus $1.00 postage and handling. For parents. Offers understanding and advice on helping children cope with learning disabilities at home and in school. Suggestions for dealing with home problems include setting aside a special time each day for extra help or just talking, establishing routines for homework, TV, and meals, and establishing basic rules for discipline. Suggestions for dealing with school problems include teaching specific study skills and leading younger children through the process of completing assignments the first few times. Osman's suggestions and techniques are intended to build confidence and to ease frustration.

Learning Disabilities: Basic Concepts, Assessment Practices, and Instructional Strategies, by Patricia I. Myers and Donald D. Hammill, 1982, 481 pages. Pro-Ed, 5341 Industrial Oaks Boulevard, Austin, TX 78735, $19.00. For professionals. Describes the major types of learning disabilities including spoken and written language, arithmetic, and reasoning. Discusses and critiques remedial and habilitative methods.

Learning Disabilities Explained, by Stanley S. Lamm and Martin L. Fisch, 1982, 247 pages. Doubleday and Company, Inc., 501 Franklin Avenue, Garden City, NY 11530, $16.95 prepaid. For parents and professionals. Describes the approach used to treat children with learning disabilities at the Lamm Institute. Information of general interest is also included. Answers frequently asked questions such as "Who is considered a learning disabled child?" "What does IQ really mean?" and "Is medication a recognized way to treat hyperactivity?" Also provides an explanation of the brain's role in learning disabilities.

Learning Disabilities: Theories, Diagnosis, and Teaching Strategies, by Janet W. Lerner, 1985, approximately 540 pages. Houghton Mifflin Company, College Division, Wayside Road, Burlington, MA 01803, $28.95 plus $1.50 postage and handling. Study guide $10.95 plus $1.50 postage and handling. For professionals. Provides an overview of the field of learning disabilities including definitions, history, and the role of the medical profession. Also covers assessment, teaching strategies, and educational services required by law. The special needs of preschoolers and adolescents are discussed.

Learning Disabilities: The Struggle from Adolescence toward Adulthood, by William M. Cruickshank, William C. Morse, and Jeannie S. Johns, 1980, 285 pages. Syracuse University Press, 1600 Jamesville Avenue, Syracuse, NY

13210, $9.95. For educators and parents. Part I provides theoretical background on the learning disabled adolescent. Part II contains interviews with five learning disabled youths who have had varying degrees of success with personal and community adjustment. Part III describes a basic approach to teaching the learning disabled adolescent reading, organization, study skills, and written language.

The Learning Disabled Child: Ways Parents Can Help, by Suzanne H. Stevens, 1980, 196 pages. John F. Blair, Publisher, 1406 Plaza Drive, S.W., Winston-Salem, NC 27103, $11.95 hardcover; $6.95 paperback. Provides explanations and advice intended to help parents become well-informed and assertive. Lists typical learning disability symptoms and describes the frequency that each occurs. Suggests adjustments that should and should not be made for learning disabled children at school and at home.

Learning-Disabled/Gifted Children: Identification and Programming, edited by Lynn H. Fox, Linda Brody, and Dianne Tobin, 1983, 297 pages. University Park Press, 300 N. Charles Street, Baltimore, MD 21201, $23.00. For educators. Provides guidelines for identifying and teaching the learning disabled/gifted child. Covers adaptive teaching methods and techniques, including computers. Discusses model educational programs, the influence of parents, and the future for research and practice. The text is an outgrowth of a research study at Johns Hopkins University by experts in the fields of learning disabilities and giftedness.

Legal Rights Primer for the Handicapped: In and Out of the Classroom, by Joseph Roberts and Bonnie Hawk, 1980, 141 pages. Academic Therapy Publications, 20 Commercial Boulevard, Novato, CA 94947, $6.00 plus $1.50 postage and handling. An easy to understand guide to the legal rights of the handicapped for families, counselors and other advocates. Covers education, work, marriage, parenthood, and socialization. Discusses landmark cases and explains legal terminology. Appendix includes text of the Education for All Handicapped Children Act (P.L. 94-142) and suggestions on "How to Move Bureaucracies."

The Misunderstood Child: A Guide for Parents of Learning Disabled Children, by Larry B. Silver, 1984, 214 pages. McGraw-Hill Book Company, 1221 Avenue of the Americas, New York, NY 10020, $14.95. Designed to make parents "informed consumers" and "assertive advocates" for their learning disabled children. Provides background information on learning disabilities, including definitions and causes. Describes normal psychological, emotional, and social development and the special developmental problems of learning disabled children. Explains diagnosis and treatment processes and discusses controversial therapies. Also helpful is a review of important aspects of P.L. 94-142, the Education for All Handicapped Children Act.

No Easy Answers: The Learning Disabled Child, by Sally L. Smith, 1980. Bantam Books, Inc., 414 E. Golf Road, Des Plaines, IL 60016, $3.95 plus $1.25 postage and handling. For parents. Describes the learning problems, behavior, and development of learning disabled children. Offers suggestions to parents on what they can do to help their LD children. Discusses the problem of socialization in adolescents and lists typical academic problems of children. Also of value is a short article on the constructive use of television.

No One to Play With: The Social Side of Learning Disabilities, by Betty B. Osman, 1982, 170 pages. Random House, Inc., 201 E. 50th Street, New York, NY 10022, $12.50. For parents and professionals. Offers practical advice on coping with the social aspects of learning disabilities. Suggestions range from how to deal with immaturity to how to use group situations as practice for social relations. Discusses the special problems of siblings and learning disabled adolescents and adults. Provides insight into the difficulties that a crisis such as divorce or death causes for the learning disabled child. Also includes techniques for dealing with crankiness, temper, and other behavior problems.

Parents' Guide to "Teacherese": A Glossary of Special Education Terms, by Nancy O. Wilson, 1981, 96 pages. Special Child Publications, P.O. Box 33548, Seattle, WA 98133, $7.50 plus $1.00 postage and handling. A glossary for parents. Explains more than 600 terms either related to developmental disabilities, or frequently used in parent-professional communications.

The Powerful Parent: A Child Advocacy Handbook, by David M. Gottesman, 1982, 169 pages. Appleton-Century-Crofts, 25 Van Zant Street, East Norwalk, CT 06855, $6.95. Designed to teach parents to be advocates for their children. Covers the educational, legal, physical, and psychological needs of children. Outlines how to evaluate professionals including teachers/schools, doctors, lawyers, and therapists. Provides general information on where and how to obtain services.

Smart But Feeling Dumb, by Harold N. Levinson, 1984, 236 pages. Warner Books, Inc., 666 Fifth Avenue, New York, NY 10103, $18.50. A layman's guide to Levinson's theories on the diagnosis and treatment of dyslexia. Comprised largely of case histories that support his assertion that dyslexia is caused by a dysfunction of the inner ear. He contends that dyslexia can be treated with anti-motion-sickness and related medications. Also available on audio cassette.

Something's Wrong With My Child, by Milton Brutten, Sylvia Richardson, and Charles Mangel, 1979, 248 pages. Harcourt Brace Jovanovich, Inc. Bookstore, 1255 "A" Street, San Diego, CA 92101, $6.95. For parents. Explains how to recognize a child with learning disabilities. Covers movement and perceptual development, language and thought development, emotional and social development, activity levels, and attention span. Tells how and where to get help and describes what learning disabilities professionals do.

Your Child Can Win, by Joan Noyes and Norma Macneill, 1983, 257 pages. William Morrow and Company, Inc., Six Henderson Drive, West Caldwell, NJ 07006, $11.95. For parents. A major section describes home games to improve visual and auditory disabilities, strengthen language skills, and improve spatial concepts, motor skills, and tactile senses. The focus of each activity is stated and detailed directions given. Also lists commercial games that Noyes and Macneill found useful with learning disabled children.

Your Child's Education: A School Guide for Parents, by Mark Wolraich, Landis Fick, and Nicholas Karagan, 1984, 163 pages. Charles C Thomas, Publisher, 2600 S. First Street, Springfield, IL 62717, $14.75 plus $2.25 postage and handling. Designed to make parents effective advocates for their children. One section is devoted to learning disabilities. Contains a historical overview of public education, suggestions for getting the most information out of parent-teacher conferences, and guidelines for selecting an appropriate preschool program. Explains the roles of school personnel, curriculum, special services, P.L. 94-142, and assessment tests.

DIRECTORIES AND GUIDES

Campus Access for Learning Disabled Students: A Handbook for a Successful Postsecondary Education, by Barbara Scheiber and Jeanne Talpers, 1985, 100 pages. Closer Look/Parents' Campaign for Handicapped Children and Youth, 1201 16th Street, N.W., Washington, DC 20036, $17.95. For parents and professionals. Covers selection of an appropriate college or other postsecondary program, the admissions process, course accommodations and support services, and tips on personal adjustment.

The Directory for Exceptional Children, Tenth Edition, 1983-84, 1382 pages. Porter Sargent Publishers, Inc., 11 Beacon Street, Boston, MA 02108, $40 plus $1.50 postage and handling. For parents and professionals. A comprehensive guide to programs for children with a wide range of special needs. More than 140 academic programs for the learning disabled are listed. Program descriptions include information on costs, enrollment, staff, and special programs and services.

Directory of College Facilities and Services for the Handicapped, edited by Charles S. McGeough, Barbara Jungjohan, and James L. Thomas, 1983, 373 pages. The Oryx Press, 2214 N. Central at Encanto, Phoenix, AZ 85004, $80.00 prepaid. For parents and professionals. Lists institutions in the U.S., Canada, Pacific Islands, Puerto Rico, and the Virgin Islands with facilities and services for the handicapped, including the learning disabled.

Directory of Facilities and Services for the Learning Disabled, 11th Edition, 1985-86, 96 pages. Academic Therapy Publications, 20 Commercial Boulevard, Novato, CA 94947-6191, free, $1.50 for postage. For parents and professionals. Lists information on more than 500 reading clinics, remedial centers, and day and residential schools in the United States and Canada. Includes information on the nature of the facility, age and grade levels served, and types of services offered. Updated every two years.

A Directory of Summer Camps for Children with Learning Disabilities, 1985, 60 pages. ACLD, Inc., 4156 Library Road, Pittsburgh, PA 15234, $2.00 plus $1.00 postage. For parents. Lists camps and other summer programs throughout the United States. Brief descriptions of each program and the services provided are included. Updated annually.

Finding A School For Your Child in San Francisco and Marin, by Vera Obermeyer and Suzanne Warren, 1984, 105 pages. The Bookplate, 2080 Chestnut (at Steiner), San Francisco, CA 94123, $12.95 plus $1.00 postage and handling. For parents and professionals. A guide to private, parochial, and alternative public schools in San Francisco and Marin County. One section is devoted to special education schools. Also contains guidelines for evaluating schools, including a list of questions to ask school personnel.

Guide to College Programs for Learning Disabled Students, 1985, scheduled for publication September, 1985, approximately 24 pages. National Association of College Admissions Counselors, 9933 Lawler Avenue, Suite 500, Skokie, IL 60077, $5.00 plus $1.00 postage. For parents and learning disabled adults. Describes college and university programs for the learning disabled. A detailed description of each college's support program is included. A quick reference checklist summarizes the services offered at all the colleges.

A Guide to Colleges for Learning Disabled Students, edited by Mary Ann Liscio, 1984, 489 pages. Academic Press, Inc., 6277 Sea Harbor Drive, Orlando, FL 32887, $24.95 prepaid. For parents, learning disabled adults, and professionals. Lists two and four-year accredited U.S. colleges that offer special services for the learning disabled. Information provided in listings includes special facilities and services, contact person, admissions requirements, school size, tuition, and majors offered. Also included is a list of questions to ask college personnel when inquiring about a program.

Guide to Summer Camps and Summer Schools, 23rd edition, 1983, 476 pages. Porter Sargent Publishers, Inc., 11 Beacon Street, Boston, MA 02108, $15.00 paperback; $20.00 hardcover plus $1.50 postage and handling. For parents and professionals. Describes over 1100 summer camp and academic programs in the U.S. and Canada. Contains a section on programs for the learning disabled. Classified lists provide easy reference to programs that emphasize computer education, tutoring, math, science, remedial work, and study skills.

The Handbook of Private Schools, 65th edition, 1984, 1496 pages. Porter Sargent Publishers, Inc., 11 Beacon Street, Boston, MA 02108, $35.00 plus $1.50 postage and handling. For parents and professionals. Lists 1,900 U.S. elementary and secondary boarding and day schools. One section covers schools for the "underachiever." Provides information on curriculum, enrollment, facilities, and fees. A directory of summer academic programs and camps and a list of schools that offer a postgraduate year are also included.

Handbook of Trade and Technical Careers and Training 1984-85, 74 pages. National Association of Trade and Technical Schools, 2251 Wisconsin Avenue, N.W. Washington, DC 20007, free. A useful resource for anyone interested in a trade or technical career, including the learning disabled. Lists 98 careers that can be learned in two years or less and schools that provide the training. Suggestions on how to choose a career are included.

Lovejoy's College Guide for the Learning Disabled, by Charles T. Straughn and Marvelle S. Colby, 1985, 192 pages. Simon and Schuster Inc., 1230 Avenue of the Americas, New York, NY 10020, $9.95. For students, parents, and professionals. Profiles some 380 colleges and universities with programs for students with learning disabilities. Includes admissions criteria, support services, degrees offered, and tuition and other costs.

The National Association of Private Schools for Exceptional Children 1985 Membership Directory, scheduled for publication June, 1985, approximately 400 pages. NAPSEC, 2021 "K" Street, N.W., Suite 315, Washington, DC 20006, $16.00. For parents. Lists schools that are members of the National Association of Private Schools for Exceptional Children (NAPSEC). Member schools subscribe to a code of ethics. A table provides easy reference to schools that serve the learning disabled. Each listing includes information about areas of need served, types of services offered, and admission procedures.

A National Directory of Four Year Colleges, Two Year Colleges and Post High School Training Programs for Young People with Learning Disabilities, 1984, approximately 94 pages. Partners in Publishing, P.O. Box 50347, Tulsa, OK 74150, $15.95 plus $1.00 postage. For parents and learning disabled adults. Lists and describes nearly 200 colleges, universities, technical/vocational schools, and other facilities that provide services for learning disabled students.

1984-1985 Resource Guide to Organizations Concerned with Developmental Handicaps, prepared by the American Association of University Affiliated Programs for Persons with Developmental Disabilities, 186 pages. AAUAP, 8605 Cameron Street, Suite 406, Silver Spring, MD 20910, free. For parents and professionals. Learning disability is one of the developmental disabilities covered. Lists university affiliated programs including research centers and hospitals, government agencies and programs, advocates, and interest groups.

Peterson's Guide to Colleges with Programs for Learning-Disabled Students, edited by Charles T. Mangrum II and Stephen S. Strichart, scheduled for publication in August, 1985, approximately 400 pages. Peterson's Guides, 166 Bunn Drive, P.O. Box 2123, Princeton, NJ 08540, $13.95. Provides information about LD programs at some 300 four-year colleges and universities. Information includes special fees, staff, admissions requirements, housing, auxiliary aids and services, counseling, academic advisement, testing, and support services such as tutoring, basic skills remediation, and special courses. Also offers guidelines and a checklist for selecting a college program.

Schooling for the Learning Disabled: A Selective Guide to LD Programs in Elementary and Secondary Schools Throughout the United States, compiled and edited by Raegene B. Pernecke and Sara M. Shreiner, 1983, 173 pages. SMS Publishing Corporation, P.O. Box 2276, Glenview IL 60025, $9.95 plus $1.05 postage. For parents. Provides comprehensive descriptions of 50 school programs for the learning disabled. Each program was evaluated during on-site visits by a trained evaluation team. Evaluators observed classes, appraised special interest and physical education programs, and inspected the physical setup of each facility.

The SpecialWare Directory: A Guide to Software Sources for Special Education, by LINC Associates, Inc., 1983, 97 pages. LINC Associates, Inc., 46 Arden Road, Columbus, OH, 43214, $13.95. For parents or professionals. A guide to computer software for the handicapped, including the learning disabled.

What Do You Do After High School?, by Regina Skyer and Gil Skyer, 1982, 357 pages plus 93 page 1984-85 update. Skyer Consultation Inc., P.O. Box 121, Rockaway Park, NY 11694, $29.95. For parents and learning disabled adults. A guide to residential, vocational, social, and college programs for adolescents and adults with learning disabilities. Six types of post high school programs are covered: vocational and skills training, residential/independent living, diagnostic tutoring and counseling, college, recreation and summer programs, and organizations and networking.

PAMPHLETS, BROCHURES, AND BOOKLETS

Academic Therapy Publications Parent Brochures, Academic Therapy Publications, 20 Commercial Boulevard, Novato, CA 94947-6191. Sampler Set 1 (twelve titles) for parents of elementary school children, $2.00. Sampler Set 2 (seven titles) for parents of teen-aged school children, $1.50. Sampler Set 3 (five titles) for parents of children of any age, $1.00. Individual titles available in bulk at $3.00 per 50 copies. For parents. Brief, informative brochures that offer suggestions for helping children with special learning needs. Titles in Set 1 include "Preparing for a School Conference on Your Child," and "Helping Your Young Child with Socialization." Titles in Set 2 include "Helping Your Child with General Study Tips," and "Helping Your Child Make Career Decisions." Set 3 includes "Parent's Rights Under Public Law 94-142" and "How to Get Help for Your LD Child."

Attention Deficit Disorders, by Larry B. Silver, M.D., 1980, 10 pages. Available from CIBA, 556 Morris Avenue, Summit, NJ 07091, free on written request. May be available from your physician or pediatrician. For parents. An overview of attention deficit disorders (ADD), a term frequently used by physicians to describe the academic and behavioral problems of learning disabled children. Describes specific problems experienced by children with ADD, such as visual perception and language disabilities. Offers suggestions on what parents can do to help.

ERIC Digests, ERIC Clearinghouse on Handicapped and Gifted Children, Council for Exceptional Children, 1920 Association Drive, Reston, VA 22091, free. For parents. One-page information sheets on each of several aspects of learning disabilities. Titles include "Learning Disabilities," "Postsecondary Options for Learning Disabled Students," and "Serving the LD Student in a Vocational Education Classroom."

Fact Sheets from CACLD, 20 N. Main Street, South Norwalk, CT 06854, prices vary. Titles include "Do's and Don'ts in Managing Children with Learning Disabilities," "Identifying Characteristics of the Learning Disabled Adolescent," "Questions for Parents to Ask Concerning Services for the Child with a Learning Disability," and "Suggested Questions to Ask Admissions Offices of Colleges Under Consideration by the LD Applicant." A list of summer camps in the eastern United States is also available.

Fact Sheets from HEATH Resource Center, One Dupont Circle, N.W., Suite 670, Washington, DC 20036, free. For parents and learning disabled adults. Titles include "Learning Disabled Adults in Postsecondary Education," "Vocational Rehabilitation Services: A Postsecondary Student Consumer's Guide," and "Measuring Student Progress in the Classroom: A Guide to Testing and Evaluating Progress of Students with Disabilities."

Fact Sheets from National Information Center for Handicapped Children and Youth (NICHCY), P.O. Box 1492, Washington, DC 20013, free. For parents and professionals. Titles include "Parent Groups: Parents Helping Parents" and "The Teacher/Parent Relationship." Other fact sheets provide concise definitions of specific disabilities, bibliographies, and lists of resources.

A Home-School Cookbook: Parents and Teachers Guide to Learning Disabilities, by Helen Ginandes Weiss and Martin S. Weiss, 1985, 40 pages. Treehouse Associates, P.O. Box 1992, Avon, CO 81620, $4.50. Booklet contains home teaching guidelines and activities for parents of learning disabled children. Also of use to teachers or teacher aides. Includes a list of LD symptoms and causes, suggestions for working with the learning disabled, and a checklist on learning styles. One chapter describes home tasks and games to help remediate specific problem areas.

I Can Jump the Rainbow, by Barbara Scheiber, 1982, 20 pages. Published by Closer Look/Parents' Campaign for Handicapped Children and Youth, 1201 16th Street, N.W., Washington, DC 20036, $3.00. Provides general background information about learning disabilities. Developed by the Pennsylvania Federation of Women's Clubs and intended for distribution to parent groups and community organizations.

Know Your Rights and Use Them, by Barbara Scheiber, 1981, 8 pages. Published by Closer Look/Parents' Campaign for Handicapped Children and Youth, 1201 16th Street, N.W., Washington, DC 20036, $4.00. For parents. A step-by-step guide to obtaining appropriate school services for handicapped children under the provisions of P.L. 94-142. A checklist of do's and don'ts for parents to use when planning their child's education is also included.

Orton Dyslexia Society Information Packet, the Orton Dyslexia Society, 724 York Road, Baltimore, MD 21204, $1.00. Pamphlets in the packet include "What is Dyslexia?," "Guidelines for Seeking Help," "Guidelines for Assessment of Reading, Writing, Spelling, and Written Expression," and "Guidelines for Reviewing and Understanding a Psychological and/or Educational Evaluation."

A Parent's Guide to Learning Disabilities, by Alice C. D'Antoni, Darrel G. Minifie, and Elsie R. Minifie, 1978, 63 pages. The Continental Press, Inc., 520 E. Bainbridge Street, Elizabethtown, PA 17022. Cost: one to four copies, $2.10 each plus postage; five or more copies, $1.50 each plus postage. For parents. An introductory booklet that uses illustrations and simple text to present an overview of learning disabilities. Offers suggestions, games, and activities for dealing with specific listening, speaking, seeing, moving, and behavior problems. Designed as a handout for parent groups and other organizations.

Research Reports from Institute for Research in Learning Disabilities, Coordinator of Research Dissemination, 313 Carruth-O'Leary Hall, The University of Kansas, Lawrence, KS 66045. Most reports and papers are $3.00 prepaid. For professionals. Describes studies conducted by, or under the auspices of, institute researchers. Titles include: "Behavioral Assessment of Occupational Skills of Learning Disabled Adolescents," "Teaching Job-Related Social Skills to Learning Disabled Adolescents," and "Major Research Findings of The University of Kansas Institute for Research in Learning Disabilities."

Steps to Independence for People with Learning Disabilities, by Dale Brown, 1980, 48 pages. Closer Look/Parents' Campaign for Handicapped Children and Youth, 1201 16th Street, N.W., Washington, DC 20036, $5.00. Written specifically for learning disabled adolescents and adults.

Describes the various aspects of living with learning disabilities, including locating diagnostic services, achieving independence, and dealing with family life, education, and employment problems. Hints for improving social skills and coping with specific disabilities are also included.

Taking the first step... to solving learning problems, ACLD, Inc., 4156 Library Road, Pittsburgh, PA 15234, $2.00. For parents. Provides an overview of learning disabilities. Includes definitions and checklists of symptoms and behaviors associated with learning disabilities, hyperactivity, and dyslexia. Also describes an Individualized Education Plan (IEP) and the procedures for a due process hearing.

Treehouse Reprint Series, by Martin S. Weiss and Helen Ginandes Weiss. Treehouse Associates, P.O. Box 1992, Avon, CO 81620, $2.75 each; two or more $2.25 each. For parents and professionals. Titles include "Survival Alternatives for the LD Adolescent," "Training Kids to Be Winners," "Education's Castaways: The Link between Learning Disabilities and Juvenile Delinquency," "Resource List for Life After High School," and "A Summary of the Orton-Gillingham Approach to Language."

MAGAZINES AND OTHER PERIODICALS

Academic Therapy, published five times per year by Academic Therapy Publications, 20 Commercial Boulevard, Novato, CA 94947-6191. Subscription: $15.00. Primarily for teachers and other professionals, but often contains articles useful to parents. Article selection based on whether the information contained can be put to immediate use by the reader. Topics include tips for building self-concept, hints for peer tutoring, and the use of parents in behavior management.

ACLD Newsbriefs, published five times per year by ACLD, Inc., 4156 Library Road, Pittsburgh, PA 15234. Subscription: $5.00. Newsletter for ACLD members, parents, and professionals. Contains information on recent developments in the field of learning disabilities, book reviews, announcements of upcoming conventions and other events, resources, and news of ACLD branches.

The Exceptional Parent, published eight times per year by Psy-Ed Corporation, 605 Commonwealth Avenue, Boston, MA 02215. Individual subscription: $16.00. For parents and professionals. Contains ideas and practical information about children and young adults with disabilities. Contains articles on parent-professional relationships, parent rights, family relationships, and managing financial resources. Much of the information applies to all disabilities. "Reader's Forum" and "What's Happening" sections allow exchange of ideas, information, and personal experiences.

Journal of Learning Disabilities, published ten times per year by The Professional Press, Inc., 11 E. Adams Street, Chicago, IL 60603. Individual subscription: $36.00. Primarily for professionals, but also of interest to parents. Contains articles on current research and practice, meeting announcements and reports, book and educational computer software reviews, opinion articles and interviews with important people in the field.

Journal of Reading, Writing and Learning Disabilities International, published quarterly by American Library Publishing Co., Inc., 275 Central Park, West, New York, NY 10024. Individual subscription: $55.00. For school administrators, teachers, and parents. Information on research, remedial techniques, and resources in the field of learning disabilities. Designed as a forum for new ideas and developments. Covers the latest topics including legal questions, diagnosis, and technology. Includes journal abstracts, book reviews, and a calendar of events. Lists audiovisual materials, special education software, clinics, and schools.

Newsletter, published approximately every two months by Learning Disabilities Consultants, P.O. Box 716, Bryn Mawr, PA 19010. Free. For parents, professionals, and learning disabled adults. Information is currently weighted towards the New York, New Jersey, and Pennsylvania areas, but contains some information on national events, programs, and organizations.

PIP College "HELPS" Newsletter published monthly by Partners in Publishing, P.O. Box 50347, Tulsa, OK 74150. Subscription: $25.00. Covers educational and social issues of interest to college students with learning disabilities. Lists information about schools and colleges that provide support services or special programs. A special feature spotlights successful learning disabled people.

The Pointer, published quarterly by Heldref Publications, 4000 Albemarle Street, N.W., Washington, DC 20016. Subscription: $30.00. A journal for educators, parents, and others concerned about students with special needs, including the learning disabled. Articles are written by teachers, teacher educators, and parents, and are based on school and home experiences.

Their World, published annually by the Foundation for Children with Learning Disabilities (FCLD), 99 Park Avenue, New York, NY 10016,

$2.00. For parents and professionals. Contains real-life stories about how families cope with learning disabled children. Includes practical tips, hints, and suggestions. Describes innovative support programs in sports, recreation/summer camps, and cultural institutions. Articles are written by people with learning disabilities or professionals who work with LD children.

Note: In 1985, three manuals funded by grants from the Foundation for Children with Learning Disabilities will become available to assist advocacy attorneys, juvenile and family court judges, and police and probation officers recognize and help learning disabled youth at risk in the juvenile justice system. Information on how to obtain these manuals is available from:

American Bar Association, Child Advocacy and Protection Center, 1800 "M" Street, Washington, DC 20036. Contact: Matthew Bogin. Telephone: (202) 331-2250.

National Council of Juvenile and Family Court Judges, P.O. Box 8978, 900 W. First Street, Reno, NV 89507. Contact: James Toner. Telephone: (702) 784-6012.

Research and Development Training Institute, Inc., P.O. Box 15112, Phoenix, AZ 85060. Contact: Dorothy Crawford. Telephone: (602) 956-8334.

FCLD, through a grant to the American Library Association (ALA) has initiated a national effort to make local public libraries resource centers for information and programs that assist parents and teachers who work with learning disabled children. For more information, librarians, parents, and teachers can contact:

American Library Association, Division of Services to Children, 50 E. Huron Street, Chicago, IL 60611. Telephone: (312) 944-6780.

A Dictionary of LD Terms

The words, terms, acronyms, and abbreviations defined in this dictionary are frequently used in parent-professional communications and in a wide range of material related to learning disabilities. Words or terms printed in *boldface italics* are separately defined.

ACLD—Association for Children and Adults with Learning Disabilities; ACLD, Inc.

adaptive physical education—a special physical education program developed to fit the limits and disabilities of persons with handicaps.

agnosia—inability to recognize objects and/or events through the senses. There are several types of agnosia. A person with auditory agnosia does not recognize nonverbal sounds such as the ring of an alarm clock or a siren. A person with auditory-verbal agnosia is unable to understand spoken words. A person with tactile agnosia cannot recognize objects by touch. A person with visual agnosia cannot recognize people, places, or objects by sight.

amphetamines—a group of drugs used to stimulate the *cerebral cortex* of the brain. Sometimes used to treat *hyperactivity*. (See also *Dexedrine* and *Ritalin*.)

anomia—inability to recall the names of people, places, or objects.

aphasia—inability to express oneself through speech, writing, or signs, or to comprehend written or spoken language. Individuals with aphasia may know what they want to say but are unable to say it.

apraxia—inability to do *fine motor* acts such as drawing shapes and figures or copying words and letters. A person with apraxia cannot produce and sequence the movements necessary to perform these kinds of tasks.

attention deficit disorders (ADD)—a term frequently used by physicians to describe the academic and behavioral problems of children with *learning* *disabilities*. Formerly called *minimal brain dysfunction* or hyperkinetic *syndrome*.

attention span—the length of time an individual can concentrate on a task without being distracted or losing interest. (See also *distractibility*.)

auditory discrimination—the ability to hear similarities and differences in sounds. For example, to recognize the difference in sound between *p* and *b* or *pail* and *bail*.

auditory memory—the ability to remember sounds, syllables, and words.

auditory perception—the ability to interpret and understand what is heard. Some learning disabled persons cannot differentiate between similar sounds or pick out one specific sound from several other sounds.

behavior modification—a technique intended to change behavior by rewarding desirable actions and ignoring or "negatively rewarding" undesirable actions.

binocular fusion—the blending of separate images from each eye into a single meaningful image.

catastrophic reaction—extreme terror, grief, frustration, or anger without apparent cause. May be triggered by changes in routine, unexpected events, or overstimulation. Children reacting in this manner may throw or break things, scream uncontrollably, or burst into tears.

CEC—Council for Exceptional Children.

central nervous system (CNS)—the brain and spinal cord.

cerebral cortex—the outer layer of the brain; controls thinking, feeling, and voluntary movement.

CNS—See *central nervous system*.

cognitive style—a person's typical approach to learning activities and problem solving. For example, some people carefully analyze each task, deciding what must be done and in what order. Others react impulsively to situations.

COH—Committee on the Handicapped.

conceptualization—the process of forming a general idea from what is observed. For example, seeing apples, bananas, and oranges and recognizing that they are all fruit.

congenital—a condition existing at birth or before birth. Congenital does not imply that a condition is hereditary.

coordination—the harmonious functioning of muscles in the body to perform complex movements.

cross dominance—a condition in which the preferred eye, hand, or foot are not on the same side of the body. For example, a person may be right-footed and right-eyed but left-handed. Also called mixed dominance.

decoding—the process of getting meaning from written or spoken symbols.

developmental lag—a delay in some aspect of physical or mental development.

Dexedrine—trade name for one of several stimulant drugs often given to modify *hyperactivity* in children.

disinhibition—lack of restraint in responding to a situation. A child exhibiting disinhibition reacts impulsively and often inappropriately.

distractibility—the shifting of attention from the task at hand to sounds, sights, and other stimuli that normally occur in the environment.

due process—the application of law to ensure that an individual's rights are protected. When applied to children with *learning disabilities*, due process means that parents have the right to request a full review of any educational program developed for their child. A due process hearing may be requested to ensure that all requirements of *Public Law 94-142* have been met.

dysarthria—a disorder of the speech muscles that affects the ability to pronounce words.

dyscalculia—inability to understand or use mathematical symbols or functions. A child with dyscalculia may be able to read and write but be unable to perform mathematical calculations.

dysfunction—any disturbance or impairment in the normal functioning of an organ or body part.

dysgraphia—inability to produce legible handwriting.

dyslexia—impairment of the ability to read. The impairment may be due to *learning disabilities*, emotional or developmental problems, or other factors. A dyslexic sees printed words upside down, reversed, blurred, backwards, or otherwise distorted. Some authorities feel that the term is misused and reading problems must be described more specifically.

early intervention program—a program specially designed to assist developmentally disabled infants and preschool children. The purpose of this type of program is to help prevent problems as the child matures.

electroencephalogram (EEG)—a graphic recording of electrical currents developed in the *cerebral cortex* during brain functioning. Sometimes called a "brain wave test." A machine called an electroencephalograph records the pattern of these electrical currents on paper.

encoding—the process of changing oral language into written symbols.

etiology—the study of the cause or origin of a condition or disease.

expressive language—communication through writing, speaking, and/or gestures.

eye-hand coordination—the ability of the eyes and hands to work together to complete a task. Examples are drawing and writing.

FCLD—Foundation for Children with Learning Disabilities.

figure-ground discrimination—the ability to sort out important information from the surrounding environment. For example, hearing a teacher's voice while ignoring other classroom noises.

fine motor—the use of small muscles for precision tasks such as writing, tying bows, or zipping a zipper.

gross motor—the use of large muscles for activities requiring strength and balance. Examples are walking, running, and jumping.

handicapped—any person with any physical and/or mental disability who has difficulty in doing certain tasks such as walking, seeing, hearing, speaking, learning, or working. Federal law defines handicapped children as those who are "mentally retarded, hard of hearing, deaf, speech impaired, visually handicapped, seriously emotionally disturbed, orthopedically impaired, other health impaired, blind, multihandicapped, or as having specific *learning disabilities*" and who require special educational services because of these disabilities.

hyperactivity (or hyperkinesis)—disorganized and disruptive behavior characterized by constant and excessive movement. A hyperactive child usually has difficulty sticking to one task for an extended period and may react more intensely to a situation than a normal child.

IEP—See *Individualized Education Plan*.

impulsivity—reacting to a situation without considering the consequences.

Individualized Education Plan (IEP)—a written educational prescription developed by a school for each *handicapped* or learning disabled child. Sometimes called an Individualized Education Program. School districts are required by law to develop these plans. An IEP must contain:

—the child's present levels of educational performance.
—annual and short-term educational goals.
—the specific *special education* program and related services that will be provided to the child.
—the extent to which the child will participate in regular education program with non-handicapped children.
—a statement of when services will begin and how long they will last.
—provisions for evaluating the effectiveness of the program and the student's performance. This evaluation must occur at least once a year.

IQ—intelligence quotient. The ratio between a person's chronological age (measured in years) and mental age (as measured by an intelligence test), multiplied by 100.

kinesthetic—pertaining to the muscles.

kinesthetic method—a way of teaching words by using the muscles. For example, a student might trace the outline of a word with a finger while looking at the word and saying the word aloud.

laterality—the tendency to use the hand, foot, eye, and ear on a particular side of the body. For example, many people use their right hand when eating and their right foot when kicking.

LD—learning disability, learning disabled, *learning disabilities*.

LEA—local education agency.

learning disabilities (LD)—disorders of the basic psychological processes that affect the way a child learns. Many children with learning disabilities have average or above average intelligence. Learning disabilities may cause difficulties in listening, thinking, talking, reading, writing, spelling, or arithmetic. Included are *perceptual handicaps*, *dyslexia*, and developmental *aphasia*. Excluded are learning difficulties caused by visual, hearing, or motor handicaps, mental retardation, emotional disturbances, or environmental disadvantage.

learning disorder—damage or impairment to the nervous system that causes a learning disability.

learning style—the channels through which a person best understands and retains learning. All individuals learn best through one or more channels: visual, auditory, motor, or a combination of these.

lesion—abnormal change in body tissue due to injury or disease.

mainstreaming—the practice of placing *handicapped* children with special educational needs into regular classrooms.

maturation lag—delayed maturity in one or several skills or areas of development.

milieu therapy—a clinical technique designed to control a child's environment and minimize conflicting and confusing information.

minimal brain dysfunction (MBD)—a broad and unspecific term formerly used to describe *learning disabilities*.

mixed dominance—See *cross dominance*.

modality—the sensory channel used to acquire information. Visual, auditory, *tactile*, *kinesthetic*, olfactory (odors), and gustatory (taste) are the most common modalities.

multidisciplinary team—in education, a group made up of a child's classroom teacher and several educational specialists that evaluates the child's handicap and prepares an *Individualized Education Plan* for the child.

multisensory—involving most or all of the senses.

neurological examination—testing of the sensory or motor responses to determine if there is impairment of the nervous system.

norm-referenced test—See *standardized test*.

ombudsman—an official appointed to investigate complaints and speak for individuals with grievances.

organicity—a disorder of the *central nervous system*; brain damage.

Orton-Gillingham approach—a method for teaching individuals with *learning disabilities*. The technique, devised by Dr. Samuel Orton, Anna Gillingham, and Bessie Stillman, stresses a *multisensory* approach to learning.

perceptual handicap—an inability to process or interpret sensory information.

perceptual-motor—muscle activity resulting from information received through the senses.

perseveration—the repeating of words, motions, or tasks. A child who perseverates often has difficulty shifting to a new task and continues working on an old task long after classmates have stopped.

phonics—a method of teaching reading and spelling that stresses symbol-sound relationships.

Public Law (P.L.) 94-142—the federal Education for All Handicapped Children Act that became law in 1975. P.L. 94-142 requires each state to provide free and appropriate public education to all *handicapped* children between the ages of 3 and 21. The law also requires that an *Individualized Education Plan* be prepared for each handicapped child, that parents must have access to their child's school records and are entitled to a *due process* hearing if they are dissatisfied with the educational plan.

Rehabilitation Act of 1973—the Civil Rights Act for the *Handicapped*. The act prohibits discrimination on the basis of physical or mental handicap in all federally-assisted programs. Section 504 of the act stipulates that handicapped people are entitled to:

—the same rights and benefits as non-handicapped applicants and employees.

—all medical services and medically-related instruction available to the public.

—participate in vocational rehabilitation, senior citizen activities, day care (for disabled children), or any other social service program receiving federal assistance on an equal basis with non-handicapped persons.

—an appropriate elementary and secondary education for physically or mentally handicapped children.

reversal—the tendency to reverse the position of letters, syllables, or words in reading or writing. For example, a child may write *b* for *d* or read *bat* for *tab*. See also *transposition*.

Ritalin—trade name for one of several stimulant drugs often given to modify *hyperactivity* in children.

SEA—state education agency.

self-concept—how a person feels and thinks about himself or herself. Sometimes called self-image.

sensorimotor—relationship between sensation and movement. Sometimes spelled sensory motor.

SLD—See *specific language disability*.

Slingerland method—a highly structured, *multisensory* teaching method designed for group instruction of persons with *learning disabilities*. Named for its developer, Beth Slingerland.

special education—instruction specifically designed for *handicapped* children.

specific language disability (SLD)—difficulty in some aspect of learning how to read and write.

standardized test—a test that compares a child's performance with the performance of a large group of similar children (usually children of the same age). Also called a *norm-referenced test*. *IQ* tests and most achievement tests are standardized.

structure—a calibrated, consistent use of rules, limits, and routines. The use of structure reassures a child with *learning disabilities* that the environment is somewhat predictable and stable.

syndrome—a set of symptoms that indicates a specific disorder.

tactile—having to do with the sense of touch.

transposition—changing the sequence of letters, syllables, or words when reading or writing. For example, reading *sing* as *sign* or *little red engine* as *red little engine*. See also *reversal*.

VAKT—acronym for visual, auditory, *kinesthetic*, *tactile*. A *multisensory* approach to teaching developed by Grace Fernald. A child might look at a word and say it out loud while tracing it in the air or on paper.

visual discrimination—the ability to perceive similarities and differences in shapes, colors, numbers, letters, and words.

visual memory—the ability to remember what is seen. For example, children with visual memory problems often have difficulty in developing a sight vocabulary.

visual-motor—related to the ability to integrate visual information with appropriate body movement.

visual perception—the ability to correctly interpret what is seen. For example, a child sees a triangle and identifies it as a triangle.

WISC-R—Wechsler Intelligence Scale for Children, Revised. A test measuring intelligence in the areas of language and performance. Often used to assess children who may need *special education*.

word attack skills—the ability to visually and phonetically analyze unfamiliar words.

Index

Index

ABCS Little Canyon School, 66
Abraham Baldwin Agricultural College, 149
Academic Achievement Center, 141
*Academics and Beyond: Volume 4, The Best
    of ACLD*, 366
Academic Therapy, 379
*Academic Therapy Publications Parent
    Brochures*, 376
Academy of Our Lady Learning Center, 159
Academy School, 153
Accotink Academy, 348
Achievement Center, The, 347
Achievement School, Inc., The, 286
ACLD, Inc., 5, 46
ACLD, Inc., Youth and Adult Section, 37
ACLD Learning Center, 299
ACLD Newsbriefs, 14, 379
ACT (American College Test), 27
Activity and Development Center, 310
Adams State College, 119
Adaptive Learning Center, 329
Adelphi University, 271
Adirondack Community College, 272
Adriel School, 294
Adult Programs and Services
    National Organizations and Services, 36-38
    State and Regional Programs and Services,
        38-44
Adventure Bound School, 345
Adventure Challenges, 318
Advocates for Children of New York, Inc., 257
Advocates for the Quiet Minority, Project
    LIFT (Living Independently for
    Tomorrow), 38
AFL-CIO Human Resources Development
    Institute, 37
Aiken Technical College, 322
Aims Community College, 120
Akron Reading and Speech Center, 298
ALABAMA, 63-64
Alabama A & M University, 63
ALASKA, 64-65
Albert Einstein College of Medicine, Yeshiva
    University, 278
Alcorn State University, 228
Aldar Academy, 84
Algonquin Reading Camp, 360
Allendale School, 162
Almansor Education Center, 74
Aloha Camps, 342
Alpha School, Dayton, OH, 293

Alpha School, Lakewood, NJ, 247
Alternative High School Program, Project
    Second Start, 242
Alternative School, 259
Amarillo College, 332
American Bar Association, Child Advocacy
    and Protection Center, 381
American College Test, see ACT
American International College, 208
American Library Association, Division of
    Services to Children, 381
American University, 134
Anastasi Family Counseling, 115
Anderson College, 172
Anderson School, The, 267
Andrus Children's Home, 284
Annals of Dyslexia, 49
Anson Technical College, 286
Antelope Valley Community College, 91
Antioch University, 313
Appalachian State University, 287
Apple Tree Learning Center, 124
Archild, Inc., 71
Archway School, 245
Arena School, 88
ARIZONA, 65-70
Arizona State University, 68
ARKANSAS, 70-73
Arkansas Children's Hospital, 72
Arkansas State University, 71
Armstrong State College, 149
Arrowhead West, Inc., 182
Art Academy of Cincinnati, 294
Asbury College, 184
Aseltine School, 85
Assessment, 16
Assessment and Resource Center, 115
Assessments Unlimited, 318
ASSETS School, 154
Assistance League School, 82
Association for Neurologically Impaired Brain
    Injured Children (ANIBIC), 281
Association for the Learning Disabled of the
    Genesee Valley (ALD), 257
Association on Handicapped Student Service
    Programs in Post-Secondary Education
    (AHSSPPE), The, 46
Astor Day Treatment Center, The, 265
Astor Learning Center, The, 283
Atlanta College of Art, 149
Atlanta Speech School, Inc., 146

Atlantic Conference on Learning Disabilities, 51
Atlantic County Association for Children and Adults with Learning Disabilities, 254
Atlantis Academy, 138
Attention Deficit Disorders, 376
Attic Reading Center, The, 115
Auburn University, 64
Augsburg College, 222
Aurora Education Center, 159
Austin Community College, 222
Austin Peay State University, 327
Aveyron Day Care Center, 326
Avila College, 232

Bacone College, 301
Bailin-Mann Associates, 282
Bakersfield College, 91
Ball State University, 172
Bancroft School, The, 247
Banyan School, The, 136
Barat College, 164
Barclay School, The, 146
Barnard College, 272
Barton County Community College, 180
Basic Language Kit, The: A Teaching-Tutoring Aid for Adolescents and Young Adults, 366
Bassett Army Community Hospital, 65
Bates College, 191
Bay Cove Adolescent Programs, 200
Bay de Noc Community College, 216
Bay Medical Center, 219
Beacon Therapeutic School, 159
Beaver College, 313
Becket Academy, 124
Beech Brook, 294
Beechwood Individualized Parent-Child Program, Inc., 131
Bee County College, 333
Bellarmine College, 184
Bellwether School, 231
Beloit College, 360
Benchmark School, 309
Benny Bronz Academy, The, 126
Bentley College, 209
Bergen Center for Child Development, Inc., 247
Berkshire Learning Center, 205
Bethel College, 222
Bethesda Hospital Association, 122
Beth Israel Medical Center, 279
Bethune-Cookman College, 141
Betty Jane Nursery School, 293
Beverly Center School, 79
Beyond High School: Alternatives for LD Adults, 25-45
Big Lakes Developmental Center, Inc., 182
Big Springs School, 84
Black Hills State College, 324
Bloomsburg University of Pennsylvania, 314
Bluefield State College, 356
Blue Ridge Community College, 348
Bodine School, The, 326

Boise State University, 156
Bond Street School, 85
Books and Other Materials, 366-381
Books on Tape, Inc., 55
Boston College, 209
Boston School Serving Deaf and Aphasic Students, 205
Boston University Medical Center-University Hospital, 212
Bowie Therapeutic Nursery Center, 193
Bowling Green State University, 294
Boys' Village School - Boys' Village Inc., 299
Bradford College, 209
Bradley University, 164
Brandeis University, 209
Brandon Hall School, 146
Brehm Preparatory School, 159
Brenau College, 149
Brescia College, 184
Brevard Community College, 142
Bridgeport Academy, 123
Brigham Young University, 339
Brislain Learning Center, 113
Brochures, 376-379
Brookfield Learning Center, 358
Brooklyn College of the City University of New York, 272
Brooklyn Community Counseling Center, 282
Broward Community College, 142
Brown University, 320
Brush Ranch School, 255
Buena Vista College, 177
Buford Academy, 346
Burbank Hospital, 212

Cabrillo Community College, 91
Calabasas Academy, The, 75
Caldwell College, 251
CALIFORNIA, 73-118
California Center for Educational Therapy, 118
California Lutheran College, 91
California State Polytechnic University-Pomona, 91
California State Polytechnic University-San Luis Obispo, 91
California State University-Chico, 92
California State University-Dominguez Hills, 92
California State University-Fresno, 92
California State University-Fullerton, 92
California State University-Hayward, 92
California State University-Long Beach, 92
California State University-Los Angeles, 93
California State University-Northridge, 93
California University of Pennsylvania, 314
California Vision and Learning Institute, 117
CALLED, Inc. (The College Association for Language, Learning, and Educational Disabilities), 47
Calvin College, 216
Camarillo Reading Clinic, 112
Cambridge Montessori School, 201
Cameron University, 301

Camp Algonquin, 163
Camp Allen, Inc., 243
Camp Anna Behrens, 215
Camp Bendito, 190
Camp Betashire, 312
Camp Bluesprings, 149
Camp Buckskin, 221
Camp Can Do, 313
Camp Choconut, 312
Camp Courage, 221
Camp Fairlee Manor, 196
Camp Frank Rand, 255
Camp Green Shores, 184
Camp Happy Hollow, Inc., 215
Camp Huntington, 270
Camp Ikhananchi, 63
Camp Ketcha Day Camp, 190
Camp Kingsmont, 208
Camp Kysoc, 184
Camp Lakeland, 269
Camp Lee Mar, 313
Camp Linden, 215
Camp Mary Mac, 154
Camp Mishemokwa, 286
Camp Mitigwa, 176
Camp Niobe, 214
Camp Niwana, 353
Camp Northwood, 270
Camp Nuhop, Inc., 294
Camp NYABIC, 269
Camp Onanda, 269
Camp Radalbek, Inc., 269
Camp Ramah, Conover, WI, 360
Camp Ramah, Ojai, CA, 90
Camp Sacajawea, 176
Camp Shalom, 127
Camp Stuther, 176
Camp Tautona, 90
Camp Tonuco, 256
Camp Triangle, 270
Camp Twin Pines, 269
Campus Access Kit for Learning Disabled
    Students: A Handbook for a Successful
    Postsecondary Education, 372
Camp Wagon Wheel, 332
Camp Wahanaha, 164
Cañada College, 93
Canadian Association for Children and Adults
    with Learning Disabilities (CACLD), 50
Canadian Organizations Concerned with
    Learning Disabilities, 50-51
Canisius College, 272
Cantwell Academy, Inc., 138
Canyon Verde School, 77
Capistrano by the Sea Hospital, 110
Cardinal Glennon Memorial Hospital for
    Children, 235
Cardinal Stritch College, 360
Career Development Institute, 40
Carl Albert Junior College, 301
Carl M. Walton Center for Independent
    Living, 281
Carroll-Hall School, 199
Carroll School, The, 203

Carteret Technical College, 287
Cary Medical Center, 192
CASOLS: California School of Learning
    Systems, 87
Castle School, 201
Castleton State College, 342
Catholic Children's Home, 158
Catonsville Community College, 196
C.B. King Memorial School, 71
CEC Information Center, 51
Cedar Valley College, 333
Cedu School, 84
Center Academy
    Pinellas Park, 139
    St. Petersburg, 140
    Tampa, 141
Center for Alternative Education, 200
Center for Dyslexia, 351
Center for Education, 77
Center for Individualized Training and
    Education, Inc., 319
Center for Neurodevelopmental Studies, Inc.,
    69
Center for Prevention of Learning Difficulties,
    114
Center for Teaching/Learning of Mathematics,
    213
Center for Unique Learners, 198
Center School, The, Chevy Chase, MD, 194
Center School, The, Warren, NJ, 251
Centers for New Horizons Day School, 160
Central Michigan University, 216
Central Missouri State University, 232
Central Piedmont Community College, 287
Central State University, 301
Central Washington University, 354
Centreville School, 131
Cerebral Palsy Association of Middlesex
    County, 246
Cerebral Palsy Center of Greater Baton
    Rouge, 189
Cerebral Palsy Foundation of Southern
    Arizona, 70
Cerritos Community College, 93
Cerro Coso Community College, 94
CES Associates, 118
Chabot College, 94
Chaffey Community College, 94
Chaminade University of Honolulu, 154
Chancellor Academy, 249
Chapel Haven, Inc., 39
Chapel Hill-Chauncy Hall School, 206
Chapman College, 94
Charles Armstrong School, The
    Belmont, CA, 74
    Fremont, CA, 76
Charles L. Shedd APSL Research Academy,
    The, 183
Charles River Academy, 201
Charlotte Rehabilitation Hospital, Inc., 289
Chase House, Inc., 160
Chatham Academy, Inc., 148
Chelsea School, The, 195
Chemeketa Community College, 305

Cheryl Louise Educational Center, 76
Chicago City-Wide College, City Colleges of
    Chicago, 164
Chicago Clinic for Child Development, 169
Child and Family Center of Atlanta, 152
CHILD Center, The, 78
child, etc., 114
Childhaven, 230
Childhood League Center, The, 293
Children Rehabilitation Unit, 230
Children's Beach House, Inc., 132
Children's Center of Riverside, The, 84
Children's Community Center, Inc., 359
Children's Evaluation and Rehabilitation
    Center, 278
Children's Garden, 190
Children's Home Society of South Dakota, 324
Children's Home Therapeutic Treatment
    Center, The, 298
Children's Hospital and Health Center, San
    Diego, CA, 111
Children's Hospital at the Washington
    University Medical Center, 235
Children's Hospital of Buffalo, 279
Children's Hospital, Cincinnati, OH, 297
Children's Hospital of Philadelphia, The, 316
Children's Hospital of Pittsburgh, 317
Children's Hospital of San Francisco, 111
Children's Hospital, The, Denver, CO, 122
Children's Hospital, Topeka, KS, 181
Children's House, The, 262
Children's Language Institute, Inc., 203
Children's Medical Center, Dayton, OH, 298
Children's Memorial Hospital, Chicago, IL,
    168
Children's Rehabilitation Center, 293
Children's Resource Center, 139
Child School, The, 262
Child Study Center, The, Billings, MT, 238
Child Study Center, Fort Worth, TX, 338
Chipola Junior College, 142
Chi Rho Camp for Learning Disabled
    Children, 221
Christ Church Child Center, 193
Christ Hospital, 169
Christian Learning Center, 214
Churchill School and Center for Learning
    Disabilities, The, 262
Churchill School, The, 230
Circle Pines Center, 214
Circle Preschool, 83
Citrus College, 95
City College of New York, 272
City College of San Francisco, 95
City University of New York, 274
Clackamas Community College, 305
Clark University, 209
Classworks, The, 182
Clayton Junior College, 149
Clearing, The, 344
Clearview School, Los Angeles, CA, 79
Clearview School, Wayne, NJ, 251
Clearway School, 207
Clemson University, 322

Cleta Harder Developmental School, 79
Cleveland Institute of Art, The, 295
Cleveland State University, 295
Cliffwood School, The, 331
Closer Look/Parents' Campaign for
    Handicapped Children and Youth, 51
    LD Teenline, 51
Coe College, 177
College and the Learning Disabled Student: A
    Guide to Program Selection, Develop-
    ment, and Implementation, 366
College and University Special Programs and
    Services (see also individual state listings),
    25-30, 57-365
College of Alameda, 95
College of Charleston, 322
College of Great Falls, 237
College of Idaho, 157
College of Lake County, 164
College of Mount Saint Joseph, 295
College of New Rochelle, 272
College of St. Scholastica, The, 222
College of Saint Thomas, 223
College of Staten Island, Sunnyside Campus,
    The, 272
College of the Canyons, 95
College of the Desert, 96
College of the Ozarks, 72
College of the Redwoods, 96
College of the Sequoias, 96
COLORADO, 118-123
Columbia College, 273
Columbia Community College, 96
Columbia University, Barnard College, 272
Columbia University, Columbia College, 273
Columbia University, Teachers College, 273
Columbus College, 150
Columbus High School, 176
Columbus Technical Institute, 295
Community Action Agency Lewis-Clark Head
    Start, 156
Community College of Allegheny County-
    Allegheny Campus, 314
Community College of Allegheny County-
    Boyce Campus, 314
Community College of Philadelphia, 314
Community High School, 246
Community Memorial Hospital, 363
Community Preschool Therapeutic Nursery,
    200
Community School, Newtown Square, PA, 309
Community School of Bergen County, Inc.,
    The, 250
Community School, Orange, NJ, 249
COMPASS, 200
Compton Community College, 97
Computer Learning Resources, 70
Concord-Assabet School, Inc., 201
Concordia College, Moorhead, MN, 223
Concordia College, Seward, NE, 239
Concordia High School, 82
CONNECTICUT, 123-130
Connecticut College Program for Children
    with Special Needs, 126

Converse College, 322
Cooper Hospital/University Medical Center, 253
Coordinating Council for Handicapped Children, 158
Coppin State College, 196
Cornell University, 273
Cosumnes River College, 97
Cottleston Hall Montessori, 194
Council for Exceptional Children (CEC), 47
Council for Learning Disabilities (CLD), 47
Counseling and School Psychological Services, 289
Cove School, Inc., 161
Covina Psychological Group, 113
CPC Horizon Hospital, 111
Crafton Hills College, 97
Creative Education, 220
Creighton University, 239
Crescent Academy, Edmond, OK, 300
Crescent Academy, New Orleans, LA, 187
Crestwood Hall, Inc.-The Dyslexia School of North Carolina, 285
Crisman Preparatory School, 331
Crossroads Rehabilitation Center, 171
Crossroads School, Fort Lauderdale, FL, 136
Crossroads School, The, Paoli, PA, 309
Crotched Mountain Rehabilitation Center School, 242
Crystalaire, 215
Curry College, 210
Cypress College, 97

Dakota Wesleyan University, 325
Dallas Academy, 329
Dannen School, The, 78
Darrow School, 262
David T. Siegel Institute for Communicative Disorders, The, 169
Davison School, Inc., The, 147
Day Camp Shakoda, 176
Day Habilitation Munadnock Workshop, 42
Daytona Beach Community College, 142
Day Treatment and Tutorial Programs of the Child Guidance Clinic, Inc., 289
Day Treatment Center, 292
Day Treatment Unit Services/Rochester Mental Health Center, 265
Dean School, Inc., 330
De Anza College, 97
Dearborn Elementary School, 199
DeKalb Community College-Central Campus, 150
DELAWARE, 130-132
Delaware Elwyn Institute, 39
Del Mar College, 333
Delta School, The, 309
Delta State University, 228
De Neuville Heights School for Girls, 326
Denver Academy, 119
Denver Auraria Community College, 120
De Paul Community Health Center, 235
dePaul Dyslexia Association, Inc., 187
de Paul School, The, Louisville, KY, 183
dePaul School of Northeast Florida, 137

de Paul School, The, Scranton, PA, 311
DePaul University, 165
Desert Occupational Therapy Services, 113
DeSisto at Howey, 137
Developmental Achievement Center, 227
Developmental Learning Center, 145
Developmental Resource Center Day School, 136
Devereux Foundation-California, The, 117
Devereux Foundation, The, Devon, PA, 318
Devereux Foundation, The, Victoria, TX, 332
Devereux Glenholme, 126
Devereux School, 205
Diablo Valley College, 97
Diagnosis and Intervention, 236
Diagnostic and Remedial Reading Clinic, 338
Diagnostic Learning Center, 283
Dictionary of LD Terms, A, 382-390
Directories, 372-376
Directory for Exceptional Children, The, 373
Directory of College Facilities and Services for the Handicapped, 373
Directory of Facilities and Services for the Learning Disabled, 373
Directory of Summer Camps for Children with Learning Disabilities, A, 373
Discrimination Complaint, Filing a, 23
DISTRICT OF COLUMBIA, 133-135
District One Technical Institute, 361
Dr. Gertrude A. Barber Center, 308
Doctors Hospital, 298
Dominican College, 98
Dordt College, 177
Douglas County Hospital, 225
Drake University, 177
D.T. Watson Rehabilitation Hospital, 317
Dubin Learning Center, The, 117
Due Process, 22
Due Process in Special Education, 367
Duke University, 287
Dundalk Community College, 196
Dunn School, 81
Du Page Easter Seal Treatment Center, 170
Duquesne University, 314
Dutchess Community College, 273
Dynamic Springs Prep School, 309

Eagle Hill School, Greenwich, CT, 124
Eagle Hill School, Hardwick, MA, 202
Eagle Village Camp, 215
Early Adolescence to Early Adulthood: Volume 5, The Best of ACLD, 33, 367
Early Childhood Learning Centers of New Jersey
    Morristown, NJ, 248
    Ridgefield, NJ, 250
Early Education Center, 227
Early Learning Center, 347
East Carolina University, 287
East Central Oklahoma State University, 301
Easter Seal Center: Alternative Beginnings for Children (ABC) Program, 170
Easter Seal Children's Clinic and Preschool, 356

Easter Seal Demonstration School, Miami, FL, 138
Easter Seal Rehabilitation Center, Lancaster, PA, 308
Easter Seal Rehabilitation Center, Oakland, CA, 114
Easter Seal Rehabilitation Center, San Antonio, TX, 338
Easter Seal Society for Disabled Children and Adults, Inc., 133
Easter Seal Society of Allegheny County, The, 310
Easter Seal Society of Del-Mar, Camp Fairlee Manor, 196
Eastern Connecticut State University, 127
Eastern Maine Medical Center, 191
Eastern Montana College, 237
Eastern Nebraska 4-H Center, 238
Eastern New Mexico University, 256
Eastfield College, 333
East Mountain Center, 207
East Tennessee Children's Hospital, 328
East Texas State University, 333
Edgar County Children's Home On Site/Treatment and Learning Center, 163
Edgemont Hospital, 110
Edgewood Children's Center, St. Louis, MO, 230
Edgewood Children's Center, San Francisco, CA, 85
Educating Exceptional Children, 5
Educational Center, Fort Lauderdale, FL, 145
Educational Clinic, Inc., The, 299
Educational Development Center of Psychiatric Institute of Richmond, 346
Educational Guidance Services, Inc., 145
Educational Service, Inc., 132
Educational Services Center, 254
Education Center, The, 228
El Camino College, 98
El Centro College, 333
eLDA Reading and Math Clinic, 226
Elim Christian School, 163
Elizabeth Brown Day School, 125
Elizabeth Seton College, 273
Elizabeth W. Pouch Center for Special People, 284
Elk Grove Learning Center, 113
Elk Hill Farm, Inc., 351
El Paso Community College, 334
Embry-Riddle Aeronautical University, 142
Emma Pendleton Bradley Hospital, 320
Employment
  Entering the Work Force, 32-36
  Job Accomodations, 34-36
  Vocational Training, 13, 30-32
Emory University, 150
Endeavor Learning Center, 198
Englewood Learning Center, 170
Epworth Village Educational Therapy Program, 238
ERIC Clearinghouse on Handicapped and Gifted Children, 51
ERIC Digests, 377
Erskine College, 322

ESCALON, 74
Essex Community College, 196
Evergreen State College, The, 354
Evergreen Valley College, 98
EWT School of Experiment With Travel, Inc., The, 206
Exceptional Children's Foundation, 79
Exceptional Children's Opportunity School, 80
Exceptional Opportunities, Inc., 176
Exceptional Parent, The, 379
Experimental Education Unit, University of Washington, 353

Fact Sheets, (CACLD, HEATH, NICHCY), 377
Fairhaven School, 154
Fairhill School, 330
Fairleigh Dickinson University, 251
Fairview Hospital, 225
Fairview School, Inc., 139
Families of Children with Special Needs: Early Intervention Techniques for the Practitioner, 367
Family Service Center Daycare, 163
Favorite, 208
Feather River College, 98
Felician School for Exceptional Children, The, 248
Fernald School, 80
Finding A School For Your Child in San Francisco and Marin, 373
First Baptist School, 84
Fisher Foundation School, 67
Fitkin Hospital, 253
FLOC (For Love of Children) Learning Center, 133
FLORIDA, 135-145
Florida A & M University, 142
Florida Atlantic University, 143
Florida International University, 143
Florida Junior College at Jacksonville, 143
Forman School, 125
Forsyth Psychological Associates, 290
Forsyth Technical Institute, 288
Fort Lauderdale Oral School of Nova University, 136
Foundation for Children with Learning Disabilities (FCLD), 4, 48, 51, 62, 257, 381
4H Wilderness Experience, 286
Fox Valley Technical Institute, 361
Franklin College of Indiana, 173
Franklin County Special Education Cooperative, 55
Fraser School, 221
Fresno City College, 98
Fresno Pacific College, 99
Friendship House Children's Center, 311
Frontier Day Camp for Children with Learning Disabilities, 294
Frostburg State College, 197
Frost School, The, 195
Fullerton College, 99
Furman University, 323

Gables Academy, Atlanta, GA, 147
Gables Academy, Baton Rouge, LA, 187
Gables Academy, Miami, FL, 138
Gables Academy/New Orleans, 187
Gainesville Junior College, 150
Garden Sullivan Hospital of Pacific Medical
    Center, 112
Gateway School, 250
Gateway School of New York, The, 263
Gateway Technical Institute, 361
Gavilan College, 99
George Halas, Jr. Vocational Center, 40
George Mason University, 348
George Washington University, 134
GEORGIA, 146-153
Georgia College, 150
Georgiana Rodiger Center, 115
Georgia Southern College, 150
Glenville State College, 357
GOALD (The Georgia Organization for
    Adults with Learning Disabilities), Inc.,
    40
Golden West College, 99
Gompers Rehabilitation Center, 66
Good Samaritan Hospital, 281
Good Shepherd School for Children, 231
Goodwill Industries of Lancaster County,
    Inc., 43
Goodwill Industries of the Greater East Bay,
    39
Goodwill Industries-Sun Coast, Inc., 40
Governor Center School, 319
Gow School, The, 267
Graceland College, 177
Gramon School, The, 248
Grand Rapids Junior College, 216
Grand Valley State College, 216
Grand View College, 177
Green Chimneys School, 259
Greenville College, 165
Greenville Technical College, 323
Greenwood School, The, 341
Grove School, Inc., 125
Groves Learning Center, The, 221
Growing Mind School, The, 74
Guardian Angel Home, 162
Guides, 372-376
Guide to College Programs for Learning
    Disabled Students, 373
Guide to Colleges for Learning Disabled
    Students, A, 374
Guide to Summer Camps and Summer
    Schools, 374
Gulf Coast Education Center, 227
Gundersen Clinic, Ltd., 364
Gunston School, The, 193

Hackensack Medical Center, 253
Half Moon Camps, Inc., 208
Hallen School, The, 262
Hamilton Center, Inc., 175
Hamilton McGregor Technical High School,
    136
Hampton University, 348

Hancock County Children's Center, 192
Handbook of Private Schools, The, 374
Handbook of Trade and Technical Careers and
    Training 1984-85, 374
Hannah Neil Center for Children, 299
Happiness House Rehabilitation Center, Inc.,
    140
Happy Hill Farm Children's Home, Inc., 331
Harbor School, 246
Harbour North Clinic, Ltd., 226
Hartnell Community College, 99
Hastings College, 239
Havern Center, Inc., 119
HAWAII, 153-155
HEATH Resource Center, 52
Helping Children with Specific Learning
    Disabilities: A Practical Guide for Parents
    and Teachers, 367
Helping Hands, Inc., 312
Helping Hands School, 71
Henry Ford Community College, 217
Henry Heywood Memorial Hospital, 212
Heritage School, Jackson, MS, 228
Heritage School, The, Calistoga, CA, 75
Herkimer County Community College, 274
HighCroft School, The, 207
Highland Heights, 125
High Valley, 260
Hill Learning Development Center, 285
Hillside School, The, 307
Hillside Treatment Center, 152
Hill Top Preparatory School, The, 311
Hocking Technical College, 295
Holmstead School, The, 250
Holy Names College, 100
Holyoke Hospital, Inc., 212
Home-School Cookbook, A: Parents and
    Teachers Guide to Learning Disabilities,
    377
Homme Home for Boys, 360
Honolulu Community College, 155
Hoosac School, 261
Hope Center for the Developmentally
    Disabled, Inc., 123
Hope Consolidated Services, Inc., 311
Horizon Mental Health Center, 181
Hospital Clinics, 57-365
Housatonic Community College, 127
House of Learning, 139
Houston Child Guidance Center, 338
Houston Speech School, 148
Howard Community College, 197
Howard School, Inc., The
    Atlanta, GA, 147
    Macon, GA, 148
How to Get Services by Being Assertive, 368
How to Organize an Effective
    Parent/Advocacy Group and Move
    Bureaucracies, 368
How to Raise Your Child to Be a Winner, 368
How to Use This Guide, 1-4
How to Write an I.E.P., 368
Hoyleton Children's Home, 161
Hudson Valley Community College, 274

Human Resources Center, 42
Hunter College-City University of New York, 274
Huntsville Achievement School, 63
Husson College, 191

I Am Learning Center/Academy, 85
I Can Do Camp, 222
I Can Jump the Rainbow, 377
IDAHO, 156-157
Idaho State University, 157
IEP, see Individualized Education Plan
I.H. Schwartz Children's Rehabilitation Center, 213
ILLINOIS, 158-170
Illinois Central College, 165
Illinois State University, 165
Imperial Valley College, 100
INDIANA, 171-175
Indiana Central University, 173
Indiana State University, 173
Indiana University, 173
Indiana University East, 173
Indiana University-Purdue University at Indianapolis, 174
Individualized Education Plan (IEP), 11, 16, 18-21, 22
Infant and Child Development Services, 130
Information Center for Individuals with Disabilities, 52
Information Centers, 51-54
Institute for Child and Family Development and Research, 153
Institute of Learning Research, 326
Institute of Logopedics, 180
Intensive Education Center, Inc., 127
International Reading Association (IRA), 48
IOWA, 175-179
Iowa Lakes Community College, 178
Iowa Western Community College, 178
Islands Community College, 65
ITOP Center for Learning, 87

James Madison University, 349
James Whitcomb Riley Hospital for Children, 175
Jane Wayland Center, 66
JCC Camp, 141
Jeanine Schultz Memorial School, 163
Jefferson Academy, The, 286
Jefferson-Gumbel Vocational Training Centers, 41
Jefferson Technical College, 296
Jemicy School, The, 194
Jerry Davis Early Childhood Center, 245
Jersey City State College, 252
Jersey Shore Medical Center, Fitkin Hospital, 253
JESPY House, Inc., 42
Jewish Hospital of Cincinnati, The, 298
Joan Davis School for Special Education, 230
John F. Kennedy Institute School, The, 193
John F. Kennedy Medical Center, 253
John F. Kennedy University, 100

John G. Leach School, 131
John Jay College of Criminal Justice, City University of New York, 274
Johns Hopkins University, 197
Johnson County Community College, 180
Johnson State College, 342
Jordan Diagnostic Center, 303
Journal of Learning Disabilities, 6, 27, 28, 380
Journal of Reading, Writing and Learning Disabilities International, 380
Journal of Rehabilitation, 25, 34
Joy Education Center, 294
Julia Ann Singer Center, 80
Julian Psychological Associates, 289
Julie Billiart School, 293

Kaiser Permanente Medical Center, 111
Kalevala School, 135
Kankakee Community College, 165
KANSAS, 180-182
Kansas City Kansas Community College, 181
Kansas State University, 181
Kapiolani Community College, 155
Karafin School, The, 262
Karum School, 352
Kauai Community College, 155
Kean College of New Jersey, 252
Keene State College, 243
Kellogg Community College, 217
Kelter Center, The, 114
Kemmerer Village School, 158
Kennedy Learning Clinic, 282
Kennedy Memorial Hospital for Children, 212
Kent State University, 296
KENTUCKY, 182-186
Keystone Area Education Agency, 179
Keystone Junior College, 315
Kildonan School, 258
Killgore Children's Psychiatric Center, 337
Kingsborough Community College, 274
Kingsbrook Academy, 249
Kingsbury Center, The, 134
Kings County Hospital Center, 278
Kingsley School, The, 200
Kings River Community College, 100
Kingsway Learning Center, 247
Know Your Rights and Use Them, 378
Kohler Child Development Center, 251
Kolburne Schools, Inc., The, 204
Krebs School Foundation, 203

Laboratory School of Natural Sciences, 77
Labouré College, 210
Lab School of Washington, The, 134
Lad Lake, Inc./Lakewood School, 359
Lafayette Academy, 345
Lake City Community College, 143
Lake Grove School, 261
Lake Land Community College, 165
Lake Tahoe Community College, 100
Lamar Community College, 120
Lambuth College, 327
La Mel Children's Center, 115

Landmark College, 25, 343
Landmark School, 205
Landmark West School, 76
Lane Community College, 306
Lane's Learning Center, 114
Laney College, 100
Language Associates, 78
Language Development Program of Western
    New York, 268
Lansing Community College, 217
Laporte Therapy Center, 172
Laredo Junior College, 334
Larkin Home for Children, 170
Lassen College, 101
LAUNCH, Inc., The Coalition of LD Adults,
    37
Laurel School, The, 86
Lawrence Hall School for Boys, 160
LD Hotline, 257
LD Teenline, 51
Learn and Play Preschool, 321
Learning and Counseling Center, The, 118
Learning and Language Specialists, 226
Learning Associates, 116
Learning Center for Exceptional Children,
    The, 246
Learning Center of Catawba County, Inc.,
    The, 285
Learning Center, The, 318
Learning Clinic, Inc., The, 124
Learning Consultants, Inc., 235
Learning Disabilities: A Family Affair, 369
Learning Disabilities: Basic Concepts,
    Assessment Practices, and Instructional
    Strategies, 369
Learning Disabilities Center, The, 116
Learning Disabilities Consultants, 317
Learning Disabilities Explained, 369
Learning Disabilities: The Hidden Handicap,
    5-15
Learning Disabilities: Theories, Diagnosis,
    and Teaching Strategies, 369
Learning Disabilities: The Struggle from
    Adolescence toward Adulthood, 369
Learning Disability Information Centers,
    51-54
Learning Disabled Child, The: Ways Parents
    Can Help, 370
Learning Disabled/Gifted Children:
    Identification and Programming, 370
Learning Foundations, 282
Learning Incentive, The, 130
Learning, Inc., 337
Learning Place, A, 112
Learning Services of Northern California, 116
Leary School, Inc., 344
LeeBil School and Learning Center, 87
Leeward Community College, 155
Leeway School, 266
Legal Rights Primer for the Handicapped: In
    and Out of the Classroom, 370
Leland Hall, 204
Lenox Baker Children's Hospital, 289
Lenox Hill Hospital, 280

Lesley College, 210
Lexington Community College, 184
Lexington Hearing and Speech Center, 183
Life Adventure Camp, 184
Lighthouse Point Academy, 137
Lighthouse School, 204
Lincoln College, 166
Lincoln Trail College, 166
Linden Hill School, 204
Lindenwood College, 232
Little Friends School, 162
Little Keswick School, Inc., 346
Little People's/Learning Prep School, 207
Little Village School, 261
Lockport Education Center, 162
Long Island College Hospital, 279
Long Stretch Learning Center, 194
Lon Morris College, 334
Lord Stirling School, 245
Loretta Heights College, 120
Lorge Lower School, The, 263
Lorge Upper School, The, 263
Los Angeles City College, 101
Los Angeles Mission College, 101
Los Angeles Pierce College, 101
Los Medanos College, 101
LOUISIANA, 186-189
Louisiana State University-Baton Rouge, 188
Louisiana Technical University, 188
Lourdes Camp, 271
Lovejoy's College Guide for the Learning
    Disabled, 374
Lowell School
    Bayside, NY, 259
    Fresh Meadows, NY, 260
Lowell Upper School, 260
Loyola Marymount University, 101
Loyola University, 197
Lutheran School for the Deaf, 213
Lycoming College, 315
Lycoming County Crippled Children's Society,
    Inc., 312
Lynchburg College, 349

Macalester College, 223
MACLD Apartment Residence/STILE
    (Success Through Independent Living
    Experience) Program, 42
Macomb Community College, 217
Madisonville Community College, 185
Madonna Heights Services, 261
Magazines, 379-381
Maimonides Medical Center, 279
MAINE, 189-192
Main Line Speech Consultants, 318
Mandarin Learning Center, 137
Manhattan College, 274
Manhattan Day School, 263
Manhattanville College, 275
Mankato State University, 223
Manuals, 381
Maplebrook School, Inc., 258
Maple Valley School, 206
Marburn Academy, 293

Mardan Center of Educational Therapy, 76
Marian Health Center, 179
Marianne Frostig Center of Educational
    Therapy, The, 80
Marin Child Development Center, 88
Marin Diagnostic and Remedial Center, 116
Marin School for Learning, The, 88
Marin Puzzle People, 37
Marion College, 174
Marist College, 275
Marquette University, 361
Marshall University, 357
Martin de Porres School, 267
Mary Dore Private School, 285
MARYLAND, 192-199
Mary McDowell Center for Learning, 259
Mason/Thurston Community Action Council,
    44
MASSACHUSETTS, 199-213
Massasoit School, Inc., 205
Mathoms Program, 200
Mayville State College, 290
McNeese State University, 188
Meadowview School, 332
Medical Center at Princeton, The, 254
Medical College of Pennsylvania Hospital,
    The, 316
Meher Schools, 79
Melmed Reading Clinic, Inc., 114
Melwood Farm, 194
Memorial Hospital of Burlington County, 253
Memphis Academy for Learning Disabilities,
    326
Memphis Academy of Arts, 327
Memphis State University, 327
Menotomy, 243
Merced College, 102
Mercer University, 151
Mercy Hospital, Davenport, IA, 179
Mercy Hospital of Watertown, 281
Mercy Hospital, Urbana, IL, 169
Meridian-Markoff School, 87
Merrimack Valley Rehabilitation Center, 41
Merritt College, 102
Mesa College, 120
Mesa Community College, 68
Mesa Lutheran Hospital, 69
Methodist Hospitals of Memphis, 328
Metropolitan Technical Community College,
    239
Miami-Dade Community College-North
    Campus, 143
Michael Reese Hospital and Medical Center,
    168
MICHIGAN, 213-220
Michigan State University, 217
Michigan Technological University, 218
Middlesex Community College, 210
Middlesex County College, 252
Midland School, The, 249
Mid-Michigan Community College, 218
Mid-State United Cerebral Palsy, Inc., 190
Midway School, 248
Midwest Computer Camp, Inc., 172

Milton S. Hershey Medical Center, 316
Mineral Area College, 232
Minneapolis Children's Medical Center, 225
MINNESOTA, 220-227
Minot State College, 290
Mira Costa Community College, 102
Miriam School, The, 231
MISSISSIPPI, 227-229
Mississippi State University, 228
Mississippi University for Women, 229
MISSOURI, 229-236
Misunderstood Child, The: A Guide for
    Parents of Learning Disabled Children,
    370
Mitchell College, 128
Modesto Junior College, 102
Monmouth Medical Center, 253
MONTANA, 236-238
Montana State University, 237
Montclair State College, 252
Montefiore Medical Center Speech and
    Hearing Center, 281
Monterey Peninsula College, 102
Montgomery College, 197
Montgomery Dyslexia Research Foundation,
    Inc., 64
Montgomery Preschool Achievement Center,
    195
Moorpark Community College, 103
Morehead State University, 185
Morning Sky Residential School, 81
Morning Star School
    Jacksonville, FL, 137
    Tampa, FL, 141
Morning Star School of Pinellas Park, 140
Morningside, 44
Morningside Learning Center, 353
Morton College, 166
Morton Plant Hospital, 144
Mott Children's Health Center, 219
Mott Community College, 218
Mountain View College, 334
Mountain West Clinic for Neuro-therapy, 340
Mt. Diablo Rehabilitation Center, 83
Mt. San Antonio College, 103
Mt. San Jacinto College, 103
Mount Sinai Hospital, Hartford, CT, 129
Mt. Sinai Hospital, New York, NY, 280
Mount Vernon Nazarene College, 296
Mount Wachusett Community College, 210
Mt. Washington Pediatric Hospital, Inc., 198
Multidisciplinary Institute, 186
Murray State University, 185

Napa Valley College, 103
National Association of Private Schools for
    Exceptional Children (NAPSEC), 152
National Association of Private Schools for
    Exceptional Children 1985 Membership
    Directory, The, 375
National Association of State Directors of
    Special Education, 54
National Association of Trade and Technical
    Schools, 30

National Council of Juvenile and Family
Court Judges, 381
*National Directory of Four Year Colleges, Two
Year Colleges and Post High School
Training Programs for Young People with
Learning Disabilities, A,* 375
National Easter Seal Society, 48
National Information Center for Educational
Media (NICEM), 53
National Information Center for Handicapped
Children and Youth (NICHCY), 53
National Information Center for the
Association of Radio Reading Services, 56
National Library Service for the Blind and
Physically Handicapped, 55
National Network of Learning Disabled
Adults, 37
National Organizations, 36-38, 46-49
National Rehabilitation Information Center
(NARIC), 53
Natividad Medical Center, 111
Naval Hospital, Oakland, CA, 111
NEBRASKA, 238-240
Neuropsychology Services, 226
NEVADA, 240-241
New Community School, The, 347
New Dominion School, Inc., 346
New England Memorial Hospital, 212
New England Trade and Technical Institute,
42
New Foundation School, The, 67
Newgrange School, The, 247
NEW HAMPSHIRE, 242-244
New Hampshire College, 244
New Hope Center, 41
New Hope Guild Centers, 282
New Hope Learning Center, 231
New Hope School, 139
New Horizons Center for Learning, 240
New Horizon School and Learning Center, 89
Newington Children's Hospital, 130
NEW JERSEY, 244-254
NEW MEXICO, 255-256
New Path Montessori School and Center, 310
New River Community College, 349
New School for Child Development, 89
New School in the Lost Forest, The, 147
Newsletter, (Learning Disabilities
Consultants), 380
New Way School, 67
NEW YORK, 257-284
New York State University College-Oneonta,
275
New York Testing and Guidance Center, 283
New York University, 275
New York University Medical Center, 280
Niagara County Community College, 275
*1984-1985 Resource Guide to Organizations
Concerned with Developmental
Handicaps,* 375
92nd Street YM-YWHA, 283
*No Easy Answers: The Learning Disabled
Child,* 371
*No One to Play With: The Social Side of
Learning Disabilities,* 371

Normandale Community College, 223
Norman Howard School, The, 265
Northampton County Area Community
College, 315
NORTH CAROLINA, 284-290
North Carolina State University, 288
North County Learning Associates, 113
NORTH DAKOTA, 290-291
North Dakota State School of Science, 290
North Dakota State University, 291
North Dakota State University-Bottineau, 291
Northeast Child Development Center, 353
Northeast Consultants Group, 254
Northeastern Junior College, 120
Northeastern State University, 302
Northeast Iowa Technical Institute, 178
Northeast Louisiana University, 188
Northeast Parent and Child Society, 266
Northern Arizona University, 68
Northern Illinois University, 166
Northern Kentucky University, 185
Northern Michigan University, 218
Northern Montana College, 237
Northern Virginia Developmental Preschool,
346
North Hills Services for the Handicapped,
Inc., 71
North Idaho Children's Home, Inc., 156
North Iowa Area Community College, 178
North Kansas City Memorial Hospital, 235
North Lake College, 334
Northland College, 362
North Shore Community College, 211
North Shore Learning Center, 283
North Shore YM and YWHA Day Camp, 271
Northside Day School, 263
Northwestern Michigan College, 218
Northwestern State University, 188
Northwestern University, 166
Northwest Georgia Regional Hospital, 152
Northwest Missouri State University, 232
Northwest Nazarene College, 157
Northwest Reading Clinic, 363
Northwest Suburban Child Development
Clinic, Inc., 169
Northwood Children's Home, 226
Northwood Sports Camp, 270
Norwich University-Military College of
Vermont, 343
Notre Dame College, 244
Notre Dame College of Ohio, 296
Nova University, 143
Nueva Learning Center, 78

Oak Creek Ranch School, 68
Oakes Children's Center, Inc., 86
Oak Hill School, Scotia, NY, 266
Oak Hill School, Sepulveda, CA, 89
Oakland Community College, 218
Oakland School, 345
Oakton Community College, 166
Oakwood School, 345
Ochsner Clinic, 189
Odyssey Academic Camp, 90
Oesterlen Services for Youth, 299

Office of Civil Rights regional offices, 23-24
Offices of Organizations Concerned with
    Learning Disabilities, 57-365
OHIO, 291-300
Ohio University, 296
Ohio University-Zanesville, 296
Ohlone College, 104
Ojai Center for Learning Disabilities, 115
OKLAHOMA, 300-304
Oklahoma Children's Memorial Hospital, 303
Oklahoma State University, 302
Oliver Holden Academy, 201
Olympic Community College, 354
Olympus Center, The, 299
One-to-One Learning Center, The, 170
Open Book School, 86
Open Meadow Learning Center, 305
Operation Discovery School, 230
Oral Roberts University, 302
Orange Coast College, 104
Orchard School, The, 284
Order Form, 409
OREGON, 304-307
Orton Dyslexia Society, The, 49
Orton Dyslexia Society Information Packet,
    378
Other Services, 57-365
Our Lady of Angels Special School, 292
Our Lady of Providence Children's Center,
    Inc., 207
Our Lady of the Elms Special Education
    School, 292
Our Lady Queen of Peace, 214
Oxnard College, 104

PACE School, Longwood, FL, 138
Pace School, Pittsburgh, PA, 310
Pacific Lutheran University, 354
Pacific Oaks Children's School, 83
Palmer Learning Systems, Inc., 117
Palmer School, 88
Palomar Community College, 104
Pamphlets, 376-379
Pan American University, 334
PARA-Educator Center for Young Adults,
    The, 43
Parent's Guide to Learning Disabilities, A, 378
Parents' Guide to "Teacherese": A Glossary of
    Special Education Terms, 371
Parish School, The, 331
Park Century School, 80
Parkland College, 166
Parsons Child Family Center: The Neil
    Hellman School, 281
Pasadena Cerebral Palsy Center Pre-School, 83
Pasadena City College, 104
Pasadena Guidance Clinics, 115
Pathfinder School, 70
Pathways Center, 195
Pathway School, The, 308
Patterson School, The, 285
Pediatric Pavilion, Los Angeles County-
    University of Southern California Medical
    Center, 110
Pediatric Therapy Center: First Steps, 352

Pembroke State University, 288
Peninsula Children's Center Children and
    Youth Services, Inc., 283
PENNSYLVANIA, 307-318
Pennsylvania State University, 315
Periodicals, 379-381
Peru State College, 239
Peterson's Guide to Colleges with Programs
    for Learning-Disabled Students, 375
Phelps School, The, 308
Phoenix Children's Hospital, 69
Piedmont College, 151
Pilot School, The, 132
Pima Community College, 68
Pine Haven Boys Center, 242
Pinehenge School at Elan, The, 190
Pine Meadows School, 77
Pine Ridge School, Inc., 342
Pinewood Academy, 359
PIP College "HELPS" Newsletter, 380
Pittsburg State University, 181
Plateau Home School, 327
Plumfield School, 124
Pointer, The, 380
Portland State University, 306
Poseidon School, 81
Potential School for Exceptional Children, 160
Potomac State College of West Virginia
    University, 357
Powerful Parent, The: A Child Advocacy
    Handbook, 371
Precious Blood, 214
Pre-School at Elk County Society for Crippled
    Children and Adults, 311
Prescott Child Development Center, 70
President's Committee on Employment of the
    Handicapped, 50
Presley Clinic, Inc., 388
Preston Hollow Presbyterian Week Day
    School, 330
Primary Children's Medical Center, 340
Primavera School, 67
Princeton School for Exceptional Children,
    250
Private and Day Schools, 57-365
Programs for Learning, 236
Project ABLE (Alternatives for a Better
    Learning Experience), 32, 39
Project Triangle, Inc., 41
Providence College, 320
Providence Speech and Hearing Center, 82
Provo Canyon School, 339
Psychoeducational Diagnostic Services, 337
Public Law 94-142, 5, 6, 16, 18, 19, 49
Pueblo Community College, 120
Purdue University, 174
Purdue University-Calumet, 174

Queensborough Community College, 275
Queens Hospital Center, 279
Quinebaug Valley Community College, 128

Radford University, 349
Rainbow Bridge Center, 78

Rainbow Center for Communicative
    Disorders, 229
Rainbow Lodge Youth Care Center, 304
Ramapo Anchorage Camp, 271
Ranch Hope/Strang School, 245
Rancho Del Mar School, 76
Range Center, Inc., 226
Rapid Learning Systems, 236
Raskob Day School, 82
Raskob Learning Institute, 114
Reach for Learning, 112
Reading Group, The, 170
Reading Research Council, The, 112
Reading Research Foundation, 187
Recording for the Blind, Inc. (RFB), 54
Rectory School, The, 126
Red Rocks Community College, 121
Reece School, 264
Reed Academy, 202
Re-Ed West Center for Children, Inc., 85
Regina Caeli Center, 187
Regis College, Denver, CO, 121
Regis College, Weston, MA, 211
Rehab Associates, Inc., 145
Rehabilitation Act of 1973, 30
Rehabilitation Center of Cattaraugus County,
    258
Reinhardt College, 151
Research and Development Training Institute,
    Inc., 381
Research Reports, (Institute for Research in
    Learning Disabilities), 378
Resource Educational Tutoring and Testing,
    153
Resources for Children with Special Needs,
    Inc., 53, 257
Resurrection Children's Center, 345
RHODE ISLAND, 319-321
Rhode Island College, 320
Rhode Island Hospital, 320
Richards Educational Therapy Center, 115
Richland College, 334
Ricks College, 157
Rights of Children with Learning Disabilities,
    The, 16-21
Rincon Center for Learning, 113
Rio Hondo College, 105
Rivendell Academy, 140
Riverside City College, 105
Riverside School, Inc., 347
Riverview School, 202
Riverview School of Sunburst Youth Homes,
    364
Rivier College, 244
Robert J. Mosby and Associates, Inc., 236
Robert Louis Stevenson School, 264
Rochester Community College, 223
Rock Brook School, The, 246
Rock Creek Farm, 313
Rockford College, 167
Rockhurst College, 233
Rockland Psychological and Educational
    Center, 283
Rock Point School, 341

Rocky Mountain Child Development Center,
    122
Rosary College, 167
Rose F. Kennedy Center for Research, 278
Rossier Educational and Assessment Center, 77
Round Lake Camp, 313
Russell Sage College, 276
Rutgers University, 252
Ruthe B. Cowl Rehabilitation Center, 331

Sabin-McEwen Learning Institute, Inc., 75
Saddleback College, 105
Sagamore Psychiatric Center for Children and
    Youth, 279
St. Ann's Home, Inc., 203
St. Cloud Children's Home Program, 227
St. Cloud Hospital, 225
St. Cloud State University, 224
Saint Edward School, 75
St. Francis Children's Activity and
    Achievement Center, 359
St. Francis Day School, 148
St. Francis Hospital and Medical Center,
    Hartford, CT, 129
St. Francis Hospital of Evanston, 168
St. Francis Hospital, Poughkeepsie, NY, 280
St. Francis Medical Center, Pittsburgh, PA,
    317
St. Francis Medical Center, Trenton, NJ, 254
St. Gregory's College, 302
St. John's Hospital, 112
St. Joseph College, 128
St. Louis Community College at Forest Park,
    233
St. Louis Community College at Meramec,
    233
St. Louis University, 233
St. Luke's Hospital, Kansas City, MO, 235
St. Luke's/Roosevelt Hospital Center, 280
St. Martin's Hall, 332
St. Mary's College, 105
St. Mary's Hospital and Medical Center, 112
St. Mary-Corwin Hospital, 122
St. Michael's Farm and School for Boys, Inc.,
    228
St. Olaf College, 224
St. Peter Learning Center, 116
St. Peter's Child Development Center, 310
St. Rose Residence and Day Education, 359
St. Thomas Aquinas College, 276
St. Vincent's Hospital and Medical Center of
    New York, 280
Saint Xavier College, 167
Salem College, 357
Salem State College, 211
Sam Houston State University, 335
San Bernardino Valley College, 105
Sandhills Academy, 322
San Diego Mesa College, 105
San Diego Miramar College, 106
San Diego State University, 106
San Fernando Valley Child Guidance, 81
San Francisco Hearing and Speech Center, 86
San Joaquin Delta College, 106

San Jose Children's Health Council, 116
San Jose City College, 106
San Jose State University, 106
Santa Ana College, 106
Santa Barbara Center for Educational
    Therapy, 117
Santa Barbara City College, 107
Sargent Rehabilitation Center, 319
SAT (Scholastic Aptitude Test), 27
Scenic Land School, 325
Schenck School, The, 148
Schenectady County Community College, 276
Scholastic Aptitude Test, see SAT
Schoolcraft College, 218
School for Contemporary Education, 348
*Schooling for the Learning Disabled: A
    Selective Guide to LD Programs in
    Elementary and Secondary Schools
    Throughout the United States*, 375
Schreiner College, 335
Scott Center, 159
Scottish Rite Children's Hospital, Atlanta,
    GA, 152
Scottish Rite Learning Center of Western
    Texas, 338
Scottsdale Community College, 68
Seattle Central Community College, 354
Seattle Learning Center, 353
Seattle Seguin School, The, 353
Seattle University, 354
Seminole Community College, 144
Serendipity Academy, 305
Seton Hall University, 252
Sewickley Valley Hospital, 317
Shadybrook Language and Learning Center,
    127
Shady Trails Camp, 215
Sheridan College, 365
Shipley Day Treatment Center, 171
Shippensburg University, 315
Shoreline Community College, 355
Shore Training Center, 41
Shriners Hospital for Crippled Children,
    Philadelphia, PA, 317
Sierra College, 107
Sierra Consultants, 115
Sierra School Language Arts Development
    Center, 85
Silver Creek Montessori School, 267
Simmons College, 211
Sinclair Community College, 297
Siskin Preschool Center, 325
Skylake Ranch Camp, 90
Sky Ranch for Boys, 324
Slauson Learning Center, 81
Slippery Rock University of Pennsylvania, 315
Smart But Feeling Dumb, 371
Snow College, 340
Solano Learning Center, 113
SOL School, 160
Somerset Medical Center, 254
Something's Wrong With My Child, 372
Sonoma State University, 107
Sources of Information and Help, 46-56

Southampton College of Long Island
    University, 276
SOUTH CAROLINA, 321-323
SOUTH DAKOTA, 323-325
Southeast Community College-Lincoln, 239
Southeastern Community College, 178
Southeastern Louisiana University, 188
Southeastern Massachusetts University, 211
Southern Illinois University, 167
Southern Maine Vocational Technical
    Institute, 41
Southern Methodist University, 335
Southern Nevada Memorial Hospital, 241
Southern Oregon State College, 306
Southern School, 161
Southern Seminary Junior College, 349
Southern Vermont College, 343
Southwestern Academy
    Rimrock, AZ, 67
    San Marino, CA, 87
Southwestern Oklahoma State University, 302
Southwestern Technical College, 288
Southwest Missouri State University, 233
Southwest State University, 224
Southwood Psychiatric Hospital, 110
Sparks Center for Developmental and
    Learning Disorders, 38
Special Lutheran Classes, 231
Special Materials for the Learning Disabled,
    54-56
SpecialNet, 54
*SpecialWare Directory, The: A Guide to
    Software Sources for Special Education*,
    376
Specific Diagnostic Studies, Inc., 198
Specific Language Disability Center, 220
Spectrum Center for Educational and
    Behavioral Development, Inc., 73
Speech and Language Center of Northern
    Virginia, 351
Speech and Language Development Center, 74
Speech-Hearing-Learning Center of Crippled
    Children's Society, 117
Spokane Falls Community College, 355
Springdale School, 321
Springer Educational Foundation, 292
Springfield College Day Camp, 208
Squirrel Hollow, Inc., 148
Stanford Schools, The, 352
Stark Technical College, 297
Starpoint School, 331
State-by-State Listings, 57-365
State Department of Education Learning
    Disabilities Personnel, 57-365
State University College-Geneseo, 276
State University of New York Agricultural and
    Technical College, 276
State University of New York-Albany, 277
    PreKindergarten Program, 258
State University of New York Canton
    Agricultural and Technical College, 277
State University of New York Cobbleskill
    Agricultural and Technical College, 277
State University of New York-Cortland, 277

State University of New York-Farmingdale, 277
State University of New York-New Paltz, 277
State University of New York-Oswego, 277
State University of New York-Stony Brook, 278
Stephen Gaynor School, 264
STEP, Inc., 161
Stepping Stone School, 249
Steps to Independence for People with Learning Disabilities, 34, 378
Sterne School, 86
Stetson School, Inc., 199
Stetson University, 144
Stratford Friends School, 308
Strauss Learning Center, 175
Strong Memorial Hospital, 280
Student Learning Center, 125
Studio for Academic Achievement, The, 118
Suffolk Child Development Center, 267
Suffolk County Community College-Ammerman Campus, 278
Summer Camps and Programs, 57-365
Summer Education Extension Program, Camp NYABIC, 269
Summit Camp Program, 312
Summit School, Upper Nyack, NY, 268
Summit School, Inc., Dundee, IL, 161
Summit Travel Camp, 43
Sunrise Academy, 139
Sunset Community School, 86
Suomi College, 219
Swain Learning Center, The, 356
Switzer Center, 89
Syracuse University, 278

Taking the first step... to solving learning problems, 379
Tamarack Learning Center, Inc., 304
Tampa General Hospital, 144
Tampa Reading Clinic and Day School, 141
Tarkio College, 233
Tarrant County Junior College-Northeast Campus, 335
Tarrant County Junior College-Northwest Campus, 335
Tarrant County Junior College-South Campus, 335
Taylor University, 174
Teachers College, Columbia University, 273
Temple University Laboratory School, 307
TENNESSEE, 325-329
Testing and Remediation Center, 145
TEXAS, 329-338
Texas A & M University, 335
Texas Scottish Rite Hospital for Crippled Children, 337
Texas Southern University, 336
Their World, 380
Thomas County Community College, 151
Thomas Jefferson University Hospital, 316
Thoms Rehabilitation Hospital, 289
Tikvah Program at Camp Ramah, The, 360
Timberline Trails, 119
Timber Ridge, 348

Timberridge Institute, 300
Time Out to Enjoy, Inc., 14, 38
Tot Haven Center, 88
Town and Country School, 301
Townsend Reading and Learning Center, 298
Towson State University, 198
Treatment Centers, The, 195
Treehouse Reprint Series, 379
Treetops, Mid-Cities Learning Center, 330
Trenton State College, 252
Tri-County Mental Health and Counseling, Inc., 298
Trident Academy, 322
Trinity Bible College, 291
Trinity College, 128
Trinity Pawling School, 265
Trinity School, 301
Tripler Army Medical Center, 155
Truman College, 167
Tulsa Junior College, 302
Turning Point Academy, 131

Umpqua Community College, 306
United Cerebral Palsy Association of Greater Suffolk, Inc., 260
United Cerebral Palsy Association, Rochester, NY, 266
United Cerebral Palsy Center, Barneveld, NY, 258
United Cerebral Palsy League of Union County, 251
United Cerebral Palsy of Northeastern Maine, 192
United Cerebral Palsy of Northeast Pennsylvania, 311
United Cerebral Palsy of North Jersey, Inc., 246
United Cerebral Palsy of Southwest Missouri, 231
United Cerebral Palsy Preschool for Children with Learning Differences, 220
Unity College, 191
University of Alabama, 64
University of Alabama-Huntsville, 64
University of Alaska-Anchorage, 65
University of Arizona, 69
University of Arkansas, 72
University of Arkansas for Medical Sciences, 72
University of California-Berkeley, 107
University of California-Los Angeles, 108
University of California-Riverside, 108
University of California-San Diego, 108
Medical Center, 111
University of Central Arkansas, 72
University of Colorado, 121
University of Connecticut, 129
University of Dayton, 297
University of Delaware, 132
University of Denver, 121
University of Georgia, 151
University of Hartford, 129
University of Hawaii-Manoa, 155
University of Idaho, 157

University of Illinois, 167
University of Illinois-Chicago, 168
University of Iowa Hospitals and Clinics, 179
University of Kansas, 181
University of Kentucky, 185
University of Louisville, 185
University of Maine, 191
University of Maine-Augusta, 191
University of Maryland-College Park, 198
University of Massachusetts, 211
University of Massachusetts Medical Center, 212
University of Miami, 144
University of Michigan, 219
University of Minnesota, 224
University of Minnesota-Crookston, 224
University of Minnesota Hospitals and Clinics, 225
University of Minnesota-Morris, 224
University of Minnesota Technical College-Waseca, 225
University of Missouri-Columbia, 234
University of Missouri-Kansas City, 234
University of Montana, 237
University of Montevallo, 64
University of Nebraska Medical Center, 240
University of Nevada-Las Vegas, 240
University of Nevada-Reno, 241
University of New Hampshire, 244
University of New Mexico, 256
University of New Mexico Mental Health Center, 256
University of New Orleans, 189
University of North Carolina-Charlotte, 288
University of North Carolina-Wilmington, 288
University of Northern Colorado, 121
University of Northern Iowa, 179
University of North Florida, 144
University of Notre Dame, 174
University of Oklahoma, 303
University of Oklahoma Health Science Center, 303
University of Oregon, 306
University of Pennsylvania, 315
University of Pittsburgh, 316
University of Portland, 306
University of Rhode Island, 320
University of Richmond, 349
University of Rochester Medical Center, 280
University of San Diego, 108
University of Santa Clara, 108
University of Science and Arts of Oklahoma, 303
University of South Carolina, 323
University of South Dakota, 325
University of Southern California, 108
  Medical Center Pediatric Pavilion, 110
University of Southern Colorado, 122
University of Southern Maine, 191
University of Tennessee Center for the Health Sciences, 328
University of Tennessee-Chattanooga, The, 327
University of Tennessee-Knoxville, 328

University of Texas-Austin, 336
University of Texas-Dallas, 336
University of the District of Columbia, 134
University of Tulsa, 303
University of Utah, 340
University of Vermont, 343
University of Virginia, 350
University of Virginia Children's Rehabilitation Center, 350
University of Washington, 355
  Experimental Education Unit, 353
University of Wisconsin-Green Bay, 362
University of Wisconsin-La Crosse, 362
University of Wisconsin-Madison, 362
University of Wisconsin-Milwaukee, 362
University of Wisconsin-Oshkosh, 362
University of Wisconsin-Platteville, 363
University of Wisconsin-River Falls, 363
University of Wisconsin-Stevens Point, 363
University of Wyoming, 365
Up The Ladder, 283
Ursuline College, 297
Ursuline-Pitt School, 183
U.S. Department of Education, 9
  Office of Special Education and Rehabilitative Services (OSE), 12, 49
U.S. Government Agencies, 49-50
UTAH, 339-341
Utah Easter Seals Day and Residential Camp, 339
Utah State University, 340

Valdosta State College, 151
Valencia Community College, 144
Valley Children's Hospital, 110
Valleyhead, Inc., 202
Valley View School, 204
Valparaiso University, 174
Vanderbilt Child and Adolescent Psychiatry School, 328
Vanderheyden Hall School, 268
Vanguard School of Coconut Grove, Florida, Inc., The, 135
Vanguard School, The, Lake Wales, FL, 137
Variety Club School, 154
Variety Pre-Schooler's Workshop, 268
Ventura Community College, 109
VERMONT, 341-344
Vermont College of Norwich University, 344
Victor Valley Community College, 109
Villa Esperanza, 83
Villa Maria Education Center, 126
Villa-Oasis School, 66
VIRGINIA, 344-351
Virginia Center for Psychiatry, 351
Virginia Commonwealth University, 350
Virginia Home for Boys, 347
Virginia Polytechnic Institute and State University, 350
Virginia Western Community College, 350
Vista Learning and Diagnostic Center, 317
Vocational Center, Virginia Home for Boys, 347
Vocational Rehabilitation, 31-32

Vocational Rehabilitation Center, Pittsburgh, PA, 43
Vocational Training, 13, 30-32

Wabasso, 243
Walker Home and School, 203
Walters Developmental School, 188
War Bonnet for Boys, Inc., 243
WASHINGTON, 351-356
Washington State University, 355
Washington University-St. Louis, 234
Webster University, 234
Westchester Association for Children with Learning Disabilities, 257
Westchester Exceptional Children's School, 265
Western Carolina University, 288
Western Illinois University, 168
Western Kentucky University, 186
Western New York Association for the Learning Disabled, 282
Western Oregon State College, 306
Western State College of Colorado, 122
Western Washington University, 355
Western Wisconsin Technical Institute, 363
West Georgia College, 152
West Hills College, 109
Westland Medical Center, 219
Westminster College, 234
Westminster School, 326
West Oaks Psychiatric Institute of Houston, 337
Westside Family Mental Health Clinic, 220
West Texas State University, 336
West Valley Center for Educational Therapy, 75
West Valley College, 109
WEST VIRGINIA, 356-358
West Virginia State College, 357
West Virginia University, 357
West Virginia Wesleyan College, 358
What Do You Do After High School?, 376
Wheeler Clinic, Inc., 130
Wide Horizons Ranch, 82
Wightwood School, Inc., 138
Wildwood School, 266
Wilford Hall Medical Center, 337
William Beaumont Hospital System, 219
William Rainey Harper College, 168
Williamsport Area Community College, 316
Willow Hill School, 206

Wilshire West School, 88
Wilson School Supplementary Department, The, 248
Windward School, 268
Winston Preparatory School, The, 264
Winston School, Dallas, TX, 330
Winston School, The, Summit, NJ, 250
Winthrop College, 323
WISCONSIN, 358-364
Wiser Institute, The, 44
Wo Kan Da Day Camp, 90
Woodbourne School, 193
Woodland Hall Academy, 140
Woodlands Academy, 162
Woodlawn Center, 172
Woodrow Wilson Rehabilitation Center, 43
Woods Psychiatric Institute, 336
Woodstock Learning Clinic, 342
Woodward Mental Health Center, 260
Wordsworth Academy, 308
Workshops, Inc., 38
Work Training Program, Inc., 39
World is a Learning Place, The: Adults Who Have Made It Against The Odds, 32
Wright State University, 297
Wyalusing Academy, 364
Wyndham Lawn Campus School, 261
WYOMING, 364-365
Wyoming State Hospital, 365
Wytheville Community College, 350

Xavier University, 297

Yakima Valley Community College, 355
Yale University, 129
Yeshiva University, Albert Einstein School of Medicine, 278
Ygnacio Learning Center, 118
Yoder Day School, The, 264
York Day School, 259
Young Horizons, 77
Young Peoples Day Camp of Staten Island, 271
Your Child Can Win, 372
Your Child's Education: A School Guide for Parents, 372
Yuba College, 109
YWCA Camp Onanda, 269

Zonta Children's Center, 87

ORDER FORM for Additional Guides

Dear FCLD:

Please rush _____ copies of the current edition of *The FCLD Learning Disabilities Resource Guide* to the address below. Enclosed is payment of $15.00 for each copy ordered ($10.00 tax deductible donation and $5.00 to help defray publishing costs. Any additional tax deductible donation would be appreciated.)

_____

Name (please print)

_____

Title (if applicable)

_____

Mailing Address

_____

City   State   ZIP

(_____)_____

Area code   Telephone number

_____

Signature   Date

Mail completed order form with payment to:

        FCLD
        Box 2929
        Grand Central Station
        New York, NY 10163